FDR

AN INTIMATE HISTORY

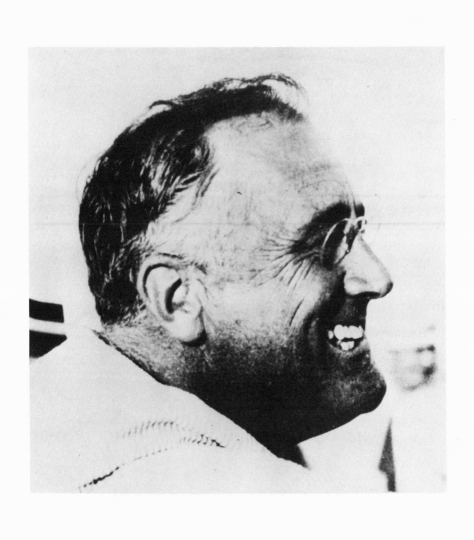

FDR
AN INTIMATE HISTORY

Nathan Miller

1983
Doubleday & Company, Inc., Garden City, New York

Library of Congress Cataloging in Publication Data

Miller, Nathan, 1927–
FDR, an intimate history.

Bibliography: p. 533
Includes index.
1. Roosevelt, Franklin D. (Franklin Delano), 1882–
1945. 2. Presidents—United States—Biography. I. Title.
E807.M54   973.917′092′4 [B]
ISBN 0-385-15108-X   AACR2
Library of Congress Catalog Card Number 80-2977

To
The Memory
of
My Father
Always an FDR Loyalist

FOREWORD

"The President is dead!"

The news of Franklin D. Roosevelt's death came to Americans in varying ways that warm April afternoon in 1945. A breathless announcer breaking into a radio soap opera . . . . a sudden telephone call from a friend . . . a snatch of conversation overheard on the street or in a shop. The shock was magnified by the fact that even though almost everyone realized that Roosevelt was in failing health, he had developed an aura of invulnerability, an air of immortality that made death unthinkable.

For Americans of my generation—I was just short of eighteen—Roosevelt's passing was like a death in the family. We could remember no other President. He dominated our lives as no political leader has been able to do since. We gathered about the radio to listen to the mellifluous voice of the Fireside Chats, and his face dominated the newspapers, magazines, and newsreels that were part of every show at the neighborhood movie theater. And during the worst of the Great Depression, most of the people who patronized my parents' grocery store, in South Baltimore, were kept from starving only by New Deal relief programs.

Experiences such as these lead me, like so many others, to measure all Presidents against Roosevelt's long shadow and all administrations by the New Deal. Thus, the writing of this book has been a voyage of discovery into my own past, an opportunity to test the memories and impressions of my youth against my research. The results have sometimes been unsettling.

This is the first full-scale one-volume biography of FDR since that of Rexford G. Tugwell, which appeared a quarter century ago. While *The Democratic Roosevelt* was an excellent piece of work, it was colored by the author's official relationship with the subject and by Roosevelt's ultimate rejection of Tugwell's dream of a planned economy. Considerable scholarship has also appeared over the intervening years, broadening our knowledge of FDR and his policies. In fact, the volume of material that has been published since 1957 makes such a synthesis as this all the more imperative.

Although Roosevelt's name can still evoke a wistful look in the eye or a hard set of the jaw in some quarters, most of the emotional fire generated by the New Deal has burned out. To younger Americans, Roosevelt is merely a figure in grainy film clips, and they have little understanding of the passions he stirred nearly a half century ago. My book is an attempt to bring FDR to life for this audience. I have tried to paint a portrait that is fair and unflinching in its realism, a portrait that captures all sides of this flawed but essentially great man. In particular, I have tried to show how a man regarded by most of his contemporaries as little more than an amiable country squire became the trustee for all those who put their faith in the maintenance of humane, decent, and civilized values.

No book of the magnitude of this one could be written without the generous assistance of others. I am most grateful to Dr. William R. Emerson and the staff of the Franklin D. Roosevelt Library, at Hyde Park; to Alice S. Creighton, of the Nimitz Library, at the U. S. Naval Academy; to the staffs of the Manuscript and Loan divisions of the Library of Congress and the National Archives. A special debt of gratitude is owed my good friend Dr. Kenneth J. Hagan, Associate Professor of History at the Naval Academy, who read the entire manuscript and made countless suggestions for improvements, and to Dr. Elliot A. Rosen, Professor of History at Rutgers University, who read and commented upon certain chapters. As usual, Judy Spahr performed wonders in typing a difficult manuscript.

I would also like to thank Donald Larrabee, of the Roosevelt Campobello Park Commission, for arranging a visit to Campobello. Harry Stevens, the park superintendent, and his wife and staff, especially Mrs. Linnea Calder, who, as a young girl, served the Roosevelt family, made it a memorable and informative stay. Emily Wright, of the National Park Service, provided a valuable private tour of Eleanor Roosevelt's Val-Kill cottage, which is in the process of restoration. I also wish to thank the many people who provided reminiscences and anecdotes about FDR and his family. My editor, Lisa Drew, and her assistant, Anne Hukill, were generous with their time, talent, and encouragement. Most of all, I wish to express my appreciation to my wife, Jeanette, for her support.

Nathan Miller

Chevy Chase, Maryland

CONTENTS

I still hold to the faith that a better civilization
than any we have known is in store for America.

FRANKLIN D. ROOSEVELT
October 28, 1936

FDR

AN INTIMATE HISTORY

PROLOGUE

THE WEATHER MATCHED the mood of the nation.

Inauguration Day—March 4, 1933—dawned dour and cheerless and the Washington sky was as gray as the marble façades lining Pennsylvania Avenue. Rain had fallen off and on and sleet clung to the trees. Tugging at the flags and bunting hanging from buildings and lampposts, the raw wind chilled the spectators who had been gathering since early morning to see Franklin Delano Roosevelt installed as thirty-second President of the United States. Some stamped their feet to keep warm; others warded off the numbing cold by standing on newspapers, torn and grimy sheets that told of a country in the grip of the severest depression in history. It seemed a destructive force beyond human control.

Upwards of fifteen million Americans—more than a quarter of the work force—drifted hopelessly from factory gate to factory gate in search of jobs that no longer existed. Statistics had failed; the number of jobless may have totaled as high as seventeen million.

Panicked depositors besieged the banks, vainly trying to withdraw the savings of a lifetime before the banks closed—or collapsed.

Out on the high plains, bands of grim-faced, taciturn men protected their farms and homes, at gun point, from foreclosures and sheriff's sales.

Unemployed Pittsburgh steelworkers sent their children out to beg stale bread from the bakeries; in New York City sweatshops, girls worked for twenty cents a day. "A job, any job, seemed like the ultimate success," a young Midwesterner named Ronald Reagan later recalled.

Iowa farmers poured unsalable milk out on the highways and burned corn and wheat for fuel; while, in Chicago, the hungry scavenged the garbage dumps for scraps. One widow carefully took off her glasses before picking up rotting meat so she wouldn't see the maggots.

America's anguish was everywhere. It was in the sad eyes of women as love and laughter vanished from their lives. It was in the face of a Baltimore grocer who saw the store fixtures for which he could no longer pay carried away. And it was in the desperation of the thousands of young people who were riding the rails and roaming the highways because their families could no longer care for them.

Not since 1861, when Abraham Lincoln had assumed the leadership of the nation as an insurgent army mobilized across the unquiet Potomac, had a new President faced such a serious crisis. Yet Roosevelt appeared the most buoyant person in the troubled capital. Tall, broad-shouldered, and aristocratic, he projected an overwhelming confidence and assurance not seen in Washington since his distant cousin Theodore Roosevelt had departed from the White House. At fifty-one, he was so dynamic that people forgot that his legs had been wasted by polio.

The President-elect began Inauguration Day by attending prayers at St. John's Protestant Episcopal Church, across Lafayette Square from the White House. The Reverend Endicott Peabody, headmaster of Groton, Roosevelt's old school, read the prayer for grace and help for "Thy servant, Franklin, about to become President of these United States." The members of Roosevelt's Cabinet were invited to attend, and Frances Perkins, the Secretary of Labor-designate, said, "Everybody prayed. . . . We were Catholics, Protestants and Jews, but I doubt that anyone remembered the difference." The press was not invited, and no pictures were taken.

By eleven o'clock, when Roosevelt arrived at the north portico of the White House to be joined in an open automobile by his predecessor, Herbert C. Hoover, the entire country had ground to a halt. Because of his infirmity, the President-elect did not call upon the President but waited for him in his car. The façade of the old mansion had not been painted in some time, as an economy measure, and Roosevelt noted that the columns were peeling badly. Hoover had spent his last night in office helplessly watching the collapse of the nation's financial system. Five thousand banks had failed, wiping out the savings of nine million depositors. To head off runs on the remaining banks, governor after governor had ordered them closed. The final blow had come at 4 A.M., when Governor Herbert H. Lehman had forbidden the New York banks to open that morning. "We are at the end of our rope," the weary President had murmured to an aide. "There is nothing more that we can do."

The giddy prosperity of the twenties had shriveled and crumbled in Hoover's hand, and he was departing from office a scorned and reviled man. Brilliant engineer, self-made millionaire, organizer of the World

War I relief effort that had saved the lives of millions, and originator of the phrase "the American way of life," he had seen his name transformed into a symbol of derision: Encampments of shacks erected by the homeless on the edges of the cities were "Hoovervilles," broken-down automobiles pulled by mules were "Hoover wagons," and empty pockets turned inside out were "Hoover flags." He was the butt of a hundred bitter jokes: On one occasion, the President dedicated a monument and received a twenty-one-gun salute. "By gum, they missed him," said an old man. Or so the story went.

Hoover sat motionless, eyes lowered, on the ride down Pennsylvania Avenue to the Capitol. The President-elect struggled to make conversation with his somber companion, no easy task even for Roosevelt, who prided himself on a mastery of small talk. In desperation, he called Hoover's attention to the framework of the new Department of Commerce building, which rose gaunt against the tumbling clouds. His eldest son, James, riding in the car's front seat, heard his father exclaim: "My dear Mr. President, aren't those the nicest steel girders you ever saw!" Finally giving up, Roosevelt began to acknowledge the scattered applause from the spectators pressing against the ropes strung out along the curb, raising his silk hat and nodding his leonine head. "I said to myself, 'Spinach!'" he later told Grace Tully, his secretary. "Protocol or no protocol, somebody had to do something."

Arriving at the Capitol, the incoming and outgoing Presidents went their separate ways. Hoover was ushered to the President's Room, just off the Senate Chamber, where he signed or vetoed last-minute bills. Roosevelt was shown to a nearby room, where he again went over his inaugural address. The speech was designed to give the American people a badly needed transfusion of hope and courage without putting a gloss on the critical situation confronting the nation. Wishing to emphasize the solemnity of the occasion, he wrote out a new opening line in his bold, slanting hand: "This a day of consecration." A delegation of senators escorted him to the Senate Chamber for the swearing in of John Nance Garner as Vice-President—a ceremony that took only a few minutes. Observers noted that Roosevelt was now subdued and seemingly lost in thought.

Forty acres of spectators crowded the plaza between the east front of the Capitol and the Library of Congress, pressed shoulder to shoulder and restlessly waiting as the dignitaries slowly took their places upon the inaugural platform. People climbed into the trees and stood on stepladders to get a better view of the proceedings. The flags that whipped in the wind over their heads flew at half-staff for Senator Thomas J. Walsh, the Attorney General-designate, who had died a few hours before. Some of the throng, believing that revolution was imminent, feared that Roosevelt might be America's last President, but the crowd was good-humored despite the tension in the air. "What are those things that look like little cages?" someone asked. "Machine guns," replied a woman with a nervous giggle.

Paralyzed legs locked in heavy braces and leaning on the arm of his son, the President-elect laboriously made his way down a maroon-carpeted ramp to the rostrum. Hoover followed him to a seat in the front row. At six minutes past one, Chief Justice Charles Evans Hughes, white-bearded and black-robed, came forward to administer the oath of office. Roosevelt placed his left hand on the old Dutch Bible that recorded more than two centuries of family births and deaths and lay open to St. Paul's Epistle to the Corinthians: *And now abideth faith, hope, charity, these three, but the greatest of these is charity*. Right arm raised, he broke with tradition by repeating the words of the oath after the Chief Justice, rather than merely saying, "I do."

The flag flying over the Capitol was raised to the top of its pole as the new President gazed momentarily over the sea of faces spread out before him. This was the first inaugural to be widely broadcast over the radio, and Americans in homes, in shops, and in hotel lobbies and speakeasies huddled over their sets, seeking guidance and hope in Roosevelt's words. Parents had their children listen so that one day they could tell *their* children about this historic occasion. The President sounded hoarse at first, but his audience found themselves unexpectedly galvanized by the confident and vibrant voice that proclaimed in the lordly accent of Groton and Harvard:

> This is pre-eminently the time to speak the truth, frankly and boldly. Nor need we shrink from honestly facing conditions in our country today. This great Nation will endure as it has endured, will revive and will prosper. So, first of all, let me assert my firm belief that the only thing we have to fear is fear itself. . . .

Bareheaded and unsmiling in the light drizzle that had begun to fall, Roosevelt presented a realistic appraisal of America's plight: "Values have shrunken to fantastic levels . . . the means of exchange are frozen in the currents of trade; the withered leaves of industrial enterprise lie on every side; farmers find no markets for their produce; the savings of many years in thousands of families are gone . . . a host of unemployed citizens face the grim problem of existence, and an equally great number toil with little return. . . . Yet our distress comes from no failure of substance. . . . Plenty is at our doorstep, but a generous use of it languishes in the very sight of the supply. Primarily this is because rulers of the great exchange of mankind's goods have failed, through their own stubbornness and their own incompetence, have admitted their failure and abdicated. . . . The money changers have fled from their high seats in the temple of our civilization. . . .

"This Nation asks for action, and action now," Roosevelt declared amid the first burst of sustained applause from the subdued crowd. "Our greatest primary task is to put people to work. This is no unsolvable problem if we face it wisely and courageously. It can be accomplished in part by . . . treating the task as we would treat the emergency of a war. . . . We must act and act quickly." Responding to the excitement that crackled through his audience at the promise of action, Roosevelt outlined his plan for dealing with the crisis, speaking with a rising lilt in his voice and emphasizing his words with movements of his head.

Public works projects would be launched to employ the jobless, farm prices stimulated, funds made available to stem the tide of farm and home foreclosures, government spending curbed, banking and credit subjected to strict supervision to prevent speculation, and a sound currency guaranteed. Roosevelt regarded international relations as secondary to restoring the domestic economy, and he touched upon world policy only once, to "dedicate this Nation to the policy of the good neighbor—the neighbor who resolutely respects himself and, because he does so, respects the rights of others." Congress would be immediately summoned into special session to approve the measures required to get the stricken nation moving again. But Roosevelt raised the specter of dictatorship if Congress failed to act quickly on these recommendations:

"I shall ask the Congress for the one remaining instrument to meet the crisis—broad Executive power to wage war against the emergency, as great as the power that would be given me if we were in fact invaded by a foreign foe," he concluded. The American people "want direct, vigorous action. They have asked for discipline and direction under leadership. They have made me the present instrument of their wishes. In the spirit of the gift I take it."

The crowd roared its approval. The new President tossed back his head in a soon-to-be-familiar gesture and his face brightened with an incandescent smile. As he entered his car to lead the inaugural parade back to the White House, he responded to the cheering by clasping his hands over his head in the gladiator's gesture of triumph.

The Roosevelt Revolution had begun.

I
A FAMILY ALBUM

YOUNG FRANKLIN ROOSEVELT was awakened by a strange light outside his bedroom window. Grotesque shadows danced on the ceiling of his room, and he could hear a far-off murmuring that seemed to be coming closer. Throwing off his covers, the boy, then nearly eleven, raced to the window to see a line of torches flickering in the brisk wind blowing off the Hudson River. The red glare revealed a large crowd, some walking, some on horseback, some in creaking farm wagons, coming up the driveway to Springwood, the Roosevelt family estate, about two miles south of the village of Hyde Park, New York. It was Election Night, 1892, and the local Democrats were celebrating the reelection of Grover Cleveland at the home of James Roosevelt, the President's good friend and leading supporter in the district.

Without waiting to put on a robe, Franklin ran downstairs to join his father on the porch as he welcomed his happy neighbors. Someone threw the lad an old buffalo robe from a wagon to ward off the chill and, blue eyes reflecting the flames, he experienced the never-to-be-forgotten excitement of his first political torchlight parade. "I had a perfectly grand evening," he recalled more than a half century later.

Yet James and Sara Roosevelt had no intention of their only son's ever going into politics. Running for office was not a career for gentlemen, even though James's distant cousin Theodore had startled the family by getting elected to the state legislature in 1880. In fact, the year before his son's birth, James had gone to a New York State Democratic convention to *prevent* his neighbors from nominating him for Congress. "Did I ever think when he was little that Franklin might be President?" his mother once replied to an interviewer's query. "Never, oh never! That was the last thing I should have imagined for him or that he should be in public life of any sort." She hoped that he would become a country squire like his father and grandfather, content to live a quiet life beside the Hudson. "The highest ideal I could hold up before our son [was] to grow to be like his father, straight and honorable, just and kind, an upstanding American."

Franklin Roosevelt was born at Springwood on January 30, 1882. Throughout his life he was a fighter, but he almost lost his first fight, the fight for life itself. Sara Roosevelt's birth pangs had started on the night of the twenty-ninth, and she writhed in labor all the next day, her moans mixing with the wind whistling about the old house. As the lamps were being lit in the upstairs bedroom, James Roosevelt pleaded with Dr. Edward H. Parker to do something to ease his wife's agony. Taking desperate measures, the physician placed a cone over Sara's face and administered a dose of chloroform; when it did not provide relief, the dosage was increased. Suddenly her lips turned blue, her pulse flickered, and she sank into a coma. The cone was hurriedly snatched away—but it was feared that both mother and child had already been lost.

Nevertheless, at twenty-eight, Sara's heart was strong, and about an hour later she gave birth to a son. The baby was limp and blue and the customary slap across the rump was not sufficient to set him bawling in protest. Years later, Sara recalled that "the nurse said she never expected the baby to be alive and was surprised to find that he was." Gradually, he began to stir, and uttering a lusty cry, seemed none the worse for his hesitant entry into the world. As soon as mother and child were resting comfortably in the big mahogany bed, the doctor went downstairs to assure the anxious father that all was well. Exhausted but elated, James took out his wife's diary and wrote: "At quarter to nine my Sallie had a splendid large baby boy. He weighs 10 lbs without clothes."

Recovering rapidly from her ordeal, Sara—known to family and friends as Sallie—found her son "plump, pink and nice." Although at first afraid of dropping the infant, she insisted on feeding and bathing and dressing him herself. "Every mother ought to learn to care for her own baby," she once said, "whether she can afford to delegate the task to someone else or not." Because of the difference in their ages—the fifty-four-year-old James was twenty-six years older than his wife—they realized that he would probably be their only child and were doting and protective parents. For nearly two months, however, the boy had no name.

Playing with "Baby," as his mother called him, Sara and James discussed possible names for their son. James wished him christened Isaac, after his father, thereby continuing a cycle of James-Isaac traditional since 1692 in his branch of the Roosevelt family. Sara usually acquiesced in her husband's wishes, but she "detested" the name Isaac and insisted that Baby be called Warren Delano, after her father. She would have had her way except for the objection of her brother, Warren Delano, Jr. His son and namesake had recently died, and he wrote his sister that he "could not bear it" to hear another child called by that name. And so, on March 20, 1882, the boy was christened Franklin Delano Roosevelt, for Sara's favorite uncle, Franklin Hughes Delano, at the chapel of St. James' Episcopal Church, in Hyde Park.* Franklin's godparents were William H. Forbes, Sara's brother-in-law, and her good friends Eleanor Blodgett and Elliott Roosevelt, who was also James's fourth cousin. "Baby was quite good and lovely . . . we were all proud of him," she wrote in her diary.

Sara breast-fed Franklin for a year, and all her attention was focused upon him. She continued to call him Baby, and her diary proudly records every stage of his development. At three months, he was vaccinated by Dr. Parker, a process that had to be repeated eight times before it was successful. Not long afterward, Franklin was put into short dresses which "were more comfortable as he likes to kick and feel free to move about." And then she noted that he had "cut two little teeth that show just a little." The entries now came with increasing rapidity. "Baby . . . laughs all the time. . . . Baby went to his first party yesterday. . . . Baby wanted to dance and I could hardly hold him. . . . Baby tries to imitate Budgy [the dog] and the cats, and manages to say a semblance of Papa and Mama." That was on November 11, 1882. Two months later, Sara noted that as she and James were preparing for a trip, "Baby takes quite an interest in our packing and stands up against the trunks." And on May 17, 1883, she wrote: "Baby walked quite alone. He is quite proud of his accomplishment."

By the time of Franklin's birth, several generations of Roosevelts had made their homes in the Hudson River Valley or were linked to it by ties of blood and marriage. The family's beginnings in America are shrouded in mystery, however. "All I know about the origin of the Roosevelt family in this country," Franklin, one of the clan's more assiduous genealogical students, once said, "is that all branches bearing the name are apparently descended from Claes Martenszen van Rosenvelt, who came from Holland sometime before 1648—even the year is uncertain. Where he came from in Holland I do not know nor do I know who his parents were. . . ."

Like many immigrants to America before and since, Claes shed all his yesterdays on the Atlantic passage. No one knows whether he was tall or short, light or dark, or how old he was when he arrived in New Amster-

---

* FDR was christened in the chapel in the village of Hyde Park rather than the church itself, which was unheated during the winter months.

dam, the straggling Dutch settlement at the tip of Manhattan. Because of the mystery surrounding the family's founding father, some Roosevelts—always flippant about their ancestors—have suggested that he may have been a rogue "two leaps before the bailiff," as Alice Roosevelt Longworth once said. Asked upon one occasion if the family might not have originally been Jewish, Franklin replied: "In the dim, distant past, they may have been Jews or Catholics or Protestants. What I am more interested in is whether they were good citizens and believers in God. I hope they were both."

One of the few clues to Claes's past is his name, which, rendered into English, is Nicholas, son of Martin, of the Rose Field. In those days, Dutchmen took in addition to their baptismal name that of their father and the locality from which they came. The family name, which was spelled in a dozen different ways in the old records—Roosinffelt, Rosewelt, Rosvelt, and Rasswelt among others—indicates that the ancestral home of the Roosevelts was on the island of Tholen, at the mouth of the Rhine, where there was once a tract of land known as the *rosen velt*, or field of roses, and where there once lived a Van Rosevelt family, which was prominent in the district. Their family motto, *Qui Plantavit Curabit* —He Who Has Planted Will Preserve—has been adopted by the American Roosevelts.

Soon after their arrival, Claes and his wife, Jannetje, believed to be the daughter of an Englishman named Thomas Samuels who had emigrated to the Netherlands, bought a 48-acre farm, or *bouwerie*, a few miles beyond the wooden pallisade that gave Wall Street its name and nestled against the slopes of Murray Hill. Claes and Jannetje had six children, five of whom grew to adulthood. Nicholas, their sole surviving son and the last common ancestor of both Theodore and Franklin Roosevelt, was the first of the family to be linked with the Hudson Valley where he became a fur trader. With the profits earned from the fur trade, he returned to New York, opened a flour mill, began buying real estate and, entering politics, was elected alderman. It was also during this period that the "van" disappeared from the family name and its various spellings were standardized as Roosevelt. Nicholas had two sons, Johannes, or John, progenitor of the Oyster Bay branch of the family, and Jacobus, or James, founder of the Hyde Park branch.

Isaac, the fifth son of Jacobus, who was born in 1726, was the most widely renowned member of the family until Theodore Roosevelt charged up San Juan Hill into the White House. Banker, businessman, politician, and member through marriage of the Hudson River aristocracy, he risked his neck and fortune for the cause of American independence in contrast to many members of his class who remained loyal to King George III. Known in the family annals as "The Patriot," he was not in the first rank of the Founding Fathers, but performed some of the day-to-day tasks that made independence a reality. He served in the New York Provincial Congress, which took over the reins of government in 1775, and was one of the city's first two state senators. When independence was won, he was an outspoken supporter of the Constitution and a leader in the fight for ratification.

Isaac's son James set his branch of the family on the road to Hyde Park. Like his father, he devoted himself to the family sugar refinery, expanding and managing his extensive real estate holdings, but he lacked the acquisitiveness and vision of the older man. James loved country life, and in 1818 he bought an estate, Mount Hope, situated on the east side of the Albany Post Road, just north of Poughkeepsie, where he had studied law as a young man. James spent his summers there while his bachelor son Isaac lived at Mount Hope the year round.

This second Isaac Roosevelt was an anomaly for the family—a shy and retiring Roosevelt. He had studied medicine but did not practice, because, it was said, he could not stand the sight of blood. The enormous vitality of the Roosevelts seemed to have waned in James and completely played itself out in his feckless and hypochondriacal son. Gerald W. Johnson, one of Franklin Roosevelt's biographers, apparently had James and Isaac in mind when he wrote of the President's ancestors: "They were simple, worthy people, intelligent without genius, decent without saintliness, educated without erudition, not slothful in business, but not titans of industry—in short, admirable, but not inspiring."

And then, in 1827, Dr. Isaac surprised everyone by taking a wife, at the age of thirty-seven. His bride was nineteen-year-old Mary Rebecca Aspinwall, niece of his father's third wife and a member of one of America's most vibrant families. Unlike James and Isaac Roosevelt, who were content to live on inherited wealth, the Aspinwalls were merchant princes who sent their ships around the world. As Franklin Roosevelt was to point out, it was through such marriages as this that the Roosevelt family "stock [was] kept virile and abreast of the times," while many of New York's old families lost their dynamism. It also reduced the percentage of Dutch blood in the Roosevelt veins, and although the President's aides used to say that his "Dutch was up" when he was angry, it has been calculated that he was only about 3 percent Dutch.

In 1828, a year after their marriage, the couple's first son was born at Mount Hope and named James. More than a half century later, he fathered a future President. Now blessed with a family, Dr. Isaac decided that the time had come to establish his own home and purchased property to the north of Mount Hope and on the river side of the Post Road. He called the place Rosedale and built a house shrouded in the trees, where the family lived in seclusion. Young James Roosevelt had a rather lonely childhood. He was an only child until a brother, John, was born, when he was twelve; and his father had a morbid determination to avoid contact with his neighbors. A bright and conscientious student, he was graduated from Union College, in Schenectady, in 1847, at the age of nineteen.

Supported by his mother, he overcame Dr. Isaac's objections and departed on a grand tour of Europe during the revolutionary year of 1848. In Italy, according to a family tradition, James joined Giuseppe Garibaldi's Red Shirts, who were struggling for the unification of the country. As his son later told the story, James became friendly with a mendicant priest with whom he spoke only Latin, and together they had gone on a walking tour of Italy. "They came to Naples and found the city besieged by Garibaldi's army," Franklin Roosevelt told an aide. "They both enlisted in the army, wore a red shirt for a month or so, and tiring of it, as there seemed to be little action, went to Garibaldi's tent and asked if they could receive their discharge. Garibaldi thanked the old priest and my father and the walking tour was resumed by them."

Byronic adventuring done, James entered Harvard Law School upon his return home—the first Roosevelt to do so—and was graduated in 1851. He did not long practice law, abandoning it for the coal-and-railroad business. Vice-president of the Delaware and Hudson Railroad, head of a shipping company that operated steamers on Lake Champlain and Lake George, and owner of considerable real estate near Duluth, James appeared the model of a conservative businessman. But he was also a daring gambler—a trait inherited by his son. He took part in several speculative ventures that would have placed him in the front rank of American moguls had they succeeded. The most ambitious plan involved building an inter-ocean canal through Nicaragua. Fund raising and preliminary construction got underway, but work on the waterway was halted after investment capital dried up in the wake of an economic depression. When the canal was finally built, it was constructed in Panama, rather than Nicaragua—and by another Roosevelt.

Following a common practice among the Dutchess County branch of the Roosevelt family, who married Howlands and Aspinwalls, James chose twenty-two-year-old Rebecca Howland as his bride, in 1853. Upon the death of his father, ten years later, James inherited Mount Hope, but he and Rebecca were not happy with the place. The problem was resolved for them when the house was destroyed by fire while the owners were on a visit to Europe. James sold the property to the state of New York, which added it to the grounds of the Hudson River State Hospital—the "Lunatic Asylum," as it was known locally. Moving two miles up the Post Road, he purchased Springwood and the surrounding 110 acres along the Hudson in 1867. Originally built in 1826, the commodious clapboard house, with its three-story tower, stained-glass windows, and overhanging eaves was a typical example of the style known as Hudson River Bracketed. Over the years, James increased his holdings to some thirteen hundred rolling and wooded acres. From the veranda of his home, the view extended over the tall treetops to the long reach of the river and the purple Catskills beyond.

The illusion of English country life that prevailed along the river fitted James Roosevelt as snugly as his pearl-gray gloves. With his muttonchop whiskers, urbane and unruffled manner, and ever-present riding crop, he might have stepped full-blown from Anthony Trollope's Barsetshire novels. Herds of fat dairy cattle grazed on his land, and there were undulating fields of grain surrounded by low stone walls and a garden famed for its roses. James prided himself on his fine stable, liking nothing better than to drive over the Dutchess County roads behind one of his fast trotters. He bred Gloucester, the first horse to trot a mile in less than two-twenty, but becoming convinced that racing was crooked and no longer a sport for gentlemen, he sold Gloucester to Senator Leland Stanford, of California.†

James had the same aversion toward politics, but with a country squire's sense of community responsibility he took a paternalistic interest in the affairs of the district. He served on the Hyde Park school board, was a member of the board of managers of the Asylum, and although baptized in the Dutch Reformed Church, was a vestryman and warden of St. James' Episcopal Church. James Roosevelt not only belonged to the best society, he set the standard for belonging as one of the sponsors of New York City's exclusive Patriarch's Ball. Not everyone was charmed, however. "He tried to pattern himself on Lord Lansdowne, sideburns and all," one disapproving relative has been quoted as saying, "but what he really looked like was Lansdowne's coachman."

After a year of marriage, Rebecca gave birth to their only child. They decided to name the boy after his father, but James, who disliked the appendage "Junior," gave him the distinctive name of James Roosevelt Roosevelt. Throughout most of his life he was known to family and friends as Rosy Roosevelt. Rosy was a handsome and intelligent youth who graduated from Columbia with honors. He studied law but never bothered to finish, because he married Helen Astor, daughter of *the* Mrs. Astor. Needless to say, Rosy Roosevelt and his wife were among the Four Hundred of New York's social elite who could be accommodated in the ballroom of her Fifth Avenue mansion. Shortly before her son's marriage, Rebecca's

† Gloucester was killed in a railroad accident before he ran a single race under Stanford's colors. Years later, someone gave FDR the horse's tail, and he hung it in his bedroom in the White House.

health began to fail and she died in 1876. With his wife dead and his son married, James was at loose ends—until he met Sara Delano.

The Hyde Park and Oyster Bay branches of the Roosevelt family were much closer in those days than they were to become, and James was a frequent guest at the home of the widowed Mrs. Theodore Roosevelt, Sr., in New York. In fact, he was considered a possible suitor for the hand of Mrs. Roosevelt's eldest daughter, Anna. Invited to a small dinner party one night in the spring of 1880—Mrs. Roosevelt's elder son Theodore was preparing for his graduation from Harvard, and Elliott, her youngest, was away on a hunting trip—he was captivated by Anna's friend Sara Delano. "He talked to her the whole time," Mrs. Roosevelt noted with amusement after her guests had gone. "He never took his eyes off her!"

And Sara Delano was well worth looking at. Tall and stately, she had dark eyes, an abundance of auburn hair, and classic features marred ever so slightly by a strong chin—indicative of stubbornness. A few years later, she might have served as a model for Charles Dana Gibson's coolly elegant idealization of the American girl. James and Sara were distantly related, and although they had never met, he had undoubtedly heard of the five beautiful Delano girls, of whom Sara, at twenty-five, was next to youngest. James was, however, acquainted with her father, Warren Delano, through joint service on various corporation boards. He invited Sara to visit Springwood, and before her week-long stay was over they had reached an understanding—even though James was twice Sara's age and had a son as old as she.

In later years, Sara often insisted that her son Franklin was "a Delano, not a Roosevelt at all," and as he grew older his face did take on a remarkable resemblance to that of his mother. With the slightest encouragement and the ease of long practice, she could recite her family's patrician pedigree back to no less than William the Conqueror. The first of the clan in America was Philippe de la Noye, a young Huguenot who came to the Plymouth colony in 1621 with the second shipload of settlers. The Delanos were a seafaring family—whalers, merchant skippers, and privateersmen—and they sailed from New Bedford and nearby Fairhaven to ports in Europe and South America and beat their way around Cape Horn to the Orient. Warren Delano, Sara's father, made his fortune in the China trade before he was thirty. Her mother was Catherine Lyman, who came from another prominent Massachusetts family. Returning home after having accumulated a sizable fortune, Warren Delano purchased Algonac, an estate on the western side of the Hudson near Newburgh, about twenty miles south of Hyde Park, where Sara Delano was born, on September 21, 1854.

The financial panic of 1857 wiped out Delano's investments, and he returned to China to make a second—and larger—fortune in the opium trade. Within a few years, he had done so well that he brought his entire family out to join him in Hong Kong. The four-month voyage on the square-rigger *Surprise* was the high point of Sara's childhood, and her son never wearied of her tales of life at sea on the long voyage around the Cape of Good Hope.‡ She made friends with the sailors, and long afterward could still sing their chanteys in a rollicking voice. The Delano children's lives were run much as they had been at home, and the physical presence of China hardly intruded upon them. Except for the servants, they had very little contact with the Chinese, as if they were separated from the world about them by a transparent but impenetrable wall. When Sara was ten, she was sent home to complete her education. Over the next several years, the Delanos alternated between Algonac and Europe, where they lived in the glamorous Paris of the Second Empire. They had an apartment overlooking the Bois, and Sara frequently saw the beautiful Empress Eugenie riding in her carriage.

Looking back over her long life to her first visit to Springwood, Sara regarded it as the most important thing that had ever happened to her. "If I had not come then, I should now be 'old Miss Delano' after a rather sad life," she once told her son. She faced spinsterhood not through any lack of suitors, however. There was "an avalanche of young men," according to her father, but none of them met the high standards he set for his daughter. Warren Delano was a father in the classic Victorian mold; as far as he was concerned, the men who wanted to marry his daughter were not good enough for her. They were too young or too old, or lacked social standing or character, or were obvious fortune hunters interested only in the million dollars she stood to inherit. Very much the dutiful daughter, Sara did her father's bidding, and one by one dismissed her suitors*—until James Roosevelt came along. Perhaps she accepted him because he reminded her of her father.

When James announced his intention to marry Sara, Warren Delano was taken aback by this May-and-October romance but could object only on the grounds of the prospective bridegroom's age, for he met all the qualifications he had set for a son-in-law and they saw eye to eye on most matters except for politics. Delano was a staunch Republican, while

‡ FDR later purchased a model of the *Surprise* and hung a painting of the vessel in his study at Springwood.
* Stanford White, the distinguished architect, was said to have been one of them. Warren Delano called him the "red-headed trial" and disliked him. White was fatally shot in 1906 by Harry K. Thaw, who accused him of philandering with his wife, a former show girl named Evelyn Nesbit. For a fuller discussion of the relationship between SDR and White, see Nona S. Ferdon, *Franklin D. Roosevelt: A Psychological Interpretation of His Childhood and Youth*, unpublished Ph.D. dissertation, University of Hawaii (microfilm in Library of Congress).

James, after supporting the Union cause during the Civil War, had, unlike the Oyster Bay Roosevelts, returned to the Democratic faith of his fathers. This was not out of any political consciousness or sympathy with liberalism—there was little to tell the parties apart on that score—but because his views coincided with those of the southern landed gentry that had led the party before the conflict. As for Delano, he was fond of saying that while not all Democrats were horse thieves, all horse thieves were Democrats. But he liked James, having once told his daughter that Mr. Roosevelt had convinced him of the theretofore unlikely possibility that a Democrat might also be a gentleman.

And so Sara Delano and James Roosevelt were married, at Algonac on October 7, 1880. Following the ceremony, the bridal pair were driven away in the Delano coach, but at Milton, about halfway between Algonac and Springwood, they transferred to the Roosevelt carriage, which was waiting for them. Taking the reins from his coachman, James drove his bride to her new home.

Probably no President of the United States had a happier and more secure childhood than Franklin Roosevelt. "He was brought up in a beautiful frame," an aunt observed many years later. Misfortunes were passed over in silence among the Hudson River aristocracy. Money was never mentioned and neither was social ambition—although both were accepted as the norm. Achievement was taken for granted and so were shortcomings. The new in literature, art, and the theater was considered daring and not discussed. Tradesmen touched their caps and kept their place. It was a comfortable world—a world of hospitality, horses, and hounds, that flowed at the unhurried pace of the Hudson itself.

Child psychology was unheard of in that day, but the boy's mother, who was charged with the details of his upbringing, followed a program aimed at "keeping Franklin's mind on nice things, on a high level; yet . . . in such a way that Franklin never realized that he was following any bent but his own." It seemed to have worked well, for he was healthy, happy, and tractable. Except for an attack of typhoid when he was seven, he hardly ever suffered a serious illness.

Franklin's own earliest memory was of nearly drowning in a shipwreck when he was little more than three years old. The Roosevelts were on their way home from a family trip to Europe when their vessel, the White Star liner *Germanic*, was struck by a severe gale on Easter Sunday 1885. A near-tidal wave smashed bulkheads, extinguished the boiler fires, and flooded the Roosevelts' cabin. Convinced that the ship was sinking, Sara wrapped her son up in her fur coat and firmly declared: "Poor little boy. If he must go down, he is going down warm." Enjoying the excitement, Franklin later recalled that he was far more concerned about his playthings than anything else. "Mama! Mama! Save my jumping jack!" he cried as his favorite toy bobbed on the fast-rising water.

Without brothers or sisters to compete for his parents' attention, Franklin was at the center of their world. They tried not to spoil him, and his life was closely but lovingly regulated. Sara kept him in shoulder-length golden curls and dresses until he was five, and then insisted that he wear the kilts of the Murray clan, to which she was related, complete with sporran and jaunty Highland cap. Franklin was almost eight before he succeeded in persuading his mother to buy him some English sailor suits with trousers, and he was nearly nine before he was allowed to bathe himself. Throughout his childhood, he had to meet the standards established by his mother, and even after he became President, she was always warning him to dress warmly or wear overshoes in inclement weather. Sara and Franklin had a warm, loving relationship, and she provided him with the security, overwhelming self-assurance, and aura of personal inviolability that he carried with him throughout his life.

Nevertheless, the boy appears to have woven at an early age a cloak of amiability that he donned with increasing frequency to avoid clashes with his mother, and to keep his innermost thoughts and desires to himself. The first recorded appearance occurred when he rebelled against the tight schedule of activities laid down for him. He got up at seven, had breakfast at eight, studied with his governess for two or three hours, and then was dismissed until lunch, at one. Another round of lessons followed until four, when he was allowed to be on his own again. One day, Sara noted a certain sadness in Franklin's manner, and asking why he appeared so unhappy was told that he longed for "freedom." For a day, the boy was allowed to come and go as he pleased except for mealtimes. He returned home "a very dirty, tired youngster," Sara noted, but he did not say how he had spent his "freedom."

Despite his strong attachment to his mother, there was no rivalry between the boy's parents for his affection, and he idolized his father—whom he called "Popsy." Although old enough to be the lad's grandfather, James enjoyed a close relationship with him, and no question was too troublesome or too unimportant for him to answer. "His father never laughed at him," reported Sara. "With him, yes—often." Upon one occasion when Sara felt that the boy should be disciplined for some breach of the peace, she turned the matter over to her husband, who called Franklin aside and said: "Consider yourself spanked." James spent a good deal of time with Franklin and taught him to swim, to sail, to fish, and to ride. In winter, they went coasting on a nearby slope and his uncle John Roosevelt took him out in his speedy iceboat. Franklin proved to be an excellent horseman and was soon given a lively Welsh pony of his own—with the stipulation that he was to be responsible for its care and grooming. By the time he was eight and dressed like a young lord of the manor, he was riding the twenty miles from Springwood to Algonac at his father's side without tiring.

As in the case of most only children, Franklin spent much of his time in the company of adults. He was a shy but precocious child and instinctively learned the way to charm grownups. When an aunt praised him for his tact, the little boy proudly burst out: "Yes, I'm just chuck full of tacks!" Usually a good-humored lad, he would, however, get angry if he lost a game, and Sara soon decided to teach him a lesson. They were playing Steeplechase, with toy horses, and her horse won several times in succession. Franklin immediately begged for a switch in mounts, which was granted, but Sara won again. When he sulked in "furious silence," she quickly ended the game and told him that until he learned to take a beating gracefully, she would not play with him again. "It was the last indication any one ever saw of a lack of sportsmanship in Franklin," she added.

The boy's rebellion usually took a subtler form. Although the Roosevelts were religious in a conventionally Victorian way, Franklin became bored with the regularity of Sunday church services. Occasionally, he avoided attendance by pleading a sudden attack of illness—an attack that usually disappeared by afternoon. The attacks became so common that his mother once noted that "Franklin has what his dear Popsy calls a Sunday headache." Similar subterfuges were adopted to avoid piano and drawing lessons. Paradoxically, when he was really hurt, he usually kept it to himself, so as not to worry his parents.

Franklin's parents tried to instill in their son a sense of stewardship and good manners—of *noblesse oblige*—rather than an interest in the grubbier aspects of moneymaking. In those days, Sara said, "the older members of the family carefully kept away from the children all traces of sadness and trouble," and the Roosevelts followed this precept in rearing their son. Carefully compartmentalizing his life, James periodically went to New York to tend to his business affairs, but the Roosevelts never discussed money in the boy's presence. Franklin liked to tell a story that illustrated his father's attitude to the rich parvenus that had come to live beside the river. At lunch one day, Sara reported that they had received a dinner invitation from one of the Vanderbilts, who had recently completed an elaborate Renaissance-style mansion just up the road from Springwood. Having heard much about the opulence of the place, Sara was curious to see it, but James adamantly rejected the invitation. "If we accept, we shall have to have these people to our home," he declared.

From the time that he could perch on his father's shoulder, Franklin was taken by James on his daily round of the farm. When he was old enough, these expeditions were conducted on horseback. Every day, they rode over the clipped lawns and meadows, down the driveway to the Post

Road, and across to the fields that were also part of the Roosevelt holdings. Franklin learned to love the land deeply, especially the trees, for his
father would not permit one to be cut unless it was decayed. Fondly
recalling his childhood from the vantage point of the White House, he
saw "a small boy [who] took a special delight in climbing an old tree . . .
to pick and eat ripe sickle pears. In the spring of the year, he sailed his toy
boats in the surface water of the melting snow. In the summer with his
dogs he dug into woodchuck holes. And he used to lie flat between the
strawberry rows and eat sun-warmed strawberries—the best in the world."

The sea was also in Franklin's blood. He listened raptly as his grandfather Warren Delano spun out tales of clipper ships and whalers skip-
pered by Delanos, and on visits to the family's ancestral home, in
Fairhaven, pored over the canvas-backed logs of whalers and merchantmen
that he found stowed away in the attic. He haunted the old stone wharf
jutting out into the Acushnet River, where the last of New Bedford's
once-great fleet of whaling ships rocked gently on the tide, their tall
masts soaring above the granite warehouses. And Franklin thrilled to the
adventures of the Bulloch brothers, relatives of the Oyster Bay branch
of the Roosevelts, who had served in the Confederate Navy and were still
regarded by some members of the family as "pirates."† He began to
dream of attending Annapolis and a naval career.

Before he could see over the top of the wheel of his father's fifty-one-
foot schooner, the *Half-Moon*, he was taking the helm of the vessel, even
in blowing weather. At sixteen, he was given his own boat, a twenty-one-
foot knockabout, the *New Moon*, in which he explored the rugged shoreline of the Bay of Fundy, near the family summer place on Campobello Island, in New Brunswick. The Roosevelts began going there shortly after
his birth, preferring the simple life of the island to the giddy social whirl
of Newport. Years later, as assistant Secretary of the Navy, he found his
knowledge of these shorelines useful. Sailing in a destroyer to inspect
naval facilities in Frenchman Bay, on the Maine coast, Franklin suggested
that inasmuch as he knew these waters, he should pilot the vessel through
the dangerous passage between Campobello and the mainland. The destroyer's captain, Lieutenant William F. Halsey, Jr., reluctantly yielded
the conn, worried that this "white-flanneled yachtsman" might pile his
ship up on the rocks. Halsey was surprised to find that Roosevelt "knew
his business" and took the ship safely through the treacherous channel.

† James D. and Irvine Bulloch were brothers of Georgia-born Martha Bulloch,
Theodore Roosevelt's mother. James, who had been an officer in the U. S. Navy, was
chief of the Confederate Secret Service in Europe and directed the building of the *Alabama* and other raiders. Irvine sailed in the *Alabama* as a midshipman. They were
among the few Southerners denied amnesty following the end of the Civil War, and
remained in Europe.

Franklin was also an enthusiastic naturalist. When he turned eleven, his father gave him a small-caliber rifle after he had promised not to bag birds in nesting season or to take more than one of each species native to the Hudson Valley. The collection quickly grew in size and variety, and at first the boy tried stuffing and mounting the specimens himself, but he never became skilled in taxidermy, so the work was turned over to a professional. Delighted by his grandson's interest in birds, Warren Delano gave him a life membership in the American Museum of Natural History. The gold-edged membership card was put to unexpected use one summer in London. Franklin and his tutor, Arthur Dumper, had gone on a visit to the South Kensington Museum to see the elaborate bird collection but were told the place was closed to the general public. The Prince of Wales, the future King Edward VII, was expected shortly to dedicate a new wing, and admission was by invitation only. Thinking quickly, Franklin produced his membership card in the New York museum and slipped it to Dumper, who flashed it before one of the doormen. Impressed, he waved the Americans in and they were treated like visiting dignitaries.

Franklin grew up without much companionship from children of his own age. His half niece and half nephew, Helen and Taddy (James Roosevelt Roosevelt, Jr.), the children of Rosy Roosevelt, who resided nearby, were occasional playmates. Various Roosevelt and Delano children visited Hyde Park, among them a painfully shy little girl named Anna Eleanor Roosevelt, the daughter of Franklin's godfather, Elliott Roosevelt, and his beautiful wife, the former Anna Hall. Nearly three years younger than Franklin, she stood bashfully in a doorway sucking on a finger until the exuberant boy set about entertaining her by crawling "around the nursery . . . bearing me on his back," as she later recalled. But there were periods when he had no playmates, and one wonders at his thoughts as he rode with his father past the village children playing in the road. One of them later said that he was "an object of sympathy," because he spent most of his time with his parents.

Franklin's closest friend was Archie Rogers, the son of Archibald Rogers, one of John D. Rockefeller's associates, who lived a mile and a half away at an estate called Crumwold. Together, they rambled over the fields in summer and built tunnels and fortifications in the snow during the blizzard of 1888. Archie died of diphtheria the following year, and this was Franklin's first brush with the reality of death. No one knows what the lonely child's reaction was to the death of his closest friend, but Archie's younger brother, Edmund, became Franklin's companion. They built a tree house among the hemlocks which they pretended was the deck of a ship on a voyage to far-off lands, and launched a raft that promptly sank, taking their fishing equipment to the bottom of the Hudson along with it. When he did have visitors, Franklin habitually ordered his playmates about, which prompted Sara to suggest that the other children be also allowed to give orders. "Mummie," he replied, "if I didn't give the orders, nothing would happen."

By the time he was five, he could write English well enough—with the aid of someone to spell the words for him—to send his mother a hand-delivered note which read:

> Dear Sallie
> I am very sorry you have a cold and you are in bed I played with Mary today for a little while I hope by tomorrow you will be able to be up I am glad tosay that my cold is better your loving
>
> Franklin Delano Roosevelt

The youngster's formal education began in October 1888, when he was invited to join the Rogers boys in studying German with their governess for two hours each day at Crumwold. Franklin picked up basic German from these classes, and his knowledge of the language was improved by a Fräulein Reinsberg, the first of a line of governesses to be installed at Springwood. He soon spoke the language with some facility and wrote his mother in German script: "I will show you that I can already write in German. But I shall always try to improve it, so that you will really be pleased." Fräulein Reinsberg, an intense, humorless woman who later had a nervous breakdown, was followed by Jeanne Sandoz, a young French-speaking Swiss, who proved to be Franklin's favorite teacher.‡

"More than anyone you laid the foundations of my education," he wrote Mlle. Sandoz many years later. The task was not always an easy one. Having outgrown his shyness, Franklin enjoyed playing the comedian. But Mlle. Sandoz was a talented teacher, and as she told the boy's mother, she was convinced "Frankie will distinguish himself." During the two years young Roosevelt was in her charge, she not only succeeded in providing him with a sound grounding in French* and other subjects but also injected a slight sense of social responsibility into a student sheltered from the harsh economic and social realities of the day. A hint of it showed through the breeziness of a composition written about ancient Egypt. "The working people had nothing," Franklin wrote. "The kings made them work so hard and gave them so little that by wingo! they nearly starved and by jinks! they had hardly any clothes so they died in the quadrillions."

‡ Mlle. Sandoz left the Roosevelts to marry, and Fräulein Reinsberg entered a sanitarium, so FDR often joked that he had driven one governess insane and another to matrimony.
* Although his accent was shaky, during World War II, he managed a forty-five-minute conversation with Gen. Charles de Gaulle, who refused to speak anything but French.

The boy was not only an omnivorous reader but soaked up information easily. Sara recalled reading aloud to him one day while Franklin lay sprawled at her feet, seemingly absorbed in his stamp collection. Suddenly, she snapped the book shut. "I don't think there is any point in my reading to you any more," she declared. "You don't hear me anyway." To prove her mistaken, Franklin unhesitatingly repeated word for word the entire last paragraph that his mother had read. When she expressed surprise, he replied: "Why, Mama, I would be ashamed of myself if I couldn't do at least two things at once."

Having read the usual books for boys, Franklin ransacked Springwood's well-stocked library. He liked books about the sea and naval affairs and, as a teenager, read Captain Alfred Thayer Mahan's books on sea power. He was also fond of Mark Twain, Kipling, and Parkman, and his appetite for facts was insatiable. He pored over copies of the *Illustrated London News*, which brought to Hyde Park the pageantry of a Europe ruled by unchallenged dynasties. One rainy afternoon, his mother discovered him propped up in bed reading his way through Webster's Unabridged Dictionary. The boy also had a passion for mechanical gadgets and photography; and as one writer has said, his mind was "like a jackdaw's nest, full of shiny bits of unrelated knowledge."

Franklin's knowledge of the world gained through reading, and his stamp collection was buttressed by considerable travel abroad. By the time he was fourteen, he had accompanied his parents on eight trips to Europe and had made repeated visits to England, France, Holland, Germany, and Italy. As James Roosevelt grew older and his health began to fail, the family went to the spa at Bad Nauheim with increasing frequency. In 1891, when Franklin was nine, he was enrolled at the local school for six weeks, his only experience of ordinary school life. "I go to public school with a lot of little mickies," he wrote a cousin. "We have German reading, German dictation, the history of Siegfried, and arithmetic in which I am up to '14 $\times$ 71', on paper, and I like it very much." Franklin was particularly interested in a course in map reading and military topography which had recently been instituted in the German schools at the order of Kaiser Wilhelm II. The German schoolmaster reported that he was "an unusually bright young fellow" with "an engaging manner" and was "one of the most popular children in the school."

Franklin also saw far more of his own country than most boys of his age. As a ranking railroad official, his father was entitled to his own private rail car—the corporate jet of the day—and often took his son along on inspection trips as far as upper Wisconsin, where the elder Roosevelt owned property. The high spot came in 1892, when James was appointed a New York commissioner to the Chicago world's fair. As soon as the family alighted from their private car, they were met by a conspicuous figure in full coachman's livery, including a tall hat and a long whip. "Cousin Jimmy, I am your cousin Clinton," said the man, who turned out to be a member of a branch of the Roosevelt family that had gone West. Now the proprietor of a large livery stable, he had the concession to provide transportation for official visitors to the fair. Cousin Clinton insisted on getting up on the box to personally drive his relatives to the hotel—and an aide to whom Franklin told the story guessed that the President's father enjoyed the experience more than his dignified mother.

When Franklin was five, James took him to the White House to meet his good friend President Cleveland. The President had offered James the post of Minister to Holland in return for his services to the Democratic party, but Roosevelt declined the appointment. Much to his satisfaction, his elder son, Rosy, who had made a handsome contribution to the party's coffers, was named by Cleveland as first secretary of the American Embassy in Vienna, and was later rewarded with a similar post in London after making a ten-thousand-dollar donation. Young Franklin remembered the President as being careworn and depressed. As James and his son rose to go, Cleveland put his hand on the boy's head and said: "My little man, I am making a strange wish for you. It is that you may never be President of the United States."

Sara Roosevelt kept Franklin under her wing as long as she could, but when the boy turned fourteen, in 1896, she was finally persuaded by her husband that the time had come to send him away to school. In fact, most boys of his social class went to boarding school at twelve. Thirteen years before, when Franklin was only a year old, his parents had visited James Lawrence, an old friend who lived at Groton, Massachusetts, about thirty-five miles north of Boston. Lawrence had told them about a new school that was being organized there and suggested they register their son for admittance when he was old enough. Impressed by the qualifications of the Reverend Endicott Peabody, headmaster of the proposed school, and the prominence of his backers, who included J. Pierpont Morgan, they put Franklin's name down even before the school was opened.

Before going off to Groton, Franklin went on a cycling trip through the Rhineland with his tutor, Arthur Dumper, in which his increasing proficiency in German was put to the test. One day they were arrested four times in succession for minor infractions of the strict laws of the German Empire: picking cherries from a tree overhanging the highway; taking their bicycles into a railroad station; riding into the fortified city of Strassburg after nightfall; and running over an unlucky goose, which cost them a five-mark fine. This put a crimp in their budget, for they had allowed only four marks a day for expenses. Living on black bread and cheese and sleeping in cheap country inns and peasant cottages, the travelers managed to stretch their remaining money to cover the trip, and Franklin proudly reported that he still had some cash on hand when he met his parents at Bad Nauheim.

In September 1896, shortly after the family's return from Europe, Sara and James sadly accompanied Franklin to Groton. They remained overnight to help him unpack and arrange his things in the spare quarters that were to be his home for the next four years, and left him in the care of the Reverend Mr. Peabody. "It is very hard to leave our darling boy," his mother confided to her diary after their return to the now strangely hushed rooms of Springwood. "James and I feel this parting very much."

II

OLD SCHOOL TIES

I AM GETTING along finely both mentally and physically,"
Franklin Roosevelt wrote his parents from Groton on September 18, 1896,
a few days after they had left him at school. Over the next several weeks,
similar assurances were received at Hyde Park—"I am getting along very
well with the fellows. . . . I have not had any warnings, latenesses or
[black] marks"—but Groton was a jolt for the boy. Without warning,
he had suddenly been plucked from the love and security of his family
and plunged into the casual brutalities of boarding school. For the first
time, he was not the center of a circle of admirers, but merely another of
a hundred or so brawling boys.

Roosevelt did not make an overwhelming impression upon Groton,
but the school had a lasting impact upon him. He spent four of his most
malleable years there, and throughout his life retained a cordial and respectful association with its headmaster, Endicott Peabody. At Harvard,
most of his friends were youths he had met at Groton, and he made periodic visits to the school. When he married, Peabody performed the ceremony, and when he was inaugurated as President, the Rector was called
to Washington to say a prayer. All four of his sons attended Groton, and
for many years he gave the debating prizes at the school. In future years,
many of Roosevelt's former schoolmates were to regard him as "a traitor
to his class" and the ideals of Groton, but as he later told Peabody:
"More than forty years ago you said in a sermon in the Old Chapel, something about not losing boyhood ideals in later life. Those were Groton
ideals—taught by you—I try not to forget—and your words are still with
me."

Groton's secluded setting was the only thing about the place that was comfortably reassuring to an uncertain and homesick youngster raised in the rolling Hudson River Valley. The handful of red-brick Georgian buildings—a dormitory, schoolhouse, gym, chapel, and a "fives" (handball) court—were laid out on three sides of a grassy plateau that sloped sharply down to the Nashua River. To the northward and westward, there was the blue haze of mountains, and except for a glimpse through the trees of Groton village, some two miles to the east, the school seemed cut off from the rest of the world.

Groton offered a muscular Christianity and a Spartan life. At Springwood, Franklin had a comfortable room overlooking the lawn, while at school he was lodged in a six-by-ten cubicle fitted with only the barest essentials and a curtain across the entrance, rather than a door. Each morning, the boys were awakened at seven o'clock by the steady clanging of a bell, and amid the shouted commands of the dormitory prefects, they plunged into a cold shower no matter what the season. Faces scrubbed, hair brushed, and nails clean, they trooped to breakfast at seven-thirty. Morning chapel followed at eight-fifteen, from which the boys went to their classes. The main meal of the day was served at noon—Franklin thought the food left something to be desired, writing home soon after his arrival that "we have [had] sausages or sausage-croquettes for the last three days." Classes and compulsory athletics filled the rest of the afternoon. Following another cold shower, the boys donned stiffly starched white collars and patent-leather shoes for supper, evening chapel, and study period.

From morning chapel to an evening handshake with each of the boys, Endicott Peabody reigned over the school like a benign despot. "You know he would be an awful bully if he weren't such a terrible Christian," Averell Harriman, who graduated from Groton nine years after Roosevelt, wrote his father. Born in 1857, the Rector was the product of one of New England's most prominent families. When his father moved to London after becoming a partner in Peabody & Morgan, a banking firm operated by George Peabody, of Baltimore, a distant relative, and J. P. Morgan, the boy was enrolled at Cheltenham, an English public school, and then went on to Trinity College, Cambridge. Rejecting a business career after a brief trial, young Peabody entered the Anglican ministry, but before his ordination, he accepted a call to Tombstone, in the Arizona Territory, where he was a great success as the town's Episcopal minister.

After six months in Tombstone, Peabody returned home to be ordained and to found Groton, which he patterned after Cheltenham and the other great English public schools. For fifty-six years, until his retirement, at the age of eighty-four, he ran the place as a reflection of himself. His model was Thomas Arnold, the headmaster of Rugby, as portrayed in

Tom Brown's School Days, and his mission was to reverse the decline of moral standards in post-Civil War America by producing a new class of patrician leaders inculcated with a strong sense of social responsibility. "Serve the Lord with gladness" was Peabody's message, and to the sons of the nation's social elite he preached this gospel of service—service to God, service to country, and service to mankind. "If some Groton boys do not enter political life and do something for our land, it won't be because they have not been urged," he declared.

With the exception of his parents, no one had a greater influence on the young Roosevelt than the Rector. Vigorous, hearty, and projecting a robust spirituality similar to that of his good friend Theodore Roosevelt, to whom he once offered a teaching post at Groton, he regarded the boys entrusted to his care as part of his family. Having little patience with skepticism and arguments over the finer points of theology, he transmitted to them a religious faith notable for its simplicity. Peabody "had a mind that was content with absolutes," according to Frank D. Ashburn, his biographer. "It is doubtful if the necessity for proof of the existence of God ever seriously troubled him." Young Roosevelt accepted this mixture of messianic idealism and simple pragmatism without difficulty, and throughout his life was content to follow the familiar litanies he had learned from the Rector. The dignified Anglicanism of Groton and St. James' in Hyde Park, which required no outward display of emotion, appealed to his own instinct to keep his innermost thoughts and feelings to himself.

Omnipotent and omnipresent, Peabody dominated Franklin Roosevelt's life during a critical stage in his development. One need not indulge in Freudian speculation to surmise that he assumed in the boy's mind the place of his father, who was receding into a twilight of old age and poor health. "I count it among the blessings of my life that it was given to me in my formative years to have the privilege of your guiding hand and the benefit of your inspiring example," he wrote Peabody after he became President. ". . . For all that you have been and are to me I owe a debt of gratitude."

Roosevelt is usually portrayed as an indifferent scholar, but at Groton he always ranked in the upper fourth or fifth of his class of nineteen. The course of study was rigidly classical, the masters taught by rule and rote, and paradoxically for a school designed to produce national leaders, American studies were almost ignored. Peabody and the masters did make an effort to acquaint the boys with the English classics by reading aloud to them each evening. In his first year, Franklin took Latin, Greek, English, and French literature, Greek and Roman history, Algebra, Science, and Sacred Studies. His first report card shows a creditable average of 7.79 out of a possible score of ten, and he received a perfect mark for Punctuality and 9.68 for Neatness. "Very good," wrote the Rector under Remarks. "He strikes me as an intelligent & faithful scholar & a good boy."

Out of his orbit for the first time, Franklin was not a leader at Groton. Having entered the school two years after his fellow third formers, he had difficulty in breaking into the established pattern of friendships. "When Father went to Groton at fourteen," said his daughter, Anna, "he no more knew how to get along with boys of his own age than the man in the moon." To make matters worse, his schoolmates thought he spoke with a sissified English accent—a souvenir of his travels abroad.*

Athletic prowess, rather than scholastic achievement, was the key to recognition at the school. "Instinctively, [Peabody] trusted a football player more than a non-football player, just as the boys did," Ashburn wrote. Franklin struggled to fit in, to enjoy an easy intimacy with his fellows, but he was only a spindly five feet three inches tall, too slight for football, baseball, or crew, the only sports that really mattered at Groton. Tennis and golf, at which he excelled, were not considered important.

Eager to conform and to prove he had the proper school spirit, he cheered himself hoarse at football games—informing his parents that he was "ready to stand on my coconut!" after a victory over St. Mark's—and accepted the thankless task of manager of the baseball team. The one sport in which he distinguished himself was the high kick, a game peculiar to Groton. A tin pan was suspended from the roof of the gym, and each of the fifteen contestants kicked at it as it was gradually raised. Franklin won with a kick of seven feet, three and a half inches, or two feet over his head. "At every kick I landed on my *neck* on the left side so the result is that the whole left side of my body is sore and my left arm is swollen," he wrote home.

One of Franklin's major problems at Groton was his nephew, Taddy, who was in the form ahead of him and was always getting into trouble. It did nothing for the boy's prestige to be known as Taddy's "Uncle Frank" —but as he said, "I would sooner be Uncle Frank, than Nephew Rosy." Peabody had forbidden "fagging" at Groton, the system which allowed the bigger boys to lord it over their juniors, but the boys had developed their own swift punishments for those who deviated from what was considered the norm. The offender was given the "bootbox" (painfully doubled up inside a small locker by his seniors) or "pumped" (bent face upward over a lavatory trough while buckets of water were flung over him until he felt as if he were drowning). Taddy was "bootboxed" and "pumped," but not Franklin. Whatever his inner struggles, his quicksilver charm ensured acceptance, and he cultivated an acceptable accent with a

* Eleanor Roosevelt said he also had difficulty in pronouncing "Schenectady" and "Poughkeepsie."

broad "a" and disappearing "r" at the end of words. Sensing that the good behavior that won the approval of adults and the Punctuality Prize was doing him no good with his fellows, he carefully made a show of testing school discipline. It was almost with a note of triumph that he wrote home: "I have served off my first black mark today, and I am very glad I got it as I was thought to have no school-spirit before."

Peabody often invited outside speakers to Groton to expose his students to the outside world. Among them was a Mr. Walker, a black attorney from the Hampton Institute, in Virginia, who told the boys "of what good Hampton is doing among the negroes." Franklin, who had probably never before seen a black who was not a servant, was impressed by the fact that Walker "has argued before the Court of Appeals in Washington and is very prominent in his own state." Following his visit, the boys contributed $124 from their allowances for Hampton. Not long afterward, Theodore Roosevelt, the newly appointed assistant Secretary of the Navy, gave "a splendid talk on his adventures when he was on the Police Board," Franklin enthusiastically informed his parents. "He kept the whole room in an uproar for over an hour, by telling us killing stories about policemen and their doings in New York."

Franklin idolized Cousin Theodore, and when he was invited to visit Oyster Bay over the Fourth of July the invitation was eagerly accepted, even though his mother, then on a yearly visit to Germany, objected to this display of self-assertion. Life at Sagamore Hill was far more boisterous than the restrained pace of Springwood. Cousin Theodore enjoyed nothing better than leading a ragtag band of his own children and their myriad cousins and friends on strenuous cross-country "scrambles" that were more obstacle course than nature walk. These outings usually ended with a picnic and an overnight stay in the woods. The elder Roosevelt entertained the group with ghost stories while they were gathered around the campfire—and would pounce on an unwary listener with a bloodcurdling yell as the fitting climax for a terrifying tale. Sometimes they would all go up to the Gun Room, on the top floor of the rambling house, where Cousin Theodore would read aloud.

Franklin was also a regular at the annual Christmas party for the younger members of the family given by Corinne Roosevelt Robinson, Cousin Theodore's younger sister. At one of these affairs, in 1898, he again met Eleanor Roosevelt. Plain and awkward and with prominent teeth, she found these gatherings more pain than pleasure. Both of her parents were dead and she had been left in the care of her rigidly strict grandmother, who insisted she wear long black stockings and short dresses. "I knew, of course, that I was different from all the other girls and if I had not known, they were frank in telling me," she observed.

Franklin, who enjoyed parties and bantering with girls, took pity on the pathetic wallflower and asked Eleanor to dance. Forty years later, she still remembered her gratitude.

Not long afterward, Franklin wrote his parents suggesting that Eleanor and Theodore Douglas Robinson, Cousin Corinne's son, be invited to a house party at Hyde Park. "They would go well and help fill out chinks," he said. He must have spent some time with her, for it was about this time that he supposedly observed to his mother that "Cousin Eleanor has a very good mind."

By and large, Roosevelt's last three years at Groton followed the pattern established during his first year. Slender and handsome and with his hair parted in the middle like two wings over his high forehead, he had developed a jaunty self-assurance. Having taken boxing lessons from an instructor who came up from Boston twice a week, he participated in a school tourney. Both Franklin and his more experienced opponent came out of the two-round match with bloody noses and cut lips, but the other fellow was awarded the decision. He also joined the Debating Society, where Sherrard Billings, the Senior Master, emphasized good delivery and clear enunciation. Franklin took the affirmative on such issues as the independence of the Philippines and—as expected of a disciple of Mahan— favored an increase in the strength of the Navy.

Roosevelt and two of his schoolmates almost made their own contribution to the latter proposition. Swept up in the patriotic fervor accompanying the outbreak of the Spanish-American War, they planned to run away from Groton and enlist. Having heard that the Navy was accepting recruits in Boston, Franklin, Lathrop Brown, his closest friend, and another boy plotted to bribe the pieman, who sold cakes and pies to the boys, to take them to town in his wagon. By the time that their absence was discovered, they hoped to be on a transport bound for Charleston. Before the scheme could be carried out, however, the conspirators came down with scarlet fever and were placed under quarantine in the school infirmary. The task of upholding the Roosevelt honor was left to roughriding Cousin Theodore.

Hurrying to Groton, Sara Roosevelt found her son wan and looking "like a *reconcentrado*," or one of the starving Cubans in the Spanish concentration camps. She was unable to enter the sickroom because of the contagious nature of the disease, so the indomitable Sara had a tall stepladder placed under a window and she sat upon it for hours conversing with Franklin and keeping him and the other boys supplied with delicacies and games.

Theodore Roosevelt returned from the "splendid little war" to a hero's welcome and election as Governor of New York. Despite his poor health and Democratic loyalties, James Roosevelt campaigned along with Archibald Rogers for his cousin's election and succeeded in carrying Hyde Park for him. "We were all wild with delight when we heard of Teddy's election," Franklin wrote home from school. ". . . The whole dormitory went mad. How splendid that even Hyde Park gave him a majority of 81. I think Papa and Mr. Rogers must have worked pretty hard to have such a good result." The following January, he accompanied his parents to Albany for Theodore's inauguration. Not long afterward, the new Governor again spoke at Groton, and Franklin was profoundly impressed by his remarks: "If a man has courage, goodness, and brains, no limit can be placed to the greatness of the work he may accomplish. He is the man needed today in politics."

In his last year at Groton, Franklin was named a dormitory prefect. This gave him the luxury of a private study and the task of keeping order among the younger boys, prompting such Olympian sentiments as "All is confusion and Babel; the new infants are like the sands of the sea." He was considered a good prefect, and one of his admiring charges said he was "gray-eyed, cool, self-possessed, intelligent and had the warmest, most friendly and understanding smile." Some of his own classmates, however, considered him cocky and argumentive. To correct his nearsightedness, he began to wear a pince-nez and adopted the habit of throwing his head back to get a better view of the person to whom he was speaking, which sometimes gave people the impression that he was looking down his nose at them.

Throughout his years at Groton, Franklin was active in religious and charitable work, in keeping with the social gospel preached by Peabody. He was elected to the Missionary Society, which conducted religious services in nearby rural communities, and helped operate the St. Andrew's Boys Club, for poor boys in Boston, and a camp for them on Asquam Lake, in New Hampshire, where he served as a counselor during part of one summer. The Missionary Society appointed him and another boy to care for a Mrs. Freeman, an eighty-four-year-old black woman and widow of a Civil War drummer. They were to visit her several times a week to make certain that she had coal and water and to dig her out in case of a snowstorm. "It will be very pleasant as she is a dear old thing, and it will be a good occupation for us," he explained to his mother.

As graduation neared, Franklin expressed an interest in attending the Naval Academy, but his parents objected. They pointed out that, as an only child, he would have a considerable estate to manage and other responsibilities that made such a choice impossible. Harvard and then probably law school were the prescribed path for his future. Besides, as a participant in Groton's "anticipation" plan, he was all but formally enrolled as a Harvard freshman, anyway. Under this program, Franklin had taken fifteen hours of the university's first-year courses, which would permit him to complete the requirements for a bachelor's degree in three years.

Roosevelt's career at Groton ended on a note of triumph. On Prize Day, June 25, 1900, he was surprised to learn that he had won the Latin Prize, a forty-volume set of Shakespeare, and described himself as "rather tickled." Nostalgia was mixed with delight as he prepared to leave the school that had been his home for four years. " 'The strife is o'er, the battle won!' " he wrote in his last letter home from Groton. "What a joyful yet sad day this has been. Never again will we hold recitations in the old school, and scarce a boy but wishes he were a first former again. . . ." He had a B average, and in his final report the Rector said that he "has been a thoroughly faithful scholar & most satisfactory member of the school throughout his course. I part with Franklin with reluctance."

Endicott Peabody intended that the precepts taught at Groton remain with its graduates throughout their lives, and carefully watched to see that their performance measured up to the school's standards. In 1932, the old man voted for Herbert Hoover on the ground that he was "an abler man" than Roosevelt. But in 1936, and again in 1940, he was an enthusiastic Roosevelt supporter. Replying to an Old Grotonian who wrote that he had known Roosevelt even longer than the Rector and "I have always felt that his lack of sincerity has been the weak point in his character," Peabody said: "I am not at all convinced of Franklin's insincerity. He was at Groton for four years and as far as I can remember there was no suspicion of untruthfulness or insincerity during his entire course; nor did I hear of anything against his reputation at the University."

Franklin Roosevelt may have made only a limited impression at Groton, but this was an oversight that he was determined to remedy at Harvard. The quintessential Big Man on Campus, he bounded into Harvard Yard with the limitless energy and zest for battle that marked Theodore Roosevelt. He engaged in a wide range of social, athletic, political, and extracurricular activities, climaxed by election to the highly coveted position of president, or editor in chief, of the *Crimson*, the college newspaper. Such enthusiasm annoyed the languorous young men who set the tone of Harvard and later dominated its affairs from the boardrooms and legal offices of Boston's State Street.

The Yard was enjoying its golden age when Roosevelt came up from New York, on September 25, 1900. Entering the fourth and final decade of the presidency of Charles W. Eliot, who had revolutionized the American university with his system of free electives, the school had been transformed from a small provincial college into a great university. The faculty was studded with such bright names as Josiah Royce, William James, George Santayana, Frederick Jackson Turner, Edward Channing, George

Pierce Baker, George Lyman Kittredge, and Charles Townsend Copeland, among others. The students, numbering about 1,750, ranged from aristocratic drones who protested in the privacy of their clubs about the aggressiveness of "pushy" Jews and Westerners, to brilliant outlanders who were to add to Harvard's renown. These two worlds revolved on different axes, coming in touch with each other only in the classroom or the playing field.

Young Roosevelt's position was firmly fixed among the gilded products of Groton, St. Mark's, St. Paul's, and similar schools. In contrast to the austerity of Groton, he shared a three-room apartment with Lathrop Brown, his old friend from prep school, in one of the luxurious dormitories on the Mount Auburn Street "Gold Coast," favored by the wealthier students. They ate at a Groton table in one of the Cambridge eating houses described by Franklin as "great fun & most informal." Less-affluent students dined in the Commons for sixteen cents a meal. The young aristocrats often passed their evenings among the clicking balls and tobacco haze of Sanborn's billiard parlor and smoke shop, on Massachusetts Avenue.

As a Roosevelt, Franklin was immediately taken up by the hostesses of Beacon Hill and Cambridge, with some believing he was the nephew of the dashing Theodore Roosevelt, then running for Vice-President on a ticket headed by McKinley. Handsome and charming, the young man looked like the square-jawed heroes of Richard Harding Davis' popular novels and was much sought after by society "mamas." He kept a horse and runabout and there was hardly a weekend when he was not attending a dinner, a dance, or a party.

The rising star of Theodore Roosevelt may have already been beckoning him into public life, and whether by design or not, he followed a course of study that was eminently suited for a career in politics. Choosing from among the smorgasbord of courses laid out before him, he majored in history and government, with English and public speaking as minors. He also took courses in Latin and French, geology, and economics —although he later said, "I took economics in college for four years and everything I was taught was wrong." It was a schedule that was, as the *Harvard Alumni Bulletin* later described it, "anything but a snap." Roosevelt was no grind, however. Bored by an uninspiring and nearsighted professor's lecture on English history, he joined his classmates in slipping, one by one, out a window and down a fire escape. He studied under many of the great names of Harvard, but none of them succeeded in creating a thirst for learning. In fact, he dropped out of Josiah Royce's philosophy course after only three weeks.

Most of Franklin's grades were in the gentlemanly range of low B and C, and unlike Theodore Roosevelt, who had graduated from Harvard in 1880 with honors, his Phi Beta Kappa key was honorary, rather than earned. Considering his course load and the weight of the other activities he enthusiastically embraced, it is surprising that he did not do worse. In later years he was, like the elder Roosevelt, to be dissatisfied with the education he received at Harvard—blaming it on the failure of the faculty to stimulate the students. As he told Lathrop Brown, his courses had little connection with the reality existing beyond the gates of Harvard Yard. They were "like an electric lamp that hasn't any wire. You need the lamp for light but it's useless if you can't switch it on."

Roosevelt made few attempts to switch on the lamp himself, for he was usually too busy with outside activities to take much interest in his classes. If a subject interested him, however, he attacked it with enthusiasm. One such course was American History, in which his sophomore thesis was "The Roosevelt Family in New Amsterdam." "I have been in the library constantly looking up old records, but nothing much is to be found," he wrote his mother. "Do please copy for me all the extracts in our old Dutch Bible & send them to me. . . . I must have them as soon as possible." Writing of the family's "progressiveness and true democratic spirit" in this paper, he observed:

> One reason—perhaps the chief—of the virility of the Roosevelts is this very democratic spirit. They have never felt that because they were born in a good position they could put their hands in their pockets and succeed. They have felt, rather, that being born in a good position, there is no excuse for them if they did not do their duty by the community.

By emphasizing the family's "true democratic spirit," Franklin provided a rationale for going into politics. This "spirit" was not democratic in the sense of identifying with the masses or asserting the fundamental equality of mankind. Rather, it was Jeffersonian in tone: a command to the rich and wellborn to direct their energies into working for the "community," instead of into mere moneymaking. Thus, Roosevelt was beginning to develop his own view of his spiritual inheritance, which, added to the example of Theodore Roosevelt and the exhortations of Endicott Peabody, helped propel him into public service.

Franklin was less impressionable than when he was at Groton, and none of his Harvard professors stood in the same relation to him as the Rector. Eleanor Roosevelt said, however, that Charles Townsend Copeland was foremost among the personalities at Cambridge who influenced her husband—particularly his speaking style. She said her husband often mentioned the enthusiasm with which he and his classmates gathered to hear "Copey" read from the Bible and the English classics. Copeland's readings had overtones of theater and were "so vivid, so completely an expression of the author read, that nobody could forget him," wrote Rollo

Brown, one of Roosevelt's contemporaries at Harvard. Copeland also required his students to read their own themes aloud. Although usually bathed in cold sweat when they began, Brown added, they found their tongues freed "so that they expressed themselves with a clearness and certainty that they did not know they could command." Such exercises helped Roosevelt to perfect his ability to read aloud and to speak in public.

As at Groton, athletics were a source of frustration for Roosevelt. Six feet one and a half inches tall but never weighing more than 146 pounds while at Harvard, he was quickly cut when he went out for freshman football and had to settle for playing end on one of the intramural teams. The same thing happened in crew. Roosevelt made his mark instead in extracurricular activities, particularly on the *Crimson*. Competition was keen and the work demanding, but he won one of the managing editorships, assisted by a scoop resulting from luck and family connections. Learning that Cousin Theodore, now the Vice-President, was visiting Boston, he telephoned to see him. Don't bother, Theodore said, because he was coming to Harvard in a few days to lecture one of the political-science classes. "That was a beautiful piece of news and the neatest scoop in the world," Franklin later recalled. The *Crimson* ran the story on its front page.

A year earlier, Franklin had begun his political career by joining the Harvard Republican Club, despite the Democratic leanings of his branch of the family. He pitched in enthusiastically to help elect the McKinley-Roosevelt ticket, although he was still too young to vote. Shortly before the election, he marched in a giant torchlight parade along with about a thousand Harvard and Massachusetts Institute of Technology students. "We wore red caps & gowns & marched by classes into Boston & thro' all the principal streets, about 8 miles in all," he wrote home. "The crowds to see it were huge all along the route & we were dead tired at the end."

Still, there were setbacks. Franklin suffered his first social rejection at Harvard, which, according to his wife, left a deep psychological scar. In his sophomore year he was elected to the Institute of 1770, which took about 20 percent of his class and was the key to membership in the more exclusive clubs. The social elite of this group were automatically chosen for Delta Kappa Epsilon, or "Dickey." The initiation rites were called "running for Dickey" and consisted of the performance of humiliating stunts in public. The clubs then made their selection from the members of "Dickey," with Porcellian, of which Theodore Roosevelt had been a member, ranked as the most snobbish. Franklin entered into the process with enthusiasm and with the fullest expectation that he would make Porcellian. "I am about to be slaughtered but quite happy, nevertheless," he told his mother. Later, he added, "My back is a bit raw but I am through the first ordeal O.K."

Much to his surprise, he was passed over by Porcellian and had to settle for Fly, or Alpha Delta Phi, the next-ranking club. Later, he told W. Sheffield Cowles, Jr., a distant cousin, that his failure to make Porcellian was "the greatest disappointment he ever had." What had been responsible for this rejection? Perhaps it was the result of the activities of his nephew Taddy, who was using Harvard as a springboard from which to dive into New York's fleshpots. The recipient of a forty-thousand-dollar-a-year income from the Astor estate, Taddy eloped with Sadie Meisinger, an ornament of the Haymarket, generally acknowledged as New York's most notorious house of assignation, where girls were openly auctioned off to the highest bidder. The yellow press had a field day with the marriage of "Dutch Sadie" and a Roosevelt who was also a grandson of *the* Mrs. Astor. "It will be well for him . . . to go to parts unknown . . . and begin life anew," wrote a disgusted Franklin. Taddy and his bride went to Florida, but it may not have been far enough to preserve Franklin's social prestige in the eyes of the fastidious members of Porcellian.†

Perhaps his contemporaries' perceptions of Franklin had something to do with this rebuff. Some of his classmates regarded him as too aggressive and too eager to be liked and were put off by his breezy manner. In Roosevelt's defense, it should be pointed out that until he entered Groton, he had had little contact with people his own age. Wishing desperately to be accepted, he masked his natural reserve and mistrust of intimacy with an adolescent buoyancy. As Mike Reilly, a Secret Service agent who saw Roosevelt almost every day in the White House, put it, he always wanted to be "one of the boys." "He never was 'one of the boys' although he frequently made a good try," Reilly observed. "It was such a good try that it never quite came off." Marguerite LeHand, his longtime secretary, agreed, saying he "was really incapable of a personal friendship with anyone."

Still, Roosevelt enjoyed Harvard despite the unsettling rejection by Porcellian. As librarian of Fly and Hasty Pudding, he indulged his passion for books, buying for the club libraries and his own collection. Following the advice of a friendly book dealer who suggested that he concentrate on a single aspect of Americana, he began collecting books, prints, and manuscripts concerned with the Navy, and over the years he built up a notable

---

† Everyone expected the marriage to break up quickly, but Taddy and Sadie remained together until her death, in 1940. Taddy became a recluse and lived over a garage in the Forest Hills section of New York City. When asked by the trustees of the Astor estate about what should be done with his income, which had grown to $60,000 a year, he told them not to bother him. Taddy died in 1958 and left his millions to the Salvation Army.

collection. And the young man's high spirits, vigor, and easy affability attracted many friends. "His charm and ease of manner were apparent in those early days," said Herbert Burgess, a classmate. And W. Russell Bowie, who worked with him on the *Crimson*, observed that he managed other people with "a kind of frictionless command."

Midway in Roosevelt's freshman year, his father died, at the age of seventy-two. For several years, James Roosevelt had suffered from a bad heart, and all through 1900 his condition had steadily deteriorated, so his passing was not unexpected. Early in December, while James and his wife were staying at their apartment in the Hotel Renaissance, on West Forty-third Street, in New York City, he had another serious attack. Both Franklin and his half brother, Rosy, were summoned to the bedside to make their farewells to their father, on December 7. He died early the next morning. "At 2.20 he merely slept away," the heartbroken Sara confided to her diary. "As I write these words, I wonder how I lived when he left me." James bequeathed a $120,000 trust fund to each of his sons, which provided an annual income of about $6,000; Springwood and the residue of the estate went to his widow, who had inherited about $1.3 million at the death of her father, two years before.

To help his mother ease her loneliness, Franklin accompanied her on a European tour that summer in company with Theodore Douglas Robinson, a Harvard classmate. While cruising in one of the Norwegian fjords, they came upon the yacht of Kaiser Wilhelm II. Some of the travelers were invited on board the vessel when the Kaiser was ashore, and Franklin later declared he had come away with a souvenir: a pencil bearing the royal tooth marks. They were in Paris when they heard that President McKinley had been shot while attending the Pan American Exposition, in Buffalo, but he seemed to be recovering. Landing in New York twelve days later, they learned that McKinley had died and Theodore Roosevelt was President of the United States. At forty-two, he was the youngest man ever to hold the office.

With Franklin back at Harvard, Sara found Springwood intolerably lonely. But she was only forty-six and life had to go on. "I try to keep busy, but it is hard," she wrote. "I had all of F's birds out to dust and air. . . . One day is much like another." For twenty years, she had divided her love between James and Franklin, and now she centered all of it on her son. James had stipulated in his will that he wanted Franklin "under the supervision of his mother"—and she immediately assumed this role. As soon as her affairs were in order, Sara moved to Boston, where she took an apartment to be near her son—"near enough to the University to be on hand should he want me and far enough removed not to interfere in his college life."

Sometimes Franklin gave parties at her flat; other times he almost ignored her presence completely. Imperious and iron-willed, she tried to
dominate all those about her, including Franklin. Young girls drawn to
the handsome young Harvard man by the prestige of the Roosevelt name
and his good looks were put off by his mother's influence over him. Some
considered him a "mama's boy" whose superficial self-assurance covered a
perennial adolescence, and they said "F.D." stood for "feather duster," or
lightweight.

This was a complete misreading of the young man's character, however. Although deeply attached to his mother and unfailingly kind and
considerate to her, Franklin had learned to manipulate her. He obeyed
her commands only so long as it suited him; if not, he listened without argument and went his own way. Sara Roosevelt never penetrated the inner
recesses of his mind, and if by chance she happened to see something that
did not suit her, she pretended it did not exist. Besides, Franklin was not
the frivolous young snob for which he was often mistaken. A strong sense
of duty toward those less fortunate than himself had been instilled in him
by his parents and by Rector Peabody and was augmented by the patrician's sympathy for the underdog. He continued to work with the poor
boys at the St. Andrew's Boys Club and organized a campaign at Harvard
to raise funds for the relief of Boer women and children held in British
concentration camps in South Africa. This campaign brought him to the
attention of the Boston newspapers, which mistakenly identified him as a
nephew of the President. One described him as having "many of the
qualities that have put his uncle at the front," but comments about his
prominence, wealth, and democratic manner were embarrassing. They
"make me excessively tired," he said.

Living in the reflected glory of the First Family had its advantages,
and he was invited in January 1902 to the glittering coming-out party
given by the President and his wife, Edith, for their eldest daughter,
Alice. Pretty, fun-loving, and quick-witted, Princess Alice, as she was
quickly dubbed by the press, was the first media superstar and attracted
more attention than any member of the family except her father. Americans could not get enough of Alice. The papers were filled with articles
about her: where she went, whom she met, what she said, and especially
what she wore. Her favorite, blue-gray color became known as "Alice
blue," and songs were written about her. Six hundred young men and
women flocked to the White House for her debut, and although Alice
complained that punch was served, rather than champagne, Aunt Corinne
noted that her niece "had the time of her life" with "men seven deep
around her all the time." Enjoying himself immensely, Franklin described
the dance as "Great fun & something to be always remembered."

From Cambridge, Franklin watched with admiring fascination as Theodore Roosevelt brought to the White House—a name that he made official—a star quality that it had lacked for decades. Pugnacious, exuberant, and bubbling over with missionary zeal, he was a cross between St. Paul and St. Vitus. Waving a "big stick" abroad and promising a "Square Deal at home," he captured the popular imagination. Unlike McKinley and his post-Civil War predecessors, who had all but abdicated national leadership to Congress, Roosevelt believed that the President should exercise the ultimate authority in government. "It was not only his right but his duty to do anything that the needs of the nation demanded, unless such action was forbidden by the Constitution," he declared.

Roosevelt's elevation to the presidency coincided with a revival of the crusading spirit that has periodically swept the United States. Reformers and muckraking journalists were exposing what William Allen White, the Kansas editor, called "the alliance between business and government for the benefit of business." The new President enthusiastically embraced the tenets of progressivism: antitrust legislation, child-labor laws, railroad rate reform, conservation, wildlife preserves, a moderate policy of uplift for blacks, workmen's compensation, income and inheritance taxes, and pure-food-and-drug laws.

Little more than a month after Franklin's visit to Washington, the President took the first step in exerting the power of the federal government in the marketplace. Making unprecedented use of the Sherman Anti-Trust Act, he instituted a suit designed to break up the Northern Securities Company, a combination organized by J. P. Morgan to control the major western railroads. Not long after he had successfully brandished his "big stick" under old Morgan's rubicund nose, Roosevelt intervened in a strike organized by the United Mine Workers to gain union recognition, a 10–20 percent increase in the average yearly wage of $560, and an eight-hour day. When the mine operators refused to negotiate or accept presidential arbitration and coal supplies dwindled, Roosevelt threatened to seize the mines. Fearful of the dreaded specter of "socialism," the operators agreed to accept binding arbitration by a presidential commission, which raised wages by 10 percent and reduced working hours but did not grant union recognition.

For the first time, a President had offered to help obtain a negotiated settlement of a labor dispute; for the first time, a President had proposed binding arbitration; and for the first time, a President had threatened to seize a strikebound industry. Franklin Roosevelt, whose father had invested heavily in coal mines, had doubts about his idol's action. "I think the President made a serious mistake in interfering—politically, at least," he told his mother. "His tendency to make the executive power stronger than the Houses of Congress is bound to be a bad thing, especially when a man of weaker personality succeeds him in office."

As a result of the advanced work he had taken at Groton, Roosevelt finished the requirements for a bachelor of arts degree in three years. But in order to take advantage of his election as president of the *Crimson* during the upcoming fall semester, he had to remain at Cambridge for another year. So, in September 1903, he enrolled in graduate school, not with any intention of earning an advanced degree but solely to secure the editorship. "Every spare moment was taken up with the paper, and he later declared that "perhaps the most useful preparation I had in college for public service was . . . [on] the Harvard *Crimson.*"

The *Crimson* of that day was a four-column tabloid of four to eight pages and was more a bulletin board than a newspaper. Editorials were written by the president and were expected to be conservative and respectful of the college administration. Young Roosevelt had been provided with his first opportunity for leadership, but he was no boat rocker and made few alterations in the paper's viewpoint or content. To the incoming freshmen, he preached the doctrine of service, saying a Harvard man owed "responsibility to the University, to his class and to himself. . . . The only way to fulfill this is to be always active. The opportunities are almost unlimited." After having run the gamut from athletics to religious work, he added that "many other interests . . . are bound to exist"— presumably even including scholarship. Perhaps the only editorial that looked to the world beyond Harvard Yard was a suggestion to the Political Club that it venture across the Charles River and examine the exotic political jungle that flourished in Boston. "It would be easy to send in parties, under the guidance of some experienced man, which in one day could learn more than through the means of lectures," Roosevelt wrote.

Many of his editorials were devoted to football and school spirit, however. Lathrop Brown, his roommate, was manager of the football team and may have influenced these choices of topics. With Rooseveltian strenuousness, he called upon Harvard men of sufficient brawn to turn out for practice; for louder and better-organized cheering—going so far as to lead the cheering at one game even though he "felt like a D . . . F . . ." and fumed over the "wretched showing" when the team lost. Following complaints from some readers, including Henry James II, about the overabundant vitriol, Roosevelt toned down his editorials.

Roosevelt ended his editorship by taking on the Harvard Corporation on the issue of adequate fire protection for the Yard's aging dormitories. Thirteen days after the editorial appeared, the Iroquois Theatre, in Chicago, caught fire and 588 people, mostly women and children, were killed. Someone sent an unsigned letter to the editor implying that the

Corporation was guilty of the same criminal negligence displayed by public officials in Chicago, but Franklin objected, probably believing that reforms are best achieved by responsibility on the part of the reformers. In restrained terms, he continued to demand more fire-protection equipment for the dormitories, and in May he saw his campaign become a success when it was installed.

Having been easily elected permanent chairman of the Class Committee after losing a race for class marshal, he was seated on the ceremonial platform with the dignitaries on Commencement Day 1904. But he was more impressed by Prize Day at Groton, to which he hurried after the ceremony. "Much has been given you," Theodore Roosevelt told the boys arrayed before him on Groton's green lawn. "Therefore, we have the right to expect much from you." Franklin Roosevelt listened to these words with more than usual interest, for he had asked Eleanor Roosevelt, the President's niece, to marry him.

III

"CALL IT LOVING"

W HO CAN EXPLAIN the chemistry of love? On the surface, it would seem almost impossible to find two more dissimilar young people than Franklin and Eleanor Roosevelt. Handsome and vigorous, Franklin was determined to drink deeply of the wine of life. Eleanor was repressed and a self-described "ugly duckling." Franklin loved to dance, dressed with a stylish flair, and was something of a ladies' man. Eleanor was serious to the point of humorlessness and appeared destined for spinsterhood and a life of good works. To the shy and introverted girl, Franklin must have seemed like a dashing cavalier, laughing and tossing a sword into the air.

They had renewed the acquaintanceship that was to ripen into love early in the summer of 1902. Walking through a New York Central day coach as the train sped up the Hudson shoreline, Franklin saw a tall, willowy girl whom he recognized as his distant cousin sitting alone. He stopped to chat and Eleanor told him that she had recently returned from three years at school in England and was on her way to spend the summer at her grandmother's estate at Tivoli, to the north of Hyde Park. Franklin enjoyed talking with her, and before the train arrived at Poughkeepsie, he invited Eleanor into an adjoining parlor car to meet his mother. The girl was dazzled by Sara Roosevelt. Although her husband had died a year and a half before, "Cousin Sallie" was still dressed in unrelieved widow's black and sweeping veil, which strikingly accented her classic beauty.

Following this chance encounter, Franklin and Eleanor met at parties and dances at country houses along the river and in New York City, and he found himself drawn to her. Undoubtedly, part of her attraction was that she was the niece of the President of the United States, but Eleanor was intelligent and not without a certain physical appeal. She had a good figure, masses of golden hair, and luminous eyes. Attractive to women and enjoying their company, Franklin had had flirtations with several girls, among them his cousin Muriel Delano Robbins, Helen Roosevelt (his niece), Mary Newbold, and Frances Pell. At Harvard, he dated two girls from old Boston families, Dorothy Quincy and Frances Dana.* But Eleanor's name began to appear in his diary with increasing frequency, and during a Christmas shopping trip to New York with his mother, he slipped away for "tea with Eleanor."

Almost as if by design, they were thrown together in Washington that winter. Eleanor had been invited by Uncle Ted to spend the holidays at the White House, while Franklin was asked by Mrs. Anna Roosevelt Cowles, Eleanor's Aunt Bye and Sara Roosevelt's good friend, to spend New Year's at her home at 1733 N Street. Eleanor was Aunt Bye's favorite niece, and she may have divined the girl's growing interest in Franklin. He was invited to tea at the White House with Eleanor and Alice Roosevelt, and on New Year's Day 1903 stood in the "inner circle" with the rest of the family, fascinated as the President enthusiastically shook hands with thousands of well-wishers. After dinner, they all went to the theater, where Franklin sat near Eleanor. "Very interesting day," he noted in his diary.

Eleanor was among the guests invited a month later to celebrate Franklin's twenty-first birthday, at Hyde Park. She was asked back several times and came to Campobello that summer after Franklin returned from a European tour. They took long walks in the woods, went sailing, picnicked together, and read to each other by firelight. Intimacy soon blossomed into love, for despite their surface differences, Franklin and Eleanor were alike in many ways. Products of the same society, they had a similar education, believed in the same values, and looked at life in the same way. And beneath his mocking, debonair manner, Franklin was sometimes as insecure as Eleanor, wishing desperately to be accepted by his contemporaries. As for Eleanor, she was delighted and a little astonished that such a princely young man should be attracted to her. Franklin's vitality may have reminded her of her beloved father, providing a haven, and she opened her heart to him.

A Campobello neighbor observed what was happening, and later, when their engagement was announced, told Eleanor it had come as no surprise. "The first summer at Campo I saw most clearly how Franklin ad-

* James Roosevelt has written that his father "nearly married" Frances Dana, whose grandfathers were Richard Henry Dana, author of *Two Years Before the Mast*, and Henry Wadsworth Longfellow. He states that FDR was talked out of it by his mother, who pointed out that Frances was a Catholic. It is James Roosevelt's opinion, however, that his father would have ignored his mother's objections and married the girl had he really wanted.

mired you," observed Mrs. Hartman Kuhn. But Sara Roosevelt either failed to recognize that the young people were becoming serious or chose to ignore the signals. She continued to regard "dear, sweet Eleanor" as just another of the girls who were attracted to her son. Franklin kept up the pose. Writing his mother from England, he told her that he had been invited to a party and "as I knew the uncivilized English custom of never introducing people . . . I walked up to the best looking dame in the bunch & said 'howdy?' Things at once went like oil & I was soon having flirtations with three of the nobility at the same time." We do not know what he wrote to Eleanor, for she burned all the letters of their courtship, perhaps because they contained pledges of lasting constancy that later became too painful.

Eleanor was profoundly impressed by the happy and stable family life of the Hyde Park Roosevelts and their Delano relatives, for her own childhood had been Dickensian in its bleakness. In her memoirs, she paints a portrait of a sensitive child full of fears—"afraid of being scolded, afraid that other people would not like me"—hungering for praise and affection from her mother and secure only in the company of her beloved but erratic father, Elliott Roosevelt.

Eleanor described her mother, Anna Hall Roosevelt, as "one of the most beautiful women I have ever seen," but saw in her mother's eyes only disappointment in her daughter's plainness. Anna preferred her two younger children, Elliott, Jr., and Hall, and she showed it. Perhaps she projected some of her disappointment in her husband upon Eleanor, who reminded her of him. Because of the little girl's grave solemnity, Anna told visitors that she was "old-fashioned" and called her "Granny." Upon these occasions, Eleanor recalled, "I wanted to sink through the floor in shame." The child's relationship with her father was far different, however. "He dominated my life as long as he lived, and was the love of my life for many years after he died," she declared.

Yet, as Eleanor's need for her father grew, he became an increasingly shadowy figure. Plagued with excruciating head pains, Elliott drank heavily and spent considerable time in sanatoriums, seeking a cure for alcoholism, only to emerge for fresh bouts with the bottle.† Upon one occasion, his wife and his elder brother, Theodore, tried to have him declared insane. Early in 1892, Elliott, in an effort at reconciliation, promised Anna that he would take another cure and establish himself in a steady occupation. Anna, however, had heard this litany before and stipulated a year of separation to see if Elliott could keep his promises. Missing her father desperately and understanding little of the reason for his absence,

† Some members of the Roosevelt family now believe that Elliott suffered from an undiagnosed brain tumor.

Eleanor blamed her mother for the separation. She lived for Elliott's letters to his "Little Nell" and carried them about with her as a talisman.
Shortly before the end of 1892, when Eleanor was eight, Anna Roosevelt
died of diphtheria. The girl's reaction to her mother's death is revealing:

> I can remember standing by a window when Cousin Susie [Mrs. Henry
> Parish] told me that my mother was dead. She was very sweet to me,
> and I must have known something terrible had happened. Death meant
> nothing to me, and one fact wiped out everything else—my father was
> back and I would see him very soon.

Elliott did return, but not to carry her away, as she so often fantasized. Anna had designated her own mother as the children's guardian,
and Mrs. Hall did not believe that Elliott could be trusted with them.
When they had been installed at her brownstone on West Thirty-seventh
Street, Elliott came to see his daughter. Taking her in his arms, he told
her that "someday I would make a home for him again, we would travel
together, and do many things which he painted as interesting and pleasant, to be looked forward to in the future. . . . There started that day a
feeling which never left me—that he and I were very close together, and
some day we would have a life of our own together."

Young Ellie died a year after his mother, also of diphtheria, and
Eleanor was now even more alone. All her thoughts were on her father.
"He rarely sent word before he arrived, but never was I in the house, even
in my room two long flights of stairs above the entrance door that I did
not hear his voice the minute he entered the front door," she said.
"Walking down the steps was far too slow. I slid down the banisters and
usually catapulted into his arms before his hat was hung up." One of
these visits culminated in a shattering experience. Elliott called for his
daughter and took her for a walk, along with his dogs. He stopped off at
the Knickerbocker Club and deposited the child and the dogs with the
doorman while he went into the bar. The little girl huddled for six hours
on a chair in the cloakroom, forgotten, along with the dogs, until her
drunken father was carried past her. She was taken home by the doorman.

On August 14, 1894, Elliott Roosevelt died in a fit of delirium
tremens. "I simply refused to believe it," said Eleanor. "While I wept
long and went to bed still weeping, I finally went to sleep and began the
next day living in my dream world as usual." Because her grandmother
did not allow Eleanor or Hall to attend the funeral, "I had no tangible
thing to make his death real to me. From that time on I knew in my
mind that my father was dead, and yet I lived with him more closely,
probably than I had when he was alive." Eleanor retained this idealized
picture of her father, and when she married, measured her young husband
against it.

For the next five years, until she was fifteen, Eleanor was shunted between the house on West Thirty-seventh Street and the Hall family estate at Tivoli. Solemn and lonely, she grew up a tall, gawky girl who lived "in a dream world in which I was the heroine and my father the hero." Corinne Robinson, her cousin, has said her mother often tried to persuade her to visit Eleanor, but she was reluctant to do so. "I remember the Thirty-seventh Street home as the darkest, most desolate house I have ever seen," she said. The situation at Tivoli was equally grim. Valentine Hall, Jr., Eleanor's uncle, drank heavily and she was afraid of him. There were no children of her own age for companionship, and with Uncle Vallie becoming increasingly difficult to handle, none were invited. Visiting her Aunt Corinne, Eleanor burst into tears one day and cried, "Auntie, I have no real home."

Grandmother Hall tried to discourage any contact between Eleanor and her father's relatives, fearing that she and her little brother might slip out of her control. Upon one or two occasions, however, she was permitted to pay summer visits to Uncle Ted and Aunt Edith at Sagamore Hill. Although Alice was the nearest in age of her cousins, Eleanor stood "in great awe of her," because she was "so much more sophisticated and grown-up." Quicksilver Alice regarded Eleanor as far too serious to be fun. "She was full of duty, never very gay, a frightful bore for the more frivolous people like ourselves." But Uncle Ted's affection was gargantuan. Upon her arrival, he "pounced" upon her like a bear, hugging her to his chest "with such vigor that he tore all the gathers out of Eleanor's frock and both button holes out of her petticoat." When Uncle Ted learned that she could not swim, he immediately set out to remedy the situation in his usual no-nonsense manner. He told her to jump off the dock, which she did with her eyes shut—coming up gasping and sputtering—fear of displeasing him overcoming her fear of the water. Aunt Edith saw something in Eleanor that escaped others. "Poor little soul, she is very plain," she wrote Mrs. Cowles. "Her mouth and teeth have no future. But the ugly duckling may turn out to be a swan."

Suddenly, in 1899, when Eleanor was fifteen, the world opened up for her. Her mother had intended the girl to be educated in Europe, and Mrs. Cowles persuaded Eleanor's grandmother to send her to a school, operated by Mlle. Marie Souvestre. Thirty years before, Mrs. Cowles had attended the school, which was then outside Paris. Following the Franco-Prussian War, Mlle. Souvestre had moved the school, now called Allenswood, to Wimbledon, near London.

From Mlle. Souvestre, Eleanor received the understanding and affection which she had sought so unavailingly at home, and regarded the three years she spent at Allenswood as "the happiest years of my life." Known to everyone as "Tottie," she made friendships that lasted a lifetime, was recognized for the first time as a leader and was one of the headmistress' favorites. Her dress and grooming were improved, and to her surprise she made the first team in field hockey—"one of the proudest moments in my life." Above all, she was "shocked into thinking" by the liberal doctrines expounded by Mlle. Souvestre, who was pro-Boer, a Dreyfusard, and an atheist. Of Eleanor, Mademoiselle wrote: "She is full of sympathy for all those who live with her and shows an intelligent interest in everything she comes into contact with." Eleanor wished to remain at Allenswood for another year, but her grandmother insisted that she return to New York to make her formal debut into society.

"Coming out" was an ordeal even for girls more socially gifted than Eleanor; for her it was "utter agony." She knew few unattached men, and although friends of the family were pressed into service to fill this gap, Eleanor recalled that "by no stretch of the imagination could I fool myself into thinking that I was a popular debutante." One escort recalled that "she was too tall for most of the young men, but she was an interesting talker. And she was always gracious and pleasant." Eleanor found that life at Tivoli had grown even more grotesque in her absence. Uncle Vallie was drinking more heavily than ever, and sometimes sat in an upstairs window with a rifle taking pot shots at anyone who wandered into range. One of her aunts who had gone through a number of disappointing affairs with men, was in a state of almost permanent hysteria, and Eleanor had been saddled with the responsibility for her brother Hall's education. "When people have asked me how I was able to get through some of the very bad periods in my . . . life," she once said, "I have been able to tell them honestly that, because of the early discipline I had, I inevitably grew into a really tough person."

Even as a child, Eleanor had shown traces of the lacerating social conscience that was to be both a trial and a triumph. "Very early I became conscious of the fact that there were men and women and children around me who suffered in one way or another," she said. Her father had taken her to visit such Roosevelt family charities as the Newsboys' Lodging House, in West Eighteenth Street, for homeless and abandoned children, and the New York Orthopedic Hospital. "Of course I did not really understand many of the things I saw," Eleanor observed, "but I still think I gained impressions that have remained with me all my life." Upon her return to New York she put this strong need to help those less fortunate than herself to work and joined the newly organized Junior League. She was sent to a settlement house on Rivington Street, on the Lower East Side, where she taught dancing and calisthenics to the slum children.

As in the case of many upper-class girls, settlement-house work was more of an education for her than for those she tried to teach, for it opened her eyes to the living conditions endured by the city's poor.

Eleanor joined the Consumers League and was assigned to investigate conditions in sweatshops where artificial flowers and feathers were made. Overcoming her shyness, she trudged up dark flights of stairs and down tenement halls and was appalled by what she found. "I saw little children of four or five sitting at tables until they dropped with fatigue. . . ."

In the meantime, Franklin and Eleanor continued their courtship under the rigid conventions of the day. "You knew a man very well before you wrote or received a letter from him," Eleanor recalled. "You never allowed a man to give you a present except flowers or candy or possibly a book. To receive a piece of jewelry from a man to whom you were not engaged was a sign of being a fast woman, and the idea that you would permit any man to kiss you before you were engaged to him never even crossed my mind." Franklin came to call for her at the settlement house upon several occasions, and the girls wanted to know if the handsome young man was her "feller." Once, Eleanor took him with her when she went to visit one of her students who was sick. Nothing in Franklin's sheltered life had prepared him for what they found. "He was absolutely shaken when he saw the cold-water tenement where the child lived, and kept saying he simply could not believe human beings lived that way," she said.

On November 21, 1903, Eleanor came to Cambridge at Franklin's invitation to attend the Harvard-Yale football game—at which he led the cheering—and on the following day, he joined her at Groton. She had gone there to visit Hall, who was now enrolled at the school. "After lunch I have a never to be forgotten walk to the river with my darling," he wrote in code in his diary.‡ On that quiet Sunday as they walked about the familiar grounds, Franklin asked her to marry him. Eleanor did not give him an immediate answer, but returned to New York, where she told her grandmother about Franklin's proposal. Mrs. Hall asked her if she were really in love and Eleanor "solemnly answered 'yes.'" Later, she confessed "that it was years . . . before I understood what being in love was or what loving really means." Four days afterward, she wrote Franklin a lengthy letter quoting a poem by Elizabeth Barrett Browning she had tried to recall when he proposed which summed up her view of marriage:

> *Unless you can swear, "For life, for death!"*
> *Oh, fear to call it loving!*

Franklin must have sworn—"For life, for death!"—for she agreed to marry him.

Roosevelt had always sought to avoid direct confrontations with his mother, but having made the most important decision of his life, he

‡ The coded entry remained unbroken for nearly seventy years. New York *Times,* Jan. 22, 1972.

wasted no time in breaking the news to her. As soon as he received Eleanor's assent to the marriage, he hurried to the Delano family home at Fairhaven, Massachusetts, where the clan had gathered for a traditional Thanksgiving reunion. "Franklin gave me a startling announcement," a stunned Sara Roosevelt noted in her diary on Thanksgiving Day. The shock was aggravated by the circumstances surrounding it. Franklin had not asked her permission or even sought her advice; he had flatly stated his intention to marry Eleanor as soon as possible. Sara saw all her plans for the future suddenly lying in ruins at her feet. Ever since the death of her husband, three years before, she had looked forward to having her son all to herself when he graduated from Harvard. Now she was being called upon to give him up—and she did not surrender easily.

Immediately after returning to Cambridge, Franklin tried to soften the blow with a soothing letter to "Dearest Mama":

> I know what pain I must have caused you and you know I wouldn't do it if I could really have helped it. . . . That's all that could be said—I know my mind, have known it for a long time, and know that I could never think otherwise: Result: I am the happiest man just now in the world; likewise the luckiest—And for you, dear Mummy, you know that nothing can ever change what we have always been & always will be to each other —only now you have two children to love & to love you—and Eleanor as you know will always be a daughter to you in every true way. . . .

And from Eleanor, Sara received a tender letter, carefully emphasizing Franklin's suggestion that she was not losing a son but gaining another child to love her:

> I know just how you feel & how hard it must be, but I do so want you to learn to love me a little. You must know that I will always try to do what you wish for I have grown to love you very dearly during the past summer. It is impossible for me to tell you how I feel toward Franklin. I can only say that my one great wish is always to prove worthy of him.

Sara Roosevelt did not dislike Eleanor. If she had picked out a bride for her son, it would probably have been someone like her. As a Roosevelt and the President's niece, she had the proper background and, although no beauty, was an intelligent and pleasant girl. If anything, she was almost too pathetically eager to please. But the old lady didn't want Franklin to marry anyone at this point.* Wisely realizing that it would be useless to try to prevent the marriage by direct assault, she adopted a

---

* Sara Roosevelt made no mention of it, but she may also have been concerned about Eleanor's bizarre family heritage. Not only were her father and uncle confirmed alcoholics, but the Oyster Bay Roosevelts had a history of physical problems. Uncle Ted and Aunt Corinne both suffered from asthma; Aunt Bye was almost a hunchback, and as children, Eleanor and Alice Roosevelt had orthopedic problems which necessitated the wearing of uncomfortable leg and back harnesses.

more subtle strategy. She pointed out that they were very young to be taking such a serious step; Franklin was just short of twenty-two, and Eleanor had recently turned nineteen. Sara's own father had waited until he was thirty-three and was "a man who had made a name and a place for himself, who had something to offer a woman when he married." Franklin's inheritance from his father produced only a modest six thousand dollars annually, which was not enough to keep him and Eleanor in the style to which they were accustomed. He would not enter law school until the following autumn, and it would be several years before he earned his own living. Until then, he would be dependent upon her for support. Besides, how could they be certain that they were in love? Perhaps it would be wiser to keep the engagement a secret until they had had time to think it over?

Reluctantly, the young couple agreed to Sara's suggestion, with the hope that she would cease her resistance to the marriage once she had lived with the idea for a time. For the next month, Franklin led a hectic life. In addition to spending as much time as possible in New York with Eleanor and trying to smooth his mother's ruffled feathers, he completed his final weeks as editor of the *Crimson*, attended classes, and led an active social life. "I have been up every night till all hours, but am doing a little studying, a little riding & a few party calls," he wrote home in mid-January. "It is dreadfully hard to be a student[,] a society whirler[,] a 'prominent & democratic fellow' & a fiancé all at the same time." When his mother offered him a five-week Caribbean cruise as a change of scenery—and the secret hope that it would get his mind off Eleanor—he quickly accepted.

Franklin, Sara, and Lathrop Brown departed on February 6, 1904, on a voyage to St. Thomas, Puerto Rico, Martinique, Barbados, Trinidad, Venezuela, Curaçao, Jamaica, Cuba, and Nassau. "F is tired and blue," his mother noted as the ship sailed. Two days before, he had said good-bye to Eleanor (who was apparently not consulted about his decision and resented his absence) with the promise that he would meet her in Washington, where she was to visit Aunt Bye. "I wonder if you know how I hated to let you go," she wrote him after his departure. ". . . Five weeks seems a long time and judging by the past two days they will be interminable."

The trip was leisurely and interesting. At Martinique they viewed the ruins of St. Pierre, which had been recently destroyed by an earthquake. Sara was shocked to see several of her fellow passengers poking about in the debris for the bones of the victims for souvenirs. They heard Caruso sing *Pagliacci* in Caracas, and at San Juan were entertained by the governor. In Cuba, Franklin and Lathrop explored the battlefields outside Santiago, where, only six years before, Theodore Roosevelt had charged up

San Juan Hill into the public imagination. They rented a launch and went out to photograph the rusting hulks of the Spanish cruisers that had been sunk by the guns of the U. S. Navy. "Sad sights," wrote Sara. "They will soon disappear." The travelers left the ship at Nassau, proceeding by boat to Florida and train to Washington, but not before Franklin, much to the annoyance of his mother, had a shipboard flirtation with an attractive older Frenchwoman.†

Franklin had greatly enjoyed the cruise, but if it was intended to make him forget Eleanor, it was a failure. When he returned, he spent almost all his time in Washington with her. Sara, however, had another card to play. She went to Joseph Choate, an old family friend and then American ambassador to Britain, who was in Washington, with the request that he take Franklin back to London with him as his secretary. Choate told her that he already had a secretary, and besides, Franklin was too young and inexperienced for the post. With this rebuff, she returned to Springwood and, recognizing defeat, wrote her son:

> I am feeling pretty blue. You are gone. The journey is over & I feel as if the time were not likely to come again when I shall take a trip with my dear boy. . . . I must try to be unselfish & of course dear child I *do* rejoice in your happiness, & shall not put any stones or straws ever in the way of it. . . .

Eleanor had won the test of wills but was poignant in her desire for Sara to accept her as a real daughter. "I knew your mother would hate to have you leave her, dear," she wrote Franklin, "but don't let her feel that the last trip with you is over. We three must take them together in the future. . . . I hope that she will love me and I would be very glad if I thought she was even the least bit reconciled to me now."

Uncle Ted was among the first to congratulate the young couple after the formal announcement of their engagement. Telling Franklin of his "great rejoicing" at the news, he wrote: "I am as fond of Eleanor as if she were my daughter; and I like you, and trust you, and believe in you. . . . May good fortune attend you both, ever." He not only promised to attend the wedding, set for March 17, 1905, but also agreed to give the bride away. Eleanor asked Alice Roosevelt to be a bridesmaid, and despite the uneasy relationship between the cousins, Alice accepted with enthusiasm. "I should love to above anything. It will be much fun. . . . Really you are a saint to ask me."

---

† The "beautiful French lady" became something of a family legend—much embroidered in the retelling. FDR, who, as his son James writes, rarely forgot anything, remembered that the enchantress had moved to Trinidad. In 1936, while on his way back from a trip to South America, he wrote his mother that he might stop at the island and "perhaps I may meet the French lady."

Two months before, Franklin had entered the Columbia University School of Law, rather than Harvard, which his father had attended, to be closer to Eleanor. He lived with his mother in her rented townhouse at 200 Madison Avenue. On weekends he went to Hyde Park and to Tivoli, from where he reported that Eleanor's alcoholic uncle "Vallie has been exemplary—I seem to have a good effect on him." It was at Hyde Park that he voted for the first time in a presidential election, casting his ballot for Theodore Roosevelt. "I thought he was a better Democrat than the Democratic candidate," he later declared. "If I had it to do all over again I would not alter that vote." Uncle Ted defeated Alton B. Parker by a landslide 2.5 million votes, and on Election Night proudly told his wife: "My dear, I am no longer a political accident." Along with the rest of the family, Franklin and Eleanor went to Washington for the inaugural, on March 4, 1905. "Much has been given us and much will rightfully be expected from us," the President told the American people. "We have duties to others and duties to ourselves and we can shirk neither." After dancing at the Inaugural Ball, Eleanor and Franklin returned to New York, with Eleanor remarking that "I never expected to see another inauguration in the family!"

"You know you don't learn much law at the best of our law schools," Franklin was to say in later years. "You learn how to think." But there are few signs that he learned either at Columbia. Like Theodore Roosevelt, who had attended the same school for a year a quarter century before, Franklin was bored and restless, seeing little connection between what he was being taught and the realities of legal practice. Writing to Dr. Peabody to invite his old headmaster to officiate at the wedding—"It wouldn't be the same without you"—he indicated a lack of enthusiasm for law school. "I am . . . trying to understand a little of the work and of course I am going to keep right on," he said. The problem seemed to be a lack of interest, rather than one of understanding, however. Roosevelt found the study of law bloodless, and unlike his years at Harvard, he did not have the editorship of the *Crimson* or his other extracurricular activities for stimulation. Eleanor accurately diagnosed the situation. Franklin "will not find himself altogether happy with the law he is studying at Columbia unless he is able to get a broad human contact through it," she told Aunt Bye.

The problems of law school were soon submerged by the excitement of the long-awaited wedding, which took place on St. Patrick's Day. The afternoon was warm, and the windows of the adjoining brownstones at 6 and 8 East Seventy-sixth Street, owned by Eleanor's relatives, had been thrown open, so the strains of "Oh, Promise Me" were almost drowned out by "The Wearin' o' the Green" filtering in from the annual parade on Fifth Avenue. The newspapers had reported that the President was to give his niece in marriage after reviewing the march, and a crowd had been gathering in the street since early morning. Waving flags and hand-kerchiefs, they broke through a police cordon and surged about the arriving Burdens and Winthrops. Shortly before 3:30 P.M., a shrill cry of "Hooray for Teddy!" was heard, and with a flash of famous teeth, the President dashed up the steps of one of the houses with a shamrock in his buttonhole.

Nervously awaiting the ceremony, Franklin sat in a small anteroom, reminiscing about Groton with Dr. Peabody and Lathrop Brown, substituting as best man for Rosy, who had been taken sick. They were so absorbed that someone had to warn them to take their places, because the wedding march had started and the President was approaching the altar, which was surrounded by pink roses and palms, with the bride on his arm. Eleanor had never looked more attractive, reminding some of the guests of her mother. She wore a lace-trimmed gown of stiff, white satin with a long train, and her veil was fastened with a diamond crescent that had belonged to her mother. Around her neck she wore a short string of pearls—a gift from Sara Roosevelt. A society reporter noted that she was considerably taller than the President.

Following the ceremony, which had been limited to immediate members of the family, the sliding doors between the two houses were thrown open for a reception, and the guests crowded around the bride and groom with congratulations. "Well, Franklin," said Uncle Ted in his high-pitched voice, "there's nothing like keeping the name in the family." But Franklin and Eleanor soon found themselves alone. Like a Pied Piper, the President had carried most of the guests along with him into the library, where refreshments were being served. "The room in which the President was holding forth was filled with people laughing gaily at his stories which were always amusing," Eleanor recalled. There was nothing else for the newlyweds to do but follow along in his wake.

A full-scale honeymoon had to be postponed until Franklin finished the spring term at law school, so the young couple spent only a week alone at Springwood, which had been placed at their disposal by his mother. Upon their return to New York, they took a small apartment in the Hotel Webster, on West Forty-fifth Street, where, said Eleanor, "I did not have to display the depths of my ignorance as a housewife." In June, they sailed on the *Oceanic* for a three-month grand tour of Europe. A half dozen Japanese naval officers who were on their way to England to take charge of two battleships being built for use by the Imperial Navy in the Russo-Japanese War attracted Franklin's attention. Trying to find out something about their country, he had "several interesting talks with them" but finally realized that he was "giving out more information than I received."

Wherever the young couple went, they received lavish treatment because of their relationship to Theodore Roosevelt, which worried Eleanor and delighted Franklin. "We were ushered into the royal suite, one flight up, front, price $1,000 a day—a sitting room 40 ft. by 30, a double bedroom, another ditto and a bath," he wrote from Brown's Hotel in London in a teasing letter to his mother. "Our breath was so taken away that we couldn't even protest and are now saying 'Damn the expense. Wot's the odds!'" They shared the task of writing to the old lady. "You are always just the sweetest, dearest Mama . . . and I shall look forward to our next long evening together, when I shall want to be kissed all the time," Eleanor wrote at one point. ". . . Goodbye dearest and a thousand thanks and kisses," she said in another note. "I feel as though we . . . have such long arrears of kisses and cuddly times to make up when we get home."

Franklin had often been to Europe more or less on his own, but, for the first time in her life, Eleanor was free to do all the things she had always desired. In London and Paris, she "trotted from shop to shop" for clothes, while "Franklin bought books, books, everywhere we went." They reveled in the theater and "dined in strange places, ordering the specialties of any particular restaurant, whatever they might be." Franklin began to call her Babs—short for "Baby"—and used the nickname for the rest of their lives together. In Paris, a clairvoyant told the amused young man that "I am to be President of the U.S. or the Equitable, I couldn't make out which!" At Cortina, in the Dolomites, an incident occurred that foreshadowed their future relations: Franklin went climbing with an old friend, a Miss Kitty Gandy, while Eleanor stayed behind, "jealous beyond description," as she later put it. He thought nothing of amusing himself with a friend while she seethed inwardly, afraid to say anything about it.

In the closed world in which the American upper class moved in the years before World War I, everyone knew everyone else, and Franklin and Eleanor encountered relations and acquaintances wherever they went. They visited friends in Scotland, and Franklin purchased Duffy, the first of many Roosevelt Scotch terriers.

On the passage across the Atlantic, Eleanor had discovered that her husband walked in his sleep—once almost leaving their cabin before he was halted by her cry—and in Scotland she found he was subject to nightmares. One night after he had spent a hard day tramping on the moors, "I was awakened by wild shrieks in the neighboring bed," she said. "Franklin sat bolt upright, pointing up at the ceiling. 'Don't you see it?' he cried. 'Don't you see the revolving beam?'"

Midway in the couple's travels, Franklin received some disturbing news when his law-school grades caught up with him. Although he had passed most of his courses with B's, he had failed Contracts and Pleading. "It certainly shows the uncertainty of marks, for I had expected much lower marks in some of the others and failure in one, and thought I had done as well on the two I failed as in those I passed with B," he wrote his mother, somewhat puzzled. He asked her to send him the textbooks for these courses and intended upon his return to New York to take makeup examinations. Eleanor noted that he was "sad" about the failure, and while she agreed with his plan to take the examinations again, "I am not very confident about his passing but it won't hurt him to try."

Venice was the most memorable part of the trip. "We had a delightful gondolier who looked like a benevolent bandit and kept us out on the canals a good part of the nights," Eleanor said. They glided along some of the smaller canals to gaze through the grilled entrances at the gardens that lay beyond the fronts of the pink palaces and visited some friends of Sara Roosevelt who lived in one of them. At the glassworks at Murano, they ordered a set of glasses with the Roosevelt family crest. They sat in the sun at the little tables around the Piazza San Marco and fed the pigeons as Eleanor had done as a little girl. They toured churches until Franklin rebelled and "would look no more." This idyll came to an end early in September, for Franklin had to be back in New York by the end of the month for the start of law school.

Always a poor sailor, Eleanor was miserable during the entire voyage home. When her illness persisted, she went to see a doctor and found she was pregnant. "It was quite a relief," she said, "for little fool that I was, I had been seriously troubled for fear that I would never have any children, and my husband would . . . be much disappointed." Sexually naïve and constrained, she confessed she had never been kissed by Franklin before they were engaged, and was to tell her daughter that "sex was an ordeal to be borne."

IV
"THE MESSY BUSINESS
OF POLITICS"

UPON THEIR RETURN to New York, Franklin and Eleanor went to live in a narrow little house—only fourteen feet wide—at 125 East Thirty-sixth Street. Rented for them by Sara Roosevelt while they were in Europe, it was just three blocks from her own home, at 200 Madison Avenue. She had decorated and furnished the place and had even chosen the young couple's three servants. Literally adopting Franklin's suggestion that his marriage meant she now had "two children to love & love you," Sara was determined to bond them both to her. Franklin was accustomed to his mother's adhesive affections and had established his defenses, but Eleanor fell completely under her domination. Knowing little about how to run a household or to manage servants, she was helpless and dependent. "For the first year of my married life, I was completely taken care of," Eleanor said later. "My mother-in-law did everything for me."

Now a family man, responsible for a wife and with a child on the way, Franklin settled down in law school. He passed his makeup examinations in Contracts and Pleading with flying colors and completed all his second-year courses with respectable grades. The following year, in the early spring of 1907, he passed the New York State Bar Examination and didn't bother to return to Columbia to finish the requirements for a degree. "You will never be able to call yourself an intellectual until you come back . . . and pass your law exams," Nicholas Murray Butler, the university's president, later joked. "That just shows how unimportant the law really is," Roosevelt replied with a laugh.

Through family influence, he obtained a clerkship at the conservative Wall Street firm of Carter, Ledyard & Milburn, which paid no salary for the first year. This was not a hardship, as the young couple had an annual income from trust funds of about twelve thousand five hundred between them at a time when sweatshop workers earned five dollars a week. Carter, Ledyard represented the Astor estate, of which Franklin's half brother, Rosy, was one of the beneficiaries, and was trustee for J. P. Morgan. The firm was also one of the leading defenders of the trusts attacked by Theodore Roosevelt, handling the dissolution of Standard Oil and the American Tobacco Company so deftly that little real competition was created and its clients were only slightly inconvenienced. None of this appeared to trouble Franklin, despite his progressive sympathies, for, like his father, he had developed the ability to keep his life rigidly compartmentalized.

Under no illusions about his status, he described himself as "a full-fledged office boy," and he was assigned to research precedents for the partners, keep dockets, and perform other menial tasks. Poking fun at himself, he drafted a mock advertisement calling attention to his willingness to carry on any type of legal business: "Unpaid bills a speciality. Briefs on the liquor question furnished free to ladies. Race suicides cheerfully prosecuted. Small dogs chloroformed without charge. Babies raised under advice of expert grandmother etc., etc." The difference between the classroom and the real world was quickly brought home to him at the firm, and he later commented:

> I went to a big law office in New York, and somebody the day after I got there said, "Go up and answer the calendar call in the Supreme Court tomorrow morning. We have such and such a case on."
> I had never been in a court of law in my life, and yet I was a full-fledged lawyer. . . . Then the next day somebody gave me a deed of transfer of some land. He said, "Take it up to the County Clerk's office." I had never been in a county clerk's office. And there I was, theoretically a full-fledged lawyer.

Along with its more important legal work, Carter, Ledyard handled considerable minor litigation for the American Express Company and similar clients. Legal fledglings such as young Roosevelt were detailed to fend off small claims against them in the Municipal Court. Matching wits with often unscrupulous lawyers working on a contingency basis kept him on his toes, but he did well in this rough-and-tumble world. For the first time, he rubbed shoulders with ordinary folk and learned something about their thinking and the way they lived. Most of all, he learned how to handle himself in situations that he had never before encountered in his sheltered life. It was excellent training for the give-and-take of politics, and as he later told a colleague, "I often think my Municipal Court work laid the foundation for politics better than any other factor in my life."

In one such case, Franklin was opposed by a law-school classmate who represented a poor woman with a claim against one of his corporate clients. The actual loss involved was eighteen dollars, but the lawyer, desperately in need himself, had taken the case on a fifty-fifty split and offered to settle, first for three hundred dollars, and then for one hundred fifty dollars. Agreeing, Roosevelt went to the attorney's combined home and office on the Lower East Side to negotiate the final amount. The attorney was away, but his mother broke down and told Franklin the whole story. Roosevelt left a note offering to settle the claim for thirty-five dollars, and his personal check to cover a one-hundred-fifty-dollar loan.

After about a year of general apprenticeship, Franklin was assigned to the firm's admiralty division, which seemed a good choice in view of his interest in ships and the sea. Nevertheless, he was often bored. Lewis C. Ledyard spotted him idling one day and fired some questions at him. Amiable as always, the young man absently answered, "Yes, sir, yes, sir." Seeking information, rather than agreement, the senior partner angrily stalked off after snapping: "Roosevelt, you're drunk!"

By then, the pattern of Franklin's life was becoming clear: He was a competent if not brilliant lawyer, and even old Ledyard regarded him as "promising." With his background and easygoing manner, he could be relied upon to bring in clients and could look forward to a lucrative partnership in time. He was a member of the most exclusive clubs, including the Knickerbocker and the New York Yacht Club, golfed in the eighties, sailed, played poker on Saturday afternoons at the University Club, and lent his name to a few select charities. At Springwood, where the family often spent the weekends, he conducted experiments in scientific tree farming on land he had purchased himself when his mother refused to consider his proposals, and was a member of the Eagle Engine Company and the Rescue Hook and Ladder Company as well as serving as vestryman of St. James' Episcopal Church. Young Roosevelt seemed to be drifting effortlessly with the tide, undergoing what Erik H. Erikson would later call a "psychosocial moratorium." "Everybody called him Franklin and regarded him as a harmless bust," recalled a friend. But ambition fermented behind this placid façade, awaiting the opportunity to bubble over.

While Franklin was learning his way about the municipal courts, Eleanor, awaiting the birth of their first child, was drawn into her mother-in-law's orbit. Every day, she went for a drive through Central Park in Sara's rented electric brougham, and she took at least one meal with her. Following a difficult pregnancy marked by much pain and nausea, she gave birth to a baby girl on May 3, 1906, who was christened Anna Eleanor for her mother and her maternal grandmother. Over the next ten years, Eleanor was, as she said, "always getting over a baby or having one." Anna was followed by James, in 1907; the first Franklin, Jr., who was born in March 1909 and died before the year was out; Elliott, in 1910; the second Franklin, Jr., in 1914; and John, in 1916.

"I had never had any interest in dolls or in little children, and I knew absolutely nothing about handling or feeding a baby," Eleanor said. "I was completely unprepared to be a practical housekeeper, wife or mother." Having heard that fresh air was good for babies, Eleanor had a small, cage-like box made and, placing Anna in it, hung the contraption out a rear window. The baby began to cry so loudly an irate neighbor telephoned Eleanor and threatened to report her to the Society for the Prevention of Cruelty to Children. "This was rather a shock to me, for I thought I was being a most modern mother," she recalled. Wire guards were tied to the children's thumbs to prevent sucking, and when Anna was three or four, her hands were tied to the bars of the crib to keep her from masturbating as she slept.

Like his own father, Franklin left the rearing of the children to his wife. "Father's attitude on nurses and other household affairs was strictly hands off," his son James has written. Because of Eleanor's ignorance and Sara's interference, her offspring inadvertently had a childhood that in some respects resembled her own. "One of the hazards of life during the period for Anna, Elliott, Franklin, Jr., and me—Johnny escaped it by virtue of his tender years—was the procession of proper English nannies foisted on our household by well-meaning Granny," says James. This constant stream of nurses and governesses meant that affection was capriciously offered and withdrawn. "I was not allowed to take care of the children, nor had I any sense of how to do it," Eleanor said. "Actually, as I was terribly inexperienced about taking responsibility of any kind whatever, I was frightened to death of the nurses, and I always obeyed every rule they made."

These nannies were not unkind to their charges, except for a woman whom James called "Old Battleaxe," who once pushed Anna to the floor, knelt on her chest, and slapped her face to impress upon the child the need to conduct herself as a lady. "Old Battleaxe" locked little Franklin in a closet for several hours, giving the boy a permanent case of claustrophobia. She saved her most exquisite tortures for Jimmy. She made him eat an entire bottle of hot English mustard spoon by spoon, on which he later blamed his recurrent stomach problems. Convinced that Jimmy was fibbing when he told her that he had brushed his teeth, she forced him to dress in his sister's clothes, hung a sign reading I AM A LIAR about his neck, and set him to walking up and down in front of the house to the jeers of his playmates. "Old Battleaxe" was finally dismissed by Eleanor—not for mistreating the children, but only after her dresser was found to be full of empty whiskey and gin bottles.

"If I had it to do over again, I know now that what we should have done was to have no servants those first few years," Eleanor later acknowledged. "I should have acquired knowledge and self-confidence so that other people could not fool me either as to the housework or as to the children. However, my bringing up had been such that this never occurred to me. . . . Had I done this, my subsequent troubles would have been avoided and my children would have had far happier childhoods. As it was, for years I was afraid of my nurses, who . . . ordered me around quite as much as they ordered the children."

When the children had grown older, Franklin enjoyed romping with his increasing brood, taking the "chicks" riding at Hyde Park and sailing at Campobello. All inherited the Delano good looks, and pretty, blond Anna was her father's favorite. "Father was fun," she said. "He would sometimes romp with me on the floor or carry me around atop his shoulders." The children adored their "Pa," who seemed much warmer than their harried, straitlaced mother, and vied for his attention. He was like a favorite uncle who periodically entertained them, while Eleanor was the disciplinarian. Too embarrassed to talk to his sons about sexual matters, he left this instruction to his wife. Typically, she read to them from a learned book which meant as much to them, James noted, as if she had been reading Homer's *Iliad* in the original Greek.

The death of the first Franklin, Jr., in 1909, cast a pall over the family. Eleanor described him as "the biggest and most beautiful of all the babies," but shortly before he was eight months old, he caught flu, which turned into pneumonia. The children were at Springwood under the care of a nurse, while their parents were in New York. Learning that the baby was sick, Eleanor dashed to Hyde Park with a New York doctor in tow, but there was nothing that could be done. On a bleak day in November, the grief-stricken parents followed the tiny coffin to the Hyde Park churchyard. "How cruel it seemed to leave him out there alone in the cold," said the anguished Eleanor.

A few months later, she was pregnant with Elliott. Morbid and plagued with guilt about the baby's death, she plunged into one of her recurrent "Griselda" moods, in which she maintained a silence that frustrated everyone. "I made myself and all those around me most unhappy," she remarked. "I was even a little bitter against my poor young husband who occasionally tried to make me see how idiotically I was behaving." Elliott suffered from weak legs, which made braces necessary, and had a pugnacious disposition—for which Eleanor blamed herself. Possibly because of the circumstances surrounding his birth and because he reminded her of her father, for whom he was named, he was her favorite child.

To add to Eleanor's problems, she had to stand virtually alone against her mother-in-law's interference. Sara Roosevelt dominated the household through smothering love and control of the purse strings. Although the Roosevelts' income was adequate to meet their expenses, it was not enough to support Franklin's costly stamp, book, and print collecting and the growing number of children. "It's hard nowadays for a man with five children and eleven servants to make a living" was a favorite joke.* Although Franklin's mother did not increase his share of the estate, to keep him dependent upon her, she always stood ready, checkbook in hand, to provide any needed funds. "She thought she was manipulating her son, but he was only being a diplomat," James Roosevelt has written. "She gave to him, and he took from her . . . as long as it suited him, but [when] he set his own course . . . neither his mother, nor her money, could make him change his mind." Sara also had the habit of referring to her grandchildren as her children and tried to buy their affection just as she bought Franklin's, offering gifts their parents would not or could not give them. "Your mother only bore you," she said. "I am more your mother than your mother is."

Only rarely, if at all, during their early life together did Franklin sit down with Eleanor and analyze the state of their marriage. Anna Roosevelt once said that her father had a "lack of desire to face what might prove disagreeable" in his personal relationships. And the sensitive antennae that were Roosevelt's great political asset did not extend into his private life. Although he regarded his wife with affection, he would not—or could not—allow her to penetrate the defenses he had erected about his private thoughts. Requiring complete devotion from those about him, he was unable to give unreservedly of himself in return. He accepted their devotion and loyalty but hid his inner self so well that, as Rexford G. Tugwell has said, "No one could tell what he was *thinking*, to say nothing of what he was *feeling*."

Over the years, Roosevelt developed the ability to disarm those about him by seeming to agree with them. He rarely had to resort to stronger tactics to repel attempts to pierce his defenses. Upon one occasion, however, Eleanor would not be so easily brushed off. With her usual earnestness she asked him what should be done about the children's religious education. Should they be taught a formalized Christianity or should they be left free to make their own choice when they grew older? "He looked at me with his amused and quizzical smile," she reported, "and said he thought they had better go to church and learn what he had learned. It could do them no harm." Having imbibed a skepticism from Mlle. Souvestre that caused her to question religious orthodoxy, Eleanor replied: "But are you sure that you believe in everything you learned?" He answered: "I really never thought about it. I think it is just as well not to

* To arrive at this total, FDR included the servants and farmworkers employed at Hyde Park by his mother.

Left: Franklin Roosevelt at sixteen months with his father, James Roosevelt. (Courtesy FDR Library) Right: Franklin Roosevelt (aged 5) is wearing the tartan of the Murray clan in this picture taken with his mother, Sara Roosevelt. (Courtesy FDR Library)

Six-year-old Franklin (left) and a playmate at the helm of James Roosevelt's yacht in a stiff Bay of Fundy breeze. (Courtesy of FDR Library)

Endicott Peabody, headmaster of Groton. (Courtesy FDR Library)

Franklin Roosevelt (center, first row) at Groton. (Courtesy FDR Library)

Springwood, the Roosevelt home at Hyde Park, before the alterations of 1915. (Courtesy FDR Library)

The house at Hyde Park after the alterations of 1915. (Courtesy FDR Library)

Harvard man. FDR at the age of twenty-one.
(Courtesy FDR Library)

FDR's room at Harvard. (Courtesy FDR Library)

think about things like that too much." That was that. But, as Eleanor noted, it was she who took the children to church on Sunday, while he played golf.

Relations between Franklin and Eleanor were complicated by the ambiguous nature of his attachment to his mother. Although he was sometimes angered and frustrated by her possessiveness, mother and son had a warm relationship, and he never completely separated himself from her. Even after he married, she was the central figure in his life and remained so until her death, in 1941. As a result, he sometimes appeared insensitive to his wife's needs and ignored her unhappiness under Sara's hand. Both mother and son disregarded Eleanor in the making of family plans. For example, when the house on Thirty-fifth Street became too small for the growing family and the neighborhood too commercial, Sara announced she was having adjoining town houses built at 47 and 49 East Sixty-fifth Street, one for herself and one for the children. "A Christmas present to Franklin and Eleanor from Mama," she wrote on a crude sketch of the proposed property.

Completed shortly before the end of 1908, the houses had sliding doors between them so that drawing and dining rooms could be thrown together, and there was a connecting door on the fourth floor. Franklin enthusiastically joined in planning and supervising construction, but Eleanor, who was not keen on being in such close proximity to her mother-in-law, showed her displeasure by remaining aloof. Not long after they moved into their house, at 49 East Sixty-fifth Street, her rigid self-possession broke down. Sitting in front of a dressing table which had been chosen for her by her mother-in-law, she burst into tears one evening. When her husband asked, "What on earth is the matter?" she replied that she didn't want to live in a house that was not hers, that she had not planned, and that did not express her taste. Franklin professed bewilderment at this outburst. "Being an eminently reasonable person, he thought I was quite mad and told me so gently, and said I would feel different in a little while."

Franklin Roosevelt liked to say that his political career began when he was "kidnapped" off the streets of Poughkeepsie by some local Democratic politicos and asked to address a Dutchess County policemen's picnic. Perhaps so, but encouraged by Uncle Ted's example and repeated suggestions that the younger Roosevelts should take an active role in politics, he had been considering following in his distinguished relative's footsteps for some time. Grenville Clark, one of his fellow law clerks, remembered Roosevelt saying "with engaging frankness that he wasn't going to practice law forever, that he intended to run for office at the first opportunity, and that he wanted to be and thought he had a real chance to be President."

The course to the White House that the young attorney charted for himself duplicated that followed by Theodore Roosevelt: First, he would win a seat in the state legislature, secure an appointment as assistant Secretary of the Navy, and be elected governor of New York. "Anyone who is Governor of New York has a good chance to be President with any luck," Franklin told the other clerks as they sat in the bullpen that surrounded their desks. "I do not recall . . . any of us deprecated his ambition or even smiled at it," Clark added. "It seemed proper and sincere; and moreover, as he put it, entirely reasonable."

Always under the Roosevelt spell, Franklin was ready to take the offensive against slurs aimed at the President. Frances Perkins recalled that the first time they met, at a tea dance at a Gramercy Park mansion, someone spoke with scorn of Teddy Roosevelt's "progressive" ideas. "A tall young man named Roosevelt, I didn't catch his first name on introduction, made a spirited defense of Theodore Roosevelt." Following his marriage to Eleanor, they were frequent guests at the White House or Aunt Bye's nearby home. At Alice Roosevelt's glittering wedding, in 1906, to Nicholas Longworth, a Republican congressman from Ohio, Franklin gallantly arranged the bride's train for the official photographer.† These visits provided the opportunity to see Uncle Ted in full cry, and Franklin had a favorite story about the elder Roosevelt which he often told. Pacing angrily before a White House fireplace, the President denounced some congressmen who had blocked a conservation bill he had recommended because they couldn't see any advantage to their districts. "Oh, if I could only be President and Congress for just ten minutes!" Uncle Ted declared.

> I remarked that I had heard him express that wish before and asked him what he would do. He replied, "I would pass an amendment to the Constitution requiring every candidate for the House or Senate to file an affidavit that he had travelled in every state of the Union and had visited foreign countries at least once."

The President's problems with Congress stemmed in part from a pledge he had made on Election Night 1904 that "under no circumstances" would he be a candidate for renomination four years later. This statement deprived him of his club over Congress, which refused to approve Roosevelt's demands for inheritance and income taxes and other reform legislation, charging that such measures were unconstitutional. In words that were to be echoed three decades later by the younger Roosevelt, the President declared that the Constitution should be "interpreted not as a strait-jacket . . . but as an instrument designed for the life and

† Eleanor was pregnant with Anna and did not attend the wedding.

healthy growth of the nation." But if Theodore Roosevelt was unable to prod a reluctant Congress into approving his program, he convinced the vast majority of Americans that he was their champion against predatory forces in business and government. Thus, he was able to dictate the nomination and subsequent election of his hand-picked successor, William Howard Taft.

Conservatives in both parties breathed a sigh of relief as he departed the White House, in March 1909, to bag big game in Africa and crowned heads in Europe. J. P. Morgan expressed the hope of Wall Street that the lions would do their duty. Critics might question Roosevelt's sincerity and effectiveness as a reformer, but he understood that the greatest task facing any political leader is to educate the public. The White House, as he was fond of saying, was "a bully pulpit." And by his example he convinced many able young men to enter politics—among them Franklin Roosevelt.

Franklin's opportunity arrived early in the spring of 1910, when John E. Mack, the Democratic district attorney for Dutchess County, brought some papers to his office on Wall Street to be signed. When their business had been completed, the talk turned to the political situation in the county. Mack noted that Lewis Stuyvesant Chanler, the incumbent state assemblyman from the Second District, appeared to be wearying of the office and might be persuaded to run for state senator from the Twenty-sixth District, consisting of Columbia, Dutchess, and Putnam counties, lying one above another along the eastern bank of the Hudson. If so, was Roosevelt interested in filling the assembly seat? Franklin almost bowled him over in his eagerness to accept the proposal. Although he had cast his first presidential vote for Theodore Roosevelt, he regarded himself as a Democrat, just as his father had been. Mack, who had known James Roosevelt and liked his son, set the wheels in motion for Roosevelt's selection by the local Democratic leaders.

Most of upstate New York was solidly Republican. Although there were Democratic enclaves, such as Poughkeepsie, the Democrats had little success in electing candidates in the farming areas and villages. The normal procedure adopted by party leaders was to offer the nomination to a member of a prominent county family, who would at least add tone to the ticket and was able to finance his own campaign. Once in a while, these gentlemen-politicians scored an upset, as Chanler had in 1906, when he was elected lieutenant governor of New York. Two years later, he was defeated for the governorship by Charles Evans Hughes, but enjoyed politics so much that he had accepted the humble office of assemblyman.

To give the party workers an opportunity to look him over, Roosevelt came up to Poughkeepsie in August to address a rally. "On that joyous occasion of clams and sauerkraut and real beer I made my first speech," he later declared, "and I have been apologizing for it ever since." Exuding friendliness and energy—"call me Franklin," he told everyone—Roosevelt made a favorable impression upon the rank and file as well as the leaders, with the exception of Edward E. Perkins, the Democratic state committeeman and an ally of Charles F. Murphy, the boss of Tammany Hall. Perkins disliked "political dudes," claiming that they could not be trusted to stay on the reservation, but acknowledged that Roosevelt ought to be good for a sizable amount of campaign cash.‡ With the Second Assembly District overwhelmingly Democratic, it appeared as if Roosevelt could count on going to Albany—taking the first step on the road to the White House that he had described to his fellow law clerks.

But Chanler decided to keep his safe seat in the assembly, rather than make a hopeless race for state senator in a solidly Republican district in which only one Democrat had been elected since 1856. The sole opportunity that now lay open to young Roosevelt was to run for the state senate himself. Despite the slim chance of defeating the incumbent, Senator John F. Schlosser—in fact, John Mack put his chances at one in five—Franklin decided to take the gamble. Undoubtedly, he did so to gain experience, to become known to the voters, and to secure a future lien upon the party leadership. Back in 1886, Theodore Roosevelt had chosen to make a similar seemingly futile run for mayor of New York City for the same reasons.

Most of the family, including Franklin's mother, tried to persuade him to keep out of what she called "the messy business of politics," but Eleanor, pregnant with Elliott, played no role in her husband's decision. "I listened to all his plans with a great deal of interest," she said. "It never occurred to me that I had any part to play. I felt I must acquiesce in whatever he might decide and be willing to go to Albany." Before taking the final plunge, Franklin, who had his own misgivings, decided to sound out Uncle Ted, recently returned from his triumphant postpresidential African and European tour. He asked Aunt Bye to find out if the former President would speak against his candidacy in Dutchess County, for that would be a fatal blow. "Franklin ought to go into politics without the least regard as to where I speak or don't speak," the elder Roosevelt wrote his sister. The young man was "a fine fellow" he added, although he regretted that he was not a Republican.

Three days before the Democratic nominating convention was to meet, at Poughkeepsie on October 6, a conference of party leaders was held in Ed Perkins' law office, in Poughkeepsie, to give the prospective candidates a final inspection. Summoned from Springwood, Franklin ar-

‡ "I guess several people thought that I would be a gold mine," FDR said later, "but, unfortunately, the gold was not there." The Roosevelt family and his friends did contribute more than $2,500 to the campaign, however.

rived bareheaded and dressed in riding breeches and boots. Looking him up and down with undisguised contempt, Perkins sourly observed: "You'll have to take off those yellow shoes and put on some regular pants."

Franklin entered the race with a Rooseveltian zest. "I accept this nomination with absolute independence," he told the convention delegates. "I am pledged to no man; I am influenced by no specific interests; and so I shall remain. . . . In the coming campaign, I need not tell you that I do not intend to stand still. We are going to have a very strenuous month." The appearance of a Democratic Roosevelt did not unduly alarm the Republicans, who believed that his dandyish clothes and patrician accent would not go down well with the local farmers. The Poughkeepsie *Eagle* consistently misspelled his name as "Franklyn" when it bothered to mention him at all, and indicated that he owed his nomination to a campaign contribution that "goes well above four figures." Even the Poughkeepsie *Evening Enterprise*, a Democratic paper, noted that "Mr. Roosevelt . . . is more a stranger than either of the other nominees."

True to his promise of a "strenuous month," Roosevelt startled everyone by campaigning in a bright-red Maxwell touring car bedecked with flags, the first time that an automobile had been used in a local campaign.* Some of Franklin's supporters feared that the gaudy vehicle would frighten farmers' horses and cattle. But it permitted him to visit every part of the sprawling district in the few weeks before Election Day, which could not have been done with a horse and buggy. Accompanied by Richard E. Connell, perennial Democratic candidate for the congressional seat then held by Representative Hamilton Fish,† he set out on a whirlwind campaign.

Organization Democrats in Poughkeepsie and the other towns could be relied upon to deliver their votes, so the candidates carried the fight to the rural areas. Bouncing over hills and rutted roads, covered with dust, bone-tired, and soaked by rain, for the Maxwell had no top or windshield, they touched at every country store and stopped at every crossroads hamlet. Young Roosevelt seemed to thrive on the excitement of his first campaign. "When we met a horse or a team—and that was about every half-mile or so—we had to stop, not only the car but the engine as well," he recalled.‡ These unplanned pauses provided opportunities for talks with farmers and teamsters. If there were no scheduled meetings, the candidates bought drinks for all comers at the local saloon or country inn.

* The Maxwell was rented for $20 a day, or a total cost of $560 for twenty-eight days.
† Hamilton Fish was the father of the Hamilton Fish who held the seat during FDR's presidency and was one of Roosevelt's bitterest critics. The son of that Hamilton Fish now holds the seat.
‡ Under New York State law, automobiles had to stop and draw off to the side of the road if the driver of a horse-drawn vehicle raised his whip as a signal.

Meeting a gang of Italian railroad workers, Roosevelt quickly began "chattering away as if he were a native," as John Mack remembered. The candidate covered some two thousand miles of back road despite frequent breakdowns and blowouts. Even a painful fall failed to slow Roosevelt down. After soaking a badly cut knee in disinfectant, he limped off on the campaign trail. Once, the candidates got so carried away, they overshot the New York State line and harangued voters in neighboring Connecticut.

Dick Connell was the star of the show. A fiery stump speaker, he climaxed each appearance with a pyrotechnic appeal to patriotism. Whipping out an American flag from somewhere inside his flapping Prince Albert coat, he would wave it over his head and declaim: "The same old flag that waved at Lexington; the same old flag that Sherman carried on the march to the sea. . . ." Connell liked to speak to groups of children, explaining that they not only took campaign literature home to their parents, but themselves grew up to be voters.

Franklin picked up several useful tips about public speaking from the old professional, including the genial greeting "My friends," which became his trademark. Advised by his companion that his pince-nez glasses made him look cold and distant, he took them off before addressing an audience. To Eleanor, hearing her husband speak for the first time, he appeared "high strung and, at times, nervous. . . . He spoke slowly, and every now and then there would be a long pause, and I would be worried for fear that he would never go on." But go on he did, and whatever Roosevelt lacked in fervor, he made up in an earnestness that convinced listeners of his sincerity. Making as many as ten speeches a day, he improved his style and tailored a set speech to suit each place it was delivered:

> Humboldt, the great traveller, once said: "You can tell the character of the people of a house by looking at the outside" [he would begin]. This is even more true of a community—and I think I can truthfully say that of all the villages of Dutchess County, and I have been in pretty nearly every one, there are very few that appear as favorably as Pleasant Valley. . . .

Espousing a vague progressivism, Roosevelt made "bossism" and good government the key issues of his campaign. He also paid obeisance to the district's rural interests, by condemning the protectionist Payne-Aldrich Tariff, imposed by the Taft administration, which farmers claimed forced them to sell their produce cheaply and pay exorbitant prices for finished goods. And he subtly emphasized his relationship to Theodore Roosevelt—who spoke in Dutchess County but did him the favor of not mentioning him—by interlarding his speeches with the word "bully." Sometimes he was even more direct. "I am not Teddy," he told one rally, amid much laughter. "A little shaver said to me the other day that he knew I wasn't Teddy—I asked him 'why' and he replied: 'Because you don't show your teeth.'"

The political neophyte's link to the former President was an important campaign asset. The Republicans were bitterly divided in 1910 on both the national and the local levels—and as was to be expected, Theodore Roosevelt was in the center of the political storm. Only fifty-two years old when he returned from his travels, he was anxious to resume an active role in politics and quickly became convinced that Taft had betrayed his policies. Well-meaning, placid, and conservative, the new President believed the time had come to relax the reformist pressures of his predecessor. An open split between Taft and Roosevelt soon followed, and the schism between its leaders divided the Republican Party into two wings: the Old Guard, loyal to the President, and the Insurgents, who rallied around the Rough Rider.

Looking about for a platform, Roosevelt chanced upon a book by Herbert Croly, *The Promise of American Life,* which refuted the Jeffersonian ideal of the least government being the best government. Croly called for a "New Nationalism"—an America organized to achieve its "national historical mission" of improving the welfare of mankind. A strong central government was the keystone of the structure envisioned by Croly—a government so strong that it could stand as a countervailing power against the trusts. Rather than viewing the trusts as inherently evil, Croly believed that they contributed to economic efficiency and should be carefully regulated, rather than dissolved by government action.

Croly's ideas appealed to the former President, and he took over his program along with the slogan "the New Nationalism." Speaking at Osawatomie, Kansas, on August 31, 1910, he defined the movement: "The New Nationalism puts the national need before sectional or personal advantage. . . . This New Nationalism regards the executive power as the steward of the public welfare. It demands of the judiciary that it shall be interested primarily in human welfare rather than property, just as it demands that the representative body shall represent all the people rather than any one class or section of people."

The most violent intraparty clashes between the Insurgents and the Old Guard occurred in New York State, where the Republican Governor, Charles Evans Hughes, had been sabotaged in his efforts to make reforms by William Barnes, Jr., his own party's boss, as well as by Tammany's stalwarts. Weary of the struggle, Hughes had accepted an appointment to the U. S. Supreme Court. Following a bruising fight, Roosevelt seized control of the state convention from Barnes and his myrmidons and dictated the nomination of Henry L. Stimson to succeed Hughes. Angered, the Old Guard retaliated by sitting on their hands during the campaign, and it appeared that John A. Dix, the conservative and colorless businessman nominated by the Democrats, would be elected governor in November.

Turning the situation to his own advantage, Franklin Roosevelt told the Republican farmers that they had been sold out by their leaders in Washington and Albany, and suggested the best way to strike a blow for Teddy Roosevelt was to vote Democratic. Having received the endorsement of the Hughes Republicans, he charged that his opponent, Republican Senator Schlosser, had helped wreck Hughes's reforms in Albany and was an errand boy for Lou F. Payn, Boss Barnes's chief lieutenant in the area.* With a rhetorical flourish that was to become familiar in future years, Roosevelt declared: "I do know that he hasn't represented me and I do know that he hasn't represented you."

Regarding Roosevelt's flamboyant campaign as a circus, the Republicans ignored the young man until they suddenly realized he was making headway among the farmers. A hasty counterattack was mounted, with Representative Fish charging that Roosevelt was not really a resident of the district but made his home in New York City. Efforts were also made to link him to Wall Street. The Poughkeepsie *Eagle*, which had all but refused to mention him throughout the campaign, now warned its readers that "Franklyn D. Roosevelt represents just the opposite of what Theodore Roosevelt stands for," and emphasized his links to Carter, Ledyard. "It is well for the electors of this Senatorial District to bear in mind that this firm are the lawyers for some of the great trusts. . . ."

Beginning a tradition he was to follow in later elections, Roosevelt closed out the campaign with an appearance before his friends and neighbors in Hyde Park. "You have known what my father stood for before me, you have known how close he was to the life of this town," he reminded them, "and I do not need to tell you that it is my desire always to follow in his footsteps." Election Day dawned gray and rainy, but the Democrats regarded it as a good omen, because bad weather would keep the Republican farmers at home. Franklin voted early, at the Hyde Park town hall, and returned to Springwood to await the results.

The outcome of the election was a personal triumph for Roosevelt. Much to everyone's surprise, he defeated Schlosser—15,708 votes to 14,568—an unprecedented majority for a Democrat. And he ran well ahead of the rest of the ticket not only in the urban precincts of

---

* In 1900, when he was governor of New York, Theodore Roosevelt had dismissed Payn from his post as state superintendent of insurance because he had borrowed nearly $500,000 from a trust company whose directors were also officials of an insurance company regulated by his office. Accused of "voting tombstones" in another case, Payn replied that he had cast the ballots the same way the deceased would have voted if alive. "We always respect a man's convictions," he said.

Poughkeepsie but in the rural areas as well. The Democratic avalanche was complete everywhere. John Dix won the governorship, as expected; the Democrats gained control of both houses of the New York legislature for the first time in almost two decades; and Dick Connell squeaked past Fish to win the seat in Congress he had sought so long.† These victories were part of a national tide of protest against the hapless President Taft. The Democrats won a majority in the House of Representatives and more than half the governorships, including New Jersey, where Woodrow Wilson, the president of Princeton University, was elected.

Republican disunity had catapulted Franklin Roosevelt into his first electoral victory, but his victory was more than a matter of sheer luck. He had paved the way to success with careful groundwork, and when opportunity occurred, he was in a position to seize it.

† Unhappily, Connell died during his first term in Washington.

V

TWISTING THE TIGER'S TAIL

LUCK AND OPPORTUNITY accompanied Franklin Roosevelt to Albany, and before he had voted on a single bill, he was one of the most widely known political figures in New York. A freshman state senator, traditionally ranked "somewhere between . . . a janitor and a committee clerk," according to a sardonic newsman named Louis McHenry Howe, but the "second coming of a Roosevelt" to the stage where Theodore Roosevelt had won fame thirty years before was hardly to be ignored. Reporters hastened to file feature stories about the intense-looking young aristocrat in high collar and gold-bowed pince-nez. W. Axel Warn, the veteran New York *Times* correspondent in Albany, described his debut, on January 4, 1911, as follows:

> Franklin D. Roosevelt stepped lightly into the Senate Chamber on the opening day of the present session. He had a certificate entitling him to a reserved seat, and he had come to claim it. Unobtrusively, he sank into the big leather upholstered chair behind a desk marked "26" in white lettering. It was the seat of whoever happened to represent the Columbia-Putnam-Dutchess district in the Senate. . . . That desk and the man behind it has been in the glare of the limelight ever since.
>
> Those who looked closely . . . saw a young man with the finely chiseled face of a Roman patrician, only with a ruddier glow of health on it. . . . Senator Roosevelt is less than thirty. He is tall and lithe. With his handsome face and his form of supple strength he could make a fortune on the stage and set the matinee girl's heart throbbing with subtle and happy emotion. . . .

Big Tim Sullivan, the boss of the Bowery, cast a much less admiring glance his way, however. "Well, if we've caught a Roosevelt, we'd better take him down and drop him off the dock," he told Charles F. Murphy, Grand Sachem of Tammany Hall. "The Roosevelts run true to form, and this kid is likely to do for us what the Colonel is going to do for the Republican party—split it wide open." Not long afterward, both Murphy and Sullivan had cause to wish they had given this suggestion serious consideration.

Elevated from the common herd of neophyte politicians by the magic of his name, Franklin was also greatly assisted in making his mark by his wealth. Most members of the legislature—paid fifteen hundred dollars a session plus whatever petty graft that stuck to their fingers—spent only a few days of each week in Albany. The more prosperous lived in the Ten Eyck Hotel, while the smaller fry crowded the back-street boardinghouses. Having left Carter, Ledyard & Milburn to form a new law firm with two friends, Henry Hooker and Langdon Marvin, and having promised the voters of his district that he would be a full-time senator, Roosevelt rented a three-story brownstone at 248 State Street at a cost of four hundred dollars a month. The entire family moved in on New Year's Day: Franklin, Eleanor, Anna, James, and baby Elliott, as well as three servants "besides the nurses." Within a brisk walk of the capitol and containing ample room for entertaining, the house was to prove an important political asset to Roosevelt.

Albany was a provincial town of low red-brick and brownstone buildings, with a skyline dominated by bristling church steeples and the massive structures on Capitol Hill. There were broad avenues, tree-shrouded streets, and gracious parks and squares where Eleanor and the nurses strolled with the children. Society moved at an easy pace and was ruled by a few old families of Dutch lineage, who welcomed the Roosevelts. Eleanor found the small-town atmosphere a surprise and a delight. Not long after the family had moved in, she was startled when stopped by a lady on the street who said: "You must be Mrs. Roosevelt, for your children are the only children I do not know."

In its long history, Albany had not seen such revelry as marked the return to power of the Democrats after twenty years in the political wilderness. Tammany stalwarts, conservative Cleveland men, progressives, upstaters, and downstaters milled about in the hotel lobbies and stood elbow to elbow in the crowded saloons. Among those on hand to see "democracy in action" were Boss Murphy, pot-bellied and bullet-headed; John H. McCooey, whose word was law in Brooklyn; and such reformers as William Church Osborn, of Putnam County, and Thomas Mott Osborne, former mayor of Auburn and founder of the Democratic League.* Roosevelt contributed to the merriment by inviting his constituents to attend the festivities, and they did—some four hundred strong along with

* An organization designed to rescue the party from Tammany's clutches.

the Hyde Park fifers and drummers and a brass band. Following the inauguration of Governor John Dix, there was to be an open house at the senator's new home.

Much to Franklin's "horror," as he put it, the opening prayer at the inaugural "was almost 'drowned out' by the discordant notes of what I easily recognized as my Hyde Park Fife and Drum Corps . . . in the street below." After the ceremony, he hurriedly left the Capitol, "and when a block from home was met by the sight of a dense cheering mob in front of the house—it was the delegation from the Senatorial District. . . . The band and Fife and Drum Corps were working overtime, but [all] managed to get into the house, shaking hands as they passed into the Dining Room." "For three solid hours" people "wandered in and out," said Eleanor, partaking of the chicken salad sandwiches, coffee, beer, and cigars that had been ordered from a caterer. "E.R. . . . made a hit with the whole delegation," observed Franklin. When the last guest had departed for the railroad station, Governor Dix telephoned to invite the Roosevelts to the Executive Mansion for "a little informal dancing." They had "a delightful evening," Franklin wrote in his diary. "It was almost a family party, only the military aides, two or three Albany girls and ourselves being there."

Politics had as much to do with the invitation as social affability, for Dix regarded Roosevelt as a natural ally during the forthcoming session. Franklin's father and half brother had been Cleveland Democrats, and it was expected that the young man would follow in their footsteps. Roosevelt picked up some useful information that night. Dix informed him that, as a conciliatory gesture, Boss Murphy had agreed to dump Thomas F. Grady, the longtime president pro tempore of the Senate. Able but alcoholic, Grady was the only member of the current legislature who had been in Albany when Theodore Roosevelt had appeared on the scene. Dix held out the prospect to Franklin that he might be elected in Grady's place. While Franklin confided to his diary that "the decision to throw over Senator Grady is splendid," he brushed aside the governor's proposal that he replace him. Grady was a skilled parliamentarian and likely "to raise Hell generally" after being deposed.

In place of Grady, Murphy selected Robert F. Wagner, a thirty-three-year-old German-born immigrant, as Democratic leader of the Senate; thirty-seven-year-old Alfred E. Smith, born on the Lower East Side and educated in the Fulton Fish Market, was named the party's leader in the Assembly. Although both were veteran Tammany men, they were able and popular. In fact, reformers often overlooked the ability of the old-fashioned political machines such as Tammany to produce leaders of unquestioned ability when required by circumstances. Roosevelt, who seconded the nomination of Wagner on behalf of the upstate delegation, said, "Wagner will be fairly good I think. He has good intentions; the only obstacle is the pressure of his own machine."

Reins firmly in hand, Boss Murphy now turned to the most important business of the session: the election of a United States senator.† The term of Senator Chauncey M. Depew, a Republican and mouthpiece of the Vanderbilt railroad interests, was to end on March 4, 1911, and Murphy had handpicked William F. Sheehan to replace him. "Blue-eyed Billy" Sheehan had gotten his start as a machine politico in Buffalo, but in more recent years, he had risen in the world. Working with Thomas Fortune Ryan, a notorious Wall Street operator, he became a millionaire in traction and utility speculation and a law partner of Alton B. Parker, the unsuccessful Democratic nominee for President in 1904. He was a member of the best clubs and resided on East 65th Street not far from the Roosevelts.

Once Murphy had bestowed his blessing upon Sheehan, his election seemed assured. The U.S. senator would be chosen by a simple majority of the two hundred members of both houses of the legislature, in which the Democrats controlled one hundred fourteen seats, thirteen more than needed to win. In reality, the choice could be made by as few as fifty-eight members—a bare majority of the Democratic caucus. Murphy had, in effect, the power to personally appoint the senator, for he had more than a majority of the Democratic legislators in his pocket.

Sheehan had been generous with funds during the previous campaign, and as a New York *Times* correspondent noted, "at least a half a dozen Democratic legislators have drifted into the capital bubbling over with gratitude." No worse than the average politico of the period, Sheehan wished to crown his career with a U.S. senatorship, but others were less enchanted with him. Most of the dissidents supported Edward M. Shepard, former mayor of Brooklyn, legal counsel for the Pennsylvania Railroad, and a moderate progressive. Franklin Roosevelt was among them. "Shepard is without question the most competent to fill the position, but the Tammany crowd seems unable to forgive him for his occasional independence and Sheehan looks like their choice at this stage of the game," he noted in his diary shortly after arriving in Albany. "May the result prove that I am wrong! There is no question in my mind that the Democratic party is on trial. . . ."

Roosevelt's decision to resist Sheehan's election was based upon several factors. Although Franklin found him "delightful personally," he was angered by the undemocratic fashion in which Murphy's choice was to be rammed down the throats of legislative Democrats. Such friends as William Osborn, Thomas Osborne, and John Mack, who had given him

† Before the ratification of the Seventeenth Amendment to the Constitution, in 1913, the legislatures, rather than the voters, chose the two senators allotted each state.

his start in politics, were all unhappy with the choice of Sheehan. Family tradition also played a role in his decision, as Sheehan had been anathema to Cleveland Democrats such as his father. And there was the example of Theodore Roosevelt. Fully realizing that his election in a predominantly Republican district was something of a fluke, the younger Roosevelt understood that if he wished to remain in politics he would have to make a reputation that would guarantee his reelection in 1912. Uncle Ted had solved a similar problem three decades before by defying party discipline to delve into a shady traction deal that brought him to public attention and made his reputation as a reformer.

Having no wish for an open break with the party, Roosevelt went to Al Smith, the newly installed assembly leader, informed him of his opposition to Sheehan, and along with some other insurgents sought guidance on procedure. With a candor that Franklin remembered many years later, Smith told them: "Boys, I want you to go into the caucus, and if you go in, you're bound by the action of the majority. That's party law. But if you're serious about this fight, keep your hands clean and stay out. Then you're free agents."

Despite these distant rumblings, Sheehan was brimming with confidence on the evening of January 16 as the Democrats began filtering into the Assembly Chamber for their caucus. Reporters crowded about asking him for his views on the issues that would come before him as a senator. "Not now," he replied. "If you call on me tomorrow I may talk." But at nine o'clock, when the caucus was to be gaveled into session, it was discovered that a number of legislators were absent. The meeting was postponed for an hour to allow the party whips to dragoon the missing members.

Meanwhile, the insurgents, including Roosevelt, gathered in a hotel room under the leadership of Edward R. Terry, a Brooklyn assemblyman and Yale classmate of President Taft, with the intention of preventing Sheehan from receiving enough votes for election. Roosevelt and Terry had arrived first, to find themselves alone. "For ten long minutes that seemed like hours," Terry said, "we assured each other that there was no doubt of the speedy arrival of the other eighteen." When the latecomers appeared, Roosevelt was elected chairman, and they awaited the outcome of the caucus up on Capitol Hill. Sheehan received sixty-two votes, Shepard eighteen, and there were a few scattered ballots for other candidates. All those who voted were bound to Sheehan, but they totaled only ninety-one members—ten fewer than needed for endorsement by the caucus.

Roosevelt issued a manifesto in the name of the insurgents explaining they had refused to attend the party gathering because "they believed the votes of those who represented the people should not be smothered in the caucus; . . . the people should know just how their representatives vote . . . and that any majority secured for any candidate should be credited to the representatives in Legislature and not some one outside the body." The manifesto made headlines and Roosevelt's name figured prominently. Some of the insurgents supported Shepard, while others backed various candidates, Roosevelt explained, but all "have decided to stand to a man and to the end against William F. Sheehan." They were "fighting against the boss rule system" and would never yield.

All legislative business ground to a halt, and the deadlock lasted for ten weeks. Murphy did not at first appear to take the insurgency seriously. While Sheehan threatened revenge in a private meeting with Roosevelt, the Boss was affability itself. Roosevelt said they talked about the weather for five or ten minutes, and he quoted Murphy as saying he was "entirely convinced" that the opposition to Sheehan was "a perfectly honest one." Most party leaders took the position that when suitable enticements were dangled in front of this band of upstarts, the ten or so votes needed for Sheehan's election would be forthcoming. As soon as they had received enough publicity, they would return to the fold.

Roosevelt, the guiding spirit behind the revolt, if not its leader, was contemptuously dismissed by machine politicos as a "college kid" and "a calf still wet behind the ears." Some of the Old Guard even claimed that he was a Trojan horse, bent on splitting the party under instructions from Theodore Roosevelt. But the young man was elated by the slash and parry of political combat. "There is nothing I love as much as a good fight," he told a reporter, with evident glee. "I never had as much fun in my life as I am having right now."

The struggle brought Roosevelt national attention, for progressives in all parts of the nation were demanding direct election of U.S. senators in an effort to end bossism. In New Jersey, the newly elected governor, Woodrow Wilson, was waging a similar fight to prevent James Smith, Jr., boss of the Newark-Essex County machine, from being appointed to the Senate. Wilson's victory established him as one of the country's major progressive leaders and put him on the road to the White House. "I am delighted with your action & told Woodrow Wilson today of how he & you are serving the nation," William Grosvenor, a prominent clergyman, wrote Roosevelt. From Sagamore Hill, Franklin received a hastily scrawled note: "Just a line to say we are all really proud of the way you handled yourself. Good luck to you! Give my love to dear Eleanor."

The New York *Times* listed the names of the insurgents on a "roll of honor" and placed young Roosevelt's name at the top. And the Cleveland *Plain Dealer* commented: "Theodore Roosevelt as a young man merely took advantage of all opportunities to keep himself in the public eye, and to strengthen the impression that he was a fighter. . . . Franklin D. Roosevelt is beginning his public career fully as auspiciously. If none of the colonel's sons turn out to be fit objects for public adoration, may not it be possible that this rising star may continue the Roosevelt dynasty?"

Although many observers regarded him as the "head and shoulders" of the revolt, the New York *Sun* suggested that Roosevelt was more the chairman of the board of the insurgency than its actual leader.

Roosevelt's home provided a combined headquarters and social club. The excitement of the opening stages of the battle was soon replaced by routine. Day after day, week after week, between twenty and thirty men gathered at the State Street house each morning, and at 10 A.M. marched up to the Capitol, where they went through the futile gesture of casting ballots for a U.S. senator. At 5 o'clock, they returned to Roosevelt's home to gather around the crackling fire in the large library for the rest of the evening. These meetings were more hand-holding sessions than strategy meetings. "There is very little business done at our councils of War," Roosevelt said. "We just sit around and swap stories like soldiers at the bivouac fire."

Reporters also dropped in to pick up tidbits of news, of which Roosevelt seemed to have an inexhaustible supply. Among them was Louis Howe, the gnarled little Albany correspondent of the New York *Herald*. Howe took particular notice of a coat of arms carved over the blazing hearth—a hand holding a club—and thought at once of Teddy Roosevelt's Big Stick. At first, he sized up the younger Roosevelt as "a spoiled, silk-pants sort of a guy," but later came to admire his spirit. "Mein Gawd! The boy's got courage," he declared in the mock German he affected.

These meetings also marked the beginning of Eleanor Roosevelt's political education. For her, the move to Albany had provided an escape from the domination of Sara Roosevelt, and she indulged her lively intellectual curiosity. As the wife of the most talked-about young political figure in Albany, she met people of diverse background and learned to accept the unexpected without becoming flustered. "The rights and wrongs of the fight" against Sheehan's election "meant very little to me at first," she said, but soon she began to hover in the background as the insurgents gathered at her home, and learned how politics really worked. When she thought the time for departure had come, she brought out beer, cheese, and crackers as the signal for everyone to eat, drink, and go home.

Five-year-old Anna, a pretty little girl with flaxen hair, had vivid memories of this period that demonstrate the deep-seated love of the Roosevelt children for their father and their ambivalence toward the political world that was already luring him away from them. "It seemed to me that on many too many occasions Father would come home from work and shut himself up in a room with a lot of other men," she recalled. "I was forbidden to interrupt. But curiosity got the best of me and one day I sneaked into the room, *with* Father and his political cohorts. I had sense enough not to utter a sound, so no one bothered me. But pretty soon, I noticed that the air began to smell and was filled, right up to the ceiling, with smoke. It wasn't long before I began to cough, rub my smarting eyes and wish I could get away. Of course, I was discovered. I still associate cigar smoke with politics." Ultimately, the blue haze of tobacco smoke seeped into the nursery above the library, and the children had to be moved up another flight to keep them from "slowly choking to death."

Perhaps the most trying time for Eleanor came early in February, when Franklin suddenly announced that Sheehan and his wife were coming to State Street the next day. "Lunch was not so bad for I had my husband to carry the burden of the conversation," she said. "But after lunch we two women sat and talked about the weather and anything else inconsequential that we could think of, while both of us knew quite well that behind the door of my husband's study a really important fight was going on." Finally, the antagonists emerged, both looking grim. After the Sheehans were gone, the greatly relieved Eleanor asked if any agreement had been reached. "Certainly not," Franklin replied. And the battle went on.

Remaining in session while accomplishing nothing was costly to the legislators, and pressure was stepped up on the insurgents.‡ Patronage was denied them, and Roosevelt, who had been appointed chairman of the Forest, Fish, and Game Committee, saw his choice as clerk discharged. His new law firm lost a client. Even more damaging was the charge that he was anti-Irish and anti-Catholic. The Catholic bishop of Syracuse claimed that the insurgents had revived "the old spirit of Knownothingism" and in a much quoted statement declared: "You are an Irishman and that's agin you; you are a Catholic and that's agin you." Alarmed, Roosevelt and several of his associates hastily denied any taint of anti-Catholicism and emphasized that some of the insurgents were Irish Catholics and a few were even members of the Knights of Columbus.

Other rebels, more vulnerable financially than Roosevelt, were severely clawed by the angry Tammany tiger. Hints were dropped of called loans and mortgage foreclosures. The owner of a rural newspaper who depended upon government printing was warned that if he did not fall into line he would lose the contract when it came up for renewal. Some of the little group were told their political careers were over, for they would not be renominated. Resolutions from their constituents fomented

‡ According to a story told by Louis Howe, one of the insurgents went home for a weekend and began to look through the newspapers. "Suddenly he blanched with horror at the front-page streamer headline, 'Eight insurgents killed.' He was wondering whether to flee the country while the whole thing blew over when he noticed that the dateline was a town in Mexico where a revolution was taking place."

by Sheehan's partisans around the state piled up on the desks of the recalcitrants. Ed Perkins, the Democratic state committeeman in Poughkeepsie, always antagonistic to Roosevelt, circulated a petition demanding that he follow the wishes of the caucus. Recognizing that some of the 265 names were in the same handwriting, Roosevelt dismissed it as "a fizzle." And he found that his stand against Tammany was popular with the heavily Republican voters of his district. But the situation was not so easy for many of the insurgents, and several times it appeared as if the coalition would break up. "They say that the road of the transgressor is hard," declared a weary Edward Terry. "The transgressor's path is pleasant compared to that of a legislator trying to do what he regards as his duty. His way is beset with temptations on every side."

Politics abhors a vacancy in any office. As soon as it was evident that Sheehan could not be elected to the Senate, Murphy, reasoning that he had paid his debt to "Blue-eyed Billy," advised him to gracefully withdraw. He quietly began to line up support for Daniel F. Cahalan, his chief lieutenant and son-in-law, who had been his secret choice for the post all along. The Boss apparently believed that the opposition to both Sheehan and Shepard would be so violent that Cahalan would be acceptable to all parties as a compromise candidate. Inscrutability had always been Murphy's chief stock-in-trade. A reporter once asked an aide why the Boss had not joined the crowd at a political rally in singing The Star-Spangled Banner. "Perhaps he didn't want to commit himself," was the reply.

In a desperate move to prevent a collapse of the insurgency, Roosevelt sought to strike a deal with William Barnes, the Republican boss. He proposed that the Democratic rebels and the Republicans agree on a candidate acceptable to both sides. Barnes rejected this proposal—deciding it was good politics to let the Democrats tear themselves apart.

It took a fire that gutted the Capitol to break the deadlock. On the night of March 29, the legislative chambers were seriously damaged, forcing the members to meet in the cramped Albany City Hall. Tempers worn raw by the long-drawn-out struggle finally snapped under the physical discomfort. Wagner and Smith anxiously informed Murphy that unless a solution was found quickly they would be unable to hold their forces in Albany. They were ready to vote for anything or anyone so they could get out of town. Already worried that Roosevelt's maneuverings with the Republicans might produce an alliance, the Boss grabbed the first train to Albany—a milk train, which crept up along the Hudson—arriving early in the morning, exhausted and covered with cinders. He put forward the name of Justice Victor J. Dowling, of the State Supreme Court, as a compromise candidate. Two days of sparring followed before a majority of the insurgents, personally promised by Wagner and Smith that there would be no reprisals for their defection, reluctantly agreed to accept Dowling.

Just as they were preparing to leave the Roosevelt house for the caucus, the insurgents learned they had been soundly outgeneraled. Dowling had declined the nomination, and in his place, Murphy had submitted the name of Justice James A. O'Gorman, a former Grand Sachem of Tammany Hall. This not only filled the senate seat with someone more to his liking than Sheehan but also opened a vacancy on the state Supreme Court for Dan Cahalan, his son-in-law. Angrily denouncing the move, Roosevelt wanted to continue the siege, but it was a futile gesture. The insurgents could not afford to reject O'Gorman. Since his elevation to the bench, he had kept out of politics and enjoyed a good reputation as a jurist. Even more important in view of the charge that the insurgents had been motivated by anti-Catholicism in opposing Sheehan, he was not only an Irish Catholic but a former president of the Friendly Sons of St. Patrick. With reports filtering in that Boss Barnes was about to make a deal with Murphy to elect Sheehan if O'Gorman was rejected, a majority of the rebels decided to vote for O'Gorman. The rest, including Roosevelt, agreed to vote for him in the legislative session but declined to take part in the caucus.

A cacophony of cheers and hoots greeted Roosevelt and the other holdouts as they filed into the Council Chamber on the evening of March 31 to cast their ballots. Someone started to sing the Tammany victory song—"Tammanee . . . Tammanee . . . Swamp 'em, Swamp 'em . . . Get the wampum"—and it was taken up by the rollicking crowd. Legislators and spectators milled about, shouting and hugging each other and paying no attention to the frantic pounding of the gavel. When the speaker managed to at last create a semblance of order, Edgar Brackett, the Republican minority leader, taunted the insurgents. "God moves in a mysterious way," he observed. "Far be it from me to add to the humiliation of the Democrats if I could. They have now accepted a man infinitely more potent in the councils of Tammany Hall than the man they rejected." Taking the floor amid groans and hisses, Roosevelt attempted to salvage a few shreds of dignity from the debacle. "Two months ago a number of Democrats felt that it was our duty to dissent from certain of our party associates in the matter of selecting a United States Senator," he declared. " . . . We have followed the dictates of our consciences and have done our duty as we saw it. I believe that as a result the Democratic party has taken an upward step. We are Democrats—not irregulars, but regulars. I take pleasure in casting my vote for the Hon. James A. O'Gorman."

Everyone agreed that the scalps of Roosevelt and his fellow insurgents dangled from the belts of the Tammany braves as they happily returned to New York City for a brief recess. Murphy was "exultant" and hailed the election of O'Gorman as a triumph for majority rule and the party caucus. Roosevelt tried to put up a bold front, however, telling newsmen that the rebels had not been trying to elect a senator of their own but to prevent Sheehan from going to Washington. "The minority never assumed to dictate the choice of the majority," he said. Once the Sheehan express had been derailed, the insurgents were solely interested in electing "a suitable man," so "the only credit Charles F. Murphy can claim in ending the senatorial deadlock" is that he eventually put forward the name of such a man. If the Boss had suggested O'Gorman's name in the beginning, Roosevelt claimed, the insurgents would have accepted him. "We all believe him to be a man of absolute independence. . . ." But at their annual dinner a few weeks later, the legislative correspondents mercilessly lampooned him:

> What's the matter with Roosevelt and his Plan?
> All the other reformers have them on the pan.
> Fattened them up with printer's ink.
> Then handed them the rinky dink.
> What's the matter with Roosevelt?
> Got the can.

Nevertheless, the deadlock had mixed results. The insurgents were forced to swallow O'Gorman, but they had prevented the election of Sheehan. Although Murphy had triumphed in the end, he had been bloodied in the struggle. And the cause of direct election of U.S. senators had been dramatized and advanced. As for Roosevelt, the "Sheehan business," as he called it, provided him with a short course in practical politics. In this rough school, he had learned to intrigue and maneuver, to balance conflicting ambitions and intricate relationships, and to turn the insatiable need of journalists for colorful copy to his own advantage.

Worried about the effect of O'Gorman's victory upon his constituents, Roosevelt hurried down to Hyde Park. The voters had supported his role in the insurgency, but he was concerned that they might view the outcome as a capitulation to Tammany. He was delighted to find that there was little grumbling and that his constituents "did not feel that the victory belonged at all to Murphy." Thus armed, he transformed a humiliating defeat into victory, with a masterful exhibition of political sleight of hand. Roosevelt shrewdly emphasized that the dragon of corruption and bossism had been dealt a serious blow, and claimed a personal victory before a public that wished to believe him. Before long, the details of the "Sheehan business" were forgotten, and all that could be readily recalled of the episode was that Franklin Roosevelt had twisted the tail of the Tammany tiger. Six months after he had entered politics, Roosevelt was already a figure to be reckoned with, and his name was being linked to that of Woodrow Wilson, the progressive choice for the Democratic presidential nomination in 1912.

VI

THE EDUCATION OF
A PROGRESSIVE

Woodrow Wilson's first recorded mention of Franklin Roosevelt was in a conversation with Joseph F. Guffey, a Democratic boss from Pennsylvania.

"The young man just elected as state senator from a safe Republican district in New York will bear watching," Wilson told Guffey. "His name is Roosevelt."

"Professor, I thought all the Roosevelts were Republican," Guffey replied.

"No, Guffey, this one comes from the Democratic branch of the family, and he is the handsomest young giant I have ever seen."

The meeting between Wilson and Roosevelt occurred toward the end of 1911. Along with many other Democrats, Roosevelt made the pilgrimage to the statehouse in Trenton to take the measure of the scholar-politician who had suddenly become an exciting new force in the party. In the governor's chair for only a few months, Wilson had won national renown by transforming boss-ridden New Jersey into a model of progressivism. He had forced measures through a reluctant legislature long dreamt about by reformers: an employer's liability law, a direct-primary law, a corrupt-practices act, and laws tightening the regulation of railroads, utilities, and other corporations. For several hours, the two men discussed progressive legislation and the prospects for Wilson's nomination at the Democratic national convention to be held the following June in Baltimore. Later, accompanied by Joseph P. Tumulty, the Governor's devoted secretary, they continued their conversation on the short train ride between Trenton and Princeton, where Wilson made his home.

As the train rumbled into the gathering darkness, Roosevelt was awed by the brilliance of the man seated opposite him. Twenty-six years older than his visitor, the stern and austere Wilson was the personification of the intellectual. His long and bony face was dominated by a powerful jaw that thrust forward in a challenging manner, and his penetrating blue-gray eyes had a way of narrowing that gave him a stern, almost grim expression. No man could have been more different in personality from the ebullient and impulsive Theodore Roosevelt, until now the young man's political hero, but he unhesitatingly enlisted in Wilson's cause. For the first time, as Frances Perkins later observed, Roosevelt had come into contact with someone who "arrived at convictions by intellectual rather than emotional processes."

Later explaining his support of Wilson—and why other progressives should vote for him—Roosevelt described him as in the vanguard of the movement "to remedy conditions which the American people will no longer tolerate." Wilson was "keenly alive to the social and industrial welfare of the great body of workers," Roosevelt continued, and could be counted upon to fight for "better conditions of life for people of all kinds." Wilson's position on the great issues of the day—the tariff, control of trusts, and conservation of natural resources—was an encouragement to all progressives, and he was a successful leader in the struggle to clean up politics and raise it to a higher moral plane.

Roosevelt told Wilson there was mounting sentiment in New York among both progressive and old-line Cleveland Democrats for his nomination to the presidency. Pressed to estimate how many votes this would mean at the convention, he was forced to acknowledge that such support could not be translated into delegates. While about a third of the ninety delegates allotted to New York—the largest single bloc at the convention—were for Wilson, the delegation would be bound by a unit rule that would give all the votes to the candidate supported by a simple majority. Most of the delegates were under Tammany's thumb, and New York would eventually have to cast its ballots for Champ Clark, of Missouri, the conservative speaker of the House of Representatives, because Boss Murphy disliked Wilson intensely.

Roosevelt had just felt the power of Tammany in action—and the sobering experience was one of the reasons he had decided to hitch his wagon to Wilson's rising star. Convinced that Tammany would spare no effort in bringing his own political career to a quick end in 1912, Roosevelt saw a way to escape the machine's hostility by entering national politics. By hopping onto the Wilson bandwagon early, he could hope for an appointment to a position in Washington if his candidate won the presidency—effectively removing himself from Tammany's vengeance.

For the most part, Roosevelt's service in Albany was far less spectacular following the fight against Sheehan. Having entered politics with only a rudimentary understanding of progressivism—in fact, he defined politics as "a question of honesty . . . a fight for good government"—he was ill at ease with philosophical speculation, with abstract ideas. As Eleanor noted, he was more interested in people and the interplay of personalities than in the science of government. Like Theodore Roosevelt, he believed that control of the government must be returned to the people and that it should support the "public interest" over greedy "self-interest" —although these terms were only vaguely defined by both Roosevelts. Products of a buoyant and optimistic age, they were convinced their goals were not only feasible but attainable by merely tinkering with the machinery of government, rather than radically overhauling the basic political and economic system.

Young Roosevelt adopted the whole battery of mechanical reforms that had long been a staple of progressivism. The first step was easy: Before the legislature had deadlocked over the "Sheehan business," he had introduced a resolution urging New York's congressional delegation to support a constitutional amendment providing for direct election of U.S. senators. Shortly after the April recess, the resolution came to the floor and, following a five-hour debate led by Roosevelt, the Senate approved it, twenty-eight to fifteen. Four days later, the resolution was easily passed by the Assembly. It was only advisory in nature, and Senator Edgar Brackett, the minority leader, taunted Roosevelt, saying, "He is pleased with a smaller rattle and tickled with a smaller feather than I'd thought."

Few of Roosevelt's guerrilla campaigns against his party's leadership were so fruitful, however, usually garnering more in newspaper headlines than legislative accomplishment. His attempt to enact a direct-primary law was a failure. Both the Republicans and the Democrats had endorsed the direct primary in their platforms of the previous year, but the party bosses, not yet realizing they would have as little trouble dominating primaries as they had conventions and caucuses, had no intention of allowing any law to be enacted that would interfere with their control of the nominating process. As a pious gesture, Tammany produced a bill that would keep the convention system intact where it counted the most: in the choice of national convention delegates and nominees for statewide office. Roosevelt "dropped a bomb," as he put it, by forcing a vote on a proposal previously submitted by Governor Dix that called for a genuine direct-primary law. The move provoked a heated three-hour debate in which "I was called some choice names," he told his mother, but the measure was roundly defeated.

Nevertheless, Roosevelt seemed to be more realistic about the effect of the direct primary upon the electoral process than the machine politicians. While they openly feared reform, he expected the bosses to keep control of the system by fielding their own candidates and turning out organization voters. Still, as he told a constituent, the direct primary would make it possible for candidates not supported by the machines to be elected if enough ordinary citizens were aroused to come out and vote. In the end, he was forced to vote for the Tammany bill as better than none, but during the following year joined some progressive Republicans in an effort to obtain a more satisfactory law.

Roosevelt also went down to defeat in an attempt to block a Tammany plan to reorganize the state highway commission. Model-T Fords were beginning to pour from the production lines of Detroit, and with highway improvements likely to consume an ever-growing portion of the state budget, the farsighted Murphy wished to ensure a greater share of the loaves and fishes for the organization. Denouncing the bill as "vicious," "ill-conceived," and an encouragement to institutionalized corruption, Roosevelt managed to stir up enough opposition so that it passed by only a one-vote margin. Even in defeat Roosevelt attracted the attention of the press, for he had a debonair way of shrugging off setbacks. "This is the last straw on the camel's back," he told reporters upon one occasion. "We are going to get a new camel!"

To emphasize the Roosevelt difference, he even took the unprecedented step of voting against a pork-barrel project for his own district, thereby setting heads to shaking all over Albany. "I hope that the stenographer will not fail to record the protest made by the Senator from Dutchess," commented Senator Harvey D. Hinman when Roosevelt rejected an appropriation of $381.54 for repairs to a bridge over Wappinger's Creek because it wasn't necessary. "It will stand as a monument greater than any that has ever been or will be erected to perpetuate the achievements of his illustrious relative." A more succinct comment came from Big Tim Sullivan, who declared: "Frank, you ought to have your head examined."

Roosevelt's constituents allowed him to play the role of quixotic crusader and to tilt at Tammany as long as he was sensitive to their requirements. As chairman of the Forest, Fish and Game Committee and later of the Agricultural Committee, and a gentleman farmer himself, he was a vigorous protector of the district's agrarian interests and a supporter of conservation measures, particularly those relating to timber resources. Progressivism was basically a middle-class doctrine, and the substantial farmers and business and professional men who held the balance of power in his district were sympathetic to the movement and opposed the machinations of Tammany Hall. Nevertheless, Roosevelt was careful not to get too far in advance of his constituents. Because most of his constituents were opposed to votes for women, his first reaction to woman suffrage was equivocal, although Vassar College, a center of feminism, was in his district. When he finally supported it, Eleanor was shocked.* "I had never given the question really serious thought, for I took it for granted that men were superior creatures and still knew more about politics than women," she said. ". . . I cannot claim to have been a feminist in those early days."

Roosevelt's air of prim self-righteousness infuriated organization men like Al Smith, Robert Wagner, and Tim Sullivan. "Awfully arrogant fellow, that Roosevelt," Sullivan told Frances Perkins—already a leading reformer—then in Albany lobbying for approval of a bill limiting the working week for women to fifty-four hours. Senator James J. Walker thought he acted as if he were on a slumming expedition. And "Packy" McCabe, the senate clerk and a leading Albany politico, spoke for many of his colleagues when he angrily denounced Roosevelt as among "the snobs in our party . . . political accidents . . . fops and cads who come as near being political leaders as a green pea does a circus tent."

When the Tammany regulars refused to vote out a fifty-thousand-dollar appropriation for protection from forest fires, one of Roosevelt's pet projects, he warned that "hundreds of thousands of dollars' worth of property is likely to go up in smoke at any time." Pointing an accusing finger at Senator James Frawley, he declared, "Here . . . is one of the men responsible for this situation!"

"Senator Roosevelt has gained his point!" shouted Wagner, pounding his gavel for order. "What he wants is a headline in the newspapers. Let us proceed to our business."

Miss Perkins was unimpressed by young Roosevelt at this point, saying he seemed to have little, if any, concern for ordinary people or their welfare. "I have a vivid picture of him operating on the floor of the Senate," she recalled. "Tall and slender, very active and alert, moving about the floor, going in and out of committee rooms, rarely talking with the members, who more or less avoided him, not particularly charming (that came later), artificially serious of face, rarely smiling, with an unfortunate habit—so natural that he was unaware of it—of throwing his head up. This, combined with his pince-nez and great height, gave him the appearance of looking down his nose at most people. . . . He had a youthful lack of humility, a streak of self-righteousness, and a deafness to the hopes, fears, and aspirations which are the common lot." On the other hand, Eleanor Roosevelt laid her husband's seemingly austere manner during his Albany years to uncertainty and shyness, rather than any lack of human sympathy. "You know," Roosevelt told Miss Perkins many

---

* FDR often told the story that he had been persuaded to join the suffragist cause by Inez Milholland, a prominent reformer of the day, who converted him while sitting on his desk in the Senate. But Eleanor later said her husband had decided to support votes for women two months before Miss Milholland's visit.

years later with a wry smile, "I was an awfully mean cuss when I first went into politics."

Although spawned by the same upper-class environment that produced Roosevelt, Miss Perkins was intrigued by the rough Tammany politicos and discovered they had more social consciousness than many of those who talked about reform as an abstraction. "Me father and me mother were poor and struggling," Sullivan told her in offering support for the fifty-four-hour bill. "I seen me sister go out to work when she was only fourteen and I know we ought to help those gals by giving 'em a law which will prevent 'em from being broken down while they're still young." Paradoxically, by accepting social-reform legislation, the urban machines eventually put themselves out of business. Social security and unemployment insurance did more to end the power of Tammany and similar organizations than all the reform legislation passed by the progressives.

Young Roosevelt's reaction—or lack of it—to the catastrophic Triangle Shirtwaist Company fire illustrated his early limitations. Late on the afternoon of March 25, 1911, pedestrians crossing Washington Square, in downtown Manhattan, heard a muffled explosion and saw smoke billowing from the eighth floor of the Asch Building, off the east side of the square. The fire did not appear serious, and the gathering crowd thought the shop was closed until what looked like a bale of dress goods came tumbling out a window. "They're trying to save the best cloth," someone said. But as the wind pulled the bundle open, a cry of horror rose from the spectators. It had revealed the form of a girl hurtling toward the pavement like a shot bird. Another body quickly followed . . . and another . . . until 146 people, mostly Jewish and Italian girls, had either jumped to their deaths to escape the flames, suffocated behind doors that had been locked to prevent minor pilferage, or died when the only fire escape collapsed into a tangle of twisted iron. Fire officials had repeatedly warned of the existence of such deathtraps, but a court held that Triangle's owners were not liable for the holocaust.†

To meet the outcry from an outraged citizenry, the legislature established a Factory Investigating Commission, to look into working conditions around the state and devise new laws dealing with safety, health, hours, and other aspects of factory work. Al Smith and Robert Wagner were members of the commission and Frances Perkins its chief investigator. Inspectors crawled, crept, and pried into dark corners that had been hidden for decades, and as a result of the commission's work, New York's labor laws were rewritten and extended. Roosevelt took no part in the commission's work, and if he made any comment about the Triangle fire

† The Asch Building itself was fireproof, and it is now used for classrooms by New York University.

or its aftermath, it has not been found in his public or private correspondence.

Roosevelt's attitude toward labor was basically paternalistic. He
wished to improve the lot of working people out of a sense of noblesse
oblige but resisted giving organized labor the power to wring concessions
from employers. Reflecting the rural views of his district, he opposed
union boycotts while supporting the use of the National Guard or the
police to enforce injunctions against unions in labor disputes. Roosevelt
was also hesitant about the fifty-four-hour bill being lobbied by Miss
Perkins, because it was unpopular among the agricultural interests of his
district. The canneries employed large numbers of women, and the
farmers were convinced that a shorter work week would hinder operations
and reduce demand for their produce. "I took it hard that a young man
with so much spirit did not do so well in this," Miss Perkins said.

Sheltered from the dark realities of the Industrial Revolution, Roosevelt had little grasp of the impersonality of relations between employers
and employees, the intense competition for subsistence-level jobs, and the
grinding boredom of most unskilled work. He believed the plight of the
workingman was more the result of natural law than the fruit of laissez-
faire capitalism. But, to his credit, the young man was capable of growth
and understanding. He took an active part in trying to improve hazardous
conditions in the Adirondack iron mines and supported the factory safety
measures proposed by the commission after the Triangle fire. In a move
that appealed to churchgoers in his district, as well as organized labor, he
sponsored a bill for "One Day's Rest in Seven" and eventually supported
the fifty-four-hour bill, with Louis Howe claiming that a Roosevelt filibuster secured passage of the measure.

The bill had been defeated by a single vote, and the Senate was
about to adjourn, when another vote was found. But Tim Sullivan, one of
the bill's backers, had departed for the night boat to New York City. Roosevelt volunteered to keep the Senate in session until Sullivan returned,
and launched into a painstakingly detailed account of the birdlife of
Dutchess County. Protesting loudly, the Republicans pointed out that
this learned ornithological dissertation was not germane to the bill. "I am
trying to prove that Nature demands shorter working hours and what better example can I use than the birds of the air who go to their well-earned
rest as soon as darkness falls?" Roosevelt replied amid laughter. He kept
talking until Sullivan came puffing into the chamber to cast the deciding
vote.‡

Outlook broadened by such experiences, Roosevelt learned that in
the imperfect world of politics there is not so often a choice between right

‡ Frances Perkins, who had a vital interest in the matter, makes no mention of FDR's
having saved the bill with his late-hour filibuster, however.

and wrong as a trade-off between two evils. He developed the insight and ability to define and clarify policy that made others look to him for leadership. And with maturity came an appreciation of his Tammany colleagues as more than cynical grafters. Years later, when Frances Perkins brought an immigration problem to the Oval Office, he unexpectedly observed: "Tim Sullivan used to say that the America of the future would be made out of the people who had come over in steerage and who knew in their own hearts and lives the difference between being despised and being accepted and liked." And with a touch of sadness the President added, "Poor old Tim Sullivan never understood about modern politics, but he was right about the human heart."

Shortly after pledging his allegiance to Woodrow Wilson, Roosevelt made what was for him an unparalleled intellectual effort by attempting to shape a comprehensive statement of his political and economic views. Presented in a speech before the People's Forum, of Troy, New York, on March 3, 1912, it revealed the first shadowy outline of some parts of the New Deal. Roosevelt accepted a greatly expanded role for government in regulating the economy to provide the greatest good for the greatest number, and made a carefully worded assault on the sanctity of private property when its use is in conflict with the public welfare. Paradoxically, the speech owed more to the New Nationalism, of Theodore Roosevelt and Herbert Croly, than to Wilson, his new political mentor.

Convinced that the traditional concept of individual liberty was incapable of dealing with the social unrest prevailing in contemporary America, he called for a new doctrine to meet this challenge. "Competition has been shown to be useful up to a certain point and no further, but cooperation, which is the thing we must strive for today, begins where competition leaves off," Roosevelt said. Unwilling to describe cooperation as "community of interest," because of its socialist overtones, or the "brotherhood of man," because that sounded too idealistic, he defined it as "the struggle for the liberty of the community," rather than for the liberty of the individual. "The right of any one individual to work or not as he sees fit, to live to a great extent where and how he sees fit is not sufficient. . . ."

Drawing upon his experience in the field of conservation, Roosevelt pointed out that in eighteenth-century Germany, landowners were free to use their property as they wished, even to denuding the land of trees. A hundred and fifty years later, however, trees could be harvested only in a scientific manner established by the state to serve the needs of the community, rather than merely those of the individual landholder. Thus, the German people had "passed beyond the liberty of the individual to do as he pleased with his property and found it necessary to check this liberty

for the benefit and freedom of the whole people." The same thing had occurred in New York State. "We are beginning to see that it is necessary
for our health and happiness of the whole people of the state that individuals and lumber companies should not go into our wooded areas like the
Adirondacks and the Catskills and cut them off root and branch for the
benefit of their own pocket."

If the state could compel an individual to use his timber only in a
certain, prescribed manner, could it not do so in the case of other productive resources? Readily accepting the consequences of his proposal, Roosevelt supported government direction of the economy:

> As it is with conservation of natural resources so also is it bound to be-
> come with the production of food supply. The two go hand in hand, so
> much so that if we can prophesy today, that the state (in other words the
> people as a whole) will shortly tell a man how many trees he must cut,
> then why can we not, without being called radical, predict that the state
> will compel every farmer to till his land or raise beef or horses. After all, if
> I own a farm of a hundred acres and let it lie waste and overgrown, I am
> just as much a destroyer of the liberty of the community—and by liberty
> we mean happiness and prosperity—as the strong man who stands idle on
> the corner, refusing to work, a destroyer of his neighbor's happiness, pros-
> perity and liberty.

"Cooperation" would also resolve the struggle between capital and
labor and the problem of the trusts, according to Roosevelt. "Neither can
capital exist without the cooperation of labor, nor labor without the cooperation of capital," he declared. "Therefore, I say there is no struggle between the two, not even a dividing line." And echoing Theodore Roosevelt, he declared that the mere size of a corporation did not make it
inherently evil, opting for strict government regulation of big business,
rather than trust-busting.

The Troy speech had a certain naïve superficiality, particularly in
Roosevelt's argument that there is no essential conflict between capital
and labor. The mere fact that they must cooperate to produce goods does
not obviate the possibility of serious conflict over wages and working conditions. He also appeared oblivious to the totalitarian overtones of his proposal, for he imposed no limits on the power of the state to compel the
best use of private property.

Roosevelt was neither a delegate nor an alternate to the Democratic
convention of 1912. Tammany saw to that, freezing him out at the state
convention, which met in New York City on April 12 to pick delegates.
Boss Murphy's control was so absolute that only three of the twenty upstate Democrats Roosevelt invited to a pro-Wilson dinner the night before agreed to attend. Setbacks to Wilson's candidacy in New York and in

other parts of the nation caused Roosevelt to doubt Wilson could win the nomination, and, worried that he himself could not be reelected state senator, he gave serious thought to dropping out of politics. Two years before, he had won election only because of a Republican split, and despite the fratricidal struggle between President Taft and Theodore Roosevelt, it was unlikely that lightning would strike twice. Nevertheless, before leaving on a month-long vacation trip to Jamaica and Panama with Hall Roosevelt, Eleanor's brother, he joined Thomas Mott Osborne and eighty-four other Democrats, two from each congressional district, in founding a New York State Wilson Conference to drum up support for the New Jersey governor's candidacy.

Returning to New York in May, Roosevelt found a pro-Wilson organization in place. William G. McAdoo, a prominent businessman; Senator O'Gorman, who had broken with Tammany on the Wilson issue; and Dudley Field Malone, O'Gorman's son-in-law and a Wilson adviser, were its guiding spirits, while Thomas Osborne provided much of the financing. Roosevelt was named chairman of the executive committee. There was little the group could do except issue Wilson propaganda and tell delegates from other states that the governor had the best chance of any candidate of carrying New York, but Roosevelt accepted the position, saying, "We may do some good and certainly can do no harm." Looking about for someone to handle publicity, he settled upon Louis Howe, whose ability and cynical wit appealed to him. Later he sent Roosevelt some samples of the pro-Wilson articles and letters he had planted about the state and joked: "As masterpieces of the English language, you better have them framed."

Roosevelt's gloomy view of Wilson's prospects was reinforced by the New Jersey governor's poor showing in the primaries. Wilson would arrive at the Baltimore convention with only 248 delegates, while Champ Clark had 436—only 109 short of a majority. Political pundits pointed out that not since 1844 had a Democratic convention operating under the two-thirds rule failed to nominate the candidate who received a majority. And then came the Republican convention, which completely transformed the election.

Ever since his break with President Taft, supporters of Theodore Roosevelt had flocked to Oyster Bay "like iron filings mobilizing to the pull of a revitalized magnet," urging him to seek the presidential nomination. Roosevelt's supporters were an odd lot: progressive idealists, long-time admirers, ambitious politicians, and representatives of big business and high finance who believed the New Nationalism would sanctify monopoly. Early in 1912, the Colonel gave his answer—and added another memorable phrase to the political lexicon: "My hat is in the ring." What had begun as a misunderstanding between friends had developed into a bitter struggle for the leadership of the Republican party and the presidency.

With the Taft forces in control of the party machinery, Theodore Roosevelt had to contest every one of the state primaries in order to win delegates to the convention to be held in Chicago in mid-June. Roosevelt won a clear victory—278 votes to only 48 for Taft—and garnered nearly double the popular vote, reinforcing his claim to be the choice of the rank and file. Nevertheless, as a result of their control of the state conventions, the Taft forces had a razor-thin majority of the delegates that poured into Chicago. The nomination rested on control of 254 contested seats. Securely in the hands of the Old Guard, the National Committee ruled, as expected, in the President's favor on most of the contested seats, awarding 235 to Taft and 19 to Roosevelt. Angrily shouting, "Thou shalt not steal!" and promising revenge, Roosevelt's supporters bolted the convention, leaving the now worthless nomination to Taft.

Two months later, they returned to Chicago to organize the Progressive party. Exuberantly proclaiming himself "as strong as a bull moose," Roosevelt appeared before the fifteen thousand red-bandanna-waving delegates, who cheered him for nearly an hour, to accept the new party's presidential nomination. When the crowd had finally quieted, he unveiled what George Mowry, a leading historian of the progressive movement, has described as the most sweeping charter for reform that had ever been presented by a major candidate: direct election of U.S. senators, preferential primaries in presidential election years, initiative, referendum, and recall, votes for women, a strict corrupt-practices act, a federal securities commission, trust regulation, reduced tariffs, unemployment insurance, old-age pensions, a minimum wage for women, abolition of child labor, and pure-food-and-drug laws. "We stand at Armageddon and we battle for the Lord!" thundered Roosevelt.

The splintering of the Republican party made it inevitable that the candidate nominated by the Democrats would be elected in November. But would it be Clark or Wilson? Although some Democrats said they could now win with almost anybody, Franklin Roosevelt warned that the Republican schism reinforced the necessity for the party to nominate Wilson. "Unless the Democrats nominate a strong progressive," he declared, [Theodore] Roosevelt will cut into the Democratic progressive vote." To assist in bringing about the New Jersey governor's nomination, he led a group of one hundred fifty Wilson boosters to Baltimore. The rebels set up an office in the Munsey Building, across the street from the Emerson Hotel, where both Wilson and Clark had their headquarters; but, without official standing, there was little they could do except cheer for Wilson from the gallery.

Some twenty thousand people crowded into the castle-like Fifth Regiment Armory, on the fringes of downtown Baltimore, on the afternoon of June 25 to hear James Cardinal Gibbons open the convention with a prayer for "righteousness and wisdom." This was the lull before the storm. Ballot after ballot followed with tedious monotony in which Clark held a commanding lead over Wilson and a handful of favorite sons. Sweltering in the clammy heat of a Baltimore summer, the delegates stripped to shirt sleeves and galluses and tried to stir up a breath of air with palm-leaf fans distributed by a local undertaker. Tempers flared and fistfights broke out on the floor and in the galleries. Eleanor Roosevelt had accompanied Franklin to the convention, leaving the "chicks" at Hyde Park with their grandmother. Wilting in the heat, understanding little of what was occurring, and "appalled" by the disorder, she returned home after a few days to take the children to Campobello. "I decided that my husband would hardly miss my company, as I rarely laid my eyes upon him," she said.

Roosevelt, however, was in his element. Sometimes leading his pro-Wilson claque, which had finagled a block of seats together, sometimes moving about the convention floor, he made the acquaintance of leading Democrats from all over the country. In years to come, they would recall the pleasant young man who was a Roosevelt and a Democrat. Among them was the benign-looking Josephus Daniels, editor of the Raleigh *News and Observer*, national committeeman from North Carolina, and one of Wilson's chief advisers. "He was in a gay humor and I thought he was as handsome a figure of an attractive young man as I have ever seen," Daniels recalled. "At that convention Franklin and I became friends—a case of love at first sight."

On the tenth ballot, the inscrutable Murphy, who had ordered New York's ninety votes cast for Governor Judson Harmon, of Ohio, released them to Clark, touching off a pandemonium. Clark now had a majority of the 1,088 votes needed for the nomination and the momentum to carry him to the two thirds required for victory. The nomination hung in the balance. To stampede the convention, Clark supporters had arranged for two or three hundred Baltimore ward heelers to dash out onto the floor at this critical moment, unfurling banners and chanting: "We want Clark! We want Clark!" Roosevelt had discovered that the doorkeepers had been instructed to admit all who wore Clark buttons to the floor, so he pinned similar emblems on his cohorts and led them into aisles on the heels of the Clark forces to drown them out with cries of "We want Wilson! We want Wilson!"

Murphy's switch failed to set off the expected stampede, and Clark picked up only a handful of new votes. On the fourteenth ballot, William Jennings Bryan, his great bald dome glistening with perspiration, dramatically announced that he could not vote for a man who had accepted the support of Tammany, and switched from Clark to Wilson, taking the Nebraska delegation with him. Bryan's denunciation of Clark did not produce an immediate groundswell for Wilson, but the tide slowly began to run in his favor. Clark's support stabilized and then began to erode, while Wilson's totals crept upward. On the forty-third ballot, he won a majority, and on the forty-sixth, was named the Democratic nominee for President of the United States. Completely exhausted, the delegates remained in town only long enough to nominate Thomas R. Marshall, of Indiana, as the vice-presidential candidate—placing control of the Democratic party firmly in the hands of its progressive wing. Wildly happy, Roosevelt wired his wife: WILSON NOMINATED THIS AFTERNOON ALL MY PLANS VAGUE SPLENDID TRIUMPH.

Roosevelt had ample reason to be elated. Although he had only a minor role at best in securing this triumph, he was one of Wilson's earliest supporters in upstate New York, taking a stand in favor of the governor at a time when it involved considerable political risk. If, as expected, Wilson won the presidential election, he could expect an ample reward. Once again, he had seized an opportunity and made the best of it. When news of Roosevelt's success in Baltimore reached him, Louis Howe wrote him a letter of congratulations that began with the playful salutation "Beloved and Revered Future President."

Before he could grasp this glittering prize, Roosevelt had to make certain that Wilson carried New York and he himself was renominated and reelected. Within a few weeks after the convention, Roosevelt and Osborne had transformed the Wilson Conference into the Empire State Democracy, which was to be a permanent progressive organization. Once again, Howe was called in to churn out publicity, while Osborne served as financial angel and Roosevelt scurried about the state lining up support for Wilson and to make certain that progressive candidates were nominated for local offices. The young man was mentioned as a possible choice for governor, but he had just turned thirty, he was politically inexperienced, and even he regarded such talk—pleasing to his ego as it was—as premature. The Empire State Democracy was short-lived, however, because Osborne ran short of funds and Roosevelt was taken sick with a severe case of typhoid.

Before his illness, he had won renomination to the state senate. Following visits to various Democratic "henchmen" in the district, he wrote "Dearest Babbie" in Campobello that "Tammany and the 'Interests' are really making an effort to prevent my renomination." They raked up the Sheehan affair and, emphasizing his role in the Empire State Democracy, blamed him for sowing "discord." But he was popular with the rank and file, and even the Poughkeepsie *Eagle* said, "It hardly seems possible that the local Democratic bosses can be in earnest in their efforts to turn down Senator Franklin D. Roosevelt." On August 24, he was unanimously renominated—with the bosses devoutly hoping that he would get his just deserts on Election Day.

Immediately afterward, Roosevelt joined his family, who had seen little of him that summer at Campobello. Two years before, Mrs. Hartman Kuhn, a neighbor, had died, and in her will expressed the desire that Sara Roosevelt have first option to buy her cottage for five thousand dollars if she agreed to give the place to Franklin and Eleanor. It was the first home that they owned, and Eleanor regarded it as a refuge from servitude to her mother-in-law. She had her own servants and could do as she pleased without being criticized by the old lady. Although the place had thirty-five rooms, it was plainly furnished to meet the needs of an energetic and active family. Franklin became reacquainted with the children, taking them sailing and climbing along the cliffs facing the sea. "We came back from these expeditions with high color, gasping for breath, but happy," recalled Anna. "My mother was always surprised to find us all in one piece." On Sundays, they marched to St. Anne's Church, where Franklin would sit at the end of the family pew with Sara Roosevelt next to him.

Refreshed and eager to launch his campaign, Roosevelt stopped briefly at Sixty-fifth Street but came down with a high fever that was diagnosed as typhoid. On the boat from Campobello, both Franklin and Eleanor had brushed their teeth with contaminated water. Eleanor nursed him herself until she, too, became ill. She was soon up on her feet again, but her husband was "still in bed and feeling miserable and looking like Robert Louis Stevenson at Vailima." Lying helplessly in bed, Roosevelt could see his bright political future fading away. If he could not campaign, he would not be reelected and would lose his chance to obtain a place in the new Democratic administration likely to come to power in Washington. Twisting and turning in frustration, he remembered Louis Howe.

Someone had once called Howe "a medieval gnome," and he gloried in the description. Wizened, barely five feet tall, and with a face furrowed like a plowed field, he looked more like the dragon than St. George—but he came to the rescue of Franklin Roosevelt's political career. Racing to the sick man's bedside, he eagerly unfolded a strategy for a campaign without a candidate. Like most political reporters, Howe was convinced he could run a better campaign than those he had covered, and for years had been searching for a man to whom he could offer his expertise and experience. Soon after his first encounter with Roosevelt, in Albany, he sensed that the handsome and ambitious young senator was the man whom he had been seeking. Many years later, Howe told James Roosevelt that early on he had worked out a detailed plan for making his friend President of the United States. "We hit the timetable right on the button. He didn't know the details. No one did. I've never talked about it. But I worked out in my mind when the right times to make our moves might be, and we made them at those times and we were successful."

At forty-one, a time when most men are well launched into their chosen careers, Howe knew only failure. He was a petty political manipulator and backstairs conspirator, familiar with the eddies of upstate politics and journalism, living with his family on the shabby edge of poverty. Frequently unemployed and debt-ridden, he dreamed of power, status, and prominence. Life had played a cruel joke on Louis Howe, for he would have liked to run for office, himself, but his physical appearance and acerbic manner made such a dream impossible.

The Howes were of old New England stock, but Louis' father, Edward Porter Howe, had moved to Indianapolis before the Civil War. Emerging from the conflict as a captain in the Union Army, he had married Eliza Blake Ray, a widow nine years his senior and a banker's daughter. Captain Howe prospered in real-estate speculation, and when the couple's only son, Louis McHenry Howe, was born, in 1871, he owned an entire business block and was building a sizable mansion in the fashionable part of Indianapolis. This world of wealth and social position crumbled in the Panic of 1873, leaving Howe sixteen thousand dollars in debt. The family took refuge in Saratoga, New York, where the husband of Mrs. Howe's half sister managed a sanitarium, and the elder Howe got a job as a reporter for the *Saratogian*, the local Republican weekly.

Saratoga was then at the height of its vogue as a spa. For several months a year, the rich, the powerful, and the renowned lounged on the verandah at the fashionable Grand Union Hotel, strolled elm-shrouded Broadway, and took the waters, which were reputed to have great restorative powers. During the racing season, the resort was a gaudy mecca for gamblers, touts, and horse lovers, who rubbed shoulders at night with Astors and Vanderbilts in Richard Canfield's elegant casino. In 1881, after six years of scrimping and saving, Captain Howe bought the weekly *Saratoga Sun*, turning it into the Democratic mouthpiece of Saratoga County. The paper's existence was precarious, and it was not until seven years later, when Louis was seventeen, that his father could afford to buy a home for his family.

From birth, Louis was a wan and sickly child, puny and asthmatic. Because of his poor health, he spent much of his early life indoors and was an omnivorous reader. Early on, he became an admirer of Thomas Carlyle and a believer in the role of the hero as a prime mover in history. Louis had spindly arms and legs and a head that seemed too large for his body, but he was a sociable boy. He took up golf and tennis and was an ardent cyclist even though forced to wear a clumsy truss because of a weak spine. Out riding one day, he caught his foot in the spokes of his bicycle and was thrown to the gravel. For the rest of his life his face was pitted with black scars resulting from the fall. Even so, he had a gaiety and charm that belied his grotesqueness, was a good dancer, and was active in amateur theatricals. Not surprising, with his deft mind, he was an expert card player, and even though his funds were limited, was a frequent visitor to Canfield's casino. Horse racing also captivated him, and he could never resist making small bets.

Captain Howe had hoped to send his son to college, preferably to Yale, but by the time Louis graduated from the Saratoga Institute, the financial burden was too great. The youth joined the *Sun* as a reporter and printing salesman. The old man's health began to fail, and Louis gradually took over the paper, developing an intimate knowledge of local politics in the process. His father had served as Saratoga "stringer" for the New York *Herald*, and the job passed to the son.

"I am one of the four ugliest men, if what is left of me can be dignified by the name of man, in the State of New York," Howe once said of himself. "I am wizened in the Dickens manner. My eyes protrude from too much looking. Children take one look at me on the street and run." But Grace Hartley, a Vassar student from Fall River, Massachusetts, whose mother was a Borden, saw something in Howe that others didn't. She met him during a visit to Saratoga during the summer of 1896, and two years later they were married. "Beauty and the Beast," said some acquaintances. Swallowing her disapproval of her new son-in-law, Mrs. Hartley bought the newlyweds a house in Saratoga and furnished it with antiques from Fall River.

With the Republicans firmly in power in New York State, the Democratic *Sun* was setting, and Howe was forced to mortgage his new home to keep the paper alive. Before long, his creditors moved in and he was demoted from editor to ten-dollar-a-week reporter, just as Grace gave birth to their first child. In September 1901, he was fired. For a time he tried gambling for a living, winning $258 at faro and small amounts at the race track. Howe's sheet anchor was his job as "stringer" for the New York *Herald*, which brought him a few dollars a week for covering the races and providing tidbits of Saratoga gossip. He also free-lanced feature articles and book reviews to anyone who would take them.

Howe's luck turned five long years later, in 1906, when the *Herald* named him assistant to its correspondent in Albany. The job paid the then princely sum of forty dollars a week, but only during the legislative session, which sometimes was as short as two months. Howe was a "digger," and his colleagues in Albany called him the "water rat" because of the vast amount of time he spent in the capitol cellars, ferreting out political secrets from piles of documents. To pick up extra cash, he went to work for Osborne, who had organized a political organization aimed at wresting control of upstate New York from Tammany, serving him as speech writer, idea man, and underground political agent. Osborne was an erratic source of income, however. In 1908, he fired Howe with one week's notice. Louis was desperate. He had just been told by his doctor that because of a bad heart he had only a few months to live, and begged Osborne to be taken back. Out of pity, Osborne returned him to the payroll at his old salary. Sarcastic, acerbic, prematurely old, and contemptuous of appearances, Louis Howe would have remained a peripheral character in Albany, forgotten soon after his death, had he not seen in Franklin Roosevelt the political leader he would have been himself.

Eleanor Roosevelt took an immediate dislike to Howe. She felt excluded from the intimacy shared by the two men and the affectionate bantering that passed between them. Howe always looked dirty and disheveled and was periodically wracked by fits of asthmatic coughing that was aggravated by chain-smoking. "I felt that his smoking spoiled the fresh air that my husband should have in his bedroom, and I was very disapproving whenever he came down to report on the campaign," she confessed. "I lost sight entirely of the fact that . . . without him my husband would have . . . probably lost the election. I simply made a nuisance of myself over those visits and his cigarettes. I often wonder how they bore with me in those days."

Placed on the Roosevelt payroll at fifty dollars a week—he was hardly ever to be off it again—Howe set up headquarters in a hotel in Poughkeepsie. Making agriculture and "bossism" the main issues of the campaign, he flooded the district with "personal" letters from Roosevelt, ran full-page advertisements in the newspapers playing up the candidate's accomplishments and promises of more if reelected, and launched an attack on his Republican rival. Leaving nothing to chance, he carefully distributed five-dollar bills to campaign workers on Election Day. "I'm having more fun than a goat," he reported. "They will know they have been in a horse race before we are done!"* Howe's greatest coup, which he labeled the "great farm stunt," was the proposal of a bill designed to protect farmers from gouging by New York City commission merchants. Copies

---

* FDR later discovered that Howe did not know how to use a checking account. At the start of the campaign, he gave him a checkbook and put some money into the account to cover expenses. Whenever he reported to FDR, Howe insisted that he had plenty of money in the account, much to Roosevelt's surprise. Eventually, the bank notified the candidate that the account was greatly overdrawn. Looking over the statements, FDR found that whenever Howe had written a check, he added the amount to the balance instead of deducting it.

of the measure were circulated among the farmers along with a letter from Roosevelt requesting comments and promising that if reelected he would fight for passage of the bill. Stamped envelopes were included in the package so the farmers could send in their comments.

While Roosevelt lay flat on his back, the presidential campaign developed into a two-man fight between Theodore Roosevelt and Wilson as they both ignored the hapless Taft. Except for their personalities, there was little to distinguish the two candidates as the campaign began. Both were pledged to progressivism and social justice, although Roosevelt sounded more radical, because he was willing to accept a stronger role by government in human affairs. But under the influence of Louis D. Brandeis, a longtime opponent of monopoly, Wilson was persuaded to make the trusts the key issue of his campaign. Calling his program the New Freedom, Wilson attacked Roosevelt's New Nationalism for its willingness to accept monopoly with a touch of governmental regulation. He emphasized the predatory and monopolistic aspects of big business and the obstacles these practices created for the small businessman. "I take my stand absolutely, where every progressive ought to take his stand, on the proposition that private monopoly is indefensible and intolerable," Wilson declared.

Theodore Roosevelt was under no illusions about the outcome of the race, privately predicting that although he would run better than Taft, Wilson would win. But this did not dampen his ardor, and he conducted a strenuous campaign. As he prepared to speak in Milwaukee on October 14, an anti-third-term fanatic shot him in the chest. The bullet tore through his overcoat, spectacles case, and the folded manuscript of his speech before lodging just beyond the ribs. Roosevelt staggered for a moment, coughed to see if he would spit up blood, and stood up again. "Stand back! Don't hurt that man!" he shouted as the crowd moved to lynch his assailant. Brushing off the protests of aides and doctors, he insisted on making his speech before going to the hospital. "It takes more than that to kill a Bull Moose," he declared.

Admiration for Roosevelt's courage was widespread, but cheers were no substitute for votes. The Colonel had waged a remarkable campaign, winning the support of most progressive Republicans, but was unable to draw reform Democrats away from Wilson. Wilson piled up 6,301,254 votes to Roosevelt's 4,127,788, while Taft trailed badly with 3,485,831.† The election results clearly demonstrated that the nation was now overwhelmingly progressive in temper. Americans might disagree about

† The casualties included Nicholas Longworth, TR's son-in-law, who had remained loyal to Taft, his fellow Cincinnatian, and lost his Ohio congressional seat. "May I suggest to any of you who may have ambitions to go to Congress to see to it that, in the same campaign, your most eminent constituent is not contesting the presidency with your father-in-law," he told some friends.

the definition of progressivism, but whatever it was, they were ready to try it. Although some regular Democrats defected from his cause, enough Republicans crossed over to vote for him to give Roosevelt a larger majority in the district than Woodrow Wilson, without his having made a single campaign appearance.

With an ear cocked for a call to Washington, Franklin Roosevelt returned to Albany in January 1913 for the new legislative session. The Democrats had again won control of both houses, and he was appointed chairman of the Agriculture Committee, which provided him with the opportunity to push for passage of the farm legislation Howe had promised during the campaign. When these measures became law, however, Roosevelt had already left the state senate for greener pastures. Journeying to Washington for Wilson's inauguration on March 4, he met William McAdoo, the newly designated Secretary of the Treasury, and was offered the choice of becoming assistant Secretary of the Treasury or collector of the Port of New York. The collectorship was especially attractive, because the cornucopia of patronage that went with the post would provide him with the opportunity to build his own political organization. But on the morning of the inauguration, he encountered Josephus Daniels, who had been tapped for Secretary of the Navy, in the lobby of the Willard Hotel.

"How would you like to come to Washington as assistant Secretary of the Navy?" Daniels asked.

"I would like it bully well," answered the young man, his face beaming with pleasure, according to Daniels' recollections. "It would please me better than anything in the world. I'd be glad to be connected with the new administration. All my life I have loved ships and have been a student of the Navy, and the assistant secretaryship is the one place above all others, I would love to hold."

Two days later, Daniels discussed the selection of an assistant Secretary with Wilson. When the President told him that he had no one in mind for the post, Daniels suggested Roosevelt.

"How well do you know Mr. Roosevelt?" Wilson asked, according to Daniels' account, "and how well is he equipped?"

"I never met him until the Baltimore Convention," the Navy Secretary replied, "but I was strongly drawn to him then and more so as I met him during the campaign when I was in New York. I have admired him since the courageous fight he made in the New York State Senate, which resulted in the election of a liberal who had favored your nomination at Baltimore. Besides, I know he has been a Naval enthusiast from his boyhood."

"Very well," said Wilson. "Send the nomination over."

Daniels liked Roosevelt and believed that he and the young man would complement each other. He had no knowledge of the Navy or ships and the sea, while Roosevelt had a lifelong interest in nautical affairs; he was a Southerner and Roosevelt was a Northerner; besides, Roosevelt bore a distinguished name and Daniels may have been flattered by the idea of having a Roosevelt working for him. But Senator Elihu Root, who had served as Secretary of State under Theodore Roosevelt, had a warning for him. "Whenever a Roosevelt rides," Root declared, "he wishes to ride in front."

Nevertheless, the appointment was made, and on March 17, 1913—the eighth anniversary of his marriage to Eleanor—Franklin Roosevelt found himself for the first time at Theodore Roosevelt's old desk in the Navy Department. He had been in politics less than three years.

VII

"A ROOSEVELT ON THE JOB"

I AM BAPTIZED, confirmed, sworn in, vaccinated—and somewhat at sea!" Franklin Roosevelt wrote his mother shortly after taking up his duties as assistant Secretary of the Navy. "For over an hour I have been signing papers which had to be accepted on faith—but I hope luck will keep me out of jail."* He was not at sea very long, however. "There's a Roosevelt on the job today," the young man lightheartedly told newsmen a few days later, when Josephus Daniels went out of town, leaving him temporarily in charge of the Navy Department. "You remember what happened the last time a Roosevelt occupied a similar position." This was a none-too-subtle reminder that just before the outbreak of the Spanish-American War, in 1898, Theodore Roosevelt had, in the absence of his chief, dispatched secret orders to Commodore George Dewey instructing him to attack the Spanish fleet at Manila as soon as war was declared.

Others saw the parallel between the two Roosevelts and freely predicted that the younger man would follow the Rough Rider from assistant Secretary of the Navy to governor of New York and finally to the White House. "I rejoice heartedly in the good fortune that has come to you," wrote Randall N. Saunders, clerk of Hudson County, New York, "and hope that you may be stepping surely in the footsteps of another of your name through this position to the presidency." From Uncle Ted himself came a congratulatory note expressing delight that he was occupying "another place which I . . . once held."

Franklin Roosevelt's seven and a half years as assistant Secretary of

---

* This letter is one of the few personal notes written by FDR that is signed with his full name—no doubt done absentmindedly while signing official papers. "Try not to write your name too small, as it gets a cramped look and is not distinct," Sara Roosevelt quickly replied. "So many public men have such awful signatures and so unreadable. . . ."

the Navy was the most thorough training conceivable for his later service as a war President. Thrown into a strange environment, he worked "like a new turbine" to master his job. An assistant Secretary was far more important than today, and he ranked second only to Daniels in the Navy's chain of command. When the Secretary was away, he was acting Secretary and attended cabinet meetings. Roosevelt was in charge of the business side of the Navy, and his responsibilities included procurement, civilian personnel, budgetary matters, and management of yards and docks, thereby providing him with invaluable administrative experience. He learned how a large federal agency was run in time of crisis, how a President operated in wartime, how to work with allies to reach common objectives, and how a democracy could be reconciled with the military needs of a global war. Plunging into his new job with boyish enthusiasm, he exploded like a sixteen-inch shell upon the somnolent bureaucracy of the Navy Department, drowsing contentedly in a corner of the gingerbread building† next to the White House that in a day of limited government also sheltered the War and State departments.

Before long, the slim young man in a derby and high collar was a familiar figure to the Navy's officers and men, as he popped up everywhere to inspect ships and shore stations. He crawled through engine spaces and clambered into the rigging in his desire to see for himself. "I get my fingers into everything and there's no law against it," he cheerfully proclaimed. "I now find my vocation combined with my avocation in a delightful way." When one of the Navy's primitive submarines was lost with all hands, he immediately went out in another to demonstrate his confidence in the new weapon.

Some senior officers were taken aback by his youth, with one navy wife being shocked to find that the young man she had chided at a dinner party as a naughty boy for some irreverent remark was her husband's superior. Cocky, impulsive, and self-centered, Roosevelt meant to make a name for himself in Washington. "He is friendly as an airedale pup and young enough to want to look older," said one newsman. Glorying in the twittering of bos'ns' pipes and the crash of the seventeen-gun salute to which he was entitled—four more than a rear admiral with forty years' service—he added to the panoply by designing an assistant Secretary's flag and made certain it was broken out upon his appearance.

As President, Roosevelt regarded the Navy as his private domain and kept a well-thumbed copy of the Navy List close at hand. Based on his experience as assistant Secretary, he could comment on the merits and deficiencies of nearly every senior officer in the service. "Some were remembered favorably," writes Robert G. Albion, a prominent naval historian, "a few unfavorably, and some, who had not happened to be around the Department of the Navy in his time, were . . . not remem-

† Now the Executive Office Building.

bered at all." Among those who were remembered favorably were William F. Halsey, Jr., who was impressed with the way Roosevelt conned his destroyer through the dangerous waters about Campobello; Harold R. Stark, who refused to allow him to take over his ship; William D. Leahy, skipper of the dispatch vessel *Dolphin*, which was often used by Roosevelt as a yacht; and Husband E. Kimmel, who briefly served as his aide.

Roosevelt immediately brought Louis Howe to Washington. He had inherited Charles H. McCarthy, who had served as secretary to several of his predecessors, but wanted his own man nearby. "Dear Ludwig," he wrote, "Here is the dope, Secretary—$2,000—Expect you April 1, with a new uniform."‡ Although halfheartedly protesting that "it will break me," Howe was pleased with the appointment, for it provided a steady income and job security. "The Navy! The Navy!" cried one of the wiseacres in the Albany press room upon hearing the news. "Louis is bound to be exposed to water. Let us give him a dozen cakes of soap and maybe he'll finally come clean!" In the beginning, Howe was so inexperienced that he did little more than stand beside Roosevelt's desk and blot his signature upon official papers. But the little man quickly found a role as troubleshooter, slashing through red tape and thumbing his nose at precedent. Contemptuous of rank and tradition, he was soon singeing the admirals' beards with insolent missives such as: "The Assistant Secretary desires that the first paragraph of the attached letter to Congressman O'Brien be rewritten in such a way that he will be able to understand what is meant."

Howe's range of duties included gathering material and sometimes writing speeches for both Roosevelt and Daniels, labor relations with the Navy's civilian work force, expediting the delivery of key items for ship construction, and even investigating prostitution and gambling in navy towns. He also took charge of patronage, drafted letters to Roosevelt's former constituents in New York, wheedled postmasterships from the Administration, and doled out shipyard jobs to deserving Democrats—all with the aim of polishing Roosevelt's image and building a political machine that would be able to challenge Boss Murphy and Tammany. Completely identified with Roosevelt, he promoted and guarded his chief's reputation.* Howe lived through Roosevelt, and as Josephus Daniels

‡ FDR's own salary was $4,500 yearly.
* For example, Howe saw to it that FDR was safely out of town when the teetotaling Daniels issued a controversial order banning the officers' wine mess as of July 1, 1914. The rum ration for enlisted men had been abolished in 1862, and prohibitionist sentiment was so strong that battleships named after dry states were christened with lemonade rather than champagne. There were raucous farewell parties for John Barleycorn as the deadline for making the Navy dry drew near. Midway during the bedlam on the *North Dakota*, one officer appeared in the wardroom wearing a baseball catcher's mask and proposed a toast. "Here's to Josephus Daniels!" he declared—and was bombarded with anything handy.

observed, "he would have laid on the floor and let Franklin walk over him."

"It always made Howe extremely sore when a few others, like myself, passed through his office, without any reference to him, on our way to see the Assistant Secretary," recalled George Marvin, assistant editor of the magazine *Worlds Work* and one of Roosevelt's masters at Groton. "Howe was a vindictive, as well as an extremely astute, individual and he never forgot his earlier inferiority complexes." Daniels thought Howe "one of the strangest men I have ever met and one of the smartest." Amassing a tremendous amount of information, he knew "all the tides and eddies" of the Navy Department and national politics as well. Even in 1913, Daniels added, Howe expected Roosevelt to eventually occupy the presidency and devoted every effort to fulfilling this ambition for his friend. "He would have sidetracked both President Wilson and me to get Franklin Roosevelt to the White House," the Secretary added.

The Navy of the Wilson era was a sprawling, loose-jointed organization that was dealing with matters of increasing technological complexity, while its attitude had been fixed in the age of fighting sail. Daniels and Roosevelt had inherited a fleet of 259 vessels, including 21 battleships, manned by some 65,000 officers, sailors, and marines, which in 1913 cost the taxpayers $143.5 million—or about 20 percent of total government expenditures.† But this force was more impressive on paper than at sea. Although the fleet seemed immense to most Americans, it ranked not only behind those of Britain and Germany but of France as well and consisted of a handful of modern vessels and a mélange of hand-me-downs dating back to before the war with Spain. Promotion was slow and by seniority, so the Navy List was barnacled with officers that had reached the lofty heights of command long after their prime.

Substantially unaltered since 1842, the Navy's administrative structure was antiquated and hopelessly ensnarled in red tape. Roosevelt once sent Daniels a note expressing his pent-up fury at the bureaucracy. "I beg to report that I have just signed a requisition (with 4 copies attached) calling for the purchase of 8 carpet tacks." "Why this wanton extravagance?" replied his good-humored chief. "I am sure that two would suffice." The Navy's administrative functions were rigidly compartmentalized into bureaus charged with the procurement of ships, men, and supplies and which were to provide professional advice to the civilian secretaries. Headed by admirals or captains, the bureaus jockeyed among themselves for precedence and the largest share of the budget without consideration for overall policy. As President, Theodore Roosevelt had proposed an organization similar to the Army's General Staff to provide

† In 1982, a completely equipped guided-missile frigate cost almost $200 million.

centralized planning, but the bureau chiefs furiously resisted any change. Reform would jeopardize their power and independence, and they were assisted in blocking the proposal by congressional supporters concerned about the loss of opportunities for pork-barrel politics. Instead, a General Board, headed by the aging Admiral Dewey, now the Navy's senior officer, prepared war plans and made recommendations to the Secretary regarding the operation of the fleet.

Josephus Daniels was a surprising choice to head the Navy. An agrarian populist and pacifist, he and William Jennings Bryan, the new Secretary of State, were regarded as the most radical members of Wilson's Cabinet. The appointment was viewed as "a noble reward for services rendered" to the President, and the new Secretary made no pretense of knowing very much about naval affairs. If the bureau chiefs expected a free hand, however, they were in for a surprise. With his rumpled suits, broad-brimmed felt hat, and string tie, Daniels fooled many people, who equated his appearance with small-town innocence and provincialism. In fact, Franklin Roosevelt later recalled that his first impression of Daniels was that he was "the funniest looking hill-billy I had ever seen." But he had his clothes custom-tailored, and his cherubic face masked a political shrewdness and wide-ranging intelligence.

Immediately after his appointment, Daniels had been shown around the Navy Department by his predecessor, George von Lengerke Meyer, and the tour had ended in the Secretary's office. Rapping the top of the big mahogany desk, Meyer gave his successor some parting advice which Daniels never forgot: "Keep the power to direct the Navy *here!*" As an observer told Ernest K. Lindley, Daniels "entered the department with the profound suspicion that whatever an Admiral told him was wrong and that every corporation with a capitalization of more than $100,000 was inherently evil. In nine out of ten cases his formula was correct. . . ."

Roosevelt, in vivid contrast, was a longtime disciple of Alfred Thayer Mahan, the high priest of sea power, and a big-Navy man. Speaking before the Navy League, a group that propagandized for naval expansion, he derided a network of arbitration treaties proposed by Secretary of State Bryan to maintain the peace. "This is not a question of war or peace," Roosevelt declared. "I take it that there are as many advocates of arbitration and international peace in the navy as in any other profession. But we are confronted with a condition—the fact that our nation has decided in the past to have a fleet, and that war is still a possibility." Therefore the nation must maintain "a fighting force of the highest efficiency." Roosevelt almost became poetic as he described this fleet putting to sea to show the flag in the Mediterranean. "The big gray fellows were magnificent as they went past, with all hands at the rail," he wrote

Eleanor, "and I only wish a hundred thousand people could have seen them."

The relationship between Roosevelt and Daniels was an uneasy one; an association of opposites. The admirals were suspicious of Daniels' politics and he angered them almost immediately by rejecting a recommendation from the General Board for twenty thousand additional men and a vast increase in the fleet. Placing little store in naval tradition, he addressed ordinary sailors as "young gentlemen" and seemed to regard the service as a vast school for educating the enlisted men, rather than a fighting machine. On the other hand, Roosevelt was popular with the Navy's hierarchy. Soon the admirals found it wise to wait until Daniels was safely out of town and then come to Roosevelt for a signature or a decision.

Roosevelt came only slowly to appreciate Daniels' qualities. He was often impatient with his slow-moving, deliberate chief, and regarding him as a man who didn't know the difference between a barnacle and a bollard, made no secret of his hope that Daniels would eventually resign so he could become Navy Secretary. Nevertheless, the two men complemented each other. Roosevelt compensated for Daniels' ignorance of the Navy and its ways, while the older man, who had served as chief clerk of the Interior Department under Grover Cleveland, was a past master of the art of coaxing appropriations out of a tightfisted Congress. Through Daniels, Roosevelt became acquainted with the southern and western congressmen who dominated the congressional committees and learned something of the viewpoint of the small-town, middle-class America they represented. Daniels was the only administrative superior Roosevelt ever had, and despite the repeated challenges to his authority, showed remarkable forbearance toward his brash assistant. Rather than crushing the young man's ebullient spirit, he adopted a parental tolerance that was almost Job-like.

Not long after Roosevelt and Daniels assumed their duties, a photographer took a picture of them together on the portico of the State, War and Navy Building. When he saw the picture, Daniels asked Roosevelt why he was "grinning from ear to ear." The young man replied that he had no particular reason to smile and was merely trying to look his best. "I will tell you," replied Daniels. "We are both looking down on the White House and you are saying to yourself, being a New Yorker, 'Some day I will be living in that house'—while I, being from the South, know I must be satisfied with no such ambition."‡

‡ When Roosevelt became President, he appointed Daniels ambassador to Mexico. Shortly before FDR's death, he named the old man's son, Jonathan, to be his press secretary.

Roosevelt had little personal contact with the President, who stood, as Frank Freidel has said, "in relation to him as a sort of a super-schoolmaster, another Rector Peabody." "You know, Wilson had an uncanny understanding of the . . . moral drives of modern man," Roosevelt told Frances Perkins many years later. "He was a Presbyterian, you know, and a tough one, and he was perfectly sure that all men are sinful by nature. He figured it out that Western civilization would attempt to destroy itself through the natural sinful activities of modern man unless (and here FDR paused to trace an exclamation point with his finger) by the grace of God the decent people of Western civilization resolved to support the doctrine of the Golden Rule."

From a distance, Roosevelt studied a virtuoso performance that restored to the presidency much of the luster it had lost under Taft. Wilson believed that the President should be a strong national leader who by wisdom and eloquence would persuade the American people to embrace "the progress that conserves." He exercised strong leadership, and when opposition to his programs did materialize—as occurred during the fight to reduce the tariff—he successfully appealed to the people over the heads of his opponents. Like Theodore Roosevelt, Wilson viewed the presidency as a "bully pulpit" and dramatized his program by addressing Congress in person, the first Chief Executive since Jefferson to do so. And for all his moral fervor, Wilson understood the positive power of patronage, skillfully using it to keep job-hungry Democrats in line.

Although Wilson's remoteness caused personal difficulties with the politicians, the flood tide of progressive sentiment assisted him in obtaining enactment of a large part of the New Freedom into law during his first years in office. The nation's banking system was restructured through the establishment of the Federal Reserve System, the tariff that progressives regarded as "the mother of trusts" was reduced, trusts and monopolies were regulated, and child-labor and workmen's-compensation laws were passed. Most significant for the future was the approval of a graduated income tax, with the top level set at a modest 3 percent.

But in the frivolous Washington society frequented by Franklin Roosevelt—for the first few months following his appointment he lived a bachelor life in the Powhatan Hotel while Eleanor remained in New York City with the "chicks"—other concerns vied with the reforms espoused by the intense professor in the White House. Young couples practiced the intricacies of the tango, the bunny hug, and the turkey trot. Women smoked in public, and hemlines were creeping upward. "For generations women have been showing off their clothes," allowed one senator; "now the clothes are reciprocating."

Handsome, prominent, and, in contrast to many members of the new

ft: Eleanor Roosevelt on her honeymoon in Venice. The picture was taken by FDR. (Courtesy
)R Library) Right: Eleanor and Franklin with James and Anna in 1908. (Courtesy FDR
brary)

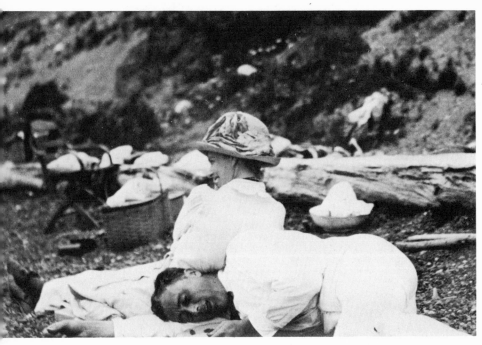

Franklin and Eleanor on a picnic at Campobello. (Courtesy FDR Library)

FDR and Josephus Daniels looking toward the White House from the Navy Department. (Courtesy FDR Library)

HINKAMP   C.W. NIMITZ   R.A. BURG

Above: Assistant Secretary Roosevelt meets Lieutenant Chester W. Nimitz in this previously unpublished photograph. (Courtesy Nimitz Library, U. S. Naval Academy) Left: Assistant Secretary Roosevelt makes an inspection. (Courtesy FDR Library)

Lucy Mercer about the time she was Eleanor Roosevelt's social secretary. (Courtesy Lyman Cotten)

administration, socially acceptable, Roosevelt was the darling of the salons. He joined the exclusive Metropolitan Club, situated a few blocks from his office, and lunched or dined there at least once a week. (Wilson was the first President not offered a membership since the club had been founded, following the Civil War.) He played golf at the equally select Chevy Chase Club and attended theater parties and late suppers at the home of Alice and Nick Longworth. And his old friend Lathrop Brown, who had just been elected to Congress from New York City, invited him for weekends amid the baronial splendors of Doughoregan Manor—the home of Charles Carroll of Carrollton, in the Maryland countryside—which Brown had leased. In later years, Roosevelt joked about the social diversions then available in Washington, which he described as "the saloon, the salon and the Salome." The "saloon" was any house where drinks flowed freely. The "salon" was a house that featured bright conversation. The "Salome" was Roosevelt's term, as an aide said, "for a mansion where the music was soft, so were the couches and the ladies were very pretty. Franklin knew them all."

The Wilson administration was none too popular among Washington's "cave dwellers," and the young man dined out on mischievous stories about his colleagues. One of his favorite tales involved a sudden visit from Secretary of State Bryan. He claimed that Bryan had rushed excitedly into his office one day and declared: " 'I've got to have a battleship. White people are being killed in Haiti, and I must send a battleship there within twenty-four hours.'

" 'Mr. Bryan,' I said, 'efficient as our Navy is, your request is impossible of fulfillment. Our battleships are in Narragansett Bay and I could not get one to Haiti in less than four days steaming at full speed. But I have a gunboat somewhere in the vicinity of Guantanamo and I could get her to Haiti in eight hours if you want me to.'

" 'That is all I wanted,' Mr. Bryan answered. He paused a moment and added, 'Roosevelt, after this, when I talk about battleships don't think I mean anything technical.' "

Like the memsahibs of Kipling's India, the wives and children of Washington's officialdom abandoned the muggy town during the summer, and Eleanor followed the family's usual practice of going to Campobello, rather than coming to her new home. Roosevelt joined the family for a few weeks, and much to the surprise of his neighbors, ordered the battleship *North Dakota* to Eastport for the Fourth of July celebration. He came on board for an inspection in open shirt and summer flannels but requested that a salute be fired, because the townspeople would be expecting it. The officers were entertained by the Roosevelts at their cottage, and one remembered him as "awfully nice—as nice as could be."

In the autumn of 1913, the Roosevelts rented Aunt Bye's old home, at 1733 N Street, which was within walking distance of his office.* Small by the standards of official Washington, the red-brick house had a post-age-stamp-sized lawn in front and a little garden in the back with a rose arbor, where the family often dined in the heat of summer. Bow windows looked out upon the tree-lined street. The house was still lighted by gas, and most of the furniture was heavy Victorian stuff that Aunt Bye had inherited from her father, Theodore Roosevelt, Sr. Eleanor's move to Washington was something of a mass migration. Besides the three children, she brought a car and chauffeur from Hyde Park, four servants, and a nurse and governess to the place that Aunt Bye and her husband, retired Admiral W. Sheffield Cowles, had maintained with two black servants.

Because of their relationship to Uncle Ted, the Roosevelts were warmly welcomed by the older generation of Washington society. Among their first invitations was to the monumentally ugly British Embassy, a few doors away, at the corner of Connecticut Avenue and N Street. The ambassador, Sir Cecil Spring-Rice, had been the best man at Uncle Ted's wedding to Edith Carow, in 1886, and it was he who had dryly observed to a friend: "One thing you must always remember about Roosevelt is that he is about seven years old." Jules Jusserand, the French ambassador, who had for the honor of France once forded a stream with the former President while wearing nothing but his gloves, opened his home to them. Senator Henry Cabot Lodge of Massachusetts, another big-Navy man, was a frequent host, and they often dined with Justice Oliver Wendell Holmes. Roosevelt attended the Sunday luncheons at the Justice's home at which the younger men of the Administration met to discuss the topics of the day. They also lunched with crusty old Henry Adams at his home, just across Lafayette Square from the White House. One day, Franklin mentioned a problem that was causing him deep concern, and Adams fiercely replied: "Young man, I have lived in this house many years and seen the occupants of that white house across the square come and go, and nothing that you minor officials or the occupant of that house can do will affect the history of the world for long!"

The Roosevelts' most intimate friends were William Phillips, the third assistant Secretary of State, and his wife; and Interior Secretary and Mrs. Franklin K. Lane and Lane's assistant, an economist named Adolph C. Miller, and his wife. Phillips, whose office was near Roosevelt's, had been secretary to Joseph Choate, the American envoy to Britain at the time Sara Roosevelt tried to persuade Choate to take Franklin to London. They organized a dinner group which met every two weeks during the Roosevelts' years in Washington, with the hostess of the eve-

* They rented their own home in New York to Thomas W. Lamont, a Morgan partner.

ning being allowed to invite another couple. "We put formality behind us these evenings, and did not even seat the Secretary of the Interior according to his rank," as Eleanor recalled. The convivial Lane enlivened these occasions with gossip about the inner workings of the Administration. On Sunday nights when the servants were off, Eleanor made it a practice to invite friends for conversation and cold cuts, cocoa and scrambled eggs—her sole culinary attainment.

People who knew Roosevelt during this period commented on his charm and vitality, but they observed few signs of future greatness. Preferring to sop up information by conversation, rather than by reading reports, he maintained a wide circle of friends. He collected ideas the way he collected stamps: from all quarters; and then he decided what use was to be made of them. "Young Roosevelt is very promising but I should think he'd wear himself out in the promiscuous and extended contacts he maintains with people," Newton D. Baker, who became Secretary of War in 1916, told Frances Perkins. "But as I have observed him, he seems to clarify his ideas and teach himself as he goes along by that very conversational method." William Phillips described his friend as "likeable, attentive but not a heavyweight, brilliant but not particularly steady in his views. . . . He had tremendous vitality, an eagerness and interest in everything and he certainly made a very effective Assistant Secretary of the Navy. He was always amusing, always the life of any party, but he did not seem fully mature."

Lean-muscled and superbly fit, Roosevelt's appearance had begun to approach the figure that Americans were to know in later years. Miss Perkins observed that his habit of looking down his nose at people was now hardly noticeable, and the toss of his head had become a gesture of cheerfulness, rather than of arrogance. "He smiled when he did it," she said. People discovered that he had a fine tenor voice. The observant also noted that one eye was slightly larger than the other. He developed the beginnings of the heavy blue shadows under them that he inherited from his mother, and his hands had a slight tremor—another family characteristic.

James Roosevelt has described his father as "the handsomest, strongest, most glamorous, vigorous, physical father in the world," and his children adored him. He joined them in pillow fights, picnics, and games of hares and hounds. Like his own father, Roosevelt was not much of a disciplinarian, even when his offspring dropped paper sacks full of water on the heads of arriving guests. Punishment was left to Eleanor, and if she insisted that her husband do it, "the punishment simply was not administered," according to James. Sometimes he took the children along with him to the Navy Department, where James and Elliott were fascinated by the elaborate ship models lining the halls. "There is only one thing that interferes with their perfect enjoyment," their father remarked, "and that is my inability to take the boats out of the 'windows,' as they call the glass cases, and sail them in the bathtub or the river." The boys were instructed to face the stern upon visiting a ship and salute the colors, but Anna was so frightened by the seventeen-gun salute to which her father was entitled she buried her head in her mother's lap. Nevertheless, shadows fell across the children's relations with their father. Increasingly busy as his star ascended, Roosevelt was often away from home, and when there, was too preoccupied to deal with his children on their own terms or to discuss their hidden fears and hopes.

Shy and somewhat remote, Eleanor was overshadowed by her ebullient husband. She saw her role as helping to advance his career and assumed the heavy burden of social obligations which his position entailed. "I was really well schooled now, and it never occurred to me to question where we were to go or what we were to do or how we were to do it," she said. "I simply knew that we had to do what we did, and that my job was to make it easy." William Phillips thought she had a steadying influence upon Franklin. The two couples shared a suite during a visit to San Francisco, and at breakfast one morning, he recalled that Eleanor had asked Franklin if he had received a letter from a certain party. Helping himself to the coffee and toast, Roosevelt acknowledged that he had.

"Well, have you answered it?"

"No, but I will answer it."

"Don't you think, Franklin, that you should answer it promptly?"

"Oh, I'll answer it promptly," he said with the air of a man whose coffee is getting cold, "I'll attend to it."

"Don't you think, Franklin, that it would be best if you answered it now?"

"All right," Roosevelt replied, "I'll answer it now."

Roosevelt immediately wrote out a reply to the letter, observed Phillips, who thought he would have ignored it without Eleanor's prodding.

Before coming to Washington, Eleanor had questioned Aunt Bye as to what was expected of her as the wife of the assistant Secretary of the Navy. While Mrs. Cowles impressed upon her niece the necessity of following the Navy's strict protocol, including the endless round of duty calls, she also gave her other advice: "You will find that many of the young naval officers' wives have a hard time because they must keep up their positions on very small pay. You can do a great deal to make life pleasant for them while they are in Washington, and that's what you should do." Eleanor dealt with luncheons, teas, receptions, and dinners, all the while going from house to house dropping off her card and repeating the ritual words, "I am Mrs. Franklin D. Roosevelt. My husband has just become assistant Secretary of the Navy." In one week alone, she made sixty calls and envied the independence of Alice Longworth, who was "too much interested in the political questions of the day to waste her time calling on women." At first, she tried to make do without a social secretary, but her obligations were so heavy that she finally hired a young lady to help her three mornings a week. Her name was Lucy Page Mercer.

As tall as Eleanor, pretty and vivacious at twenty-three, Lucy was a member of an impoverished branch of the Carroll family of Maryland and as much a patrician as the Roosevelts. She had lived as a child at 1761 N Street, a few doors away from the house where she was now employed, and was listed in the Washington and New York social registers. One of the few ways in which a distressed young lady of her background could earn a living was as a social secretary, and she was able and efficient, swiftly putting her employer's affairs in order. She was paid twenty-five dollars a week. "When I was 10 or 11 I remember feeling happy and admiring when I was greeted one morning at home by Miss Lucy Mercer," Anna Roosevelt recalled in an unpublished magazine article found among her papers. "I knew she sat at a desk and wrote on cards, and I knew that I liked her warm and friendly manner and smile." Eleanor sometimes invited Lucy to dinners and parties when an extra woman was needed, and she made a good impression on everyone. Even Sara Roosevelt was full of praise for her. "Miss Mercer is here, she is so sweet and attentive and adores you, Eleanor," she wrote her daughter-in-law upon one occasion.

Most mornings when Roosevelt was in Washington, Louis Howe, who lived with his family in an apartment on P Street, stopped by to pick him up for the walk down Connecticut Avenue to the Navy Department. Some days they met Miss Mercer as she arrived for work. Raising his hat, Roosevelt would call out a greeting to the "lovely Lucy" and stride off, with Howe hurrying along at his side like a pet terrier.

On these walks, Howe expounded on one of his favorite themes: Roosevelt should become personally involved in contract negotiations with the Navy's civilian labor force. Realizing that the upwards of one hundred thousand employees could be molded into a potent political weapon, Howe pressed Roosevelt into dealing with union leaders himself, rather than spending his spare time playing golf with his aristocratic friends. Roosevelt's contacts with organized labor filled a large gap in his political education. When he stepped down from his post, he could boast that in the seven and a half years in which he had been in charge of the Navy's labor relations, there had not been a single strike or serious work stoppage.

Whenever a strike threatened, Howe acted swiftly and sometimes secretly—but always in Roosevelt's name—to head off trouble. Naval officers were infuriated by Howe's unkempt appearance, lack of respect, and pro-labor bias, but their criticism rolled off his back. The workers had the votes, and the admirals did not. Early on, Roosevelt outlined his labor policy to the workers at the Washington Navy Yard:

> We want cooperation. We want to get down and talk across the table with you, and to right your wrongs. . . . I hope that any of the men of the Navy Department will come to the office of the Secretary of the Navy or the Assistant Secretary of the Navy and talk things over concerning the Department anytime they want. . . . We want you to talk to us as human beings.

Despite his offhanded manner, Roosevelt exhibited remarkable talent in the role of executive. He had the ability to listen, to decide, to cut bureaucratic knots, and to appear to come up with some favorable action, thereby placing himself at the center of events and in a position to take full credit for whatever worked out well. Flexibility was the key to Roosevelt's activities. Every problem facing him involved a mixture of policy, technique, and politics, and his usual reaction was to make a move and see what happened. Early in 1913, workers at the Boston Navy Yard, in Charlestown, threatened to strike over a proposal to introduce the Taylor system of scientific management into the yard's operations. While management regarded Taylorism as the key to productive efficiency, the unions viewed it as an inhumane speedup certain to result in wage cuts and lost jobs. Roosevelt made a personal inspection and although privately impressed with the Taylor system, left the workers with the impression that the two officers who had proposed the plan would be transferred. Back in Washington, he learned that the men had been responsible for substantial cost reductions, and Felix Frankfurter, a recent Harvard Law School graduate employed by the War Department, told him that Taylorism was being successfully applied at the Watertown Arsenal. Caught in these crosscurrents, the assistant Secretary bided his time until Congress resolved the problem for him by forbidding the Navy Department to use the Taylor system.

Suspecting collusion and often finding their suspicions confirmed, Daniels, Roosevelt, and Howe scrutinized every contract awarded by the department. Daniels once demanded an explanation of why a contract for oil had been let to a firm bidding ninety cents a barrel, rather than to one bidding eighty-nine cents. Within a year, he boasted, such vigilance was saving the taxpayers ten thousand dollars each day. It was no surprise, then, that the old populist tangled with the three steel companies—Carnegie, Midvale, and Bethlehem—that had a monopoly on the production of armor plate for the Navy. In August 1913, contracts were advertised for armor for the battleship *Arizona*, and all three firms submitted identical bids, of $454 per ton.

Upon learning that Bethlehem Steel habitually sold armor plate abroad at prices considerably lower than those charged the U. S. Navy, Daniels angrily rejected the bids and ordered them resubmitted on a genuinely competitive basis. In the meantime, Roosevelt had the Department of Justice comb its files for evidence of collusion by the armor trust. Once again the companies submitted identical bids, and once again they were rejected. Hinting that he might award the contract to a foreign firm, Daniels instructed Roosevelt to open negotiations with a British steel company that offered lower prices. Fearing they might lose the contract, the American firms lowered their prices substantially. Enforced competitive bidding reduced the cost of the *Arizona*'s armor by $1.1 million, according to Daniels.

Roosevelt also campaigned against monopoly on his own. Paradoxically, he chose the coal industry for his target, although his father had been a heavy investor in coal mines. Instead of putting out competitive bids for coal—still the major fuel for its ships despite the increasing use of oil—the Navy kept a short "approved list" of contractors with whom it dealt. Most were West Virginia firms. This "approved list" and the fact that the bids were almost always identical raised suspicions of collusion in Roosevelt's mind. "The passage of a camel through the needle's eye was a considerably easier journey than the route of . . . independent coal on its way to the accepted list," he observed.

Early in 1914, Roosevelt rejected the bids submitted by the West Virginia companies and had Howe rewrite the specifications. Some Pennsylvania firms offered coal at a reduced price, and these tenders were accepted. But, for once, Howe had slipped up. No coal expert, he drafted specifications containing errors that allowed the Pennsylvania mines to supply inferior coal. Naval engineers complained that some of it refused to burn completely, slowing their ships down. Prodded by the coal brokers, the West Virginia congressional delegation demanded an investigation, and Roosevelt was called before the House Naval Affairs Committee for some rough questioning. "I have about come to the conclusion that there is an awful lot of luck in this game," he later declared.

As a big-Navy man, Roosevelt was far more militant than most of the Wilson administration in the two international crises that erupted soon after it assumed office. The first occurred in April 1913, following approval by the California legislature of a bill aimed at preventing Japanese from owning land in the state. Angry anti-American demonstrations broke out in Japan, and there were fears, fanned by jingoistic newspapers in both countries, that war was imminent. The Joint Board of the Army and

Navy, the top military planning agency, made plans for the defense of the Philippines and suggested that for safety's sake the five old cruisers of the Asiatic Squadron stationed in the Yangtze River off Shanghai be immediately withdrawn to Manila. Rear Admiral Bradley A. Fiske, Daniels' aide for operations, fanned the flames by sending a secret memorandum to the Secretary, with a copy to Roosevelt, warning of a possible surprise attack by the Japanese. "War is not only possible but even probable," he declared.

Believing that the transfer of the ships would not only be provocative but also ineffective, Daniels rejected Fiske's advice. President Wilson agreed and forbade the Joint Board from meeting again. The storm blew itself out, but Roosevelt, firmly on the side of the militants, was convinced that the decision to ignore the Joint Board's recommendations was a serious mistake. Writing to Admiral Mahan, he complained about the decision to leave the ships in the Yangtze. "I did all in my power to have them return to their base," he said.

Roosevelt was far less reserved in his public statements during a crisis with Mexico in April 1914. Nearly four years before, the aging Mexican dictator, Porfirio Díaz, had been swept out of power by a revolution, and in the kaleidoscopic violence that followed, a strongman named Victoriano Huerta had seized control of the nation. Proclaiming a desire for "an orderly and righteous government in Mexico," Wilson refused to recognize the "unspeakable" Huerta, and a squadron of warships took up station off the Caribbean coast of Mexico to protect the lives and property of U.S. citizens. Some forty thousand Americans resided in Mexico, and American investments were valued at about a billion dollars. On April 9, several unarmed seamen went ashore at Tampico to load previously purchased supplies and were taken hostage by the Mexicans. The men were quickly returned, but Rear Admiral Harry T. Mayo, acting without authority, demanded an apology and a twenty-one-gun salute to the American flag. Profuse apologies were forthcoming, but Huerta balked at the salute unless assured that the Americans intended to render similar honors to the Mexican colors—assurances that Mayo declined to provide.

The situation deteriorated quickly. Wilson opposed Taft's legacy of "Dollar Diplomacy" and wished to improve relations with Latin America but made the autonomy of these nations conditional upon the establishment of "orderly processes of just government based upon law." In an attempt to bring down Huerta, he asked Congress to take "such action as may be necessary to enforce the respect due to the nation's flag." Before such authorization was granted, word was received that a German steamer had arrived off Veracruz with a sizable shipment of arms for Huerta, including two hundred machine guns. On orders from the President, eight hundred sailors and marines were landed on April 21 to capture the customs house and seize the ship. Three thousand more men were put ashore the following day and met strong resistance. By the time the naval brigade had won control of the streets of Veracruz, 126 Mexicans and nineteen Americans had been killed.

Roosevelt was on the West Coast, inspecting naval facilities—an area much alarmed by developments in Mexico. Reacting to the excitement and eager to take an active role, he created the impression that he was mobilizing the Pacific Fleet for operations off the Mexican coast. A request for information from Washington placed a damper on his activities, however. Having no desire for a repetition of Theodore Roosevelt's attention-getting insubordination of 1898, Daniels ignored the request for information and indicated that his assistant was needed in Washington. As Roosevelt's train rolled eastward, the Wilson administration, shocked by the bloodletting at Veracruz, sought a way out of the debacle. When Argentina, Brazil, and Chile offered to mediate, the President accepted.

But Roosevelt, lacking knowledge that the threat of war was rapidly receding, offered belligerent statements at each stop. In Minneapolis, a reporter asked what the crisis meant and he replied: "War! And we're ready!" The following day, he reached Milwaukee, and although the newspapers now had reports of the Administration's acceptance of the mediation offer, Roosevelt's bellicosity was still unchecked. "I do not want war, but I do not see how we can avoid it." "Sooner or later, it seems the United States must go down there and clean up the Mexican political mess. I believe that the best time is right now." In Chicago a few hours later, Roosevelt, growing cautious, was reluctant to state his own views and attributed the bellicosity to others. "The war spirit is sweeping the West like a prairie fire," he said. "The general opinion is that since the United States has finally started military activities they should be carried through to a finish with no compromise. Many persons and newspapers are openly advocating annexation as the only solution to the Mexican problem. The sentiment appears to be growing."

Back in Washington, where the Secretary of the Navy impressed upon Roosevelt the limits of his authority, the statements abruptly ceased. "He was young then and made some mistakes," Daniels would say in a fatherly fashion in later years. The whole episode turned out to be a study in futility. The U. S. Navy had no right to hold the German munitions ship and she unloaded her cargo at another Mexican port. Huerta, who was deposed a few months later, never ordered the salute demanded by Admiral Mayo. And within a few months, the landing at Veracruz faded into insignificance as Europe was engulfed by the bloodiest war in history.

VIII

A HOUSE OF SWORDS

THESE ARE HISTORY-MAKING days," Franklin Roosevelt observed on August 1, 1914, as the Old World plunged headlong into the fiery cataclysm of World War I. "It will be the greatest war in the world's history." Over the years, conflicting nationalisms and dynastic rivalries had transformed Europe into a house of swords so delicately balanced that the assassination of Archduke Franz Ferdinand, heir to the throne of the Austro-Hungarian Empire, brought the whole edifice crashing down on the heads of all. Two alliances were pitted against each other: one of Britain, France, Russia, and Serbia, later joined by Italy; the other of Germany, Austria-Hungary, and Turkey. Americans, whose attention had been fixed on Mexico, watched with stunned fascination as four decades of European peace were shattered by the clash of armies.

Galvanized by the prospect of action, Roosevelt rushed to the Navy Department from an out-of-town trip* on the morning Germany declared war on Russia, only to find "everyone was asleep and apparently oblivious to the fact that the most terrible drama in history was about to be enacted," he told Eleanor, at Campobello awaiting the birth of their fourth child. Along with Admiral Bradley Fiske, the aide for operations, he tried to persuade Daniels to order the fleet home from Veracruz, but noted that the Secretary "totally fails to grasp the situation," and the fleet remained where it was. Daniels seemed "very sad that his faith in human nature and similar idealistic nonsense was receiving such a rude shock, so

* FDR had been in Reading, Pennsylvania, where he had presented an anchor recovered from the sunken battleship *Maine* and testified to its authenticity. This was required because so many relics of the ship had been distributed around the country that rumors had spread that some were fakes. One town in Ohio got the captain's bathtub.

I started in alone to get things ready and prepare plans for what *ought* to be done by the Navy end of things."

In his letters to "Dearest Babs," Roosevelt expressed joy in being at the center of things—"Alive and very well and keen about everything. . . . I am *running* the real work, although Josephus is here. . . . Gee! But these are strenuous days!"—and was contemptuous of those who, like Daniels and Bryan, believed the nation could remain aloof from the rapidly spreading conflict. "These dear good people . . . have as much conception of what a general European war means as Elliott has of higher mathematics," he declared. "They really believe that because we are neutral we can go about our business as usual."

He was particularly scornful of a proposal by Daniels to dispatch the fleet to Europe to bring stranded American tourists home. "Aside from the fact the tourists (female etc.) couldn't sleep in hammocks and that battleships haven't got passenger accommodations, he totally fails to grasp the fact that this war between the other powers is going inevitably to give rise to a hundred different complications in which we shall have a direct interest," he angrily told his wife. "Questions of refugees, of neutrality, of commerce are even now appearing and we should unquestionably gather our fleet together and get it into the highest state of efficiency. . . . Today we are taking chances and I nearly boil over when I see the cheery 'mañana' way of doing business."

Roosevelt tended to exaggerate his own importance and Daniels' passivity, but the little that was being done to prepare the Navy to meet the emergency was done at his direction. Engaged in a vigorous and long-running struggle with his pacifist-minded chief over naval preparedness, his aggressiveness was noted by outsiders, among them Admiral Mahan.† "I wrote to you because I know of no one else in the Administration to whom I should care to write," the old strategist said in sending some suggestions for fleet operations. At Daniels' order, he was placed in charge of censoring wireless communications and represented the Navy Department on two cabinet-level boards that dealt with the maintenance of the neutrality proclaimed by President Wilson and the problems of Americans stranded abroad.

Roosevelt's heritage, associations, and long-standing suspicions of what he regarded as Germany's imperialistic ambitions in the hemisphere led him to be pro-Allied from almost the opening moments of the war. "I hope England will join in and with France and Russia force peace *at Berlin!*" he wrote Eleanor early in the struggle, and within a few days he

† FDR was concerned that the opening of the Panama Canal would cause residents of the Pacific coast to demand that the battle fleet be divided between the Atlantic and the Pacific to meet the threat of Japan. He asked both Theodore Roosevelt and Admiral Mahan to write magazine articles deploring such a move, and they complied. "Halve the fleet, and it is inferior in both oceans," Mahan argued.

was hailing the landing of British troops to stem the German advance through Belgium. Having lunch one day at the Metropolitan Club with Sir Cecil Spring-Rice, the British ambassador, Roosevelt noted that Count Johann von Bernstorff, the German envoy, was seated at the next table, trying to eavesdrop on the conversation. "I just *know* I shall do some awful unneutral thing before I get through," he said. These sentiments were at cross-purposes with those of President Wilson, who, in a famous phrase, commanded Americans to be "neutral in fact as well as in name, impartial in thought as well as action."

Throughout the early months of 1914, the New York political mill buzzed with rumors that Franklin Roosevelt might be a candidate for governor or United States senator. Tammany was on the ropes, having been defeated in recent elections, and the state's Democratic leadership was in disarray. It seemed the opportune time for someone to wrest control of the party from Boss Murphy, and the devious hand of Louis Howe was soon observed at work. The campaign began with a Howe-inspired trial balloon in the New York *Sun* stating that if Governor Martin H. Glynn did not cut his ties to Tammany, the Wilson administration would support Roosevelt for the gubernatorial nomination. Roosevelt, following the time-honored political practice, whetted public interest in his candidacy by repeatedly denying that he was available, while stepping up attacks on Tammany. "There can be no compromise with criminals, no alliance with grafters," he declared.

Before he could announce his candidacy, however, he had to have the support of President Wilson. As a member of the Administration, he could not act contrary to Wilson's wishes, and the President's patronage and support would be required if he was to make a creditable run against Tammany. By the end of March, Roosevelt could no longer put off a decision, and he sought "a five minute talk" with Wilson to discuss the New York political situation. The President did not grant the interview but sent him a note: "My judgment is that it would be best if members of the administration could use as much influence as possible but say as little as possible in the politics of their several states," particularly in New York, where "the plot is not clear." That put an end to any immediate plans that Roosevelt may have had to declare his candidacy, but he continued to put out feelers, even making an overture to the Progressive party with the hope of winning both the Progressive and the Democratic nominations if Theodore Roosevelt did not become the Bull Moose candidate. "I will not run against him," the young man explained. "You know blood is thicker than water." Perhaps so, but Uncle Ted neither ran nor chose to help Franklin secure his party's nomination.

Tammany launched an attack on the other flank. Representative

John J. Fitzgerald, chairman of the House Appropriations Committee and a Tammany leader, warned Wilson that the Democratic congressmen from New York City would no longer stand for being slandered as "representatives of crooks, grafters, and political buccaneers" by someone regarded as an authorized administration spokesman. Wilson, who could not afford to alienate senior congressmen if he wished his legislative program enacted into law, immediately issued a conciliatory statement. Reading the handwriting on the wall, Roosevelt gave up his gubernatorial candidacy late in July, and Howe went off on a Cape Cod vacation. And then, on August 13, Roosevelt unexpectedly announced that he was a candidate for the senate seat being relinquished by the retiring Elihu Root. "My senses have not yet left me," he telegraphed Howe and added that an "important political development" had caused him to take this step.

It is unclear what inspired this sudden turn of events. Ernest K. Lindley later said Roosevelt was "under the impression that it was Wilson's positive wish." Daniels thought that William G. McAdoo, the Secretary of the Treasury and the President's son-in-law, had passed the word. For his own part, the Navy Secretary stated that he tried to dissuade his assistant from making the apparently futile race because he had "a hunch" that he could not win the primary, and if he did, would be beaten in November. On the other side, there was considerable pressure upon him from upstate Democrats to be the running mate for their candidate for governor, a flashy Irish newspaperman named John A. Hennessy, who claimed to have the goods on Tammany in a little black book. Having beat the drums of reform, Roosevelt could hardly refuse to lead the charge.

Roosevelt also believed he had a fighting chance to win the senatorial nomination, because this was to be the first New York senatorial election held under the direct-primary system. Many voters credited him with helping make this reform possible through his fight against Sheehan, and he believed he would have their support. "I had no more idea or desire of offering myself as a 'white hope' than I had of attempting to succeed Kaiser Wilhelm," he told a friend. "I protested, but finally agreed to be the goat. Now I am going into the fight as hard as I can. . . ." Howe had serious misgivings about the wisdom of Roosevelt's decision but hastened to New York to organize a campaign. He concentrated on the strongly anti-Tammany rural areas, and using some of the tricks that had worked so well during the 1912 campaign, flooded the state with "personal" letters from the candidate. There was also a fresh touch: circulars containing endorsements from the navy-yard union leaders, which were handed out at factory gates.‡

‡ Much to Howe's embarrassment, some of the circulars did not have the union label.

But, once again, Howe had no visible candidate. Roosevelt remained at Campobello until well after the birth of the couple's fourth surviving child, Franklin D. Roosevelt, Jr. The boy was born by the light of an oil lamp in an improvised delivery room in the Roosevelt cottage. There was no telephone, so at the start of Eleanor's labor pains, her husband set off by boat to fetch Dr. E. H. Bennett from Lubec, Maine, but by the time he returned the baby had been delivered by the housekeeper. An anguished Howe prodded the absent candidate with needling messages: "For the love of Mike, stop seeing if the kid has cut a tooth and drop me a post card. . . . I suppose the baby talks quite fluently by this time. . . . Are you waiting for your son to be old enough to act as your stenographer before writing me?"

For a brief time, it appeared that Roosevelt might be unopposed or that Tammany would choose William Randolph Hearst, who had repeatedly been discredited in the eyes of the voters, as its candidate. "The truth is that they haven't anything to say against you and no one is very anxious to bell the cat," declared an optimistic Howe. "Particularly when they have the idea that the President occasionally pats him on the back and calls him 'pretty pussy' and gives him a nice saucer of warm patronage milk to drink!" For his own part, Roosevelt fervently hoped that Hearst would run for the nomination. "I have been offering up my prayers" that the rumors about his nomination "may come true," he said. "It would be magnificent sport and also magnificent service to run against him."

And then Murphy unveiled a candidate that jolted Roosevelt and Howe. Rather than choosing Hearst or some unsavory political henchman, he selected James W. Gerard, a liberal and wealthy businessman with ties to Tammany, who was serving as American ambassador to Germany. With a single blow, Murphy had knocked the props out from under Roosevelt's candidacy. Pleading the necessity of remaining at his post in Berlin, where he was assisting stranded Americans, Gerard was an all but impossible target. Roosevelt could not openly attack one of Wilson's diplomatic representatives, nor could he plead for the Administration's open support or claim to have its secret backing.

Although now pessimistic about his chances, Roosevelt took leave of his post as assistant Secretary of the Navy and conducted a strenuous campaign that took him into every corner of the state. Unable to attack Gerard, who remained at his post in Berlin but in the news, he campaigned against Murphy and bossism. "I have only one possible opponent," he told an audience in Buffalo, "an opponent who works in the dark underground passages of the crookedest political byways, an opponent who with a few trustworthy lieutenants, has for years used the Democratic voters of this state to further his own selfish ends. I refer to

Charles F. Murphy. . . ." Actively campaigning for only the second time
in his career, Roosevelt still had much to learn, as the editor of a Republican newspaper pointed out:

> He is quiet and unassuming, has the demeanor and poise of the student,
> and with his youthful scholarly face and soft accent, he gives no indica-
> tion of the stubborn attitude that his friends claim he can assume on oc-
> casion. . . . Some of his utterances were planned with the skill of an old
> campaigner, [but] when his speech was finished his listeners knew no
> more about his attitudes on the great questions of the day than they did
> before he began. . . . The great personal forces and magnetism necessary
> to push forward great national issues seem to be entirely lacking in him.

Roosevelt's defeat on Primary Day—September 28, 1914—was as
complete as Boss Murphy could have desired. Gerard won the nomination
with 210,765 votes to only 76,888 for Roosevelt. Hennessy, who had failed
to back up his charges of Tammany corruption and was laughed at by
upstaters because of his brogue and flamboyance, was crushed by Governor
Glynn. Howe blamed Hennessy for the disaster and bitterly observed that
he "ruined us and will sink any ship on which he is a passenger." Licked
by four to one in New York City, Roosevelt took consolation in the fact
that he had carried twenty-two of the state's sixty-one counties. To
strengthen his credentials as a Democratic team player, he campaigned for
Gerard but was "not entirely surprised" when the Democratic slate was
swamped by the Republicans in November.

This setback taught Roosevelt lessons that he would never forget. He
learned that it takes more than a few weeks to organize an effective campaign. He learned to pace himself in a statewide campaign, to conserve
his voice and his energy. And he learned how to accept defeat. But the
major lesson of the 1914 campaign was that he could not openly defy
Tammany and expect to carry New York State; if the Democrats were to
win, both progressives and organization men had to work together.
Murphy and Roosevelt remained wary of each other, but the coating of
respectability achieved by Tammany as it supported reformist factory and
labor legislation, and Roosevelt's increasing emphasis on party regularity,
made possible a meeting of minds. In 1915, Roosevelt endorsed the candidacy of Al Smith for sheriff, and the following year, he helped obtain the
postmastership of New York City for Robert Wagner. Roosevelt would
never again campaign on an anti-Tammany platform.

Returning to the Navy Department, Roosevelt joined Theodore Roosevelt, General Leonard Wood, and Senator Henry Cabot Lodge in beating the drums for American preparedness. Zealous to the point of insubordination, Roosevelt launched a flood of speeches and magazine articles
emphasizing the need for a strong Navy. "Our national defense must ex-

tend all over the western hemisphere, must go out a thousand miles into the sea," he declared. "We must create a Navy not only to protect our shores and our possessions, but our merchant ships in time of war, no matter where they may go." He drafted plans for a naval reserve of fifty thousand men and devised a program to commission civilian college graduates after they had taken a short course at Annapolis.

Late in October 1914 when Daniels was out of town, Roosevelt, as acting Secretary, issued a memorandum stating that the Navy was short eighteen thousand men and was unable to keep thirteen second-class battleships in commission. The statement made the headlines, but as he told Eleanor, it was "the truth and even if it gets me into trouble I am perfectly ready to stand by it. The country needs the truth about the Army and Navy instead of a lot of the soft mush about everlasting peace which so many statesmen are handing out to a gullible public." Roosevelt also provided congressional supporters of preparedness, such as Representative Angustus P. Gardner, Lodge's son-in-law, with ammunition and eagerly testified before the House Naval Affairs Committee when it examined the state of naval readiness. Everyone was impressed with Roosevelt's candor and mastery of the facts, and the New York *Sun* observed that "he exhibited a grasp of naval affairs that seemed to astonish members of the committee."

Such outspoken criticism of an administration of which he was a member might have left Roosevelt in an exposed position had not public opinion shifted to preparedness. The European conflict bogged down into a bloody war of attrition as the trenches stretched from neutral Switzerland to the English Channel and the belligerents attempted to starve each other into surrender through naval blockade. Unable to contest Britain's command of the sea, the Germans retaliated with the only weapon available to them: the submarine. Relations between the United States and Germany deteriorated after February 1915, when Berlin announced that the waters around Britain were thenceforth to be regarded as a war zone and that enemy ships would be torpedoed without warning. Using strong language to protest these "unprecedented" measures, Wilson warned the German Government that it would be held to "strict accountability" should any American lives be lost. The U-boats piled up an increasing number of "kills" in British waters, but despite repeated German warnings, Americans continued to travel into the war zone on Allied vessels.

On May 7, 1915, the Cunard liner *Lusitania* was torpedoed off Ireland, with the loss of 1,198 lives—including 128 Americans. Though the ship carried munitions in her cargo, German attempts to justify the sinking were unavailing. Americans were outraged by what they regarded as "wanton murder on the high seas," and an angry Theodore Roosevelt spoke for them as he declared that it was "inconceivable that we can refrain from taking action . . . for we owe it not only to humanity but to our own national respect." "It is a deed for which a Hun would blush, a Turk would be ashamed, and a Barbary pirate apologize," said *The Nation*. Billy Sunday, the evangelist, cried, "Damnable! Damnable! Absolutely hellish!"

Privately, Wilson was just as angered, but he was determined to keep the United States out of war. "There is such a thing as a man being too proud to fight," he declared, and dispatched a series of protest notes to Berlin. The first vigorously upheld the right of American citizens to sail the high seas and demanded an indemnity for the loss of American life. The German reply was unacceptable, and was followed by a second note, demanding an end to unrestricted submarine warfare. Bryan, who regarded the note as so provocative in tone as to threaten war, resigned as Secretary of State on June 9, 1915, rather than sign it.

The resignation created a sensation. Bryan was assailed for "unspeakable treachery . . . to the President and the nation," and critics, expressing opinions heard often in later times of crisis, charged that he had created the impression abroad of a divided country and weakened the President's hand. Franklin Roosevelt was among them. "What d' y' think of W. Jay B.?" he asked Eleanor. "I can only say I'm disgusted clear through."* This disgust apparently included Daniels, whose views were similar to those of Bryan, for he added: "J.D. will *not* resign." Some of the admirals had expected the Secretary to leave also, with Admiral Fiske telling Roosevelt that he should be prepared to assume the office "if J.D. gets canned." To Wilson, Roosevelt sent a handwritten letter of support: "I want to tell you simply that you have been in my thoughts during these days and I realize to the full all that you have had to go through—I need not repeat to you my own entire loyalty and devotion—that I hope you know. But I feel more strongly that the Nation approves and sustains your course and that it is *American* in the highest sense."

The Germans eventually paid an indemnity for the American lives lost in the sinking of the *Lusitania* and ordered U-boat skippers to spare passenger liners. Nevertheless, the episode heightened anti-German sentiment in the United States. Increasing numbers of Americans were now convinced that the victory of German absolutism was a menace to their liberties and to democratic institutions everywhere. But the major significance of the *Lusitania* crisis was that it focused the attention of many Americans upon the military and naval impotence of their country.

* Twenty years later, FDR took a different view. Impressed by the evidence, gathered by the Nye Committee, indicating that Wall Street and the munitions makers had helped propel the United States into World War I, he told Daniels: "Would that W.J.B. had stayed on as Secretary of State—the country would have been better off."

Woodrow Wilson was among them. Fearing that the Republicans might seize control of the preparedness movement—as well as worrying about the consequences of a German victory—the President became a reluctant convert to the cause of preparedness.

Roosevelt was convalescing at Campobello from an appendectomy when Daniels informed him that, on July 21, President Wilson had instructed the Secretaries of War and Navy to draft plans for a massive increase in the strength of their services and to have them ready for Congress when it reconvened, in November. Elated, he returned to Washington in mid-August to serve as acting Secretary while Daniels vacationed and to work on plans for the most effective utilization of the navy yards in the new program. "Things will hum," he promised Howe. The General Board produced a sweeping recommendation that called for the construction of 156 ships at a cost of $500 million. This armada was to include ten battleships, six battle cruisers, ten scout cruisers, fifty destroyers, and sixty-seven submarines, along with a concomitant increase in the Navy's manpower. The plan, which was approved by Wilson, set a new standard of naval power for the United States—a navy "second to none," including that of Britain. Even the Navy League could not have asked for more. Although enthusiastically supported by the pro-preparedness forces, the General Board's recommendations came under intense attack from the progressive-pacifist movement, which warned that the plan was the work of an unholy alliance of imperialists, militarists, monopolists, and bankers. Anti-preparedness sentiment was particularly strong in the Middle West, and congressmen from the area placed stumbling blocks to quick approval of Wilson's program.

Unable to budge Congress after several months of lethargic committee hearings, Wilson took the case for preparedness to the people. In January and February 1916, he campaigned westward from New York to Kansas City. "Have you ever let your imagination dwell upon the enormous stretch of coast from the [Panama] Canal to Alaska—from the Canal to the northern corner of Maine?" he asked an audience in St. Louis. "There is no other navy in the world that has to cover so great an area of defense as the American navy, and it ought, in my judgment, to be incomparably the greatest navy in the world."

Roosevelt applauded these statements from the sidelines at Atlantic City, where he had gone, at the insistence of his wife and his physician, to cure a persistent throat infection. While there, he followed speculation in the newspapers—undoubtedly inspired by Louis Howe—that he was under consideration by Wilson for the post of Secretary of War. The incumbent, Lindley Garrison, had resigned when the President rejected his call for universal military training. Roosevelt had the support of a scattering of officers, businessmen, newspapers, and labor leaders, mustered by Howe, but Wilson apparently did not consider him for the job. A few days after Roosevelt's return to Washington, Eleanor gave birth to their last child, named John Aspinwall Roosevelt, for Franklin's uncle.

For the next year, until the United States entered the war, in April 1917, Roosevelt was among the most ardent advocates of preparedness. "A great many nations and peoples are jealous of us," he warned. "The question comes down to this: if you believe there is any possibility of an attack upon our country, whether upon our shores or our island possessions, of our trade with foreign lands, then you become at once a believer in adequate national defense." Agreeing that the $500 million sought for naval expansion was indeed a sizable sum, he claimed it was not exorbitant. "Why, we spend more money per year for chewing gum . . . than we do to keep our Army, more money is spent for automobile tires than it costs to run the Navy."

Military aviation was in its infancy, but, early on, Roosevelt was convinced that no nation that neglected the new weapon could be considered fully prepared for war. Upon taking over the assistant Secretary's desk, he had tried to expand and improve the Navy's small air arm. An air station was established at Pensacola, Florida, and aircraft were integrated into fleet exercises and served with the force involved in the Mexican operation. Following the outbreak of the war, he detailed naval officers to observe developments in Europe and sent agents abroad to procure engines and aircraft for study in this country. When the naval attaché at the American embassy in London complained about the difficulty of meeting this order, he told him he wanted a complete seaplane and didn't care how it was obtained.

Impressed with the camp established by Theodore Roosevelt and Leonard Wood at Plattsburg, New York, in 1915 to drill a civilian elite in the rudiments of military life, Roosevelt wished to organize a naval counterpart. He proposed that yachtsmen be invited to participate in a training cruise on the Navy's battleships, but Daniels, concerned that the plan would appeal only "to college boys, rich young men, well-to-do yachtsmen, etc.," was wary. He gave reluctant approval only after receiving assurances that the cruise "would be carried out on absolutely democratic lines," and in his assistant's absence, baptized it as the John Paul Jones Cruise. The response was overwhelming. More than nineteen hundred men participated in the twenty-five-day cruise during the summer of 1916. They received training in navigation, seamanship, and gunnery, and 80 percent of them were awarded commissions in the U. S. Navy after the United States entered the war.

In addition to organizing the training cruise, Roosevelt rode herd on the long-delayed naval expansion bill, while Daniels campaigned for the reelection of Woodrow Wilson. "I am trying though I fear in vain to eliminate a number of fool features in it and to get into it a few more really constructive items," he wrote Eleanor at Campobello. Unexpected help was received when the fleets of Britain and Germany fought the greatest naval battle in history, off Jutland on May 31, 1916. In driving the Germans back to their harbors, the Royal Navy suffered severe losses, and there was considerable anxiety in the United States as to whether or not Britain could maintain her traditional command of the sea. Spurred on by this uncertainty, Congress not only approved the expansion bill, which was signed by the President on August 29, 1916,† but speeded up the five-year building program sought by the General Board to three years.

Family anxieties dimmed Roosevelt's enjoyment of the passage of the long-delayed naval expansion bill. During the summer of 1916, the nation was ravaged by a severe poliomyelitis epidemic, in which more than seven thousand victims died. Worried that his own children might be stricken, he insisted they remain at Campobello until the epidemic subsided. Visiting the island briefly in July, he spent hours swatting flies, which were then thought to be carriers of polio. "*Please* kill all the flies I left," he wrote his wife upon returning to Washington. "I think it really important."

Throughout the summer, the anxious father followed the spread of the disease with alarm. "There is much I.P. [infantile paralysis] in Boston, Springfield, Worcester, etc., and even in Rockland and other Maine points," he told Eleanor. He would not allow the children to return home by train and noted that it would be difficult to come to Hyde Park by automobile, because panicked villagers all over the eastern seaboard were blocking the passage of motorists with children. Roosevelt wished to send the Navy Department yacht *Dolphin* to pick up his family and bring them up the Hudson to Hyde Park, but Daniels was reluctant to give permission. Elections were to be held in Maine, and he was concerned that the Republicans might make private use of the vessel a campaign issue. "He is scared blue and *Dolphin* won't be allowed within 1000 miles of Maine till after September 11," Roosevelt said. The vessel was finally dispatched to Campobello in October.

Roosevelt played only a minor role in the 1916 presidential cam-

† The Naval Appropriations Act of 1916 also strengthened the recently organized office of Chief of Naval Operations, which was designed to provide central strategic planning in the mold of the long-sought general staff. Daniels, fearing that such a change would give the admirals too much control over naval policy at the expense of civilian leadership, resisted the change, charging that it would "Prussianize" the Navy, while Roosevelt supported it. Admiral Fiske seemed likely to be chosen as the first Chief of Naval Operations, but his uncompromising stand for preparedness had angered the Secretary and he was passed over.

paign, in which Wilson was opposed by Charles Evans Hughes, who had resigned his seat on the Supreme Court to accept the Republican nomination. The President's reelection looked uncertain, for, unlike 1912, when the Republicans were divided, Theodore Roosevelt had abandoned the moribund Progressive party and supported Hughes despite a personal distaste for him. As belligerent as ever, the elder Roosevelt denounced Wilson's failure to declare war on Germany after the sinking of the *Lusitania* as "weak" and "cowardly" and derided the President's "too proud to fight" declaration. The cautious Hughes would not go that far but acknowledged he would have been "firmer" in dealing with the Germans. Banking on the fact that a majority of the voters were still opposed to America's entry into the conflict, the Democrats campaigned for Wilson with the slogan "He kept us out of war."

Privately, Franklin Roosevelt found himself in sympathy with Hughes, but he knew where his political future lay. Counterattacking Republican assaults on the Navy's lack of readiness under Wilson and Daniels, he charged that the fleet inherited from President Taft had been a hollow shell. In 1912, when a review was held in New York Harbor, some vessels had to be towed to their stations and others were kept afloat only by continuous pumping. Under the Wilson administration, he claimed, "the navy is growing; it must grow more. It is using the appropriations wisely and honestly. All it needs now is boosting and not knocking."

Wilson ran a forceful campaign, but on Election Day, November 7, bookmakers were laying odds of ten to six in favor of Hughes. That night, Roosevelt attended a dinner given by Henry Morgenthau, Sr., chairman of the Democratic Finance Committee, at the Biltmore Hotel, in New York City. The early returns cast a pall over the gathering. The faces of the assembled Democrats grew longer as every eastern state except New Hampshire went for Hughes. Roosevelt remained jovial, even jokingly laying plans with Frank Polk, the State Department counselor, to open a law practice. Both the New York *Times* and the New York *World* bannered the election of Hughes, and when Roosevelt left the Biltmore at midnight to take the train to Washington, it appeared as if his days as assistant Secretary of the Navy were drawing to a close.‡

But when Roosevelt went to the Navy Department in the morning, everything was topsy-turvy. Returns from the midwestern and far-western states, where German-Americans and antiwar sentiment were heavily concentrated, had swung the pendulum back toward Wilson. At noon "of

‡ There is a story, perhaps apocryphal, that Hughes had gone to bed believing himself elected. When the returns began running toward Wilson, a reporter called Hughes's home, only to be told that the "President-elect" was asleep and couldn't be disturbed. "Okay," replied the reporter, "when he wakes up tell him he isn't the President-elect any more."

the most extraordinary day of my life," he excitedly wrote Eleanor at Hyde Park that "Wilson may be elected after all. It looks hopeful. . . ." Wilson carried California and its thirteen electoral votes by fewer than four thousand votes—and with it the election. The President had 277 electoral votes to 254 for Hughes, and the popular vote was 9,129,606 to 8,538,321. Jubilant over the outcome, Roosevelt declared that it was rumored that "a certain distinguished cousin of mine is now engaged in revising an edition of his most noted historical work, *The Winning of the West.*" And shaking his head over the rigid conservatism of his Delano relations, he fervently told Eleanor: "I hope to God I don't grow reactionary with advancing years."

"It is a curious thing," Franklin Roosevelt once observed, "that as soon as I go away we seem to land Marines somewhere." He had been on the Pacific coast in 1914 when the Marines landed at Veracruz; a year later, while he was recovering from his appendectomy at Campobello, they had been dispatched to Haiti, because the Wilson administration feared that Germany might use one of the periodic revolutions as an excuse to seize control of a naval base within striking distance of the Panama Canal. As a result of his frequent vacation trips to the West Indies, Roosevelt had a keen interest in the Caribbean, and when Daniels suggested he make a trip to Cuba, Haiti, and the Dominican Republic to inspect the American occupation forces, he accepted with alacrity. Like Wilson, he was opposed to imperialism merely for the sake of economic gain, but believed stability was required for democracy and progress in Latin America—even if it was secured at the point of an American bayonet.*

Accompanied by Major General George Barnett, the Commandant of the Marine Corps, and several friends, including George Marvin, his old Groton master and a magazine editor, Roosevelt sailed into the harbor of Port-au-Prince, the cheerfully ramshackle capital of Haiti, on the destroyer *Wainwright* on January 26, 1917. "I have never been in Naples," he later said, "but this Bay with its wonderful setting must be the equal of anything in Italy." The ships of the Atlantic Fleet had been drawn up for review in two parallel lines nearly three miles long, and the destroyer steamed down the lane between them. Salutes boomed out, marine guards snapped to attention, and the band of the flagship crashed into the national anthem. "It was an unforgettable picture in the opalescent light of a tropic morning, framed in the wide amphitheater of blue Haitian mountains," George Marvin later recalled. "Franklin stood alone on the bridge [with the *Wainwright's* skipper] taking the salutes. On all such occa-

---

* The ever-protective Sara Roosevelt reminded her son to wear dark glasses and take a pith helmet with him.

sions he appeared to very great advantage, always a graceful, dignified figure."

In a holiday mood, Roosevelt was delighted and stimulated by his trip to Haiti. Unlike many of the marine officers, he spoke French and was seemingly without racial prejudice and careful of the sensibilities of the Haitians—all of which made him popular with the local elite. He sprinkled his speeches with anecdotes and references to Haitian history supplied by Marvin, who had previously visited the island. When General Smedley D. Butler, the marine commander, tried to block the Haitian President from entering his limousine so the assistant Secretary could go first, Roosevelt politely raised his hat and stepped aside with an *"Après vous, Excellence."*

The highlight of the visit was a four-day expedition on horseback through the mountains to Cap-Haïtien, on the island's northern coast. Armed revolutionaries, regarded by the Americans as bandits, were known to be in the area, so the column was heavily guarded by an escort commanded by Major Henry Latrobe Roosevelt, a distant cousin. "Franklin was the life of the pilgrimage," said Marvin. "It was a tough ride—tropic heat, rough trails. . . . We forded rivers, climbed elevations, slept *al fresco*. . . . Of all the party . . . Franklin stood the journey best. He was always gay and animated, enormously interested in all he saw, in his numerous interviews with local officials . . . and never tired." Roosevelt picked up the recipe for a powerful cocktail made from strong, dark Haitian rum, brown sugar, and orange juice, which he always called "my Haitian libation." He shot a dove at one halt, and had himself photographed with it, later claiming in Washington that it was a "Great Haitian Shrink Bird," which, when shot, fades away unless immediately plunged into a pot of boiling water. At another point, the party went swimming in a stream and attracted an attentive group of black women who had never seen a naked white man before.

The marines made certain that Roosevelt and his party saw only what they wanted them to see, and the visitors were duly impressed. Roosevelt was particularly pleased by Butler's road-building program, which constructed an all-weather highway from Port-au-Prince to Cap-Haïtien in little more than two years and at a cost of less than $250,000 a mile. The secret of Butler's success was forced labor, which had been introduced to Haiti by the French in colonial times. Gangs of workmen were rounded up and put to work on the roads for little or no money. When the highway was finished, later that year, the assistant Secretary cabled a "Well done" to Butler and arranged for him to be awarded the Medal of Honor for capturing a rebel stronghold. Roosevelt, convinced that the Haitians were pleased with the progress being brought to them, considered investing in a vacation resort on the island and a chain of variety stores in both

Haiti and the Dominican Republic. Butler's strong-arm methods resulted
in an insurrection, however, and in 1918 the marines were nearly driven
from the country.

While Roosevelt and his companions were enjoying themselves in
the tropics, relations between the United States and Germany had
reached a crisis. The Battle of Jutland, although hailed as a great victory
by the Germans, had in reality demonstrated the inability of the Central
Powers to break the Allied blockade by conventional means. In a desperate attempt to starve Britain into submission, Germany resumed unrestricted submarine warfare as of February 1, 1917. One concession was
made to the United States—a concession that could only be regarded as
insulting. Each week, a single American ship would be permitted to sail a
specified course through the war zone, provided it carried no contraband
and was painted with wide red and white stripes. The German High
Command fully realized that the resumption of unrestricted submarine
warfare would probably bring the United States into the conflict on the
side of the Allies but gambled on winning the war before American resources could be mobilized. Meanwhile, Wilson went before Congress on
February 3 to announce that the German ambassador had been given his
passport, signifying a break in relations.

That evening, Roosevelt was being entertained at the handsome old
palace at Santiago, in the Dominican Republic, by the local marine commander and his wife. Near the end of dinner, an aide brought him a cable
from Secretary Daniels. He left the table with General Barnett, the Commandant of the Marine Corps, and went to the adjoining room to read it.
It read: BECAUSE OF THE POLITICAL SITUATION PLEASE RETURN TO WASHING-
TON AT ONCE. AM SENDING SHIP TO MEET YOU AT PUERTO PLATA TOMORROW
EVENING. Returning to the dining room, Roosevelt's long face made it
clear to the others guests that something had happened. He said that he
and his party would have to leave immediately, and although he did not
know what had happened, said the recall was based on "political considerations."

"What can political considerations mean?" asked his hostess. "It
must be that Charles E. Hughes has led a revolution against President
Wilson."

"My dear lady," replied Roosevelt, "you have been in the tropics too
long!"

Roosevelt and his companions returned to the United States on
the collier *Neptune*, under considerable tension. Cut off from the outside world, they were convinced that the United States had declared war
on Germany. "No lights were showing, the guns were manned and there
was complete radio silence," Roosevelt recalled. A sharp lookout was

maintained for German submarines. Thus, it was something of a letdown when they landed at Fortress Monroe, at the entrance to Hampton Roads, on the morning of February 8 to find there was no war. "Late that afternoon we were back in Washington," Roosevelt added. "I dashed to the Navy Department and found the same thing—no diplomatic relations with Germany broken off, no excitement, nor preparations, no orders to the Fleet at Guantanamo to return to their home yards on the East Coast."

The decision for peace or war hung in the balance for the next two months. Wilson, convinced that war was inevitable but unable to move faster than public opinion would allow, bided his time. Frustrated after his dash from the Caribbean and impatient for action, Roosevelt had little insight into Wilson's problem until he faced a similar dilemma, two decades later. At that time, however, he vividly recalled a visit to the White House during the twilight period between peace and war:

> I went to see the President and I said, "President Wilson, may I request your permission to bring the Fleet back from Guantanamo, to send it to the Navy Yards and have it cleaned and fitted out for war and be ready to take part in the war if we get in?" And the President said, "I am very sorry, Mr. Roosevelt, I cannot allow it." But I pleaded and he gave me no reason and said, "No, I do not wish it brought north." So, belonging to the Navy, I said, "Aye, aye, sir," and started to leave the room. He stopped me at the door and said, "Come back." He said, "I am going to tell you something I cannot tell the public. I owe you an explanation. I don't want to do anything . . . by way of war preparations that will allow the definitive historian in later years to say that the United States had committed an unfriendly act against the Central Powers."

Unmollified, but at least aware that the question facing Wilson was not *whether* the United States would enter the conflict but *when*, Roosevelt surged ahead with the war preparations that he could accomplish with the approval of the President or the Secretary of the Navy. "I have any amount of work to do," he told Eleanor, "and J.D. is too damned slow for words—his failure to decide the few big things holds me up all down the line." As an ardent yachtsman, he was convinced that small craft would have an important role in antisubmarine patrols along the coast and laid plans to mobilize them as soon as war was declared. Angered by the high price charged by the American company that monopolized the importation of nitrate, used in the manufacture of explosives, he bypassed the State Department and upon his own authority entered into a contract with the Chilean Government for five million pounds of nitrate. It turned out not only to be cheaper than that supplied by the American company but "the finest nitrate ever shipped to the United States."

Roosevelt claimed after the war that he had broken enough regulations to put him in jail "for 999 years." Contracts were let without authority, and suppliers were told to send the bill to the Navy Department. There were stories that he conspired with naval officers to expand the "boot" camps, notably the one at Great Lakes, without the Secretary's knowledge. Daniels later denied that anything had been slipped over on him and said he had been fully aware of all of Roosevelt's actions. The assistant Secretary also openly consorted with the Administration's critics, attending a dinner in New York at which his companions included Theodore Roosevelt, Leonard Wood, Elihu Root, and J. P. Morgan. Root was inclined to praise Wilson's course, but as the young man noted, "T.R. wanted more vigorous demand about future course—less indorsement of the past. I backed T.R.'s theory."

American entry into the war followed swiftly. To meet the threat of the U-boats, shipowners urged the Navy to provide guns and armed guards for their vessels. Roosevelt searched the Navy's stockpile and found a half dozen six-inch guns and determined that under an old law they could be loaned to the steamship companies by executive order. Always the legalist, Wilson refused to take advantage of this loophole and asked Congress to approve legislation authorizing the arming of merchant ships. The bill was filibustered to death by what Wilson called "a little group of willful men, representing no opinion but their own." As soon as Congress adjourned, Wilson ordered the guns mounted, by executive order. The Germans replied by torpedoing three American vessels, with heavy loss of life. And so, with a heavy heart, Wilson called a special session of Congress for April 2, at which he was expected to ask for a declaration of war.

A soft rain was falling as Franklin and Eleanor Roosevelt left their new home, at 2131 R Street, for the Capitol early that evening.† Everyone wanted to hear the President's historic address, and Roosevelt had obtained a ticket for his wife only with some difficulty. Troops guarded the mist-shrouded building, and Secret Service agents prowled the halls to prevent pacifists from staging a demonstration. By 8:30 P.M., the members of the House were in their seats, the Supreme Court sat directly in front of the Speaker's desk, the Cabinet was to the side and behind them, and the diplomatic corps, in full evening dress, occupied a place on the floor for the first time in memory. The senators filed in, two by two, most carrying tiny American flags. Moments later, the doorkeeper announced: "The President of the United States!" The crowd rose to its feet, and for three minutes cheered and applauded with an intensity never before seen in the chamber.

† The N Street house had become overcrowded after the birth of John Roosevelt, and the family had moved to larger quarters in the autumn of 1916.

"I have called the Congress into extraordinary session," Wilson began matter-of-factly, "because there are serious, very serious choices of policy to be made, and made immediately." He briefly recited the facts of the controversy with Germany and described German submarine warfare against commerce as "warfare against mankind." Armed neutrality proved impracticable, the President continued, and the alternative to war was submission. "With a profound sense of the solemn and even tragical character of the step I am now taking and the grave responsibilities which it involves . . . I advise that the Congress declare the recent course of the Imperial German Government to be in fact nothing less than war against the Government and the people of the United States; that it formally accept the status of a belligerent which has been thrust upon it. . . . The world must be made safe for democracy."

Led by Chief Justice Edward D. White, a Confederate veteran and long-time Allied sympathizer, the entire assemblage leaped to its feet, the Roosevelts among them, to applaud and cheer at the top of their lungs. Tears furrowed White's face, and some of the audience excitedly clutched their neighbors or pounded them on the back. Eleanor, who had "listened breathlessly" to the speech, was "half-dazed by the sense of impending change." When the Roosevelts returned home, Franklin prepared some remarks for the press. "No statement about American national honor and high purpose more clear or more definite . . . could be made," he said in a try for Wilsonian eloquence. "It will be an inspiration to every true citizen no matter what his political faith, no matter what his creed, no matter what the country of his origin."

IX
WAR TO END WAR

RISING AND FALLING on the long Atlantic swells, a half dozen storm-beaten destroyers steamed through an opening in the antisubmarine nets guarding the British naval base at Queenstown,* on the south coast of Ireland. Cheers and whistles echoed from the green hills surrounding the harbor as the vessels let go their anchors. It was May 4, 1917, and the first American fighting ships had arrived in European waters to join the battle against the U-boats. With his ships safely moored, Commander Joseph K. Taussig reported to Vice Admiral Sir Lewis Bayley, under whom the flotilla was to serve. Asked by Bayley when he would be ready for sea, Taussig unhesitatingly replied: "We are ready now, sir."

These words struck a chord of appreciation on both sides of the Atlantic—and no one better exemplified this spirit than Franklin Roosevelt. As soon as the United States formally declared war on Imperial Germany, he threw himself into the task of mobilizing the Navy. Seemingly everywhere, he pressed for the enlistment of large numbers of men, ordered training camps expanded, placed contracts for vast amounts of matériel and equipment, and was free with advice whether it was sought or not. "See young Roosevelt about it," was a byword in wartime Washington. Such efficiency brought him to the attention of the White House. Not long after the declaration of war, he was summoned to a meeting with President Wilson and General Hugh Scott, the Army's chief of staff. "Mr. Secretary, I'm very sorry but you have cornered the market for supplies," the Chief Executive told him with a twinkle in his eye. "You'll have to divide up with the Army."

Nevertheless, like Theodore Roosevelt in 1898, the young man had

* Now Cobh.

no intention of fighting a war from behind a desk in the Navy Department. Although he had five small children, he planned to resign as assistant Secretary and get into uniform—not only out of patriotism but because that was the route Uncle Ted had followed to the presidency. The old Rough Rider repeatedly encouraged Franklin to join up, much to Eleanor's dismay, but Wilson and Daniels persuaded him that he was more valuable to the war effort where he was. The conflict had placed a high premium on the qualities that the thirty-five-year-old assistant Secretary possessed—energy, flexibility, self-confidence, and the willingness to take a chance—and they did not wish to lose them. Leonard Wood added his voice to those urging him to remain at his desk. "Franklin Roosevelt should under no circumstances think of leaving the Navy Department," he declared. "It would be a public calamity to have him leave at this time."

At the first sound of the bugle, the elder Roosevelt characteristically hastened to Washington with military ardor aroused. Even though he was fifty-nine years old, blind in one eye, and weakened by a tropical fever picked up during an expedition into the Amazonian jungle, he bombarded the War Department and the White House for permission to raise a division of volunteers and lead it to fight in France. Franklin and Eleanor spent much time with him and found he was "completely preoccupied" with the quest for adventure.

Franklin was convinced that the Colonel's proposal would be good for morale at home and abroad, and assisted in paving the way for a meeting with the President at the White House. Outwardly cordial, the longtime political rivals were tense and wary of each other. Wilson told the ex-President there was no room in modern war for gallant gestures and said the nation would rely upon a conscript, rather than a volunteer, army. Roosevelt agreed to support the draft—or selective service, as it was to be called—but emphasized that a volunteer division could be quickly organized and would show the Allies "what was on the way." Wilson promised to give the matter the consideration it deserved, and the interview was over. "I really think the best way to treat Mr. Roosevelt is to take no notice of him," the President later told an aide. "That breaks his heart and is the best punishment that can be administered." The old lion never forgot the slight.†

"Force, Force to the utmost, Force without stint or limit" was Wilson's clarion call to the nation, but there was complete confusion on

---

† TR's four sons immediately joined the Army. "It's rather up to us to practice what father preaches," said Quentin, the youngest, who became a fighter pilot and was killed in aerial combat. Ted, Jr., won the Distinguished Service Cross, and he and Archie were wounded. Kermit, who served in the British Army, was awarded the Military Cross.

the Potomac as to the magnitude of America's contribution to the defeat of Germany. The general assumption was that the United States would offer financial and material assistance to the Allies and perhaps a small naval force. No one suspected that within eighteen months the United States would have four million men under arms, about half that number in France, and American industry would be performing unprecedented feats of production. The Navy Department entered the conflict without a war plan, and the one finally promulgated, in mid-April, involved little more than a defensive patrol by battleships and cruisers on the American side of the Atlantic while a sizable fleet remained in the Pacific to keep a watchful eye on Japan. Under such circumstances, it was too much to expect that the friction between Josephus Daniels and Franklin Roosevelt would be immediately reduced. Neither man could transform his personality overnight. The cautious Daniels urged restraint; Roosevelt craved action—and obviously thought himself better fitted to lead the Navy into war than his superior.

Events played into the younger man's hands. German submarines were sinking Allied merchantmen faster than they could be replaced, and Britain, with only a three-week supply of grain on hand, was on the brink of being starved into submission. Rear Admiral William S. Sims, one-time naval aide to Theodore Roosevelt, was one of the people who understood the gravity of the situation. Under an assumed name, Sims was sent to London by the Navy Department shortly before the declaration of war. He arrived at the Admiralty on April 10, 1917, to confer with an old friend, Admiral Sir John Jellicoe, the First Sea Lord. With scarcely a word, Jellicoe handed him a memorandum that revealed the ravages being made by the U-boats: In the first three months of the year, the Germans had sunk about 1.3 million tons, or 6 percent of all available Allied and neutral shipping. The toll for April was expected to be nine hundred thousand tons, and if the hemorrhage was not stanched, by October there would not be enough vessels left to sustain the lifeblood of Britain.

Before reporting this shocking news to Washington, Sims spent a few days trying to learn everything he could about the crisis. Much to his astonishment, he discovered that the British had refused to organize convoys. The Admiralty claimed convoys were defensive, and the U-boats could only be defeated by offensive measures: sending out destroyers to hunt them down, mining the approaches to submarine bases, and arming merchantmen. Besides, it was argued that merchant vessels were too undisciplined to maintain convoy formation, and destroyers could not be spared for escort duty from the vital task of screening the battleships of the Grand Fleet. Sims launched a two-pronged attack on the problem: He urged the Navy Department to send every destroyer it could lay its hands on to European waters for antisubmarine patrol. "We cannot send too soon or too many," he declared. And abetted by David Lloyd George, the British Prime Minister, and some junior officers, he persuaded the Admiralty to give the convoy system a fair trial. In May, experimental convoys sailed to Britain from Hampton Roads and Gibraltar with the loss of only one vessel, convincing the Admiralty that the long-sought weapon for dealing with the U-boat menace had been found.

Sims had had better luck in London than with his superiors at home. Both Daniels and Admiral William S. Benson, the Chief of Naval Operations, were skeptical of his warnings. Benson had wagged a cautionary finger under Sims's nose on the eve of his departure and warned: "Don't let the British pull the wool over your eyes. It's not our business pulling their chestnuts out of the fire." Fearing that German submarines would soon appear off the American coast, the Navy Department resisted sending more than Taussig's token force of destroyers to Europe. To do so, it was argued, would strip the Atlantic Fleet of its protection and prevent it from operating as an entity. In reality, the Germans had only a few U-boats with the range to cross the Atlantic.

Roosevelt sided with Sims and was active in the fight to send every available destroyer to aid the Allies. Nevertheless, it required high-ranking British and French missions to convince the reluctant Daniels and Benson that Sims was not exaggerating the seriousness of the situation. Roosevelt, who met the French at Hampton Roads and conducted them to Washington on the presidential yacht *Mayflower*, urged them to request the fullest assistance from the United States—which they did. By July 1917, thirty-five American destroyers and two tenders were based at Queenstown, and before the war ended, a total of eighty-five vessels were operating from British and French ports. "That decision was momentous," Roosevelt later commented, "because it involved complete abandonment of [the] conception of [the] Atlantic Fleet operating as a complete naval unit."

Once President Wilson had made the critical decision to pour American troops into Europe, it was the task of the Navy to get them there. Vast amounts of shipping were required—four times as much tonnage was needed to carry an army division's equipment and supplies as was needed for the soldiers themselves. The ships did not exist, because the American merchant marine had suffered decades of neglect, and it was necessary to start almost from scratch. The Emergency Fleet Corporation was established to mass-produce merchantmen, and to fill the gap, the Navy seized the some six hundred thousand tons of German shipping that had been lying idle in port since 1914, including the fifty-six-thousand-ton luxury liner *Vaterland*, which became the troopship *Leviathan*. The first convoy of American troops arrived in France in June 1917, and by the summer of the following year, men were disembarking on the docks of

Brest and other French ports at a rate of ten thousand a day—all without the loss of a ship or a man. The Navy also underwent an astonishing growth of its own. At the end of 1917, it mustered 269,000 officers and men, as compared to sixty-seven thousand when war was declared, and by the war's end, total strength numbered nearly a half million men and women. For the first time, the Navy accepted women in its ranks, and about 11,275 volunteered as "yeomanettes"—including Lucy Mercer, Eleanor Roosevelt's social secretary.

Throughout the initial period of the conflict, Franklin Roosevelt fumed about what he regarded as the super caution of Daniels and Benson and their failure to react promptly to the crisis facing the Allies. Memos flowed from his office verging on the impertinent if not the insubordinate: "The days, and the weeks and the months, are piling up and I should very much like to see some definite action. . . . If we are going to build any more destroyers, no matter what type, *the estimates should go in now.* . . . I am sorry to say that conditions are to all intents and purposes no better. . . . We have left undone these things which we ought to have done. . . ." Early in July 1917, he told Admiral Cowles: "Things here are going on in a disgustingly routine way. We have no offensive naval policy, and it is only because we have had enormous luck in our operations that the country persists in believing that the Navy is living up to its best traditions. I feel there will be some horrible jolts in the future." These jeremiads were not confined to private letters and interoffice communications, for he made the same points in speeches and articles. "It is time that the Administration, that members of the Senate and the House of Representatives . . . appreciate more fully that our task is now and not tomorrow," he told the Navy League. "It is time that they insist on action at once. Action that will give us something definite—definite ships, definite men—on a definite day."

Once again, luck was on Roosevelt's side. He won an ally in his crusade against lethargy and delay in the person of Winston Churchill, a popular American historical novelist. Churchill, a graduate of the Naval Academy some twenty years earlier and a friend of President Wilson, had offered his services to the Navy, and Roosevelt eagerly accepted his proposal to write syndicated articles popularizing the service. But he also saw an opportunity to use the novelist to further his own ends and encouraged him to do more than "turn out mere 'write-ups' or recruiting posters of Navy life." Talking to officers and digging into the Navy's activities, Churchill was disturbed by the low morale and sluggishness he found. "Our Navy Department . . . is suffering from the hookworm—certainly not through any fault of yours," he told Roosevelt. Encouraged by the assistant Secretary, he decided to prepare a private memorandum for Wilson.‡ Although he tried to be scrupulously fair to Daniels, praising his dedication and intentions, Churchill's report was a serious indictment. He said naval officers of all ranks were sharply critical of the Secretary's "dilatoriness, of his unwillingness to act on great matters and small, the result of which has been to delay and at times almost to paralyze the activities of the Naval service. . . . The officers of the Navy are not concerned with his personality; all they ask is that, for the good of the Service, of the country and the world, the Department be made more efficient."

The President was impressed by the memorandum and talked personally with the novelist. But if Roosevelt hoped that his conspiracy would lead to Daniels' ouster from the Cabinet or his resignation, he was disappointed. Wilson merely sent the Navy Secretary a copy of Churchill's memorandum and a note, which he typed himself, suggesting that younger and more active men be placed in charge of procurement and operations. Roosevelt soon detected a more aggressive tempo in the Navy Department, and following a meeting with the President in mid-August, remarked to Eleanor that "I am encouraged to think that he has *begun* to catch on." But he added that "lots more of the Churchill type of attack" would be needed to maintain momentum. Nevertheless, as the war went on, he abated the storm of criticism leveled at Daniels, although there were periodic rumblings.

After Franklin Roosevelt became President, observers often commented upon his willingness to adopt any policy or program that looked as if it might have a chance of success, and if it didn't work, to obliterate the failure with bold new plans. It was a trait first noted during World War I, when he pressed ahead with bold schemes for dealing with the submarine menace. "He was a great trial and error guy," according to Admiral Emory S. Land, a leading naval constructor in both wars. Two proposals captured Roosevelt's imagination in 1917, and he worked doggedly to bring them to reality: a fleet of small craft for antisubmarine patrols and a gigantic wall of mines stretching across the North Sea to prevent the U-boats from reaching the shipping lanes. Both were regarded as impractical by the experts—but by a combination of hard work, persistence, and subtle maneuver on Roosevelt's part, these projects became a reality. The results were mixed, however.

‡ Kenneth S. Davis, in *FDR: The Beckoning of Destiny 1882–1928* (New York: G. P. Putnam's Sons, 1971), states that in his eagerness to force Daniels' resignation, Roosevelt prepared a ten-page memorandum for Churchill's confidential use detailing "charges of disastrous confusion and delays" for which he held Daniels responsible. A search of the files of the FDR Library in 1980 failed to turn up the document, however.

In the summer of 1917, Roosevelt was genuinely concerned that U-boats might appear momentarily off the American coast to attack shipping and to shell unprotected harbors. "If by any perfectly wild chance a German submarine should come into the bay and start to shell Eastport or the Pool, I want you to grab the children and beat it into the woods," he warned Eleanor at Campobello. "Don't stay to see what is going on. I am not joking about this, for while it is 500 to one against the possibility, still there is just that one chance. . . ." To avoid just such an emergency while waiting for destroyers to be built, he pressed the construction of 110-foot, wooden-hulled submarine chasers for use on inshore patrols. More than four hundred of these craft were built, and they turned out to be such excellent sea boats that a substantial number crossed the Atlantic. Mostly manned by reservists whose first experience at sea often was the Atlantic crossing itself, the "splinter fleet" saw useful service from Murmansk to the Mediterranean.

Roosevelt also fought for the construction of fifty-foot patrol craft, but both Daniels and the General Board put up strong resistance, claiming that these craft would be useless except in good weather. Wedded to the idea of small boats because of his own experience as a yachtsman, Roosevelt pressed ahead, imaginatively spinning off tasks that the fifty-footers could perform, including police work, checking on rumors of secret enemy wireless stations, and even attacking submarines taking shelter in secluded inlets. Whether with or without Roosevelt's knowledge, is unknown, but pressure was applied to some officers who opposed the project, and Louis Howe approached Captain Hugh Rodman with the veiled suggestion that if he was more cooperative his career might advance at a faster pace. Rodman, anxiously awaiting promotion to admiral and command of five battleships that were to be sent to reinforce the British Fleet, almost threw him out of his office.* Worried about the possibility of a U-boat attack on American shores, Daniels' resistance to small craft weakened. "How much of that sort of junk should we buy?" he wearily confided to his diary. The boats proved to be useless, however, and Roosevelt's insistence on ordering them later aroused suspicions of conflict of interest. They were powered by engines produced by Sterling Motors, a British firm represented by Arthur P. Homer, a swashbuckling promoter who had the ear of the assistant Secretary.

Roosevelt's persistence showed to better advantage in his fight for the North Sea mine barrage. "Why don't the British shut up the hornets in their nests?" Wilson often complained about the failure to prevent the U-boats from getting to sea. "We are hunting hornets all over the farm and letting the nest alone." The President had no specific plans in mind,

---

* Rodman received his promotion and commanded the Sixth Battle Squadron, which served with the British Fleet.

but soon after the war began, Roosevelt envisioned a wall of mines extending two hundred forty miles across the North Sea from Scotland to Norway, a wall so dense that no submarine could safely penetrate or dive underneath it. The plan was discussed with the British, who had by the use of mines, nets, and destroyer patrols made some progress in closing the narrow Dover Strait to submarines. The Admiralty turned thumbs down on the North Sea project, citing the vast area to be covered, the depth of the water, and the lack of effective mines. It was estimated that four hundred thousand mines would have to be sown to close the northern passage—a task viewed by the Admiralty as impossible. Besides, it was feared that the barrage would interfere with free movement of the British Fleet in those waters.

New life was breathed into Roosevelt's scheme when a Massachusetts inventor named Ralph C. Browne came forward with a device that made the antenna mine possible.† Unlike the mines in general use, it did not have to come in direct contact with a vessel's hull in order to explode but would detonate if the craft merely brushed a long wand, or antenna, that extended from it. The new mine meant the North Sea could be closed with one hundred thousand mines, or a fourth of the number originally estimated for the job. With the support of Wilson and Daniels, Roosevelt again sent the plan to the Admiralty, which only reluctantly gave its approval. The tactics used to win final approval for the barrage were typical of Roosevelt's promotion of his pet ideas. If his proposal was rejected, he would take it from official to official until he found someone to whom it appealed and then would use this support to beat down the objections of those who had originally turned down his proposal.

Roosevelt, by now a veteran of the bureaucratic wars, nailed his victory down with a sharply worded memorandum to Daniels. Recalling the delays in getting the barrage approved, he urged that the project be carried out "with a different spirit from any of the operations up to now. . . . This is a bigger matter than sending destroyers abroad or a division of battleships, or building a bunch of new destroyers—it is vital to the winning of the war." A copy was also sent to Wilson with a covering letter explaining that it had required six months to gain approval of the barrage from all parties concerned. "It is my duty to tell you that if the plan is put into execution with the same speed and method employed in the past other priceless months will be wasted and the plan will be jeopardized," Roosevelt told the President. At the end of the day, he summed

---

† In 1928, FDR, with his penchant for dressing up a story, described Browne to a reporter as "a typical inventor . . . with a beard and a regular inventor's bag. . . . [He] looked like a crank. . . ." The inventor, who in reality had been recommended to the Navy Department by qualified scientists, protested the description, and Roosevelt apologized.

up his activities in a note to "Dearest Babs": "I have . . . given the Sec'y a very stinging memorandum and sent a copy to the President. Some day they will be interesting reading!"

Under Roosevelt's eager prodding, antenna mines, each containing three hundred pounds of TNT, were soon pouring from the production lines. Actual mining began in June 1918, under the direction of Rear Admiral Joseph Strauss, and by October, some seventy thousand mines had been sown, about 80 percent by the U. S. Navy, the rest by the British, at a cost of $80 million. The war ended before the effectiveness of the North Sea Barrage could be fully tested. U-boats continued to pass through the North Sea, but six are thought to have been destroyed, and most authorities believe that fear of the deadly mine field contributed to the decline in morale of the submarine crews, which led to a mutiny that spread to the rest of the German Fleet.

World War I marked the beginning of the huge concentration of administrative power in the hands of the federal government that reached its climax under the New Deal. Franklin Roosevelt was not a major figure in bringing about this process, but he supported it. Profoundly impressed by the effectiveness of the German war machine, he had urged the President to organize a Council of National Defense, to draft plans for industrial mobilization before the United States entered the war. Wilson, not wishing to "rattle the sword," had put off the proposal until the eve of the declaration of war. A multitude of powerful agencies sprang from the brow of the Council of National Defense, each of which held more authority over its segment of the economy than had ever before been entrusted to any federal administrative body. Before the war ended, Wilson had more power concentrated in his hands than any war leader, including the Kaiser.

The War Industries Board, which regulated all industries that produced war matériel and organized new sources of supply, was the most important. Bernard Baruch, the Wall Street speculator who headed the WIB, was for two years virtual dictator of the nation's economy. Everything from the amount of metal used in women's corsets to the number of stops made by elevators were regulated to save steel and coal. The Food Administration, headed by Herbert C. Hoover, the engineer who had fed the starving people of Belgium, brought the war home to the American public more than any other government agency. "Wheatless" Mondays, "meatless" Tuesdays, and "porkless" Thursdays all became part of national life. "Hooverizing" enabled the United States to triple the normal amount of foodstuffs available for export to its allies. The Fuel Administration introduced daylight saving time, raised the price of coal to bring marginal mines back into use, and established "fuelless" Mondays. When the railroads broke down under the unprecedented demands placed upon them, they were taken over by the government and operated by Treasury Secretary McAdoo as a unified system. Never before, experts said, had the railroads been operated so efficiently.

In the Navy Department, Roosevelt worked toward centralization of the decision-making process. He dealt with a mountain of paper, met the press twice a day, attended meetings of the various agencies and commissions at which he represented the Navy, and gave the impression of being on top of his job. Inevitably, he was given credit for all sorts of achievements, whether deserved or not. One naval aviator recalls that the "scuttlebutt" at his base was that "in Washington most of the business was done in the Navy Department by Assistant Secretary Roosevelt on weekends when the Secretary of the Navy was away." Always an advocate of physical exercise, he invited Walter Camp, the Yale football coach, to Washington to set up a conditioning program for everyone in the Navy Department. Four days a week he left home at 7:15 A.M. for physical exercises with other officials and congressional leaders under Camp's direction.

Once in his office, Roosevelt would lean back in his chair, head back, eyes intent upon the wall, and reel off reams of correspondence with "clear enunciation, perfect English and everything that goes with it," recalled R. H. Camalier, his wartime stenographer. Camalier would take dictation for about fifteen minutes, and an assistant would exchange the notebook in which he had been writing for another. The assistant typed these letters while Roosevelt was still dictating, and the first batch of letters would be ready for signing before Camalier left the room. Camalier described Roosevelt as a no-nonsense chief but said he readily forgave honest mistakes. "He was a man of few words, modest and unassuming," the stenographer added. "He was exceedingly human—never too big to mix with the common man. If it was after hours he wouldn't hesitate to play cards or smoke cigarettes with you"—Roosevelt already used the long cigarette holder that was to become a trademark.

But Roosevelt's easygoing manner ceased when delays were encountered in procuring supplies or equipment, and he was not above commandeering the required item if necessary. Upon learning that a generator was needed to complete a plant designed to produce vital fittings for destroyers, and General Electric could not supply one for at least three months, he assigned Louis Howe to track down a generator. One was located in the Philadelphia freight yards, and it was seized and diverted to the plant. Sometime later, the Navy Department received a letter stating that this had delayed the opening of the Hotel Pennsylvania for three months.

Joseph P. Kennedy, the tough young assistant manager of Bethlehem

Steel's Fore River shipyard, at Quincy, Massachusetts, also found Franklin
Roosevelt more than "just another rich man's son with nothing more to
do than dabble in politics," as he first regarded him. The Fore River yard
had constructed a pair of battleships for Argentina at the request of the
Navy Department. But when the vessels were completed, the Argentines
were unable to make payment, and Charles Schwab, Bethlehem's boss, refused to release them. Roosevelt asked for a meeting, and Schwab sent
Kennedy in his place.

"Don't worry about this matter," Roosevelt told him. "The State Department will collect the money for you."

"Sorry, Mr. Secretary, but Mr. Schwab refuses to let the ships go
until they are paid for."

"Absurd," laughed Roosevelt.

"Not at all absurd, sir," Kennedy replied. "Positively no ship will be
delivered until it is paid for."

Ushering his visitor to the door, the assistant Secretary thanked him
for calling and said that unless the battleships were released, he would
send a detachment of marines to the yard to seize them.

Kennedy reported to Schwab, telling him that he thought Roosevelt
"a smiling four-flusher," and the two men agreed to call "this youngster's
bluff." Not long afterward, four Navy tugs loaded with armed marines
pulled into the shipyard, commandeered the battleships at bayonet point,
and towed them to where Argentine crews waited to receive them. "Roosevelt was the hardest trader I'd ever run up against," a chastened Kennedy said years later when he and the "rich man's son" had become uneasy allies.

Early in June 1918, Roosevelt was approached by an emissary from
Boss Murphy with a proposal that he run for governor of New York, a
proposal that had widespread support among reform Democrats. This
offer was the culmination of the process of conciliation between Tammany Hall and Roosevelt. Relations between them had progressed to the
point where Roosevelt had been invited to make the annual Fourth of
July oration to the Society of St. Tammany in 1917. The speech went
over well, and Roosevelt and Murphy were photographed together, the
Boss resplendent in his badge of office. The picture placed the seal on a
treaty of mutual assistance from which they both hoped to reap benefits.
The Republican Governor, Charles S. Whitman, was running for a third
two-year term, and Murphy believed he could be beaten by a candidate
who could attract the support of progressives, while Tammany delivered
the New York City vote—and Roosevelt eminently fitted the role. Even
the President encouraged him to run, with the hope of strengthening the
Democratic ticket in the off-year elections, which he made a referendum

on his policies. Daniels was instructed to "tell Roosevelt he ought not to decline to run for Governor if it is tendered to him."

Nevertheless, Roosevelt, with Howe's advice, decided against making the run for governor, believing that 1918 would be a Republican year. "I have made my position entirely clear that my duty lies in my present work —not only my duty to you and to the country but my duty to myself," he told Wilson. "If I were at any time to leave the Assistant Secretaryship it could only be for active service." To resign and actively campaign for office while the war was still on would be an admission that his duties were only of peripheral importance and would leave him open to attack for deserting his post when the first opportunity for higher office had come along. Public reaction would be disastrous for his future political career if he quit before the war was won. And in June 1918, the Allied cause was in crisis and the end of the war looked far away.

Roosevelt later claimed that upon his refusal to run, Murphy asked him to suggest other upstate candidates for the gubernatorial nomination. Instead, he suggested Al Smith, then president of the New York City Board of Aldermen. Roosevelt obviously expected Smith to win the nomination but to be beaten in the general election, which would have left him with an open field for 1920. Much to his surprise, however, Smith defeated Whitman, although the Republicans captured both houses of Congress—causing irreparable damage to Wilson's prestige. On the face of it, Roosevelt's rejection of the nomination in 1918 appeared a grave mistake, but if he had been elected governor at that time, in all probability he would never have become President. As governor, he would probably have been nominated by the Democrats for President in 1920. But that was a Republican year, and so were 1924 and 1928, which meant that in 1932, when the Democrats had their first good shot at the White House in a dozen years, he would undoubtedly have been shunted aside in favor of someone else. Besides, Roosevelt was not ready for the governorship; at thirty six, he still lacked the maturity and stature for the job. Yet, if he had realized in June that the war would be almost over by Election Day and he would never see active service as a naval officer, he probably would have accepted Murphy's invitation.

With the Navy Department finally organized to conduct operations efficiently, Roosevelt suggested that either he or the Secretary visit the war zone for a personal inspection of naval facilities. "One of us ought to go and see the war in progress with his own eyes," he told Daniels, "else he is a chess player moving his pieces in the dark." Just as he hoped, Daniels was unable to make the trip, because Wilson wished his counsel, so the assignment went to Roosevelt. Characteristically, he crossed the Atlantic in a newly commissioned destroyer, the *Dyer*, sailing with a convoy from New York on July 9, 1918. It was his twenty-first Atlantic crossing.

Roosevelt recorded his adventure in a long diary-letter kept for Eleanor, and it reveals his vitality, high spirits, and love of the sea. The first evening out, five large transports were silhouetted against the western sky, "black shapes, no motion, no life, yet peopled like a city and moving on. . . . Tomorrow morning they will reappear in all their details of camouflage and bow wave and wake and a thousand khaki points along the rail & on the forecastle—that is if a submarine doesn't run amuck at the critical period of dawn. . . ." But a destroyer is not a pleasure craft, and soon the *Dyer* was rolling and pitching like a living thing. Roosevelt gloried in it all. "One has to hang on all the time, never moving without taking hold with one hand before letting go with the other. Much of the crockery smashed; we cannot eat at the table . . . have to sit braced on the transom and hold the plate with one hand. Three officers ill, but so far I am all right."

During a gun drill, a green youngster accidentally fired a 4-inch gun mounted on the superstructure that was trained almost directly forward. Roosevelt, on the bridge with the vessel's skipper, Commander Fred H. Poteet, reported, ". . . the blooming thing went off at the back of our heads and the shell went by only a few feet outboard, we thought the end had come." Later, alarm bells sounded throughout the ship as a lookout reported sighting a periscope. The *Dyer*'s gunners opened up on the suspected periscope before discovering it was a floating keg with a tiny flag on it that had probably been dropped over the side by another ship for use as a target. A few days later, the destroyer signaled farewell to the convoy, raised the assistant Secretary's flag, and headed for the Azores to refuel. But her engines overheated, and she was forced to lay to for six hours off the breakwater at Ponta Delgada, a perfect target for a U-boat. Later, it was learned that a submarine had indeed been lurking in the area—and as he recounted the tale over the years, Roosevelt brought it ever closer to his ship.

Repairs completed, the *Dyer* arrived in Portsmouth, England, on July 21, where Roosevelt was greeted by Admiral Sims and ranking officials from the Admiralty. For the next ten days, he was busy with a hectic round of briefings and inspections of British and American naval installations. The visit to Britain was climaxed by an audience with King George V in Buckingham Palace, and Roosevelt, always fascinated by European royalty, was enthusiastic about the meeting.

"The King has a nice smile and a very open, quick and cordial way of greeting one," he wrote Eleanor. "He is not as short as I had expected, and I think his face is stronger than photographs make it appear. This is perhaps because his way of speaking is incisive, and later on when he got talking about German atrocities in Belgium his jaws almost snapped." When Roosevelt remarked that while at school in Germany he had observed the early stages of German preparations for war, the King replied that he, too, had gone to school in Germany. "You know I have a number of relations in Germany," he added with a twinkle, "but I can tell you frankly that in all my life I have never seen a German gentleman."‡

Roosevelt then crossed the English Channel to Dunkirk. There he had his first look at the devastation of war, for the town had been bombed almost every night for three years and there was "not a whole house left in the place." The young man was tremendously impressed by the French Premier, the seventy-seven-year-old Georges Clemenceau. "I knew at once that I was in the presence of the greatest civilian in France. . . . He almost ran forward to meet me and shook hands as if he meant it; grabbed me by the arm and walked me over to his desk and sat me down about two inches away." After discussing the advance being made by French and American troops, Clemenceau "launched into a hair-raising description of the horrors left by the Boche in his retreat." He told Roosevelt of something he had seen while following just behind the advance: "A Poilu and a Boche still standing partly buried in a shell hole, clinched in each other's arms, their rifles abandoned, and the Poilu and the Boche were in the act of trying to bite each other to death when a shell had killed both—and as he told me this he grabbed me by both shoulders and shook me with a grip of steel to illustrate his words, thrusting his teeth forwards toward my neck."

On August 4, the start of the fifth year of war for the French, Roosevelt departed for the front, only to learn that the American naval attaché had planned a safe visit to the rear areas. Much annoyed, he angrily scrapped the schedule and ran the trip himself, getting close to the actual fighting. "The members of my staff have begun to realize what campaigning, or rather sightseeing, with the Asssistant Secretary means," he noted. He led them into Belleau Wood, where, not long before, two marine regiments brigaded into the U. S. Army's 2nd Division had helped blunt a German advance on Paris in some of the bloodiest fighting of the war. The way was marked with "water-filled shell holes, . . . hastily improvised shelter pits, rusty bayonets, broken guns, emergency ration tins, hand grenades, discarded overcoats, rain-stained love letters, crawling lines of ants and many little mounds, some wholly unmarked, some with a rifle bayonet stuck down in the earth, some with a helmet, and some, too, with a

‡ That evening, FDR attended a dinner at Gray's Inn at which Winston S. Churchill, the former First Lord of the Admiralty, was present. Later, Roosevelt recalled the meeting to Churchill, but the Prime Minister could not remember it.

whittled cross with a tag of wood or wrapping paper hung over it and in a pencil scrawl an American name. . . ."

Farther up the line, they entered the village of Mareuil-sur-Ay, which had been captured by American troops only hours before. "There were a number of dead Boche in the fields and in one place a little pile of them awaiting burial." The smell of decaying flesh hung in the air. Roosevelt discovered a battery of American 155-millimeter guns nearby and gleefully accepted an invitation to pull the lanyard of one aimed at a German-held railroad junction. The next day, he inspected a battalion of the 5th Marines before it went back into the front-line trenches. The majority of the men were wearing army khaki, their own olive-green uniforms having worn out in two months of heavy fighting. To distinguish them from army troops, Roosevelt issued an order allowing them to wear the Marine Corps insignia on their collars.

At the barrier fortress of Verdun, where in 1916 nearly a half million men had been killed in a limitless horror, Roosevelt came under German artillery fire. The party had halted to photograph the site of the village of Fleury, which had been totally obliterated, and they were hurried on by a French officer who said they had been spotted by German observation balloons. One or two minutes later, Roosevelt heard "the long whining whistle of a shell followed by the dull boom and puff of smoke of the explosion at the Dead Man's Corner we had just left." Standing atop the citadel of Verdun, he was horrified by the unparalleled scene of devastation spread out before him, and it was branded upon his imagination for the rest of his life.

Five days in Italy followed, in which he tried to persuade the Italian Navy to launch aggressive operations against the Austrians in the Adriatic and to achieve agreement on a unified Allied naval command in the Mediterranean. This essay into coalition warfare ended unhappily. The Italians were determined to preserve their capital ships from harm so that they would be a force in the Mediterranean after the war. The proposal for the supreme naval command foundered on the question of which nation would supply the commander in chief. Roosevelt proposed a general naval staff with Admiral Jellicoe as its chief, but the French objected and made their unhappiness known in Washington. President Wilson was irked and complained that "too many men go over[seas] assuming to speak for the Government."

Roosevelt's most useful contribution to the war effort occurred during an inspection of the port of Pauillac, at the mouth of the Gironde River, where the U. S. Navy had established a base for assembling seaplanes arriving from America by ship. Although large numbers of aircraft had arrived, not a single one was in condition for active service. Hundreds of hours of overhaul were required to correct defects. One Liberty engine that had been certified as ready to run was found to contain two pounds of sand in the cylinders; there were only two self-starters for a hundred planes, and fuel pumps on most of the engines were defective. Roosevelt described the situation as "scandalous" and urged Daniels to take drastic action to correct conditions. Roosevelt blamed the failure on the Navy Department's administrative system. Unless improvements occurred swiftly, he warned, the Navy would lose control of its aircraft to a unified air force, as had just happened in Britain, with disastrous results for the future.*

The rest of the trip was a kaleidoscope of action. From Brest he wrote Eleanor that "it has been a frightfully busy week—on the road each day from 6 a.m. to midnight—and we have done all manner of interesting things, all the way from south of Bordeaux to here—all by auto—flying stations, ports, patrols, army stores, receptions, swims at French watering places, etc., etc." In St.-Nazaire, he encountered a unit under the command of Admiral Charles P. Plunkett that was mounting fourteen-inch naval rifles upon special railway cars that were to be shunted up and down the Western Front to bombard strategic points behind the German lines. These guns could lob fourteen-hundred-pound shells as far as twenty-four miles. Roosevelt saw the battery as a solution to his dream of being a naval officer and serving at the front. He requested permission to join the unit, and the Admiral asked "if I could swear well enough in French to swear a French train onto a siding and let his big guns through. Thereupon, with certain inventive genius, I handed him a line of French swear words, real and imaginary, which impressed him greatly. . . ." Plunkett offered him the rank of lieutenant commander upon the spot, and Roosevelt resolved to submit his resignation as assistant Secretary as soon as he returned to Washington.

The trip ended with a sweep into the Allied-held sector of Belgium, where he met King Albert, witnessed a fight just off the coast between destroyers and a U-boat, and again came under enemy fire. Even Roosevelt's tremendous energy was not up to the pace he had set, and worn out by his exertions and with a fever of 102 degrees, he boarded the *Leviathan* in Brest on September 8 for the voyage home. He collapsed into his berth with influenza that developed into double pneumonia. Fever left him so weakened that when the ship reached New York he had to be carried on a stretcher to an ambulance, which took him to his mother's house on Sixty-fifth Street. He was not able to return to Washington until mid-October, when he submitted a report recommending sweeping reforms in naval operations overseas, a report called "clear, concise, and illumi-

---

* In 1921, to fend off the demands of General "Billy" Mitchell for an independent air force, the Navy finally created the Bureau of Aeronautics—the first new bureau since the Civil War.

nating" by Daniels. No longer content to confine himself to his desk, he asked the President to accept his resignation, but it was already too late for dreams of military glory. Wilson informed Roosevelt that peace was at hand—and on November 11, 1918, "the war to end war" was over.†

While Franklin was recovering from pneumonia, Eleanor made the shocking discovery that her husband was having an affair with Lucy Mercer. Gathering up his personal possessions after he had been taken from the *Leviathan*, she found some letters from her former social secretary. "The bottom dropped out of my own particular world," she told Joseph Lash a quarter century later. "I faced myself, my surroundings, my world, honestly for the first time." It seemed to confirm what she had always believed: She was unattractive and unloved. Exactly when the relationship between Lucy and Franklin bloomed is unknown, but by the summer of 1917 Eleanor was uneasy, for gossipmongers were only too eager to play upon her gnawing suspicions. Lucy had left her employ in April to join the Navy as a yeomanette, but she worked in the Navy Department and lived in the Decatur Apartments, on Florida Avenue, just around the corner from the R Street house. Reluctant to make the annual pilgrimage to Campobello with the "chicks," Eleanor postponed her departure, certain that her husband was anxious to get rid of her. Apparently wishing to make amends after she had left, Franklin wrote "Dearest Babs" on July 16, 1917: "I really can't stand the house all alone without you, and you were a goosy girl to think or even pretend to think that I don't want you here all the summer because you know I do!" The following day he added: "It seems years since you left and I miss you horribly and hate the thought of the empty house."

But whatever guilt Roosevelt may have felt was eased by a New York *Times* article based on an interview with Eleanor. The conservation section of the Food Administration, it said, had selected the Roosevelt home with its seven family members and ten servants as the model for other large households. "Mrs. Roosevelt does the buying, the cooks see that there is no food wasted, the laundress is sparing in her use of soap, each servant has a watchful eye for evidence of shortcomings on the part of the others," the article continued. " 'Making the ten servants help me do my saving has not only been possible but highly profitable,' " Eleanor was quoted as saying.

† For the rest of his life, FDR was sensitive about his failure to go on active duty during World War I. When a plaque was erected at Groton bearing the names of those who had served during the conflict, he wrote: "Though I did not wear a uniform, I believe that my name should go in the first division of those who were 'in the service,' especially as I saw service on the other side, was missed by torpedoes and shells and had actual command over 'materiel' navy matters in Europe, while I was there."

Franklin greeted the story with a mixture of derision and amusement. "All I can say is that your latest newspaper campaign is a corker and I am proud to be the husband of the Originator, Discoverer and Inventor of the New Household Economy for Millionaires!" he wrote his wife. "Please have a photo taken showing the family, the ten cooperating servants, the scraps saved from the table. . . . Honestly you have leaped into public fame, all Washington is talking of the Roosevelt plan. . . ." Eleanor suffered an agony of embarrassment. "I do think it was horrid of that woman to use my name in that way and I feel dreadfully about it," she replied. ". . . I never will be caught again that's sure and I'd like to crawl away for shame."

Following this exchange, Roosevelt's protestation of loneliness gave way to letters about expeditions down the Potomac on a presidential yacht and long drives in the country with groups of friends that included Lucy Mercer. Possibly to allay Eleanor's suspicions, her name was usually linked with that of Nigel Law, a young British diplomat and Franklin's good friend.‡ But there were those who spotted Franklin and Lucy out together alone. "I saw you 20 miles out in the country," Alice Longworth told him one day. "You didn't see me. Your hands were on the wheel but your eyes were on that perfectly lovely lady." "Isn't she perfectly lovely," Roosevelt happily replied. Alice mischievously encouraged the romance, inviting both Franklin and Lucy to dinner at her home. One day, Eleanor encountered Alice at the Capitol and, as she told Franklin, her cousin seemed anxious to let her in on a "secret," but she refused to listen. "She inquired if you had told me and I said no and that I did not believe in knowing things which your husband did not wish you to know so I think that I will be spared any further secrets."

Eleanor was more self-assured than when she had first come to Washington, but she was serious to the point of humorlessness, sometimes puritanical with herself and others, and unable to let down her guard. When excited, her high-pitched voice spiraled into "shrill arpeggios." Lucy, on the other hand, was feminine, charming, and had the southern gentlewoman's talent for putting men at their ease. "She was tall and stately and quiet in manner," according to a relative. "Her features were regular, her skin exquisitely fine, and her smile was the most beautiful and winning that I have ever seen." Weighed down with the heavy responsibility of mobilizing the Navy and often "unreasonable and touchy," as he acknowledged, Roosevelt sought gayer and more yielding companionship than his wife. As for Lucy, she was attracted by his good looks and position. James Roosevelt states that his mother later obtained

‡ In later years, Law paid Roosevelt an Englishman's ultimate compliment: "He was a perfect example of the English Country Gentleman."

evidence that they once checked into a Virginia Beach hotel as man and wife and spent the night.

Varying versions exist of what happened after Eleanor confronted Franklin with Lucy's letters, but the account of Anna, their daughter, based upon on what her mother told her, seems most logical. Bitter at being discarded, after thirteen years of marriage and five children, for a younger and more beautiful woman, she offered him a divorce. But, according to Anna's unpublished article, she "asked that he take time to think things over carefully before he gave her a definite answer. . . . He voluntarily promised to end any 'romantic relationship' and seemed to realize how much pain he had given her." Several reasons have been advanced for this decision. The effect of a divorce on the children, the possibility that Lucy, a devout Catholic, might be reluctant to marry a divorced man, a threat from his mother to cut him off if he left Eleanor, and the fatal impact of a divorce on his political career all made this outcome inevitable. One of Lucy's relatives later said Lucy had told her the decisive factor was that "Eleanor was not willing to stand aside." Telling her this may have been Franklin's way of resolving the situation.*

Eventually the Roosevelts reconciled, but the relationship between them was never again the same. Eleanor could forgive but not forget, and she nursed her wound, never letting it completely close, for the remainder of her life. She became more independent: less a reflection of her husband and with her own life to live. "My mother had an iron stubbornness of her own," Elliott Roosevelt said recently, "and she was bound and determined that she would have nothing to do with my father, even though he was quite abject in seeking to rehabilitate himself in her eyes. . . . Through the entire rest of their lives, they never did have a husband-and-wife relationship, but . . . they struck up a partnership arrangement. This partnership was to last all the way through their life; it became a very close and very intimate partnership of great affection—never in a physical sense, but in a tremendously mental sense. . . . But there were very few light moments. . . . The never enjoyed *anything* in the way of light-heartedness in their lives."

* Not long afterward, Lucy was employed as a governess by Winthrop Rutherfurd, a wealthy sportsman and dog breeder, whose wife had recently died leaving him with the care of five teenage children. They married, in 1920. Lucy was twenty-nine, Rutherfurd fifty-eight.

X

KEEPER OF THE FLAME

PEACE BROUGHT NEW responsibilities for Franklin Roosevelt. As the transport *George Washington** eased out into the Hudson River on January 2, 1919, and headed for the open sea, he and Eleanor were among those who watched the pewter-gray towers of Manhattan drop below the horizon. Officially, the assistant Secretary of the Navy was bound for Europe to supervise the disposal of the holdings accumulated by the U. S. Navy—an empire that included several radio stations, fifty-four shore bases, and 359 ships, manned by some eighty thousand officers and men. Unofficially, he had finagled a return trip overseas with the hope of catching a glimpse of the Peace Conference, to open ten days later in Paris. President Wilson, the first Chief Executive to leave the country during his term of office, had sailed for Europe three weeks before.

One of Roosevelt's most remarkable traits was the ability to shift gears as circumstances demanded, and as soon as the Armistice went into effect, he quickly turned his attention from the problems of waging war to those of demobilization. And just as he had been dissatisfied with what he regarded as Josephus Daniels' lethargy in mobilizing the Navy for war, he was critical of his failure to organize an efficient dispersal of the Navy's surplus property. Particularly irritating was the Navy Secretary's decision to leave the matter to Admiral Sims and his staff. He pointed out that Congress, which after March 4 would be controlled by the Republicans, would hold the Navy's civilian administrators responsible for any errors, and he, for one, was unwilling to place his political future at the mercies

* Like the *Leviathan*, the *George Washington* had been seized from the Hamburg-Amerika Line when the United States entered World War I.

of navy career officers. Roosevelt was so vehement on the subject that he told Daniels that unless he was permitted to take personal charge of the disposal of navy property abroad, he would dissociate himself from the entire demobilization process.

Apparently coming to the conclusion that Roosevelt's arguments had merit, Daniels authorized him to undertake a new mission to Europe. Eleanor was permitted to accompany her husband, ostensibly to make certain there was no recurrence of his illness but actually as much in furtherance of their marital truce as anything else. Since his break with Lucy Mercer, Franklin had tried to make amends, devoting more attention to his wife, spending time with the children and shepherding the family to St. Thomas' Episcopal Church on Sunday mornings, rather than playing golf at the Chevy Chase Club. Much to his surprise, this show of unexpected piety resulted in his being named a church vestryman.

On January 6, the ship's radio brought word of the death of Theodore Roosevelt. Worn out by sixty years of strenuous living, he brushed off warnings that if he did not slow down he would have to spend the rest of his life in a wheelchair. "All right! I can work like that, too!" he had replied and was widely touted as the leading Republican candidate for the presidency in 1920. Plunging into a bitter attack on Woodrow Wilson's proposal for a League of Nations as inimical to the interests of the United States, he underscored the rejection of the President's policies by the voters in the November 1918 elections. Indeed, Wilson had departed for Paris with the imprecations of the Rough Rider resounding across the land. "Mr. Wilson has no authority whatever to speak for the American people at this time," he warned. "His leadership has just been emphatically repudiated by them." Reporters accompanying Wilson on a visit to Italy noted that his first reaction to his old rival's death was one of surprise, then pity, and finally "transcendent triumph."[†]

Franklin and Eleanor were saddened by the news. "My cousin's death was in every way a great shock for we heard just before leaving that he was better—and he was after all not old," Franklin wrote Daniels. "But I cannot help think that he himself would have had it this way and that he has been spared a lingering illness of perhaps years." Eleanor not only grieved at the loss of her beloved Uncle Ted but also saw in his death the passing of an important American symbol. "Another big figure gone from our nation," she said, keenly feeling "the loss of his influence and example." One of the guiding spirits of Franklin Roosevelt's life was now gone, but the vigorous personality of the Rough Rider continued to be an example to him. In years to come when others used the spirit of Theodore Roosevelt to buttress conservatism or nationalism, the younger

† "Death had to take him sleeping," said Vice-President Thomas Marshall, "for if Roosevelt had been awake, there would have been a fight."

'DR chats with President and Mrs. Wilson during the voyage home from the Paris Peace Confer-
nce in 1919. The young officer between them is W. Sheffield Cowles, Jr., Franklin's aide and
listant cousin. (Courtesy FDR Library)

FDR is greeted by his daughter, Anna, upon his return from Europe in 1919. (Courtesy FDR
Library)

FDR campaigns with James Cox in 1920. (Courtesy FDR Library)

The last photograph of FDR walking unassisted. It was taken on July 27, 1921, during a visit to a
Boy Scout encampment at Bear Mountain, New York. (Courtesy FDR Library)

The Roosevelt cottage at Campobello. (Courtesy FDR Library)

FDR at Warm Springs in 1926. The contrast between his thin legs and powerful upper body is vividly shown. (Courtesy FDR Library)

Friends. FDR and Al Smith in the governor's office in Albany. (Courtesy FDR Library)

Roosevelt emphasized his progressivism and dynamic view of the presidency.

Roosevelt arrived in Europe to find the work of demobilization and settlement of claims well underway. In Britain, little more was required than approval of the agreements reached by Admiral Sims and his agents, but the atmosphere was tense in France. The French were hard bargainers, obviously hoping that if they stalled long enough in paying for the bases, equipment, and supplies the Americans were anxious to unload, they would pick them up for nothing. Looking through a pile of French contracts on his desk, he told R. H. Camalier with a downward sweep of his head, "Camy, I'm going to pay them that much." In such an acrimonious atmosphere, Roosevelt's affability was an asset.

The "biggest deal" arranged by the assistant Secretary was the sale of the Lafayette Radio Station, near Bordeaux, to the French Government. Built to assure communications between American forces in France and the United States, the station had only been partially completed by the time the war ended. Despite weeks of negotiations before Roosevelt's arrival, the French had delayed in reaching a settlement. Roosevelt flatly informed them that if they did not immediately agree to purchase the station on what the Americans regarded as fair terms, he would have it dismantled and the equipment shipped home. Bluff called, the French put up the cash. "Roosevelt knows how to handle the French," remarked a naval officer who had been unsuccessfully dealing with the matter.

With the Peace Conference underway, Paris was in a carnival mood. Every great hotel flaunted the flag of some foreign potentate, and the city teemed with supplicants from all corners of the globe—Macedonians, Serbs and Montenegrins, Croats, Slovenes, Slovaks and Czechs, Arabs in flowing robes chaperoned by a sharp-featured little Englishman named Lawrence, Zionists, Armenians, Azerbaijanis, and little men from Indochina with wispy beards—all wishing something at the expense of their neighbors. Adventurers hovered about peddling oil concessions and diamond mines; pretenders to nonexistent thrones proliferated along with Russian grand dukes who drove taxis, secret agents, pimps, prostitutes, and cranks with shortcuts to Utopia in their briefcases. Paris tingled with expectation as it awaited a new world to be born in the Salon de l'Horloge, the gathering place of the victorious Allied leaders. Woodrow Wilson might have suffered a rebuff at home, but he dominated the conference. Delirious throngs turned out to greet the prophet from the West, feeding what his many critics called the President's messiah complex. In some places, peasants burned candles before his picture.

The Covenant of the League of Nations assumed a mystical

significance for Wilson. The other leaders insisted that the peace treaty was the most pressing business of the conference, but he feared that if the League was not approved at the start of the conference, it would be lost in the scramble for spoils. The President had to expend much of his prestige and make vital concessions to gain acceptance of the League as part of the treaty. Despite the promise of the Fourteen Points, announced in January 1918, with its declaration of "open covenants . . . openly arrived at," the conference met behind closed doors, and those not directly involved in the deliberations—such as Franklin Roosevelt—knew next to nothing of the proceedings. Not until February 15, when he and Eleanor were on the train carrying them to Brest and the *George Washington* for the trip home did they see a copy of the League Covenant. "What hopes we had that this League would really prove the instrument for the prevention of future wars," Eleanor recalled many years later. "How eagerly we read it through! Little did we dream at the time what the future held."

Having spent a month at the conference, Wilson was also returning to the United States on the *George Washington* to report to the American people on his accomplishments in Paris and to sign pending legislation before the 65th Congress adjourned. The President remained aloof from the rest of the passengers for the first several days of the voyage, and Roosevelt, who had hoped to discuss the Covenant with him, despaired of the opportunity. But, much to his delight, he and Eleanor were finally invited to lunch with Wilson in his cabin. The conversation turned to the League of Nations, and Wilson made a remark that the younger man never forgot: "The United States must go in or it will break the heart of the world, for she is the only nation that all feel is disinterested and all trust."

The trip did have its lighter moments, however. Wilson was persuaded to attend an entertainment put on by the crew, which included a chorus line of sailors. At the end of a song, the "girls" flounced out into the audience and one lad genially chucked the startled President under the chin. "I thought Captain McCauley [the vessel's skipper] would have apoplexy and everyone held his breath," Eleanor recalled. "You almost heard the unspoken order: 'Put him in irons on bread and water.'" Later, Wilson sent the captain a message to the effect that he hoped the young man would not be punished.

The day before the *George Washington* was to arrive at Boston, the vessel was shrouded in fog and the navigator was unable to take her position. Suddenly, bells sounded throughout the ship and the engines stopped. "We are almost on the beach," someone told Eleanor. Her husband dashed to the bridge to find Captain McCauley confused by the sighting of land where no land was supposed to be. Roosevelt guessed that they were near Marblehead—and when the fog lifted it was discovered that he was correct.‡ The ship and its accompanying destroyers had nearly run aground on Thatcher Island, just off the tip of Cape Ann.

Wilson arrived in Boston to a tumultuous greeting. "We could see the President and Mrs. Wilson ahead of us, the President standing up and waving his hat at intervals to the crowds which lined the streets," said Eleanor, who rode with her husband only a few cars back in the line. "Everyone was wildly enthusiastic. . . ." Even the Republican Governor of Massachusetts, the laconic Calvin Coolidge, said he was "sure the people would back the President" on the League.

Nevertheless, Wilson had already been betrayed by his own pride. He had failed to consult with the Republican majority in the Senate, which by law was to ratify the peace treaty. Although his personal antipathy for Henry Cabot Lodge, the new chairman of the Senate Foreign Relations Committee, was intense, he had rejected the opportunity to mollify the opposition by inviting such pro-League Republicans as Elihu Root or former President Taft to accompany him to Paris. Wilson and his opponents confronted each other for the first time at a White House meeting at which he explained the League covenant to the congressional committees concerned with foreign affairs. "I feel as if I had been wandering with Alice in Wonderland and had tea with the Mad Hatter," observed one Republican senator. The opposition showed its teeth with a round robin signed by thirty-nine senators and senators-elect—more than the one third plus one needed to reject the treaty—in which they announced they could not accept it in its present form.

Thus, Wilson returned to Paris to continue negotiations with his prestige tarnished. For the next two months, he labored for a just peace against the demands of the Allies for revenge and reparations from Germany. Georges Clemenceau, the French Premier, was his bitterest foe. "Mr. Wilson bores me with his Fourteen Points," said the "Tiger" of France. "Why, God Almighty has only Ten!" Twice in less than a half century, France had been invaded by the Germans, and the French demanded a security that could be obtained only from a prostrate Germany. With all his eloquence, Wilson tried to convince the French that security was unattainable by imposing intolerable burdens on the vanquished. He had insisted upon a peace without punitive damages, but, worn down by ill health and fatigue, compromised his Fourteen Points to obtain acquiescence in the treaty. Presented to the Germans on the point of a bayonet, the treaty was signed at Versailles on June 28, 1919—the fifth anniversary of the assassination of Archduke Franz Ferdinand.

In the beginning, most Americans favored ratification of the Ver-

‡ Legend has it that FDR took over the helm of the *George Washington* and steered the vessel to safety, but his role was far less dramatic.

sailles Treaty but thought there should be changes to bring the League in conformance with the Constitution and American practice. Article X of the Covenant of the League, which pledged the United States to send troops abroad to uphold the "territorial integrity" and "political independence" of any member nation, was a vexing problem, because it allegedly infringed on congressional authority to declare war. Wilson's shrewd political judgment failed him completely. Although he had accepted numerous compromises to obtain British and French approval of the League, he stubbornly refused to give a single inch to win over moderates and isolate the "irreconcilables." By refusing to accept even the simplest of reservations—such as one reaffirming that the Constitution should be paramount in cases where it came in conflict with the Covenant—Wilson did more than Cabot Lodge to ensure that the United States would not join the League of Nations.

Franklin Roosevelt was a strong and active supporter of the League, but sensing the changing mood of the American people, he devoted serious attention to the objections of critics. As a realist, he had originally viewed the League as "merely a beautiful dream, a Utopia"; but he explained that his visits to the European battlefields had convinced him of the necessity of some sort of international organization to maintain world peace. "This is a time of idealism, a time when more ideals are properly demanded of us," he declared. "Over there on the other side, every man, woman and child looks to us to make good the high purpose with which we came into this war."

Unlike Wilson, however, he made no claim that the Covenant was perfect, that it could not be improved. The League was an experiment, and there was no reason to expect the Covenant to be any more perfect than the Constitution, which had been often amended. "I have read the draft of the League three times and always find something to object to in it," he told one audience. Yet "to go backwards toward an old Chinese wall policy of isolation" would result in a "grievous wrong . . . to all mankind." Without the participation of the United States, the League would merely be "a new Holy Alliance" that was hostile to the United States and would be unable to stem the tide of Bolshevism rolling in upon Europe in the wake of the Russian Revolution.

The fight over ratification of the Versailles Treaty raged through the summer of 1919, with both Wilson and his opponents stubbornly refusing to make concessions. Alice Longworth, in the forefront of the struggle against the League, cajoled, advised, and succored the oppositionist "Battalion of Death" and helped devise its strategy and tactics. Her home on Massachusetts Avenue became their headquarters, and no task was too insignificant for Alice if it promoted the anti-Wilson cause. Day after day, Alice haunted the Senate gallery like a latter-day Madame Defarge, grimly noting on her blacklist the names of those who supported the League or wavered in their opposition. She revealed an infinite capacity for hatred and viperish comment.

The long-drawn-out struggle over the League, spiraling inflation, high unemployment, labor unrest, failing farm prices, race riots, and the specter of Bolshevism created a climate of hysteria that has become known as "the Great Red Scare." Radicalism was equated with Communism, tempers were inflamed by the press, and gross violations of civil rights and personal freedom became commonplace in the name of Americanism. A. Mitchell Palmer, the Attorney General, saw in this chaotic situation the opportunity to further his presidential ambitions by launching a crusade against alien radicals. An antiradical General Intelligence Division was established within the Department of Justice's Bureau of Investigation, and a young bureaucrat named J. Edgar Hoover was placed in charge. Hoover played upon the Attorney General's fears and exploited the issue of radicalism to enhance his agency's power and prestige. Palmer, in pursuit of alleged radicals, conducted a series of lawless raids in which several thousand aliens were rounded up for deportation. Most were innocent of any crime.

Although Franklin Roosevelt was perturbed by the threat of radicalism and favored limitation on free speech,* he forewent the opportunity to grab easy headlines. In September 1919, while acting Secretary in the absence of Josephus Daniels, he received a request from Governor Coolidge that the Navy assist in breaking a strike by Boston policemen. Roosevelt calmly replied that he would follow the orders of the President if federal assistance was authorized. Although the strike was settled through the efforts of Andrew Peters, Boston's mayor, Coolidge manipulated it to catapult himself into the national spotlight.

Just a few months before, Roosevelt had had an encounter with radicalism that would have turned a more timorous man into a raving Red-baiter. On the evening of June 2, 1919, as Franklin and Eleanor were parking their car a block or so from their house on R street, a tremendous explosion shattered the front of Mitchell Palmer's home, directly across from their own. Windows were blown out all over the neighborhood, and eleven-year-old James Roosevelt, the only child at home, narrowly escaped death or serious injury from flying glass. The terrorist had failed to kill the Attorney General but had blown himself up. Roosevelt, seeing the bloody pieces of the corpse lying on his front steps, feared that it might be the body of his son. "I'll never forget how uncommonly unnerved Father was when he dashed upstairs and found me standing at the window in my pa-

---

* FDR condoned a move by the commandant of the Boston Navy Yard to dismiss a worker for distributing literature advocating the overthrow of the government, but stopped him from firing others simply because they were Socialists.

jamas," Jimmy said. "He grabbed me in an embrace that almost cracked my ribs."

In September 1919, with the Versailles Treaty still bottled up in the Senate Foreign Relations Committee, Wilson decided to take his case to the people. He was a persuasive and eloquent speaker, and such tactics had always worked before. Traveling through the Middle West, the heartland of the opposition, he delivered twenty-five speeches in twenty-two days to increasingly enthusiastic crowds. In Pueblo, Colorado, where he spoke on September 25, the audience rose and cheered for ten minutes as he pleaded for his beloved League with tears in his eyes.† That was the high-water mark for Wilson. Soon after, he suffered a serious stroke and returned to the White House, a hopeless invalid. Two months later, the Senate rejected the treaty.

Wilson's humiliation at the hands of Congress had a lasting impact upon Roosevelt. He resolved never to make the same mistakes when he became President. From Wilson's tragic experience, he learned that foreign policy could not be successfully carried out on a partisan basis. Wherever possible, he tried to conciliate Republican partisans and involve them in the preliminaries of negotiation. As he told Eleanor during the great debate over the League:

> This business of the President and the Secretary of State negotiating and signing a treaty, and then handing it cold to the Senate is all wrong. The number of treaties—good treaties—that have been turned down in the course of our history is appalling. If I were doing it, I'd take the Senate, and maybe the House, into my confidence as far as I could. I'd get them committed to a principle and then work out the details in negotiations. In that way the thing could be secured.

Early in 1920, Mrs. Charles S. Hamlin, an old Roosevelt friend, met him walking on R Street and was surprised by the absence of his usual buoyance. "He has had his tonsils out and has been ill too," she wrote in her diary. "He looks rather poorly for him. He had two of his boys and a dog with him and we walked along together. Several of the children have had or are having chicken pox—James is to have his appendix out—Eleanor was getting out 2000 invitations for Navy teas. . . ." Roosevelt's low spirits mirrored the national mood. The Wilson era was drawing to a close, with the disabled President a virtual prisoner in the White House, and the government was being run by his wife and his personal physician, Dr. Cary T. Grayson. The American people were spiritually exhausted

---

† The outcome of the struggle might have been different had Wilson been able to take advantage of radio or television during his crusade. Rather than being able to address millions of people, he was forced to expend his energies to deal with only a few thousand at a time.

and disillusioned with Wilsonism and great moral crusades—whether for reform at home or for international order abroad. Weary of appeals to idealism and visionary talk of the nation's mission, they wanted nothing more than to shape their own affairs without interference from the government. The Republicans appeared almost certain to win the presidency in November.

Roosevelt's own malaise had both personal and professional overtones. After seven years of federal service, he was in a financial pinch aggravated by the runaway inflation which struck the United States following the World War. By November 1919, the cost of living was 82.2 percent above the 1914 level, and six months later, it hit 104.5 percent. The expense of maintaining a large family in Washington was becoming burdensome, and his income barely exceeded expenses. "I am honestly a fit candidate for a receiver," he wrote a friend.‡ Food, rent, education, and medical care were his responsibility, while Eleanor used her independent income for clothing for herself and the children, and they shared the cost of charitable donations. Later, he would tell an aide that his salary "just went"—he didn't know where. But his collector's instincts were unabated. While he still wore his father's jackets, kept suits until they were threadbare, and stubbornly refused to pay more than two dollars for a shirt, he would go after a stamp or a book or a print he coveted no matter what the cost.*

Sara Roosevelt came to her son's financial rescue—as was often the case—with an extra-large check for his thirty-eighth birthday. "You are not only an angel which I already knew, but the kind which came at the critical moment in life!" he told her. "For the question was not one of paying Dr. Mitchell for removing James' insides, the Dr. can wait . . . but of paying the gas man and the butcher lest the infants starve to death, and your cheque which is much too much of a Birthday present will do that. It is so dear of you." To William McAdoo, who had resigned as Secretary of the Treasury and was practicing law in New York, he wrote: "I do not see how I can afford another winter in Washington, and I think there is enough law business in New York to warrant me in assisting you to get some of it away from our Republican friends."

Professionally, he was plagued by a congressional investigation of the Navy Department's conduct during the war. The inquiry stemmed from the dissatisfaction of Admiral Sims with the honors recommended by Secretary Daniels following the Armistice. Sims, who had returned to his post

‡ According to an account book now in the FDR Library, Roosevelt's income for 1919 was $26,725.70, while his expenditures were $24,401.78, but the value of his "Principal Account," consisting of stocks, bonds, and other holdings, declined from $276,490.25 at the beginning of the year to $272,971 at the end.
* Ironically, in view of his later illness, FDR had a weakness for expensive, handmade English shoes.

as president of the Naval War College at Newport, angrily rejected the Distinguished Service Medal he was awarded as inadequate and complained about the brevity of the honors list. Roosevelt agreed with him. "Strictly between ourselves, I should like to shake the Admiral warmly by the hand," he wrote Mrs. Sims. Sims, however, broadened his assault with an attack on the Navy's state of preparedness in 1917. Eager to uncover scandals in an election year, the Republicans happily leaped upon the Admiral's sensational disclosures to discredit the Wilson administration. Roosevelt had made similar charges, but he realized that any criticism of the Navy was certain to rub off on him as well as the Secretary. His opinion of Sims and other "gold-braided gentlemen" shifted to disdain and he supported Daniels out of a sense of mutual defense.

Nevertheless, Roosevelt tried to put some distance between himself and the Secretary in case the congressional sleuths began sniffing around his door. Efficiency in government had become his new cause, and he supported the creation of institutions that would help the government operate in a more businesslike manner. "Reform" and "idealism" disappeared from his public statements, because, as he told a friend, they conjured up "visions of pink tea artists who dabbled in politics one day a week for perhaps two months in the year." During the course of one of his numerous speeches in support of governmental efficiency, at the Brooklyn Academy of Music on February 1, 1920, he openly boasted of the risks he had taken to prepare the Navy for war—inadvertently confirming the charges being made by Sims. Wilson was angered, and, for once, he had gone too far even for the ever-patient Daniels, who considered asking for his resignation. Roosevelt quickly issued an "explanation" to the press, but it never caught up with his original comments. Much to his relief, he managed to avoid being called before the Senate committee investigating Sims's charges, by indicating that if summoned he would "drop a bomb" by laying the blame for naval unpreparedness in the lap of Congress—where it truly belonged.

Roosevelt's winter of discontent was by no means over, for he was soon embroiled in scandals that brought his personal integrity into question. The first resulted from Daniels' desire to reform the naval penal system. Shocked by the harsh conditions at the Portsmouth Naval Prison, in New Hampshire, the old Populist had wished to transform it from "a scrap heap" to "one of humanity's repair shops." Thomas Mott Osborne, Roosevelt's reformer friend who had achieved renown as an enlightened warden at Sing Sing Penitentiary, was placed in charge with the rank of lieutenant commander and given a free hand. Most of the inmates were disciplinary, rather than criminal, offenders, and Osborne felt justified in humanizing conditions at the prison. Some officers objected that under the new regime, confinement at Portsmouth was less arduous than sea duty.† They also complained that Osborne's "graduates" were being returned to the fleet after they had served their sentences instead of being given the customary dishonorable discharge, which permitted them to contaminate other enlisted men. Captain Joseph K. Taussig, who had commanded the first destroyers to arrive at Queenstown in 1917 and was subsequently detailed as Director of Enlisted Personnel, objected so strenuously to this policy he was relieved and transferred to the Naval War College.

Not long afterward, Taussig was angered by an article in the *Army and Navy Journal* stating that the Navy's younger officers, particularly destroyer skippers, endorsed the policy of returning Portsmouth "graduates" to active duty. He fired off a letter stating that to his personal knowledge it was untrue. Taussig's letter was printed along with an editorial note stating that the article had been written by assistant Secretary Roosevelt. Much annoyed, Roosevelt retorted that Taussig had presented "a wrong impression of the actual facts" and leaped upon an assertion by the officer that Osborne was sending homosexuals back to the fleet. Roosevelt claimed this had occurred in only two cases and both involved special circumstances. Fearing his career was in danger of being blighted, Taussig requested a court of inquiry. Roosevelt was worried about the political consequences of a long-running controversy and invited Taussig to Washington. Following a two-hour meeting behind closed doors, he issued what was supposed to be a joint statement papering over the dispute. But Taussig had refused to sign it, saying the challenge to his veracity had not been withdrawn, and pressed ahead with a demand for an inquiry. Daniels declined to accede to his request, and the unhappy Taussig was left to fume in frustration.

This incident had hardly faded from public attention when John R. Rathom, the publisher of the Providence *Journal* and an ally of Admiral Sims, launched a sensational attack upon Roosevelt that was also entwined with homosexuality. During the war, the Navy had discovered that the training center at Newport was plagued with bootlegging, drugs, and sodomy, and Roosevelt had, as acting Secretary in the spring of 1919, authorized a special vice squad to clean up the unsavory situation. It was designated "Section A—Office of the Assistant Secretary." Before the year was out, Roosevelt learned that, in gathering evidence, some of the vice-squad members had engaged in homosexual relations themselves. He immediately ordered the squad disbanded and launched a secret investigation of its operations. The whole sordid business was leaked to Rathom,

† "No man will be a sailor who has contrivance enough to get himself into a jail," Samuel Johnson once observed. "Being in a ship is being in a jail with the chance of being drowned. . . . A man in jail has more room, better food and commonly better company."

who held Roosevelt personally responsible for the outrageous conduct of the investigators.

These charges were political dynamite, and Roosevelt launched a vigorous counteroffensive. He claimed that such statements were "dishonorable" and "morally dishonest" and, claiming he had had nothing to do with the vice squad, explained that its official designation was merely an administrative convenience. He also tried to persuade newspaper editors around the country not to reprint the *Journal's* articles as a patriotic duty, because they were detrimental to recruitment. "Any average citizen reading [them] must be led to believe that the Navy as a whole is a pretty rotten institution," he wrote. Finally, he asked the Senate Naval Affairs Committee to conduct a full investigation of Rathom's charges. Hearings were delayed by the inquiry stemming from the Sims controversy, and the affair hung like a threatening cloud over Roosevelt as his career took a new and important turn.

Paradoxically, Roosevelt's personal fortunes and position within the Wilson administration were at their lowest ebb at a time when his standing among progressive Democrats was at its highest. This enthusiasm stemmed directly from a speech before the Democratic National Committee in Chicago on May 29, 1919—a speech that marked his arrival as a leader of the party's liberal wing. Just as his speech in Troy seven years before was an expression of his economic philosophy, the Chicago speech crystallized his vision of the Democratic party as the party of reform and progressivism.

For twenty-five years, Roosevelt said, the history of American politics had been the struggle between the forces of "safe conservatism" and "sane liberalism" for control of the Republican and Democratic parties. This battle was now over, and the Republicans, having purged themselves of their progressive wing, were clearly the conservative party, while the Democrats had rid themselves of conservative elements and were the liberal and progressive party. The Republicans, he said, were "a party devoted to the policies of conservatism and reaction, to the principles of little Americanism and jingo bluff." Domestically, the new Republican Congress was concerned only with increasing the tariff for "pet groups of manufacturers," revising the income tax "to lighten the burden of those unfortunate individuals who have incomes of $1,000,000 a year or more," and discrediting every act of the Wilson administration by mudslinging, slander, and misrepresentation. Republican foreign policy was even less constructive, Roosevelt continued, and was based on little more than automatic opposition to Wilson's policies.

Roosevelt's announcement of the demise of the Democratic party's conservative wing was premature, but the Chicago speech attracted national attention. It stole the headlines from the keynote address of Attorney General Palmer, who had planned to use the occasion to strengthen his bid for the presidential nomination, and was warmly praised by liberal Democrats. "It was a humdinger!" wrote the editor of the Detroit *News*. "I already can see the Democrats of this state running around in circles trying to discover whether the new bird is an eagle or a hawk. . . ." Among those impressed by Roosevelt's remarks was Governor James M. Cox, of Ohio, another leading contender for the presidential nomination. In New York, there was talk of running Roosevelt for senator if Al Smith should opt for another term in Albany, or for governor should Smith choose to run for senator. There was even a "Roosevelt for President" movement, which he nipped in the bud. "Being early on the job is sometimes wise and sometimes not," he wrote an overzealous supporter. "I sometimes think we consider too much the good luck of the early bird, and not the bad luck of the early worm."

Roosevelt was convinced that 1920 was a Republican year, and any candidate likely to be fielded by the Democrats for the presidency—whether Palmer, Cox, Smith, or McAdoo—was certain to meet the fate of the early worm. Both he and Louis Howe were alert to prevent a draft that would push him into a hopeless race that year. "Do not believe everything you hear about me running for Senator or Governor or dog catcher," he confided to a friend. "I do not propose to make an early Christian martyr of myself this year. . . ."

As far as Roosevelt was concerned, only one man could turn the tide for the Democrats: Herbert Hoover. Hoover's hero had been Theodore Roosevelt, and he was generally regarded as a progressive, but his exact political affiliation was something of a mystery. Nevertheless, in the over-all disillusionment following the war, he was one of the few leaders who still had the admiration of the American people. "Hoover is certainly a wonder and I wish we could make him President of the United States," Roosevelt wrote Hugh Gibson, a mutual friend. "There could not be a better one." And according to Louis B. Wehle, a wartime associate and college friend, Roosevelt acquiesced in a plan for a Hoover-Roosevelt ticket. "You can go to it as far as I am concerned," Wehle has quoted him as saying. "Good luck!" But Hoover opted for the Republican party. "I knew no Democrat could win in 1920 and I did not see myself as a sacrifice," he later explained to a friend. Roosevelt went to the San Francisco convention pledged to the favorite-son candidacy of Al Smith, along with the rest of the New York delegation.

"Take wine, women and song, add plenty of A-No. 1 victuals, the belch and bellow of oratory, a balmy and stimulating climate and the whiff of patriotism, and it must be obvious that you have a dose with a

powerful kick in it." So wrote H. L. Mencken in fond recollection of the
Democratic national convention of 1920. The convention seems to have
had a similar effect upon Roosevelt. Frances Perkins remembered him as
"tall, strong, handsome and popular . . . one of the stars of the show." He
once vaulted over a row of chairs in his hurry to get to the podium, she
said. Perhaps some of his enthusiasm stemmed from the fact that he was
being widely mentioned as a candidate for the vice-presidential nomination. Professing surprise, he later claimed it was his intention to announce
his candidacy for either governor or U.S. senator upon his return home. "I
am wondering who started the fool Vice-Presidential boom," he told his
law partner, Langdon P. Marvin. "I am not at all sure that I care for it."

Nevertheless, Roosevelt had brought an entourage with him to San
Francisco far larger than required by a mere delegate. Not only had he
persuaded a reluctant Josephus Daniels to come, but he also urged his
chum Lathrop Brown, and John E. Mack and Thomas Lynch, old
loyalists from Dutchess County politics, to be on nd. To restore his
tarnished luster as a reformer, he had again challe   the Tammany-su
ported unit rule. This was an obvious exerc   imagery, beca   he
knew he did not have enough votes and the co   tion was likely to abolish the unit rule anyway. And with Howe's help, he had also drafted a
mixed bag of platform resolutions designed to emphasize his own progressivism.

Echoing his state-senatorial campaign of 1912, one of these resolutions advocated government action to reduce the high cost of food and
other necessities by regulating the middleman. "We believe it to be a
proper governmental function to exercise the full powers of the National
Government for the elimination of this parasite upon American business,"
it read. Other Roosevelt-Howe proposals included easier credit for farmers
and a similar policy for urban home builders, reorganization of the railroads, increased federal aid for highway construction, a guarantee of labor's rights to organize, tax reform to differentiate between earned and
unearned income, and deficit spending by the government in time of
depression to create jobs. This last recommendation called for the authorization of "Prosperity Bonds," or short-term notes, to finance roads and
reclamation and land-settlement projects—and was the forerunner of the
antidepression measures of the 1930s.

By the time the delegates were gaveled to order, Democratic prospects seemed less bleak, thanks to the Republicans. Meeting in Chicago,
they had bypassed such favorites as General Leonard Wood and Governor Frank O. Lowden of Illinois, as well as Herbert Hoover, to nominate
Senator Warren G. Harding, a silver-haired mediocrity from Ohio, as
their presidential candidate, and the equally conservative Calvin Coolidge
as his running mate. William Allen White, a distinguished Kansas editor,

later said he never seen a convention "so completely dominated by sinister predatory economic forces"—particularly the oil industry. Harding's nomination is usually presented as the work of a cabal of party leaders meeting in a "smoke-filled room," but in reality he was the candidate who best suited the mood of the delegates. Once the convention had deadlocked over Wood and Lodge, Harding's nomination was inevitable, because he aroused no strong opposition among any segment of the party and could be relied upon to take advice, rather than give orders.

In San Francisco, where his friends were buttonholing delegates and drumming up support for his vice-presidential candidacy, Roosevelt was alert for any opportunity to gain prominence. He did not have long to wait. The convention opened with the unfurling of a huge portrait of the absent President Wilson, which touched off a demonstration that sent most of the delegates swirling into the aisles with their state standards before them. But the New York delegation, firmly under control of Boss Murphy, who, like most of the city bosses, disliked Wilson, pointedly remained in their seats. Unable to bear the taunts of the demonstrators, Roosevelt scuffled with the Tammany stalwart clutching the state's standard and carried it away in triumph into the parading mob, much to the delight of pro-Wilson southern delegates. He also attracted favorable attention with a brief but rousing seconding speech for Smith. "The nominee of this convention will not be chosen at 2 A.M. in a hotel room," he declared in a jibe at Harding that touched off a wave of applause. "In the Navy we shoot fast and straight. Governor Smith, in that respect, is a Navy man. . . ." As a band broke into the Smith theme song, "The Sidewalks of New York," Mencken, covering the convention for the Baltimore *Sun*, grabbed a baton, climbed onto a chair, and enthusiastically kept time.

Throughout the early balloting, the New York delegation held firm for Smith, until Murphy, knowing full well that the Governor could not be nominated because he was a Catholic, was opposed to Prohibition, and was a representative of urban America, ordered a switch to Cox, the candidate of the city bosses. Most of the delegates followed instructions, but with the unit rule having been upset earlier in the convention, a bloc of twenty led by Roosevelt shifted to McAdoo. Ballot after ballot followed in which the strength of both Palmer and McAdoo waned and early in the morning of July 6, Cox won the nomination, on the forty-fourth ballot.

Roosevelt was chosen as the vice-presidential candidate as something of an afterthought. Following the eighteen-hour session in which Cox had been nominated, Edward H. Moore, Cox's campaign manager, telephoned the Governor in Dayton and asked his preference for a running mate. "I told him I had given the matter some thought and that my choice would be Franklin D. Roosevelt of New York," Cox recalled in his memoirs. "Moore inquired, 'Do you know him?' I didn't. In fact, so far as I knew, I had never seen him; but I explained to Mr. Moore that he met the geographical requirement, that he was recognized as an Independent and that Roosevelt was a well-known name."

Aware of Murphy's antipathy toward Roosevelt, he told Moore to clear the nomination with the Tammany chieftain. "Murphy had gone to bed but Moore delivered the message," Cox continued. "I can quote Murphy's exact words: 'I don't like Roosevelt. He is not well known in the country, but Ed, this is the first time a Democratic nominee for the presidency has shown me courtesy. That is why I would vote for the devil himself if Cox wanted me to. Tell him we will nominate Roosevelt on the first ballot as soon as we assemble.'"

Murphy was as good as his word. But just as Roosevelt's name was to be placed in nomination, Judge Timothy T. Ansberry, another Cox aide, recalled the constitutional provision that the Vice-President must be at least thirty-five years old and was not sure whether the youthful-looking prospective nominee met this qualification. As someone was telephoning the Navy Department, in Washington, for the information, Ansberry encountered Roosevelt:

"How old are you?" he asked.

"Thirty-eight. Why do you want to know?"

"I'm going to nominate you."

"Do you think I ought to be around when you do?"

"No, I'd leave the hall."

Several favorite sons had been placed before the convention when Ansberry came to the platform to nominate Roosevelt, whom he described as a man young in years but of "very large experience as a public official." Al Smith and Joseph E. Davies of Wisconsin seconded the nomination. The favorite sons quickly withdrew and Roosevelt was nominated by acclamation. "Roosevelt! Roosevelt! We want Roosevelt!" chanted the cheering, stomping delegates, but the nominee had left the hall in keeping with tradition, and Josephus Daniels spoke in his place. With words designed to allay any suspicion of discord between them, he declared that it was "a matter of peculiar gratification that the convention unanimously has chosen as candidate for Vice President that clearheaded and able executive and patriotic citizen of New York, the Assistant Secretary of the Navy, Franklin D. Roosevelt."

Roosevelt's nomination was a logical step for the Democrats. Although Theodore Roosevelt was dead, the family name still had political magic; he had made a good record as assistant Secretary; as a New Yorker, he provided geographic balance to a ticket headed by a Midwesterner; he straddled the Prohibition issue,‡ while Cox was a "wet," and as a Wilsonian, he would dispel the taint of machine support that clung to Cox despite his record as a progressive governor. In fact the President, like most of the nation, interpreted the nomination of Cox as a direct slap at himself and greeted the news with a torrent of obscenities. Wilson sent only the coolest of congratulatory telegrams to the new ticket, with Roosevelt's merely stating: "Please accept my warm congratulations and good wishes."

But the choice of Roosevelt was popular with a broad spectrum of Americans. Herbert Hoover told him that although as a Republican he could hardly wish him success, "as an old friend, I am glad to see you in the game in such a prominent position. . . . It is a contribution to the good of the country that you have been nominated." Walter Lippmann, an associate in the wartime bureaucracy and editor of *The New Republic*, wired him that "your nomination is the best news in many a long day. . . . When parties can pick a man like Frank Roosevelt there is a decent future in politics." The New York *Times* observed that Roosevelt's "fine record" in Albany and Washington, "together with the impression which he has given to the public of uniting unusual intelligence with sterling character, renders the ticket of Cox and Roosevelt one full of strength and purpose. The convention could not have made a better choice." One of the few carping voices was that of the Chicago *Tribune*, published by his fellow Grotonian Colonel Robert R. McCormick, which warned old Bull Moosers not to be fooled by the Roosevelt name: "The characters of the two Roosevelts are about a hundred times further removed than their relationship, which is about fifth cousin. The name is inspiring; the candidate is not."*

Returning home from San Francisco, Roosevelt stopped off at the Ohio statehouse, in Columbus, to meet Cox for the first time and to lay strategy for the coming fight. Along the way, he pledged an active campaign, in contrast to the "front porch affair" that was promised by Harding. "The voters have the right to see, as far as possible, the men who are in the race," he declared. Benign and shrewd, Cox resembled Josephus Daniels, and he, too, was impressed with the young man. "I liked him from the outset," recalled Cox. "His mind was alert and he was keenly alive to the conditions that would bear on the campaign." Roosevelt made only one suggestion at this meeting: that Cox announce that the

‡ Before the effective date of Prohibition, FDR had laid in as large a private stock of potables as he could afford.
* Arthur Woods, a former New York police commissioner who had known FDR at Groton and Harvard, told the New York *Sun* on July 7, 1920, that Roosevelt had shown no particular leadership qualities at school. "He was one of several score of darn nice fellows with lots of native ability and manliness but no more brilliance than the average darn nice fellow with lots of native ability and manliness."

Vice-President would sit with the Cabinet if the Democrats won in November. Cox rejected the proposal, saying that the Senate, jealous of its prerogatives, would resent being presided over by "a White House snoop." Nevertheless, in order to show his confidence in his running mate, Cox invited him to attend a meeting with Wilson at the White House a few days later.

Both Cox and Roosevelt were shocked when they saw the President on July 18. Ushered out onto the south portico, they found Wilson, in a wheelchair, frail and shriveled. Despite the stifling heat of a Washington summer, his left shoulder was covered with a shawl, which concealed his paralyzed left arm. Two decades later, Roosevelt recalled that Cox had tears in his eyes. Wilson did not seem to realize their presence until Cox approached and warmly greeted him. "Thank you for coming," the President replied in a weak voice. "I am very glad you came." Following a few minutes of desultory conversation in which Wilson's head was down, Cox said: "Mr. President, we are going to be a million per cent with you and your Administration and that means the League of Nations." Looking up, the President replied in a voice that was barely audible, "I am very grateful. I am very grateful."

Following this dramatic meeting, Cox issued a statement committing the Democratic candidates to making the League of Nations the paramount issue of the campaign. Although some writers have claimed this was the result of the emotional visit to the White House, Cox said it was a step he had intended to take all along despite warnings from some of his advisers that it was politically unwise. "I wish that every American could have been a silent witness to the meeting between these two great men," said Roosevelt. "Their splendid accord and their high purpose are an inspiration." To Eleanor, who had remained at Campobello with the children throughout these momentous events, he wrote that it "was a wonderful experience. . . . I miss you so so much. It is very strange not to have you with me in all these doings."

Clearing up some last-minute details, Roosevelt submitted his resignation as assistant Secretary of the Navy. An estimated two thousand workers gathered at the door of the Navy Department to present him with a loving cup and to bid him farewell. There was an affectionate exchange of letters with Daniels in which Roosevelt wrote: "This is not to say goodbye—that will always be impossible after these years of closest association—and no words I write will make you know better than you know now how much our association has meant. . . ." In his diary, Daniels expressed his personal thoughts: "He left in the afternoon, but before leaving wrote me a letter most friendly & almost loving which made me glad I had never acted upon my impulse when he seemed to take sides with my critics."

The campaign formally began, on August 9, with Roosevelt's acceptance speech, delivered from the front steps of Springwood to a crowd of some five thousand people, including party bigwigs, friends and neighbors, and a sizable delegation from Tammany Hall. "I sympathized with my mother-in-law when I saw her lawn being trampled by hordes of people," Eleanor said. When a reporter inquired about her own political views, she had to stop and think before replying: "My politics? Oh yes, I am a Democrat but I was brought up a strict Republican and turned Democrat. I believe that the best interests of this country are in the hands of the Democratic party for I believe they are the most progressive."

The speech established the twin themes of his campaign: the need for American participation in the League of Nations, and for reorganization of the federal government to increase its efficiency: "Two great problems will confront the next administration," he declared, "our relations with the world and the pressing need of organized progress at home." In international affairs, the United States could not "build an impregnable wall of costly armaments and live, as the Orient used to live, a hermit nation, dreaming of the past. . . . We must open our eyes and see that modern civilization has become so complex and the lives of civilized men so interwoven with the lives of other men in other countries as to make it impossible to be in this world and out of it." The League of Nations was "a practical solution of a practical situation," he continued, although he supported reservations to establish the supremacy of the U. S. Constitution.

Turning to domestic policy, Roosevelt called for major surgery to deal with the problem of governmental inefficiency. Congressional procedures that had not been altered in decades had to be streamlined, governmental departments and agencies reorganized, and the pay of efficient civil servants raised, while those who failed to meet higher standards should be dismissed. Efficient government also included planning for intelligent use of national resources—including America's people. Women and children should be protected from exploitation and abuse, the some five million illiterate living in the United States should be provided with educational programs, and immigration laws should be tightened to bar the physically and mentally unfit.

Not long before, Harding had declared that "America's present need is not heroics, but healing; not nostrums but normalcy";† and Roosevelt assailed this as a retreat into the past: "Some people have been saying of late: 'We are tired of progress, we want to go back to where we were before; to go about our own business; to restore "normal" conditions.' They are wrong. This is not the wish of America. We can never go back. The

† Frederick Lewis Allen states in *Only Yesterday* that Harding had meant to say "normality" but stumbled over the word.

'good old days' are gone past forever. . . . We cannot anchor our ship of state in this world tempest, nor can we return to the placid harbor of long years ago. We must go forward or flounder."

The speech was well received and clearly showed how far Roosevelt had advanced over the hesitant and fumbling candidate of a decade before. Roosevelt "gets . . . the last ounce of appeal power out of each sentence," wrote a reporter for the New York *Post*. "The physical impression leaves nothing to be asked—the figure of an idealized college football player, almost the poster type in public life . . . making clean, direct and few gestures; always with a smile ready to share. . . . He speaks with a strong clear voice, with a tenor note in it which rings—sings, one is tempted to say—in key with . . . [an] intangible, utterly charming and surely vote-winning quality."

Two days later, Roosevelt embarked on a whirlwind campaign that carried him to thirty-two states in the next three months. He barnstormed with a small staff in a private railroad car, the Westboro, which was attached to regular trains on a carefully planned schedule. The campaign began without Louis Howe, who remained in Washington until late in September, vainly hoping to be named assistant Secretary of the Navy in Roosevelt's place. Charles McCarthy, once Roosevelt's secretary, was placed in charge of the candidate's New York office, and a competent and attractive young woman named Marguerite LeHand was hired as a thirty-five-dollar-a-week assistant. Marvin H. McIntyre, a former Navy Department public relations man, served as Roosevelt's speech writer and press aide, and his secretary, R. F. Camalier, also went along. Stephen T. Early, an old journalistic friend of Howe's who had covered the Department for the Associated Press, was given a job that suited his name: advance man. Arriving before the candidate in towns and cities where Roosevelt was to speak, he rode herd on the local politicians in arranging for a crowd, prepared publicity, and gathered intelligence on the mood and attitude of local voters. Tom Lynch paid the campaign's expenses from a slim war chest that was augmented by five thousand dollars of Roosevelt's own money and a three-thousand-dollar donation from his mother.

The Democratic ticket was clearly doomed to defeat, but Roosevelt made a fight of it. In all, he made nearly a thousand speeches and appearances, and his campaign was the most extensive that had ever been waged by a candidate for national office. It was the last campaign before radio, and he spoke anywhere from six to twenty times a day as he swung from Chicago out to the Pacific Northwest down into California, back through the Middle West and up into New England, then westward again, this time by a southerly route. Sometimes he traveled by auto and at least once took the revolutionary step of using an airplane. Everywhere, he pleaded for support for the League and hammered away at Harding's evasiveness on the issue—a calculated ambiguity designed to placate both pro- and anti-League sentiment. To vary the diet, Roosevelt also invoked the progressive reforms of the New Freedom and appealed for the votes of independents.

"I voted for your father!" and "You're just like the Old Man!" people shouted, believing him to be Theodore Roosevelt's son. This was too much for the Oyster Bay Roosevelts, who looked upon this Roosevelt as an upstart and regarded the Rough Rider's eldest son, Theodore, Jr., as his legitimate political heir. The Republican National Committee dispatched Ted, Jr., as a one-man "truth squad" to dog Franklin's footsteps throughout the West. "He is a maverick," Ted said of his distant cousin. "He does not have the brand of our family." Eleanor was deeply hurt by the attack and refused to speak to Ted for years afterward. Franklin struck back by bitingly recalling that "in 1912 Senator Harding called Theodore Roosevelt first a Benedict Arnold and then an Aaron Burr. This is one thing, at least some members of the Roosevelt family will not forget."

Buoyed by the enthusiastic reception he was receiving, Roosevelt apparently began to believe there was a possibility of an upset victory. Having breakfast one morning with Tom Lynch about halfway through the campaign, he said he wanted him to come to Washington with him in March.

"Listen, Frank," Lynch replied, "you're not going to Washington."

"Why not?"

"While you've been speaking, I have been getting around in the crowds. They'll vote for you, but they won't vote for Cox and the League."

Women were voting for the first time in 1920, so Eleanor, having first placed James at Groton, joined her husband on the campaign trail. Unprepared for the organized chaos of campaigning, she had difficulty in adjusting. There was little for her to do except appear to be listening with rapt attention to speeches she had heard over and over again and to effusively greet total strangers, no matter how tired she was. And her husband had little time for her. He was either preparing speeches, plotting strategy, or relaxing around the poker table with his companions. The one person who took an interest in her was Louis Howe. Realizing that she wanted to take an active role in the campaign, he began coming to her at night to discuss speeches, points of political strategy, and the vagaries of the press. "I was flattered and before long I found myself discussing a wide range of subjects," she later recalled. For the first time, Eleanor sensed the keen intelligence behind Howe's prickly personality, to understand the relationship between him and her husband, and she no longer resented the intimacy between them.

Vice-presidential candidates are not supposed to make headlines, and Roosevelt violated that rule only once. Speaking in Butte, Montana, on his first swing through the West, he tried to answer the argument that the British Empire would have six votes in the Assembly of the League of Nations while the United States would have but one. In actuality, he said, the United States would have a dozen votes, because no one seriously doubted that Cuba, Haiti, the Dominican Republic, Panama, and Nicaragua would refuse to follow the lead of the United States. Not satisfied with this cynical but realistic assessment, he carelessly boasted, according to an Associated Press reporter: "I have something to do with the running of a couple of these little Republics. Until last week I had two of these votes in my pocket. . . . One of them was Haiti. I know, for I wrote Haiti's Constitution myself, and if I do say it, I think it was a pretty good Constitution." Harding immediately took advantage of the blunder and declared that if he were elected President, he would never empower an assistant Secretary of the Navy to impose a constitution, on a small, helpless nation, with the aid of marine bayonets. Roosevelt hastily backtracked by claiming he had been misquoted.

The Newport vice scandal also came back to haunt him in the closing days of the campaign. The Republican National Committee released a letter from John Rathom accusing Roosevelt of lying when he denied having removed from the Navy Department files the records of a man convicted of a morals charge. Roosevelt angrily refuted the allegation and filed a five hundred thousand dollar libel suit—but in both cases his candidacy was damaged.

Awaiting the results of the election at Hyde Park, Roosevelt expected defeat, but the disaster was greater than even he had foreseen. The Harding-Coolidge ticket won nearly 61 percent of the popular vote, and received 404 electoral votes to 127 for Cox and Roosevelt. Not for a century had any presidential ticket suffered such a lopsided defeat. The Republicans also added to their margins in both houses of Congress. "It wasn't a landslide," said Joe Tumulty, President Wilson's secretary. "It was an earthquake." In New York, the Democrats lost every state office contested, and Al Smith was ousted from the governorship by Nathan L. Miller. Most commentators have laid the defeat of the Democratic ticket to their support of the League of Nations, but a disaster of such magnitude could only have resulted from the rejection of everything the Wilson administration represented, rather than mere antipathy to American participation in the League of Nations. Harding won because he was identified in the public mind with peace and prosperity and a return to national balance and safety. There might not be any such word in the dictionary as "normalcy," but that undefined condition is what the American people craved in 1920.

Franklin Roosevelt did not seem dismayed or angered by the outcome of the election. He accepted the "overwhelming defeat . . . very philosophically" and within a few days was good-humoredly referring to himself as "Franklin D. Roosevelt, Ex. V.P., Canned. (Erroneously reported dead.)" Examining his situation, he found that indeed he had lost little. He had received national political exposure for the first time, had developed a national following, had improved his campaigning skills, and had built a team of dedicated assistants who added their expertise to that of Louis Howe.‡ Writing to Steve Early shortly after the debacle, he said: "Thank the Lord we are both comparatively youthful!"

‡ FDR gave each of his associates a set of gold cuff links as a souvenir of the campaign and arranged annual dinners for what became known as the Cuff Links Club. His initials were engraved on one link and those of the recipient on the other.

XI

CRISIS . . . AND COURAGE

Y EARS BEFORE Warren Harding became President, his father had an inkling of the disaster that lay in the future. "Warren, it's a good thing you wasn't born a girl because you'd be in a family way all the time," allowed the old man. "You can't say no." Friendly and gregarious, Harding brought with him to the White House as jolly a gang of small-town sports and backroom fixers as were to be found in any Ohio county courthouse. Big-bellied and good-natured, they wasted no time in trying to pry the dome off the Capitol. Franklin Roosevelt was not surprised. "Every war brings after it a period of materialism and conservatism; people tire quickly of ideals," he observed. "We are now repeating history."

Out of political office for the first time in a decade and faced with the necessity of supporting and educating a large family,* Roosevelt became active in the law firm of Emmet, Marvin & Roosevelt. But his heart was not in the rather staid practice it offered, for in law and business as well as politics, he liked adventure. The twenties were the heyday of the speculator, the plunger, and the smart operator, and Roosevelt followed the gravitation of power to Wall Street. "America's business is everybody's business," Harding declared, while Calvin Coolidge offered a fervent amen: "The business of the United States is business." Roosevelt appeared to agree. Having emulated Theodore Roosevelt and Woodrow Wilson for ten years, he now tried to be a successful businessman, like his father.

* Financially, 1920 had been a bad year for FDR. His income was $26,227.78, while he spent $38,390.37, political expenses accounting for $8,939.58 of this. Reflecting poor business conditions, his investments also dropped in value, from $272,971 to $269,240.94.

From several job offers, Roosevelt chose a vice-presidency of the Fidelity & Deposit Company of Maryland, one of the nation's largest surety bonding firms. He was paid twenty-five thousand dollars yearly, five times his salary as assistant Secretary of the Navy, to head its New York office. Van-Lear Black, major stockholder in the company and owner of the Baltimore Sunpapers, was a longtime friend and, like Roosevelt, an enthusiastic yachtsman and practitioner of the strenuous life. Although the company's directors had wanted a man with more experience in the insurance business, Black persuaded them that Roosevelt's name and widespread contacts in Washington and Albany and among organized labor would be an asset to the firm.

The arrangement was ideal for Roosevelt. Having again taken up residence on Sixty-fifth Street with his family, he spent his mornings working for Fidelity & Deposit at 120 Broadway and his afternoons in his law office at 52 Wall Street. "I am delighted to get back into the real world again," he told Felix Frankfurter. "The two varieties of work seem to dovetail fairly well." Weekends were spent at Hyde Park, which remained his voting address. The children now ranged in age from five to fifteen, and he made every effort to get to know them again. Eleanor had also outgrown the genteel life of teas and sewing circles she had known before the war. No longer the timid girl of fifteen years before, she took courses in typing and shorthand, learned to cook, became active in the League of Women Voters, sat on the boards of several charities, and became friendly with social workers and activists. Sara Roosevelt was distressed that she was no longer available to pour tea for her friends or to keep her company, but following the Lucy Mercer affair, Eleanor had declared her own independence. "I was thinking things out for myself and becoming an individual," she said.

Meanwhile, Franklin immersed himself in business. To an interviewer, he described himself as "one of the younger capitalists" and glamorized the bonding business as "a balance wheel of industry," because it prevented dishonesty and fraud. Just how valuable Roosevelt was to the company is a matter of dispute,† but Black described the performance of the New York office as "world beating" during February 1921, Roosevelt's first full month on the job.

Fully realizing that no one fades faster than a defeated vice-presidential candidate, Roosevelt kept his name in the limelight by participating in a wide array of political and civic causes. He helped organize the Woodrow Wilson Foundation, led a $2 million fund-raising drive for the Lighthouse for the Blind, became chairman of the Greater New York

† An old F. & D. employee has told the author that when FDR was inaugurated President, her boss, who had worked with Roosevelt, refused to close the Baltimore office so the staff could go to Washington for the ceremony, and angrily denounced him as a "glad-hander" and "a back-slapper."

Committee of the Boy Scouts, and was a member of the Board of Over-
seers of Harvard. He issued political statements and maintained a voluminous correspondence that kept him in touch with acquaintances from the
Wilson years and the 1920 campaign. He urged Democratic leaders
throughout the country to cooperate in drawing up a liberal domestic
agenda in preparation for the 1922 elections.

Following the collapse of Wilsonism, the party had lapsed into sectionalism, split between its urban northern and eastern wings and the predominantly rural South and West. Roosevelt's objective was the creation
of a vigorous national organization that was moderately progressive in outlook. In his own area, he laid plans to revive the shattered Democratic organization in upstate New York, to prepare for the upcoming campaign in
which he was likely to be a candidate for either governor or senator. The
party was to be reorganized from the bottom up, with every Democrat in
good standing to pay a small membership fee to keep the machinery oiled
and running.

There was but a single cloud on the horizon: the long-running inquiry into the Newport scandal by a subcommittee of the Senate Naval
Affairs Committee. It was composed of two Republicans and a Democrat,
so Roosevelt had no illusions about the outcome. Shortly before leaving
office himself, Josephus Daniels had told him: "You may be happy you
got out of here 'while the going was good.' Congress is out for blood and
the hearings are not as agreeable as in better days." Roosevelt had been
promised an opportunity to testify in his own behalf, but in mid-July he
learned that the subcommittee intended to release its final report without
hearing him. Cancelling plans for a much-needed vacation with the family
at Campobello, he rushed down to Washington on July 18. "I found all
the cards stacked, only worse than I thought," he wrote Eleanor. The Republican members brushed off his demand for an opportunity to present
his defense, saying they had already read his testimony before an earlier
inquiry. As a sop, they gave him a few hours to examine the six thousand
pages of testimony and agreed to wait until 8 P.M. to receive a statement
from him.

Perspiring in the sultry heat of a Washington summer, Roosevelt
worked feverishly against the clock with the assistance of Steve Early to
prepare a statement covering twenty-seven pages of legal foolscap. He was
convinced that the Republicans intended to smear him and that his political future was at stake. Roosevelt's worst suspicions were confirmed when
newsmen told him at 4 P.M. that the subcommittee had distributed its report to the press for release the following afternoon without even waiting
for his defense. With rising fury, he turned the pages of the report, which
charged that the vice squad had been under the assistant Secretary's "direct supervision" when it had engaged in sodomy to gather evidence

against homosexuals and described this as "a most deplorable, disgraceful and unnatural proceeding." The sole Democrat on the subcommittee absolved him of any wrongdoing, however, underscoring the partisan nature of the charges.

Recognizing the futility of expecting fair treatment, Roosevelt presented his statement to the subcommittee that evening, anyway. Once again, he flatly denied responsibility for the vice squad's activities and emphasized that as soon as he had learned of them, he had ordered an immediate halt. "Insinuations that I must have known, that I supervised the operations, that I was morally responsible, that I committed all sorts of high crimes and misdemeanors, are nowhere supported by the evidence directly or indirectly," he declared. And turning the tables on his accusers, he accused them "of deliberate falsification of evidence, of perversion of facts, of misstatements of the record, and a deliberate attempt to deceive" —all in the name of "cheap ward politics."

Throughout the next day and night, Roosevelt anxiously waited to see how the press would handle the subcommittee's report and his comments on it. Opening the New York *Times* on the morning of July 20, he was shaken by a headline:

LAY NAVY SCANDAL
TO F. D. ROOSEVELT

Senate Naval Sub-Committee
Accuses Him and Daniels in
Newport Inquiry.

DETAILS ARE UNPRINTABLE

Roosevelt's denials were buried in the *Times* article, but he was relieved to find that most other newspapers had given prominent play to his rebuttal. The bias of the subcommittee's report was clearly obvious, and the furor quickly faded without doing much damage to Roosevelt's reputation. The resentment rankled, however, and in the files of the library at Hyde Park, there is a handwritten note to the subcommittee chairman, Senator Henry W. Keyes of New Hampshire, that reveals the depth of Roosevelt's anger. "I have had the privilege of knowing many thousands of Harvard Graduates. Of the whole number I did not personally know of one whom I believed to be personally and willfully dishonorable. I regret that because of your recent despicable action I can no longer say that. My only hope is that you will live long enough to appreciate that you have violated decency and truth and that you will pray your

Maker for forgiveness." Written on the envelope are the words: "Not sent. What was the use? FDR."

Worn out by the heat and his anxieties, Roosevelt yearned to join the family on the cool shores of Campobello for his first real vacation in years, but there were obligations to be met. On July 27, he went up to Bear Mountain to inspect a Boy Scout encampment, and a newspaper photograph shows him in dark jacket and white trousers leading a procession of dignitaries and looking thin and strained. It was the last picture taken in which he is walking unassisted.

Roosevelt arrived at Campobello on a foggy morning early in August at the helm of the *Sabalo*, Van-Lear Black's 140-foot yacht. Black had invited him to come up to the island along with some other friends, and he had eagerly accepted, to avoid the long train trip. Marguerite LeHand, his new secretary, wrote Eleanor that he "looked tired when he left." The *Sabalo* ran into dirty weather off the coast of Maine, and Roosevelt took over the task of navigating the vessel, because Black's captain was not familiar with those waters. For several hours, he piloted the vessel northeastward through Frenchman Bay and Machias Bay, nosing into the Grand Manan Channel and past the treacherous Lubec Narrows. The charts were useless, and familiar landmarks had vanished in the swirling mist, and Roosevelt navigated by the echo of bell buoys and the muffled sound of foghorns. Even Black, an experienced sailor, was nervous, so Roosevelt assured him that he had once taken a high-speed destroyer through these same waters without mishap. All the same, it was exhausting work, and he was relieved when the *Sabalo* anchored in Welshpool Harbor. Eleanor and the "chicks" greeted him on the dock, along with Louis Howe, who had come to Campobello to discuss the prospects for the 1922 elections.

The following day was sunny and warm and Roosevelt took his guests out in the *Sabalo*'s motor tender for some promised cod fishing in the Bay of Fundy. Playing the role of the salty islander, he insisted on baiting their hooks himself. The work was strenuous, requiring him to walk back and forth between the boat's bow and stern cockpits on a three-inch varnished plank that passed close to the engine, and he was soon dripping with sweat. Suddenly Roosevelt lost his balance and tumbled overboard. Even though he was quickly pulled out, he still remembered the shock a dozen years later. "I've never felt anything so cold as that water! I hardly went under, hardly wet my head, because I still had hold of the side of the tender, but the water was so cold it seemed paralyzing. This must have been the icy shock in comparison to the heat of the August sun and the tender's engine." Roosevelt joined the others in laughing at his mishap and went back to work wearing his wet clothes, which were dried by the sun and the heat of the engine.

Most of the visitors soon left, and Roosevelt plunged into a typically active vacation, swimming, playing tennis and baseball with the children, and climbing with them on the rocks. On August 10, they went sailing in the twenty-four-foot sloop *Vireo*. Sighting a cloud of blue smoke rising from a small island, the Roosevelts landed and joined in fighting a forest fire, flailing away at the flames with evergreen branches. "It was a terrifying sight," according to Anna. "And it was a terrifying feeling to be standing next to a fir tree, suddenly have it catch fire, and hear the awful roar of the flames as they enveloped the whole tree." Late in the afternoon, the blaze was finally brought under control. "Our eyes were bleary with smoke; we were begrimed, smarting with spark-burns, exhausted," Roosevelt recalled. He suggested a swim and led a two-mile jog across Campobello to Lake Glensevern, a freshwater pond, where the party took a dip and topped it off with a plunge into the icy waters of the bay, which had always been an invigorating tonic. Much to Roosevelt's surprise, he "didn't feel the usual reaction, the glow I'd expected."

Back at the cottage, he found the mail had arrived bringing fresh newspapers, and he sat down on the porch in his wet bathing suit to read them. After a while, he felt a chill and was too tired to dress for dinner. "I'd never felt quite that way before," he said later. Complaining of chills and aches, Roosevelt went to bed early, believing he had lumbago. During the night, he got up to go to the bathroom, and Eleanor found him crawling on his hands and knees. The next morning, he greeted Anna, who had brought him his breakfast on a tray, with a cheerful smile and a wisecrack, but when he swung out of bed to shave, his left leg was weak. "I tried to persuade myself that this trouble with my leg was muscular, that it would disappear as I used it," he said. "But presently, it refused to work, and then the other."

"I don't know what's wrong with me, Louis," Roosevelt muttered to Howe over and over again a few days later. "I just don't know." Pain and desperation were etched on his face. Dr. E. H. Bennett, the country physician summoned by the worried Eleanor, diagnosed his illness as a heavy cold and was puzzled when the patient's condition rapidly deteriorated. Severe pains spread through Roosevelt's back and legs, and soon he was unable to move the muscles below his chest. Even the weight of the bedclothes on his limbs was painful. His temperature shot up to 102 degrees, and he temporarily lost control of his bodily functions. The children and other guests were sent on a three-day camping trip to get them out of the way, while Howe and Eleanor nursed him.

When the pain and numbness spread to Roosevelt's shoulders, arms, and fingers, Howe and Dr. Bennett scoured nearby resorts in Maine with the hope of finding a vacationing specialist. Dr. William W. Keen, a leading Philadelphia diagnostician, was persuaded to come up from Bar Harbor. After examining the patient, he concluded that Roosevelt was suffering from a blood clot in the lower spinal cord, and then, changing his mind, said it was lesion. He prescribed massage and sent Eleanor a bill for six hundred dollars.

For two nightmarish weeks, Eleanor slept on a cot in her husband's room, nursing him night and day. She bathed him, fed him, and tried to keep up his spirits, while her own anxiety was made worse by the frightening inability of the doctors to determine even the nature of Franklin's illness. The only person to whom she could turn for help was Louis Howe. Refusing several job offers, he remained with his friend. "From that moment on he put his entire heart into working for my husband's future," Eleanor said. Following the misguided advice of Dr. Keen, they massaged the prostrate man's limbs for hours on end, only to later learn that besides being painful, it further damaged his already weakened muscles.

Roosevelt was undergoing mental as well as physical agony. Overnight, he had been transformed from a lithe, active man of thirty-nine, with a brilliant future, into a bedridden cripple completely dependent upon others for the simplest service. Lying in bed during those bleak August days, able only to stare at the wallpaper with its yellow flowers and leaves, he was nearly crushed. Many years later, he told Frances Perkins that he had been "in utter despair" during the first days of his illness, "fearing that God had abandoned him." Nevertheless, his buoyant spirit prevented him from giving up hope, and before long he was bantering with Eleanor and Howe in his usual flippant manner despite the ever-present pain. "Yesterday and today his temperature has been normal and I think he is getting back his grip and a mental attitude though he has of course times of great discouragement," Eleanor wrote Franklin's half brother, Rosy, after the first week. "We thought yesterday he moved his toes on one foot a little better which is encouraging."

Two weeks after Roosevelt had been stricken, his uncle, Frederic Delano, acting on information provided by Eleanor, sent Dr. Robert W. Lovett, a Boston specialist on poliomyelitis, to Campobello. From what he had been told, Lovett suspected that Roosevelt was a victim of infantile paralysis; an examination of the patient confirmed his hypothesis. A mild epidemic of polio had been noted that year, and somewhere—in New York City, in Washington, or at the scout encampment—he had been infected by the virus and, worn out by his strenuous round of activities, was unable to resist its ravages. Lovett thought, however, that the attack was a mild one and told Eleanor that her husband's chances for a full recovery were excellent.

Treatment would require months, Lovett cautioned, and there was little medical science could do to hurry recovery along. He ordered an immediate end to the painful massage but said that except for bromides for sleeplessness, drugs were of little or no value. Hot baths were recommended, "as it is really helpful and will encourage the patient, as he can do so much more under water with his legs." Particular stress was placed on keeping up Roosevelt's spirits, because "there is likely to be mental depression and sometimes irritability in adults. . . ." As a result, everyone exuded optimism for his benefit, including his mother, who returned from her annual trip to Europe at the end of August. "I realized that I had to be courageous for Franklin's sake," she said of her first visit to his bedside, "and since he was probably pretending to be unworried for mine, the meeting was quite a cheerful one."

Roosevelt was deeply concerned about the effect of his incapacity upon his children. They knew only that their father was gravely ill in an upstairs room, where the shades were always drawn, and their mother was tense and worried. "We children were allowed only a few glimpses of him, a hurried exchange of words from a doorway," says James. "Yet from the beginning, even before the paralysis had receded fully from the upper reaches of his body, Father was unbelievedly concerned about how *we* would take it. He grinned at us, and he did his best to call out, or gasp out, some cheery response to our tremulous, just-this-side-of-tears greetings." Learning that the doctors who examined her father were to hold a consultation in her room, Anna hid in a clothes closet but was unable to understand much of what was said except for the dreaded word "polio." No one outside the family was allowed to know that Roosevelt was paralyzed, however. "Mother told us not to talk about polio, as so many people were scared of it," Anna explained. "But rumor travels fast; we found that many of our friends had been told by their friends not to go near the Roosevelt children as 'they might have polio.'"

Roosevelt's illness created a public-relations crisis for Howe. Realizing full well that the words "polio" and "paralysis" would be devastating to his friend's political future—if he still had one—he wanted to keep all mention of the attack out of the papers until it could be combined with an optimistic report on Roosevelt's condition. Rumors of something afoot on Campobello soon reached the outside world, but Howe, who had built a reputation for leveling with newsmen, provided little substantial information to a wire-service reporter who came over from Eastport. The first story on Roosevelt's condition did not appear until August 27, and it stated that the former vice-presidential candidate was "now improving" after a serious illness. There was no mention of infantile paralysis.

In mid-September, Howe adroitly stage-managed Roosevelt's transfer to Presbyterian Hospital, in New York City. Uncle Fred arranged for a private railroad car to pick him up at Eastport and take him all the way to New York without having to change trains in Boston. Under the direction of Captain Franklin Calder, an old family friend, he was brought down from the upstairs bedroom on an improvised stretcher and carried down the steep slope to the Roosevelt dock, where he was placed in the bottom of a motor launch, which ran him across the channel to Eastport. Every step of the way resulted in excruciating pain, but when Roosevelt caught a glimpse of seven-year-old Franklin, Jr., he managed a wave, and "his whole face burst into a tremendous sunny smile." To prevent the reporters and well-wishers from seeing Roosevelt while he was lying helpless on a stretcher, Howe told them the launch would land at a pier at the far end of town, and then signaled to have him brought ashore at the near end. The stretcher was passed through a window into the waiting railroad car, and before the crowd was aware of what was happening, he was comfortably settled in bed. "Mr. Roosevelt was enjoying his cigarette and said he had a good appetite" when visited by a reporter for the New York World. "Although unable to sit up, he says he is feeling more comfortable."

Tom Lynch was on hand to meet the train at Grand Central Terminal. Hearing Lynch's voice cautioning the porters as he was again being lifted on a stretcher through a car window, Roosevelt called out in his usual cheery way, "Hello, Tom!"

When the stretcher was free of the window, he added: "Come on and ride with me. There are some things I want to talk to you about."

Lynch watched as Roosevelt was carried down the platform and into a freight elevator but did not follow. Shortly afterward, Eleanor came back to say that her husband was calling for his old friend and would not allow the ambulance to leave until he arrived.

"Tell him you can't find me," said the shaken Lynch, turning his head away. "I'll go up and see him tomorrow."

Upon his arrival at the hospital, Roosevelt was placed under the care of Dr. George Draper, one of Lovett's associates, whom he had known at Harvard. For the first time, Howe acknowledged to the press that Roosevelt had been stricken with polio and his legs paralyzed, but he coupled the news with an optimistic bulletin from Draper. "He will not be crippled," the physician declared. "No one need have any fear of permanent injury from the attack." After reading this statement on the front page of the New York Times, Roosevelt wrote its publisher, Adolph S. Ochs, that although his doctors had told him the same thing he had been suspicious that they were trying to build up his morale. "But now that I have seen the same statements officially made in the New York Times I feel immensely relieved because I know of course it must be so."

Further examination forced Draper to the realization that his earlier optimism, based on Dr. Lovett's reports, was unwarranted. In fact, Draper was worried that Roosevelt would never be able to sit up again, let alone stand by himself or walk. Nevertheless, aware that the state of his patient's morale was vital to his physical condition, Draper kept his misgivings to himself. To Lovett he wrote: "He has such courage, such ambition, and yet at the same time such an extraordinarily sensitive emotional mechanism that it will take all the skill which he can muster to lead him successfully to a recognition of what he really faces without crushing him."

The next several weeks were a dismal period for Roosevelt as he faced the full consequences of his illness. Sweat streaming down his face, he spent hours concentrating on trying to wiggle his big toe. His eyesight failed temporarily and his right knee tightened, causing the leg to jack-knife so badly that both legs had to be put in plaster casts to keep them straight. Every day, a wedge was tapped a little farther into each cast at the joint to force the tendons to unlock, as if Roosevelt were being stretched on a medieval torture rack. But the man who had often been regarded as a playboy and grown-up boy scout had hidden reserves of courage. Presently, there were a few small signs of improvement. Both his arm and back muscles became stronger, and the day came when he could sit up.

Visitors found that he cheerily brushed aside any hint of condolence. Josephus Daniels reported that as he approached Roosevelt's bedside, his former assistant surprised him with a blow that almost sent him reeling. "You thought you were coming to see an invalid, but I can knock you out in any bout," Roosevelt said with a laugh. By the time he was discharged from the hospital, late in October, he could with the aid of a strap suspended from the ceiling, swing himself from his bed into a wheelchair if the chair was held steady by someone else. Still, there was a certain finality about the last entry on his hospital chart: "Not Improving."

With stubborn courage and incorrigible optimism, Roosevelt either refused to recognize the grim fact that he would be crippled for life or chose to ignore it. Early in December he told a friend that he expected "to be walking on crutches in a very few weeks. The doctors say that there is no question but that by this Spring I will be walking without any limp." Two months later, in February 1922, he first put on the leather and steel braces that he wore for the rest of his life. Weighing seven pounds each, they were cumbersome and painful if worn for any length of time, and stretched from his hips to his ankles. They locked at the knees and turned his lower extremities into stilts. With braces and crutches, Roosevelt could "walk" by maneuvering himself with his torso and arms, but at first he often tipped over and the crutches pained his arms.

While Roosevelt struggled to regain his feet, a behind-the-scenes battle of wills raged between his wife and his mother over his future. Raised voices and sharp words were rarely exchanged, but the conflict was acrimonious and the emotional scars deep all the same. Eleanor later described that period as "the most trying winter of my life." She and Howe wished Franklin to remain active in business and politics and to lead, as far as possible, a normal life. Believing that he would wither if treated as an invalid, they brought interesting people to the house on Sixty-fifth Street to stimulate his imagination with the hope that it would assist in his recovery. They knew that when Franklin finally realized he was crippled for life, politics would be the only existence left to him. In politics, his mind would matter, not his body. Howe kept up a busy correspondence with politicians all over the country in Roosevelt's name and urged him to issue periodic statements to show his interest in public affairs. And he pushed Eleanor out into the world to keep her husband's name before the public. "I am only being active till you can be back again," she told Franklin.

But Sara Roosevelt was convinced that Franklin's career was finished and protested that they were burdening him unnecessarily. She believed he should retire to Hyde Park, where, under her adoring eye and protective wing, he could lead the quiet life of a country gentleman, overseeing the estate, indulging in his hobbies, perhaps even writing the books he always talked about. There was even a family precedent for such a move. A century before, one of Franklin's ancestors, James Henry Roosevelt, was stricken with polio as a young man and had withdrawn from active life. He had remained at home, skillfully playing the stock market, and upon his death in 1863, left the money to found Roosevelt Hospital in New York City. Franklin Roosevelt may have found the prospect of retiring into a life of genteel invalidism momentarily alluring, but he had no intention of spending the rest of his days quietly beside the Hudson. Even before leaving Campobello, he had accepted membership on the State Democratic Committee.

Meanwhile, Sara Roosevelt was determined to break up the alliance between Louis Howe and Eleanor and get her son under her care. She particularly resented the constant presence of Howe, who had moved into the Roosevelt home and been given Anna's bedroom, a large sunny room on the third floor, while the girl had been "banished" to a smaller room in the back of the house. She detested his general air of sloppiness, his careless manners, his hacking cough, and the incense he burned in his room to relieve his asthma. Most of all, he represented everything that she wished Franklin to renounce. Howe talked to Franklin about politics and brought a steady stream of vulgar men to his bedside, turning the

Roosevelt home into a political clubhouse. She often provoked Franklin to cold fury by calling Howe that "dirty ugly little man"—but despite all her objections, he stayed.

Having been repulsed in a direct attack, the old lady played upon Anna's resentment at having had to give up her room to Howe. At fifteen, the girl was at the difficult stage. She was doing poorly in school, was feeling unloved, and there were times when she fled from the dinner table in tears. "Granny's needling finally took root; at her instigation I went to Mother one evening and demanded a switch in rooms," Anna recalled. "A sorely tried and harassed mother was naturally anything but sympathetic; in fact, she was very stern with her recalcitrant daughter." Years later, Eleanor blamed herself for the situation. "She was an adolescent girl and I still treated her like a child. . . . It never occurred to me to take her into my confidence and consult with her about our difficulties."

Eleanor's stoic self-possession gave way. While reading to two of the boys, she suddenly broke down without warning and began crying uncontrollably. "I could not think why I was sobbing, nor could I stop," she said. "I sat on the sofa in the sitting room and sobbed and sobbed." Finally, she pulled herself together by going into an empty room. "That is the one and only time I ever remember in my entire life having gone to pieces in this particular manner." Eleanor's breakdown did have a beneficial effect upon her relations with Anna. Perceiving her emotional stress for the first time, they began to reach out to each other.

Fearing that the children would brood about his condition if they were not taken into his confidence, Roosevelt openly discussed his physical problems with them. Throwing back the covers, he showed them his legs and taught them the anatomical names for the muscles he was trying to exercise to prevent them from atrophying. "He would give us progress reports as a little life returned to various areas, and we would cheer jubilantly, as if at a football game, when Pa would report, say, a slight improvement in the muscles leading from the *gluteus maximus*," says James Roosevelt. "How we loved to talk about Pa's *gluteus maximus!*"

Within a few months after being disabled, Roosevelt was getting down on the floor to Indian-wrestle with his sons, but their relationship had been changed forever. A curtain had dropped on the vigorous outdoor life of Hyde Park and Campobello; never again would he lead them on cross-country hikes or onto the tennis court and the skating pond. Although Roosevelt never spoke about this loss, he revealed his feelings in subtle ways. From a bedside window he could see a nearby street corner, and he asked Elliott, who skated to school each morning, to cross at that corner so he could watch him. Eleanor said he never mentioned golf to her after his illness, and he avoided a return to Campobello, with its painful memories, for a dozen years.

Roosevelt regarded the challenge of learning to walk again as similar to his campaign against hopeless odds for the state Senate in 1910 or his efforts to mobilize the Navy's resources for war. He had won those battles and was determined to win this one—if only his "somewhat rebellious legs" would cooperate. Except for the black despair that engulfed him when he was first stricken, he looked to the future. With the coming of spring, he went to Hyde Park to begin the struggle in earnest. He had a pair of parallel bars set up on the south lawn, one placed higher than the other, and practiced thrusting his body along on them, back and forth, for hours on end. One of the goals he set for himself was to reach the Post Road, a quarter of a mile from Springwood. Each day, he hobbled down the driveway on his crutches, struggling a few more feet toward the highway than the day before. Sometimes he fell and lay waiting on the ground until someone came along to help him up. Anna vividly recalled this battle, seeing "the sweat pouring down his face" and hearing him say, "I must get down the driveway today—all the way down the driveway."

Roosevelt's most harrowing fear was being trapped in a fire, and he learned to crawl down the long halls and stairways of the house by the strength of his hands and arms. He was proud of this accomplishment and showed no embarrassment in demonstrating it. While dining with the Charles Hamlins one evening, he pushed back his chair and said: "See me get into the next room." He dropped down on the floor and crawled into the room and pulled himself into another chair. "My husband was so overcome at such courage and seeing that superb young fellow so pleased by being able to do this—that on the plea of hearing the telephone—he went into his den for a while."

Yet Roosevelt himself refused to engage in self-pity and was remarkably patient and good-humored, considering his plight. "Now I don't want any sob stuff," he told a reporter who interviewed him about his illness. Sheffield Cowles, Jr., who visited him soon after he was stricken, recalls that they spent the evening together discussing naval history and looking at Roosevelt's extensive collection of naval prints. "I remember feeling very sorry that now obviously his life was through, but Franklin showed no signs of depression nor did he talk about his illness."

Sometimes he even made jokes about it. When a firm that was making special arch supports for his shoes wrote to ask if he walked with "a cain," he scrawled a note along the side of the letter: "I cannot walk without a *Cain* because I am not *Abel*." To another correspondent, he wrote, "I have renewed my youth in a rather unpleasant manner by contracting . . . infantile paralysis." Something comic might be described as "funny as a crutch," and when finishing a conversation, he would often say, "Good-bye, I've got to run."

Anna Roosevelt could recall only one occasion when her father lost his patience. She was up on a ladder arranging the books in the library at Hyde Park while he directed her from his wheelchair. Suddenly, an armload of books slipped from her grasp and crashed to the floor, causing Roosevelt to flinch in surprise. He angrily accused her of carelessness and she fled the room in tears. She sobbed out the story to her mother and said she didn't see why he had been so angry at a simple mistake. "Mother told me of the battle Father was fighting against great odds; of the naturalness of his nervous reaction; how lucky we were to have him alive and to be able to help him get well; how much more patience and grit he had to have than we; until I felt very sheepish and even more ashamed—but in a different way, more adult understanding way. Back I went to the library where, of course, I found not only forgiveness but also a sincere and smilingly given invitation to resume my place on the library ladder."

Dr. Lovett suggested that Roosevelt take up water therapy. Before a pool was built at Hyde Park, he swam three days a week in the heated indoor pool at Vincent Astor's estate, in nearby Rhinebeck. He would crawl to the edge and then lower himself into the water, while Louis A. Depew, his mother's chauffeur, stood on the edge to haul him in when he was ready. "The legs work wonderfully in the water, and I need nothing artificial to keep myself afloat," Roosevelt told Dr. Draper. "I see cautious improvement in my knees and feet." "One day, he hollered to me—he was out there swimming," Depew remembered, "and he says: 'The water put me where I am and the water has to bring me back.'"

Roosevelt liked to sit in an easy chair on the verandah at Springwood with Louis Howe, making model sailboats from balsawood and oiled paper. They went out onto the Hudson in a rowboat with Depew at the oars to launch their creations, and Roosevelt was excited when one sailed across the wide river in little more than ten minutes. He worked on his stamp collection, catalogued his books, and read, if not systematically, deeply in American history, politics, and biography, and developed the habit of reading himself to sleep with detective stories. As he grew stronger he liked to read aloud to his family. "I would almost rather read to someone than read to myself," he told Frances Perkins. There is no evidence, however, that he read any of the speculative writers whose ideas permeated the twenties—Marx, Freud, Spengler, Whitehead, Parrington, Beard—or that he used this period of enforced idleness for intensive study, except for the subject of infantile paralysis. He read everything he could find on the disease and discussed it at length with his physicians, becoming in time something of an authority.

Roosevelt had regained his old vitality and energy—his joy in living, his ability to obtain happiness in little things—but he never walked again without braces and the support of crutches or someone's arm. The muscles of his legs continued to atrophy until they were so withered he could raise his legs by the crease of his trousers. Paradoxically, the stern program of exercise that he imposed upon himself developed the massive shoulders, deep chest, and bull neck which, when sitting, gave him the appearance of immense strength. Jack Dempsey, the boxing champion, once said Roosevelt had the most impressive shoulder muscles he had ever seen. The lithe young man who had graced Harvard Yard and the salons of Washington had vanished, to be replaced by a bulky figure who exuded authority.

Roosevelt's progress was marginal, but he remained optimistic beyond all reality. "The combination of warm weather, fresh air and swimming has done me a world of good," he wrote James Cox. "The legs are really coming along finely, and when I am in swimming, work perfectly. That shows that the muscles are all there, only require further strengthening. I am still on crutches but get along quite spryly." Not until the end of 1923, more than two years after he had become paralyzed, did he resign as an active member of the Dutchess County Golf and Country Club.

In the fall of 1922, Roosevelt returned to work at the Fidelity & Deposit Company. At first he appeared at the office two days a week, then three, and finally four. Van-Lear Black had generously kept him on the payroll during his convalescence and took on Howe as his assistant. The need to return to work was pressing. Roosevelt not only required the stimulus of business and the opportunity to prove to others that he was not a hopeless cripple, but he was concerned about the heavy expense of his illness and the cost of maintaining his family in its usual style.‡ He did not become active in his law firm, however, partly through lack of interest and partly because the Wall Street building in which it was situated had a flight of stairs at its front entrance, which would have required him to be carried inside. This was a personal humiliation, and he agreed with Howe that it would be "bad politics" to be seen in such a helpless state.

Even though 120 Broadway, where the F. & D. had its offices, had only a single step, a man in Roosevelt's condition had no easy time even there. D. Basil O'Connor, a young attorney with offices in the building,

‡ In 1921, FDR's income was $48,542.12 and his expenses totaled $41,321.32. His mother gave him $6,008.69 to help defray medical costs of $7,075.62. His investments were worth $19,074.61 more at the end of the year than the beginning, or $288,324.55. The following year, his income was $42,110.82 and his expenses were $40,001.38. His investments increased in value by $25,526.13, to $313,850.68.

never forgot his first encounter with his future law partner. Arriving one morning at the same time as Roosevelt, he watched with sympathetic concern as the big man was helped out of a car by his chauffeur, heaved himself up on his crutches, and made his way across the sidewalk and through the door. Suddenly, as Roosevelt was proceeding cautiously over the polished marble floor of the lobby with the chauffeur at his elbow, one of his crutches splayed out from under him and he crashed to the floor. With considerable difficulty, he drew himself up to a sitting position and, looking at the shocked and pitying faces of the onlookers, began to laugh as if it were all a big joke. Unembarrassed, he asked a brawny young man to assist the chauffeur in helping him up and, restored to his feet, made his way to the bank of elevators as if nothing had occurred.

Roosevelt's day began at 8:30 A.M., when he saw Howe and other visitors while still in bed. Two hours later, he was at the office and worked straight through to five o'clock, having had lunch at his desk. In the morning, he worked at F. & D. business; afternoons were usually devoted to private affairs. He came home for tea, exercise, and more meetings with visitors, which lasted until dinnertime. Black had expected him to bring in new bonding business through his name and contacts, and he and Howe crossed the line between business and politics with agility. Writing to an executive of a company with which he had done business during the war, Roosevelt said the news of an award of a contract to the firm for gun forgings "brought to my mind the very pleasant relations we had during my term as Assistant Secretary of the Navy. . . . I wondered if you would feel like letting my company write some of the contract bonds that you are obliged to give the government." And Howe, whose ties with organized labor had remained close, recalled past favors to persuade the unions to throw their bonding business to Fidelity & Deposit.

Howe became Roosevelt's legs, taking his place at political and philanthropic meetings—Roosevelt still held memberships in a sizable number of organizations—buying prints and stamps for him at auction, and running family errands. Missy LeHand, now a member of Roosevelt's inner circle, assisted Howe in protecting the Boss's interests. Sometimes even Louis balked at the demands upon him. "Lord knows, I have acted as your alter-ego in many weird commissions," he told Roosevelt upon one occasion, "but I must positively and firmly refuse to risk my judgment on neckties, watches and pajamas."

The return of Al Smith to the Executive Mansion at Albany in 1922 provided a windfall for Fidelity & Deposit. Out of office for two years, Smith had been reluctant to leave a job as president of a trucking firm, with a salary of fifty thousand dollars a year, for the governorship, which paid ten thousand dollars. William Randolph Hearst saw an opportunity and seized it. The publisher declared himself a candidate for the Democratic gubernatorial nomination and began spreading money around the state. Fearing a disaster if Hearst was nominated, party leaders put pressure upon Smith to run. With only a week remaining before the deadline for nominating petitions to be filed, Smith agreed to make the race if publicly requested by the leadership.

As the best-known Democrat in the state after the former governor himself, Roosevelt was chosen to make the appeal. "There is no question but that the rank and file of Democrats want you to run," he wrote in a "Dear Al" letter. Smith accepted in a "Dear Frank" letter, and Hearst's balloon was punctured. Before the Democratic convention met, Roosevelt invited Smith to Hyde Park, where party workers not only got a chance to meet the candidate but to see how well Roosevelt had progressed in fighting off the effects of polio. In both cases, they liked what they saw. Smith asked him to run for the Senate, but Roosevelt declined. Eleanor, making her debut in politics, attended the convention as a Smith delegate and led the Dutchess County delegation in demonstrating for him. Smith won the election handily—making him a leading contender for the presidential nomination in 1924.

Smith appointed George Shuler, one of Howe's friends, as state treasurer—in fact, Howe wrote press releases for him—and he established a policy of depositing state funds in local banks that made loans to farmers. Banks serving as depositories for such funds required surety bonds, and Shuler made certain that Roosevelt's firm got a significant share. Within a year, Roosevelt was boasting to the home office that F. & D. had gained over $3 million of this business, while the shares of all but one of its rivals had dropped. And when James J. Walker, Smith's candidate for mayor of New York City, was elected, a drive was launched to land more city business. He urged his colleagues to go after the really "big men" who had contracts to hand out. "Things in the office are going well, exceedingly well," Roosevelt happily informed Van-Lear Black, "and we are getting a lot of new business through my political connections."

Two years after having been stricken, Roosevelt was still searching for a cure. Medical opinion in that day was practically unanimous that any improvement in muscle condition had to occur fairly soon after the attack, but he refused to accept it as gospel. He made inquiries about a Kansas City doctor who recommended "aero-therapeutic" treatment, looked into the deep heat lamp therapy, and even expressed an interest in the positive-thinking approach of Dr. Émile Coué, who claimed cures by having his patients endlessly chant: "Day by day, in every way, I am getting better and better." Well-wishers suggested all kinds of cures. In February 1923, he wrote to Dr. Draper about the "latest quack medicine" which "may be monkey glands or perhaps it is made out of the dried eyes of the extinct three-toed rhinoceros. You doctors have sure got imagination. . . . I am going to Florida to let nature take its course—nothing like Old Mother Nature anyway!"

Following the sun to Florida, he chartered a houseboat, the *Weona II*, and spent several enjoyable weeks cruising among the Florida Keys. He loafed, fished, and swam in the buoyant salt water and was convinced that sunlight had a beneficial effect upon his muscles. He could stand unassisted in water up to his shoulders. "Except for the braces, I have never been in better health in my life," he wrote Senator Carter Glass, of Virginia.

The following winter, Roosevelt bought a houseboat in partnership with John S. Lawrence, a Boston merchant whom he had known at Harvard and who was also crippled. They christened it the *Larooco*, an acronym of Lawrence, Roosevelt and Company. The double o and the seven letters of the name were supposed to bring good luck, but the craft proved to be in poor shape and was always breaking down or running into trouble. Accompanied by a small party that included Missy LeHand— Eleanor was already too busy with her various projects to take time off—he placed the *Larooco* in commission at Jacksonville on February 2, 1924, for a cruise down the Florida coast to Miami. Three days later, the houseboat entered the harbor of St. Augustine to find the flags at half-staff to mark the death of Woodrow Wilson. Roosevelt ordered the *Larooco*'s own ensign lowered for thirty days. At Palm Beach, which he had not visited since 1904, he went ashore, but his patrician sensibilities were repelled by its gaudy, boom-town atmosphere. "I found the growth of mushroom millionaries' houses luxuriant. The women we saw went with the place—and we desired to meet them no more than we wished to remain in the harbor even more than necessary."

For the next two months, Roosevelt spent an idyllic time in South Florida. Writing to his mother, he described a typical day: "[We] took a motorboat to an inlet, fished, got out on a sandy beach, picnicked and swam and lay in the sun for hours. I know it is doing the legs good, and though I have worn the braces hardly at all, I get lots of exercise crawling around and I know the muscles are better than ever before." He kept up his political contacts through a wide-ranging correspondence, and among his visitors were James Cox and William Jennings Bryan, now lending his oratorical talents to promoting Florida real estate.

To help pass the time, Roosevelt began work on a history of the United States and a biography of John Paul Jones but did not get far on either project. Although he had a strong sense of history, he lacked the staying power and concentration required to produce lengthy books. Roosevelt's uncompleted writings became something of a rueful joke both to himself and his friends. Invited to collaborate on an article about international affairs, he replied perceptively: "In regard to my own actual pen to paper possibilities I am always in the delightful frame of mind of wanting to say 'Yes' to anything in the way of writing, be it a magazine article or a 12 volume history of the Navy—always provided that the writing is to be done next week or the week after (Miss LeHand who is taking this is nodding her head and saying 'Too true—too true!')."

Roosevelt did, however, complete work on a plan for world peace which he intended to submit to a $100,000 prize competition held by Edward Bok, a prominent magazine publisher. Basically, his plan created a society of nations free of the objections that caused the American people to reject the League of Nations. "We seek not to become involved as a nation in the purely regional affairs of groups of other nations," he declared in the preamble, nor would the United States commit itself to "undertakings calling for or leading up to the use of armed force without our full and free consent, given through our constitutional procedures." As far as Roosevelt was concerned, the important thing was to convince the American people to join an organization that could maintain international peace, rather than to worry about the strings on such participation. He did not submit the plan to the Bok competition, because Eleanor became a member of the prize jury, but in later years he often referred to it and used some of its parts in organizing the United Nations.

What effect did Franklin Roosevelt's struggle against infantile paralysis have on his personality and political career? He could not do such simple things as walk about a room, switch easily from one chair to another, climb steps, pick up a book he had dropped, stand up to signal the end of a conversation, or kneel in prayer. Conversation became an outlet for his suppressed energies. It became his golf and tennis. He not only gained information by meeting new people and asking questions but relieved tensions by gossiping and dredging up stories from an inexhaustible fund of ancedotes. "I've often thought that the impression some people got . . . that Father talked to his guests more than he ever allowed them to talk to him came from an unconscious habit formed when he realized he could not make an excuse and leave people because he was sedentary," Anna Roosevelt once said. "And it was, therefore, his responsibility to give them as good a time as possible while they were with him."

Roosevelt's physical inactivity had certain compensations, however. Polio gave him a serenity that he had lacked. Anyone who spends months concentrating on moving his big toe develops an infinite amount of patience. He had always been restless, dashing about in search of firsthand information, and with a thousand interests. Now compelled to remain in one place, he could concentrate all his physical energy and vitality on the work at hand. "Suddenly, there he was flat on his back, with nothing to do but think," Louis Howe once recalled. ". . . His thoughts expanded, his horizon widened. He began to see the other fellow's point of view. He thought of others who were ill and afflicted and in want. He dwelt on many things which had not bothered him much before. Lying there, he grew bigger day by day."

People came to see him, and he did not have to waste time going to see them or moving from one conference to another. Thus, he was relieved of many of the petty irritations and the nervous wear and tear that often make life difficult. And if his judgment or instinct told him that some decision or course of action might not be wise or in his best interests, he had an excellent reason for avoiding it. Above all, Roosevelt's illness kept him on the sidelines throughout the years the Republicans dominated American politics.

Legend has it that polio transformed him from a frivolous young aristocrat into a humanitarian with a compassion and understanding for the downtrodden that ultimately led him to the White House. Frances Perkins, for one, believed it: "Franklin Roosevelt underwent a spiritual transformation during the years of his illness," she wrote. "I noticed that when he came back that the years of pain and suffering had purged the slightly arrogant attitude he had displayed on occasion before he was stricken. The man emerged completely warmhearted, with humility of spirit and with a deeper philosophy. Having been to the depths of trouble, he understood the problems of people in trouble. . . . He believed that Divine Providence had intervened to save him from total paralysis, despair, and death."

This implies a mystical metamorphosis—a spiritual rebirth akin to being born again—but Roosevelt was too much the pragmatist to be a mystic. Behind his lighthearted banter was a vaulting ambition that had caused him to seek important position in public life. The struggle against polio gave him a depth he lacked as a young man, a compassion for the afflicted, and added shadows to an outwardly sunny personality; yet it did not transform him. Since he came close to death, Roosevelt's victory over polio reinforced his private religiousness, but it did not alter his ideas, his basic philosophy, or his view of life.

Prolonged illness can lead to narcissistic self-absorption, and it would have been easy for Roosevelt to give up his political aspirations and retire to the comfortable life of Hyde Park. His refusal to bid farewell to a normal life testifies to his courage and determination—and the strength of his ambition. This iron core of will, this stubbornness, rather than any alteration in character resulting from the crisis, enabled him psychologically to survive the shattering ordeal. And those who look for a sickbed conversion to liberalism and concern with the plight of the common man overlook his longtime admiration of Theodore Roosevelt and his commitment to the idealism of Woodrow Wilson.

James Roosevelt probably had the clearest view of the impact of infantile paralysis upon his father when he wrote that although polio broadened his compassion for human suffering, it did not make him President. "Indeed, I believe that it was not polio that forged Father's character but that it was Father's character that enabled him to arise above the affliction. I believe his path would have led him to the White House regardless of polio. . . ."

XII
THE HAPPIEST WARRIOR

EARLY IN JUNE 1924, Moses Smith, one of the Roosevelt tenant farmers, came upon him sitting on a blanket in the grass near Springwood, dictating to Missy LeHand. "Moses, what do you think I'm doing?" Roosevelt called out in greeting. "I'm writing a nominating speech to nominate Al Smith for President." The speech to the Democratic National Convention meeting later that month in New York City was Louis Howe's idea. The time had come for Roosevelt to show the world that he had emerged victorious from his ordeal, and, to convince doubters, an extra bit of drama was added: He planned to walk to the platform on the arm of his son James and then propel himself to the rostrum under his own power.

Shortly after Roosevelt returned from the cruise of the *Larooco* Boss Murphy suggested he join in lining up delegates from other states behind Smith's candidacy. Smith had started his campaign late, and his major opponent, William McAdoo, Woodrow Wilson's son-in-law and former Secretary of the Treasury, was far ahead in pledged delegates. Roosevelt and Howe were by no means convinced of Smith's chances of victory, because of his ties to Tammany, his Catholicism, and his "wringing wet" opposition to Prohibition, but they had little alternative except to go along with New York's favorite son. Besides, Howe, operating with his usual deviousness, saw an opportunity to advance Roosevelt's political fortunes.

Murphy had appeared in excellent health, but a few days after the meeting at Roosevelt's home, suffered a fatal heart attack. "New York has lost its most powerful and wisest leader," said Roosevelt of the man whom he had once described as working "in the dark underground passages of the crookedest political byways." Smith's supporters were dismayed at the loss of the Governor's most important backer, but Murphy's passing was a blessing in disguise. The albatross of Tammany had been lifted from Smith's shoulders, and he was now the unchallenged leader of the state Democratic political machine.

Roosevelt also benefited from Murphy's death. Two of Smith's closest advisers, Belle Moskowitz and Judge Joseph M. Proskauer, suggested that he be named to head up the campaign, because he would give it balance and broad appeal. Roosevelt had a national reputation, was free of Tammany's taint, was an upstate Protestant, had antagonized no one on the Prohibition issue, and could appeal to liberals suspicious of McAdoo, who had accepted the support of the resurgent Ku Klux Klan. Moskowitz and Proskauer felt that Roosevelt, as a cripple, would be unable to interfere in their direction of the campaign. And like Al Smith, they viewed the patrician in politics with contempt, regarding Roosevelt as little more than a handsome piece of window dressing.

Smiling benignly at Moskowitz and Proskauer, Roosevelt accepted the offer, but he had no intention of sitting idly by and allowing them to run the show. The alliance was a two-way street. By assuming the chairmanship of Smith's campaign, Roosevelt was able to plunge back into national politics and to broaden the contracts he had made in the 1920 campaign. Howe maintained a wide-ranging correspondence with political leaders all over the country—whether they supported Smith or not—and his intelligence network reached deep into each state. Only a handful of delegates were won for Smith in the process, but it added to Roosevelt's stature, particularly when he called upon Smith workers to refrain from stirring animosities that would last beyond the convention. "I do not believe in a campaign for nomination which leaves scars in our party," he later declared. The last suspicions of anti-Catholicism that had clung to Roosevelt's name since his battle against "Blue-eyed Billy" Sheehan, in 1911, were dissipated by his active role in the Smith campaign, making it easier for the predominately Irish Catholic city bosses to support him in the future.

The campaign also marked Eleanor's assumption of a leadership role in Democratic politics. She was named chief of the Women's Division of the Smith organization, and Cordell Hull, the chairman of the Democratic National Committee, appointed her to head a subcommittee assigned to draft planks on social welfare legislation. She organized a staff that included her good friends Marion Dickerman and Nancy Cook; Elinor Morgenthau, the wife of Henry Morgenthau, Jr., a Dutchess County neighbor; and acquaintances from the settlement houses and the labor movement. Overcoming her shyness, she spoke before women's clubs, parent-teacher groups and statewide conferences. Howe went along with her a few times and sat in the back so he could provide a personal critique of her performance. To break Eleanor of a nervous giggle, he imitated her so she could see how it sounded. "Have something you want to say, say it and sit down," he advised her. Under Howe's tutelage, she developed a highly refined reportorial skill, and the information she brought back was invaluable to him and his machinations.

On the face of it, 1924 should have been a Democratic year. Not only had Smith won the governorship two years before, but the Democrats had carried several other states and reduced the Republican majorities in Congress to the vanishing point. The odor of corruption hung over the Republican administration in Washington. Warren Harding had died the previous August, universally mourned by the American people as the most genial of Presidents, but no sooner had Harding been succeeded, by Calvin Coolidge, than Teapot Dome and other scandals tumbled out of the White House closet. The hapless Harding had not stolen so much as a nickel, but friends, associates, and members of his Cabinet were discovered in cahoots with crooked businessmen. Harding's Secretary of the Interior became the first cabinet officer to go to jail; his Attorney General only narrowly escaped a similar fate, and his Secretary of the Navy was forced to resign because of a mixture of stupidity and criminal negligence. Fraud in the Veterans Bureau, graft in the Office of Alien Property Custodian, and conspiracy in the Justice Department were all part of Harding's legacy.

The most notorious of these scandals involved the naval oil reserves at Teapot Dome, in Wyoming. Private oil companies had been trying to gain access to the reserves since their inception, under the Wilson administration. Josephus Daniels recalled that during the close of one congressional session, "Mr. Roosevelt and I remained at the Capitol all night long watching the legislation . . . fearing that some act might be passed that would turn over these invaluable oil reserves to parties who laid claim upon them without even decent show of title." Albert B. Fall, the impecunious new Secretary of the Interior, had long been eyeing the reserves at Elk Hills, California, and at Teapot Dome, and persuaded Harding to remove them from the Navy Department and turn control of them over to him. Fall awarded a lease to the Elk Hills reserve to a company headed by Edward Doheny,* and not long after, Doheny's son presented Fall with a little black bag containing $100,000. Teapot Dome went to Harry Sinclair for little more than $300,000 and negotiable bonds. Word of the oil leases soon leaked, and a Senate committee launched an inquiry. But the Republicans were loath to investigate their own administration, and

---

* Doheny's name had been put in nomination for the vice-presidency at the Democratic convention in 1920. He withdrew in FDR's favor.

the leadership passed by default to Senator Thomas J. Walsh, a Montana Democrat. With patient thoroughness and grim determination, Walsh pursued Fall through a jungle of conflicting documents and lying witnesses. Ultimately, Fall was sent to prison for taking bribes, but Doheny and Sinclair, who had given him the money, escaped punishment.

The Democrats were unable to take advantage of this political opportunity. For one thing, Coolidge projected an image of Puritan rectitude. Even though he had avoided action against the malefactors until Walsh and other investigators ferreted them out, he got the credit for fighting corruption. It was, as Roosevelt observed, a repetition of the Boston police strike, in which the city's mayor had settled the dispute and Coolidge then reaped the accolades. The Teapot Dome inquiry also revealed that McAdoo was on retainer as Doheny's lawyer, tarring him with scandal even though he had nothing to do with the oil leases. And there was Coolidge prosperity. The stock market had begun a dizzying upward spiral that was not to end until 1929, and most Americans, except for the farmers who had not recovered from the recession of 1920–21, were enjoying the fruits of a high tariff, low taxes, and government support for business and industry. Production and employment were rising, and if workers complained that wages lagged, they could console themselves with relatively stable prices.

Perhaps the greatest obstacle to a Democratic victory was the divided state of the party itself. While political trends at both the state and the local levels were running in favor of the Democrats, the party was split by regional rivalries and conflicting moralities. There were two major factions: one urban and northeastern, of immigrant stock, opposed to Prohibition and primarily Catholic; the other rural and predominately western and southern, ardently dry and Protestant. These differences were aggravated by the racial and religious bigotry that had swept the country in the wake of the Red Scare. Grounded in biblical fundamentalism, anti-Catholicism, and anti-Semitism, it fed on rural America's fear of political and cultural dominance by the immigrant rabble of the cities. Such tensions provided fertile ground for the resurrected Ku Klux Klan, and by 1924, the Invisible Empire reached beyond the South and was a powerful political force in Oregon, California, Oklahoma, Kansas, and Indiana.

Al Smith's candidacy became a lightning rod for all these animosities. With his ever-present brown derby, cigar, and rasping New York accent, he symbolized everything that rural America hated and feared. Smith was a progressive governor—his "little welfare state" was responsible for improved educational opportunities, housing-law reform, aid for dependent children, the rebuilding of hospitals, an expansion of the parks system, salary increases for teachers, and the reorganization of the state government

—but to rural voters his candidacy conjured up the dreaded specter of rum and Romanism.

Realizing that Smith was doomed to defeat unless he could broaden his base, Roosevelt counseled him to water down his opposition to Prohibition and to appeal to the economically distressed farmers. At Roosevelt's urging, Smith issued a statement designed to take the edge off his opposition to Prohibition: "No matter what we may think of the Volstead Law, it is the law of the land and we must support it." No one was fooled by this charade, however. Roosevelt had even less luck in persuading Smith to take an interest in agricultural affairs and farm relief. Roosevelt later described an incident that illuminated Smith's parochialism. While he was conferring with a group of Kansas delegates, Smith entered the room "like a breeze, in a swallowtail coat, a silk hat at a rakish angle, and with the usual cigar in his mouth. 'Hello, hello, my boy, and how's things?' the candidate called out. 'Hello, boys,' said Smith, shaking hands with Roosevelt's callers. 'Glad to see you. Y'know, the other day some boys were in from Wisconsin, and I learned something. I always thought Wisconsin was on the other side of the lake. It's on this side. Glad to know it. Glad to know more about the place where the good beer comes from.' And this to delegates from a strong Prohibition state."

Louis Howe sardonically predicted disaster. "The leading candidates will be trotted out one after another for enough ballots to make it evident that they cannot secure the nomination, and after that they will hold a conference in a back room amongst the leaders of the largest blocks of votes at which some unguessable and perhaps unknown John Smith will be picked," he declared. "Mr. Roosevelt is sitting perfectly tight and not even talking about any second choice in case Smith does not get through."

Howe proved to be a remarkably accurate prophet. Storm warnings fluttered over Madison Square Garden as the Democratic convention opened, on June 24, 1924. Every prejudice, every animosity in American society simmered in the unbearably humid hall. The explosion was not long in coming. Shortly after the convention was gaveled to order, by Senator Thomas J. Walsh of Montana, the permanent chairman, it split wide open over a platform plank specifically denouncing the Klan. In an effort to conciliate the rural Protestant factions, Roosevelt urged Smith's followers to support a compromise denouncing all secret organizations but mentioning none by name. Angry words, fistfights, and shouted obscenities punctuated the bitter debate that ended with the defeat of the hardline plank by a single vote. Only the presence of a special detail of a thousand New York City policemen prevented a full-scale riot when the tally was announced.

Under normal circumstances, campaign managers do not make nominating speeches, but Bourke Cockran, the silver-tongued Tammany orator who would have placed Smith's name in nomination, had died unexpectedly. Smith auditioned several prominent Democrats as replacements but was dissatisfied with them all. Eventually, he gambled on Roosevelt, who already had a reputation as an effective speaker. "I'll do it if you dispense with the tryout," Roosevelt told him. Smith grinned and gave his assent. Judge Proskauer prepared a speech with a quotation from William Wordsworth that likened Smith to the "Happy Warrior," but Roosevelt objected strenuously. "You can't give poetry to a political convention," he said, and produced a draft of his own.

"So I took Herbert Bayard Swope, the editor [of the New York World] with me to Roosevelt's place up the Hudson so that we could work it out," Proskauer later recalled. "Swope made the mistake of the century. He picked up Roosevelt's speech, turned to me and said, 'Joe, this is awful. It's dull. It won't do.' And he flung it on the floor. Then he picked up my 'Happy Warrior' speech. 'This is great, Frank,' he said to Roosevelt. 'You've done it just the way it ought to be.' Well, Roosevelt damn near went through the roof. We fought and fought. Finally I told him, 'Frank, I have this message from the Governor: Either you give this speech or you don't nominate him.'"

Unwilling to be seen in a wheelchair, Roosevelt walked to his seat on the floor of the Garden on crutches before most of the delegates arrived. As a concession to his infirmity, he had an aisle seat with arms so he could lower himself into it. The scattered spectators who observed the daily ritual of his arrival greeted him with applause. Sixteen-year-old James Roosevelt carried messages for his father and hovered about during demonstrations to make certain that he was not injured. At day's end, after the other delegates had left, Roosevelt was helped into a wheelchair and whisked out of the hall. The nominating speech was the real test of his comeback, however, for no one knew if, balanced on his steel braces, he could hold an audience.

"As we walked—struggled, really—down the aisle to the rear of the platform, he leaned heavily on my arm, gripping me so hard it hurt," James recalled more than a half century later. "It was hot, but the heat in that building did not alone account for the perspiration which beaded on his brow. His hands were wet. His breathing was labored. Leaning on me with one arm, working a crutch with the other, his legs locked stiffly in his braces, he went on his awkward way." Thunderous cheers greeted Roosevelt's arrival on the platform, and flash bulbs flickered across the Garden like heat lightning. Before venturing forward, he asked Joe Guffey, a Pennsylvania politico, to "go over and shake the rostrum" to make certain that it would support him when he leaned against it. Guffey complied; the rostrum appeared solid. Relaxing his grip on his son's arm, Roosevelt took up his other crutch and swung himself forward, step by step, as the delegates and spectators held their breath, fearing that the gallant figure might stumble or fall. He reached the rostrum and, braced against it, cast aside his crutches. With a toss of his classic head he drew himself erect and smiled triumphantly into the glaring spotlights.

The crowd went wild. Several minutes passed before the cheering stopped to allow Roosevelt to speak. Skillfully pacing himself, Roosevelt dominated his audience, and playing upon it as if it were a giant organ, he brought his listeners to their feet with a call for unity. "You equally who come from the great cities of the East and from the plains and hills of the West, from the slopes of the Pacific and from the homes and fields of the Southland, I ask you in all seriousness . . . to keep first in your hearts and minds the words of Abraham Lincoln—'With malice toward none, and charity for all.'" And then he turned to praise of Al Smith. "He has a power to strike at every error and wrongdoing that makes his adversaries quail before him. He has a personality that carries to every hearer not only the sincerity but the righteousness of what he says. He is the 'Happy Warrior' of the political battlefield. . . ."

The lid blew off the Garden and the cheering lasted for an hour and thirteen minutes. Connoisseurs of political oratory universally agreed that it was by far the best speech of the convention. Following this display of courage and eloquence, Roosevelt was probably more popular than any of the candidates, and most observers believed the image of the "Happy Warrior" better suited him than Smith. But no speech could prevent the Democrats from committing suicide, and the deadlocked 1924 convention became a classic example of a political calamity. The balloting droned on for two weeks, with neither Smith nor McAdoo able to obtain the 732 votes needed for a two-thirds majority. Red-eyed, unshaven, and drunk with bootleg booze and fatigue, the delegates often came to blows. This was the first convention to be broadcast, and the cry that began every roll call—"Alabama casts twenty-four votes for Oscar W. Underwood!"—resounded across the nation like a drumbeat.

Throughout the proceedings, Roosevelt counseled compromise and tried to prevent the party from tearing itself apart. As ballot followed weary ballot, Earle Looker, a columnist for the New York *Herald Tribune,* said the delegates cast "lingering looks at him over their shoulders." Roosevelt was "the one man whose name would stampede the convention were he put in nomination. . . . From the time Roosevelt made his speech in nomination of Smith . . . he has been easily the foremost figure on floor or platform. . . . Without the slightest intention or desire to do anything of the sort, he has done for himself what he could not do for his candidate." And as the New York *Evening World* observed: "No matter whether Governor Smith wins or loses, Franklin D. Roosevelt stands out as the real hero of the Democratic Convention of 1924. Adversity has lifted him above the bickering, the religious bigotry, conflicting personal ambitions and petty sectional prejudices. It has made him the one leader commanding the respect and admiration of delegations from all sections of the land."

Following the ninety-third ballot—Smith had received 355½ votes and McAdoo 314—Roosevelt returned to the rostrum as rumors swept the Garden that a break was imminent. Roosevelt pointed out that although Smith led in the balloting it was clear that neither of the frontrunners could win the nomination, and for the sake of unity, Smith would withdraw if his rival would do the same. But McAdoo stubbornly refused to give way. Slowly, votes began to shift to John W. Davis, of West Virginia, who had been Wilson's Solicitor General and envoy to Britain before becoming a prominent Wall Street lawyer. On the 103rd ballot, he was nominated as a compromise candidate. Charles W. Bryan, brother of the Great Commoner, was chosen as the vice-presidential nominee in an attempt to appease the West, angry over the choice of the attorney for the House of Morgan to head the ticket.

The nomination was worthless. Radio and the newspapers had carried the hatreds and passions of the Garden into the homes of the voters; nothing that Calvin Coolidge might have said or done could have damaged the Democrats more. And Davis offered little in the way of an alternative to Coolidge. Although an able and intelligent man, he was as conservative as his opponent. He often sounded more like the Republican candidate than Coolidge. The real opposition to Coolidge was offered by Senator Robert M. La Follette, of Wisconsin, candidate of the Independent Progressive party. An alliance of insurgent Republicans, Socialists, the Farmer-Labor party, and the railroad brotherhoods, its members charged that the two major parties had turned their backs on the farmer and the workingman. Sensing a disaster and fearing La Follette might throw the election into the House of Representatives, Roosevelt pleaded ill health and did not actively campaign for Davis.

Eleanor, however, took an active role in Al Smith's campaign for reelection as governor. His opponent was Theodore Roosevelt, Jr., who as assistant Secretary of the Navy under Harding had been bespattered by the fallout from Teapot Dome through no fault of his own. "Of course he [Smith] can win," she declared, in a seconding speech at the Democratic State Convention. "How can he help it when the Republican convention . . . did everything to help him." This thrust against her first cousin was loudly applauded. Still smarting from Ted's attack on her husband four years before, she was persuaded by Louis Howe to tail him about the state with a giant-size teapot that spouted real steam mounted on the roof of her car to remind the voters of Teapot Dome. "It was a pretty base thing for her to do," declared an angry Alice Longworth. Years later, Eleanor tended to agree. "In the thick of political fights one always feels that all methods of campaigning are honest and fair, but I think now that it was a rough stunt." Ted lost the governorship by 108,000 votes, although Coolidge carried New York by nearly 9 million votes and won the election by a lopsided majority.†

Roosevelt was undeterred by the magnitude of the defeat suffered by the Democrats. "In 1920 . . . I remarked . . . that I did not think the nation would elect a Democrat again until the Republicans had led us into a serious period of depression and unemployment. I still [think] that forecast holds true, for much as we Democrats may be the party of honesty and progress the people will not turn out the Republicans while wages are good and the markets are booming," he declared.

Throughout the Coolidge era, much of Roosevelt's attention was consumed by the struggle to walk again. During the next two winters, he again cruised off South Florida in the *Larooco*, but Florida had begun to pall on Roosevelt. The water was often not warm enough for him to swim, there was the ever-present danger of sharks, sand beaches were not plentiful, and a houseboat was not very practical, with the difficulty of transferring to the launch that carried him ashore. Returning from a fishing trip shortly after the *Larooco* left Miami in February 1925, he fell and tore the ligaments in his right knee so badly that he could not exercise for a month. Missy LeHand later told Frances Perkins he was sometimes so depressed that, unable to face his guests with his usual gaiety, he remained in his room until noon.

John Lawrence, the *Larooco*'s co-owner, rarely used the boat, so most of the considerable operating cost was borne by Roosevelt at a time when his expenses were outrunning his income.‡ Cash was so short that he suggested that Eleanor cut monthly household expenses by three hundred dollars and let one of the servants go, because his frequent absences from New York meant smaller food bills and less work. He also sold some of his naval prints, for $4,537—which may not have compensated him for the unhappiness of giving them up. Lawrence agreed they should put

† Coolidge won 54 percent of the popular vote; Davis had 28.8 percent and La Follette 16.5 percent.
‡ FDR's income in 1923 was $40,059.51 and his expenses $43,553.68. His investments dropped in value from $313,830.68 to $299,742.06. Expenses again exceeded income, by $9,454.36, the following year, but his investments increased in value by $10,461.04. In 1925, he spent $9,625.16 more than he took in, while the value of his investments increased by $13,601.19. During 1925, the last year for which detailed figures are available, his income was $53,766.85, as compared to expenses of $74,588.64. Reflecting Coolidge prosperity, his investments increased in value from $323,801.29 to $377,712.47.

Larooco on the block, but there were no buyers, and she was finally wrecked by a hurricane in September 1926.

Roosevelt had already found a substitute. In the summer of 1924, George Foster Peabody, a prominent philanthropist and financier, had told him about a remarkable pool at a resort which Peabody owned at Warm Springs, in western Georgia, that had helped cure a young man who had been paralyzed by polio from the waist down. After three years of exercises in the buoyant water, the youth, Louis Josephs, was able to walk with only a cane, Peabody said. Immediately interested, Roosevelt decided to visit Warm Springs while on his way to Florida. That October, he, Eleanor, and Missy LeHand arrived there to find a shabby summer resort that consisted of a dilapidated old hotel, a handful of whitewashed cottages, and a large outdoor swimming pool—all set amid the red clay hills of Georgia. The place had been an important spa before the Civil War—Henry Clay and John C. Calhoun had been among the visitors— but had long since fallen out of fashion. Although there was some striking scenery, much of the surrounding area was eroded and dotted with the neglected shacks of black and white sharecroppers. It seemed poor country compared to the well-tended Hudson River Valley, and the Roosevelts probably looked at each other and silently concluded they had come on a wild-goose chase.

But as soon as Roosevelt lowered himself into the mineral-laden waters of the pool, he was immediately enchanted by the "heavenly warmth" that flowed over his withered legs. "How marvellous it feels!" he cried. "I don't think I'll ever get out!" Because of the 88-degree temperature of the water and its buoyancy, he was able to remain in the pool for hours—swimming, floating, and kicking his legs without becoming enervated.* He also met Louis Josephs that morning and conferred with Dr. James Johnson, the young man's physician. Johnson told him that Josephs had begun to show progress after only three weeks of daily and prolonged immersion in the pool. Roosevelt began his own course of exercise that day, and for the first time since he had been stricken, three years before, he felt life in his toes. "The pool," he wrote his mother, "is really wonderful."

Eleanor Roosevelt returned to New York City after a few days. Although the nearby town had been named Bullochville, for her paternal grandmother's family, she was appalled by the poverty and neglect all about her. She startled the wife of Thomas W. Loyless, the lessee-manager of the resort, by asking why blacks were not admitted to the

---

* The Warm Springs pool is fed by a subterranean spring created by rain that falls on Pine Mountain, about five miles away, and then runs down 3,800 feet to a deep pocket of rock, where it is warmed and returned to the surface at a rate of 800 gallons a minute. If the feat were to be duplicated by mechanical means, engineers estimated at the time, it would require twenty tons of coal every twenty-four hours.

resort. She was impressed, however, by the kindness of the people. Hardly a day passed when the Roosevelts did not receive a gift of wood for the fireplace, a chicken, or flowers from the neighbors.

Mornings were spent in the pool and sunbathing; in the afternoon, Roosevelt kept up with his voluminous correspondence, played rummy with his secretary, or worked on his stamp collection. Sometimes, Loyless drove him around the countryside, over the pine-studded mountains to Greenville, the county seat of Meriwether County, and on to the villages of West Point and Hamilton. Cheerful and friendly as always, Roosevelt not only talked to business and political leaders but had Loyless stop so he could chat with farmers they passed on the road. Roosevelt and Loyless became good friends, and he learned that Loyless had twice been driven from the editorships of Georgia newspapers because of his outspoken attacks on the Ku Klux Klan.

One day, Roosevelt invited several of his new friends to a cocktail party at his cottage, a party that had to be discreet because of Prohibition. Missy and Loyless' sister were bringing in a tray of drinks from the kitchen when there was a knock on the door. Missy nonchalantly opened it to find herself suddenly confronted by the local Baptist preacher. The cocktails were hastily covered with an apron as Roosevelt almost doubled up with laughter.

Basil O'Connor came down during the latter part of Roosevelt's stay to put the finishing touches on plans to form a law partnership to be known as Roosevelt & O'Connor. Shortly before departing for Georgia, Roosevelt had told Van-Lear Black of his intention to sever his relationship with Emmet, Marvin & Roosevelt. "The other partners are dear delightful people, but the type of law business does not in the least appeal to me as it is mainly estates, wills, etc., all of which bore me to death." Roosevelt also had an ulterior motive in inviting O'Connor. He was already considering investing in Warm Springs and converting it into a center for the treatment of the victims of polio and similar diseases and wanted his advice. O'Connor advised him not to take the plunge—but this did not affect Roosevelt's enthusiasm. By the time he left, at the end of October, he joyfully reported that he was able to walk in water only four feet deep without braces "almost as well as if I had nothing the matter with my legs."

Returning in April 1925 from Florida, Roosevelt found that his first visit had put Warm Springs "on the map." The Atlanta *Journal* had reported that he was "swimming his way back to health and strength" and, reprinted nationally, the story attracted other polio victims to the resort in search of a cure. Several were on hand when he arrived and more were on the way, although the resort was ill-equipped and ill-prepared to help them. A few years later, Roosevelt described the situation:

We did not know what to do with them, so I sent for Dr. Johnson. He came over and looked them over and guaranteed that they did not have heart trouble or some thing from which they would suddenly die, and he recommended cream and fattening diets for some and he recommended very little food for some of the others.

. . . I undertook to be doctor and physiotherapist, all rolled into one. I taught Fred Botts to swim. I taught them all at least to play around in the water. I remember there were two quite large ladies; and when I was trying to teach them an exercise I had really invented, which was the elevating exercise in the medium of water, one of these ladies found great difficulty in getting both feet down to the bottom of the pool. Well, I would take one large knee and I would force this large knee and leg down until the foot rested firmly on the bottom. And then I would say, "Have you got it?" and she would say, "Yes," and I would say, "Hold it, hold it." Then I would reach up and get hold of the other knee very quickly and start to put it down and then number one knee would pop up. This used to go on for an hour and a half at a time; but before I left in the spring, I would get both knees down at the same time.

Like many of Roosevelt's stories, there was some exaggeration to this tale, but "Dr. Roosevelt," as his fellow "polios" called him, was in some ways a pioneer therapist. He had picked up considerable lore about infantile paralysis and its treatment and, along with Dr. Johnson, worked out charts for measuring muscle growth and strength, developed special therapeutic exercises, and was the laughing, zestful leader of games of water polo. After an hour or so of exercise or games, Roosevelt would call out, "All right now, everybody stay in the sun for an hour!" Resting beside the pool, the "polios" compared notes and discussed their progress. "Dr. Roosevelt" offered advice based on his own experience. "You've got to *know* you're going to improve," he often said, cigarette holder at a jaunty 45-degree angle. "Keep yourselves mentally alert; don't lose contact with the things you enjoyed before infantile paralysis."

Some of the regular guests who returned to Warm Springs with the opening of the season were put off by the cripples, with their wheelchairs and braces. Afraid of catching the dread disease, they shunned the "polios" and demanded they be banned from the pool and dining room. Roosevelt was angered by this unfeeling prejudice, but he realized that Loyless needed the money provided by these guests. He suggested that the basement of the hotel be converted to a dining room for his "gang" and had a smaller pool dug about thirty feet away from the larger one and hidden from sight by a shed. Loyless' health had begun to fail—he would be dead in a year from cancer—and he asked Roosevelt to temporarily take over the column he wrote three times a week for the Macon *Telegraph*. It would be easy, Loyless assured him, and was an opportunity to test out his views on current affairs on the public.

Between April 16 and May 25, 1925, Roosevelt wrote eight columns for the *Telegraph*, which published them on its editorial page under the standing headline, "Roosevelt Says."† Basically a restatement of themes already presented in speeches, these columns, like his editorials in the Harvard *Crimson* two decades before, were bland and avoided controversy. Roosevelt thought enough of his columns to offer them for syndication, but no paper showed an interest except the Atlanta *Constitution*.

Still in search of the elusive cure, Roosevelt investigated all avenues to health, and in August 1925 went to Marion, Massachusetts, to work with Dr. William McDonald, a prominent neurologist, who had devised a "walking board" for polio patients. Roosevelt's natural optimism was buoyed by McDonald's promise to have him walking without braces. As at Warm Springs, he swam every morning, but the water was colder than in Georgia, so he could not stay in as long. For two or three hours a day, he went around and around on an oblong board, pulling himself along by the railing and dragging his legs behind him. "This time I think I have hit it," he declared, and instead of spending a month with McDonald, as intended, he remained in Marion until nearly the end of the year. In December, he walked nearly a block with only a brace on his left leg and a cane. Believing himself to be on the verge of walking unaided, he returned the following summer, but despite valiant efforts this was the high point of his cure.

In April 1926, Roosevelt purchased Warm Springs from George Peabody for $195,000, with $25,000 down and the balance payable over ten years. It was a considerable burden for a man with a son on the "Gold Coast" at Harvard, three more at Groton, and a daughter to marry off. Basil O'Connor, who drafted the agreement, advised against making the purchase, and his mother refused to invest in Warm Springs.‡ For his money, Roosevelt received the rundown resort hotel, the handful of cottages, the pool, twelve hundred acres of surrounding woodland on the side of a mountain—and a dream. He saw Warm Springs as a center for the treatment of polio victims and a resort for prosperous vacationers, and enthusiastically threw himself into an extensive and expensive program of rebuilding and renovating. Always eager to improve desolate landscapes— Eleanor said that he once told her that after his years in the White House were over he would like to go to some desert land in the Middle East and make a garden bloom—he began building new cottages, had new pools dug, hacked out new roads, and planned a nine-hole golf course.

† The money received by FDR for the columns went to Loyless, who badly needed it.
‡ FDR received a financial windfall in 1927 when his half brother, James Roosevelt Roosevelt, died at the age of seventy-three and left him a legacy of $100,000.

Worried about the magnitude of the financial obligation assumed by her husband, Eleanor had strong reservations about Warm Springs. "I know you love creative work, my only feeling is that Georgia is somewhat distant for you to keep in touch with what is really a big undertaking," she wrote him. "One cannot, it seems to me, have *vital* interests in widely divided places, but that may be because I'm old and rather overwhelmed by what there is to do in one place and it wearies me to think of even undertaking to make new ties. Don't be discouraged by me; I have great confidence in your extraordinary interest and enthusiasm. It is just that I couldn't do it."

Roosevelt brought in Dr. Leroy W. Hubbard, an orthopedic surgeon who had just retired from the New York State Board of Health, to direct the medical program, and Helena Mahoney, a graduate nurse, and a few physiotherapists, to assist him. Warm Springs had difficulty in winning professional acceptance, however. Learning that the American Orthopedic Association was meeting in Atlanta, a short drive away, Roosevelt sought permission to appear at the convention and report on the beneficial effects of underwater treatment upon polio victims. He was quickly rebuffed as a layman. Refusing to be put off, he telephoned a convention official, who also told him he could not appear. Three hours later, he showed up at the meeting and lobbied the members from his wheelchair. Roosevelt's appeal resulted in unofficial approval of the continuation of the water treatment at Warm Springs on an experimental basis, while three orthopedists investigated the program and Roosevelt's claims of success. The committee observed the treatment of twenty-three cases during the summer and autumn of 1926 and after improvement was noted in each case, recommended the establishment of a permanent hydrotherapeutic center at Warm Springs.

Nevertheless, Roosevelt's plan for a combined resort and therapeutic center foundered on friction between the "polios" and the able-bodied vacationers. Early in 1927, he decided to concentrate on rehabilitating victims of infantile paralysis, and the profit-making corporation that had been organized the year before was replaced by the nonprofit Georgia Warm Springs Foundation. Roosevelt was named president, O'Connor became secretary-treasurer, and Louis Howe was made a trustee. Expenses were heavy and the income received from patients did not begin to cover costs, so Roosevelt found himself writing checks and signing notes with abandon. Some of the pressure was eased after Warm Springs' renown grew and prominent people began to make charitable contributions to the foundation. Edsel Ford, son of Henry Ford, gave twenty-five thousand dollars for the construction of a glass enclosure for the large pool so it could be used the year around. Within a few years—primarily because of Roosevelt's increasing prominence—Warm Springs became an international center for the study of infantile paralysis and the treatment of its victims.

But, more than a place where Roosevelt hoped to win a final victory over polio, Warm Springs became his second home, as beloved as Hyde Park. He had a cottage built for his use* and purchased a 1,750-acre farm on the side of Pine Mountain, where he tried experiments aimed at proving to southern farmers that cotton was not the only crop that would pay. He bought pure-blooded cattle and loaned sires to his neighbors and looked for the best and quickest-growing longleaf pine to substitute for the weedy and worthless second-growth jack pine that covered the area. But the farm did not prosper, and the losses were considerable before Roosevelt ended his experiments.

Roosevelt loved the warm Georgia sun, the smell of peach blossoms, and the carpet of treetops stretching to the horizon. No miracles were to occur at Warm Springs, but he certainly benefited from the relaxed atmosphere and the easy pace of life. An ingenious mechanic rigged a small Ford so that it could be controlled by hand, and Roosevelt spent part of each day exploring the back roads and visiting neighboring farmers. From these casual conversations, he learned much about the farmers' problems and grievances. Warm Springs also marked a turning point in his relations with his wife. Never having gotten over the cultural shock of her first visit and increasingly busy with her own work, Eleanor seldom came to Georgia, and Missy LeHand presided over the Roosevelt cottage. For the rest of their lives, the Roosevelts were to be apart much of the time, pursuing their own goals.†

In need of money, Roosevelt engaged in a wide range of business activities that brought him into conflict with his personal philosophy. On the one hand, he believed business must be socially responsible, while he also hoped to make a financial killing in the booming economy. In most cases, the lure of a quick profit prevailed. The projects in which he took a flyer were usually highly speculative, in companies offering new products or services that promised a large return or none at all. But the buoyant optimism that served him well in his fight for physical recovery played him false in business. Most of his investments were unprofitable, and

---

* The Little White House, the cottage in which FDR died, was not built until 1932.
† Elliott Roosevelt raised the possibility of a love affair between FDR and Missy LeHand in *An Untold Story: The Roosevelts of Hyde Park* (New York: Dell Publishing Co., 1974). His sister and brothers issued a statement disassociating themselves from the book, and James Roosevelt flatly denied the charge in *My Parents*. "Missy adored father, as he adored her," he wrote. "I suppose you can say they came to love one another, but it was not a physical love." The one real romance in her life, according to James Roosevelt, was William C. Bullitt, a prominent diplomat, but he broke off their engagement. Bullitt's first wife was Louise Bryant, the widow of journalist-revolutionary John Reed.

some endangered his reputation. He engaged in business in the same way
he played poker: preferring seven-card stud with deuces wild to more staid
versions of the game.

Roosevelt remained fascinated by Arthur P. Homer, the slick super-
salesman whose luck in selling the Navy small-boat engines during the
war had stirred conflict-of-interest charges against Roosevelt. Before Roosevelt stepped down as assistant Secretary of the Navy, Homer broached a
plan for an oil refinery that he claimed would provide the Navy with a de-
pendable supply of fuel that would be free from market pressures. The
refinery was to be built in Fall River, Massachusetts, conveniently the
home town of Louis Howe's wife. Roosevelt pushed the scheme through
despite the objection of Josephus Daniels and some skeptical admirals.
They turned out to be correct, for no sooner had the refinery been completed than oil prices plunged, turning the plant into a white elephant.
Both Roosevelt and Howe, who invested in the project, sold their holdings at a loss. Five years later, Homer was back with a plan to corner the
lobster market. Once again the company failed, costing Roosevelt twenty-
six thousand dollars. That finally ended Homer's magic as far as he was
concerned, but it did not dull his appetite for get-rich-quick schemes.

A few of Roosevelt's investments had a certain farcical aspect about
them. Intrigued by giant dirigibles such as the *Graf Zeppelin*, he
helped organize a company that was to offer airship service between New
York and Chicago, but it never got off the ground. He planned to sell advertising in taxicabs, and to market maté, an Argentine herb tea, in the
United States. He invested in an oil company that wildcatted in Wyoming and struck sulphur instead of petroleum. "Why not go into the
sulphur bath industry—look at Hot Springs!" Howe needled. He planned
a chain of resorts from Lake Placid to Warm Springs and tried to interest
General Electric in an elaborate scheme to develop the tidal power of Pas-
samaquoddy Bay. He was a director of the Compo Thrift Bond Corporation, which was to sell small-denomination bonds through savings banks.
The firm went broke, costing Roosevelt his twenty-five-hundred-dollar investment. Some of these activities prompted a letter from the Society for
Promoting Financial Knowledge expressing concern "about the use of
your name to further the sale of stock in new promotions that . . . are
business risks of the more hazardous type. . . ."

Living comfortably on inherited wealth, he cared little about money
for its own sake and, unlike Al Smith, who had risen from the Fulton
Fish Market, he did not regard money as power. Independent wealth had
greatly assisted his political career and he was fully aware of what money
could buy in the way of gracious living and, in his own case, medical care,
but he was not competitive about money. He never believed that the business ethic should be dominant in American society or that any restriction

on business was a threat to the American way of life. He regarded moneymaking as an adventure; if he ever considered the social implications of his activities, he had no trouble convincing himself that he was providing capital for new and adventuresome businesses that would not have been financed by conservative capitalists.

Not all of Roosevelt's investments were failures, however. Taking advantage of the skyrocketing inflation in Weimar, Germany, he became president of United European Investors, a Canadian corporation, which bought up devalued marks and used them to buy shares in German industry. The syndicate eventually declared a 200 percent profit, and Roosevelt made about five thousand dollars on his investment. Later, critics charged that he had made money on the miseries of the German people, but he pointed out that the company had funneled a hundred thousand marks into a shaky economy. He also made money by investing in Photomaton, Inc., which placed quarter-in-the-slot automatic cameras in some eight thousand locations, and in the Sanitary Postal Service Company, which marketed postage stamps through vending machines.‡ These two companies were merged into the Consolidated Automatic Merchandising Company, which operated clerkless stores that sold goods through vending machines. With the onslaught of the depression, critics claimed that Camco contributed to unemployment, but Roosevelt explained that he had become a director only because his two companies had been merged into Camco, and he had soon resigned anyway.

One of Roosevelt's adventures provided an education in business self-regulation and cast a long shadow. In 1922, he became president of the American Construction Council, organized by contractors, architects, engineers, and the construction unions to create stability in the building industry and to improve its image. The position paid no salary and over the next six years caused him a number of headaches, but it provided Roosevelt with a platform from which to keep his name before the public. Roosevelt's position was similar to that of the baseball and movie "czars," Judge K. M. Landis and Will Hays, respectively, but unlike them, he had little authority.

Such associations were the brainchild of Herbert Hoover, Secretary of Commerce under both Harding and Coolidge. Hoover was a firm believer in "business statesmanship," convinced that businessmen could lay aside private gain for the public good under the eye of a benevolent government and that trade associations would provide self-regulation to forestall popular demand for government regulation. Rival producers would pool credit information, cost formulae, and other information and curb unfair marketing practices. But in establishing "fair" and "unfair" pricing policies, they sailed close to the Sherman Anti-Trust Act. Endorsing the

‡ FDR paid $3 a share for his Photomaton stock and sold it for $17.

Hoover doctrine, Roosevelt said: "The tendency lately has been toward regulation of industry. Something goes wrong somewhere in a given branch of work, immediately the public is aroused, the press, the pulpit call for an investigation. That is fine, that is healthy . . . but government regulation is not feasible. It is unwieldy, expensive. . . . The public doesn't want it; the industry doesn't want it."

Roosevelt's participation in the American Construction Council was consistent with his belief that in business, public service and public welfare should be as important as profits. "Our aim is solely to further the Public Good," he proclaimed. Nevertheless, he reaped little from the position except newspaper publicity. Lacking executive authority, there was not much he could do except advise and exhort. He tried to persuade the industry to cut speculative building, urged the public to take advantage of the reduced demand for materials and labor during the winter months, and despite opposition from the building-trades unions, tried to get them to relax numerical limits on apprentices. The major significance of this episode lay not in what was or what was not accomplished, but its effects on Roosevelt's thinking. Reflecting the ideas of the businessmen and promoters surrounding him, he was scornful of government regulation when he became president of the Council, but the experience convinced him that self-regulation of industry would not work without the force of law behind it.

In a glowing review of Claude G. Bowers' *Jefferson and Hamilton* written at the end of 1925, Roosevelt observed that Hamilton was "a fundamental believer in an autocracy. . . . Jefferson brought the government back to the hands of the average voter. . . . I have a breathless feeling . . . as I wonder, if, a century and a quarter later, the same contending forces are not again mobilizing. Hamiltons we have today. Is a Jefferson on the horizon?" Obviously, he thought there was—and his name was Franklin Delano Roosevelt.

Based upon his extensive if unorganized reading of American history, Roosevelt saw the 1920s as a repetition of the struggle between progressivism and conservatism. As a longtime progressive, he looked upon himself as a modern follower of Jefferson. Recognizing that conditions had been greatly altered since the last decade of the eighteenth century, he did not blindly accept Jefferson's philosophy. The task for contemporary Jeffersonians was to match Jeffersonian idealism with the imperatives of the machine age. "We have today side by side an old political order fashioned by a pastoral civilization and a new social order fashioned by a technical civilization," he wrote. "The two are maladjusted. Their creative interrelation is one of the big tasks ahead of American leadership."

In many respects, this same conflict was present in Roosevelt's own political, economic, and social views. Like Jefferson, he believed rural and small-town life was superior to the city, and ever since his political debut, in 1911, had worked for improved conditions for the farmer. And like Jefferson, he opposed a privileged position for the wealthy and supported a government that worked for the best interests of the ordinary citizen. These convictions had been reinforced by his service under Woodrow Wilson and his relations with such agrarians as Josephus Daniels. Yet, in his belief in centralism, Roosevelt's views paralleled those of Hamilton, rather than of Jefferson. To bridge this gap, Roosevelt created a Jeffersonianism that was not what the Sage of Monticello would have conceived it to be, but what Roosevelt thought was demanded by the requirements of modern society. The Jeffersonian belief in freedom from government was altered to freedom to use government to solve social problems.

Immediately following the rout of John Davis, in 1924, he and Louis Howe set out to revitalize the battered and demoralized Democratic party with a dose of this new Jeffersonianism—and with the practical goal of improving his own political prospects. Roosevelt had no official position in the party—he was merely a defeated vice-presidential candidate twice removed—but there was a vacuum of leadership to be filled. National headquarters consisted of "two ladies occupying one room in a Washington office building," and Clem Shaver, Davis' hand-picked choice as national chairman, was out imploring multimillionaires to endorse notes to pay off the party's debts. "Could anything be much more of a farce?" Roosevelt demanded. "We have no money, no publicity, no nothing!—not even any *plans* for having an organization." Letters were sent out to some three thousand leading Democrats, including all the delegates to the recent convention, urging an end to sectional feuding and suggesting reforms designed to give the party a liberal cast in contrast to Republican conservatism. "We are unequivocally the party of progress and liberal thought," he declared and sought ideas "to make the Democracy a stronger and more militant organization nationally." Roosevelt's own suggestions included an end to factionalism and localism, putting the national organization on a sound financial basis, meetings between Democratic leaders in the House and Senate to coordinate policy, and a smoother public-relations operation.

Response from the rank and file was so enthusiastic that Roosevelt wrote Senator Walsh suggesting that a national conference be called to hammer out a reform program for the party. Party conservatives saw no reason to bolster Roosevelt's position, however, and they torpedoed the proposal. Nevertheless, the seeds Roosevelt planted took root and blossomed. The national committee later created a publicity staff under the able direction of a former newsman named Charles Michelson, and Roosevelt's plea for closer cooperation between party leaders in Congress brought about a meeting to create "clear understandings" on politics and policies. Having learned the lesson of 1924, Roosevelt skirted all matters that would cause further schism. He realized that the White House would come to the Democrats only if the West and the South were rejoined with the East, and as the party's leading "harmonizer," he was the only prominent Democrat who appealed to all factions.

Roosevelt's ambitions required him to play a waiting game. He had to wait until 1928—when Al Smith would either move up to the presidency or out of political contention—before he could make his own bid for power. In the meantime, he broadened his education, assembling information from a variety of sources and adopting a more liberal position. Eleanor provided him with books that she thought he should read on the social and economic issues of the day, and if he seemed interested, invited their authors to visit. Roosevelt had a talent for making people feel comfortable in his company and getting them to talk about what they knew, and it stood him in good stead during this period. Among those whom Eleanor brought to see her husband were two friends she had met in the Women's Trade Union League, Rose Schneiderman and Maude Schwartz. Roosevelt learned a great deal from them about the inner workings of the labor movement, its ideals, and its goals. The suspicion of organized labor that had characterized his early years of politics faded, and later, a union leader would tell Frances Perkins, "You'd almost think he had participated in some strike or organizing campaign the way he knew and felt about it."

Mrs. Charles Hamlin arrived one evening to visit Roosevelt just as a young man was leaving to catch the Fall River night boat to New York. "After he had gone, Franklin told me that he was an east side Jew, a tailor, from New York. Franklin said he had a chance in this way to learn a great deal about the conditions in his life . . . at first hand. He felt he got to the bottom of situations that could and should be remedied."

Roosevelt was also weighing the advantages of public versus private power. He discussed the possibility that such great power sites as the St. Lawrence River, the Colorado River, and Muscle Shoals, on the Tennessee River, might be developed by the government to generate electric power and serve as yardsticks to measure the charges for production and transmission levied by private utilities. Such discussions led him to accept the proposals advanced by Senator George Norris of Nebraska that eventually created the Tennessee Valley Authority. To alleviate the distress of the farmer, Roosevelt supported some form of agricultural relief, looking with favor upon a plan put forward by former Governor Frank O. Lowden of Illinois. Farm prices would be raised by allowing cooperatives to purchase surplus crops and sell them abroad. Any losses on these foreign sales would be covered by an "equalization fee" paid by the farmer to the cooperative from the profits made on domestic sales, which were kept high by dumping the surplus on the overseas market.

Howe's nightmare was that Roosevelt might be induced to run for office prematurely. In 1926, Democratic leaders searching for a candidate to oppose Senator James W. Wadsworth, Jr., offered him the nomination. "There are two good reasons why I can't run for the Senate," Roosevelt declared. "The first is that my legs are coming back in such fine shape that if I devote another two years to them I shall be on my feet again without my braces. The 2nd is that I am temperamentally unfitted to be a member of the uninteresting body known as the United States Senate. I like administrative or executive work. . . ." An unstated reason for turning down the nomination was that if he campaigned for office he would have to take positions on the issues that were dividing the party, thereby stepping out of his role as mediator and damaging his future presidential prospects. The nomination went instead to Robert Wagner, who won a narrow victory over Wadsworth, and was to hold the seat for the rest of his life. Al Smith was elected to an unprecedented fourth term as governor—putting him on the springboard for another try at the presidential nomination in 1928.

Eleanor and Franklin Roosevelt announced their support for Smith as early as May 1927, and his chance to win the nomination this time seemed excellent. McAdoo had decided not to run, leaving the anti-Smith forces without a strong candidate; the power of the Ku Klux Klan was waning, disillusionment with Prohibition was growing even in rural areas, and party leaders were determined to prevent a recurrence of the 1924 fiasco. Having widened his acquaintance among southern Democrats during his visits to Florida and Warm Springs, Roosevelt did what he could to reduce religious prejudice against Smith. But he thought that even though Smith might win the nomination, he would be knifed in the November election. "I am very doubtful whether any Democrat can win in 1928," he confided to Josephus Daniels, as long as Coolidge prosperity continued. Coolidge himself chose not to run again, and the Republicans turned to Herbert Hoover, who as Secretary of Commerce was the chief apostle of the new economic age. "We in America today are nearer to the final triumph over poverty than ever before in the history of our land," he declared.

The Democratic convention in Houston was anticlimactic. Smith was nominated on the first ballot, Senator Joseph T. Robinson of Arkansas was chosen as his running mate, and a platform was adopted in a record three days. Houston officials were dismayed, because they had counted on the convention lasting at least six days. Once again, Roosevelt served as Smith's floor manager, and for the third time in eight years placed the

Governor's name in nomination for President. Low-keyed and simple in style, his speech was designed for the millions of listeners tuned in on the radio, rather than the fifteen thousand delegates and spectators at Houston, and revealed Roosevelt's early mastery of the new medium. America needs "a leader who grasps and understands not only the large affairs of business and government, but in an equal degree the aspirations of the individual, the farmer, the wage earner," Roosevelt declared. ". . . One who has the will to win—who not only deserves success but commands it. Victory is his habit—the happy warrior, Alfred E. Smith!"

But there was only a surface gloss of unity at Houston. Anti-Smith holdouts refused to make his nomination unanimous, and he received no votes in four southern states. Smith's candidacy rekindled fundamentalist fervor, and bigotry again bubbled to the surface. Bishop James Cannon, Jr., leader of the Southern Methodist Church, declared that "no subject of the Pope" would be allowed to enter the White House. Smith compounded his problems by failing to conciliate southern and western sentiment. Instead of turning to moderates like Roosevelt, who shared the confidence of Democrats in all sections of the nation, he consulted only with his own inner circle. Much to Roosevelt's dismay, he chose John J. Raskob, a "wet," a Catholic, an associate of the Du Ponts, and a General Motors millionaire, to head the National Committee. Like most self-made men, Smith was basically a conservative, and there was little in the way of issues to distinguish him from Hoover.

Roosevelt was asked by Smith to direct the Division of Commerce, Industry and Professional Activities, while Eleanor headed the women's division of the campaign. In this position, Roosevelt circulated a letter criticizing Hoover for "a most alarming desire to issue regulations and to tell business men generally how to conduct their affairs" and promised that Smith would take a hands-off attitude. He peppered the Governor with suggestions—most of which were ignored—and, bored and blocked from access to Smith by the tight little circle about the candidate, departed for Warm Springs in early September. "The campaign is working out in a way I, personally, would not have followed," he told Van-Lear Black, and added that he had no intention of becoming "one of the 'yes men'" in a campaign largely run by "the General Motors publicity and advertising staff."

Roosevelt went to Georgia with other motives than to merely continue his struggle to walk again—he wished to escape from the pressures for him to run for governor of New York. Realizing they needed to carry New York, with its forty-five electoral votes, Democratic leaders appealed to Roosevelt to accept the nomination. A torrent of letters, telegrams, and telephone calls poured in upon him, emphasizing that without his name on the ticket, Smith would be unable to carry the state. As a Protestant with upstate connections and an unblemished record, he would provide balance. Supported by Eleanor and Howe, Roosevelt remained adamant in his refusal to run.

He was convinced that his recovery from polio was so far advanced that he was on the verge of learning to walk with only a single leg brace and a cane, and wished to continue his treatment. Warm Springs was also financially shaky and needed his full support before it would be firmly established. Besides, Smith's campaign had failed to catch fire. Rumors circulated that he slept with nuns, was a drunk, and his election would mean that the Pope would be installed in the White House. "Watch the trains! The Pope may arrive perhaps on the northbound train tomorrow!" So cried a Klansman to a crowd in North Manchester, Indiana. The next day's northbound train was met by some fifteen hundred people. Howe expected Hoover to win two terms and thought Roosevelt should hold off running for governor until 1932 and be ready for the presidency in 1936. "I have had a difficult time turning down the Governorship," Roosevelt wrote his mother. "I only hope they don't try to stampede the convention . . . and nominate me and then adjourn!"

Unwilling to take "no" for an answer, Smith and his kitchen cabinet gathered in a Rochester hotel suite on October 1 to plot strategy, before the opening of the state Democratic convention. The need to nominate Roosevelt had been heightened by the choice of Albert Ottinger, the state attorney general, as the Republican candidate. Ottinger had waged an effective and well-publicized battle against consumer frauds, and as the first Jew to be nominated for governor, would have a strong appeal to New York City voters. To meet Roosevelt's objections to running, Herbert H. Lehman, an investment banker and liberal Democrat, agreed to run for lieutenant governor and assume much of the workload in Albany, while Raskob promised to underwrite financing for Warm Springs. But Roosevelt refused to accept Smith's telephone calls and left word that he was going on a picnic. Upon his return, he found a sheaf of telephone messages and telegrams, including one from his daughter, Anna,* that read: GO AHEAD AND TAKE IT, but YOU OUGHT TO BE SPANKED was his fatherly reply.

A reluctant Eleanor was pressed into tracking down her husband, and it was after midnight when they finally got him on the line.

Smith, Raskob, and Lehman took turns in beating down each of Roosevelt's reasons for refusing the nomination. "Don't you dare!" Missy LeHand kept saying to him whenever his resistance appeared to weaken. "Don't you dare!"

---

* Anna, then a tall and attractive girl of twenty, had, in May 1926, married Curtis B. Dall, a Wall Street broker, employed by Lehman Brothers, who was ten years older than herself.

"Frank, I told you I wasn't going to put this on a personal basis, but I've got to," said Smith at the conclusion of the long conversation.

Roosevelt tried to assure him that the political situation was not as bleak as it appeared and other candidates could win, but Smith pressed ahead.

"I want to ask you one more question: If those fellows nominate you tomorrow and adjourn, will you refuse to run?"

Roosevelt hesitated for a few moments before replying that he could not sanction the presentation of his name to the convention.

What would he do if he was actually nominated?

Rather than slamming the door with a flat refusal to run, he replied that he didn't know.

"All right," replied an exultant Smith. "I won't ask any more questions."

The following day, Roosevelt was nominated by acclamation as the Democratic candidate for governor of New York, and he accepted. But gloom enshrouded his friends. REGRET THAT YOU HAD TO ACCEPT BUT KNOW THAT YOU FELT IT OBLIGATORY, Eleanor telegraphed him. Louis Howe was less philosophical. BY WAY OF CONGRATULATIONS DIG UP TELEGRAM I SENT YOU WHEN YOU RAN IN SENATORIAL PRIMARIES—a reference to the ill-fated race for the Senate in 1914, which had also been made against Howe's advice. And Missy hoped that he would be defeated so he could continue his struggle to walk. But Roosevelt really had little choice. He could not have conscientiously refused a genuine draft unless he was willing to sacrifice his presidential ambitions. With so many concessions having been made to meet his personal requirements, a refusal to run might have been considered disloyal and caused trouble when he sought the White House on his own. "Well, I've got to run for governor," he said with a shrug. "There's no use in all of us getting sick about it!"

While expressing personal admiration for Roosevelt, Republican newspapers shed crocodile tears as they assailed Al Smith for heartlessly sacrificing a cripple on the altar of his ambition. To counter planted rumors that he was physically unable to campaign, Roosevelt announced he would appear before the voters in every corner of the state. "I was not dragooned into running by the Governor," he declared. ". . . I was drafted because all of the party leaders . . . insisted that my often-expressed belief in the policies of Governor Smith made my nomination the best assurance to the voters that these policies would be continued." Smith met the issue with characteristic bluntness. "A Governor does not have to be an acrobat," he told a press conference. "We do not elect him for his ability to do a double back flip or a handspring. The work of the Governorship is brainwork."

Leaving Tammany to deliver New York City—and the presence of Lehman on the ticket as lieutenant governor to counter Ottinger's appeal to Jewish voters—Roosevelt concentrated on the upstate counties. At his service was the nucleus of the staff that would later go with him to the White House: the easy-mannered, backslapping James A. Farley, new secretary of the state Democratic committee; Edward J. Flynn, boss of the Bronx; and a young secretary named Grace Tully; as well as such old hands as Henry Morgenthau and Missy LeHand. As usual, Louis Howe was in overall charge, organizing independent committees, issuing a flood of propaganda, and peppering the candidate with advice. Howe jealously guarded his relationship with Roosevelt, but despite frazzled tempers and conflicting ambitions, the new team performed well.

Recognizing that he was out of touch with state issues, Roosevelt had asked party headquarters to assign someone to assist him with campaign material and to write speeches. In mid-October, Samuel I. Rosenman, a young lawyer and former state legislator, struggled onto the Roosevelt campaign train with several suitcases crammed with red manila envelopes carefully labeled "Labor" and "Taxes" and "Public Power." His first meeting with the candidate was something of a surprise, for he had heard that Roosevelt was a playboy and weak and ineffective. "The broad jaw and upthrust chin, the piercing flashing eyes, the firm hands did not fit the description, . . ." Rosenman later recalled. "He was the country squire, dressed carefully—soft collar, loose-fitting tweed suit, well-used felt hat. He was friendly, but there was about his bearing an unspoken dignity which held off any undue familiarity."

For three days, as the train rattled westward through the tier of rich agricultural counties along the Pennsylvania border, Roosevelt ignored Rosenman and his red envelopes. He campaigned more vigorously for Smith than for himself, attacking bigotry in the heart of Klan country, and dwelled so strongly on national issues that the New York headquarters wired Rosenman: TELL THE CANDIDATE THAT HE IS NOT RUNNING FOR PRESIDENT BUT GOVERNOR. Happily for Rosenman, he did not have to pass on the message, for Roosevelt abruptly switched to state issues on his own.

Rosenman was put to digging into his envelopes for material on public power, agricultural relief, court reform, old-age pensions, and a broader health program. He was soon grinding out speech after speech, pounding away through the night at his typewriter. Roosevelt worked over the drafts at breakfast, revealing a remarkable ability to take complex facts and a forbidding array of statistics and pep them up. When he decided to speak about public power, Rosenman provided the details on Republican attempts to turn the state's hydroelectric resources over to private developers. Roosevelt glanced at the draft and dictated a new opening to a stenographer: "This is a history and a sermon on the subject of water power, and I preach from the Old Testament. The text is '*Thou shalt not steal.*'"

Wishing to have contact with more voters, Roosevelt switched from the train to an automobile for the rest of the campaign. This enabled him to make speeches at scores of crossroads and country villages that he would not have otherwise been able to reach. Two buses accompanied the caravan—one for the press and the other carrying stenographers, campaign paraphernalia, and mimeograph machines—as they rolled through the brilliant autumn foliage of the Mohawk Valley to Albany and then down the Hudson to New York City. In all, Roosevelt covered some thirteen hundred miles and gave about fifty speeches during the final three weeks of the campaign, a schedule that wore out many of his companions and laid all questions about his health and vigor to rest. "If I could keep on campaigning twelve months longer, I'd throw away my canes," he joyously proclaimed.

It was by no means easy for a crippled man to carry on this sort of campaign. Even the simple task of standing to make speeches in the back of his car and then sitting down was an effort. He could not climb stairs and sometimes had to be carried up fire escapes so he could speak in rented halls. Seeing him carried into a hall, Frances Perkins recalled that he had "accepted the ultimate humiliation which comes from being helped physically. He had accepted it smiling. He came up over that perilous, uncomfortable, and humiliating 'entrance,' and his manner was pleasant, courteous, enthusiastic. He got up in his braces, adjusted them, straightened himself, smoothed his hair, linked his arm in his son Jim's, and walked out on the platform as if this were nothing unusual. . . . I don't recall the speech at all. For me and for others who saw that episode his speech was less important than his courage."

Following his usual Election Day appearance at the town hall in Hyde Park to cast his vote, Roosevelt went to the Biltmore to receive the results. It was another dismal night for the Democratic ticket. As soon as the early returns were tallied, it was obvious that Smith was the victim of a Hoover landslide.† States that had been Democratic since before the Civil War were going Republican. Unlit cigar drooping in his mouth, Smith watched glumly as Hoover's margin mounted to 21,392,000 popular and 444 electoral votes to his own 15,016,000 and 87—the most sweeping victory scored by any candidate in the country's history. Hoover won all but eight states, cracked the Solid South, and to Smith's shock and dismay even carried New York by some one hundred thousand votes. "Well,"

† Hoover's victory touched off a boom in the stock market, and prices reached levels just short of the all-time record of March 1928.

Smith is supposed to have remarked, "the time just hasn't come yet when a man can say his beads in the White House."

Roosevelt appeared to have gone down with Smith. Many of Roosevelt's supporters drifted off, and the early editions of the newspapers reported a Republican sweep in New York State and the nation. Nevertheless, Roosevelt refused to concede. Looking over returns from some upstate districts, he told Sam Rosenman that the local politicos seemed to be up to the old trick of holding back returns to see how many votes they would have to stuff into the ballot boxes to overcome the Democratic lead in New York City. Roosevelt picked up the telephone and began calling the sheriffs in the slow counties, warning them that he would hold them personally responsible for any finagling. Ed Flynn issued a press statement charging the Republicans with fraud and announcing that the Democrats were immediately dispatching a hundred lawyers to the disputed areas. It was all bluff—but it was effective.

Returns from upstate began to come in faster, and the tide slowly turned in favor of Roosevelt. But not until morning was it certain that he had won, by only 25,564 out of some 4.25 million votes cast. Roosevelt jocularly referred to himself as the "one half of one per cent Governor," but the victory—no matter how narrow—had catapulted him into the national political spotlight. "You are," said Governor Harry F. Byrd of Virginia, "the hope of the Democratic party."

XIII

"I CAST THAT ONE VOTE!"

FLANKED BY MOTORCYCLE outriders with sirens scream-
ing, an automobile bearing Franklin and Eleanor Roosevelt swept up the
driveway to the ornate Executive Mansion in Albany on New Year's Eve
1928. "God bless you and keep you, Frank," declared Al Smith as he
greeted his successor on the front steps. "A thousand welcomes. We've
got the home fires burning and you'll find this a fine place to live." The
governor-elect was equally gracious. "I only wish Al Smith were going to
be here for the next two years," he said. The next day, Roosevelt, with a
hand resting on the family's old Dutch Bible, took the oath of office in
the crowded Assembly Chamber, thirty years to the day after Theodore
Roosevelt had been sworn in in the same room. But the cordiality that
surrounded the transfer of power veiled the tensions existing between the
new governor and his predecessor.

"I've *got* to be Governor of the State of New York and I have got to
be it MYSELF," Roosevelt had told Frances Perkins a few days earlier.
"If I weren't, if I didn't do it myself, something would be wrong." For
one thing, he had to prove to everyone that despite his crippled legs, he
possessed the will and the stamina to run the state on his own. And for
another, he suspected that Al Smith, reluctant to relinquish his grip on
the governorship to a man he regarded as a protégé, thought he could pull
the strings of the new administration from the sidelines. There were even
reports that the outgoing governor had reserved a suite in the DeWitt
Clinton Hotel, in Albany, so he could be on the scene to lend advice and
counsel. But Roosevelt quickly asserted his independence. Although he
lavishly praised Smith and promised that the new administration would

build upon his progressive record, he made clear his intentions to explore new areas, adopt new methods, and field a new team.

Smith had suggested that two ranking members of his "kitchen cabinet" be retained: Robert Moses, the aggressive and acid-tongued secretary of state, and Belle Moskowitz, his one-woman brain trust. Moses, Smith pointed out, was a dynamic administrator, was completely familiar with the newly enacted executive budget system, and was responsible for the ambitious parks and hospital construction programs that were the highlights of Smith's administration. Mrs. Moskowitz knew how to manipulate the machinery of government and, as a facile speechwriter, stood ready to begin work on Roosevelt's inaugural address. Roosevelt was aware of the amused contempt of Smith's associates for him—especially Moses, who had gibed that "he'll make a good candidate but a lousy governor"— and quickly turned thumbs down on him.* Moses remained as chairman of the state Council of Parks, however. Fearing that Mrs. Moskowitz might prove loyal to Smith, rather than to the new governor, both Eleanor and Louis Howe advised against giving her an appointment. "It will always be one for you and two for Al," said Eleanor. After some hesitation, her husband agreed.

Nevertheless, wishing to avoid an open break with Smith, he kept on most of the department heads from the former administration, and at his wife's urging, appointed Miss Perkins, chairman of the Industrial Board since 1919, to head the state's Department of Labor. Before making the appointment, he discussed it with Smith, who counseled caution, because as Roosevelt later told Miss Perkins, male employees wouldn't take orders from a woman. "You see, Al's a good progressive fellow but I am willing to take more chances," he chuckled. "I've got more nerve about women and their status in the world than Al has."

"But it was more of a victory for Al to bring himself to appoint a woman, never appointed before, when I was unknown, than it is for you when I have a record as a responsible public officer for more than ten years," she replied.

Following Roosevelt's inauguration, Smith retreated to New York City to head the company constructing the Empire State Building, not yet bitter—that was to come later—but somewhat uneasy at the unexpected stubbornness and surprising strength exhibited by the genial country squire. Eleanor Roosevelt best summed up the situation: "One of Franklin's main qualities, which Governor Smith was apparently unaware of, was that he never assumed any responsibility that he did not intend to

---

* The ill will between FDR and Moses was alleged to be rooted in the refusal of Moses to put Louis Howe on the state payroll as secretary of the Taconic State Park Commission, which was headed by Roosevelt. "If you want to pay personal debts and take care of your secretary, you can't do it in the park system," Moses later said he told FDR.

carry through." Roosevelt moved quickly to form his own inner circle of advisers. Ed Flynn, the astute Bronx leader who had been smoothly effective during the campaign, became secretary of state and chief dispenser of patronage. Sam Rosenman was named counsel to the governor, Henry Morgenthau became chairman of the Agricultural Advisory Commission and later commissioner of conservation, while Basil O'Connor, Roosevelt's law partner, was pressed into service to give advice. Missy LeHand and Grace Tully also came to Albany for jobs that put them on call twenty-four hours a day, seven days a week. Bright and ambitious young university professors from Cornell, Columbia, and Harvard found themselves drafted without pay to help "educate" the new governor in the intricacies of modern government or to ghost speeches and messages.

One familiar face was missing from what Roosevelt called his "privy council": that of Louis Howe. Temperamentally unsuited for the routine duties of the gubernatorial staff and without the technical skill to head a department or agency, he remained in New York City in charge of Roosevelt's quiet campaign for the presidency, while Jim Farley took over control of the state party. With the responsibility of office, Roosevelt had begun to outgrow his old friend. For the first time, grudgingly, Howe had to share access to Roosevelt, and his suggestions were now tossed, along with others, into the bubbling intellectual stew being concocted in Albany. Sometimes he argued so strenuously against the governor's actions that the office staff heard him shouting into the telephone: "Can't you get anything into that thick Dutch skull of yours?" Hearing that Roosevelt was going for a swim following one conversation, he yelled: "I hope to God you drown!" Unruffled as always, the governor listened in good humor and then did what he wanted to do.

The Roosevelts quickly settled down to life in the Executive Mansion, and the stuffy Victorian edifice—still outfitted with furniture going back to Grover Cleveland's time—took on the informality of Hyde Park. Home from Groton or Harvard, the boys brought their friends, who mingled with politicians and officials. Chief, Anna's German shepherd dog, frolicked in the halls. Books and magazines were strewn about haphazardly. Secretaries came and went with important papers to be signed by the governor. Meals were uproarious and everyone seemed to chatter at once. "It was the Roosevelt habit to treat all visitors as honorable," Rex Tugwell later observed, and "the most explosive gossip I ever heard was exchanged during the long meals." Every afternoon that Eleanor was in Albany—she spent three days a week in New York City teaching at Todhunter, a private girls' school she had helped organize— tea and cake was served in the family dining room and anyone in the house at the time was invited: family, friends, newsmen, secretaries, and state troopers.

Twenty-one years before, Franklin Roosevelt had told Grenville Clark that "anyone who is Governor of New York has a good chance to be President with luck." The politicians who controlled New York started out with a block of forty-five of the 266 electoral votes needed to win the White House. In nine of the fifteen campaigns between the Civil War and 1928, one or the other of the major parties had nominated a governor or former governor of New York. By winning the governorship while Smith was losing the state, Roosevelt automatically became a leading prospect for the Democratic presidential nomination in 1932, although Louis Howe was pointing toward 1936 as a more propitious year. Prospects for a Democratic victory were not all that dim, as Smith had done better in 1928 than the Hoover landslide indicated. He received six million more votes than any previous Democratic candidate and carried most urban areas. If the Democrats could hold these gains and win back states alienated by Smith's religion and opposition to Prohibition, the future might well belong to them. Roosevelt seemed most likely to be able to reconcile the feuding factions—but first he had to consolidate his power and prestige in New York State.

Roosevelt was a good governor, and in Albany he honed the skills that were to be useful in Washington. He inherited a state government from Al Smith that was in good working order, and Smith had laid the foundation for sound social reforms, so his task was primarily to carry on the work of his predecessor. Never losing sight of the White House, he took few chances with the future, but Sam Rosenman later contended that the basic philosophy and social objectives of the New Deal can be found in the speeches and messages delivered by Roosevelt during his four years in Albany. "In those messages and speeches from 1929 through 1932 you will find proposals for appropriate state action in the same fields in which he later urged action by the Congress: minimum wages and maximum hours, old-age insurance, unemployment relief through public works and other means, unemployment insurance, regulation of public utilities, stricter regulation of the banks and of the use of other people's money." Rosenman exaggerated the similarities between Roosevelt's New York programs and the New Deal, but in Albany Roosevelt did exhibit a willingness to experiment and a determination to make the fullest use of the power of government.

Roosevelt functioned confidently, as if he had been governor for years. He said that there had been so few changes since he had left the state Senate, in 1913, that it was just like renewing acquaintance with old friends. To avoid bitter wrangling, he sought the cooperation of the Assembly and, in his inaugural address, expressed the hope for an "Era of Good Feeling." This political honeymoon was short-lived, however. Within a few weeks, the Democratic governor and the Republican lawmakers clashed over the executive budget—one of the key reforms engineered by Al Smith. Although the technical details underlying the ensuing battle of the budget were complex, the basic issue was who would control the state's purse strings: the governor or the legislature. If Roosevelt was successful in piloting the first such budget through the legislature, it would add to his prestige; a defeat could destroy his political future.

Under the old system, the making of the budget rested almost entirely in the hands of the legislature. Department heads went directly to the legislature with funding requests, which were approved or denied after logrolling among the members aimed at protecting pet pork-barrel projects and paying off political debts. The governor could veto the appropriation, but he had no other role in the budget-making process. The new system empowered him to write the budget, and the legislature could only delete items. If the lawmakers wanted to make their own appropriations, they had to submit new bills to the governor, along with plans for providing the revenue to pay for them. The new system was designed to take the budget out of politics and end the legislature's indirect control of the executive branch of the state government.

Early in February 1929, Roosevelt submitted a $256 million budget, an increase of nearly 10 percent over the previous year. Most of the new funds were earmarked for improvements to hospitals, prisons, schools, and parks. Because of the extensive reorganization of the state government, launched by the Smith administration, many expenses could not be estimated in advance, so Roosevelt had sought lump-sum appropriations for these functions, rather than itemizing them. Unhappy about the budget system but unable to directly attack what was widely hailed as an important reform, the Republican leadership, mistaking Roosevelt's amiability for weakness, pounced upon his proposals. They denounced the lump-sum appropriations as a mask for Democratic patronage payoffs and charged the governor with "avarice, presumption and usurpation."

Roosevelt had not sought the battle, but he did not flinch from it. "I am getting into a grand little fight with the Legislature and from now on, for five weeks, it will be a general row," he told his son James with evident zest. Both sides claimed that they were defending the state constitution against assault by the other. "I raise the broad question affecting the division of governmental duties between the executive, the legislative and the judicial branches of the government," the governor said. "It is our duty to see that the rights of the people must be preserved from the arrogance and presumption of an overzealous executive," countered the lawmakers. For two weeks, Roosevelt delayed action on the bill containing some $56 million in lump-sum appropriations that had been amended by the legislature. He used the time to bury it under a series of proposals calling for old-age-pension reform, increased financial support for the schools, farm relief, tax reduction, a St. Lawrence Power Commission, and other popular measures.

Having thrown the legislature on the defensive, Roosevelt vetoed the amended appropriations bill presented him. "I will not assent to a precedent depriving the present Governor and future Governors of a large part of the constitutional duties which are inherent in the office of Chief executive," he declared. The bill was sent back to the legislature in its original form. Armed with legal advice from the Republican attorney general, the lawmakers again approved the budget in its amended form and hastily adjourned, pausing only long enough to kill off most of Roosevelt's other proposals. But the governor had just begun to fight. Rather than submit to legislative control of the budget or calling what was likely to be a futile special session, he decided to take the matter to the courts.

In the meantime, recalling Woodrow Wilson's effectiveness in going to the people, Roosevelt delivered a series of radio "reports" that made striking use of the new medium. Speaking in simple, uncomplicated language, he persuaded his listeners of the justice of his position. A flood of letters descended upon the offending lawmakers after each talk, and radio proved to be a valuable weapon in the governor's arsenal. Roosevelt was not yet the masterful radio speaker that he was to become—he spoke more rapidly than in later years and his audience was limited—but these speeches were the forerunner of the Fireside Chat of the White House years. Although a lower court dealt him a setback by sustaining the legislature, the Court of Appeals upheld him on every major point. The legislature was adjured to keep its hands off the budget, but even more important, the fight demonstrated that Roosevelt intended to be his own master. Like so many others, the lawmakers had been beguiled by his air of agreeable inconsequence, only to find it masked an iron will.

"You are right that the business community is not much interested in good government and it wants the present Republican control to continue just so long as the stock market soars and the new combinations of capital are left undisturbed," Roosevelt wrote a friend early in 1929. "The trouble before Republican leaders is that prevailing conditions are bound to come to an end some time. When that time comes, I want to see the Democratic party sanely radical enough to have most of the disgruntled ones turn to it to put us in power again." As governor of New York, he

devised a program designed to entrench the party within the state and to
attract favorable attention from without. Posing as a farmer (his tree-farm
and Georgia experiences were always useful) Roosevelt emphasized agricultural relief, reforestation, and development of electric-power resources
by the state—in effect a regional plan for New York that, as Daniel Fusfeld has pointed out, foreshadowed the type of planning used in the Tennessee Valley. This program was designed to redress the serious imbalance
between rural and urban life. Farmers had not shared in the economic
prosperity of the twenties and were further hobbled by increasing taxes
and higher distribution costs. Roosevelt tied the prosperity of the city and
the country together, emphasizing that the United States could not continue half prosperous and half depressed. "If the farming population does
not have sufficient purchasing power to buy new shoes, new clothes, new
automobiles, the manufacturing centers must suffer," he declared.

Roosevelt's agricultural program was hardly radical, but because of
the perennial distress of the farmers, anything that improved conditions
in rural New York would attract national attention. These proposals included a two-cent-a-gallon tax on gasoline to lift the burden of highway
construction and maintenance costs from the rural areas and to finance
the building of farm-to-market roads; rapid expansion of rural electrification; stepped-up research on farm problems; and a detailed survey of land
use. Marginal farmland was to be removed from production and diverted
to reforestation projects, thereby reducing crop surpluses and their de-
pressing effect upon prices. At the same time, a timber crop could be developed and the problems of flood control and water supply eased. The
Republican legislators, most from rural constituencies, did not dare oppose these proposals, and Roosevelt appeared as the champion of the
farmer even beyond the confines of New York. "We thought you were
acquainted only with Wall Street magnates," a Wisconsin official wrote
him after he had expounded on the gap between the prices farmers received for their produce and what the consumer paid in the corner grocery.

Cheap electricity developed from water power was an important part
of Roosevelt's program. Like the farm problem, the question of public
versus private development of water-power resources reached beyond New
York; Roosevelt's position on the issue would influence the attitude of
western political leaders toward his candidacy. The largest single source of
untapped power in New York State was the St. Lawrence River, but development had been blocked for nearly a quarter century by a deadlock
over who was to develop it. "In the brief time I have been speaking to
you," Roosevelt said during his inaugural address, "there has run to waste
on their paths toward the sea, enough power from our rivers to have

turned the wheels of a thousand factories, to have lit a million farmers' homes." The time had come to harness this resource and distribute it to consumers at the lowest possible cost. "It is our power; and no inordinate profits must be allowed to those who act as the people's agents in bringing this power to their homes and workshops."

Roosevelt's words created a flood of speculation. Because of his carefully plotted failure to come out flatly for public power, some advocates feared that he had deserted them; on the other hand, Republican legislators saw in the statement the veiled threat of public ownership. Such sphinx-like pronouncements became part of Roosevelt's stock-in-trade. While both sides tried to puzzle out his intentions, he was educating himself in all ramifications of the problem.

In March 1929, he again appeared before the legislature to present a special message on water-power development. Power plants and dams would be constructed on the St. Lawrence to generate electricity and the private power companies would be given contracts to transmit it to consumers as long as they charged reasonable prices. But the Morgan interests were in the process of merging three of the largest upstate power companies—a merger that was expected to lead to a boost in electricity rates. So, adding a new note to the water-power controversy, Roosevelt warned that if the private companies refused to transmit electricity generated by publicly owned plants to the consumer at low rates, the state might construct its own transmission lines. Expressing concern that the Public Service Commission—long dominated by the utilities—would not protect consumers, he proposed a five-member St. Lawrence Power Development Commission to draft a plan for generating power and a contract with the private firms for its distribution.

The Republicans rejected the proposal, but they had been outmaneuvered by the governor. Roosevelt had transformed the complicated issue of water-power development into something everyone could understand: a fight for cheap electricity. Louis Howe was assigned to compare the rates paid by Canadian consumers for public-generated electricity with those paid by New Yorkers, who got theirs from private utilities. As he expected, there was a wide discrepancy in charges, with the Canadian rates being substantially lower. The utility lobby, worried about the possibility that the governor, who had public opinion on his side, might interfere with the upstate power merger, persuaded the Republican leaders to give way. Roosevelt hailed legislative approval of the St. Lawrence Commission as a triumph, but proclamations of victory were premature. Although the Commission's report was substantially in agreement with his proposals, the Hoover administration, no friend of public power, dragged its feet on negotiations with Canada. More than a quarter of a century was

to pass before the swift-moving waters of the St. Lawrence were to turn
factory wheels and light the homes of New Yorkers.

Unperturbed by the stalemate in Albany, Roosevelt launched a round
of speaking engagements in the summer of 1929 carefully tailored to keep
him in the public eye. Once again following the old political maxim that
nothing makes the voters lust more for a candidate than seeming
unavailability, he denied any interest in running for the White House. "It
is probably because of the warm weather and the lack of real news that
my young gentlemen friends of the Press are inventing Arabian night tales
about the Presidential possibilities and candidates for the somewhat far
distant date of 1932," he declared. But in several commencement
speeches—including an address at Harvard, where, much to his delight, he
was awarded an honorary Phi Beta Kappa key that he had failed to win
as an undergraduate—Roosevelt sounded like a presidential candidate.

Speaking out against the growing concentration of economic and political power under the Republicans, he noted that "every day that passes
. . . a hundred small shopkeepers go out of business or are absorbed by
the new business device known as the chain store. That means that a hundred independent owners of their own businesses either transfer to some
other business or become employees of a great impersonal machine. We
see the same trend in every form of manufacture, in transportation, in
public utilities, and in banking." And as a governor, he decried the slip-
page of power to the federal government. "If there is failure on the part
of a State to provide adequate educational facilities for its boys and girls,
an immediate cry goes up that a department of education should be established in Washington. If a State fails to keep abreast of modern
[health] provisions, immediately the enthusiasts turn to the creation of
a department of health in Washington."

Roosevelt served up his remedy for dealing with the concentration of
capital and the corresponding concentration of governmental power in
fewer hands in a speech at the dedication of Tammany Hall's new headquarters, off Manhattan's Union Square, on July 4, 1929. Twelve years
had passed since he had last addressed the assembled braves, and the contrast was sharp. Then he was a junior politician seeking Tammany's blessing; now he was governor and a front-runner for the Democratic presidential nomination. "I want to preach a new doctrine," Roosevelt
declared. "A complete separation of business and government." It was an
ironic message for the future architect of the New Deal. He warned that
the existing partnership between business and government being fostered
by the Republicans—a partnership exemplified by the recently enacted
Hawley-Smoot protective tariff—created the threat of "economic feudal-

ism." If the American people were to preserve their freedom, they might have to don liberty caps like their forefathers and proclaim a new declaration of independence. This time, however, the struggle would be fought with ballots, rather than swords and muskets. Reaction to the speech was immediate. Will Rogers—a nationally syndicated humorist—mentioned it in his newspaper column, and it received favorable attention from the rebellious farmers attracted by Roosevelt's Populist rhetoric.

Roosevelt's speeches reaped a harvest of national publicity, but his first task was to win reelection as governor in 1930 by a convincing margin. Upstate New York was the key to the election, so he spent the summer of 1929 touring the area. Learning that the state owned a small boat with a glass roof designed for use on the New York State Barge Canal, the successor of the old Erie Canal, Roosevelt and his wife embarked on an inspection of hospitals, prisons, and asylums in the area. Recalling World War I, when he had dashed across the Atlantic on a destroyer, he told a friend, it "makes me laugh whenever I compare it with the old Navy days."

As his craft leisurely floated from Albany to Buffalo and then to Lake Ontario and back down the Hudson to the Champlain Canal, the governor extended a friendly greeting to the predominately Republican farmers and made votes for himself wherever he went. Upon reaching a state hospital or prison, he would climb into an accompanying car and make an inspection of the grounds. Unable to enter the buildings himself, he delegated Eleanor to serve as his eyes and ears. In the beginning, her reports were highly unsatisfactory, but based on his experience as assistant Secretary of the Navy, he taught her what to look for. "I would tell him what was on the menu for the day and he would ask: 'Did you look to see whether the inmates actually were getting that food?'" she said. "I learned to look into the cooking pots on the stove and to find out if the contents corresponded to the menu; I learned to notice whether the beds were too close together, and whether they were folded up and put in closets or behind the doors during the day, which would indicate that they filled the corridors at night."†

While Eleanor and Franklin spent the summer of 1929 touring upstate New York, the bull market soared to dizzying heights. Brokerage offices were crowded with men and women staring fixedly at the lighted screens on which an endless procession of numbers hurried past their eyes proclaiming record highs on the New York Stock Exchange. Most Americans had bought their first bonds in the wartime Lib-

† FDR liked to recall a visit to one mental hospital. As the governor's party drove up, a man who had been cutting the grass doffed his cap and bowed. Someone looked back after they had passed, and the man was still standing there—thumbing his nose.

erty loans, but, hypnotized by spiraling stock prices during Coolidge Prosperity, had turned to more speculative issues. "If a man saves $15 a week, and invests in good common stocks, and allows the dividends and rights to accumulate, at the end of twenty years he will have at least $80,000," declared John J. Raskob, voicing the unqualified optimism of the day. ". . . Anyone not only can be rich but ought to be rich."

Much of this buying was on margin, with the investor putting up as little as 5 percent of the value of his shares, while his broker advanced the rest by borrowing from the banks. As a result, about $8 billion worth of credit was sucked into the market, rather than into productive industry. Janitors put their savings into Montgomery Ward; gas-station attendants had margin accounts in American Can; and nursemaids eavesdropped on their employers in hopes of picking up the latest tip. U. S. Steel was at 261¾, Anaconda Copper at 130⅞, American Telephone at 302, General Electric at 395.

To many investors, the old laws of economics seemed to have been repealed, and what went up did not necessarily have to come down. Stock prices were no longer rooted in such tangibles as consumer demand, gains in productivity, or real earnings. Holding companies and investment trusts were pyramided one atop another, and the entire structure rested on a quagmire of unrestrained speculation.

Yet cracks in the system's foundation were evident to those who looked closely. Of course, the farmers had been in trouble for years, but the tremors had reached into other segments of the economy as well. Coal mining and textiles were chronically sick industries, wages and purchasing power lagged, unemployment was creeping upward, and production was falling. Unsold radios filled the store shelves, and cars were piling up in the dealers' garages; construction was off, and bank failures—mostly small institutions—averaged two a day nationally. Almost 78 percent of all American families had yearly incomes of less than three thousand dollars. The defeated European nations depended on American loans to pay the reparations demanded by the Versailles Treaty, and unrestrained access to American markets for their goods; if either were shut off, chaos would result. Smart operators were already getting out of the stock market.‡

As early as 1925, President Hoover, then Secretary of Commerce, had become concerned over the "growing tide of speculation." In the months and years that followed, uneasiness turned to premonition and then to

‡ In August 1929, Bernard Baruch began to sell his stocks and buy gold. But when the market continued to climb, he began to doubt the wisdom of his decision. On the way to his office on Wall Street one day, he was stopped by a panhandler, who offered him a tip on the market in exchange for a coin. That was enough to convince the master speculator that it was time to get out.

alarm at the possibility of total disaster. "There are crimes far worse than murder for which men should be reviled and punished," he said of speculation in his memoirs. But Hoover's attempts to restore a semblance of sanity to the stock market were frustrated by Coolidge and his fellow cabinet member Andrew W. Mellon, the Secretary of the Treasury. In fact, Mellon, lauded by businessmen as "the greatest Secretary of the Treasury since Alexander Hamilton," played a leading role in helping uncork the genie of speculation.

Upon assuming the presidency, Hoover tried to persuade the Federal Reserve Board to restrain speculation, and appealed to the nation's bankers to restrict credit. Richard Whitney, the debonair vice-president of the Stock Exchange, was summoned to Washington to discuss the problem.* Governor Roosevelt was urged to propose legislation tightening up on Wall Street, but the request was ignored. In August, the Federal Reserve raised its discount rate—the interest at which it lent money to member banks—from 5 to 6 percent. And still the bull market continued its rampage, smashing to a historic high on September 3, 1929. Although prices faltered and drifted down, each dip was followed by a recovery. Thomas Lamont, a Morgan partner and wartime tenant of the Roosevelt house on Sixty-fifth Street, objected to Hoover's criticism of speculation, prompting the President to observe acidly, "The only trouble with capitalism is capitalists. They're too damn greedy." Expecting the worst, Hoover instructed his own financial agent to liquidate his personal holdings, but he made no public announcement—although such an announcement would probably have given more weight to his warnings of trouble ahead.

The financial world fell apart on October 24, 1929—a date that endures in history as "Black Thursday." Following heavy selling the day before, stocks opened sharply lower, and some issues were already skidding precipitously as the opening bell was still reverberating across the floor of the exchange. Prices fell so swiftly that the ticker was unable to keep up. Ripping off collars and ties, red-faced brokers and clerks bellowed at each other in a vain attempt to be heard above the din. "A kind of madness" had seized control of the exchange, said one witness. Brokers were pinned against the trading counters by a frenzied throng that waved sell orders in their faces. A hysterical man stood at one trading post yelling orders that made no sense until friends took him by the arm and gently led him away. "Margin! More margin!" demanded the brokers. Investors unable to come up with fresh cash were sold out, pouring more shares into the

---

* In 1938, Whitney, who had become president of the Stock Exchange, was convicted of stock fraud. Handcuffed to a rapist and wearing a Porcellian Club pin on his watch chain, he was shipped off to Sing Sing, where he served a little over three years behind bars.

bottomless pit. Montgomery Ward plunged from 83 to 50 . . . RCA from 68¾ to 44½ . . . U. S. Steel from 205½ to 193½. . . .

Outside the Stock Exchange, a strange roar could be heard as a crowd gathered on Broad Street. Special police details were hurried to the financial district to keep order. A workman appeared atop an adjoining building to make repairs, and the crowd, assuming he was a would-be suicide, impatiently waited for him to jump. Wild rumors spread across the country: Stocks were selling for nothing; the Chicago and Boston exchanges had closed; at least eleven speculators had committed suicide.

The big bankers came to the rescue early in the afternoon. Forming a pool to support the market, they sent Richard Whitney to the floor to buy stocks. He put in a bid for ten thousand shares of U. S. Steel at 205 and placed similar orders for other stocks. The market steadied and prices revived. Montgomery Ward rallied to 74 and U. S. Steel to 206. The lords of finance had stopped the panic, and some experts professed to see some good in the shake-out. John Maynard Keynes thought that money formerly used for speculation would now flow into productive enterprise. "The fundamental business of the country—that is, the production and distribution of goods and services—is on a sound and prosperous basis," President Hoover told the country. Prices rose slightly on Friday but turned lower during the short Saturday session and again on Monday.

On Tuesday—October 29—the bottom fell out. Huge blocks of shares were thrown on the market for whatever they would bring. A bright messenger boy jokingly bid a dollar a share for a block of White Sewing Machine Company stock, which had opened at 11—and got it. The investment trusts that had attracted most of the small investors were horribly battered. Goldman Sachs Trading Corporation opened at 60 and dropped to 35; Blue Ridge plummeted from 10 to 3. Blue-chip stocks did little better. American Telephone and General Electric each lost 28 points; Westinghouse dropped 19 points and Allied Chemical 35. Values melted before the eyes of investors as they slumped deeper in their chairs in the brokers' offices. Some were tearful; others sat stony-eyed. Big and small, insiders and outsiders, gamblers and prudent investors were all cleaned out before the worst day in Wall Street's history finally came to an end. In a few frantic hours, stocks had shed some $10 billion in value—or twice the amount of currency in circulation at the time. This time, the bankers did not step in to save the market, creating the suspicion that they had merely stabilized it only long enough to get out themselves.

Few Americans—including Franklin Roosevelt—envisioned that the collapse of the stock market would lead to the Great Depression. In retrospect, the word "crash" has misled later generations. There was no overnight plunge from glittering prosperity to a grim world of closed factories, bankrupt shops, and breadlines. The onset of the depression was more like a slow leak in an automobile tire than a sudden blowout. Roosevelt required considerable time before he recognized the arrival of the hard times he had forecast as required to loosen the Republican grip on the White House. When asked by the New York *American* to comment on the events of "Black Thursday," the governor, then at Warm Springs, replied that he lacked detailed information but believed the economy was basically sound.

Along with President Hoover, Roosevelt regarded the "Little Flurry downtown" as just retribution for the small group of plungers and gamblers engaged in speculation, and expected the stock market to rebound as it always had. Previous experience indicated a crisis of relatively short duration. Within days of the crash, John D. Rockefeller issued an encouraging statement: "Believing that fundamental conditions in the country are sound . . . my son and I have for some days been purchasing sound common stocks." "Sure," cracked Eddie Cantor, the comedian. "Who else has any money left?"

Hoover's initial estimate was probably a fair one. To prevent distress and "maintain social order and industrial peace," he summoned the business and labor leaders to the White House ritual of reassuring the nation. From business he extracted the promise to trim profits before wages would be cut or factories closed, while the unions agreed to forgo wage increases. It was the American way—rugged individualism at work—no handouts, no favoritism, and everyone working together for the common good. Telegrams were sent to the governors of all the states and to the mayors of the larger cities urging them to undertake "energetic but prudent" construction of public works to show their confidence in the economy and to take up any slack in employment. Governor Roosevelt replied that he intended to recommend construction of new hospitals and prisons to the 1930 session of the legislature. But this was in no way an emergency program, for it had been planned before the crash and Roosevelt's prudence exceeded even that recommended by Hoover. The size of the building program would be limited to the amount of revenue that could be provided without an increase in taxes.

For Roosevelt, the major task of 1930 was to win reelection as governor by so impressive a margin that he would have a first mortgage on the Democratic presidential nomination two years thence. Beginning his second year as governor, he proposed a program attractive to both Republicans and Democrats: reform of the criminal justice system, old-age pensions, changes in the banking laws to prevent speculation with the funds of small depositors, more-stringent public-utility regulation, and cheap electricity. The effect of the stock-market collapse had not yet been felt, so there was no program to deal with unemployment, except for the $20 million in new construction already planned. He kept his eye on the jobless figures, however, frequently telephoning Frances Perkins for the latest statistics, and was delighted when she became embroiled in controversy with President Hoover about the severity of unemployment.

As part of his campaign of optimistic assurances that all was well, Hoover announced in late January 1930 that the number of unemployed had decreased. Miss Perkins, appalled because her own statistics revealed just the opposite, flatly contradicted the President without consulting Roosevelt. The statement attracted considerable attention, and when the governor called the next day, she expected to be chastized. Instead, he cheerfully congratulated her. When Miss Perkins apologized for not having cleared the statement with him in advance, he told her that it was better that she hadn't. "If you had asked me," Roosevelt said, "I would probably have told you not to do it, and I think it is much more wholesome to have it right out in the open."

By the end of the legislative session, in mid-April, Roosevelt had placed himself in an excellent position for a reelection campaign. He had either won everything he sought from the legislature or else had maneuvered the Republicans into appearing to obstruct progress and reform. Through artful use of his radio reports to the people, he created the impression that all the achievements of the session belonged to him and all the failures were the work of the opposition. Roosevelt had also begun to recognize the seriousness of unemployment in New York State. A survey of industrial centers taken in March—about the time that Hoover was earnestly proclaiming that the worst would be over in sixty days—revealed that in some places as many as 75 percent of the workers were jobless. Already vulnerable before the crash, the economy reeled under the blow it had received from Wall Street. Investment capital dried up, nervous consumers reduced spending, and factories retrenched, throwing their employees into the street. Worst of all was fear for the future.

Nevertheless, Roosevelt still believed the depression would be short-lived and the nation would be spared unusual hardship. Creeping unemployment could best be solved by relying on the leaders of industry, rather than by government interference with the operation of the marketplace. When he did act, it was merely to appoint a Committee on the Stabilization of Industry for the Prevention of Unemployment, to work out methods for dealing with *future* unemployment. Such naïveté was not uncommon in a era of laissez-faire economics, and New York was the first state to even take such a tentative step to deal with the problem of unemployment.

To further his campaign for the presidential nomination, Roosevelt happily taunted Hoover when the President's rosily optimistic forecasts of an upturn in the economy failed to materialize. Playing to the conservatives, Roosevelt all but accused Hoover of radicalism because of his reliance on public works spending to combat unemployment, and warned against unbalanced budgets—words that were to sound ironic in a few years.

But as the gubernatorial campaign approached, it was clear that the Republicans were not going to wage it upon the fundamental issues of cheap electricity, farm relief, and unemployment. They fell back upon the old standbys of Tammany corruption and Prohibition. The number of jobless mounted every day as the economy ground to a halt—in Washington some five thousand women stood in line that summer to apply for two hundred openings for charwomen in government offices, and war veterans with medals pinned to their coats sold apples on the street corners of a thousand cities and towns—but the politicians were concerned with matters entirely peripheral to the real concerns of the voters.

Since the death of Boss Murphy, six years before, the leadership of Tammany had fallen into less-deft hands, and grafters operated with open impunity in New York City. One leader made off with half of a $16-million sewer contract, and policemen openly fixed tickets in the street. The year before, Fiorello H. La Guardia, an Italian-Jewish progressive Republican congressman, had unsuccessfully run against dapper playboy mayor Jimmy Walker, charging that the city government was riddled with corruption. The Republicans tried to force Roosevelt into an investigation of Tammany, but he avoided the trap by claiming they had not come up with definite proof of wrongdoing. In 1930 the Republicans hoped to hang the sins of Tammany around Roosevelt's neck, and even if the popular governor was not defeated, he would be so tarnished as to no longer be an attractive presidential possibility.

The corruption issue put Roosevelt in a difficult position. He was on good terms with John Curry, the leader of Tammany, Tammany legislators had supported his program in Albany, and two thirds of the state's Democrats were in New York City. On the other hand, he could not remain blind to Tammany's indiscretions. The state constitution vested him with the authority to order an investigation if enough evidence was presented to him—and the Republicans were determined to maneuver him into that corner. Following an unsuccessful search for a candidate with a national reputation, the Republicans settled upon Charles H. Tuttle, the U. S. Attorney for the Southern District of New York, which includes New York City. Tuttle had received considerable newspaper publicity for rooting out crooked judges and seemed an ideal choice to wage a campaign against corruption and crime.

Prohibition proved to be a less potent issue for the Republicans than corruption. Roosevelt had always straddled it, arguing that for the sake of unity the Democrats should avoid the issue. By 1930 the Great Experiment was regarded as a failure by all but the most ardent drys, having led to racketeering and widespread contempt for the law. Learning that Tuttle was planning to come out flatly for repeal of the Eighteenth Amendment, Roosevelt beat him to the punch. In a letter to Senator Wagner, which was made public, he advocated repeal of the Prohibition amendment and its replacement by a new one giving the people of each state the right to decide whether they wanted to permit the sale of liquor by state agencies. This, he claimed, would end crime and disrespect for the law. Roosevelt's mildly "damp" stand did little damage to his candidacy among upstate drys and gave him credence as a states' righter, while Tuttle completely alienated the fanatical Republican drys. They fielded their own candidate, dimming his chances for victory.

Corruption put Roosevelt on the spot, however, when Tuttle produced evidence that Tammany was engaged in a brisk trade in appointments to the bench. But Roosevelt had not lost his magic. Under pressure to act, he surprised everyone with his zeal. The governor placed the affair in the hands of the Republican attorney general, designated a Republican State Supreme Court justice to impanel a blue-ribbon grand jury, and requested the Appellate Division to conduct an investigation of the lower courts. Samuel Seabury, a Democrat and longtime foe of Tammany, was chosen by Roosevelt to head the inquiry. Having taken these drastic steps, he then pulled back by trying to tie up the Republican investigators in red tape. When Tammany leaders declined to waive immunity after being called before the grand jury, he refused to grant its request for expanded authority. Reformers angrily accused him of expediency and dodging the issue. Replying to a critical letter from a Harvard classmate, the Reverend W. Russell Bowie, pastor of Grace Church, Roosevelt reminded him that under Anglo-Saxon jurisprudence, grand juries could not force witnesses to waive immunity. "For the love of Mike," he added, "remember that I am just as anxious as you to root out this rottenness."

The two candidates campaigned as if they were taking part in different elections. Tuttle hammered away at corruption, while Roosevelt talked about his constructive record as governor, about water power, assistance to the farmers, Prohibition, and old-age pensions. "Never let your opponent pick the battleground on which to fight," he told Rosenman. "If he picks one, stay out of it and let him fight all by himself." Howe and Jim Farley were afraid that Tuttle would score valuable points, but after an initial flurry, his campaign lost momentum when he was unable to come up with fresh charges. One voter asked why, if New York City needed cleaning up so badly, he hadn't remained there to do the job. And

Roosevelt mischievously professed to be puzzled as to whether his opponent was "running for Governor of the State of New York or for District Attorney of New York County."

The campaign was an easy one—perhaps Roosevelt's easiest. New York City was sewed up for him, for Tammany had no alternative but to support him. If Roosevelt failed to win reelection, the organization would be left to the tender mercies of Charles Tuttle. Farley had also done a remarkable job of rebuilding the upstate Democratic organization, which had been in a shambles. Wishing to swell with Republican votes the substantial majority he was expected to win, Roosevelt attacked Republican "obstructionism" in Albany and Republican "incompetence" in Washington, rather than the Republican party itself.† Howe thwarted a whispering campaign about Roosevelt's health—including a canard that he had syphilis, rather than polio—by having him examined by insurance company doctors, who, amid much publicity, approved policies totaling $560,000 on his life. The Georgia Warm Springs Foundation was the beneficiary.‡ Roosevelt actively stumped the state for two weeks, poking fun at his opponent, whom he never mentioned by name. When Tuttle was quoted as saying he wanted to "get down among the people," he dryly remarked: "I know the people will be properly flattered."

With the Republicans narrowly focusing on the crimes of Tammany, they seldom contradicted Roosevelt as he extolled his accomplishments. Deriding Hoover for his optimistic incantations that prosperity lay just around the corner, he charged that if the Administration had applied the brake to speculation in 1928 or 1929, the crash might have been averted. And instead of swift action being taken to deal with it, "nothing happened but words." No one bothered to point out that as governor of New York he could have moved to regulate the Stock Exchange. He pointed with pride to the state's public works program as an example of wise planning, and no one said it antedated the crash. And he appealed at last for unemployment relief. "It is not a matter of party," he declared. "It is a matter of good citizenship and good Americanism." In contrast, Hoover

† "There are thousands of people who call themselves Republicans who think as you and I do about government," FDR told Rosenman. "They are enrolled as Republicans because their families have been Republicans for generations—that's the only reason; some of them think it is *infra dig* [a common phrase of his] to be called a Democrat; the Democrats in their village are not the socially 'nice' people the enrolled Republicans are. So never attack the Republicans or the Republican party—only the Republican *leaders*. Then any Republican voter who hears it will say to himself: 'Well, he doesn't mean me. I don't believe in the things that Machold and McGinnies and Knight and the other reactionaries up in Albany believe in either.' "
‡ In the private part of their report, the examining physicians noted "no symptoms of *impotentia coeundi*"—or inability of the male to perform sexual functions. James Roosevelt noted, however, that it "would have been difficult for him to function sexually after he became crippled from the waist down by polio. He had some use of his lower body and some sensation there, but it was extremely limited."

was unwilling to provide direct relief, saying it was a task for local governments or private charity, that it weakened the moral fiber of the workers.

Three members of Hoover's Cabinet were dispatched to New York to assist Tuttle's bogged-down campaign: Secretary of State Henry L. Stimson, Secretary of War Patrick Hurley, and Ogden L. Mills, the under Secretary of the Treasury. Roosevelt greeted them with ridicule, noting that Hurley was from Oklahoma and knew nothing about New York, while Stimson and Mills had both run unsuccessfully for governor. "The people of this State who repudiated them are the best judges of whether or not any man is fit to be Governor," he declared. Having ignored the charge that he was condoning corruption, Roosevelt faced the issue squarely at a final rally, at Carnegie Hall on November 1. "If there are any corrupt judges still sitting in our courts they shall be removed," he told his audience. "They shall be removed by constitutional means, not by inquisition; not by trial in the press, but by trial as provided by law."

As Election Day neared, Jim Farley wanted to issue a prediction of victory by a spectacular six hundred thousand votes, but Roosevelt, fearing it would make party workers overconfident, had him tone it down to 350,000. Making his own guess in a private poll among the reporters who had covered the campaign, he forecast a margin of 437,000 votes.* But when the ballots were tallied, he won by an astounding 750,001 votes. "I cast that one vote!" cried the surprised and delighted candidate. Roosevelt had not only wiped out any lingering doubts about his narrow victory of two years before, but had doubled Al Smith's best vote-getting record. He even accomplished the seemingly impossible task of winning upstate New York, carrying counties that had not been won by a Democrat since the Civil War. The spreading depression, Tuttle's colorless campaign, the "wet" vote, Roosevelt's magnetism, Farley's smoothly oiled organization—all contributed to the victory. The Democrats won control of the House of Representatives and gained enough seats in the Senate so that along with Republican progressives they would dominate that body. Clearly, they appeared likely to win the White House in 1932—and Franklin Roosevelt was the front-runner for the nomination.

* FDR, who came closest to the final tally, disqualified himself, making John Kieran, of the New York *Times*, the next-closest with his estimate of 300,000 votes, the winner of a Brooks Brothers suit paid for by Roosevelt.

XIV
THE POLITICS OF CHAOS

"WHAT KIND OF man is Franklin Roosevelt?"

As the nation sank deeper into the grip of the Great Depression, Americans asked this question with increasing frequency, because the cheerfully expansive governor of New York might well be the next President of the United States. What really lay behind his handsome face and wonderful grin? Would he be able to open the factories and put the country to work again? Did he have the toughness to deal with the crisis? Or was he just another politician with little more to offer than unbridled ambition? Undoubtedly the most perceptive appraisal of Roosevelt on the eve was that of Raymond Moley, who had been plucked from the political-science faculty at Columbia University to serve as an adviser to the governor. Replying to a letter from his sister, Moley wrote:

> You ask what he is like and that isn't easy to answer because I haven't had the chance to confirm a lot of fleeting impressions. One thing is sure —that the idea that people get from his charming manner—that he is soft or flabby in disposition and character—is far from true. When he wants something a lot he is hard, stubborn, resourceful, relentless. I used to think on the basis of casual observation that his amiability was "lord-of-the-manor"—"good-to-the-peasants"—stuff. It isn't that at all. He seems quite naturally warm and friendly—less because he genuinely likes most of the people to whom he is pleasant (although he does like a lot of people of all sorts and varieties) than because he just enjoys the pleasant and engaging role, as a charming woman does. . . . The man's energy and vitality are astonishing. I've been amazed with his interest in things. It skips and bounces through seemingly intricate subjects. . . . I don't find he has read much about economic subjects. What he gets is from talking

to people and when he stores away the net of conversation he never knows what part of what he has kept is what he said himself or what his visitor said. There is a lot of auto-intoxication of the intelligence that we shall have to watch. . . .

Roosevelt's campaign for the Democratic presidential nomination began the morning after his landslide victory in the 1930 gubernatorial election. Collar loosened and with the ashes of a Sweet Caporal dusting his shirt front, Louis Howe gleefully crafted a press statement that was to be issued over Jim Farley's name: "I do not see how Mr. Roosevelt can escape becoming the next presidential nominee of his party, even if no one should raise a finger to bring it about." Fearing that Roosevelt would have forbidden such a statement, Howe had not checked with the Boss before issuing it, and Farley was uneasy about his reaction. As soon as Roosevelt arrived in Albany, where some five thousand people lined the streets in a cold rain to greet him with shouts of "Our next President!" Farley telephoned the Executive Mansion. "Whatever you said, Jim, is all right with me," the governor replied nonchalantly. And then he summoned the reporters for another disclaimer of interest in anything except fulfilling his duties as governor.

Roosevelt's reluctance to run openly for the nomination was not due to coyness but to the fact that campaigning for a presidential nomination is like tiptoeing through a minefield. "You can speak too often or not enough," Farley once observed. "You can speak too loud or too soft; you can be too polite or not polite enough; and again you can be too friendly or not friendly enough. Any of these extremes at any given time may be fatal." To ensure that Roosevelt made none of these missteps, Howe and Farley plotted a two-tiered campaign. They tried to create the impression that Roosevelt was not seeking the presidency but the office was seeking him. While the candidate kept a modestly low profile with the hope of preventing the other aspirants from ganging up on him in a "stop Roosevelt" movement, they waged an aggressive behind-the-scenes battle for convention delegates. For public consumption, they might boast that Roosevelt's nomination was inevitable, but every step of the way had to be carefully choreographed.

There was a bumper crop of possible Democratic nominees in 1932, in addition to Roosevelt. Looming largest was Al Smith. Was he, or was he not, out of politics? Because of the economic crisis, he convinced himself that despite his religion, his outspoken opposition to Prohibition, and his identification with the cities, he could reverse the decision of 1928. And he nursed a festering grudge against Roosevelt, whom he felt had unceremoniously shunted him aside. John Nance Garner, of Texas, the beetle-browed, cigar-chewing speaker of the House of Representatives, also harbored presidential ambitions—ambitions fed by William Randolph

Hearst, who controlled the California delegation. Newton D. Baker, Woodrow Wilson's Secretary of War, kept alive the torch of the League of Nations, while Albert C. Ritchie, the handsome four-time governor of Maryland, appealed to conservatives. Asked by a reporter if he would like to be President, Ritchie replied: "Of course I would. Who wouldn't?" Governor William Murray, known to his fellow Oklahomans as "Alfalfa Bill," hoped that agricultural discontent would swing the nomination his way. James Cox, the 1920 standard-bearer, placed himself in a position for lightning to strike again. Former Senator James Reed would have the votes of the Missouri delegation; Governor Harry F. Byrd controlled the Virginians; and Owen D. Young, of General Electric, was being mentioned as a likely alternative if the convention deadlocked.

Roosevelt made the major strategy decisions for his campaign but left day-to-day operations to Howe and Farley. The contrast between the two men was striking. Howe was wizened and hollow-eyed, often rude and astringent; Farley was a big, affable Irishman with a round, beaming face. Howe operated in the shadows; Farley was gifted with an easy charm and a remarkable memory for names and faces. Encountering some minor politico that he may have met only briefly years before, he could not only remember the man's name but was able to summon up some flattering detail about him. Such skills made him popular with the oyster-roast-and-clambake crowd, the shock troops of politics.

Farley, who was just over forty, had been born in Rockland County the son of a brickyard worker who had been kicked to death by a horse. Before he had turned twenty-one and could vote for himself, he had been elected clerk of Stony Point, his home town, even though it was Republican territory. He was an early supporter of Al Smith, and with the Happy Warrior's backing, climbed the ladder of New York politics. Attracted to Roosevelt by his charm, energy, and obvious political potential, he put his talents to work for him. "You have done a wonderful piece of work," Roosevelt wrote Farley after the 1930 campaign, "and I don't need to tell you how very appreciative and grateful I am."

Early in 1931, Howe and Farley took the first overt step toward the nomination by launching the Friends of Roosevelt as an umbrella organization for the campaign. They opened an office on Madison Avenue across from the Biltmore Hotel and staffed it largely with workers carried over from the gubernatorial campaign. From this crowded warren, they directed a political apparatus whose aim was nothing less than the seizure of the Democratic party. Maneuvering adroitly among the diverse and divided elements of a faction-ridden party, they were careful to alienate no one. In the South, Roosevelt had to appear conservative while distancing himself from the "wringing wet" stand on Prohibition associated with

Al Smith. In the East, his posture was liberal and reasonably wet; in the West, he was the White Knight of progressivism, with farm relief and public power emblazoned on his standard.

Aware of the value of the personal touch in politics, Howe and Farley launched a letter-writing and long-distance-telephone campaign that put them in touch with Democratic county chairmen all over the nation. It was reminiscent of the letter-writing mill that Howe had run in Roosevelt's race for reelection as state senator two decades before, but far more sophisticated. Births, marriages, weddings, and anniversaries were marked by warm congratulatory notes ostensibly signed by Roosevelt. Invitations to Albany and Hyde Park were extended to key politicians likely to be swayed by a personal encounter with the governor. Lesser fry received signed photographs. Pamphlets and press releases demonstrating Roosevelt's vote-getting abilities flooded the country. A steady stream of intelligence regarding local politicians and political conditions flowed back to Howe's cluttered desk on Madison Avenue. This information was assembled on pink cards that candidly evaluated the strengths and weaknesses of those with whom he was dealing. Some leading political figures were unflatteringly portrayed on Howe's cards:

Jones, Jesse
Houston, Texas
Money
Houston *Chronicle* owner
For himself first, last and all the time
Ambitious
Promises everybody everything
Double-crosser

Carter, Amon
Fort Worth, Texas
Non-committal
Powerful
King-maker type
Loud
Breaks with everyone

Connally, Tom
Marlin, Texas
U. S. Senator
Politician—no convictions
Friendly but non-committed
Tremendous influence
Key man
Delegate-at-large
Fears N.Y. situation*

* A reference to the Tammany scandals that still plagued FDR.

Roosevelt for President clubs sprouted on their own in various parts of the nation, but they mostly consisted of nonprofessionals, so Roosevelt, regarding them as premature, decided to ignore them. "I am not in any sense a candidate in 1932," he told one admirer, "partly because I have seen so much of the White House since 1892, that I have no hankering, secret or otherwise, to be a candidate." But the Roosevelt for President Club of Meriwether County, with its hometown overtones, was different, and he attended a dinner it gave in his honor. "Georgia is happy to have a favorite son to present to the next Democratic National Convention," declared the new governor, Richard B. Russell. Roosevelt parried weakly with a statement that the convention was nearly two years off and politics was such an uncertain game that the nominee might well be some person who had not yet been mentioned.

Money is the mother's milk of politics, and in a time of deepening economic crisis it was difficult to come by. Ed Flynn and Frank C. Walker, a New York attorney, were placed in charge of fund raising. Walker himself gave five thousand dollars, and when funds were low, Flynn personally picked up the tab for office expenses. Old Roosevelt friends and supporters were touched—often and hard—among them the Morgenthaus; Herbert Lehman; James Gerard; Basil O'Connor; John Mack; Colonel E. M. House, who had been Woodrow Wilson's closest adviser; Laurence A. Steinhardt; Jesse Straus, a member of the family that owned Macy's; and Joseph P. Kennedy. Newer recruits included Robert W. Bingham, publisher of the Louisville *Courier-Journal*; Joseph E. Davies, husband of Post Toasties heiress Marjorie Post; and William H. Woodin, a New York industrialist and former Republican. Most were later rewarded with cabinet appointments and ambassadorships.

Upon one occasion, Joe Kennedy expressed an interest in visiting headquarters, and Walker agreed to show him around. Suddenly remembering that Louis Howe harbored a passionate dislike for Wall Street speculators, Walker asked Howe as a personal favor to be polite to Kennedy. "Don't worry, don't worry," the little man assured him. "I'll put on my best company manners." But when Walker ushered Kennedy into Howe's office, they found him slumped over his desk, head resting on his folded arms as if he were asleep. Howe showed no sign of having heard his visitors until Walker gave an embarrassed cough, and then he merely opened an eye and stared balefully at them. Following a desultory conversation, Kennedy left fuming; but, anxious to penetrate the Roosevelt inner circle, he contributed at least twenty thousand dollars to the campaign.

Political campaigns cannot be conducted by correspondence and long-distance telephone alone, but in this early stage it was unthinkable for Roosevelt to go on the road himself. Howe frequently went to

Washington† to confer with such power brokers as Cordell Hull, now senator from Tennessee; Senator Walsh; and Senator Key Pittman of Nevada, but neither he nor Farley had much practical experience outside of New York State politics. Roosevelt wanted Ed Flynn to assume the task of traveling about the country, renewing Roosevelt's political friendships and taking the pulse of potential delegates to the convention. Flynn declined, however, pointing out that he was not an "easy mixer" or a backslapper. Besides, he had the serious liability of being known as a political boss, which would arouse anti-Tammany sentiment in the hinterland.

The job went, instead, to Jim Farley. Farley was Exalted Ruler of the Elks, and his trip to the order's annual convention, in Seattle, in July 1931, seemed an excellent pretext for him to travel across the country and sound out the political situation. One Sunday morning in June he drove up to Hyde Park with a map of the United States, a fistful of railroad timetables, and a list of Democratic state chairmen and national committeemen. Working together in the study, Roosevelt, Farley, and Howe planned an itinerary that would take him, by sleeping-car jumps, to eighteen states in nineteen days.

Leaving New York on June 29, Farley, who described himself as a "combination political drummer and listening post," engaged in a series of meetings, conferences, luncheons, dinners, and "gab-fests" with Democratic leaders. "All along the route, I talked to all sorts of people to learn everything I could about the public political temper," he later observed. Usually, he discussed party affairs with Democratic leaders in the guise of a fellow state chairman from a state with three favorite sons: Roosevelt, Smith, and Owen D. Young. But if the local politicos seemed receptive, he quickly dropped his feigned neutrality and openly sought support for his candidate. Farley's optimism blossomed with each stop, for he discovered considerable support for Roosevelt among patronage-hungry Democrats. "I'm damn tired of backing losers," the South Dakota national committeeman told him. "In my opinion, Roosevelt can sweep the country, and I'm going to support him." Farley even found a warm reception in states that fielded favorite sons, such as Missouri, where among those attending a Kansas City luncheon in his honor was a spear carrier in the Pendergast organization named Harry S Truman. "The name of Roosevelt is magic," Farley told newsmen in Seattle. Reporting to the governor, he wrote that if he continued to find such overwhelming support, he would upon his re-

† Howe also went to Kentucky to help straighten out a factional dispute, and so impressed Governor Ruby Lafoon that he made him a Kentucky colonel. Howe gruffly tried to brush it off, but he was secretly pleased, because it placed him on the same level as Colonel House, whose own rank was honorary. FDR loved to refer to his friend as "Colonel Howe" in public statements.

turn to New York issue a statement so enthusiastic that "those who read it will believe I am a fit candidate for an insane asylum."

Farley's optimism was infectious, touching everyone in the Roosevelt camp and creating visions of a first-ballot victory. But he had been misled. Most of the states through which Farley traveled were already leaning toward Roosevelt, and he was far too sanguine about states where the governor faced a serious contest—California and Illinois in particular. Having spent only a day or so in each, he was unable to sort out the conflicting loyalties that prevailed in some areas. But Farley's enthusiasm did entice some fence-sitters into supporting Roosevelt out of fear that the bandwagon might roll without them.

While Jim Farley was crisscrossing the country, selling Roosevelt's candidacy to the Democratic rank and file, economic conditions unexpectedly took a turn for the better. For a brief moment in the summer of 1931 it looked as if Herbert Hoover might be right, that the crisis was merely a temporary aberration that would work itself out if market forces were allowed free rein. Production, payrolls, and the price of shares all began to rise. The tempo of construction increased, and some of the unemployed returned to work. The worst appeared over. And then the storm, which had so tantalizingly veered away, roared back in full fury—this time rolling in from across the Atlantic and engulfing the American banking system.

The European nations, dependent upon a brisk trade with the United States as well as American loans and credits, had been hard hit by the stock-market crash. The beggar-my-neighbor Hawley-Smoot Tariff, which had been enacted by the Republican Congress in 1930, all but blocked foreign goods from entering the United States, adding to the disruption of the European economies. Fearing the collapse of Europe's financial institutions, Hoover, in an act of consummate statesmanship, ordered a one-year moratorium on the payments due on the war debts the Europeans owed the United States. But it came too late. The Creditanstalt, Austria's largest bank, failed, sending out ripples of panic and despair that triggered the collapse of the closely interlocked international financial structure.

In Hoover's words, "a nightmare" followed. With Great Britain in the lead, every important industrial nation except France and the United States went off the gold standard. American banks, already shaky due to the weakness of the domestic bonds and mortgages they held, tumbled over the brink as the price of foreign bonds in which they had invested plummeted. In September 1931, 305 banks closed; in October the tally reached 522, and Hoover was convinced that "blows from abroad" had frustrated his efforts to end the crisis just when they were beginning to succeed.

The statistical dimensions of the Great Depression are quickly sketched. At its worst, unemployment ranged upward from 15 million to perhaps as many as 17 million—a quarter of the work force. Farm prices were practically nonexistent, having dropped 60 percent of the already depressed levels of 1929. Share values on the New York Stock Exchange slumped from $87 billion before the crash to $19 billion in 1933. National income over these same years fell to almost half what it had been. Industrial stagnation was accompanied by a fever of bank failures, and as many as ten thousand banks may have closed their doors, taking the savings of small depositors with them.

But statistics do not provide a living impression of what the depression was like for ordinary Americans. There were the fruitless, never-ending search for work . . . the relentless dwindling of savings . . . the ceaseless scrimping that made life an agony . . . the selling of whatever possessions that could be sold . . . the overwhelming feeling of inadequacy and lost pride. Once-prosperous suburban families lived on stale bread. Near famine stalked the coalfields of West Virginia and Kentucky. Soup kitchens were familiar sights in the cities. As many as 2 million men and boys—and some women—sneaked rides on freight trains, headed anywhere as long as it wasn't where they had been. One writer saw a crowd of fifty men, women, and children fighting over a barrel of garbage set outside a Chicago restaurant. Amtorg, the Soviet trading agency, received one hundred thousand applications for jobs in Russia. John Maynard Keynes was asked if there had been anything like this before and he replied that indeed there had: It had lasted for four hundred years and was called the Dark Ages.

As disaster followed disaster, President Hoover, the world's greatest expert on assisting ruined nations, waited for the economic machinery to make its own adjustments. Most nights, he got little more than three hours sleep, and his eyes were red-rimmed from work and worry. But he was unable to dramatize his fight against the depression in a way to kindle the popular imagination or rally the nation's morale. He was enshrouded in gloom. "If you put a rose in Hoover's hand it would wilt," said the sculptor Gutzon Borglum. He gave the impression of looking upon human misery as an engineering problem. All the facts were carefully mustered: the hemorrhage of gold reserves figured down to the last ounce, the drop in steel production worked out to the last ton.

Hoover was the last classical liberal in the White House, the last defender of the doctrine that the government should not interfere with the marketplace. History had proved not only the efficiency but also the morality of American individualism, so the depression had to be the result of the collapse of the European economy, rather than domestic failures. Therefore, nothing was to be gained by governmental interference in the domestic economy. But even the apostle of rugged individualism was gradually forced to move closer to state socialism than any previous peacetime President. The Federal Farm Loan Bank was propped up with a billion dollars for loans to help the farmers avoid foreclosures. The Federal Reserve Board expanded the supply of credit. The Reconstruction Finance Corporation channeled $2 billion to banks, railroads, and insurance companies teetering on the brink of collapse. In the face of charges that the "trickle-down" theory constituted a dole for corporations, Hoover argued that restoring prosperity to the banks and corporations would, in turn, reinvigorate the economy.

The man who had saved the starving people of Europe never left the White House to inspect the soup kitchens or to look at the faces of the apple sellers.‡ Hoover was not unmindful of the misery faced by many Americans and was personally generous with contributions to charity. But he fought against direct relief for the unemployed, regarding it as a handout. "If we start appropriations of this character we have not only impaired something infinitely valuable in the life of the American people but have struck at the roots of self-government," the President declared.

An engineer, Hoover saw society in the abstract, as a problem in the organization of matter and energy. Once something was clear and tidy in his mind, it should conform to the blueprint. Today it is pointless to argue whether or not his efforts to end the depression would have succeeded given enough time. Americans were puzzled—and then angered—that a President who handed out relief to corporations could ignore the misery of people grubbing in garbage cans for food. No leader who followed such a policy could maintain the confidence of the public. The day had passed when workmen who had lost their jobs due to the blind operation of the system could cultivate a patch of garden or begin again on the western frontier. Now they were truly helpless, for the United States was the only major industrial nation without some form of national unemployment insurance. Unable to cope with the chilling realities of modern society, the unemployed turned in desperation for help to the agency of last resort: the federal government.

‡ In fact, Hoover never believed the apple sellers were a symbol of distress. He maintained that the apple growers' associations, stuck with a surplus and shrewdly appraising the sympathy of the public for the unemployed, established a system of selling apples on street corners, which allowed them to get higher prices for their fruit. "Many persons left their jobs for the more profitable one of selling apples," he declared. Herbert Hoover, *The Memoirs of Herbert Hoover* (New York: The Macmillan Company, 1952), Vol. III, p. 195.

Franklin Roosevelt, perhaps the most advanced of the forty-eight state governors in dealing with the depression, was, like Hoover, unable to free himself from obeisance to the totem of a balanced budget. Although he emphasized the need for an enlarged public works program to provide jobs in his annual message to the legislature in January 1931, expenditures were strictly limited by the reduced state revenues. But Roosevelt's basic instincts—the sense of *noblesse oblige* instilled in him by his parents and Dr. Peabody, as well as his belief in social justice—were carrying him beyond the boundaries of economic orthodoxy. Frances Perkins recalled a meeting in which a conservative economist tried to assure the governor that the crisis would be cured by allowing the laws of supply and demand to follow their natural course. "I shall never forget the gray look of horror on his face as he turned to this man and said, 'People aren't cattle you know!' "

Under the guidance of bright young university and labor economists who had been mustered by Miss Perkins, Roosevelt groped toward recognition that all the old solutions for the canker of depression were totally useless. "New and untried remedies must at least be experimented with," he declared in June 1931. Over a million New Yorkers were without jobs, local governments and private charities were running out of money, and during the coming winter New York City alone would need $20 million for relief. Realizing that his own political future would turn on how he dealt with the emergency, Roosevelt told Sam Rosenman that if Washington was unwilling to assume responsibility then it was up to the individual states to provide work or food for the unemployed. "Government just can't sit back and expect private charity or even local government to take care of it entirely," he declared. But Roosevelt was unable to act without approval from the legislature, and it was not due to meet until January 1932. Paradoxically, the preoccupation of the Republicans with Tammany corruption provided the opportunity he was seeking. The investigating committee requested him to convene a special legislative session so a law could be passed granting immunity to witnesses, and he complied with alacrity. "This is the time to get some direct action on unemployment relief," he informed Rosenman.

Roosevelt addressed the legislature in person, and unveiling a theme that was to be an underlying concept of the New Deal, said that it was the duty of the government to alleviate distress and promote the general welfare of its citizens. The people were the masters of the government, rather than the other way around.

> The duty of the State toward the citizen is the duty of the servant to its master. The people have created it; the people, by common consent, permit its continual existence. One of these duties of the State is that of car-

ing for those of its citizens who find themselves the victims of such adverse circumstances as makes them unable to obtain even the necessities for mere existence without the aid of others. . . . To these unfortunate citizens aid must be extended by government—not as a matter of charity but as a matter of *social duty*.

Pointing out that local governments and private charities could not meet the heavy burdens being imposed upon them, Roosevelt recommended that the state appropriate $20 million, for a Temporary Emergency Relief Administration, that was to be raised by increased state income taxes. This was to be no dole, however. The first priority of the agency would be to provide jobs for the unemployed; if work could not be found, food, clothing and shelter would be provided to the needy. Local officials were to distribute the relief funds under the guidance of a three-member state commission and an executive director.

This proposal may seem commonplace today, but in 1931 it was regarded as a challenging statement, particularly coming from a leading candidate for the presidency. Yet Roosevelt was inspired by a wish to preserve the American economic and social system, rather than to make fundamental changes in it. A year before, he had remarked that it was "time for the country to become fairly radical for at least one generation. History shows that where this occurs, occasionally, nations are saved from revolutions." In fact, Roosevelt's plan was a response to the urgings of the President for the states and local governments to assume more of the burden of relief. The governor also self-righteously criticized Hoover's resort to deficit spending rather than following Rooseveltian pay-as-you-go methods. "I am disturbed by this morning's news that the President's policy seems to be to borrow money, over one billion dollars, to pay the current treasury deficit," he told a correspondent. "This merely puts the burden of the unemployment cycle on future generations."

Instead of challenging Roosevelt on the basis of economic or social policy, the Republican leaders chose purely political grounds for an attack. They tried to enact a plan of their own designed to keep control of the machinery of relief out of the governor's hands. Roosevelt refused to accept an opposition bill that placed the administration of relief under the Department of Social Welfare (headed by a Republican) and called for the unlimited matching of local funds with state money without an increase in revenues. Assailing the Republican plan as a pork-barrel proposal that would spend the state into bankruptcy, Roosevelt threatened to veto it and immediately call another special session. The Republicans would be saddled with the blame for delaying relief and the cost of the new session. Realizing that they had been outsmarted, the opposition capitulated, and approved the governor's plan without substantial change.

Roosevelt emerged from the affair with increased national prestige and a reputation as the governor doing the most to deal with the effects of unemployment.

The Temporary Emergency Relief Administration—immediately dubbed the T.E.R.A. by the press in a forerunner of the abbreviations describing New Deal agencies—was in place by the end of 1931, with Jesse Straus, who was helping finance the Roosevelt presidential campaign, as its chairman. Straus chose Harry L. Hopkins, a young professional social worker and head of the New York Tuberculosis and Health Association, as executive director. Ignoring civil-service rules, Hopkins recruited a capable staff from private welfare agencies and launched a determined attack upon the harshest distress. But the task was overwhelming. At the beginning of 1932, there were at least 1.5 million unemployed in New York State, and the number was increasing daily. Soon the T.E.R.A. was furnishing relief to nearly 10 percent of the state's families, providing an average of about twenty-three dollars monthly. Minuscule as these payments were, they kept starvation at bay and were generous by the standards of other areas. In Detroit, relief payments averaged five cents a day per person, and coal miners in southern Illinois received $1.50 every two weeks.

It quickly became obvious that the $20 million appropriated for relief was not enough, and in March 1932, Roosevelt, declaring that no one should be allowed to go "unfed, unclothed, or unsheltered,"* requested more money for relief. The legislature appropriated $5 million to carry the program through November 1, when a referendum would be submitted to the voters for a $30-million bond issue. The gravity of the situation had forced Roosevelt to abandon his Jeffersonian abhorrence of deficit financing. "In such extraordinary times," he acknowledged, "I believe that extraordinary measures, otherwise not to be considered, are justified." He also modified his belief in states' rights, to endorse Senator Wagner's proposal for a $750-million federal unemployment relief bill, then pending before Congress. "Where the State itself is unable to successfully fulfill this obligation," he declared, "it then becomes the positive duty of the Federal Government to step in to help."

With the coming of a new year, Roosevelt dropped all pretense about his candidacy for the presidential nomination. On January 22, 1932—eight days before his fiftieth birthday—he allowed his name to be entered in the North Dakota primary in accordance with a state law that a candidate had to announce his availability before he could be placed on the ballot. This contest had been carefully chosen for Roosevelt's debut as an active candidate because North Dakota's nine delegates were safely in

* These words forecast FDR's "one third of nation" remarks in his second inaugural speech, Jan. 20, 1937.

Jim Farley's bag. On Roosevelt's birthday, Al Smith telegraphed HEARTY CONGRATULATIONS ON THE HALF CENTURY but made no mention of the announcement of the candidacy. The reason for this omission became patently clear not long afterward, when the Happy Warrior sent his familiar brown derby sailing into the ring.

Sitting in his office in the nearly empty Empire State Building—opened in 1931, hardly the best time to attract tenants—Smith had ample time to brood on the slights that he convinced himself he had suffered at Roosevelt's hands. Not long before, Ed Flynn had called upon his old friend to sound out his political intentions and Smith had assured him he was through with politics. Reaching into a desk drawer, he pulled out a sheaf of papers covered with figures and spread them before Flynn. "Ed, these are all the debts that I must clear up," Smith said. "Financially I am in an extremely bad situation." Members of Smith's family had speculated heavily in the stock market and had been wiped out in the crash, leaving him to pay off their debts. But as jealousy, resentment, and ambition gnawed at his spirit, he decided upon one more try at the White House.

The long-smoldering conflict between Roosevelt and Smith flared into public view during the off-year election in November 1931. Roosevelt had proposed an amendment to the state constitution providing for a $19-million bond issue for the purchase of non-productive land for reforestation, a project dear to his heart. Looking about for an issue that could be a test of popularity between himself and Roosevelt, Smith attacked the referendum as a giveaway to the lumber interests. Surprised by the vehemence of Smith's assault, Roosevelt mobilized the support of conservationists, and the amendment was approved handily—proof of his strength in the state. "What a queer thing that was for Al to fight so bitterly," he mused to a friend. "I cannot help remembering the fact that while he was Governor I agreed with almost all the policies he recommended but I was against one or two during those eight years. However, for the sake of party solidarity, I kept my mouth shut."

Roosevelt was concerned about Smith's belligerency, for despite an increasing conservatism and the influence upon him of such millionaire friends as Raskob, Smith was still popular with urban voters. A report from Clark Howell, publisher of the Atlanta *Constitution*, on a lengthy conversation he had had with "Alfred" heightened the concern. Howell had told Smith that he could assure a Democratic victory in 1932 by supporting Roosevelt for the presidency and that everyone believed he could not do otherwise. "The hell I can't," Smith had snapped. He added, however, that he had always put party above personality and would support "the man who seems best for the party." When Howell inquired if there was any personal hostility between himself and Roosevelt, Smith replied:

"No—socially we are friends. He has always been kind to me and my family, and has gone out of his way to be agreeable to us at the Mansion at Albany but"—and here Howell said he rose and angrily stamped his foot —"do you know, by God, that he has never consulted me about a damn thing since he has been Governor? He has taken bad advice and from sources not friendly to me. He has ignored me!"

For Roosevelt and his supporters, the winter of 1931–32 was a time of discontent. Smith's candidacy quickened the pulses of other aspirants, and Governor Ritchie, Newton Baker, and "Cactus Jack" Garner, among others, positioned themselves to reap the harvest if Roosevelt should falter. While feigning neutrality, Raskob and Jouett Shouse, director of the National Committee's Washington office, kept the political pot bubbling by subtly encouraging these candidates. Bernard Baruch was going about calling Roosevelt "the Boy Scout Governor" and praising Ritchie and Owen Young—although he denied it when confronted by Roosevelt. The "stop Roosevelt" movement received a boost with the choice of Chicago as the site of the national convention, over the objections of Howe and Farley. They feared that Mayor Anton Cermak, who was leaning toward Smith, might pack the galleries with anti-Roosevelt ward heelers. And issues were taking the place of backslapping. For two years Roosevelt had sheltered himself from controversy by calculated generalities, but now he was coming under fire for failing to take a stand on Prohibition, for avoiding comment on foreign affairs, and for appearing both conservative and liberal on the question of relief.

Worse yet, the Tammany scandals returned to haunt the governor. Among those collared by the relentless Samuel Seabury was Sheriff Thomas M. Farley,† of New York County, who had amassed a fortune of some four hundred thousand dollars over seven years on salary and expenses of eighty-seven thousand dollars. When asked where he had gotten the money, Farley said it had all come from "a wonderful [tin] box." Unamused, Seabury sent a transcript of the testimony to Roosevelt with a recommendation that Farley be summarily fired. Roosevelt was in a quandary. On one side, Tammany was seething over Seabury's inquiry and threatening to withhold its delegates; on the other, the reformers, uncertain about his capacities for the presidency, were carefully watching to see how he resolved the matter.

To add to Roosevelt's problems, he came under fire from William Randolph Hearst, Garner's chief supporter, who assailed him as an internationalist and supporter of the League of Nations. Roosevelt's first instinct was to ignore the Lord of San Simeon, but as the attacks grew more strident, Howe warned that the only way to silence the isolationist Hearst

† Sheriff Farley was not related to Jim Farley.

was to beat a retreat from the League. Yet such a reversal had been made difficult by a widely-discussed column by Walter Lippmann that portrayed Roosevelt as a charming but slippery master of the art of carrying water on both shoulders. "Franklin Roosevelt is no crusader," Lippmann wrote. "He is no tribune of the people. He is no enemy of entrenched privilege. He is a pleasant man who, without any important qualifications for the office, would like very much to be President."‡

Beset and upset, Roosevelt squirmed under these attacks from the press. But placating Hearst was more important than chancing the scorn of a columnist—even if it did lend weight to Lippmann's charges of equivocation. And so, after much soul-searching, Roosevelt, who had run for the vice-presidency a dozen years before as an eloquent advocate of the League of Nations, dramatically recanted. "The League of Nations today is not the League conceived by Woodrow Wilson," he declared. "It might have been had the United States joined. Too often through these years its major function has been not the broad overwhelming purpose of world peace, but rather a mere meeting place for the discussion of strictly European political national difficulties. In these the United States should have no part." These words were sandwiched between two conflicting statements: an attack on the Hawley-Smoot Tariff intended as a peace offering to the internationalists; and a denunciation of the Europeans for failure to pay their war debts, offered as a bone to the isolationists. All in all, it was an inconsistent, weaseling performance that shocked some of Roosevelt's friends and convinced detractors he was out of his depth in national politics. "I am devoted to Franklin but he ought to be spanked," said Mrs. Charles Hamlin.

Having appeased Hearst, Roosevelt tried to placate the reformers by removing Sheriff Farley. "Democracy is a just but jealous master," he said in a statement drafted by Raymond Moley. Public officials with wealth beyond their salaries had "a positive public duty to give reasonable or credible explanation." The statement boomeranged, however. Two prominent reformers, Rabbi Stephen S. Wise and the Reverend John Haynes Holmes, pointed out that Seabury's files contained numerous cases of a similar nature and demanded that the governor take action on them. Convinced that Seabury harbored presidential ambitions of his own, and jumpy over his recent run of bad luck, Roosevelt stepped out of character by accusing the clergymen of caring "more for personal publicity than for good government," and in essence told them to mind their own business. Howe angrily blamed Rosenman for the unfortunate wording of the state-

‡ Lippmann, then a supporter of Newton Baker, later switched to FDR. Speaking of his famous column in later years, he said: "That I will maintain to my dying day was true of the Franklin Roosevelt of 1932." Ronald Steel, *Walter Lippmann and the American Century* (Boston: Little, Brown & Company, 1980), p. 292.

ment, but the problem lay much deeper. No one could mollify Tammany and the reformers at the same time.

Roosevelt faced more than thirty-five state conventions and primaries before the Democrats would gather in Chicago in late June to choose their nominee, and he needed a staff to formulate ideas, prepare speeches and statements, and in general supply an intellectual underpinning for the campaign. Howe, Farley, and Flynn were political technicians untutored in national campaign issues, and Rosenman doubted that anyone on the staff could meet the challenge. "We'd be in an awful fix" if the campaign had to begin immediately, he warned Roosevelt one evening in March. Having caught the governor's attention, Rosenman suggested that a group of university professors be gathered to confer with Roosevelt and prepare memoranda on the complex problems of agricultural relief, tariffs, railroads, government debts, and private credit.* Moley, who had already proved to be a versatile idea man and eloquent speech writer, was selected to recruit other members and to head the team. This may have been an act of diplomacy on Rosenman's part for, unlike himself, Moley got along with Howe and would allay the little man's suspicion of anyone who had influence with Roosevelt. Presidential candidates have often had councils of advisers—usually industrialists and financiers—but hardly ever one composed of scholars. At first Roosevelt resisted the idea, contending that academics talked too much and were too pedantic, but he was intrigued, as always, with the idea of breaking new ground. Finally agreeing, he insisted on having only New Yorkers, for money was short and he wanted his advisers readily available. Because of these limitations, Moley recruited them from among his colleagues at Columbia. Young and imaginative, they represented a variety of views and opinions, and not all were admirers of the governor.

Moley himself, who had been brought into the Roosevelt circle as a specialist on criminal justice, was a conservative reformer. Rex Tugwell, who looked more like a matinee idol than an agricultural economist, believed capitalism had failed and favored a fundamental but non-Marxist reordering of the economic system. Adolf A. Berle, coauthor of the soon-to-be-published and influential book *The Modern Corporation and Private Property*, supported changes in the structure of business and was an avowed backer of Newton Baker.† Rosenman, who had been appointed

---

* Moley, however, states that FDR had already spoken to him about the need for expert, professional advice on national issues. After Rosenman came to the same conclusion, Moley says he encouraged him to believe that he was the originator of the idea. Raymond Moley, *After Seven Years* (New York: Harper & Brothers, 1939), pp. 8–9.
† " 'I want your expertise, not your vote,' Moley told Berle. 'We've got plenty of votes but we need experts.' " Quoted in a lecture by Elliot A. Rosen, "The Brain Trust," at the Smithsonian Institution, Feb. 2, 1981.

by Roosevelt to the New York State Supreme Court, and Basil O'Connor, the governor's law partner, were *ex officio* members of the group.

The existence of this circle of academic advisers was kept secret, because Howe feared that the press would poke fun at it. In fact, he was not enthusiastic himself and, according to Rosenman, derisively referred to it in a conversation with Roosevelt as "your brains trust." Sometime later, a New York *Times* man ferreted out the story and described the advisers as the "brains trust." The term caught on with the "s" dropped, and the Brain Trust became irrevocably linked with Roosevelt and the New Deal. As Howe feared, conservative papers ridiculed the Brain Trust, usually portraying its members as wild-eyed radicals. Roosevelt was stimulated and enlightened by his academic advisers, and they, in turn, were fascinated at the prospect of tutoring a presidential candidate in a time of national crisis.

The Brain Trust would usually go up to Albany on a late-afternoon train, arriving in time for dinner. The table talk would be casual, but once they gathered about the fireplace in the adjoining study,‡ Roosevelt would toss out a problem on which he was seeking information, and as Moley recalled, "we were off at an exciting and exhausting clip." Roosevelt was "a student, a cross-examiner, and a judge. He would listen with rapt attention for a few minutes and then break in with a question whose sharpness was characteristically blurred with an anecdotal introduction or an air of sympathetic agreement with the speaker. . . . But those darting questions of Roosevelt were the ticks of the evening's metronome. The intervals between them would grow shorter. The questions themselves would become meatier, more informed—the infallible index to the amount he was picking up in the evening's course. By midnight . . . the Governor, scorning further questions, would be making vigorous pronouncements on the subject we had been discussing, waving his cigarette holder to emphasize his points."

Roosevelt confronted a complex problem. As governor of New York, he had been concerned merely with the effects of the depression; now he had to raise his sights and create ideas and policy for dealing with the causes of the upheaval as well as to alleviate the distress resulting from it. The task of the Brain Trust was to provide the intellectual foundation for this readjustment. Their job was not to do his thinking but to provide options. Roosevelt was remarkably receptive to novel and unorthodox ideas—sometimes almost too receptive—as Moley noted. But there were times when he felt that the professors, in their enthusiasm at having the nation as a laboratory in which to test their theories, were trying to push

‡ Drinks were available for those who wanted them. Tugwell often wondered who FDR's bootlegger was but never asked.

too far too fast. Tugwell, in particular, pressed for a more radical program of reconstruction than the candidate was willing to accept.

More experienced in politics than his advisers, Roosevelt had a clearer grasp of the political realities and the temper of the American people. In the spring of 1932, his immediate goal was to win the nomination. Farley, Howe, and Flynn would by convention time have corralled a majority of the delegates, but Roosevelt would still be short the magic two thirds required for victory. And if he did not prevail on an early ballot, his chances of winning would fade. Under these circumstances, Roosevelt argued that it would indeed be foolhardy to risk getting too far in front of public opinion. William Jennings Bryan had, for example, aroused the American people with his ideas and passion, but he had never been elected President. Would it not be wiser, would it not show more political foresight, to win the nomination and the election, and keep proposals likely to stir up controversy under wraps until he had time to educate the voters? Berle, for one, came to accept this viewpoint: "Roosevelt chose as much of the ideas and measures we presented to him as he believed he could translate into reality," he observed many years later.

The first fruit of the Brain Trust was a ten-minute nationwide radio address, drafted by Moley, that was delivered by Roosevelt on April 7. Although the speech was presented under the auspices of the Democratic National Committee, the candidate turned it to his own advantage by laying out a positive program designed to reassure liberals of his progressivism. In words that cast a long shadow, he dismissed the "trickle-down" proposals of the Republican and Democratic conservatives and demanded a recovery program "that builds from the bottom up and not from the top down, that puts the faith once more in the forgotten man at the bottom of the economic pyramid." He called for diversion of some of the Reconstruction Finance Corporation's funds to loans to small businessmen, farmers, and homeowners facing foreclosure—all to be key components of the New Deal.

The "Forgotten Man"* speech not only created a vivid image of the millions left in economic desperation by the depression, but it came at a critical juncture in the campaign for delegates. It had an electrifying effect upon the farmers of the midwestern and southern states, where primaries and conventions were getting underway. The governor of New York became a rallying point for the distressed and dispossessed, and he won most of the delegates from the southern and western states who were not pledged to favorite sons. Conservatives in both parties were furious,

* Moley picked up the "Forgotten Man" from an article written in 1883 by William Graham Sumner. Sumner had used it to describe the middle-class citizen who bears society's most burdensome loads, not the destitute.

however, and branded Roosevelt's remarks as unmitigated demagoguery. Al Smith led the assault. "I will take off my coat and fight to the end against any candidate who persists in any demagogic appeal to the working people of this country to destroy themselves by setting class against class, and rich against poor," he declared. Later, Smith claimed that he had not been referring to Roosevelt, and the governor, accepting the disclaimer, archly told newsmen: "Wasn't that a terrible attack Al made on Alfalfa Bill Murray?"

Roosevelt toned down his appeal to progressivism in succeeding speeches but revived it in a commencement address at Oglethorpe University, in Atlanta, on May 23, 1932. This speech had a curious origin. The candidate was out picnicking at Warm Springs with several of the reporters assigned to cover him, when they began ribbing him about his wishy-washy speeches. "Well, if you boys don't like my speeches, why don't you take a hand at drafting one yourselves?" Roosevelt demanded. Ernest Lindley, of the New York *Herald Tribune*, who had recently published a Roosevelt campaign biography, took up the challenge and produced a speech, edited by several other newsmen, that provided the New Deal with its watchword:

> The country needs and unless I mistake its temper, the country demands bold, persistent experimentation. It is common sense to take a method and try it. If it fails, admit it frankly and try another. But above all, try something. The millions who are in want will not stand by silently forever while the things to satisfy their needs are within easy reach.

"Bold, persistent experimentation. . . ." Lindley may have written these words for him, but to an increasing extent, they represented Roosevelt's own thinking. In New York State, he had already exhibited a pragmatic willingness to break with tradition by establishing a program of relief for the unemployed and distressed. Obviously, his thoughts were running in the same direction as he concentrated on national problems. But clever politics decreed that he soft-pedal any discussion of sweeping change until after the Democratic convention. In fact, Louis Howe was infuriated by all this talk about experimentation. Didn't Roosevelt realize that it would scare away voters who already suspected that he might be a dangerous radical? And would it gain him a single vote that he could not already count upon?

Roosevelt heeded the warning. Having reestablished his liberal credentials, he carefully made no more statements of this kind until after the convention was safely over. But just a few days before the Oglethorpe University speech, Sam Rosenman had arrived at Warm Springs with a lengthy memorandum from Moley that outlined most of the proposals that were, in the words of Elliot Rosen, "to constitute the domestic New

Deal of the years 1933 through 1937." Moley urged that the Democratic party support liberal and humane policies designed to create a farmer-labor constituency and suggested higher taxes on corporations and the wealthy to redistribute income. He also proposed that the federal government assume direct responsibility for relief, and recommended a package of assistance and public works that would be financed by deficit spending if necessary. Other proposals included recognition of the Soviet Union to increase trade, getting jobless youths off the streets by putting them to work on conservation projects, and in a major shift of policy, dealing with the agricultural crisis by crop controls rather than by dumping surpluses abroad. Revised and modified as required, the Moley memorandum shaped the New Deal and the administration of Franklin Roosevelt.

XV

"HAPPY DAYS
ARE HERE AGAIN!"

FROM ALL POINTS of the compass, exuberant Democrats streamed into Chicago in the last days of June 1932, confident they were about to choose the next President of the United States. Any doubts had been allayed by the Republicans, who had glumly renominated Herbert Hoover, in the same city, at a convention that reminded some observers of a funeral. Little groups of Democrats clustered in the lobbies of the lakefront hotels and the higher-class speakeasies, slapping backs, trading the latest rumors, and launching conspiracies. "To the Republicans politics is a business," said Anne O'Hare McCormick of the New York Times, "while to the Democrats it's a pleasure."

Franklin Roosevelt did not go to Chicago. It was difficult for him to move about in crowds, and by remaining in Albany, he could make strategic decisions without being pressured. Louis Howe, Jim Farley, and Ed Flynn opened headquarters in the Congress Hotel, but every important move was cleared with the Boss. "We did nothing without consulting him," said Flynn. A private telephone line was established between the Executive Mansion and Howe's command post, in Room 1702. As delegates arrived, they were greeted by Farley and taken there to hear Roosevelt's cheerful voice crackling from a loudspeaker as he greeted "my friends from Nebraska" or "Indiana" or "Alabama" with a personal word and a pitch for their votes. Key leaders had extended private conversations with the governor, and they usually came away impressed.

On the verge of attaining the goal he had first envisioned for Roosevelt two decades before, Howe was tense and suspicious. He saw danger everywhere, and some of his security arrangements were comic. Margaret Durand, his longtime secretary, whom he called "Rabbit," screened all visitors to Room 1702, assisted by his son Hartley. Flynn and Farley were quartered in widely separated suites, and they kept in touch with Howe through a team of messengers that scurried along the hotel's back stairs. A young assistant was dispatched to the Chicago Stadium, where the convention was to be held, to commandeer three adjoining rooms so that the two end ones could be kept empty and locked to prevent eavesdropping on Farley when he moved his operations there. To forestall leaks, Louise "Hacky" Hackmeister was brought in from Albany to run the switchboard. Secretaries were warned against dating men who might be spying for rival candidates. Pro-Roosevelt delegates were assigned to keep tabs on the other factions within their delegations.

The various campaign headquarters were crowded together on the ground floor of the Congress—dubbed "President's Row"—and their recorded campaign songs created an ear-splitting din: "Anchors Aweigh," chosen to recall Roosevelt's association with the Navy; "The Sidewalks of New York," for Smith; "The Eyes of Texas," for Garner; "Maryland, My Maryland!" for Ritchie; and "Carry Me Back to Old Virginny," for Harry Byrd. Campaign aides swarmed about with outstretched hands and rationalizations of how their candidate was going to sweep the convention; reporters nosed around, looking for stories; pretty girls pinned campaign badges on anyone who wandered by. Roosevelt's headquarters was the liveliest and the object of the most curiosity. "I am just going around from cage to cage to look at the animals and pick out one to support," John W. Davis, the Democratic standard-bearer of 1924, told newsmen who cornered him coming out of Farley's office.

Prominently displayed in the corridor was a huge map of the United States with the states committed to Roosevelt colored red. It was designed to persuade hesitant delegates to climb on board the Roosevelt bandwagon while there was still time, although other candidates scoffed that it represented more area than votes. Farley steadfastly predicted a first-ballot victory for Roosevelt, but Al Smith dismissed these claims as "Farley's Fairy Stories." Other nose counts put Roosevelt anywhere from eighty to 150 votes short of the 768 needed for a two-thirds majority. And Mayor Frank Hague of Jersey City claimed that Roosevelt was the weakest candidate that the Democrats could possibly field against Hoover; if nominated, he would not carry a single state east of the Mississippi. Apprised of Boss Hague's fiery words, Roosevelt dictated a mild reply to be circulated by Farley that was calculated to anger no one and emphasized his role as party harmonizer and compromiser: "Governor Roosevelt's friends have not come to Chicago to criticize, cry down or defame any Democrat from any part of the country."

Roosevelt had won thirty-four states and six territories in the primaries and caucuses, most of them in the South and the West, but his control of those areas was by no means assured. Garner had corralled the large California and Texas delegations, while Mississippi was Roosevelt's by only a one-vote margin, and Senator Huey P. Long, the leader of one of two contending Louisiana delegations, was an uncertain factor. At the moment, the Kingfish was leaning toward Roosevelt, but anything could be expected from the pudgy populist. There were also two Minnesota delegations. Al Smith was Roosevelt's major problem, however. Wearing a straw hat at a cocky angle, he arrived in Chicago saying he was not interested in a "stop Roosevelt" movement but in preventing the formation of a "stop Smith" campaign. Asked by a newsman what he hoped the convention would accomplish, he unhesitatingly replied: "Write an honest, concise, clear platform and nominate me."

Roosevelt and Smith had clashed in seven states that spring. Roosevelt had won four primaries and Smith two, while they both trailed Garner in California. In Massachusetts, Smith had given Roosevelt a severe jolt by winning by a three-to-one margin,* and he had made a good showing in Pennsylvania although Roosevelt had carried the state. Roosevelt's most humiliating loss to Smith was in New York, where John F. Curry, the leader of Tammany, denied him all but a third of the delegation, all from upstate except for Flynn's loyal Bronx delegates. Tammany had exacted this revenge for the Seabury investigations, which had now engulfed Mayor Jimmy Walker. The implacable Seabury wanted to know why a New York businessman had given Walker $246,692 as his share of the profits of a stock transaction in which the mayor had not invested a penny. Why had the representative of a taxicab holding company interested in limiting the number of cabs on the city's streets given Walker $26,535 in bonds? And how had an obscure sixty-dollar-a-week bookkeeper in Walker's old law firm accumulated $961,000 in a bank account from which he paid the mayor's personal bills? The dapper Walker tried to brush off these inquiries with wisecracks and evasions that satisfied no one.

Three weeks before the start of the Democratic convention, Seabury, in a move that reinforced Roosevelt's conviction that he was out for his scalp as well as that of Walker, dropped the entire mess into the governor's lap. The press demanded that Roosevelt act at once, and both Tammany and the reformers watched closely to see how he handled the dilemma. Faced with a no-win situation, Roosevelt stalled as long as he could before sending Walker a copy of the charges pending against him. Fortunately, the mayor had the presence of mind to delay his reply until the convention was over.

* FDR's advisers had argued against entering the Massachusetts primary, a state with a large Irish Catholic vote, but their objections were overcome by James M. Curley and James Roosevelt (who had gone into the insurance business in Boston and become Curley's protégé).

"We have Roosevelt licked now!" proclaimed Jouett Shouse, openly partisan despite his position on the National Committee. Nevertheless, the "stop Roosevelt" movement had the unity of confetti and lacked the one thing it most needed to prevail: a single candidate everyone could agree on. Hearst disliked Roosevelt but despised Smith and the internationalism of Newton Baker even more. William McAdoo, leader of the key California delegation, was pledged to Garner, but he had not forgotten 1924 and, given the choice between Smith and Roosevelt, he would take Roosevelt. And Smith, by his refusal to say he would support one of his rivals if his own candidacy faltered, had alienated them. In fact, the Happy Warrior seemed to have lost his sure political touch. "The Al of today is no longer a politician of the first chop," wrote Henry Mencken. "His association with the rich has apparently wobbled him. He has become a golf player."

Just before coming to Chicago, the Roosevelt forces had met at Hyde Park to put their convention strategy in final order. Haunted by the example of Champ Clark, who had entered the Democratic convention in 1912 with a majority, only to fall victim to the two-thirds rule, they reached a tentative agreement to fight for its abolition if conditions appeared favorable. Before Farley and Flynn were ready, however, the issue got out of hand, and for one hectic afternoon it appeared as if Roosevelt's candidacy might have been sunk even before his name was put in nomination.

Three days before the convention was to be called to order, Farley summoned about sixty-five leaders of the pro-Roosevelt delegations to an organizational meeting. Several matters had been disposed of, when Huey Long proposed a resolution urging a fight against the two-thirds rule. Realizing that not all Roosevelt delegates opposed the rule, Farley tried to brush the resolution aside, saying it would be unfair to the candidate to put him on record on the issue without consulting him. But the Kingfish, making his debut on the national scene, launched into a rousing stem-winder that carried his audience by storm. Josephus Daniels, Cordell Hull, Homer Cummings of Connecticut, and others supported him, and Farley lost control of the meeting. "He looked bewildered, confused and pathetic," said Molly Dewson, head of the Women's Division. Long's resolution carried, and the Roosevelt forces were now pledged to fight for the abolition of the two-thirds rule—whether they wanted to or not.

"The incident hit me like a blow on the nose," said Farley. Southern conservatives, the backbone of Roosevelt's strength, supported the two-thirds rule, because it gave them a veto over the party's deliberations and warned that any move to abolish it would cost Roosevelt votes. A worried Farley immediately telephoned the governor, but the lines were down due to a bad storm in upstate New York and it was some time before he reached Albany. Roosevelt accepted the bad news philosophically; let matters simmer down and follow developments, he told Farley. As expected, Roosevelt's rivals assailed the resolution as an attempt to change the rules in the middle of the game. Newton Baker, now regarded as the leading "dark horse" candidate, said a nomination won under such conditions would have a "moral flaw" in the title. Senator Pat Harrison, of Mississippi, who was almost singlehandedly holding the delegation in line for Roosevelt, objected, and even some northern states, such as Pennsylvania, were on record against doing away with the two-thirds rule.

With the ranks of Roosevelt's supporters in danger of crumbling, Louis Howe told the Governor to sound the retreat. From Albany came an adroitly worded statement backing away from the resolution but holding open the face-saving option of raising the issue again. Roosevelt had withdrawn in good order, but he had lost the skirmish. Farley blamed Long for jumping the gun, which had given the opposition a rallying point. Had the plan to abolish the two-thirds rule been sprung upon the convention itself, he was convinced, it would have been approved before the "stop Roosevelt" movement could organize themselves. Be that as it may, Roosevelt's rivals had tasted blood, and as *Time* remarked, "Smith & The Favorite Sons took fresh heart."

The convention was gaveled to order by John Raskob shortly before one o'clock on the afternoon of June 27. Spread out before him, filling some two acres of the Chicago Stadium, were 3,210 delegates and alternates with 1,154 votes to cast. The galleries were packed with nearly thirty thousand spectators, nearly all vociferous supporters of Al Smith and hand-picked by Mayor Anton Cermak's underlings. To cut expenses, the Democrats had retained the decorations put up by the Republicans, and a huge portrait of George Washington gazed down upon the milling throng. Alice Longworth, no doubt hoping that Cousin Franklin would be tripped up on his way to the nomination, also remained behind. "I'm here to see the show," explained Princess Alice when asked what a rock-ribbed Republican was doing at a Democratic convention. "I've been going to conventions, both Republican and Democratic, for more than twenty-five years." The sweltering heat soon pressed down upon the delegates, crumpling collars and suits and turning the stadium into a steam bath.

For two hours, Senator Alben W. Barkley, of Kentucky, kept the delegates on their feet with a keynote address that hung the depression about the necks of the Republicans. "No fair man or woman wants to be unjust to Mr. Hoover," the white-suited Barkley declared. "But that the

Hoover Administration and the policies it has pursued have largely contributed to the disaster which has overtaken ours and the world's affairs
no intelligent observer can dispute." The speech was so long, Will Rogers
declared, because "when you start enumerating the things that the Republicans have got away with in the last twelve years you have cut your
self out a job." The delegates wanted a chance to demonstrate, and when
the Kentuckian proposed repeal of Prohibition, he touched off a wild
demonstration. Delegates poured into the aisles shouting and singing,
banners were produced, bands played, and a pipe organ boomed out campaign songs from the bowels of the hall. "It was only the beginning,"
noted Farley. "Those tunes lingered on for almost a week, repeated over
and over through long, hot weary night sessions until most of the delegates wished they had the power to throw both the organ and the bands
into nearby Lake Michigan."

The real work of the convention began on the second day, and Roosevelt's supporters did not repeat the blunders of the two-thirds rule. The
Credentials Committee recommended the seating of the pro-Roosevelt
Louisiana and Minnesota delegations, but minority reports were filed, so
the issue had to be settled on the floor. In both cases, the Roosevelt forces
prevailed by significant margins. The next test—the choice of a permanent chairman for the convention—was touch and go. The post was important because the permanent chairman could exercise enormous influence over the choice of the nominee, as Elihu Root had done at the
Republican convention in 1912, by recognizing speakers, ruling on parlia-
mentary questions, and cutting demonstrations short.

At their final strategy session at Hyde Park, Roosevelt and his advisers had settled upon Senator Tom Walsh for the job, while Jouett
Shouse was the candidate of the "stop Roosevelt" forces. They accused
Roosevelt of deviousness and bad faith, claiming that he had not objected
when, months before, the National Committee had agreed upon Shouse.
The governor's supporters noted, however, that he had agreed only to
"commend" Shouse to the convention, not "recommend" him. Tension
was so high that Farley had difficulty in finding a seat among the hostile
New York delegation even though he was an accredited delegate. He nervously kept a tally on long sheets of brown paper as the roll was called,
and never forgot his feeling of relief when Walsh won—by fewer than a
hundred votes. In Albany, where he had been working with Sam Rosenman upon his acceptance speech† in between telephone calls from
Chicago, Roosevelt was jubilant. And Arthur Krock, of the New York
Times, professed to hear the rumble of a Roosevelt bandwagon in the
near distance.

† A preliminary draft of the speech had been prepared by Moley and Rosenman, and
FDR worked from it.

"The nervous strain during this period of suspense was very close to the limit of physical endurance," according to Farley. "I was working eighteen or nineteen hours a day, conversing with hundreds of people, constantly consulting with other leaders, receiving reports from every delegation, and meeting at least twice daily with several hundred newspapermen. I ate my meals, usually consisting of sandwiches and milk, off a tray, and slept a few hours just before dawn if the opportunity offered. To add to my burdens, I was besieged on all sides for convention tickets which I did not have. Hundreds of other men were caught up in the same dizzy whirl. . . ." The torrid heat played havoc with Louis Howe's asthma. Gasping for breath, he lay on a couch near his desk, knees drawn up to his chest, a radio tuned to the convention. Lela Stiles, one of his secretaries, was afraid that he was dying. "Hell," said a newspaperman, "Louis Howe has come this far, half alive, and you know damned well he isn't going to die until he sees Franklin Roosevelt nominated for President."

The vice-presidential nomination was dangled before Ritchie, Byrd, and Garner in exchange for their support. Joe Kennedy telephoned Hearst with the warning that unless the California delegate switched to Roosevelt, the convention was likely to deadlock and finally end up nominating Newton Baker. The Lord of San Simeon replied that he would stick with Garner for at least seven ballots. Late on the evening of June 29, Farley met with Representative Sam Rayburn of Texas, one of Garner's closest friends, and raised the specter of a repetition of the 1924 convention unless the Speaker released his delegates to Roosevelt. In exchange, he promised to do everything in his power to secure the vice-presidential nomination for Garner. Rayburn listened without commenting until Farley had finished. "We have come to Chicago to nominate Speaker Jack Garner for the Presidency if we can," he drawled. "We are not against any other candidate and we are not for any other candidate. Governor Roosevelt is the leading candidate and naturally he must be headed off if we are to win. But we don't intend to make it another Madison Square Garden."

Farley was encouraged by the hint. No commitments had been made, but he was certain that Rayburn would be willing to listen to reason, and hastened to pass the word on to Howe. Howe was unimpressed, and thought that Harry Byrd was more likely to lead the break to Roosevelt than the Texans. They agreed to let Roosevelt make the choice, and he told them to continue to pursue both avenues. For Roosevelt, this discussion of events from afar must have been intolerable. "I would have given anything in the world to have been there too," he wrote later. "It was the most difficult thing for me to sit here with the telephone and get everything secondhand."

Worn out by three days of heat and oratory, nearly deafened by the organ as it swirled out its medley of theme songs over and over again, the delegates did not get down to the business of nominating a presidential candidate until the afternoon of June 30. Roosevelt's name was put in nomination by John Mack of Dutchess County, who had steered him into politics twenty years before. The candidate had wanted Claude Bowers or Senator Robert Wagner to nominate him, but Bowers was afraid to anger Hearst, his employer, and Wagner decided against antagonizing Tammany. Just before Mack was to go to the podium, Lela Stiles burst into Howe's room, where he lay upon his couch.

"Mein Gawd!" he cried. "What's the matter with you? Is the hotel on fire?"

Miss Stiles told him that most of the staff thought "Anchors Aweigh," the Roosevelt theme song, sounded like a dirge, and the best song for him would be "Happy Days Are Here Again!" "You, too!" he cried, clutching his head. Ed Flynn had also told him "Anchors Aweigh" sounded like a funeral march. "They're driving me nuts out at the hall. What'll we play? What'll we play? The organ player calls me every five minutes. I don't give a damn what they play."

Miss Stiles talked up "Happy Days," and as Howe looked on in horror, she began to sing, dancing up and down the room, snapping her fingers in time. With a groan, Howe picked up the phone and ordered the organist to play "Happy Days Are Here Again!" as soon as Roosevelt's name had been put in nomination.

Mack's speech was lackluster and poorly delivered. "Country born and country-loving this man's whole political life is an open book," he declared. "His reputation is unsullied, his character spotless. . . . The candidate of this convention shall be, must be and will be Franklin Delano Roosevelt!" As Mack reached his peroration, Al Smith came to the stadium in evening clothes. "I can go back to the hotel and listen to that on the radio," he rasped. Roosevelt's supporters poured out onto the floor, and a huge picture of the candidate was unfurled from the third balcony. In his room at the Congress, Howe lay on his couch next to the radio, and between spasms of coughing, kept saying, "Tell them to repeat 'Happy Days Are Here Again!'"

As the nominating and seconding speeches for the nine candidates droned on, Roosevelt and Rosenman continued work on the acceptance speech. "We presented a strange picture along about three o'clock in the morning there in the small sitting room of the Executive Mansion," he recalled. "The Governor, his wife, his mother and I sat listening to the radio. He was in his shirt sleeves, silent, puffing on one cigarette after another. The phone was at his side, and he used it frequently. He seemed deeply interested in the convention oratory, nodding approval of some parts, shaking his head in disapproval of others, laughing aloud when the eloquence became a bit too 'spread-eagle' in tone." Out in the garage, to the rear of the house, the reporters covering the governor had set up their wires and typewriters and listened to the convention on the radio. Coffee was sent over at Eleanor's order, and she went into the kitchen to scramble some eggs for them.

At one point, Roosevelt picked up the phone and the voice on the line said, "Hello, Franklin—this is the Kingfish."

"Hello, Kingfish, how are you?" replied Roosevelt with a laugh. He and Huey Long had never met.

"I'm fine and hope you are," replied the senator. "I have a suggestion for you which will clinch the nomination."

Roosevelt was all attention.

"I think that you should issue a statement immediately, saying that you are in favor of a soldier's bonus to be paid as soon as you become President."

A bonus has been promised to World War veterans, to be paid in 1945, but pressure was building up for immediate payment as an anti-depression measure. Thousands of veterans—dubbed the Bonus Army—had descended upon Washington to persuade Congress to approve such legislation. Roosevelt told Long that he was opposed to immediate payment because he favored a balanced budget.

"Well," said the Kingfish as he hung up, "you are a gone goose."

It was not until 4:28 A.M. that Senator Walsh banged his gavel and announced: "The clerk will call the roll!" The anti-Roosevelt forces had tried to delay the first ballot for another day to have more time to organize, but Farley insisted on an immediate vote. Most of the delegates were exhausted, and some pushed chairs together and slept, too tired to take notice of the babble about them. The stadium was rancid with the smell of sweat and stale cigars; pop bottles, old newspapers, and discarded sandwich wrappings littered the floor. Farley sat on the platform, furiously jotting down the vote of each state. The galleries jeered at every mention of Roosevelt's name. When it was New York's turn, Boss Curry demanded a poll of the delegation to put its members on record as being opposed to the governor. Jimmy Walker, seemingly indifferent to his forthcoming trial before Roosevelt, cast his ballot for Al Smith in a firmly defiant voice. He got a cheer. Farley hoped for some last-minute switches to push Roosevelt over the top before the tally was announced, but they failed to materialize. Roosevelt received a total of 666½ votes—well over a majority but 104 short of two thirds. Smith had 201¾; Garner, 90¼; Byrd, 25; and Ritchie, 21.

A second ballot followed immediately. Roosevelt had to hold tight to his delegates and to show momentum by picking up more support. Farley managed to dredge up an additional 11¼ votes, half of them from Tom Pendergast of Missouri, bringing Roosevelt's total to 677¾. The other candidates held their own, and Will Rogers received 22 votes. The Roosevelt forces wanted to adjourn before a third ballot, but the opposition, smelling blood, blocked the motion. Angry over the stubborn refusal of the convention to nominate her son by acclamation, Sara Roosevelt grimly announced that she would take no more and left Albany for Hyde Park. Munching on hot dogs, Roosevelt and his circle gathered about the radio for what might be the deciding ballot. Rosenman began to fear that the acceptance speech would never be given. Spirits ebbing, Farley told an aide this vote "will show whether I can ever go back to New York or not." McAdoo had refused to release California to Roosevelt, and Cermak would not deliver Illinois. Arkansas and Mississippi showed signs of slipping away, but Pat Harrison held his delegation in line, and Huey Long warned the Arkansans that if they defected he would personally destroy them in the next election.

Roosevelt picked up another five delegates, bringing his total to 682¾, still 87 votes short of the nomination. Smith's strength dropped to 190¼, while Garner's rose to 101¼, Ritchie's to 23½, and Baker had 8½. The edge of physical endurance had been reached, and at 9:15 A.M. Walsh adjourned the convention. Unwashed and unshaven, the army of disheveled delegates staggered out of the stadium, blinking in the bright sunshine. As they disbanded in search of breakfast and a bed, many were convinced that Roosevelt had passed his peak. Rumors circulated that Baker would be the compromise candidate when they reconvened that evening.

For the Roosevelt forces, the next few hours were crucial. Signs of defection were appearing in a dozen delegations, and if the governor did not win on the fourth ballot, only a miracle would prevent a collapse. The weary Farley returned to the Congress Hotel to confer with Howe and found him gasping on the floor of his room with a pair of electric fans playing over him. He appeared even more haggard than usual, and his voice was husky and faint. Farley got down on the floor to whisper in Howe's ear and told him that in his opinion Texas was Roosevelt's only hope. He wished to make whatever deal he could to win the delegation. Howe assented, and Sam Rayburn agreed to meet Farley in twenty minutes. Quickly getting to the point, Farley said that without the votes of the Texas delegation there would be a hopeless deadlock. Once again, he promised Garner the vice-presidency in exchange for his support. The meeting lasted only a few minutes, but Farley was elated by the result.

Rayburn gave him no commitment, but upon rising to leave, the Texan said, "We'll see what can be done."

Racing upstairs to Howe's room, Farley passed on the news that Texas would come over and the nomination was Roosevelt's. "That's fine," Howe said flatly, nodding his head. "He had labored for years for just such a moment," observed Farley, "yet his face failed to change expression or to betray the slightest sign of emotion." Farley stumbled off to get a few hours of badly needed rest, but Howe, taking nothing for granted, sent for Harry Byrd. Bluntly, he asked the Virginia governor what he wanted for his votes. Byrd replied that he wanted to be a U.S. senator. But Virginia already had two senators: Carter Glass and Claude Swanson.

"Is that your price?" Howe asked.

Byrd replied that it was.

"Very well," said Howe. "We'll put either Glass or Swanson in Franklin's Cabinet."‡

Several attempts were made to persuade McAdoo to swing California into the Roosevelt column. Daniel Roper, one of Roosevelt's floor leaders, offered him the post of Secretary of State—apparently without consulting the governor—but McAdoo turned it down. He insisted, instead, on being consulted on all appointments to the Cabinet. Roosevelt appeared willing to make the concession, but McAdoo could not deliver the delegation, because it was tightly pledged to Garner and controlled by Hearst. Joe Kennedy got the press lord on the telephone. "If you don't take Roosevelt," he warned, "you'll get Newton Baker."

Hearst moved quickly. He checked with his men in Chicago, who confirmed Kennedy's report, and then instructed George Rothwell Brown, one of his columnists, to advise Garner, who had remained in Washington, to release his delegates to Roosevelt to prevent the nomination of Smith or Baker. "Either would be disastrous," said Hearst. Brown, a close friend of Garner's, met him at the Capitol at 11 A.M. and passed on Hearst's message. There was no mention of the vice-presidency in exchange for stepping aside. The speaker stared out a window, silently considering Hearst's plea, until Brown repeated himself. "Say to Mr. Hearst that I fully agree with him," Garner finally declared. "He is right. Tell him I will carry out his suggestion and release my delegates to Roosevelt."

Later, almost everyone who worked for Roosevelt's nomination claimed to have played a key role in nailing down the victory. "Of the 55,000 Democrats alleged to have been in Chicago for the recent convention," Basil O'Connor joked to Roosevelt, "unquestionably 62,000 arranged the . . . shift." In fact, Garner's decision assured Roosevelt's nomination.

‡ Glass was offered the post of Secretary of the Treasury after the election, and when he refused it, Swanson was made Secretary of the Navy.

Why had he done it? Not for the vice-presidency, for he thought the job powerless—"not worth a pitcher of warm piss"*—and much preferred to remain speaker of the House. A good party man, Garner did not want to see a deadlocked convention and a weak compromise candidate.

Waiting until he had finished lunch, Garner telephoned Rayburn. "Sam," he said, "I think it is time to break this thing up. Roosevelt is the choice of the convention." The Texas delegation caucused at 6 P.M., and despite howls of protest from bitter-enders who wanted to stick with Garner, Rayburn gaveled through a motion to switch to Roosevelt, by a narrow margin. California followed suit. "Good—fine—excellent," Roosevelt muttered when Louis Howe telephoned the news. Placing the receiver back on the hook, he looked around the dinner table and smiled broadly. "F.D., you look like the cat that swallowed the canary," said Missy LeHand. Always tantalizing, he refused to tell anyone the news as they took their places before the radio in his study.

Most of the delegates were still unaware of what had occurred as they returned that night to the Chicago Stadium for a fourth ballot. Raymond Moley was boiling mad about a column by Heywood Broun describing Roosevelt as "the corkscrew candidate of a convoluting convention" and threatened to punch him on the nose. Rumors danced about the hall like heat lightning. Roosevelt was finished . . . Mississippi and Louisiana had cracked . . . other delegations were crumbling . . . Baker was going to be the nominee. Once again, Senator Walsh directed the clerk to begin the long-drawn-out roll call: Alabama, 24 votes for Roosevelt . . . ; Arizona, 6 votes for Roosevelt; Arkansas, 18 votes for Roosevelt. . . . Now it was California's turn. The tall, lanky figure of McAdoo appeared at the rostrum to explain his delegation's vote. Packed with Smith supporters, the galleries exploded into a hideous cacophony of boos and catcalls like that which had greeted him at Madison Square Garden eight years before. Then the mob had destroyed him; now he would destroy Al Smith. Unable to gavel the convention to order, Walsh appealed to Cermak to quiet his leather-throated henchmen. "California came here to nominate a President," McAdoo declared when he could at last be heard. "She did not come here to deadlock this convention. California casts forty-four votes for Roosevelt!"

"Good old McAdoo!" exclaimed Roosevelt as he slumped back in his chair and grinned. In Chicago, bedlam followed. Farley pushed through the crowd to pound the Californian on the back. Cermak seized the microphone to announce the release of Illinois's fifty-eight delegates. The organ boomed out the lilting rhythm of "Happy Days Are Here Again!" as, one by one, Roosevelt's rivals climbed on the bandwagon. Only Smith's

* The last word is usually given as "spit," but the stronger expression seems more characteristic of Garner.

190½ votes were denied him. Bitter and angry, the unhappy warrior bit down on his cigar and replied, "No comment!" when asked if he would support the party's nominee. Howe and his staff celebrated with champagne in paper cups. In Albany, Mrs. Roosevelt, Grace Tully, and Missy embraced each other, and John and Elliott Roosevelt tore up their tally sheets and threw them into the air. Friends, associates, and well-wishers crowded into the Executive Mansion—almost deserted for the previous five days—to shake the hand of the nominee. And in Washington, Cactus Jack Garner, who had been assured the vice-presidential nomination, told a newsman, "Politics is funny."

Traditionally, presidential nominees awaited the arrival of a committee to officially inform them of their nomination—a process that could take weeks—but Roosevelt notified the convention that he would fly to Chicago the next day to accept in person. A trivial thing in itself, it was a harbinger of things to come. Already a shrewd master of public moods, Roosevelt sensed that a dismayed, disheartened nation would welcome a startling gesture that signified a break with the past. Air travel was still a novelty, and this was the first time that a presidential candidate made a campaign trip by plane. Before Roosevelt departed for Chicago, Howe demanded that the acceptance speech be read to him over the telephone, and he had it transcribed by one of his secretaries. With a mixture of jealousy and resentment, he pronounced it unsatisfactory and spent most of the night filling page after page of lined yellow sheets with an impatient scrawl as he dashed off his own version.

At 8:30 A.M., Roosevelt and his party—Eleanor, two sons, three secretaries, two bodyguards, and Sam Rosenman—took off from Albany under lowering skies in a chartered Ford Trimotor. Sharp-eyed reporters had already spotted the plane at the airport and asked about it. "I'm going to bicycle out to Chicago," Roosevelt had replied with feigned seriousness. Strong headwinds buffeted the plane, and John Roosevelt became airsick. Despite the noise and the cold, Roosevelt and Rosenman went over the acceptance speech one last time, polishing here and trimming there. Refueling stops were made at Buffalo and Cleveland, where Newton Baker refused to join municipal officials in greeting the Democratic nominee. Because of the bad weather, the plane fell farther and farther behind schedule, and the radio reported that some of the restless delegates were leaving the stadium without waiting to hear Roosevelt. He napped during the last leg of the flight.

Nine hours after taking off from Albany, the plane touched down at Chicago, to be greeted by a vast throng. Young John staggered off first and was followed by Mrs. Roosevelt and the nominee, who emerged from the cabin with a broad smile upon his face. Anna and her two other brothers rushed up to greet him, and he embraced and kissed each of them. Any lingering doubts about Roosevelt's popularity vanished before the enthusiasm of the crowd. Spotting Farley in the surging mob, he seized him by the hand and called out, "Good work, Jim!" He waved to Moley and Tugwell. A jubilant Howe was among the first to reach him. In the excitement, Roosevelt's hat was knocked off and his glasses slid sideways on his nose, but he was unhurt. Once in the big white touring car that Cermak placed at the nominee's disposal, Howe thrust a copy of his version of the acceptance speech into Roosevelt's hands and launched into a litany of criticism of the Albany version. "Dammit, Louis, I'm the nominee!" Roosevelt protested—but realizing the importance of the speech to Howe, he leafed through it with one hand while waving to the crowds with the other as the motorcade sped through the streets of downtown Chicago.

Upon his arrival at the stadium, Roosevelt went directly to the platform. Tightly gripping the lectern to steady himself on the uneasy prop of his braces, he gazed in triumph over the wildly cheering crowd. Across the nation, some ten million Americans huddled about their radios with troubled spirits, waiting for words of hope. Howe was on the platform with Farley and the party's ranking leaders, the first and last time he allowed himself to appear in such a place of prominence. When the noise had subsided, Roosevelt began to speak, in clear and vibrant tones. Moley and Rosenman were startled by unfamiliar words—they glumly noted that he was using Howe's text—but their disappointment quickly faded, for he soon slipped easily into their carefully honed phrases. Unwilling to offend anyone, Roosevelt, in a typical gesture, had taken the first page of Howe's draft and substituted it for the first page of the prepared text. Hardly anyone noticed, for Howe had merely paraphrased the rest of the Albany version of the speech.

"I have started out on the tasks that lie ahead by breaking the absurd traditions that the candidate should remain in professed ignorance of what has happened for weeks until he is formally notified of that event many weeks later," Roosevelt declared. "You have nominated me and I know it, and I am here to thank you for the honor. Let it also be symbolic that in so doing I broke traditions. Let it from now on be the task of our Party to break foolish traditions." One tradition that he wished to maintain, however, was that of the Democratic party as the "bearer of liberalism and progress" and leader of "the country's interrupted march along the path of real promise, of real justice, of real equality for all our citizens." The good sense and the faith of the American people had prevented a descent into "wild radicalism" in the face of the economic crisis, he continued, but "a workable program of reconstruction" was mandatory to prevent the radicals from getting the upper hand.

"What do the American people want more than anything else?" Roosevelt asked. "To my mind they want two things: work, with all the moral and spiritual values that go with it; and with work, a reasonable measure of security—security for themselves, and for their wives and children. Work and security—these are more than words. They are more than facts. They are the spiritual values, the true goal toward which our efforts of reconstruction should lead." To accomplish these goals, Roosevelt proposed programs similar to those he had offered as governor of New York: federal relief for the distressed, self-sustaining public work projects to provide jobs, the repeal of Prohibition, reforestation for the better use of land, reduction of interest on home and farm mortgages, regulation of the securities industry, a voluntary crop-control program to reduce agricultural surpluses, and lower tariffs.

Rousing, crisp, and full of hope, this speech also was rife with ambiguities that were to enjoy a bizarre resonance throughout Roosevelt's years in the White House. Taxes were to be cut, budgets tidily balanced, government payrolls slashed, and public works financed by bonds rather than by deficit spending. "Government—Federal and state and local—costs too much," he asserted. "We must abolish useless offices. We must eliminate unnecessary functions of Government—functions in fact that are not definitely essential to the continuance of Government. We must merge, we must consolidate. . . ."

But it was not the contradictions of Roosevelt's remarks that captured attention; it was the nearly religious intensity with which he closed his speech:

> I pledge you, I pledge myself, to a new deal for the American people. Let all of us here assembled constitute ourselves prophets of a new order of competence and of courage. This is more than a political campaign; it is a call to arms. Give me your help, not to win votes alone, but to win in this crusade to restore America to its own greatness.

Roosevelt attached no special significance to the words "new deal," and neither had Moley or Rosenman. But, the next day, a Rollin Kirby cartoon showed a farmer leaning on a hoe, bewildered and hopeful, looking skyward as an airplane—Roosevelt's airplane—passed overhead with "New Deal" emblazoned on its wings. Within a short time it became the watchword of a fresh and vibrant political faith.†

"The campaign starts at ten o'clock tonight!"
Bubbling over with enthusiasm, Roosevelt got the battle for the pres-

---

† There was nothing new about the "New Deal." Stuart Chase had recently written an article in *The New Republic* entitled "A New Deal for America," and a few hours before Roosevelt's speech, John McDuffie of Alabama had nominated Garner for Vice-President with the declaration: "There is a demand for a new deal in the management of the affairs of the American people."

idency off to a flying start while the cheers were still resounding at the Chicago Stadium. Everyone thought he had the election wrapped up. "All you have to do is stay alive until election day," Garner told him. Louis Howe and most of his advisers agreed, urging a "front porch" campaign. But Roosevelt enjoyed the controlled madness of campaigning—the hasty conferences, the speeches, the whistle stops, the handshaking—as have few other American politicians, and he was determined to conduct an aggressive, coast-to-coast campaign like that of 1920. Besides, by showing himself to the people, he would put to rest rumors about his health and capacity to serve. "My Dutch is up," he told Farley.

Even before the nomination had been won, Howe, who handled overall political strategy, had worked out tentative itineraries and speech topics for the candidate. Farley replaced Raskob as chairman of the Democratic National Committee and meshed the Roosevelt political machine with the national organization. Charles Michelson, the brilliant publicity man inherited from Raskob, slashed mercilessly at Hoover. The scent of victory was a remarkable political tonic, and all Roosevelt's rivals, with the exception of Al Smith, who continued to sulk, fell into line. Farley's most effective innovations were an emphasis on attracting the votes of women —Eleanor played a leading role in this—and convincing county and precinct workers they were a vital part of the organization. He made certain they received periodic communications from national headquarters, often with skillfully forged Roosevelt signatures. "The fellow out in Kokomo who is pulling doorbells . . . gets a real thrill if he receives a letter on campaigning postmarked Washington or New York," he observed.

While Farley handled political operations, Moley remained in charge of research, issues, and speeches. New members were added to the Brain Trust, chief of them General Hugh S. Johnson, who was recommended by Bernard Baruch. A graduate of West Point and the author of boys' adventure books, Johnson had served on the War Industries Board during the war, had entered private industry as a Baruch protégé, and had gained some renown as an expert on agricultural problems.‡ Money was still a problem, yet Frank Walker raised some $2.2 million, about $500,000 less than the Republicans. The largest single expenditure was for radio time— recognition of Roosevelt's mastery of the medium. Once again, William Woodin, Vincent Astor, and Joe Kennedy were among the campaign's major financial angels, but Walker also wrung out sizable contributions

‡ FDR was fascinated by Johnson. When the retired general first came to Albany, he began to read aloud from a long memorandum denouncing the Hoover administration's economic policies. Moley, who had heard it all before, went upstairs to bed, but he could still hear the mighty roar of Johnson's voice. Occasionally, Roosevelt's laughter would be heard. "It's great stuff," he later told Moley. "Water it down 70 percent and make it into a speech."

from Raskob, Baruch, and Pierre Du Pont, as well as others who had formerly supported Roosevelt's rivals.

Despite the complexity of the campaign organization, all the parts of it meshed well together. "Roosevelt so ordered the various divisions of his political activity, so sharply delegated authority and so clearly maintained personal contact with each of us that there was never the semblance of conflict and never an overlapping of functions," Moley later recalled.

Having won the nomination, Roosevelt was the candidate of the entire party, not merely its liberal wing, and subject to conflicting pressures in the formulation of ideas and programs. From the right and the center, he was besieged by conservative and traditionalist Democrats like Baruch, Kennedy, and John Davis, who argued for sound money, retrenchment, and budget balancing. Garner pungently summarized their views: "Tell the Governor that he is the boss and we will follow him to hell if we have to, but if he goes too far with some of these wild-eyed ideas we are going to have the shit kicked out of us." Liberals like Felix Frankfurter, who peppered the candidate with memos from his eyrie at the Harvard Law School, and cyclonic populists like Huey Long pressed Bryan-Wilson progressivism upon him with its emphasis on trust busting, inflation, and a return to a vanished America of family farms and small businesses. And from the far left, Tugwell and others, convinced that capitalism was on its last legs, urged him to restructure the economic system, rather than patch it up. Roosevelt himself was most comfortable in the middle of the road but tacked from port to starboard as required by circumstances. "To accomplish almost anything worthwhile," he once said, "it is necessary to compromise between the ideal and the practical."

Leaving his associates to get the campaign organized, Roosevelt went fishing. Accompanied by his three younger sons, he sailed along the New England coast in a forty-foot yawl, *Myth II*, trailed by a press boat and a chartered yacht bearing contributors and advisers, who met with him each night in port. If Roosevelt's intention was to project an image of the strenuous life, he succeeded admirably, for the newspapers were filled with pictures of the buoyant candidate at the yawl's helm. "I love to be on the water," he declared. "It is great fun."

But there was no fun for the hapless President Hoover. The Bonus Army had grown to nearly twenty thousand men, some living in half-demolished buildings on Pennsylvania Avenue but most encamped in shacks and tents on the Anacostia mud flats, south of the Capitol. It reminded John Dos Passos of a wartime army camp, with its bugle calls, mess lines, and liaison officers. "There's the same goulash of faces and dialects . . . but we were all youngsters then," he wrote. "Now we are getting on into middle life, sunken eyes, hollow cheeks off breadlines, pale-looking, knotted hands of men who've worked hard with them, and then for a long time have not worked." Later, Hoover charged that many of the men were Communists or had criminal records, but, in fact, known "Reds" were given the bum's rush, and, by-and-large, the veterans were well-behaved. When the Senate overwhelmingly rejected, on June 16, a bill calling for immediate payment of the bonus, the veterans keeping vigil on the steps of the Capitol sang "America" and quietly dispersed.

Most accepted the offer of Congress of free railroad tickets home, but a few thousand men remained behind, in the capital. After all, where had they to go? Official Washington became uneasy. The gates of the White House were chained and the streets about it cleared. Federal troops were brought in and kept in readiness to move. On July 28, the police were ordered to evacuate the squatters from the buildings on lower Pennsylvania Avenue. There was a scuffle, stones were thrown, and the police opened fire. In the melee, two veterans were killed and several policemen injured. Panic-stricken local officials pleaded for help from the Army. Having waited until he got the request in writing, Hoover ordered Patrick Hurley, the Secretary of War, to move against the strikers. Resplendent in full uniform and medals, General Douglas MacArthur, the Chief of Staff, assisted by an aide, Major Dwight D. Eisenhower, took personal charge of the operation.

As some eight hundred troops—cavalry under the command of Major George S. Patton, infantry with bayonets fixed, and a handful of light tanks—approached the disputed area, they were greeted by cheers from the veterans and several thousand spectators. Suddenly there was chaos. Cavalrymen rode into the crowd with sabers drawn, infantrymen hurled tear-gas bombs, and men, women, and children were trampled and choked. Scattering veterans and spectators alike, the troops crossed the bridge to the Anacostia flats, where some veterans had already set their shacks afire, and completed the destruction. Throughout the night, the sky glowed with flames—and the Bonus Army was in full retreat in all directions. "A challenge to the authority of the United States Government has been met, swiftly and firmly," Hoover declared.

Early the next morning, Tugwell visited Roosevelt in the Executive Mansion and found him sitting up in bed with the New York *Times* on his lap. The rout of the Bonus Army dominated the headlines, and there was a full page of photographs. Spreading a hand over the pictures as if to cover them from sight, the governor said they looked like "scenes from a nightmare." He pointed to soldiers advancing through the smoking debris, or hauling resisters still weeping from the tear gas to police wagons, while women and children waited for rescue. Apologizing for having even considered Hoover as a presidential candidate in 1920, Roosevelt said there was nothing left inside the man but jelly. Perhaps there never *had* been anything. Instead of turning the veterans over to Pat Hurley and Doug MacArthur, he said, the President should have asked for a delegation to visit him in the White House and sent out coffee and sandwiches to the rest.

Roosevelt added that if he had any doubts about his chances for election they had been wiped out by the incident. In fact, if the "battle of Anacostia" had occurred earlier, Hoover wouldn't even have been renominated, he said. Tugwell suggested that perhaps a majority of the American people might consider the use of force justified, but Roosevelt questioned his judgment. He pointed out that upon several occasions the "fat cats" had wanted him to call out the National Guard in tense situations but he had refused to acquiesce. As for Hoover, he didn't feel sorry for him and wouldn't feel sorry for him in November. Either Hoover had been very different during the war years or he hadn't known him as well as he believed. Tugwell thought there was something wistful about the last remark.

Just a few months earlier, during the annual Governors' Conference, at Richmond, Virginia, Roosevelt and Hoover had met for the first time since the Wilson years. As part of the festivities, the President invited the governors to dinner at the White House, and the guests assembled in the East Room, as protocol required awaiting Hoover's appearance. Aides said he would be along shortly. But the President failed to arrive and the guests were kept standing—some said a half-hour, others said a full hour. Roosevelt laughed and joked with his fellow governors, but the pain of his crippled legs in their braces must have been excruciating. Mrs. Roosevelt was convinced that the slight had been a deliberate attempt to humiliate her husband, and as Tugwell states, Eleanor "was so enraged she could hardly be decent through the dinner."

The newspapers that told of crushing the Bonus Army also contained Jimmy Walker's reply to Seabury's charges against him: "Since the day of my birth, I have lived my life in the open," he declared. "Whatever shortcomings I have are known to everyone—but disloyalty to my native city, official dishonesty, or corruption form no part of these shortcomings." Roosevelt convened a hearing in Albany on August 11, and having mastered Walker's previous testimony, personally took charge of the interrogation. For several days he relentlessly questioned the mayor, whose denials were little different from those he had presented before Seabury. Roosevelt's stature grew as a result of his dignified cross-examination of Walker. But would he remove him? To do so would antagonize Catholic voters, already unhappy over Smith's defeat, and might drive them out of the Democratic party. Knowing Roosevelt's penchant for compromise, many observers expected him to let Walker off with a slap on the wrist. Roosevelt apparently considered the possibility. "How would it be if I gave the little Mayor hell and then kept him in office?" he asked Moley. But then he quickly added, "No. That would be weak." From that moment on, Moley was certain Walker was finished.

The hearings were recessed after a dozen sessions, and on the evening of September 1, Roosevelt discussed the case with a group of friends. The preponderance of the advice he received was to reprimand Walker but keep him in office. The argument grew heated, voices were raised, and there was considerable table pounding, according to Moley. Musing aloud, Roosevelt suggested that it was probably best to remove the mayor, because he was obviously guilty and that was the right thing to do. One of his visitors, who had just lit a cigarette, angrily threw the lighted match at the governor and shouted: "So you'd rather be right than President!"*

"Well, there may be something in what you say," replied Roosevelt.

At that moment, the telephone rang. An aide reported that Walker had just resigned as mayor.

Roosevelt received credit for getting rid of Walker without have to bear the blame of actually throwing him out of City Hall. Critics who had regarded him as vacillating on Tammany corruption were forced to eat their words. In revenge, Tammany refused to endorse Rosenman for a full term on the state Supreme Court and tried to prevent the nomination of Herbert Lehman for governor. Al Smith came to Lehman's rescue —and healed the breach with Roosevelt. Smith came up to the governor at the state Democratic convention, stuck out his hand, and according to Farley, declared, "Hello, Frank, I'm glad to see you." Pleased by this gesture, Roosevelt beamed and replied, "Hello, Al, I'm glad to see you too— and that's from the heart." Unable to hear the exchange in the bedlam, a quick-witted wire-service reporter created his own version of Smith's greeting—"Hello, you old potato!"—and it gained widespread acceptance.

The campaign, itself, was anticlimactic. Roosevelt traveled some thirteen thousand miles, making sixteen major addresses and sixty-seven minor speeches as well as countless informal talks from the rear platform of his train, the "Roosevelt Special." The aim of the campaign was to win the confidence of the American people without alienating any significant bloc of voters. "Campaigning, for him, was unadulterated joy," according to Moley. "It was broad rivers, green forests, waving corn, and undulating wheat; it was crowds of friends, from the half-dozen who, seated on a baggage truck, waved to the cheery face at the speeding window to perspiring thousands at a race track or fairgrounds; it was hands extended in wel-

* Louis Howe was not listed by Moley as among FDR's visitors, but only he could have gotten away with such conduct.

come, voices warm with greeting, faces reflecting his smile along the interminable wayside."

Beneath his usual buoyancy and optimism, Roosevelt was shocked by what he saw. Conditions were even worse than he had imagined. "I have looked into the faces of thousands of Americans," he told Anne O'Hare McCormick. "They have the frightened look of lost children." He was reminded of Europe after the Armistice and saw the same yearnings in the crowds that had greeted Woodrow Wilson. "Then they were thinking of the war. Perhaps this man, their eyes were saying, can save our children from the horror and terror we have known. Now they were saying: 'We're caught in something we don't understand; perhaps this fellow can help us out.'"

Early on, Roosevelt established the theme of his attack on the Hoover administration in four sentences:

First, it encouraged speculation and overproduction, through its false economic policies.
Second, it attempted to minimize the crash and misled the people as to its gravity.
Third, it erroneously charged the cause to other nations of the world.
And finally, it refused to recognize and correct the evils at home which it brought forth; it delayed relief; it forgot reform.

Time and again, these charges were trotted out, until in Baltimore, near the end of the campaign, Roosevelt claimed to be waging a war against "the 'Four Horsemen' of the present Republican leadership: the Horsemen of Destruction, Delay, Deceit, Despair." But those who sought a consistent pattern of future policy in Roosevelt's speeches and statements were disappointed. Upon examination, his proposals were often vague and sometimes as contradictory as the promises of a balanced budget and increased spending for emergency relief made in his acceptance speech. For example, Moley claimed that when presented with two drafts taking diametrically opposed positions on tariff policy, Roosevelt left him speechless with an offhanded "Weave the two together."†

In Columbus, Ohio, he proposed wide-ranging banking and stock-market reforms that cheered trust busters but also promised less interference in American life from a "prying bureaucracy." In Topeka, he outlined a farm policy, which had been stitched together from offerings from no fewer than twenty-five contributors, that contained the faintest hint of a voluntary domestic allotment plan to reduce surpluses while

† Elliot Rosen points out that the suggestion was really made by Senator Edward P. Costigan of Colorado, in order to leave the candidate room to maneuver on the tariff issue. Moley told his version after he had broken with FDR. *Hoover, Roosevelt, and the Brains Trust* (New York: Columbia University Press, 1977), p. 345.

promising no increase in costs to consumers. In Pittsburgh, under the prodding of conservatives like Baruch and with the endorsement of Louis Howe, he departed from his policy of avoiding commitments, to pledge a 25 percent cut in government expenditures.‡ "I regard reduction in Federal spending as one of the most direct and effective contributions Government can make to business," Roosevelt declared. In Sioux City, he berated Hoover for extravagance and expanding the bureaucracy. Foreign policy was almost totally ignored, and in Detroit he declined to discuss labor policy because it was Sunday. He reversed field so drastically on the tariff—moving from support of lower tariffs to continued protectionism—that Hoover contemptuously dismissed him as "a chameleon on Scotch plaid."

Such fundamental contradictions did not seem to bother Roosevelt, but intellectuals were frustrated. Elmer Davis, a leading journalist, said he was certain that Roosevelt favored the repeal of Prohibition but was not so sure where he stood on anything else. "You could not quarrel with a single one of his generalities; you seldom can," he wrote. "But what they mean (if anything) is known only to Franklin Roosevelt and God." Some detractors called him "a Democratic Harding," and Mencken labeled him "Roosevelt Minor." Rabbi Stephen Wise told Felix Frankfurter that he would rue his support of Roosevelt. "There is no basic stuff in the man. There are no deep-seated convictions. He is a tremendously agreeable and attractive person, but there is no bedrock in him. He is all clay and no granite." Frankfurter's reply was hardly a ringing endorsement of the candidate: "I am supporting Roosevelt fundamentally because I think the most urgent demand of the hour is to turn Hoover out. . . . Politics, perhaps you sometimes forget, is a choice of the second best." Will Rogers spoke for many Americans who despaired of the political process when he observed: "The way most people feel, they would like to vote against all of 'em if this was possible."

Nevertheless, both Rosenman and Moley later insisted that every major project of the New Deal was foreshadowed in one or more of Roosevelt's 1932 campaign speeches except for the National Industrial Recovery Act, deficit spending, and the abandonment of the gold standard. In Salt Lake City, they pointed out, he produced a plan for rehabilitation of the railroads. In Portland, Oregon, he supported public power development as a "national yardstick" and called for government regulation of

‡ The budget-balancing promise of the Pittsburgh speech became an embarrassment for FDR, as government spending far exceeded revenues during his first term. In the 1936 campaign, he decided to make another speech in Pittsburgh, and instructed Rosenman to provide an explanation of his statement of four years before. After carefully rereading the earlier speech, Rosenman went to FDR. "Mr. President," he said, "the only thing you can say about that 1932 speech is to deny categorically that you ever made it."

utilities. In Boston, he said "no one would be allowed to starve" and promised federal relief programs, unemployment insurance, and old-age pensions. Even the budget-balancing Pittsburgh speech contained a loophole: "If starvation and dire need on the part of any of our citizens makes necessary the appropriation of additional funds which would keep the budget out of balance, I shall not hesitate to tell the American people the full truth and ask them to authorize the expenditure of that additional amount." In dissent, William E. Leuchtenburg points out there is no mention in his campaign speeches of such New Deal milestones as a gigantic public works program, federal housing and slum clearance, the Tennessee Valley Authority, sharply increased taxes on the wealthy, federal sanctions to enforce collective bargaining, and massive relief programs.

Roosevelt was at his most eloquent and reached the progressive peak of the campaign in an address to the Commonwealth Club, in San Francisco. An endorsement of planning on a national scale, this speech disclosed the program and philosophy of the New Deal and Roosevelt's intention to use the state as a guarantor of the common good. Pointing out that the American economy had reached maturity, he spoke of the need to consolidate gains already made, rather than to embark upon further expansion.* Reaching back to the Troy speech of 1912 and its overtones of the New Nationalism, he emphasized that private economic power had become a public trust. If business failed to assume the responsibilities that went with power, if the market no longer provided an equilibrium, then it was the duty of the state to move swiftly to protect the public interest. "Every man has a right to life and this means that he has also a right to make a comfortable living," Roosevelt said. Government's role in society "is the maintenance of a balance, within which every individual may have a place if he will take it; in which every individual may find safety if he wishes it; in which every individual may attain such power as his ability permits. . . ."

Most Americans may have been in doubt about Roosevelt's intentions, but not Herbert Hoover. From the beginning, he perceived in his opponent's blithe promises the clear and present danger of revolutionary

---

* Both contemporaries and historians have tended to overemphasize those sections of the Commonwealth Club speech in which FDR spoke of the maturity of the American economy. As Tugwell noted a quarter century later, this probably better expressed the views of Adolf Berle, the author of the speech, than those of Roosevelt, who, pressed for time, had little opportunity to go over the speech before delivering it. FDR's own personality was far too optimistic and upbeat to seriously believe that progress had been halted and the nation had reached the zenith of its power. R. G. Tugwell, *The Democratic Roosevelt* (Garden City, N.Y.: Doubleday & Company, Inc., 1957), p. 246.

change. The philosophy espoused by the Democrats was "the same philosophy of government which has poisoned all Europe . . . the fumes of the witch's cauldron which boiled in Russia," he said. Despairing of victory, lacking Roosevelt's ease of manner and eloquence, Hoover campaigned doggedly, goaded by what he regarded as the potential of his rival for mischief. To the burdens of the presidency he added the drafting of his own speeches, turgid affairs delivered in a droning voice. Warnings against impending radicalism, justifications of past actions, and optimistic predictions of recovery were all jumbled together. Sometimes he was greeted by cheers; more often the crowds were sullen and sometimes threatening. In Wisconsin, Hoover's train was delayed when a man was discovered pulling up the spikes from the tracks. In Detroit, where there were a quarter of a million people on relief, he was greeted at the railroad station by a mob shouting, "Hang him! Hang him!" In Nevada, the governor refused to appear in public with him. Hoover had become the victim of the primitive impulse to personify misfortune in an individual—the scapegoat for the Great Depression.

"This campaign is more than a contest between two men," the President declared in his last major appearance of the campaign, at Madison Square Garden on October 31, 1932. "It is more than a contest between two parties. It is a contest between two philosophies of government." Roosevelt and his supporters were "proposing changes and so-called new deals which would destroy the very foundations of our American system." With an eloquence born of desperation, Hoover called the roll of these advocates of revolution—Huey Long, the Brain Trust, Senator George Norris, and others—who would come to power if Roosevelt was elected. "The changes proposed by all these Democratic principals and allies are of the most profound and penetrating character. If they are brought about, this will not be the America which we have known in the past." Deficit spending, an inflated currency, government involvement in business, and "the enormous expansion of the Federal Government" along with "the growth of bureaucracy such as we have never seen in our history" would be the result. ". . . The grass will grow in the streets of a hundred cities, a thousand towns; the weeds will overrun the fields of millions of farms. . . ."

Roosevelt, who heard this speech on the radio while in a Boston hotel, was indignant. "I simply will not let Hoover question my Americanism," he snapped to his aides. Only with difficulty, they persuaded him to ignore the remarks in his own speech later that evening. And so the campaign drew to an end with Roosevelt projecting an aura of decisiveness, confidence, and hope. People turned to him with expectation and a sense of excitement. But as Ernest Lindley pointed out, he was no "great popular idol" in 1932. "The country yearned for a Messiah, Mr.

Roosevelt did not look or sound like a Messiah. He was not even a Bryan. . . . Certainly there was nothing of the revolutionary in the manner or language of this charming, cultured aristocrat with his factual speeches and leaven of gay humor. He promised no utopia; he calmly asserted that he knew no patent remedies and did not believe in them. . . . But he was the one sure means of rebuking the party in power. . . ."

A thousand impressions crowded Roosevelt's mind as he closed out the campaign with the traditional election-eve appearance in Poughkeepsie: ". . . The sunset at McCook, Nebraska and the strong progressive farmers, Sioux City and Milwaukee and Chicago and Detroit . . . the stricken but dauntless miners of Butte . . . Los Angeles, the miracle of a city built—as history measures time—in a moment . . . my neighbors in my Southern home in Georgia . . . the children in wheel chairs at Warm Springs . . . and Portland and Boston and Providence. . . . Out of this unity that I have seen we may build the strongest strand to lift ourselves out of this depression. . . . To be the means through which the ideals and hopes of the American people may find a greater realization calls for the best in any man; I seek to be only the humble emblem of this restoration."

Having voted early on the morning of November 8 at Hyde Park, Roosevelt went down to New York City, where, surrounded by family and friends, he received the returns at Democratic headquarters, in the Biltmore. Only Louis Howe was missing. Gloomily expecting some last-minute mishap, he remained in his deserted office across Madison Avenue amid the debris of the campaign. Roosevelt jumped out to a quick lead, but Howe pessimistically dismissed these reports. "Losers always have a big spurt before they dwindle off to defeat," he declared. Roosevelt gleefully took the telephone calls from his field commanders himself. "You mean I'm getting votes in rock-ribbed Pennsylvania?" he chortled after being told that for the first time in sixty years the Keystone State might go Democratic. Rosenman noted that two men in dark suits slipped into the room, and during the evening took up positions near the governor. They were Secret Service agents—and for the rest of his life Roosevelt would always be under their surveillance.

Finally, even Howe was convinced Roosevelt would win by a landslide. Farley and Eleanor Roosevelt came over to persuade him to join the jubilant crowd across the street and found him poring over the returns "like a miser inspecting his gold." But he preferred to telephone his congratulations. "Hello, Franklin," he said. "I guess I've worked myself out of a job." Roosevelt summoned him to his side so he could make a public announcement: "There are two people in the United States more than anybody else responsible for this great victory. One is my old friend and associate, Colonel Louis McHenry Howe, and the other is that splendid American, Jim Farley."

Roosevelt swept to victory, 22,800,000 votes to 15,750,000.† The margin was even more decisive in the Electoral College—472 to 59—with Hoover carrying only six states, all but two of them in New England. The Democrats won substantial majorities in Congress, and Herbert H. Lehman was elected governor of New York. Soon after Hoover conceded, a buoyant Roosevelt went home to Sixty-fifth Street, where his mother embraced him at the door. "This is the greatest night of my life!" he declared. Later, as his son James helped him into bed, the same bed in which he had lain as a nearly helpless victim of polio in 1921, the President-elect was subdued and thoughtful. As James bent over to kiss his father good night, he looked up at him and said: "You know, Jimmy, all my life I have been afraid of only one thing—fire. Tonight I think I'm afraid of something else."

"Afraid of what, Pa?"

"I'm afraid that I may not have the strength to do this job."

And he asked his son to pray for him.

† FDR won 57.4 percent of the total vote, Hoover 39.7 percent. Norman Thomas, the Socialist candidate, received only 881,951 votes, or 2.2 percent.

XVI
WINTER OF DISCONTENT

PROPPED UP IN bed the morning after the election, the President-elect penciled an acknowledgment across the back of Hoover's congratulatory telegram. "I hold myself in readiness to cooperate with you in our common purpose," he wrote, thick fingers moving swiftly across the paper. But the word "cooperate" bothered him. For a moment, Roosevelt pondered, and then crossed out the phrase "in readiness to cooperate with you" and substituted "ready to further in every way the common purpose to help our country." More than a quibble was involved in this change. Who was to cooperate with whom? Unable to take office until March 4, 1933,* Roosevelt was suspicious of any attempt that might be made by Hoover to maneuver him into accepting the policies of a discredited administration. Why should he accept the responsibility for policy when he had no power to make it?

Left to his own devices, Roosevelt would have spent the interregnum resting, preparing an efficient transfer of the governorship to Herbert Lehman, and quietly organizing his administration. In fact, he considered a trip to Europe in order to stay out of the limelight, but the economic crisis would not wait four months. That winter was the low point of the depression. An upturn in the economy linked to Hoover's cautious adventure in "pump-priming" through Reconstruction Finance Corporation loans to business and industry had sputtered out. Bank failures were mounting; hunger marches erupted in New York and Chicago, and jobless auto workers rioted in Detroit. Farm prices collapsed completely, and the skies of the Dakotas, Iowa, and Kansas were dark with the acrid smoke of

* The Twentieth Amendment, which ended presidential terms as of January 20, rather than March 4, was not ratified until February 1933.

burning grain that had no market. Huey Long frightened the rich with a bellicose crusade to "Share Our Wealth," while a spellbinding radio priest named Charles E. Coughlin poured out a mixture of undigested religio-economic doctrine and populism that smacked of Fascism.

The old order was bankrupt. The nation's business leaders were summoned before the Senate Finance Committee and asked for their solutions to the crisis. The responses of these, the most powerful men in America, was dispiriting and disappointing. If there was a consensus, it was offered by Bernard Baruch: "Balance budgets. Stop spending money we haven't got. . . . Tax . . . tax everybody for everything."

Rather than wait a quarter year for the promised New Deal, some people suggested that Hoover immediately resign and turn the White House over to the President-elect. Instead, alarmed by what he regarded as Roosevelt's irresponsibility, Hoover was determined to reverse the decision of November and persuade his successor to accept his policies for combating the depression. Later, it became a cardinal article of his faith that dread of Roosevelt's accession paralyzed recovery. "Whether his policies were justified or unjustified, they immediately caused our business world to stop, wait and listen," he wrote in his *Memoirs*. "The price of commodities and securities immediately began to decline and unemployment increased."

Paradoxically, the confrontation between Roosevelt and Hoover arose from international complications, rather than domestic problems. During the campaign, the Democratic candidate had all but ignored global issues, telling Moley, "Old Hoover's foreign policy has been pretty good." Suddenly, on November 13, 1932, Roosevelt, who was down with influenza, received a telegram from the President requesting a meeting to discuss the critical question of European war debts. Britain and the other debtor nations had sent notes to Washington demanding not only a delay in payments due on December 15, when the year-long moratorium declared by Hoover would expire, but also a review of the entire war-debts question. Internationalists favored cancellation of the debts, but Hoover, along with most Americans, was opposed. Nevertheless, he believed that debt revision might be used as a lever to persuade the Europeans to return to the gold standard. Inasmuch as any agreement would have to be carried out by the new administration, he suggested that Roosevelt discuss the matter with him.

Roosevelt was wary. In agreeing to the moratorium, Congress had stated that it was not to be extended, and he saw no reason to expend prestige on debt revision that he would need in order to get his own programs approved. Besides, he regarded the proposal as a cat-and-mouse game designed by Hoover to impose his view that the depression could be ended by international financial action. Roosevelt and his advisers regarded the war debts as a peripheral issue and were convinced that the road to recovery lay through domestic reform.

Unable to openly reject a proposal for cooperation with the outgoing administration, Roosevelt telephoned Hoover on November 17 to make detailed arrangements for the meeting. Hoover had a secretary listen in on another line and make a transcript of their conversation—then an unusual occurrence—and a clear sign of the suspicion that existed between the two men.†

"Good morning, Mr. President, how are you?" Roosevelt began.

"All right," Hoover replied.

"They tell me you had a little rest."

"I have and I hope you have had too."

"I have been in bed five days. I had a real case of flu."

"That is too bad."

"I got up today, for the first time came downstairs. I want to know if it is all right for you if I come on Tuesday next."

"That will be fine."

Five days later, Roosevelt, accompanied by Moley, arrived at the White House in the late afternoon and was greeted by "Ike" Hoover, the chief usher, whom he had known from the Wilson era. He also recognized one of the doormen who helped him from his automobile and shook hands with him, a gesture that contrasted sharply with Hoover's formal manner. Roosevelt and Moley were taken by elevator up to the Red Room, where the President and Ogden Mills, the Secretary of the Treasury, awaited them.

"The governor of New York," announced the chief usher.

"I am glad to see you, Governor, and thank you for coming," said a solemn and uneasy Hoover, stepping forward to shake hands with Roosevelt.

For a few minutes there was a bantering conversation between Roosevelt and Mills, Dutchess County neighbors and Harvard classmates. Taking chairs around a small mahogany table below portraits of Grant, Jefferson, Madison, and John Adams, Hoover and Mills lit up cigars, while Roosevelt and Moley smoked cigarettes. The President, who glanced up only occasionally at Roosevelt, plunged into a nearly hour-long

† Frank Freidel published the fact that Hoover had secretly recorded his conversation with FDR in 1973, but I have since learned that the recording process was far more extensive than originally reported. In all, there are about 860 pages of transcribed telephone conversations in the Hoover Library, in West Branch, Iowa. Most of this material concerns foreign-policy discussions, particularly the debt moratorium, and includes conversations with British Prime Minister Ramsay MacDonald and Sir John Simon, the British Foreign Secretary. It is doubtful that they knew a secretary was listening in on the conversations and taking everything down. Some domestic conversations were also transcribed. Letter to the author from Dwight M. Miller, senior archivist, Hoover Library, Mar. 9, 1982.

recital of the background of the debt problem and its links to the Geneva Disarmament Conference, then underway, and the forthcoming World Economic Conference. Moley was impressed and said he showed "a mastery of detail and a clarity of arrangement that compelled admiration."

Either cancellation or default, Hoover maintained, would undermine the international credit system and would adversely affect the American economy. Looking up from the Seal of the United States that was woven into the red carpet, at which he had been staring, he addressed himself primarily to Moley, whom he obviously regarded as the more knowledgeable of his visitors. Once the Europeans had paid the installment due the following month, the President suggested, it was only fair that they be permitted to discuss the entire matter with Washington. Roosevelt indicated assent but was noncommittal on Hoover's proposal to reconstitute the Debt Commission, a body that had previously studied the problem. Periodically, he asked questions that Moley had prepared and which he had written down on small file cards. Sometimes he nodded—in agreement, Hoover thought—but in reality merely his usual way of signifying understanding.

Passionately convinced that only he could resolve the international financial crisis, Hoover regarded his task as one of educating his successor and making certain that he did not stray from the approved path. "The impression he left on my mind was [of] a man amiable, pleasant, anxious to be of service, very badly informed and [possessing] comparatively little vision," he wrote soon after the meeting. Although Roosevelt's seeming receptivity convinced Hoover that his visitor had agreed to underwrite his proposal for the Debt Commission, Roosevelt was hardly out of the White House before he told newsmen the problem was "not his baby." In a statement issued the following day, he said it would be better to negotiate any debt revision through regular diplomatic channels—a statement angrily resented by Hoover, who claimed that he had been misled by Roosevelt's attitude. So a meeting designed to encourage harmony and a united front in order to deal with the crisis, deepened the hostility between the old President and the new.

One of the great American myths—much reinforced in the telling—is that Roosevelt came to power without a program or a significant pool of ideas for dealing with the depression. Henry L. Stimson, Hoover's Secretary of State, observed that by failing to cooperate with his predecessor, he "showed a most laughable, if it were not so lamentable, ignorance of the situation." Reporters pleaded with him for policy statements, and editorial writers criticized his failure to do anything to relieve the tensions of that terrible winter. Leisurely traveling between Albany, Hyde Park, and Warm Springs, he smiled a lot and said little. Hoover often tried to persuade him to issue statements endorsing the policies of his administration in the name of restoring confidence, but Roosevelt refused. He met with congressional leaders and toured the Tennessee Valley with Senator George Norris—departing long enough from his vagueness on specific issues to promise a massive redevelopment program for the entire region.

Behind the scenes, however, Roosevelt and his advisers were working up a comprehensive legislative program that contained the basic outline of the New Deal. While the President-elect was putting the finishing touches on the gubernatorial transfer, which took place at the end of 1932, Moley functioned as a one-man cabinet. The Brain Trust had been dissolved after the election—never to meet again as a unit—and he now provided direction for a guerrilla army that showered Roosevelt with drafts of bills, memos, reports, and recommendations. An attempt was made to push as many measures as possible through the lame-duck session of Congress, in which the Democrats and Republican progressives had a majority, so the new administration would have momentum for a frontal assault on the depression.

Assignments were parceled out to a varied team: Lewis W. Douglas, an Arizona congressman of conservative bent, and Swagar Sherley, wartime chairman of the House Appropriations Committee, were given the task of slashing the budget and reorganizing the government. Henry A. Wallace, a Republican and a former editor of *Wallace's Farmer*, a leading agricultural journal; M. L. Wilson, a professor at Montana State College; Tugwell; and Morgenthau drafted a farm bill that was supposed to be passed before the spring planting season. Berle divided his efforts between farm relief and working with William Woodin and others to expedite bankruptcy procedures for ailing industries, particularly the railroads. Samuel Untermyer, a long-time advocate of stock-exchange reform, and Charles W. Taussig, a sympathetic businessman, were consulted on securities regulation.

Moley also had the delicate and time-consuming task of negotiating with prospective cabinet nominees. In making his Cabinet, Roosevelt was guided by several factors: (1) Although he had defeated Hoover by a landslide, the Democrats were a minority party, and if he was to win reelection in 1936, he had to attract Republican votes; (2) the key congressional committees that would pass on his legislative program were headed by conservative Southerners; (3) he wanted a woman in the Cabinet; (4) he had no intention of rewarding those Democratic leaders, such as Al Smith or Newton Baker, who had opposed his nomination. Early on, Roosevelt had decided upon Jim Farley for Postmaster General, the job usually given to the party's political chieftain; and Governor George Dern of Utah for Interior Secretary. Cordell Hull was offered Secretary of State, and Senator Carter Glass the Treasury. Lists of other prospects were made and discarded, and names were shifted about. Even Sara Roosevelt had her choices: "I wonder who you will take to Washington," she wrote her son. "I should try Owen Young or Newton Baker."

Taking note of Moley's increasing prominence, Sam Rayburn gave him a pointed warning. "I hope we don't have any God-damned Rasputin in this administration." There was little danger, however, of a Rasputin in an administration headed by Franklin Roosevelt—for the squire of Hyde Park was himself a master manipulator of men. Seeking the crosscurrent of ideas that the Brain Trust had previously provided, Roosevelt consulted spokesmen of varying points of view, gave a sympathetic ear to all, and selected those elements from each presentation that suited his needs. Sometimes, as Moley was to learn to his anger, he assigned the same task to several individuals or groups without telling them. There were occasions when he purposely adopted an extreme position for the sake of maneuver, and then allowed himself to be talked out of it. The policy usually adopted was the one Roosevelt had covertly supported all along, but by jockeying others into persuading him to support it, he converted them into advocates of issues to which they might have originally objected.

The way in which he maneuvered congressional conservatives into virtually demanding that he support a progressive program was an example of this policy. Visiting Roosevelt in Warm Springs a month after the election, Senator Tom Connally was surprised to find him still talking about budget balancing and constitutional limitations on presidential power. "If it was constitutional to spend forty billion dollars in a war," the Texan declared, "isn't it just as constitutional to spend a little money to relieve the hunger and misery of our citizens?" Hearing exactly what he wished from Connally, Roosevelt puffed contentedly on his cigarette and remained noncommittal. Fear of Roosevelt's apparent conservatism reached the point that even Cordell Hull urged Josephus Daniels to persuade the President-elect to appear more progressive.

Any hope that the lame-duck session of Congress that convened on December 5, 1932, would be a springboard for New Deal legislation quickly faded. Policemen armed with riot guns barricaded the Capitol as Communist-led hunger marchers paraded through the streets of Washington singing the "Internationale." The session itself was only a shade less tumultuous. Congress was burdened with 158 members who had been defeated in November, and party discipline was nonexistent. Huey Long paralyzed the Senate with a filibuster against a banking bill, and the Democrats accused the Reconstruction Finance Corporation of favoring Republican applicants for loans.

Hoover pushed for a budget-balancing national sales tax, and conservative Democrats went along until Roosevelt objected on grounds that it would be regressive. The key to the President-elect's program was the restoration of consumer purchasing power and a sales tax, reducing the amount available for spending, would be counterproductive. Roosevelt's agricultural reform plan, designed to bolster prices paid to farmers, was modified beyond recognition in committee, farm relief was tied up by wrangling, the industrial bankruptcy plan was muddled, and even the chance to immediately legalize the sale of beer was lost.‡ Unwilling to expend prestige to salvage something from the debacle, Roosevelt left his program to its fate.

The chaos in Congress mirrored the confusion and despair of the country in the cold, gray winter of 1933. Over one third of Iowa's farmland had been foreclosed, and farmers banded together, with rifles and shotguns, to protect their homes against tax sales. Apple sellers reappeared on street corners. People were said to be starving. Less than half the usual number of marriages were taking place. To save money, housewives revived the half-forgotten arts of preserving fruit and soapmaking. Uneasy about the future, depositors were withdrawing their savings from the banks. Reserves dwindled, and it was obvious that a financial crisis was in the making. A Japanese army trying to seize control of Manchuria from China was advancing on all fronts. And on January 30—while Roosevelt was celebrating his fifty-first birthday—Adolf Hitler rode through cheering crowds to become Chancellor of Germany.

Six weeks into the new year, the banks began to close. The storm broke in Michigan, where, on February 14, Governor William A. Comstock proclaimed an eight-day bank holiday to prevent the collapse of the state's financial institutions. Late the following day, Roosevelt, who had been cruising in the Bahamas on Vincent Astor's sleek yacht, the *Nourmahal*, came ashore in Miami. The tanned and happy President-elect's comments at a press conference offered little reassurance to those worried by the creeping paralysis spreading across the nation. "I didn't open [a] brief case during the entire twelve days," he declared and told reporters that he had locked up the ship's log to keep all evidence of his adolescent humor from their prying eyes. Later, he conferred privately with Moley, who had come to Miami to report on his negotiations with prospective members of the Cabinet. The meeting was cut short, for Roosevelt was scheduled to speak briefly that evening at Bay Front Park.

Seated in an open touring car en route to the park, Roosevelt led a cavalcade of automobiles onto a dimly lit boulevard lined with tall palms. Vincent Astor, riding with Moley and Kermit Roosevelt,* who had been

‡ Congress did vote to repeal the Eighteenth Amendment, but repeal (the Twenty-first Amendment) was not ratified until December 1933.
* Kermit Roosevelt, Theodore's second son, was the only member of the Oyster Bay clan friendly to FDR. Edith Roosevelt had emerged from retirement to introduce Herbert Hoover at a rally, and it was she who described FDR as "nine-tenths mush and

one of the guests on the cruise, commented on Roosevelt's accessibility to any assassin. "Anyone could shoot him in such a place as this," he said. Moley replied that during the campaign such a possibility had always existed and although danger had become commonplace, Roosevelt was not apprehensive in crowds. The President-elect himself faced the threat of assassination with equanimity. A few weeks before, John Garner had warned him of the possibility of an attempt on his life, and he had replied: "I remember T.R. saying to me, 'The only real danger from an assassin is from one who does not care whether he loses his own life in the act or not. Most of the crazy ones can be spotted first.' "†

Thousands of people crowded about Roosevelt's car as it entered the brightly lighted park shortly after 9 P.M., and he was hoisted up on the top of the back seat, where he could be seen. "I haven't been here for seven years, but I am coming back," he said. "I am firmly resolved not to make this the last time. I have had a wonderful twelve days fishing in these Florida and Bahama waters. . . . The only fly in the ointment on my trip has been that I have put on about ten pounds." Roosevelt spoke for about two minutes amid much laughter and applause and then lowered himself to the seat of the car. He refused a request by a newsreel photographer to repeat the speech and greeted Mayor Cermak of Chicago, who was visiting Miami. Cermak wanted to discuss an RFC loan for his city, and a meeting was arranged for later at the President-elect's railroad car, which was standing by to take him to New York.

"Just then I heard what I thought was a firecracker; then several more," Roosevelt later told newsmen. Moley, who was close by, thought it a backfire. A short, curly-haired man standing on a bench less than twenty feet from the President-elect was emptying a revolver at him. Mrs. Lillian Cross, a horrified spectator, grabbed the would-be assassin's arm, spoiling his aim as he fired four more shots. There were shouts and screams and a rapid blur of violence. Blood covered Mayor Cermak's shirtfront, a woman was hit in the abdomen, and three other persons, including a Secret Service agent, were slightly wounded. The assassin was wrestled to the ground by an avalanche of spectators and police.

"I'm all right! I'm all right!" Roosevelt cried reassuringly above the din. His driver started the car forward, but the President-elect, seeing Cermak tottering with a wound in the chest, ordered him to stop. Secret Ser-

---

one-tenth Eleanor." Ted, Jr., winding up a term as governor-general of the Philippines, described his relationship to the President-elect as "Fifth cousin—about to be removed."

† Theodore Roosevelt often went for brisk walks about Washington while President, usually accompanied by only a single Secret Service agent. Sometimes he packed a pistol, telling one friend, "I should have some chance of shooting the assassin before he could shoot me, if he were near me."

vice men frantically shouted for the driver to get out of the crowd, but Roosevelt countermanded the order.

> I saw Mayor Cermak being carried. I motioned to have him put in the back of the car, which be the first out. He was alive, but I didn't think he was going to last. I put my left arm around him and my hand on his pulse, but I couldn't find any pulse. He slumped forward.
> On the left of Cermak, and leaning over him, was the Miami chief of detectives. He was sitting on the rear mudguard. He said we had gone two blocks, "I don't think he is going to last."
> I said, "I am afraid he isn't."
> After we had gone another block, Mayor Cermak straightened up and I got his pulse. It was surprising. For three blocks I believed his heart had stopped. I held him all the way to the hospital and his pulse constantly improved.
> That trip to the hospital seemed thirty miles long. I talked to Mayor Cermak nearly all the way. I remember I said, "Tony, keep quiet—don't move. It won't hurt you if you keep quiet."

Cermak, cradled in Roosevelt's arms, was conscious when they reached the emergency entrance of the Jackson Memorial Hospital and was immediately rushed to the operating table. Roosevelt waited until he was brought out and spent several minutes with him. "I'm glad it was me instead of you," whispered the mayor. Before returning to the *Nourmahal*, the President-elect also visited the other shooting victims. Mrs. Roosevelt, who was in New York, returned home that evening from a speaking engagement to receive a confused account of the attempted assassination from the family butler. Eleanor remained calm as more information was provided by a reporter. "These things have to be expected," she said. After reaching her husband by telephone at Cermak's bedside, she told newsmen: "He's all right. He's not the least bit excited."

Giuseppe Zangara, the would-be assassin, had a personality profile that would become all too familiar. Friendless, hollow-eyed, and barely five feet tall, he was an unemployed bricklayer who had emigrated from Italy a decade before. Throughout his life, he had been tormented by intense stomach pains. "I want to make it clear I do not hate Mr. Roosevelt personally," Zangara told police. "I hate all Presidents, no matter from what country they come, and I hate all officials and everybody who is rich." The pistol he had emptied at the President-elect had been purchased for eight dollars at a Miami pawn shop, with no questions asked. Within a week, he was tried and sentenced to eighty years, and when Cermak died, on March 6, he was condemned to death in the electric chair. He had come within inches of altering history.

Throughout the episode, Moley noted that Roosevelt remained calm and self-possessed. The time of real testing, he thought, would come after they had returned to the yacht and the tensions of the moment had ebbed. "All of us were prepared, sympathetically, understandingly, for any reaction that might come from Roosevelt," Moley said. "There was nothing—not so much as the twitching of a muscle, the mopping of a brow or even the hint of a false gaiety—to indicate that it wasn't any other evening in any other place. Roosevelt was simply himself—easy, confident, poised, to all appearances unmoved." He went to bed about 2 A.M., but the other members of the party, their nerves shattered, talked among themselves through the night. In the morning, they questioned the Secret Service man who had been guarding the President-elect's stateroom as to whether or not Roosevelt's calm had been feigned. "I was curious myself so I stole in several times," replied the agent. "Each time Mr. Roosevelt was asleep."

Roosevelt accepted his narrow escape from death with a fatalism that had marked his life since his bout with polio. He regarded his survival as an act of Divine Providence, and was more concerned about those who had been wounded by Zangara's wild fusillade than his own fate. Such unflinching, even cheerful courage won universal admiration and resulted in a fresh surge of confidence in him. "People seemed to feel that their faith in the future was the assassin's target," said *Time*. "There *is* a star, you know," Missy LeHand quietly told Tugwell.

Immediately following his return to New York, Roosevelt was pulled into the vortex of the banking crisis. Banks failed in Cleveland, Memphis, and San Francisco. Long lines snaked around the banks in every town as depositors hurried to withdraw their money. Armored trucks ran by night from city to city, carrying cash to beleaguered banks, but they were unable to stem the spreading panic. Public suspicion was fed by disclosures before a senate committee of the gross misuse of funds by America's financial elite. People hoarded cash, hiding it under the mattress or burying it in the yard. Foreigners withdrew their deposits from the New York banks in gold; almost every ship that sailed added to the drain of bullion. Banks dared not lend money, and the nation's financial machinery froze into rigidity. The bank failed in Northampton, Massachusetts, Calvin Coolidge's home town, and the ex-President found his law partner slumped at his desk with his head in his hands. He left a check for five thousand dollars beside him and quietly shut the door.

Shortly before midnight on February 18, while Roosevelt was attending a show at the Hotel Astor sponsored by New York newsmen, a Secret Service agent handed him a lengthy, handwritten letter from Hoover. He noted that, on the envelope, his name had been spelled "Roosvelt" by the agitated President. Without attracting attention, Roosevelt hastily looked the message over and passed it under the table to Moley, who with a glance grasped its meaning: The banking crisis had gotten out of control.

A most critical situation has arisen in the country of which I feel it is my duty to advise you confidentially [the President wrote]. . . . The major difficulty is the state of public mind, for there is a steadily degenerating confidence in the future which has reached the height of general alarm. I am convinced that a very early statement by you upon two or three policies of your Administration would serve greatly to restore confidence and cause a resumption of the march of recovery. . . .

The turning point of the depression had been reached in the summer of 1932, Hoover claimed, but victory had slipped from his grasp only because of Roosevelt's failure to pledge himself to follow conservative fiscal policies. "It would steady the country greatly," he continued, "if there could be prompt assurance that there will be no tampering [with] or inflation of the currency; that the budget will be unquestionably balanced, even if further taxation is necessary; that the Government credit will be maintained by refusal to exhaust it in the issue of securities." Hoover understood full well what he was asking, for a few days later he wrote a Republican senator that if the President-elect accepted his proposals "it means the abandonment of 90% of the so-called new deal."

Meeting with his advisers early the next morning, Roosevelt described the letter as "cheeky." Fear stalked the land not because of the threat of the new administration's policies but because of Hoover's failures and a lack of confidence in the banking system. Roosevelt felt that to issue a statement promising to remain on the gold standard would have been the height of cynicism, for his advisers were suggesting he take the country off the gold standard, as most of its trading competitors had done. Devaluation had made their exports far cheaper than American goods, and they were underselling the United States in the world market. Roosevelt had already discussed the possibility of using unrepealed provisions of the Trading with the Enemy Act of 1917‡ to embargo the shipment of gold, and rather than tip his hand and raise the level of speculation to even higher levels, he remained silent about his future plans.

"I am equally concerned with you in regard to the gravity of the present banking situation," he finally wrote Hoover, "but my thought is that it is so very deep-seated that the fire is bound to spread in spite of anything that is done by way of mere statements." Either through pique or error, however, his reply did not reach the White House until March 1, ten days later.

In the meantime, Roosevelt announced his Cabinet. Cordell Hull, tall, dignified, and a leading advocate of lowered tariffs, became Secretary of State. Carter Glass, suspicious of Roosevelt's commitment to fiscal con-

---

‡ Unknown to FDR and his advisers, the same provisions of the Trading with the Enemy Act had been brought to Hoover's attention, but when their legality was questioned, he declined to make use of them.

servatism, declined the Treasury secretaryship, and it went to William
Woodin. Tom Walsh was named Attorney General, but he died before
he could assume office, and the job was given to Homer S. Cummings.
Daniel C. Roper, who had been commissioner of internal revenue under
Wilson, was named Secretary of Commerce. Roosevelt had originally intended to offer George Dern the post of Secretary of the Interior, but the
Utah governor aroused the opposition of public power advocates, and
Harold L. Ickes, a Chicago lawyer and Bull Moose Republican, was chosen in his place. Roosevelt had never met Ickes until he interviewed him
about the appointment. "I liked the cut of his jib," he said afterward.
Dern was made Secretary of War. Senator Claude Swanson of Virginia,
chairman of the senate Naval Affairs Committee, was named Secretary of
the Navy.* Swanson was old and ailing, which permitted Roosevelt to be,
in effect, his own Navy Secretary. Henry Wallace was chosen Secretary
of Agriculture, a position his father had filled under Harding and
Coolidge. Jim Farley was named Postmaster General, as originally
planned, and placed in charge of doling out patronage. Frances Perkins,
as Secretary of Labor, became the first woman ever named to a Cabinet,
and her appointment aroused considerable furor. Miss Perkins and Ickes
were the only members of the original Cabinet to last through Roosevelt's entire presidency.

Lacking political luminaries, this Cabinet was regarded as merely
competent by most observers. A mixed bag of liberals and conservatives,
Easterners, Southerners, and Westerners, it contained three senators, a
governor, an industrialist, a couple of social reformers, an agricultural expert, and a political technician. Wallace, Woodin, and Ickes were Republicans. Only Woodin and Wallace had any part in shaping the programs
they were to administer. "So far as I could see," said Moley, "there was
neither a well-defined purpose nor underlying principle in the selection."
If there was any unifying factor, it was a belief in progressivism and loyalty to the man who had appointed them, for they were all FRBC—For
Roosevelt Before Chicago.

In that day of limited government, the President did his work with a
minuscule staff, and Roosevelt quickly filled the positions open to him.
Louis Howe, neither temperamentally nor technically fitted for the Cabinet or a ranking administrative post, was made his chief secretary. "Louis
can do that job," Roosevelt remarked, "and still work behind the scenes
being the mysterious figure that he loves." Steve Early and Marvin McIntyre—two veterans of the 1920 campaign and members of the Cuff Links
Club—were brought in to handle press relations and appointments. Out

---

* Swanson's appointment permitted Louis Howe to redeem his convention pledge to
Harry Byrd. Byrd, who had stepped down as governor, was named by his successor to
fill Swanson's senate seat.

of deference to Howe, they were called assistant secretaries. Moley was made an assistant Secretary of State and Tugwell an assistant Secretary of Agriculture, but it was intended that they be available to work directly for the President. Berle declined an appointment, as did Felix Frankfurter, who was offered the post of solicitor general. Like Ed Flynn, he preferred to wield influence outside the Administration.

There was still one more bit of business: preparation of the President's inaugural address. Roosevelt had first discussed the outline with Moley following a strenuous day of campaigning in California in September 1932. He believed that he would face an emergency no less urgent than the war, and while he wished to offer encouragement to the American people, he refused to gloss over grim reality. The speech must offer warming assurance and the promise of vigorous and immediate action. Further discussions were held by Roosevelt and Moley early in February 1933, and Moley went to work on the speech. On February 27, he took a draft to Hyde Park and showed it to Roosevelt for the first time.

Shortly after dinner, the two men retired to the library, where Roosevelt seated himself in the chair he had used as governor of New York, with a bridge table before him. He carefully read over Moley's draft and approved it. But noting that Howe was coming up from New York the next day and recalling his anger over the Chicago acceptance speech, Roosevelt said he had better copy it out in his own hand. The little man would "have a fit" if he learned someone else had written the speech.

"I sat on the long couch before the fireplace, in which a bright fire was burning," Moley recalled. "Then began a long process of considering every sentence and sometimes every word. We exchanged comment, and from time to time, either Roosevelt or I decided upon a change. The discussion and writing went on to the end of my draft." They finished about 1:30 A.M., and Moley gathered up his copy from the card table and tossed it into the still-glowing embers. "This is your speech now," he said.

The next day, as expected, Howe went over the text, tightening it up and adding a new first paragraph. Howe's introduction included the sentence "The only thing we have to fear is fear itself." These words, always to be associated with Franklin Roosevelt's name, bear a striking resemblance to Thoreau's "nothing is so much to be feared as fear," but Moley discounts such a link. He recalled seeing the phrase in a department-store advertisement earlier that month and surmised that Howe, who read only detective stories and newspapers and probably never had heard of Thoreau, must have seen it there too.

Rain and sleet were falling when Roosevelt and his family arrived in Washington on the evening of March 2. With them they brought the drafts of a pair of presidential proclamations: one invoking the Trading with the Enemy Act to declare a national bank holiday, the other summoning Congress into a special session. As the train passed through the winter-scarred landscape, it was noted that no smoke poured from the factory chimneys of the nation's industrial heartland. Twenty-one states had declared partial or total bank holidays, and the rest teetered on the brink. The Federal Reserve Board reported that the gold hemorrhage had reached nearly $250 million in Hoover's last week in office and reserves were below the amount required to back the currency. The Treasury could not meet the government payroll, and the United States was technically bankrupt.

Upon his arrival at the Mayflower Hotel, Roosevelt found the bank crisis approaching a climax. The chief fiscal officers of the outgoing administration, Treasury Secretary Ogden Mills and Eugene Meyer of the Federal Reserve Board, urged Hoover to temporarily close all banks to prevent a total collapse. He refused, however, to go farther than an order prohibiting withdrawals of deposits and gold, and stipulated that Roosevelt would have to agree to the order before he would sign it. Democratic congressional leaders were summoned to Roosevelt's suite, and after considerable discussion it was decided there could be no joint action. As long as Hoover held power, the responsibility to act was his.

The next afternoon, March 3, Roosevelt, his wife, and his son James went to the White House for tea with the outgoing First Family. Traditionally, this was a formal social call, but Ike Hoover, the chief usher, whispered to the President-elect that the President had told Mills and Meyer to stand by in an adjoining room for another discussion of the crisis. Moley was hastily summoned from the Mayflower as the social amenities proceeded in a chilly fashion in the Red Room. With their aides present, Hoover and Roosevelt again sparred fruitlessly over the ultimate responsibility for dealing with the crisis.† Hoover now thought he had fathomed the reason for Roosevelt's refusal to accept joint action, and it left him bristling. Ten days before, he had been informed by an industrialist named James Rand that Tugwell had told Rand over lunch that Roosevelt's advisers believed the banking system would collapse in a few

† Forty-eight years later, Dorothy Roe Lewis, a reporter for Universal Service in 1933, wrote that following the meeting, Mrs. Roosevelt gave a private briefing to the four women journalists assigned to cover her. She related that Hoover had invited FDR into a private room for a discussion of the banking crisis but forgot to close the door, which allowed her to overhear their conversation. " 'Well,' Mr. Hoover said to Mr. Roosevelt, 'will you join me in signing a joint proclamation tonight, closing all the banks?' And Mr. Roosevelt said to Mr. Hoover: 'Like hell, I will! If you haven't got the guts to do it yourself, I'll wait until I am President to do it!' " Much to Mrs. Roosevelt's surprise, the reporters told her they were unable to print the story, asserting it would touch off a panic and they couldn't quote either President directly because it was all hearsay. The women were fond of Mrs. Roosevelt and agreed not to mention the matter. New York Times, Mar. 13, 1981.

days, "which would place the responsibility in the lap of President Hoover."

Realizing the conversation was getting nowhere, Roosevelt decided to cut it short. He bent down to lock his braces and in a polite effort to relieve the harassed Hoover of a burdensome obligation, said: "I realize, Mr. President, that you are extremely busy so I will understand completely if you do not return the call." For the first time that afternoon, as Roosevelt later told Grace Tully, Hoover looked him squarely in the eye and replied: "Mr. Roosevelt, when you are in Washington as long as I have been you will learn that the President of the United States calls on nobody." With that, Roosevelt hustled his family out of the room, certain that Jimmy wanted to punch Hoover in the eye. "I shall be waiting at my hotel, Mr. President, to learn what you decide," he said as he left.

Throughout the evening, Roosevelt and his advisers discussed the crisis. It was clear that the American banking system had reached the point where it could not stand the strain of another business day. People came and went with suggestions. The telephone rang constantly. Hoover called twice, the last time at one o'clock in the morning of Inauguration Day. Personal animosities were now so deep that agreement at this late hour was impossible and Roosevelt suggested they both go to bed. Moley and Woodin went instead to the Treasury, where Mills, Meyer, and Arthur Ballantine, the under Secretary, acting on their own, were trying to persuade governors who had not closed the banks in their states to do so before they were scheduled to reopen in the morning. All except Governor Henry Horner of Illinois and New York's Lehman had agreed. Woodin and Moley joined in, and despite the antipathy between the incoming and outgoing Presidents, their top aides worked together in harmony. They "had forgotten to be Republicans or Democrats," Moley observed. "We were just a bunch of men trying to save the American banking system." Shortly after 4 A.M., the last cogs fell into place. Governor Lehman proclaimed a state banking holiday, and almost simultaneously Horner issued a similar order.

As dawn broke over Washington, the financial heartbeat of the world's greatest nation had come to a halt. A cold wind swirled down Pennsylvania Avenue, angrily tossing the flags and bunting that lined the route of the inaugural parade.

XVII

THE ROOSEVELT WHIRLWIND

T HIS GREAT NATION will endure as it has endured, will revive and will prosper. . . . the only thing we have to fear is fear itself." The confident words crackled across the stricken land with the ring of a call to battle. "This Nation asks for action, and action now. . . . I shall ask the Congress for . . . broad Executive power to wage a war against the emergency, as great as the power that would be given to me if we were in fact invaded by a foreign foe." Rarely has a political leader so completely expressed the popular mood as did Franklin Roosevelt on that raw Saturday afternoon in March 1933. The new President's promise of bold leadership, his resolution, and his blithe optimism kindled a new spirit of national unity and purpose. Observers noted that his pledge to combat the depression with the vigor of wartime triggered the most enthusiastic response from the crowd spread out before him.

Hope seemed to revive everywhere. Here at last was a President who did not make excuses for inaction; here was a President ready to go on the attack. From the miserable lines of the hungry at the soup kitchens, from the dispossessed in the shabby Hoovervilles on the fringes of the big cities, from the rebellious farmers out on the high plains, came a wave of support. Over the next week, letters of approval poured into the White House by the thousands. Eleanor Roosevelt found the unhesitating willingness of the people to accept the prospect of dictatorship somewhat chilling. "You felt that they would do *anything*—only if someone told them *what* to do," she declared. Not long before, Roosevelt had outlined his concept of the presidency to Anne O'Hare McCormick, of the New York *Times*. "The Presidency is not merely an administrative office," he declared. "That's the least of it. It is more an engineering job. . . . It is preeminently a place of moral leadership."

To get his administration off and running, Roosevelt requested prompt senate confirmation of his Cabinet, which was rushed through without the formality of hearings. As dusk fell over Washington, the cabinet members gathered upstairs in the Oval Room of the White House to be administered the oath of office by Supreme Court Justice Benjamin N. Cardozo, an old presidential friend. Having enjoyed the five-hour inaugural parade with its jangling troops of cavalry and forty marching bands, the President was in high spirits. This "little family party" was the first time a Cabinet had ever been sworn in as a unit and the first such ceremony conducted in the White House. Shaking hands with each official, Roosevelt presented each with a signed commission and decreed that Miss Perkins was thenceforth to be known as "Madame Secretary." Following the ceremony, he went to the Red Room to greet thirteen crippled youngsters who had been invited up from Warm Springs to attend the inauguration.

The change from the sedate and formal atmosphere that had surrounded the Hoovers was sudden and complete. Colonel E. W. Starling, chief of the White House Secret Service detail, returned from seeing the departing President and his wife off at Union Station to find the old mansion "had been transformed during my absence into a gay place, full of people who oozed confidence. . . . The President was the most happy and confident of them all." As the Cabinet was being sworn in, a reporter noted that Roosevelt grandchildren romped in the halls, and coveys of visitors came and went. Eleanor invited about seventy-five relatives, including Alice Longworth and her brothers Kermit and Archie Roosevelt, to a buffet supper that evening and, breaking with tradition, greeted her guests at the door. Except for this family affair, the President attended none of the inaugural festivities that evening. He was represented by Mrs. Roosevelt, who led a happy party of family and friends from one function to another.*

Instead, he met with William Woodin, the new Secretary of the Treasury; Attorney General Homer Cummings; and Moley, to discuss the banking crisis. Roosevelt had already decided on swift action: to use the Trading with the Enemy Act to declare a bank holiday and embargo the shipment of gold, to summon Congress into special session, and to convene a meeting of leading bankers to get their ideas for dealing with the crisis. Cummings, who had spent the afternoon examining the old law's

---

* Out celebrating on his own, the President's youngest son, John, drove up to the White House gates early the next morning in a battered roadster. The guards wouldn't let him in. "Go on," they said. "No son of the President would be driving such a junk heap." Young Roosevelt passed the remainder of the night in a hotel lobby.

legislative history, told the President that in his opinion it would meet the legal test. And Woodin assured him that, come what might, the banking bill would be ready in four days, on March 9.

Woodin and Moley, who were joined by Ogden Mills and Arthur Ballantine, plunged into another grueling night. Already at the point of exhaustion, they worked into Sunday morning revising the proclamation declaring a bank holiday. Back at the White House, Roosevelt and Louis Howe conversed in the Lincoln Room until bedtime. Not long afterward, a friend told Roosevelt that if he succeeded in the task he had set for himself he would go down in history as the greatest American President, but if he failed, he would be condemned as the worst. "If I fail I shall be the last," Roosevelt quietly replied.

Roosevelt never forgot his first morning as President of the United States. He wanted to read the newspapers while having breakfast in bed, but the papers arrived late and were not the ones he wanted. After he had shaved and dressed, Irwin McDuffie, his valet, helped him into his wheelchair, took him down in the elevator, and pushed him along the terrace to the Oval Office. Bumping along the flagstones for the first time, Roosevelt looked across the lawn and recognized a big magnolia that had been planted by Andrew Jackson. The room, which Hoover had left only the day before, was bare except for the furniture. There were no pictures on the curving walls, no flags, no books on the shelves. Empty walls annoyed him. There was nothing on the big desk except incoming and outgoing trays. An empty desk annoyed him too. There he was, as he told Tugwell, in a big, empty room, completely alone.

> The nation, he supposed, was waiting breathlessly for the following up of his brave words of yesterday. There was a financial crisis, activity was congealed, and he was expected to find the means for bringing the nation's dying economy back to life. Here he was, without even the wherewithal to make a note—if he had had a note to make. And for a few dreadful minutes he hadn't a single thought. He knew that the stimulus of human contact would break the spell; but where was everybody? There must be a button to push, but he couldn't see one. He pulled out a drawer or two; they had been cleaned out. Presently, he sat back in his chair and simply shouted. That brought Missy LeHand from her office on one side and Marvin McIntyre from the reception room on the other. The day's work then began.

The Cabinet gathered again at the White House after lunch, with Vice-President Garner, speaker of the House Henry T. Rainey, Howe, and Moley. "The President outlined more coherently than I had heard it outlined before, just what this banking crisis was and what the legal problems were," recalled Miss Perkins. Cummings was formally asked when he would be ready to deliver an opinion on the validity of the Trading with the Enemy Act and replied: "Mr. President, I am ready to give my opinion now." Roosevelt then met with congressional leaders and asked if a special session could be convened on March 9. They agreed that it could. Later that evening, Roosevelt signed the necessary documents calling Congress into session and proclaiming a four-day national bank holiday. To keep from profaning the Sabbath, the holiday did not become effective until after midnight. Every bank in the country was closed, gold and silver shipments embargoed, hoarding forbidden, and violations of the order made punishable by a fine of ten thousand dollars or ten years' imprisonment. With stunning speed and decisiveness, Roosevelt had moved to fulfill his pledge of "action and action now."

Ernest Lindley said it was like "a streak of lightning out of a black sky." People woke up on Monday morning to learn that every bank in the country had been shut down by the government. The only money they could lay their hands on was in their wallets and pocketbooks. When that was spent, they wouldn't be able to get more, for no one would take checks. Yet there was no panic. Most Americans enjoyed the novelty and excitement after weeks of tension and uncertainty. One of the biggest problems was getting change for anything bigger than a five dollar bill, because storekeepers would make change only for regular customers. But people survived through ingenious improvisations: Credit and barter took the place of cash. Absolute strangers trusted each other and exchanged IOUs. Novel ways of doing business were created: A New York hotel sent clerks around to various churches to exchange large bills for the smaller currency and coins in the collection plates. Postage stamps, foreign coins, and subway tokens were all accepted for goods and services. Some municipal governments and private concerns issued scrip to cover their bills and payrolls. "This is the happiest day in three years," observed Will Rogers. "We have no jobs, we have no money, we have no banks; and if Roosevelt had burned down the Capitol, we would have said, 'Thank God, he started a fire under something.'"

In the meantime, Woodin, Moley, Mills, Ballantine, and their assistants worked around the clock to get the banks reopened. The bankers Roosevelt had asked to assist in providing answers—few people commented on the irony of this move in the light of his inaugural attack on the "money changers"—had nothing to offer. Some were on the edge of going to pieces under the nervous strain. Everyone was worried that when the banks reopened there would not be enough currency to meet minimum needs. There was talk of nationalizing the banking system, of guaranteeing deposits, and of issuing scrip. But Woodin thought there must be a better solution than issuing "funny money." He was a businessman, not a banker, and believed the problem was as much one of restoring confidence as it was of finance. "I'll be damned if I go back into those meetings until I get my head cleared," he declared late Monday night.

The following morning, Woodin rushed up to Moley, who was dourly having breakfast. "I've got it! I've got it!" he shouted. Before going to bed, he said, he had taken up his guitar and thought about the problem of scrip. "I played some more, and read some more and slept some more and thought some more. And by gum, if I didn't hit on the answer that way! Why didn't I see it before? We don't have to issue scrip! . . . We can issue currency against the sound assets of the banks. . . . And it won't frighten people. It won't look like stage money. It'll be money that looks like money." This was the simplest of all possible solutions, and Woodin and Moley dashed over to the White House to tell the President. Roosevelt was delighted and gave his immediate approval. "Then we were off," Moley added, "for forty-eight hours of wrangling over details in the meetings at the Treasury, of bill drafting, message drafting, and conferring with Congressional leaders."

The Emergency Banking Act validated the presidential proclamation closing the banks. Only the stronger banks would be allowed to reopen, and "conservators" would be appointed to administer the shakier institutions until their fate could be determined. The Treasury was authorized to issue Federal Reserve notes providing enough currency to prevent runs. "Yes, it's finished," an exhausted Woodin told a reporter as he left his office at dawn on Thursday, March 9. "Both bills are finished. You know my name is Bill and I'm finished, too."

"Vote! Vote!" cried members of the House after little more than a half hour of debate on the emergency banking bill. There had been no time for printing, and a few typewritten copies were hurried to Capitol Hill with marginal notes and corrections scribbled on them. Only the leaders had read the measure, and no committee hearings were held. "The house is burning down and the President of the United States says this is the way to put out the fire," said Representative Bertrand H. Snell, the Republican floor leader. The bill was shouted through in an atmosphere of wartime crisis and sent to the Senate, where debate was less perfunctory. Progressives such as Senator Robert M. La Follette, Jr., argued that the banks should be subjected to stricter regulation,† but the measure was

† Liberal historians have been critical of FDR for not using the opportunity presented by the emergency to nationalize the banks. But as Moley has pointed out, Roosevelt had no desire to change the system; his goal was to restore it. Besides, there was little sentiment in Congress for nationalization. Even La Follette and Senator Bronson Cutting of New Mexico, who later lamented the lost opportunity for nationalization, voted for the Emergency Banking Act. Raymond Moley, *The First New Deal* (New York: Harcourt, Brace & World, 1966), pp. 178–80.

finally approved, seventy-three to seven, shortly before 8 P.M. It was rushed down to the White House, where, as the newsreel cameras recorded the event, the President placed his signature upon the first legislative accomplishment of the New Deal.

The banks still could not open until Monday, but such a delay was fortunate, for it provided Roosevelt with the opportunity to personally explain the complicated process to the American people and persuade them to redeposit the money they had withdrawn during the panic. As governor of New York, he had often used the Fireside Chat—an informal radio address in which he explained complex issues in a way that his neighbors in Dutchess County and Warm Springs could understand—and the technique was ideally suited in this instance.

Sixty million people were gathered about their radio sets at ten o'clock Sunday evening as the President began his first report to the nation. "I want to talk for a few minutes with the people of the United States about banking. . . . I want to tell you what has been done in the last few days, why it was done and what the next steps are going to be." For twenty minutes, he discussed the banking crisis in terms that were readily grasped by ordinary citizens, and his tone was warmly reassuring. Urging his listeners to bring their savings back to the banks, Roosevelt told them "that it is safer to keep your money in a reopened bank than it is under the mattress." Finally, he returned to the theme of his inaugural. "Let us unite in banishing fear. We have provided the machinery to restore our financial system; it is up to you to support and make it work. It is your problem no less than it is mine. Together we cannot fail." The New Deal had found its voice—and it was masterful.

Heavy withdrawals were expected when the banks opened for business as usual next morning, because the country had been stranded without cash for several days, yet in every city deposits exceeded withdrawals. In New York alone, the excess that first day was $10 million. By the end of the week, about 75 percent of the nation's approximately eighteen thousand banks had reopened their doors following a massive effort by the Treasury to grade and license them.‡ Every bank in California was shaky, but Woodin personally ordered a handful opened, saying Californians had to have banks. One bank given up by its own directors was opened through error, but, as with the others, renewed confidence enabled it to weather the storm. "Capitalism was saved in eight days," observed Moley.

Seizing the momentum generated by the banking bill, Roosevelt summoned congressional leaders to the White House on the evening of March 9, only an hour after he had signed the measure into law. "Shortly

‡ Some two thousand banks had disappeared through merger and permanent closing by the time the crisis had completely run its course.

after midnight they departed," observed Lindley, "a mixture of dazed, determined and angry men." Reminding them of the Democratic campaign pledge to cut federal spending by 25 percent and to balance the budget, he had unveiled the most drastic plan for governmental economy ever put forward by a President. The work of Lewis Douglas, who had been appointed director of the Bureau of the Budget, the economy plan called for slashing veterans' benefits in half—by $400 million—and trimming government salaries, including those of members of Congress, by an additional $100 million.

The legislative leaders were stunned. The veterans' lobby was among the most powerful in the nation and had overridden every previous effort to reduce pensions and benefits. Others pointed out that slashes of the magnitude sought by the President—an estimated 13 percent of the fiscal year 1934 budget—would be deflationary at a time when the economy should be inflated. Undeterred, Roosevelt sent the economy bill to Congress the next day, on Friday, March 10. "For three long years, the Federal Government has been on the road toward bankruptcy," he said in an accompanying message. The huge deficits piled up under Hoover, running to $5 billion a year, were undermining confidence in the government, which could only be restored by frugality. "Too often in recent history, liberal governments have been wrecked on rocks of loose fiscal policy."

The bill inspired a rebellion in the House. Representative Joseph W. Byrns, the majority leader, declined to sponsor the measure, and Democratic members refused to bind themselves to support it. It passed on Saturday, 266 to 138, but only because of Republican support. Ninety-two Democrats deserted the President, but sixty-nine Republicans backed the proposal. Even more trouble appeared likely in the Senate, which was to take up the bill on Monday, and where debate was unlimited. But during dinner on Sunday, before his Fireside Chat on the banking bill, Roosevelt suddenly had an inspiration. "I think this would be a good time for beer," he declared. Louis Howe was sent in search of a copy of the Democratic platform, and as soon as he had finished his speech, the President wrote out a succinct, seventy-two-word message to Congress quoting the Democratic pledge to bring back beer and light wines. The proposal of legal beer immediately captured the headlines from the economy bill, and the House whooped it through on Tuesday along with a substantial tax that had been requested by the President. The next day, the Senate, its throat whetted for the taste of beer, cleared the economy bill by an overwhelming margin so it, too, could act on the beer bill.

It had been a remarkable two weeks. Roosevelt had turned the country around, creating a mood of excitement and optimism where there had been only torpor and fear. Using the tools that had been available to

Hoover but ignored by him, the President quickly marshaled his proposals and brilliantly merchandised them. The New York Stock Exchange and the Chicago commodity markets, which had been reopened along with the banks, recorded the biggest gains and the highest volume in months. An offering of $800 million in Treasury notes was quickly snapped up by investors. William Allen White was captivated by the Roosevelt whirlwind. "How do you account for him?" he wrote Ickes. "Was I just fooled in him before the election or has he developed? . . . He [has] developed magnitude and poise, more than all, power! I have been a voracious feeder in the course of a long and happy life and have eaten many things, but I have never had to eat my words before. I shall wait six months and . . . if they are still on the plate, down they go with a gusto. And I shall smack my lips as my Adams apple bobs."

In his first week in office, Roosevelt, ignoring Hoover's admonition that the President calls upon no one, had visited retired Justice Oliver Wendell Holmes on his ninety-second birthday. Out of high regard for Holmes dating back to the Wilson years, he undertook the difficult climb up the steep steps to the justice's home. Before leaving, the President sought his advice on dealing with the crisis. "Form your ranks and fight!" replied the Civil War veteran, his enormous white mustache bristling. After Roosevelt had gone, Holmes turned to a companion and said: "A second class intellect—but a first class temperament."

Roosevelt, however, had few illusions about what had been accomplished. No one realized more than he that his efforts had been primarily defensive. The panic had been halted, but the virus that caused it was yet to be isolated. "We still have done nothing on the constructive side," he told a press conference, "unless you think the beer bill is constructive." In fact, the bank holiday and the spending cuts would be deflationary unless countered by efforts to restore purchasing power. Originally, the President had intended to send Congress home after the banking and economy measures were approved, so the Administration, which had to rely on Hoover appointees in many key places, could organize itself and submit legislation in an orderly fashion. But noting, as Senator Burton Wheeler put it, Congress would "jump through a hoop" if he asked, Roosevelt decided to forge ahead. And so began a dazzling period of legislative accomplishment—"the Hundred Days"—that is without parallel in American history.

Relief, recovery, and reform jostled each other in the flood of bills and executive orders that poured with a staccato rhythm from the hotel rooms and the warren of government offices where the architects of the New Deal had set up shop. Lights burned late all over Washington as they drafted bills and regulations and memoranda, tore them up, and then began all over again. They inhabited a world of nervously stubbed-out cigarette butts, of sandwiches half eaten at desks, and their wives were neglected. Without a body of doctrine to serve as a guidepost, Roosevelt produced results that were experimental, contradictory, chaotic, and sometimes incoherent. But forced by events to deal with a myriad of problems, the President ignored the question of priorities and pressed ahead on all fronts.

Circumstances assisted him. As Robert E. Sherwood later remarked, Hoover was an easy act to follow. The country was at rock bottom, with no place to go but up. Every new administration has enjoyed a traditional honeymoon with the American people; in 1933, this good will was more intense than usual. Everyone, even the Republicans, wanted the New Deal to succeed. Gripped by war psychology as surely as it had been in 1917, Congress acted upon Roosevelt's requests with startling rapidity. Party loyalty was strong, the President was enormously popular, and the lawmakers readily accepted guidance from the White House.

As the atmosphere of crisis abated, however, Congress began to show a degree of independence. Its leaders were talented and rich in experience, especially the southern barons who dominated the committee structure, and they had no intention of becoming rubber stamps. Roosevelt's skills as a mediator played a vital role in winning approval of his legislative program. Blissfully free of dogmatism, he allowed Congress to put its brand upon New Deal legislation, as long as fundamentals were not endangered.

Patronage also proved to be a useful carrot-and-stick for the Democratic donkey. Thousands of deserving Democrats, out of office for a dozen years, besieged Jim Farley, the Administration's official dispenser of patronage, until he had to sneak into his office and hotel as if he were dodging a summons. The creation of New Deal agencies multiplied the number of non-civil-service jobs—and congressmen duly noted that Roosevelt had decided that the loaves and fishes would be distributed only after the special session had adjourned and each member's loyalty tested and weighed.

The firestorm of legislation began on March 16, with the Agricultural Adjustment Act. Hastily pulled together by Henry Wallace, the Secretary of Agriculture, and assistant Secretary Tugwell from the conflicting recommendations of various farm leaders, the measure was aimed at restoring farm income and reducing surpluses. Basically, it established a domestic allotment plan under which farmers were paid subsidies for restricting acreage. These payments were to be financed by a tax upon processors, such as millers who ground wheat into flour, that would eventually be passed on to consumers. Roosevelt acknowledged that this was "a new and untrod path" but emphasized that something had to be done to restore agriculture. Before the bill was enacted, on May 12, Congress added an amendment that gave the President sweeping authority to bring about inflation by reducing the gold content of the dollar or by issuing greenbacks. "This is the end of Western Civilization," moaned the fiscally conservative Lewis Douglas.

March 21—Civilian Conservation Corps. Of all the legislation of the Hundred Days, the CCC was the closest to Roosevelt's own heart. Expressing his lifelong interest in forests and conservation, it was designed to put two hundred fifty thousand unemployed young men to work in the forests and national parks on reforestation and flood-control projects. It was passed by Congress on a voice vote on March 31, and within a week the first CCC camp was opened, near Luray, Virginia, with an initial enrollment of twenty-five hundred youths.

March 21—Federal Emergency Relief Act. With this act, the federal government assumed direct responsibility for assisting the victims of the depression. The President sought an appropriation of $500 million to be distributed to the states in loans and grants for an assault on unemployment. Approved by Congress on May 12, it created the Federal Emergency Relief Administration, the precursor of many agencies evolved by the New Deal to provide relief and jobs for the unemployed. Harry Hopkins, who had headed the Temporary Emergency Relief Administration, in New York State, took a cut in salary, from fifteen thousand dollars a year to eight thousand dollars, to come to Washington to run it. "Hunger is not debatable," declared Hopkins, and he disbursed more than $5 million in his first two hours in office.

March 27—Farm Credit Administration. Organized by executive order, it merged several conflicting government agencies that were supposed to be assisting farmers, into a single organization headed by Henry Morgenthau, Jr. The Farm Mortgage Act provided loans to farmers facing foreclosure and the loss of their farms.

March 29—"Truth in Securities" Act. "This proposal," said the President, "adds to the ancient rule of *caveat emptor* the further doctrine 'Let the seller also beware.' It puts the burden of telling the whole truth upon the seller." Anyone engaged in marketing securities was required to supply the Federal Trade Commission with full information, and stiff penalties were imposed on violators. The FTC was also authorized to block the sale of misrepresented securities. Congress enacted the legislation on May 27, and the President followed up in 1934 with the Securities Exchange Act, which regulated the securities markets themselves. Joe Kennedy, an old Wall Street speculator familiar with all the methods of making a fast buck, was named chairman of the Securities and Exchange Commission. "Set a thief to catch a thief," Roosevelt told critics of the appointment.

April 10—Tennessee Valley Authority. Reflecting Roosevelt's own long-standing interest in public power and conservation, this measure set in motion the most ambitious adventure in regional planning that had yet been seen outside the Soviet Union. Senator George Norris' long campaign for a public power project on the Tennessee River at Muscle Shoals was expanded into a breathtaking plan for development of an entire watershed of some 640,000 square miles, overlapping several states. Because of its emphasis on social planning and government operation, the TVA was as close to socialism as the New Deal ever came, but it was handily approved by Congress, on May 18, and became an outstandingly successful example of regional conservation and economic development.

April 13—Home Owners' Loan Act. Enacted by Congress on June 13, this act served the same purpose for urban homeowners that the Farm Mortgage Act did for farmers. The Home Owners' Loan Corporation, with a revolving $2 billion fund raised through the sale of bonds, averted the foreclosure of tens of thousands of homes by lending their owners money at low interest rates to keep up mortgage payments. As many as one out of every five mortgaged dwellings would ultimately be refinanced by the HOLC.

April 19—Abandonment of the gold standard. Roosevelt issued an executive order permanently embargoing the export of gold—in effect taking the nation off the gold standard—for several reasons. Under persistent pressure for inflation from farm-state legislators who wanted to raise prices and ease the burden on debtors, he faced the choice of either submitting or taking the lead himself. He was also concerned about the deflationary effects of the early New Deal economy measures and decided to pursue a policy of controlled inflation. Allowing the dollar to find its own level among the depreciated currencies of the world might also give America's international trade a much-needed boost. No less a personage than the younger J. P. Morgan applauded the departure from the gold standard as a way to fight deflation. This was followed on May 26 by a congressional resolution annulling the gold clause in both public and private contracts, which called for payment of debts in dollars with a specific gold content.

May 4—Emergency Railroad Transportation Act. Perhaps no segment of American industry was in worse shape than the railroads, most of them kept on track only by loans from the Reconstruction Finance Corporation. This bill, enacted on June 16, was intended to create a coordinated rail transport system through economies, consolidation of lines and routes, and regulatory reform.

May 17—Glass-Steagall Act. Primarily the work of Senator Carter Glass, this measure, although not, strictly speaking, a product of the New Deal, received its impetus from the atmosphere of reform prevailing in

Washington. During the boom, commercial banks had created investment affiliates to cash in on the sale of securities, and the law ordered them to get out of this business, denying them the temptation to gamble with their depositors' money.* It also created the Federal Deposit Insurance Corporation, to insure savings deposits against another wave of bank failures. Although Roosevelt was only reluctantly converted to the FDIC, deposit insurance is now regarded as one of the most significant of the New Deal's monuments.

In the hectic early weeks of his administration, Roosevelt gave little thought to stimulating industrial recovery. Believing that ideas for such a far-reaching program had not had sufficient time to develop, he seemed content to depend upon a policy of controlled inflation, limited public works, and rising agricultural prices to revive the economy. But, once again, Congress forced the President's hand. On April 6, the Senate overwhelmingly approved a bill introduced by Senator Hugo L. Black of Alabama designed to spread the available work among the jobless by reducing the work week from forty-eight to thirty hours. Roosevelt doubted the constitutionality of the measure and believed it would retard recovery, because it contained no provision for maintaining wage levels, in that a marginal twelve-dollar-a-week job might be transformed into two submarginal, six-dollar-a-week jobs.

Under the gun of the Black bill, Roosevelt ordered legislation to accomplish for industry and business what the AAA was to do for agriculture. Task forces that ranged over the economic and social spectrum labored to devise a plan but, as was to be expected, produced little more than bitter wrangling. Businessmen, led by Henry Harriman, president of the U. S. Chamber of Commerce, and Gerard Swope, of General Electric, wanted a revival of the trade associations encouraged by Herbert Hoover to bring order to the chaotic marketplace and to establish higher price levels. Labor wanted federal guarantees for collective bargaining. There were demands for huge public works programs or direct relief for the unemployed. On May 10, Roosevelt called a meeting of the competing groups at the White House, which after two hours seemed to be getting nowhere. Exasperated, he appointed a drafting committee headed by General Hugh S. Johnson, the pugnacious former brain truster, and told

* Roosevelt & Son, the investment house of the Oyster Bay branch of the family, was one of the firms forced to spin off its banking operations. Sometime later, Philip J. Roosevelt, a partner in the firm, telegraphed FDR asking what should be done about some of his wife's utility investments. "I have nothing to suggest," the President is supposed to have replied. "Investments are your business, not mine." Philip bided his time and then wrote his cousin to the following effect: "We have liquidated the utility investments in question and have invested the proceeds in government bonds. Now it is your business." Author's conversation with P. James Roosevelt, Jan. 28, 1979.

its members to lock themselves into a room and not come out until they had produced a satisfactory bill. From this rough-and-tumble emerged the National Industrial Recovery Act.

Regarded by Roosevelt as the crowning achievement of the Hundred Days, the NIRA was a patchwork of Theodore Roosevelt's New Nationalism, the old War Industries Board's experience, and the trade-association movement in which Roosevelt had participated as president of the American Construction Council. The bill was the most challenging foray yet made into mass industrial planning without socialism. In his second Fireside Chat, Roosevelt emphasized, however, that the government had not taken control of business and industry but had gone into "partnership" with them—"a partnership in planning, and a partnership to see that the plans are carried out." The bill suspended the antitrust laws and allowed groups of businessmen to draw up their own rules of competition, production, and marketing—codes of fair competition—and to set maximum hours of labor and minimum wages. If no agreement could be reached in an industry, the government could impose a code. Section 7(a) of the NIRA guaranteed workers the right to collective bargaining and to decide whether or not to join a union. Title II authorized a $3.3 billion public works program to quickly pump money into the economy to provide jobs and increase purchasing power.

Loaded with something for everybody, the bill was sent to Congress on May 17, where it easily passed the House. But it ran into heavy weather in the Senate, where old-line populists and trustbusters insisted that, instead of helping the working man, the NIRA would promote the concentration of wealth and power. Shortly before adjourning, on June 16, an exhausted Senate approved the proposal by only a five-vote margin, and the bill was rushed to the President amid much fanfare. "The law I have just signed was passed to put people back to work," Roosevelt declared. "History will probably record the National Industrial Recovery Act as the most important and far-reaching Legislation ever created by the American Congress." Hugh Johnson was named to head the National Recovery Administration, which was to administer it. Harold Ickes was placed in charge of the Public Works Administration, created by Title II with the authority to build highways, dams, and federal buildings.

The Hundred Days were over. Fifteen messages had been sent to Congress demanding immediate action on the nation's problems, fifteen major laws had been steered to enactment, and Roosevelt had given ten major speeches. Most of these measures were controversial; some were of doubtful constitutionality. But Roosevelt had no intention of making a revolution or creating a new institutional structure for the nation. Rather, he was attempting to cure the temporary ailments of a capitalistic society and to nurse it back to health. Experimental cures were being tried only because the conventional nostrums no longer worked. Roosevelt had charged during the campaign that Hoover had failed to revive the economy because he had been too timid in applying available remedies. "Bold, persistent experimentation" had been the promise of the Oglethorpe University speech—and now it was being fulfilled.

Overworked and harassed aides sighed with relief as the President departed for a leisurely cruise along the New England coast to Campobello in the schooner *Amberjack II*, but he had thrived on the tension and the crisis atmosphere. Ebullient, optimistic, and always ready with a wisecrack, he surprised visitors with an obvious delight in wielding power that was a sharp contrast to the tortured self-doubts of his predecessor. Everyone remarked on his astonishing ability to relax in the midst of crisis. A swim in the White House pool complete with duckings and splashings would suddenly be interrupted by searching questions on the progress of railroad legislation. A serious evening's discussion of bank deposit insurance would turn into a leisurely night at home. The President would bring out his stamp collection; Eleanor might wander in to call his attention to a passage in a book she was reading; Missy LeHand or Grace Tully might appear with documents to be signed; perhaps Louis Howe would pop in with a story he had picked up on his grapevine. Although these quick changes of pace did not make for maximum efficiency, they were, as Moley observed, basic to Roosevelt's staying power. "Not even the realization that he was playing ninepins with the skulls and thighbones of economic orthodoxy seemed to worry him."

Piloting the *Amberjack* along the rocky Maine coast, Roosevelt enjoyed fair winds and following seas. And so did the economy. The New York *Times* Weekly Business Index, which had been at 52.3 at the time of the inauguration, reached 87.1 in mid-June, the highest level in more than two years. Factory chimneys were again belching smoke, the FERA and other relief programs were putting money into people's pockets, CCC camps were being opened, and the farmers were bringing their crops to market, rather than burning them. Beer flowed freely again. People were hopeful about the future. The depression was not over—but fear of it had been relieved. "Up go the prices of stocks and bonds," said the *Literary Digest*. "Up go the prices of wheat, corn and other commodities. . . ."

Yet, storm clouds continued to gather on the far horizon. In the Far East, Japanese troops continued their advance across Manchuria, and in Germany, Adolf Hitler, voted absolute power by the Reichstag, had launched a rearmament program in violation of the Versailles Treaty and was ghettoing the nation's Jewish citizens. Roosevelt had all but ignored international affairs in his Inaugural Address; like Moley and Tugwell, he believed the depression had been caused by a breakdown of the American economy and could best be cured by domestic action. Nevertheless, he wished the United States to regain a leadership role in world affairs. Like much else, the foreign policy of the early New Deal reflected the contradictions in the President's own views. Such measures as the AAA, which were aimed at stimulating the domestic economy, temporarily barred imports from abroad, while the expressed policy of Secretary of State Hull was the establishment of a system of economic cooperation based upon reciprocal tariffs.

Yet, as Robert Dallek has pointed out in his study of Roosevelt's foreign policy, the President saw no inconsistency in this position. Economic nationalism was regarded as merely a temporary expedient, rather than a permanent policy. Long-term recovery depended upon the opening of new foreign markets for American agricultural products won through the reciprocal trade agreements sponsored by Hull. In the meantime, Roosevelt hoped that his nationalistic monetary and economic policies would succeed in time to permit him to support stabilization and tariff agreements at the World Economic Conference, due to start in London later in the year.

As part of his plan to assume world leadership, Roosevelt sought improved relations with the Soviet Union and Latin America. The United States had never recognized the Bolsheviks, who had seized power in 1917, but the depression brought about a change of sentiment on the part of conservatives. Businessmen were now convinced that the Soviet Union represented a vast new market for American exports, and Roosevelt gingerly began negotiations with the Soviets. Having received promises from the Kremlin to refrain from spreading propaganda in this country, the United States officially recognized the Soviet Union on November 16, 1933.† Roosevelt, who had once boasted of having written the Haitian constitution, also moved to give meaning to his inaugural promise of a Good Neighbor policy in this hemisphere. Speaking at the Pan American Union a little more than a month after taking office, he emphasized the dedication of the United States to equality, cooperation, and nonintervention in the affairs of other states.

The new President's first diplomatic overtures were aimed at revitalizing the Geneva Disarmament Conference, which was on the brink of collapse because the participants could find no common ground. The French demanded security guarantees against a resurgent Germany; the Germans wanted an end to the restrictions imposed by the Versailles Treaty; the

† FDR's mother was so angered by the decision to recognize the Soviet Union that she wrote him that she would never come to the White House again. Two weeks later, however, she arrived on a visit.

British and the Americans sought limitations on offensive weapons. Worried that a breakdown would increase international tension and make economic reform even more difficult, Roosevelt sought a five- or six-week recess in which Norman Davis, the newly appointed chairman of the American delegation, could confer informally with other delegates outside the framework of the conference. As evidence of American sincerity about disarmament, he proposed reductions in the 140,000-man Regular Army—a move that would also be an economy measure. Like most Americans, the President regarded the Navy, not the Army, as the nation's first line of defense, and he earmarked $238 million of the emergency relief funds provided by the NIRA for warship construction. Naval and private shipyards that had been all but abandoned again resounded to the chatter of riveting hammers as work began on thirty-two new ships, including the aircraft carriers *Yorktown* and *Enterprise*.

Unhappy with the prospects of further cuts in their service, General Douglas MacArthur, the Chief of Staff, and Secretary of War George Dern went to the White House to protest. "Paralyzing nausea began to creep over me," recalled MacArthur. "I spoke recklessly . . . to the general effect that when we lost the next war, and an American boy, lying in the mud with an enemy bayonet through his belly and an enemy foot on his dying throat, spat out his last curse, I wanted the name not to be MacArthur, but Roosevelt. The President grew livid. 'You must not talk that way to the President!' he roared. He was of course right. . . . I said that I was sorry and apologized." MacArthur offered his resignation as Chief of Staff, but Roosevelt refused it. " 'Don't be foolish, Douglas,' he said. 'You and the budget [bureau] must get together on this.' "

While domestic affairs occupied the center ring in Washington, a stream of foreign visitors trooped into the capital, among them Ramsay MacDonald, the British Prime Minister, and ex-Premier Édouard Herriot of France. Alarmed that Roosevelt's decision to abandon the gold standard would give the United States a trade advantage, they tried to persuade the President to support currency stabilization. Roosevelt left them with the impression that he was in accord with their views, and it was agreed that the World Economic Conference would convene in London on June 12, to deal with an assortment of economic ills that included war debts and trade barriers. "We have in these talks found a reassurance of unity of purpose and method," Roosevelt and MacDonald said in a joint statement, and similar sentiments were voiced by Herriot. Overcome with the optimism of the moment, even the nationalistic Moley thought there was "good hope" that an understanding would be reached at the conference.

The President's own natural optimism was buoyed by positive developments in the disarmament negotiations. MacDonald had suggested a plan for international consultation in case of aggression and for a scaling down of weaponry and manpower that Roosevelt regarded as a major step toward world disarmament. Before MacDonald and Herriot left Washington, he assured them that if agreement were reached on arms reduction and inspection, the United States would give up its rights as a neutral and refuse to furnish supplies to any nation designated an aggressor. France was reassured by this offer, which left Germany's insistence on rearming the only stumbling block to a settlement.

Fearing that Hitler might upset the delicate balance for which he had been working, Roosevelt addressed an appeal to fifty-four heads of state on May 16 supporting "peace by disarmament" and "the end of economic chaos." "Put the old organ roll into it," the President told Moley, who was preparing the final text. Hitler replied the next day in a speech to the Reichstag. Listening in on the radio, Roosevelt remembered enough of his schoolboy German to recognize that Hitler was being conciliatory. Unwilling to accept the blame for the breakup of the Geneva conference, he declared that Germany was not only willing to sign a nonaggression pact but would dissolve its entire military establishment if other nations would also do so.

"I think I have averted a war," he told Morgenthau. But the triumph was illusory. Senate isolationists immediately objected to any proposal that would impinge on America's neutral rights, and the French, doubting Hitler's sincerity, were unwilling to trade their army for what they regarded as a paper promise of collective security. The conference bogged down and recessed again—a recess that was an adjournment in everything but name. By the end of the year, Hitler had denounced the restrictions imposed upon German rearmament by the Versailles Treaty and had walked out of the League of Nations.‡ For Roosevelt, there was a lesson in this unsuccessful adventure in international diplomacy: Never get out in front of public opinion until the ground has been well prepared.

By the time the World Economic Conference convened, in London, Roosevelt had lost much of his enthusiasm for it. The fall of the dollar was beginning to bring a faint blush of prosperity to the United States, and he now apparently wished the conference to pass a few innocuous resolutions and adjourn. Unfortunately, these views were not communicated

‡ The State Department remained officially silent regarding Nazi mistreatment of the Jews, taking the position that, as much as Americans might privately deplore such actions, the United States could not intervene in the internal affairs of another nation. When George H. Earle, the American minister to Austria, warned that Americans had little sympathy with the rising tide of anti-Semitism in that country, his remarks were regarded as a blunder in some diplomatic circles. FDR said nothing publicly, but he wrote Earle: "Strictly between ourselves, I am glad that you committed what some have suggested was a diplomatic blunder. I can assure you that it did not embarrass me at all!" FDR to Earle, Dec. 22, 1933.

to the American delegation. Headed by Secretary of State Hull, unhappy about being told by the President that the reciprocal tariff had been put on the back burner, they were an oddly assorted, somewhat zany lot. Senator Key Pittman of the silver-mining state of Nevada, was drunk much of the time, used London streetlights as targets for his six-shooter, and pursued an adviser suspected of inadequate enthusiasm for silver down a corridor in Claridge's with a bowie knife. Fearing for his life, the adviser obtained a pistol for self-protection. Warren Delano Robbins, a Roosevelt cousin and the delegation's protocol officer, lounged about wearing a monocle, and his wife, who had her hair dyed purple, described her husband to the press as "the mystery man of the conference."*

Believing that the President had committed himself to monetary stabilization in his talks with British and French leaders, the delegation supported a similar agreement, which caused prices to unexpectedly tumble on Wall Street. Quickly disowning the move, Roosevelt ordered Moley to go to London to put the delegation back on course, thus aggravating the tension. Hull was already suspicious of his assistant Secretary, who had a direct line to the President, and was angered by interference from Washington. The other delegations, believing Moley was bringing some vital message to relieve an anxious world, all but went into recess awaiting his arrival. "Moley, Moley, Moley, Lord God Almighty!" sang the reporters covering the conference.

Working with the French and British delegations, Moley eventually effected a compromise that called for acceptance of the principle of stabilization without committing the United States to anything, and opening the possibility of future agreement on other issues. Roosevelt's answer was not long in coming. From the captain's cabin of the cruiser *Indianapolis*, he fired off, on July 2, 1933, a message to London, that exploded with an impact that gave it the name of the "bombshell" message. Roosevelt not only repudiated the Moley compromise but soundly rebuked the delegates for concentrating on currency stability to the exclusion of other economic problems. "The Conference was called to better and perhaps to cure fundamental economic ills," he declared. "It must not be diverted from that effort."

Roosevelt had effectively "torpedoed" the conference, and it sank beneath the waves a few days later. The ultimatum was published on the Fourth of July, and some newspapers hailed it as "a new Declaration of Independence" from European entanglements. In London, the delegates were angered by the harshness of the President's words and his unwillingness to support stabilization after having apparently agreed to it during the preliminary talks in Washington. This seemingly impulsive

* FDR later appointed Robbins as minister to Canada, where he died in 1935.

reversal was probably prompted by Roosevelt's expectations that recovery would be further along than it actually was when the conference met, and concerned about the quickening tempo of western inflationary demands, decided to have nothing at all to do with monetary stabilization. He was already looking toward his next experiment: the creation of prosperity by manipulating the currency. Moley's increasing prominence may also have begun to irritate him. One joke had it that you had to call the President to make an appointment to see Moley. Both Howe and Eleanor, suspicious of anyone with so much influence with the President, may have helped grease the skids under the professor. In fact, before Moley went to London, Joe Kennedy warned him to "watch out" for the swish of Howe's hatchet.

Hull vehemently complained to the President about Moley's interference in London and charged that he had undercut him in the negotiations. With his white hair and ascetic face, Hull projected a saintly image, but he had the temper and vocabulary of a feuding Tennessee mountaineer. "That piss-ant Moley," he declared, "here he curled up at mah feet and let me stroke his head like a huntin' dog and then he goes and bites me in the ass!" The Secretary was far too skilled a politician to present the President with an ultimatum, but his intent was clear: Either he or Moley must go. Faced with a choice between Hull, who had considerable influence with his former colleagues in Congress, and Moley, who had no independent political base, the President's choice was obvious. Characteristically, Roosevelt, who hated to be unpleasant to anyone, said nothing to Moley, but the old camaraderie was gone. A few weeks later, the first of the brain trusters resigned.†

Some critics, gifted with 20/20 hindsight, have faulted Roosevelt's handling of the Economic Conference. Because of his infatuation with the prospects of raising domestic prices through inflation, they suggest, he helped accelerate the drift toward economic nationalism that brought about World War II. Perhaps. Yet there is considerable doubt as to whether anything substantial would have been achieved at London even if Roosevelt had not dropped his "bombshell" for the conflicts among the participants precluded agreement. John Maynard Keynes, for one, thought the President "magnificently right" in refusing to stabilize prices at an artificially low level. Roosevelt himself had no doubts about his role. "I'm prouder of that than anything else I ever did," he proclaimed.

---

† Moley became editor of *Today*, a weekly newsmagazine bankrolled by Vincent Astor, W. Averell Harriman, and Harriman's sister, Mary Harriman Rumsey, that later became *Newsweek*. For a while, he continued to serve FDR as a speech writer and adviser, but becoming increasingly disenchanted with what he perceived as the leftward drift of the New Deal, he became one of its bitterest critics.

Debate might rage over the correctness of Roosevelt's actions, but his decisiveness had captured the imagination and the loyalty of the American people. Opponents soon complained that he didn't know where he was going, but most Americans found the ride with this Roosevelt as exhilarating as the charge up San Juan Hill. Bonds had been formed between them and the President that were to endure throughout the remainder of his life.

XVIII

ON OUR WAY

WITH THE END of the first, explosive months of the New Deal, Franklin Roosevelt turned to the task of constructing an administration from the ground up. Like the leader of a freshly independent colonial nation, the President had to create a whole new regime while actually engaged in the process of governing. Only a scattering of key positions had been filled by Roosevelt appointees during that first spring, and the Administration was at the mercy of a Republican-dominated bureaucracy that looked upon the New Deal with suspicion and dismay. "We stood in the city of Washington . . . like a handful of marauders in hostile territory," Ray Moley later recalled.

The President showed remarkable skill in bringing together men and women of diverse outlook—many of whom had seen little difference between Hoover and himself in 1932—winning their loyalty and shaping often conflicting ideas into a national program. "He is the best picker of brains I ever saw," said one aide. After the demise of the Brain Trust, the bulk of the work of putting the New Deal into effect was performed by bright young lawyers and academics, who swarmed into Washington when the depression cut them off from the normal outlets for their talents, such as the prominent law firms and topflight universities. Ranging in outlook from Adam Smith conservatives to advocates of proletarian revolution, they drafted most of the New Deal legislation and manned the alphabet soup of governmental agencies spawned to administer it. Few of them had any personal contact with the President, but "he was there, a massive figure in back of his desk, his cigarette and cigarette holder rising at a jaunty angle, telling you how important was the work you were doing and how much he approved of the results," recalls John

Kenneth Galbraith, then a young economist with the Agricultural Adjustment Administration.

The cream of these new arrivals owed their positions to Felix Frankfurter, the Administration's chief talent scout. "A plague of young lawyers settled upon Washington," declared George N. Peek, administrator of the AAA. "They all claimed to be friends of somebody or other and mostly of Felix Frankfurter. . . . They floated airily into offices, took desks, asked for papers and found no end of things to be busy about. . . ." The most prominent of Frankfurter's "Happy Hot Dogs," as they were called —not always with admiration—were Benjamin V. Cohen, a thirty-eight-year-old specialist in corporate reorganization; Thomas G. Corcoran, at thirty-two already charming his way through the Washington bureaucratic and political labyrinth; and James M. Landis, a thirty-three-year-old Harvard law professor. They had no common ideology and were linked only by their relationship to Frankfurter and through him to Justice Brandeis and his longtime crusade against bigness and the money power.

Contemptuous of the bankers and big businessmen, who had been discredited by their inability to deal with the depression the New Dealers reversed the usual relationship between business and government. Power passed from the paneled boardrooms of Wall Street to the offices outfitted with battered furniture that abruptly blossomed all over Washington. These lawyers, economists, and social workers marched to a different drummer from the progressives of the previous generation. Hard-boiled, arrogant, and cynical, they made a great show of avoiding the gushy sentimentality they attributed to earlier reformers. To them, reform meant sweeping social economic change—nothing less than a redistribution of the national wealth. They adopted the easy amorality of the end justifying the means, which they identified with the President. Harry Hopkins summed it up best in a talk with a group of aides: "I want to assure you that we are not afraid of exploring anything within the law, and we have a lawyer who will declare anything you want to do legal."

If, as was often said, the New Deal had some of the overtones of a three-ring circus, Roosevelt was the undisputed ringmaster. But in those early days he had to share the spotlight with Hugh Johnson, administrator of the National Recovery Administration. Bounding onto the scene like a star-spangled acrobat, he captured the public imagination with a volcanic outburst of energy. Bulbous-nosed, raucous, and using language that was hardly housebroken, Johnson was known as Ironpants from his days as a hell-for-leather cavalryman. He had a fondness for good bourbon and would often disappear on benders for days at a time. He was under no illusions, however, about the difficulty of his task. "It will be red fire at first and dead cats afterward," he declared. "This is just like mounting the guillotine on the infinitesimal gamble that the ax won't work."

In fact, Johnson had almost turned down the job when Roosevelt, having qualms about giving him control of relief funds, had placed the Public Works Administration under Harold Ickes, the Interior Secretary.* Frances Perkins recalled that he nearly blew up at the cabinet meeting at which the announcement was made. "The blood mounted to his face, he grew purpler and purpler as the President talked. When the President had finished, Johnson spoke in a strange, low voice that came from deep within him. 'I don't see why. I don't see why,' he said." When the meeting broke up, Roosevelt beckoned Miss Perkins to his side. "'Stick with Hugh,' he said. 'Keep him sweet. Don't let him explode.'" Convinced that the NRA would be ineffective unless complete authority was vested in a single administrator, Johnson kept muttering, "'He's ruined me. I've got to get out. I can't stay.'" To keep Johnson away from the press, Miss Perkins led him to her car and took him on a drive around Washington while trying to calm him down. "Don't blow up," she pleaded. "Don't pull out." "'It's terrible. It's terrible,'" the general replied over and over again. Finally, the Labor Secretary's persistence paid off, and he agreed to remain as NRA chief.

Johnson had already begun drafting codes regulating wages, hours, prices, and fair competition even before he had been appointed. Hoping to give the NRA a tremendous lift, he had concentrated on the large industrial groups: steel, automobiles, textiles, coal mining, and construction. But he had underestimated the popularity of the codes. Almost every industry was demanding its own, and during the first months of the NRA, Johnson received requests for more than two hundred sixty different codes. The first, for the cotton textile industry, was ready for the President's signature on June 27, when it was signed with much fanfare. Ending a long history of cutthroat competition and exploitation of labor, the code stabilized production, set prices, established uniform wages and hours, and ended child labor in the mills. "That makes me personally happier than any other thing which I have been connected with since I came to Washington," Roosevelt said of the curbs on child labor.

Negotiations over codes for the other major industrial groups bogged down, however. Henry Ford flatly refused to have anything to do with the NRA, and so did the southern coal operators. Some businessmen also schemed and connived to evade Section 7(a) of the NIRA, aimed at guaranteeing labor the right to collective bargaining. This was a time for

* Bernard Baruch, Johnson's erstwhile mentor, was surprised to hear that FDR planned to make him head of the NRA. "I think he's a good number-three man, maybe a good number-two man, but he's not a number-one man," Baruch told Frances Perkins. ". . . I'm fond of him, but do tell the President to be careful. Hugh needs a firm hand." Frances Perkins, The Roosevelt I Knew (New York: The Viking Press, 1946), p. 200.

knocking heads together, but Johnson, for all his bluster, declined to do so, for he doubted the constitutionality of the NRA. The problem was compounded by the failure of Ickes to quickly approve expenditures for bridges, highways, and new public buildings, which would have pumped vast sums of money into the economy. Wishing to make certain that PWA funds were fully accounted for and honestly spent, he insisted on a lengthy planning process for each project. At the same time, congressional delays and other obstacles prevented the Agricultural Adjustment Administration from becoming effective before the spring planting season.

Conditions were particularly bad in the Farm Belt, where farmers renewed their demands for higher prices for their crops. Radicals threatened a march on Washington unless Roosevelt made immediate use of the authority granted him by Congress to inflate the economy. Before the summer of 1933 was over, the wind had been taken out of the sails of the recovery generated by the Hundred Days. Farm prices collapsed, the stock market faltered, and by October, the New York *Times* Weekly Business Index had sunk to 72. With unemployment hardly dented, another long, hard winter was in the making. Roosevelt found a scapegoat for the slowdown in the speculators who had rushed to tie up great quantities of raw materials and commodities before the codes created higher prices. If "Honest Harold" Ickes had pumped money into the economy, raising consumer purchasing power, the recovery might have been sustained until the NRA and the AAA took hold. But he doled out PWA funds with an eyedropper.

The New Dealers had scoffed at Herbert Hoover's reliance on exhortation, but Johnson now launched a public-relations crusade to enlist support for the NRA that dwarfed anything that had gone before. Motorcades, mass meetings, and parades were held in almost every community. The largest was in New York City, where more than a quarter million people marched down Fifth Avenue beneath the banner of the Blue Eagle, the symbol of the NRA, and another million and a half watched and cheered. The Blue Eagle appeared everywhere: on newspaper mastheads, in placards in shop windows, and stenciled on the backs of film starlets. Even Hoover subscribed to its principles, having not yet determined that it smacked of Fascism. Influenced by public opinion, major industries that had been resisting the NRA codes, particularly Section 7(a), joined in.†

---

† Visiting FDR in the White House to complain about the code for the steel industry, Charles M. Schwab, chairman of the board of Bethlehem Steel, explained that it was his duty to look after the interests of the stockholders. The President smiled and asked if he had been looking after the Bethlehem stockholders when he paid million-dollar-a-year bonuses to Eugene Grace, the operating head of the company. FDR's parting word to Schwab was to remind him to give his "warm regards" to his good friend "Gene," and to tell him that never again would he make a million dollars a year. Ernest K. Lindley, *The Roosevelt Revolution* (New York: The Viking Press, 1933), p. 239.

Johnson dashed into the White House one day, handed the President three codes to sign, and then raced off to catch a plane. "He hasn't been seen since," Roosevelt dryly remarked. By September, Johnson proclaimed that nearly three million workers had been put back on payrolls and that the average wage rate had been raised from forty-two cents an hour to fifty-two cents. In all, some five hundred fifty codes were approved, including those for the bottlecap manufacturers, brassiere makers, and dogfood processors. And the Burlesque Theatre Code limited each show to four striptease acts.

Nevertheless, the Blue Eagle's high-flying days were numbered. As Ellis W. Hawley points out in *The New Deal and the Problem of Monopoly*, the NRA reflected the dilemma that confronted twentieth-century America: the need to find some mechanism that would reconcile demands for industrial order while preserving the nation's democratic heritage. Offering something for everyone, the NRA tried to yoke business, industry, labor, and consumers into an uneasy alliance. Johnson's massive propaganda campaign glossed over the bitter differences that divided them, and when the euphoria faded, they began fighting among themselves.

Organized labor charged that it had received little protection from Section 7(a) and claimed that the NRA was biased in favor of management. Nevertheless, some labor leaders immediately grasped its inherent possibilities. Led by John L. Lewis, head of the militant United Mine Workers of America, they launched the Committee for Industrial Organization and, proclaiming "President Roosevelt wants you to join a union!" began organizing the unskilled workers in the mass-production industries who had been ignored by the old-line craft unions of the A.F. of L. Business fought back, using strong-arm tactics against organizers, intimidating workers, and starting company unions. The battle lines for labor conflict were drawn, and the industrial centers of the United States erupted into spasmodic violence.

Meanwhile, businessmen claimed they were being squeezed between higher costs and the freeze on prices. Consumers complained prices were going up while wages remained stationary. Small businessmen charged that the NRA codes favored the large corporations and fostered monopoly. Even Harry Harriman, the Chamber of Commerce official who had helped plan the NRA, joined the attack. Liberals charged that the NRA smacked of the Fascism of Benito Mussolini's corporate state and was retarding recovery by limiting production and raising prices. Increasingly dependent upon large doses of bourbon to keep himself going, Johnson began to falter in strength and judgment. He raged at those who refused to comply with the codes as "chiselers," and disappeared from his office for days on end.

Persistent reports reached Roosevelt that the NRA was in danger of falling apart under Johnson's erratic leadership, and aides advised him to drop the General. "But he is so tender-hearted that he has not been able to say the final words," said Ickes, a less-than-sympathetic witness. "Johnson persists in staying . . . and goes through all sorts of theatricals with the President in order to hold on." At last, however, Johnson handed in his resignation, in September 1934, and shot out of the Administration like an angry pinwheel to excoriate his former colleagues in a syndicated newspaper column. The NRA lingered in limbo for another nine months, until the Supreme Court unanimously held it unconstitutional.

By most standards of measurement, the NRA was a failure and vanished without an institutional trace. Marked by inconsistency, it gave government sanction to a host of disjointed and uncoordinated monopolistic agreements while retaining a rhetorical commitment to the competitive ethic. Johnson had neither the time nor the expertise to even attempt to control over five hundred industries, and without Ickes' vigorous cooperation, there was no strong machinery for economic expansion. Perhaps a reversal of roles would have produced a successful NRA. Ickes' caution in the making of codes, combined with freehanded spending by Johnson on public works, might well have stimulated an economic revival.

As it was, the best that is usually said of the NRA is that it did not impede recovery and may have prevented a renewal of the crisis. It may even have made some slight contribution to turning the economic corner. Between 1933 and 1935, the gross national product rose from $39.6 billion to $56.8 billion, and the national income rose apace. The NRA's most significant contribution was in the field of social innovation, where it brought about the abolition of child labor, the acceptance of federal regulation of wages and hours, and recognition of labor's right to organize and bargain collectively. But the most formidable index of misery in the United States had budged only slightly; more than 10 million Americans were still without work.

One day toward the end of July 1933, a cotton farmer from Texas named William E. Morris was invited, along with his congressman, Richard Kleberg, to the White House to meet President Roosevelt. Through some means undoubtedly divined by Kleberg's aggressive young administrative assistant, Lyndon B. Johnson, it had been determined that Morris was the first farmer to plow under part of his cotton crop in accordance with the Administration's program for reducing agricultural surpluses. Photographers crowded around as the President presented Morris with a

$517 check as his "adjustment payment" for the forty-seven acres he had taken out of production.

This ceremony marked the beginning of a radical strategy aimed at rescuing American agriculture. Under the terms of the Agricultural Adjustment Act, farmers were to be paid to reduce their acreage in crops. If there was a surplus, the government would provide a subsidy to ensure the farmer a minimum price that would be financed by a tax on processors such as millers and packers. Unfortunately, Congress had delayed the establishment of the Agricultural Adjustment Administration until cotton farmers, assured of government-supported prices, had planted record crops and hog producers vastly increased production. Having lost their race with the sun, Henry Wallace, the Secretary of Agriculture, and George Peek, the Triple A administrator, sent agents to persuade cotton farmers to plow under one quarter of their crop, about 10 million acres in all, and to buy up some 6 million breeding sows and piglets to forestall a glut in the market. Bad weather was expected to take care of the surplus wheat crop.

The slaughter of little pigs and plowing under crops at a time when people were hungry created a tremendous public outcry. Some of the pork was offered to families on relief, but most of it was inedible. Newspaper pictures of squealing piglets crowding the middle-western stockyards resulted in Wallace and Peek's being subjected to a flood of abuse, and the AAA received a black eye from which it never recovered. New Deal farm policy was denounced for trying to end want in the midst of plenty by doing away with plenty. "You'd think no one ever raised a pig except as a personal pet!" exclaimed an exasperated Wallace, who justified the willful destruction of food only as a last resort. "These were not acts of idealism in any sane society," he said later. "They were emergency acts made necessary by the almost insane lack of world statesmanship during the period 1920 to 1932."

Forelock dangling over his forehead, shy and hesitant, Wallace looked like an Iowa dirt farmer. "No swank," said Sherwood Anderson, sizing him up. In the highly politicized atmosphere of New Deal Washington, he was a puzzling phenomenon: part farmer, part scientist, part businessman, part social philosopher—all overlaid by a vague and dreamy mysticism. Wallace's practical side was underscored by his experiments that led to the development of a hybrid seed corn that produced enormous yields per acre. Through government planning and crop control, he believed, an "ever-normal granary" could be created that would break the cycle of boom and bust that afflicted American agriculture. Wallace was also given to mystical flights of ecstasy, and he once addressed the President as "the flaming one, the one with an ever upward-surging spirit." Puzzled by such rapture, Roosevelt was more comfortable discussing farm problems than mysticism with Wallace.

The Triple A became the center of social ferment within the New Deal. Rumpled old-time farm specialists who had previously dominated the Department of Agriculture found themselves shunted aside by eager young theorists and reformers who declared war on rural poverty. Today, it is difficult to recall the hope and incandescent passion of the New Dealers. With an evangelical fervor worthy of medieval crusaders, young men and women saw an opportunity to remake American society—and nowhere was this spirit greater than in such experimental organizations as the Triple A.

Such spirits were concentrated in the legal staff, headed by Jerome N. Frank, a Chicago corporation lawyer and legal scholar who had been recommended by Frankfurter and Rex Tugwell, the assistant Secretary of Agriculture. Frank recruited a staff of dedicated young lawyers and, unconcerned about their lack of practical knowledge of agrarian problems, believed they could quickly learn on the job. One of them once demanded to know what the macaroni code was going to do for the macaroni growers. Yet as a journalist wrote, "There are more brains and more real ability per pound of human flesh in the agriculture wing of the New Deal than anywhere else." No steps were taken to screen those with Communist affiliations and sympathies, and the legal staff included Lee Pressman, Nathan Witt, John Abt, and Alger Hiss, all later accused of being underground Communists. Adlai Stevenson, George W. Ball, Thurman Arnold, Abe Fortas, and Telford Taylor also served as lawyers with the Triple A.

Roosevelt had in the meantime resorted to manipulation of the price of gold to inflate agricultural prices—a proposal that had long been urged upon him by a Cornell professor named George Warren. If the government made large purchases of newly mined gold and raised the price by small amounts at frequent intervals, Warren claimed, this would lower the value of the dollar and raise the price of wheat, cotton, and other commodities. Orthodox economists discounted Warren's theory, but it offered Roosevelt an opportunity for action. Writing to Will Woodin, he said: "You and I understand this national situation and I wish our banking and economist friends would realize the seriousness of the situation from the point of view of the debtor class—i.e., 90 per cent of the human beings in the country—and think less from the point of view of the 10 per cent who constitute the creditor classes."

Beginning on October 25, 1933, Henry Morgenthau, now acting Secretary of the Treasury in the absence of the ailing Woodin, and Jesse Jones, head of the Reconstruction Finance Corporation, which did the actual gold buying, met in the President's bedroom every morning to set the price of gold. One day, Morgenthau suggested a price increase of nineteen to twenty-two cents an ounce. Roosevelt, who called Morgenthau "Henny Penny" and enjoyed pulling his friend's leg, proposed twenty-one cents. "It's a lucky number because it's three times seven," he declared with a laugh. Not long afterward, the lugubrious Morgenthau noted in his diary: "If anybody ever knew how we really set the gold price through a combination of lucky numbers, etc., I think they would really be frightened." In point of fact, Roosevelt's happy-go-lucky method was as good a way as any, for the main thing was to set a rate of increase that the speculators could not predict.

The gold-buying scheme sent shock waves through the financial community. The Chamber of Commerce denounced "monetary experimentation," and Al Smith joined in. "I am for experience against experiment," he said and attacked the "baloney dollar." The honeymoon between Wall Street and Washington was over, and Roosevelt summed up his complaints about the bankers in a letter to Colonel House: "The real truth of the matter is, as you and I know, that a financial element in the larger centers has owned the Government ever since the days of Andrew Jackson—and I am not wholly excepting the Administration of W.W. [Woodrow Wilson] The country is going through a repetition of Jackson's fight with the Bank of the United States—only on a far bigger and broader basis." Dean G. Acheson, the dapper under Secretary of the Treasury, told the President he was opposed to the plan on both legal and philosophical grounds, and his resignation was demanded. Woodin also resigned, primarily for reasons of health, although he, too, disagreed with the gold-purchase scheme.

In the end, the Warren plan failed and was abandoned. Other experiments were tried, including devaluation of the dollar and propping up the price of silver. When the pace of recovery began to quicken again, it was due to the money pumped into the economy by the various New Deal programs and a natural cyclical revival, rather than manipulation of gold prices. Roosevelt was elated, no matter what the cause. "Our troubles will not be over tomorrow," he declared, "but we are on our way."

The benefits of the Triple A were unevenly spread. Small farmers and poultry raisers complained that they were the forgotten men of American agriculture. In the South, most of the money went to large landholders and commercial farmers, while sharecroppers and tenants suffered because of the curtailment in production. With more money to be made by leaving the land fallow than growing crops, landlords got rid of their croppers and tenants, white and black alike. "I had I reckon four renters and I didn't make anything," related an Oklahoma farmer. "I bought tractors on the money the government give me and got shet o' my renters." Families tractored off the land joined the refugees, uprooted by the drought and savage dust storms that lashed the Great Plains, in a desperate migration to the already overburdened cities or to the new promised land of California.

The first of the great dust storms, blowing black and cold, swept across the plains on Armistice Day 1933. Writing from Huron, South Dakota, Lorena Hickok, a former Associated Press reporter who had been hired by Harry Hopkins as a confidential investigator, described what it was like to her friend Eleanor Roosevelt:

It started to blow last night. All night the wind howled and screamed and sobbed around the windows. When I got up at 7:30 this morning, the sky seemed to be clear, but you couldn't see the sun! There was a queer brown haze—only right above was the sky clear. And the wind was blowing a gale. It kept on blowing harder and harder. And the haze kept mounting in the sky. By the time we had finished breakfast and were ready to start out, about 9, the sun was only a lighter spot in the dust that filled the sky like a brown fog.

We drove only a few miles and had to turn back. It got worse and worse —rapidly. You couldn't see a foot ahead of the car by the time we got back, and we had a time getting back! It was like driving through a fog, only worse, for there was that damnable wind. It seemed as though the car would be blown right off the road any minute. When we stopped, we had to put on the emergency brake. The wind behind us actually moved the car. It was a truly terrifying experience. It was as though we had left the earth. We were being whirled off into space in a vast, impenetrable cloud of brown dust.

They had the street lights on when we finally groped our way back into town. They stayed on the rest of the day. By noon, the sun wasn't even a light spot in the sky anymore. You couldn't see it at all. It was so dark, and the dust was so thick that you couldn't see across the street. I was lying on the bed reading the paper and glanced up—the window looked black, just as it does at night. I was terrified for a moment. It looked like the end of the world.

The "black blizzards" grew worse over the next two years. Poor farming methods had ripped away the protective sod that had covered the great belt of grassland that pointed like a finger from the Canadian border to the Texas panhandle. Out on the high wheat lands of Kansas and the Dakotas, no rain fell and the sun baked the topsoil to a tawny grit that was whirled awry by the hot, dry winds. And as the soil blew away, the people followed. The Okies and Arkies of John Steinbeck's *The Grapes of Wrath* headed West to make a new beginning. Piling their families and household goods on old jalopies, they rattled along Highway 66 to California. Those lucky enough to find work were ensnared into a new bondage as migratory workers on the fruit ranches and lettuce farms.

The rest were kept moving like human tumbleweeds by local authorities who feared they might become the dupes of "red agitators."

Desperate appeals for help poured into Washington from farmers, ranchers, businessmen, and politicians. "You gave us beer," they told the President, "now give us water." Governor Alfred M. Landon of Kansas joined other governors in seeking federal relief funds. In May 1934, as dust sifted down on the White House, Roosevelt announced a drought-relief program. Seed and feed were rushed to the distressed area, and the government bought the remaining livestock. Until nature and conservation plans could revive the land, the farmers of the dust bowl received direct relief from the Federal Emergency Relief Administration. Subsistence homestead projects that attempted to combine small-scale farming with handicrafts were also tried, becoming almost the private preserve of Mrs. Roosevelt.‡ In April 1935, a new agency, called the Resettlement Administration, was created by Roosevelt to combine the various agricultural relief programs under one roof. Headed by Rex Tugwell, the agency provided a foretaste of the welfare state in action.

With his stubborn bias in favor of an agrarian society, Roosevelt saw the Resettlement Administration as an opportunity to reverse the flow of population to the cities and to restore the Jeffersonian ideal of the self-sufficient family farm. Promising farm families were given loans to buy and equip small farms or to pay off existing debts and upgrade their places. Experts showed them how to get the best results from their acreage, to use their new equipment, and to stretch their dollars. Many impoverished farmers were simply uprooted from submarginal lands and relocated to where the soil was better, and about 10 million exhausted acres were returned to the public domain to be converted into forests or grazing land.

Tugwell, however, saw the problem in more complex terms. In his view, commercial, rather than subsistence, farming was the key to reversing the human and physical erosion that afflicted American agriculture. If farmers were to become prosperous, they had to apply to the land the technological innovations that had revolutionized industry. This required sizable acreage, machinery, and centralized management—all the direct antithesis of the small-scale farming envisioned by the President. Tugwell experimented with rural cooperative communities where farmers banded

‡ Before coming to Washington, Eleanor had, with Nancy Cook and Marion Dickerman, established a similar project at Val-Kill to provide winter employment for Dutchess County farmers through the manufacture of reproductions of Early American furniture. Although the project ultimately failed because few of the local people had the required skills or were willing to learn them, Val-Kill furniture was well designed and finished. In recent years, it has enjoyed a vogue among collectors.

together to buy equipment for common use, organized commissaries, and marketed their crops under the guidance of experts. Startled conservatives charged that under the domination of "Rex the Red," American farmers were being "collectivized" like Russian peasants. Perhaps Tugwell's most significant contribution was the three "greenbelt" towns he built near Washington, Cincinnati, and Milwaukee—garden suburbs that were near to jobs but protected from urban blight. "My idea is to go just outside centers of population, pick up cheap land, build a whole community and entice people into it," he explained. "Then go back into the cities and tear down whole slums and make parks of them."

Substantial start-up and operating costs, a continuing shortage of money, and the perversity of American farmers who upset the best intentions of government planners by refusing to abandon their old homesteads hindered the cooperative settlements. The RA had planned to resettle five hundred thousand families; only about four thousand were actually moved. Tugwell's personality also contributed to the failure. Brusque and impatient with those he did not regard as intellectual equals —and that included leading lawmakers and businessmen—he symbolized the wild-eyed professorial Bolshevik said to be running amok in Franklin Roosevelt's Washington. In 1937, Congress passed the Bankhead-Jones Farm Tenant Act, designed to assist tenants and farm laborers in becoming landowners—and got rid of Tugwell in the bargain. The Resettlement Administration was replaced by the Farm Security Administration, which made low-interest, long-term mortgages for the purchase of family farms, loaned small sums for rehabilitation projects, and established clean, well-run labor camps for migratory workers. Particularly noteworthy was the FSA's insistence on treating blacks the same as it did whites. But the agency was kept on a short financial leash by suspicious conservatives, and it made only minor inroads on the problems of rural poverty.

New Deal farm policy achieved some measure of success, however. The amount of land taken out of cultivation—assisted by the drought and dust storms—tripled from about 10 million acres in 1933 to 30.3 million in 1935. Farm income rose 50 percent. Cotton went from a ruinous five cents a pound to a respectable twelve cents, while corn was up from ten cents a bushel to seventy cents. Small-town businessmen and mail-order houses dependent on sales to farmers and their families noted an increase in trade as crop prices advanced. Farm credit and mortgage protection engineered by the New Deal also helped preserve farm ownership. Consumers complained, however, about higher food prices resulting from the taxes on processors, and farmers were unhappy about the rising cost of machinery and fertilizer. They also claimed government regulation abridged their individual freedoms. Yet when faced in referenda with the choice between rugged individualism and government checks, they voted overwhelmingly to continue the restrictions on production.

One day, an aide in the Federal Emergency Relief Administration came to Harry Hopkins with a plan for putting the unemployed to work that was certain to be successful "in the long run." "People don't eat in the long run," snapped an exasperated Hopkins. "They eat every day." This offhanded remark summed up Hopkins' basic philosophy: In an emergency, act, don't rationalize. With anywhere up to 15 million Americans without jobs, such decisiveness appealed to Roosevelt. Having been given $500 million for direct grants to the states and local public agencies to help the unemployed and the destitute, Hopkins did not even wait until he had an office. He set up a desk in a hallway of the RFC building, where, surrounded by packing cases and enveloped in a constant cloud of cigarette smoke, he handed out money with the abandon of a Medici prince.

Lean, loose-limbed, with the "sardonic manner of a bored police court judge who has heard it all before," Hopkins was not the typical social worker. He was a zealous reformer but wore no hair shirt. The son of a shiftless Iowa harness maker and his socially conscious wife, he envied the rich, liked women, and enjoyed playing the races. "He had the purity of St. Francis of Assisi combined with the sharp shrewdness of a race track tout," observed Joseph E. Davies. Hopkins had little patience with bureaucratic niceties and red tape. When the Bureau of the Budget asked for an organizational chart for FERA, he replied that he didn't have time to draft one; if they had to have a chart, they could prepare it themselves. Having taken a salary cut from fifteen thousand dollars a year to eight thousand dollars to become head of FERA, Hopkins was always teetering on the brink of personal financial disaster, but he was scrupulously honest with public money. He spent freely for relief but kept a tight hand on operational costs, and he would not permit his staff to use relief funds for office expenses. Reporters liked his frankness and flights of sarcasm.

Roosevelt, with his optimistic faith in an eventually balanced budget, regarded FERA as a temporary operation to tide the jobless over until the NRA, the AAA, and Harold Ickes' $3.3 billion PWA started up the engine of recovery. Hopkins, however, was less certain about the prospects for putting all the unemployed back to work. Modern technology had created a permanent underclass of about seven million people, whom he believed were likely to remain unemployed even after an economic revival, and government would have to provide relief for these rejects. But Hopkins detested the idea of the dole, as soul-destroying, and was convinced that it was infinitely better to create jobs and work relief. Recipients would be productive and retain their self-respect. Hopkins' demands for quick action brought him into almost immediate conflict with Harold Ickes. Ickes' slow and cautious doling out of PWA funds ensured honesty and careful planning but infuriated Hopkins. To him, Ickes' methods smacked of the old Republican "trickle-down" theory, while he favored a "trickle-up" theory: putting money immediately into the hands of the poor, who would spend it and thereby put people to work providing more goods and services.

As the first winter of the New Deal approached—and it turned out to be among the most bitter in memory—Hopkins urged the President to launch a vast emergency program of work relief to be paid for entirely out of the Treasury. He had little hope of success, however. Roosevelt was in one of his periodic budget-balancing moods and organized labor strongly opposed government-created jobs because they offered competition for union workers. Late in October 1933, while Hopkins was in Kansas City meeting with relief officials, he received a telephone call from an excited aide. Researchers had found a statement from Samuel Gompers, the patron saint of organized labor, calling for just such a program during an earlier economic crisis. Knowing of Roosevelt's love of historical precedent and now able to defuse labor objections to his plan, Hopkins eagerly sought an appointment with the President.

As they lunched together, Roosevelt asked Hopkins how many jobs would be needed.

"About four million," he replied.

"Let's see," said the President thinking aloud. "Four million people —that means roughly four hundred million dollars."

Realizing that Congress would not approve an appropriation, and that the money had to come from somewhere, Roosevelt decided to divert unexpended funds from the PWA to the Civilian Works Administration, as the new agency was to be called. On November 15, 1933, Hopkins promised to have four million people at work before Christmas—a target he failed to meet, but by January 18, 1934, some 4.3 million men and women were on the job, more than had served in the armed forces during World War I. By early 1934, as many as 20 million Americans were dependent on federal relief of some sort for the essentials of life. In drought-stricken South Dakota, one third of the entire population were on the dole.

Racing against the weather, Hopkins hastily threw projects together, most of them offering pick-and-shovel work or its equivalent. Some were makeshift, and there were boondoggles aplenty. A research team in New York City investigated the history of the safety pin. A hundred-man squad patrolled the streets of downtown Washington with toy balloons on long strings to frighten the starlings roosting untidily on the eaves of government buildings. There were, however, solid accomplishments.

CWA workers built or improved about five hundred thousand miles of roads. Forty thousand schools were built or improved, and about fifty thousand teachers were given jobs. Some five hundred new airports were laid out and an equal number upgraded. Streets were repaired, sewers unclogged, and parks cleared of underbrush. Even more important, millions of Americans who might otherwise have festered in despair and idleness were given work.

Roosevelt has often been charged with being "so intoxicated with the pomp and privilege of power" that he was unable to delegate authority. Perhaps so, but when he found a man who could handle authority without constantly seeking advice and assurance from the White House, he delegated authority with a lavish hand—and he found such a man in Harry Hopkins. Originally, Hopkins had been closer to Mrs. Roosevelt than to the President because of their common interest in social problems, but in time the relationship between the two men ripened into friendship. Hopkins became a frequent guest at the White House and on presidential yachting trips down the Potomac. A report by Frank Walker, Roosevelt's old friend from the political wars and currently president of the National Emergency Council, a watchdog organization that kept an eye on New Deal agencies, strengthened Hopkins' standing with the President.

Walker took a trip across the country to inspect various relief projects, met with local politicians and officials, and went out on the job sites to talk with CWA workers. In his native Montana, he reported that he found old friends with whom he had gone to school digging ditches and laying sewer pipe. Unable to afford overalls and rubber boots, they wore business suits. "If I ever thought, 'There but for the sake of the Grace of God—' it was then," he said. But when he talked to them he found they were happy to be working. One man pulled a few silver coins from his pocket and showed them to Walker. "Do you know, Frank, this is the first money I've had in my pockets in a year and a half?" he said. "Up to now, I've had nothing but tickets that you exchange for groceries." Another man said: "I hate to think what would have happened if this work hadn't come along. . . ." Upon his return to Washington, Walker suggested that the President "pay little attention to those who criticize the creation of CWA or its administration. Hopkins and his associates are doing their work well. They've done a magnificent job."

With this ringing endorsement, Hopkins hoped that the life of the CWA and its work relief programs would be extended, but Roosevelt, worried about the effect on the budget and the charges of reckless profligacy leveled by conservatives, ordered it wound down as the weather improved. Such assistance was intended as an emergency measure, and he feared the creation of a permanent class dependent upon relief for a livelihood. "We cannot carry CWA through the summer," Roosevelt declared.

"We all agree that there has got to be a limit on CWA and the people must assume more or less that things are going to straighten themselves out."

Swallowing his disappointment, Hopkins loyally went back to dispensing direct relief through FERA. Monthly family allowances were increased from fifteen dollars to thirty-five dollars—still inadequate, yet a boost to national morale and purchasing power. But all during 1934, he worked on plans to replace it with a comprehensive program of federal work projects based on his experience with the CWA. The prospects for such a proposal depended upon whether the voters approved or repudiated the New Deal in the off-year congressional elections.

Roosevelt set the keynote for the coming campaign in a Fireside Chat on June 28, 1934. Reviewing the achievements of the Seventy-third Congress—and those of the New Deal itself—he made the election a referendum on his administration. "Are you better off than you were last year?" he asked. "Are your debts less burdensome? Is your bank account more secure? Are your working conditions better? Is your faith in your own individual future more firmly grounded?"

For the most part, Roosevelt's second year in the White House had been a time of national stocktaking. Having laid the foundation for sweeping changes in the relation between Americans and their government, the President, heeding the advice of Jim Farley and Vice-President Garner, decided to give the country time to catch its breath. While there was some tinkering with earlier programs, there were few major initiatives except for the establishment of the Securities and Exchange Commission and approval of Cordell Hull's long-sought Reciprocal Trade Agreements Act. But the New Deal went before the voters with a tremendous record of accomplishment. Unemployment had been reduced, farm prices were up, industrial production was increasing, homes and farms that had been threatened by foreclosure had been saved, and bank depositors no longer feared for the safety of their savings. Much remained to be done, however. Relief measures were inadequate to meet the needs of those in distress, some 10 million Americans were still jobless, and with the exception of the TVA, reform had been limited almost entirely to banking and finance. And although the New Deal was humanitarian in tone, big business and agriculture had reaped most of its benefits.

The sense of national emergency had passed, and the bankers and industrialists, having picked themselves up off the floor with the assistance of the New Deal, charged that Roosevelt and the radicals around him were wrecking the country. Expenditures for emergency relief had vastly increased the public debt, and they worried about the country's solvency. Alarmed at a perceived drift toward socialism and regimentation, they denounced the President for leading an unsuspecting nation to Communism or Fascism. Ogden Mills accused the New Dealers of "fostering revolution under the guise of recovery and reform," and the Administration was described as "the Kerensky phase of a Communist upheaval." That summer, a number of conservative Democrats, including Al Smith, John Raskob, Jouett Shouse, and a clutch of Du Ponts, helped organize the Liberty League, dedicated to the defeat of the New Deal.

Traditionally, the political party that controls the presidency loses seats in Congress in nonpresidential elections, and Farley and Howe were jittery about the outcome. Realizing that the election would be regarded as a barometer of the President's success, they urged him to take an active part in the campaign. Roosevelt, however, had decided to remain above the battle in order to cultivate a nonpartisan image. Roosevelt always believed that a sea voyage was the tonic for anything, and he spent part of the summer on a fourteen-thousand-mile cruise, on the U.S.S. *Houston*, that took him from the Caribbean through the Panama Canal to Hawaii and then to Portland, Oregon. The transcontinental train trip to Washington was a triumph. "Coming across the continent the reception was grand," the President told Garner, "and I am more than ever convinced that, so far as having the people with us goes, we are just as strong—perhaps stronger—than ever before."

The length of Roosevelt's coattails was still to be measured, however. Could he transfer his own personal popularity to Democratic candidates? Farley, who had been worried about the attacks on the New Deal from business, was buoyed by the confidential reports reaching national headquarters from all over the country. Shortly before the election, he made what Roosevelt considered a wildly optimistic prediction. Not only would the Democrats hold their own in the House of Representatives, Farley said, but they would win no less than twenty-six of the thirty-five senate seats being contested, including that of the Republican stronghold of Pennsylvania.

As it turned out, he was overcautious. Farley's prediction of a senate sweep was on the mark—including victory in Pennsylvania and the election of Harry Truman in Missouri—but in the House the Democrats added nine seats. The new Senate would have 69 Democrats to 25 Republicans; in the House, the margin was even greater: 322 to 103. The Democrats also swept the contests for local and state offices, leaving the Republicans with only seven governorships.*

This landslide was universally interpreted as a ringing endorsement of the New Deal and the policies of Franklin Roosevelt. "He has been all but crowned by the people," declared William Allen White.

---

* The Progressives won seven seats in the House, and the Farmer-Labor party had three. Each held a single senate seat.

XIX

PROFILE OF A PRESIDENT

Mr. PRESIDENT," a young reporter once asked Franklin Roosevelt, "are you a Communist?"

"No."

"Are you a capitalist?"

"No."

"Are you a socialist?"

"No."

Baffled by Roosevelt's refusal to be fitted into any of the conventional ideological pigeonholes, the reporter finally asked: "Well, what is your philosophy, then?"

"Philosophy?" replied the somewhat puzzled President. "Philosophy? I am a Christian and a Democrat—that's all."

The New Deal reflected Roosevelt's own impatience with theoretical speculation. Although it marked the zenith of reform in the United States and produced profound changes in American institutions, with a continuing impact, debate still rages over its place in the American political tradition. It altered for all time the relationship between Americans and their government. One of the few successful gradualist revolutions in history, the New Deal centralized power in the national government, and in the hands of the President in particular. The United States was transformed from a nation of individualists into a social-minded community that accepted the principle of the welfare state and the planned society. For the first time, the goal of government became a better way of life for all Americans—and nothing was out of bounds.

Like Roosevelt's own mercurial and contradictory personality, the

New Deal was compounded of naïveté, humanitarianism, practical politics, and a willingness to gamble with social and economic experimentation. Never a theorist, Roosevelt could hold two contradictory ideas in mind at the same time. He was called everything from a Fascist to a Communist, with conservatives charging that he was carrying out the Socialist platform of 1932—a charge that made Norman Thomas bridle. "Roosevelt did not carry out the Socialist platform unless he carried it out on a stretcher," snorted the Socialist leader. And Rex Tugwell observed that "with what reluctance President Roosevelt was forced into deficit spending, and how he resisted at every step—Harry Hopkins, Ickes and numerous New Deal administrators could testify."

Innovator and conservator, Roosevelt dealt the American people a new hand, but he used the old deck of cards. "The New Deal . . . seeks to cement our society, rich and poor, manual workers and brain workers, into a voluntary brotherhood of free men, standing together striving together for the common good of all," he said in 1934. If anything, he emphasized its conservatism. "It was this administration which saved the system of private profit and free enterprise after it had been dragged to the brink of ruin," he declared during the 1936 campaign. And throughout his presidency, Roosevelt exhibited a wistful longing for balanced budgets, priding himself on the fact that he held spending for ordinary governmental operations to a low level. Huge sums were spent on relief through a parallel emergency budget, he acknowledged, but only because it was necessary to prevent people from starving. Roosevelt had no wish to create a permanent army of welfare recipients, and his eagerness to return to business as usual led to a recession in 1938 that almost wiped out the gains of the New Deal.

Roosevelt told Emil Ludwig, a contemporary biographer, that his major purpose was to avoid revolution. Civilization, he said, was like a tree that produces some deadwood and rot. "The radical says: 'Cut it down.' The conservative says: 'Don't touch it.' The liberal compromises: 'Let us prune, so that we lose neither the old trunk nor the new branches.'" Regarding politics as the art of improvisation, Roosevelt likened himself to a football quarterback, who knows what the next play is going to be but can't plan beyond that because "future plays will depend on how the next one works."

Roosevelt's thinking was based on the progressive tradition of Woodrow Wilson and Theodore Roosevelt. While he lacked the intellectual brilliance of the former and the moral fervor of the latter, he convinced most Americans and many Europeans that democratic reform represented a workable alternative to totalitarianism, whether of the Right or of the Left. But the devastation created by the Great Depression propelled him beyond middle-class reformism into uncharted seas. Confronted with the most severe economic crisis in the nation's history, he had little time or inclination to be distracted by the old hobgoblins of the urban political machines and the trusts. While progressivism had been primarily concerned with ensuring competition in the marketplace and protecting the farmer and small businessman, the New Deal employed the power of the government to make sweeping social changes. Under Roosevelt's hand, as Carl N. Degler has said, the federal government became "a vigorous and dynamic force in society, energizing it and if necessary supplanting private enterprise where the general welfare required it."

Because it was hammered together to meet an emergency, and its administrators, like Roosevelt himself, rejected dogma, the New Deal's pattern of development is neither clear nor systematic. Nevertheless, it was not as rudderless as it sometimes appeared. Early in his career, Roosevelt had evolved an integrated view of American politics from which he never deviated. Taking a cyclical view of history, he saw the control of government alternating between the Hamiltonian "haves" and the Jeffersonian "have nots." He regarded himself a latter-day Jefferson, with the task of preserving American democracy against the efforts of the Hamiltonians to dominate the government for their own, selfish ends. Armed with this vision, he was untroubled about short-term doubts.

Roosevelt provided little assistance to those trying to fathom his intentions. Shortly before the legislation establishing the Tennessee Valley Authority went to Congress, Senator George Norris asked him what he would say when asked about the political philosophy behind the measure. The President laughed. "I'll tell them it's neither fish nor fowl but whatever it is, it will taste awfully good to the people of the Tennessee Valley." And midway through the 1936 presidential campaign, a local Democratic headquarters received a telephone call. "We're having an argument," said an agitated voice on the line. "Tell us just what the principles of the New Deal are." "Hold the phone," replied an official, who went off to consult his associates. There was a considerable delay before he came back on the line. "Sorry," he said, "but we're having an argument, too."

The Roosevelt White House reflected the President's breezy manner. On his first day in office, he summoned Patrick McKenna, the chief doorkeeper, for some purpose or other. McKenna stuck his head in the doorway and was cordially greeted as "Pat." He nearly fainted. He had been in the White House for some thirty years and this was the first time a President had ever called him "Pat." Within a week, Roosevelt was calling everyone on the White House staff—secretaries, clerks, and servants—by their first name or a nickname. Upon learning that the wife of his valet, Irwin McDuffie, who also worked in the White House, believed in reincarnation, the President was curious. Lizzie McDuffie, who weighed nearly two hundred pounds, told him she wanted to come back as a canary. "I love it! I love it!" roared Roosevelt.

One of the earliest orders the President circulated to his staff was that if people in distress telephoned the White House for help, the appeal was not to be shunted aside. Roosevelt said that if someone was desperate enough to call the President, then a way ought to be found, if at all possible, to help him. Many such calls were received—from farmers threatened with imminent foreclosure of their land and householders about to lose their homes—and some were taken by Mrs. Roosevelt herself. Usually a way would be found to cut red tape at some federal agency and get help for them.

Besides the President and the First Lady, the permanent residents of the White House included Louis Howe, who felt as if he were rattling about "like a pea in a pod" in the Lincoln Room and moved his bed into an adjoining dressing room; Missy LeHand, who had a room on the third floor; and Anna Roosevelt Dall and her two small children, Anna Eleanor and Curtis, known to everyone as Sisty and Buzzy.* Anna had separated from her husband, Curtis B. Dall, after six years of marriage. During the 1932 campaign, she had fallen in love with John Boettiger, a reporter for the Chicago *Tribune*. Eleanor Roosevelt, who liked Boettiger and called him "one of the people for whom I have a very special and personal feeling," encouraged the affair. Writing years later of his parents' love, Anna and John's son has written that it "may have offered Eleanor an image of the kind of intimacy she had fantasized and deeply wished but never realized." Both obtained divorces and were married in 1935, after Boettiger had left the *Tribune*, which had become the President's most strident journalistic critic.

The White House had not undergone an extensive renovation in decades, and the place was run-down and seedy. Mrs. Henrietta Nesbitt, the Dutchess County matron hired by Eleanor as housekeeper, found the antiquated kitchen infested with cockroaches and complained that it was impossible to keep the public rooms clean. Until Roosevelt's arrival, the White House did not have a library. One of the doorkeepers doubled as the presidential barber. In the dozen years the Roosevelts lived there, the second-floor living quarters took on the same comfortably cluttered look as the house at Hyde Park. Family pictures and snapshots of children and grandchildren and naval prints lined the walls, and assorted bric-a-brac and ship models took up the rest of the space. Books and magazines, often several months old, were strewn about haphazardly. The furniture, some of which belonged to the family, was more comfortable than ele-

* In later years, Curtis Roosevelt Dall dropped his last name; he is now known as Curtis Roosevelt.

gant. A few pieces, including the President's bed, had been made to order in the Val-Kill shop. Eleanor hung a portrait of her grandfather, Theodore Roosevelt, Sr., in the Monroe Room, which became the family sitting room. She had planned to leave it in the house on Sixty-fifth Street, which was to be rented out, but her husband had insisted: "You can't rent your grandfather. Take him with us."

The magnificently proportioned Oval Room, on the second floor of the White House, became the President's study. Marine paintings and naval prints from his private collection covered the walls, and there was a model of a destroyer on the mantel. One of the paintings, "The Return of the *Mayflower*," which showed the arrival of the first American warships in European waters in 1917, was a reminder of his days as assistant Secretary of the Navy. Over the door hung a portrait of Eleanor painted when she was a girl—with shimmering light hair that curled naturally, blue eyes, and creamy skin. One day, Roosevelt saw Frances Perkins studying the picture. "I always liked that portrait of Eleanor," he said. ". . . That's just the way Eleanor looks, you know—lovely hair, pretty eyes." There were two desks, one a reproduction of Jefferson's revolving desk and the other a handsomely carved affair made from the oak timbers of the *Resolute*, a vessel used by Sir John Franklin, the polar explorer.†

A connecting door led to the President's bedroom, which was rather plainly outfitted. The main pieces of furniture besides the bed were a heavy wardrobe—the White House had no closets—a rocking chair, and a night table. Jumbled together on it were a few books, a worn prayer book, stubs of pencils, notepaper, aspirin, nose drops, a glass of water, cigarettes, an ashtray, and a couple of telephones. The marble Victorian mantel held Roosevelt's collection of miniature pigs, and snapshots of the family and friends were propped up in back of them. Over the door hung the tail of Gloucester, his father's famous trotting horse.

The President's day usually began at about 8:30 A.M. Until he had his morning coffee and his first cigarette (he smoked two packs of Camels a day), he was usually in a bearish mood. The famous cigarette holder was specially designed for him with a soft tip because he had tender gums. While he breakfasted in bed, he scanned the morning papers: the New York *Times* and the *Herald Tribune*, the Washington *Post* and the *Herald*, and the Baltimore *Sun*. He paid particular attention to such columnists as Walter Lippmann and Frank R. Kent‡ and to the editorials. Howe also provided him with a digest of press comment from around the

---

† Jacqueline Kennedy later found the *Resolute* desk in the White House basement and installed it in the Oval Office.
‡ FDR had persuaded Van-Lear Black to syndicate Kent's column, which had originally appeared only in the *Sun*. It was a decision he was to rue, for Kent soon ranked among the New Deal's severest critics.

nation, which became known as the *Daily Bugle*. To ward off the chill in winter, he wore an old gray pullover sweater over his pajamas, rather than a robe, because it was easier for him to get in and out of it. The Roosevelt grandchildren were the only ones allowed to interrupt his morning ritual, and sometimes Eleanor, who occupied an adjoining suite of rooms, had to rescue him. One morning she heard shouting and calls for help coming from her husband's bedroom and discovered two little girls bouncing up and down on the bed shouting: "He's my grandfather!" "No, he isn't. He's mine!" The harried President was trying to protect his breakfast tray with one hand and holding the telephone in the other. "Wait a minute, Hacky," he was desperately telling the operator. "I can't talk to Paris just yet."

Aides would filter in as Roosevelt finished turning the pages of the newspapers—Howe, Steve Early, Marvin McIntyre, General Edwin M. Watson, the President's military aide—and the day's business and appointments would be discussed while he shaved himself. Harold Ickes recalled one such occasion:

> When I got to his study, his valet ushered me into his bedroom, telling me the President was shaving. He waved toward the bathroom and the President called out to me to come in. There he was, sitting before a mirror in front of the washstand, shaving. He invited me to sit on the toilet seat while we talked. When he was through shaving he was wheeled back to his room where he reclined on his bed while his valet proceeded to help him dress. . . . His disability didn't seem to concern him in the slightest degree or to disturb his urbanity.

If it was a Tuesday or a Friday, Early would go over points likely to come up at his news conference. Ordinarily, he worked over papers until about ten-thirty, when he would be taken down by elevator to his office in the West Wing, preceded by the ringing of a buzzer to let the staff know he was on his way. He used a small wheelchair without arms so that he could swing himself into the swivel chair behind his desk. Once there, he was imprisoned for the day.

Visitors were to be ushered in at fifteen-minute intervals, but, invariably, the President would get behind because of his delight in talking and seeing new faces. Sometimes these conversations would turn into monologues, with the visitor unable to get in more than a few words. Roosevelt's conversation was rather like a man crossing over a river on ice floes after a thaw; he skipped from one topic to another before it could sink under him. Representative Claude Pepper, then a senator from Florida, recalls going to the White House to make a plea for a pet project. Having anticipated Pepper's mission, the President pleasantly filibustered about his wife's relative Robert Livingston during the entire meeting. "I didn't make much progress on my project," Pepper recalled, "but I was the best-informed man in Washington on Robert Livingston."

Assistants were always bustling about with important business, and Henry L. Stimson, who had been Herbert Hoover's Secretary of State and was to serve Roosevelt as Secretary of War, told a friend he was amazed at Roosevelt's ability "to reach the kernel of a problem" despite the interruptions. "He could grasp the essentials, reach a decision and complete action with speed and clarity." The President disliked long memoranda, and when presented with one that could be trimmed, he would say, "Boil it down to a single page." Despite his sociability and the fact that he spent half his time on the telephone, he kept up with an enormous volume of mail, sometimes scribbling a personal note at the bottom of letters. On Christmas Day, he dictated letters of thanks for gifts while they were still being unwrapped.

At one o'clock, the President had lunch at his desk, usually with a visitor. The meal might consist of clear soup or clams, a chop or his favorite dish, broiled trout. Careful of his weight, the President took no dessert with his lunch. The flow of talk did not stop, but Rex Tugwell, for one, developed a strategy for dealing with it. He would eat lunch before coming to the White House, and while the President's mouth was full, he made his points. Perhaps the major reason for Roosevelt's garrulousness was that it compensated for his physical disability. Unable to relieve tensions by getting up and pacing about his office or by other means, he asked questions, gossiped, and told stories. One of the hazards of close association with him was having to listen to the same ancedote over and over again, often embellished in the retelling. Some aides heard these stories dozens of times.

Roosevelt's love of conversation was also a political asset, particularly when he wished to avoid a commitment or was uncertain about a course of action to be followed. The unfolding of a maddeningly long ancedote often provided him with the time to sort out his options before making a decision. Roosevelt had a marked distaste for being unpleasant face-to-face, and he sometimes left visitors with the impression that he supported their proposals when he hadn't the slightest intention of doing so. A nod and a murmured "Yes, yes" was not necessarily a sign of agreement but merely signified an understanding of what was being said—and a habit that caused some people, including his predecessor, to accuse him of duplicity.

Indeed, of all the charges leveled against Roosevelt, both in his lifetime and since his death, the one heard most often was that he was devious and lacking in candor. Some of this was the result of his seeming agreeability and desire to be gracious. Often it stemmed from the need to mask his intentions, for in official Washington, secrets are the coin of the realm. But there were times when he indulged in secrecy and subterfuge out of sheer delight in pulling rabbits out of hats. Sometimes he would announce appointments without the appointee's knowing it was coming, because he enjoyed the dramatic effect. As a result, Roosevelt's enemies charged him with deviousness and his friends never felt they could completely trust him. In fact, Ed Flynn stated flatly that "the President did not keep his word on many appointments." Once, he became so angry at what he regarded as a double cross that he hung up on Roosevelt during a telephone conversation.

"You are a wonderful person but you are one of the most difficult men to work with that I have ever seen," Ickes blurted out one day.

"Because I get too hard at times?" the President replied.

"No, you never get too hard but you won't talk frankly even with people who are loyal to you and of whose loyalty you are fully convinced. You keep your cards close up against your belly."

"Complex" and "subtle" are among the words most often used to describe Roosevelt. Seemingly the most gregarious of men, he remains, as Winston Churchill said of the Soviet Union, a riddle wrapped in an enigma. Part of Roosevelt's continuing fascination is that he is prismatic. Viewed from one vantage point, he refracts one set of colors; view him from another direction and the colors change too. "To describe Roosevelt, you would have to describe three or four men for he had at least three or four different personalities," said William Phillips, his old friend from Wilson days who became under Secretary of State. "He could turn from one personality to another with such speed that you often never knew where you were or to which personality you were talking." Frances Perkins regarded Roosevelt as "the most complicated human being I have ever known." And Henry Morgenthau, among his oldest friends, said he was "an extraordinarily difficult person to describe . . . a man of bewildering complexity of moods and motives."

The quality that most people first noticed about Roosevelt was his charm. Liking to be liked, he courted people. "If he thought you didn't like him," one aide told John Gunther, "he'd practically jump over a chair to get you." For example, in the summer of 1936, a young woman who had been invited to Hyde Park by one of the Roosevelt boys let slip the fact that she was stuffing envelopes for Alf Landon, the Republican presidential candidate. The President roared with laughter and then spent the rest of the evening trying to charm her. By the time she left Hyde Park, she had become a convinced Democrat, much to the consternation of her staunchly Republican family.

Both daring and cautious, Roosevelt could seize upon an idea and make a decision with breathtaking speed; yet, at other times, he might temporize until almost the last moment. He could be extremely flexible but had an underlying vein of steely stubbornness. He delighted in breaking precedents and loved tradition as dearly as the most conservative member of the Daughters of the American Revolution. He could be ruthless, yet, hating to fire anyone, kept appointees on long after they had become political liabilities. Loving peace and harmony, he followed policies that created controversy and contention in his official family. He mixed petty vindictiveness with Christian charity. Worldly and without illusion, he harbored a private religious faith strengthened by his close brush with death.

Roosevelt took an intense satisfaction in the effect of his inscrutability upon others. With the possible exception of Louis Howe, no one was allowed to penetrate his armor of aristocratic nonchalance. "Never let your left hand know what your right hand is doing," he once told Morgenthau.

"Which am I, Mr. President?" asked his old friend.

"My right hand," answered Roosevelt, "but I keep my left under the table."

Morgenthau thought this "the most frank expression of the real F.D.R. that I ever listened to, and the real way he works."

Politics fortified the reserve Roosevelt had cultivated throughout most of his life—first to protect himself from the domination of his mother and then against the real and fancied slights of Groton and Harvard. As a young man, he was subjected to the amused contempt of those who underrated him as a "feather-duster" living well beyond his intellectual means. He was regarded as an amiable country squire and patronized in Walter Lippmann's famous column as "a pleasant man who, without any important qualifications for the office, would like very much to be President." This attitude followed him into the White House, where longtime acquaintances found it almost impossible to reconcile the supercilious figure they had known with the dynamic Chief Executive of the Hundred Days. "There has been a miracle here," said Oswald Garrison Villard, editor of *The Nation*. "Many of us who have known him long and well ask ourselves if this is the same man."

There had been no miracle. The exercise of authority and the pressure of responsibility revealed an ambition and will to power that had always existed. Roosevelt's friends had never considered it worthwhile to probe beneath his Eagle Scout buoyancy and Ivy League diffidence. Had they done so, they would have discovered that politics was Roosevelt's passion and much of his adult life had been devoted to its study and practice. Over the years, he had developed a sensitive antenna that enabled him to make a shrewd appraisal of what was occurring in the minds of the American people. Although cut off by his physical ailment and position from shared experience with them, he had a gift for imagining human impulses, frustrations, and needs. If he had given the law or business the same prodigious attention as politics, he would undoubtedly have attained equal distinction in one of those fields. Roosevelt's background and code of conduct precluded him from providing any public evidence that he was making a serious effort to master politics, however. It was *"infra dig"* to show too much zeal.

Sir Isaiah Berlin has placed Roosevelt in the company of such aristocratic reformers as Alexander Herzen, Mirabeau, and Charles James Fox. "Their minds see large and generous horizons, and above all, reveal a unique intellectual gaiety of a kind that aristocratic education tends to produce," he declared. "At the same time they are intellectually on the side of everything that is new, progressive, rebellious, young and untried, of that which is about to come into being. . . ." In many ways, Roosevelt resembles Benjamin Disraeli. Both were aristocrats—Roosevelt by birth and Disraeli by self-identification—and both fought for reform. Both had a gift for the theatrical and brought color and excitement to politics. Both were motivated less by principle than by sheer zest for the game of politics. Loving power, they skillfully maneuvered to obtain and make use of it. Both were attacked as poseurs and inspired intense hatred as well as worship. Both were artful persuaders, understanding that political success often depends upon impression and style, rather than reason and logic. Above all else, the American President and the British Prime Minister understood that the height of political artistry is the concealment of shifts in policy behind a façade of adherence to immutable principles.

Most editorial writers had turned against Roosevelt before the end of his first term, but the President was on good terms with the bulk of the correspondents who regularly covered the White House. Before the country entered World War II, they gathered informally about his desk twice a week as the President, leaning back in his chair and with his cigarette holder at its debonair angle, nimbly fielded their questions. During his twelve years in office, Roosevelt met the press 998 times and regarded these conferences as part of the nation's educational process, along with the Fireside Chats and his more formal speeches.

Roosevelt's entry into the White House meant a New Deal for the press as well as the nation. Immediately upon taking office, the President announced the end of the written-questions-only rule established by Warren Harding, although he could not be quoted directly without specific permission. Roosevelt's relations with the press were in vivid contrast to those of Herbert Hoover. As the depression had deepened, Hoover had reacted to mounting criticism by drying up as a news source, making the work of those assigned to cover him even more difficult. Roosevelt quickly won the respect and admiration of the press by his accessibility, responsiveness, and understanding of journalistic problems and psychology. As with the White House staff, he was soon on a first-name basis with the regulars, liked their company, and enjoyed the verbal fencing with them. Roosevelt, said Heywood Broun, was "the best newspaperman who has ever been President of the United States."

Steve Early was responsible for much of Roosevelt's success with the press. Personally known to most of the White House press corps, Early urged the President to throw open the doors of his administration to them, to end the reliance on written questions, and to change the atmosphere of the White House so the correspondents would be "welcomed, as gentlemen, not suspected as spies." He was always available to answer questions and, even more important, usually knew the answers. And if he did not, he was not afraid to ask the President. Early also played an important role in grooming Roosevelt for press conferences by providing him with newsworthy announcements, briefing him on issues likely to come up, and preparing answers.

Most of the White House press corps were sympathetic to the New Deal and Roosevelt's objectives, but the basic reason for the friendly relationship between them was mutual benefit. The President's frequent press conferences meant that the reporters were plugged into an unbeatable news source. If relations remained smooth, they were in the enviable position of learning about administration policies on a background basis before they were discussed elsewhere—as in the case of lend-lease in 1941. Regular contacts with the press enabled Roosevelt to dominate the news and its presentation as no other President before him had done and to outflank the opposition of editorialists. Press conferences were often a springboard for launching new ideas, and they were an integral part of the process of mobilizing public opinion. Skillfully using background and off-the-record discussion, he made his views known to the assembled reporters so that they could write knowledgeably—and sympathetically—about forthcoming policy. Sometimes he might even try to write their stories for them. "In other words," he would sometimes say, "here is the way I would put it if I were writing the story."

A Roosevelt press conference was a virtuoso performance—"the best show in town" was the common verdict. The President explained complex policies in language the reporters could understand, and he used colorful metaphors that made good copy. John Gunther recalled that in one twenty-minute news conference, the President's face expressed amazement, curiosity, mock alarm, genuine interest, concern, and pleasure. He was always in command. Faced with the prospect of embarrassing questions, Roosevelt often adroitly avoided them by beginning a conference with announcements so newsworthy that they dominated the rest of the meeting. Sometimes he evaded questions by pretending not to hear them, or replied with a quip. The Roosevelt charm and persuasiveness were so powerful, said columnist Mark Sullivan, he "could recite the Polish alphabet and it would be accepted as an eloquent plea for disarmament."

Usually jocular but preferring to use the rapier against critics, Roosevelt could be sharp-tongued at times, particularly when the reporters tried to pry information out of him. "That's an iffy question," he might say, or "No cross examination please!" Those who transgressed what he considered acceptable behavior were told to "put on a dunce cap and go stand in the corner."* Roosevelt disliked columnists, but upon one occasion when he made some critical remarks about them, the tables were turned. "But, Mr. President," said May Craig, who represented some New England papers, "you've got one in the family!" This reference to Mrs. Roosevelt's daily column—"My Day"—broke everyone up.

The President's triumph over the press corps was so complete that some correspondents found it necessary to make a spirited defense against the charge that they had become propagandists for the New Deal. And indeed there was something of a conspiracy between the press and the White House regarding Roosevelt's paralysis. It was rarely mentioned, and few Americans realized that the President's primary means of locomotion was the wheelchair. As if by agreement, no pictures were taken of him while he was being lifted from his car like a sack of potatoes and stood on his feet, and if some photographer didn't heed this unwritten rule, the Secret Service was on guard to prevent him from taking a picture.

The informality of Roosevelt's press relations also marked his cabinet meetings. Little work was actually accomplished, because Roosevelt preferred to deal with individuals or small groups, and particularly with the heads of various agencies, such as Marriner Eccles of the Federal Reserve Board, or Harry Hopkins. The function of the Cabinet has been a subject of debate throughout American history. Should it be a consultative body or merely a staff meeting of departmental administrators? George Washington sought the counsel of his ministers, but later Presidents found

* FDR's handling of Henry Mencken was more subtle. In 1934, Mencken was invited to give the opposition speech at the Gridiron Club's annual dinner, in which he addressed the guests as "Fellow Subjects of the Reich" and lambasted the New Deal. Roosevelt's own speech turned out to be a bitter attack on the press. "A Washington correspondent is one with a special talent for failing to see what is done before his eyes," the President declared. "I have beheld a whole herd of them sitting through a national convention without once laughing." There were some embarrassed shifting in seats and snorts of anger as the tirade continued until the assemblage realized that FDR was reading from the works of Mencken. There were guffaws and nervous glances at Mencken, who was nearly apoplectic. "I'll get the son of a bitch!" he hissed to Governor Albert C. Ritchie of Maryland, who was seated next to him. Edgar Kemler, *The Irreverent Mr. Mencken* (Boston: Little, Brown, 1950), pp. 269–71.

them too specialized and concerned with the operations of their own departments to provide general advice. Nevertheless, Presidents had persisted in trying to make use of the Cabinet as a consultative body, and Roosevelt followed suit. But his experience soon paralleled that of his predecessors, and cabinet meetings were downgraded in importance.

Roosevelt was wheeled into the Cabinet Room after all the members had gathered about the table, and would usually begin talking as soon as he came into the room. Sometimes he opened with a story he had just heard, less often with a particular project he wanted to discuss. Then he would turn to the senior member, Secretary of State Hull, and cheerfully ask: "Well, Cordell, what's on your mind today?" When Hull had finished, he would continue around the table in order of precedence until everyone had been given the opportunity to speak. Only the most routine matters were discussed, and Roosevelt seldom confided in his Cabinet, because of repeated breaches of security. Vice-President Garner, who had been asked to sit in—a decision the President soon regretted—leaked information to his cronies on Capitol Hill, and anything that Harold Ickes gleaned from the meeting was likely to appear in the political gossip column written by Drew Pearson.

Most sessions were devoted to reports from the various members and there was little policy discussion. "The cold fact is that on important matters we are seldom called upon for advice," Ickes confided to his diary in 1935. "We never discuss exhaustively any policy of government or question of political strategy. The President makes all of his own decisions, and, so far as the Cabinet is concerned, without taking counsel with a group of advisers. . . . As a matter of fact, I never think of bringing up even a serious governmental issue at Cabinet meetings, and apparently the other members follow the same policy."

Jealous and suspicious of each other and constantly jockeying for position with the President, the cabinet members vied for his private ear after every session—what Garner called "staying for prayer meeting." Most of them were angry at Morgenthau's privileged position as an old friend and his standing invitation to lunch with Roosevelt every Monday. Maintaining peace in his official family consumed energy that could well have been devoted to other purposes. Professor Charles E. Merriam visited the President one day and found him bent over his desk with his head in his hands. He said that he had just finished refereeing a bout between Wallace and Ickes. "They were in here for an hour arguing over who should have a couple sticks of timber along the Cumberland River," he declared. "And do you know—neither of them controls a single vote!"

Roosevelt is usually given low marks as an administrator. Unable to bring himself to fire anyone, he tolerated more incompetence than he should have. He liked to draw elaborate organizational charts, but permitted—and even encouraged—duplication of effort, overlapping authority, and internecine feuds. Yet the day-to-day job of running the government got done. The people whom Roosevelt attracted to Washington through the force of his personality were fiercely loyal and, for the most part, able. He invested the bureaucracy with a zest and excitement it had never known before. In the final analysis, Roosevelt's unorthodox approach to government stimulated creativity and innovation—and this was more important than an orderly flow of paper.

The President relaxed between 5:30 P.M. and dinner at 9:00. He went for a swim in the pool installed shortly after he took office, and sometimes conducted business there. When his distant cousin Nicholas Roosevelt returned from Hungary, where he had served as minister under Hoover, Roosevelt received his final report while they were splashing about in the water together. After a massage and a brief nap, he was ready for the "Children's Hour": cocktails in his study. Priding himself on his skill, he mixed the drinks, favoring martinis or old-fashioneds. He limited himself to two drinks, but they were strong ones. It was said he kept two grades of gin in stock, saving the best for favored guests. The President took time out during the cocktail hour to feed tidbits to Fala, his pet Scottie, and put him through his bag of tricks.

Dinner might be either with the family in the private dining room or a more elaborate affair downstairs in the State Dining Room. On formal occasions, the President would be at the table when the guests came in. After dinner, they would leave the table when he put down his napkin, and then he would be wheeled out to join them in another room. Mrs. Roosevelt often invited people to dinner whom she thought the President should meet, and some odd characters turned up at the White House table. One official placed beside an obviously nervous young woman asked her what she did and was told: "I'm the dietician at the Brooklyn YWCA."

Neither of the Roosevelts had much interest in food—the President once said he had "a digestion like ten oxen"—and the White House cuisine reflected it. "Undistinguished" and "uninspired" were the most charitable words used to describe the menus prepared under the direction of Mrs. Nesbitt. People who stayed at the White House for any length of time claimed they could tell the day of the week by what was set before them. Ernest Hemingway, invited to dinner in 1937, described the food as "the worst I've ever eaten. . . . We had rainwater soup followed by rubber squab, a nice wilted salad and a cake some admirer had sent in. An enthusiastic but unskilled admirer." Even Roosevelt finally rebelled, and when he had important guests to entertain, he called in a chef from outside. After his mother's death, in 1941, he brought the cook down from

Hyde Park and installed her in the family kitchen, on the third floor of the White House.

Until World War II altered his schedule, the President liked to attend the movies shown in the wide, book-lined second-floor hall almost any evening. He especially liked newsreels and Mickey Mouse cartoons and was delighted by Charlie Chaplin's *The Great Dictator*. His favorite actors were Myrna Loy and Walter Huston. He was fascinated when Katharine Hepburn, having been invited to a picnic at Hyde Park, descended upon the Hudson in a seaplane and waded ashore, showing up at Springwood in slightly damp clothes and bare feet. He personally drove her to Val-Kill for the picnic. When his mother was present for a movie, he would playfully try to shock her by making ribald remarks about the physical charms of the women in the picture. If he disliked a film, his valet would assist him into his study, where he would deal with papers and reports or work on his extensive stamp collection.

The State Department had orders to send him any unusual stamps arriving in the mails, and the Post Office Department presented him with the first sheet of all new issues. He suggested subjects for new stamps, took time out to inspect their designs, even designing a few himself.† During World War II, a New Zealand official suggested that Allied forces capture a South Pacific island in which his country was interested. "No, not that island," said Roosevelt. "An island nearby called Mangareva would be better." The New Zealander had never heard of Mangareva. "Oh, it's in the Tuamotu Archipelago, in the postal administration of Tahiti," replied the President. "I know the place because I'm a stamp collector."

Roosevelt usually went to bed about midnight, but he would often chat with Eleanor or read a report or a book or a magazine for another hour or so before turning off the light. He seemed to have no trouble sleeping and told one aide: "During my waking, working hours, I give the best in me. . . . When time comes for rest, I can reflect that I could not have done it better if I had it to do all over again. . . . There is nothing left for me but to close my eyes and I am asleep."

As the years passed, Roosevelt looked forward to vacations at Warm Springs or going on a long sea voyage on a navy cruiser. But it was to Hyde Park that he always returned. It was his home, his elixir, and he cherished it with a nostalgic affection. Even after his children were grown and dispersed, it was the place where they came for summer vacations and holidays with their own offspring—especially at Christmas. The President's hearthside reading of Dickens' *A Christmas Carol* was a classic performance complete with stage voices and dramatic business that kept the smaller children on the edge of their seat. He loved to show the family

† Following FDR's death, his stamp collection was sold for $250,000.

acres to visiting friends, piloting them about in his hand-operated Ford. "Isn't this nice," he would murmur, "isn't this nice." He listed his occupation as "tree-farmer" when he voted at Hyde Park. In four presidential elections, however, he carried stoutly Republican Dutchess County only once, but romped over the opposition in Meriwether County in Georgia, where Warm Springs is situated.

Sara Roosevelt lived to be eighty-seven and delighted in her role as "Mother of the President." She was a one-woman cheering squad for her son among her staunchly Republican friends and would not stand for a word of criticism of him in her presence. As imperious as ever, she had strong views on almost everything. Questioned about the persistent hostility of the Oyster Bay Roosevelts to the Hyde Park branch of the family, she replied: "I can't imagine why unless it's because we're better looking than they are." She never became entirely used to the politicians who visited Hyde Park, however. "Who is that terrible man sitting next to my son?" she hissed while the President was entertaining Huey Long. And some of the visitors that her daughter-in-law brought home also aroused her ire. "*Where* does Eleanor get all these people?" the dowager muttered.

Eleanor Roosevelt entered upon her duties as First Lady with considerable reluctance. Having established a career as a leader in the fight for social reform and as an educator and writer, she feared becoming a captive of protocol and tradition. "I never wanted to be a President's wife," she told Lorena Hickok. Nevertheless, she put aside her misgivings and exhibited a tireless energy and warm humanity in the White House that captivated the public as much as her husband's own exuberant vitality. All her predecessors had led circumspect and self-effacing lives, but Eleanor saw no need to take the veil. Typically, she held her first news conference even before the President had met the press. "I feel that my job is to help him as much as possible and to do whatever falls within my scope," she said.

Once again, Louis Howe was instrumental in propelling her into the limelight. In the spring of 1933, the Bonus Army had returned to Washington, but instead of meeting it with troops and tear gas, Roosevelt ordered the Veterans Administration to establish a camp for the demonstrators and to feed them. Howe invited Eleanor for a drive in the country one rainy afternoon and then told her they were going to visit the veterans' encampment. Pushing her out of the car into ankle-deep mud, he said he was going to take a nap—confident that she would defuse a potentially dangerous situation. Surprised at being visited by the First Lady, the veterans welcomed her and she listened to their problems. They talked about the war and sang old songs and Eleanor helped find places in the CCC for some of the men and tickets home for the rest. "Hoover sent the Army," said one veteran, "Roosevelt sent his wife."

Eleanor was extremely interested in the social-welfare aspects of the New Deal and frequently poked around to see what progress was being made. Often she telephoned officials directly, much to their surprise. Upon one occasion, she called Walter G. Campbell, the director of the Food and Drug Administration. "This is Mrs. Roosevelt," she said, and Campbell, who couldn't believe the President's wife was calling, replied: "Yes, and this is the King of Siam."

Far from being a prisoner in the White House, she traveled some forty thousand miles during the first year, and reported to the President on what she had seen and heard. Eleanor's travels soon became part of American folklore. Radio comedians joked about where she might turn up next, and it was not long before life imitated art. *The New Yorker* published a cartoon in which a startled coal miner tells another: "Good gosh, here comes Mrs. Roosevelt!"—and before people had even stopped chuckling, Eleanor did visit a coal mine. Soon afterward, Sara Roosevelt sent a barbed comment to her son: "I hope Eleanor is with you this morning. . . . I see she has emerged from the mine." On one occasion, Eleanor left the White House early in the morning to visit a prison in Baltimore without saying good morning to the President. He asked her secretary, Malvina Thompson, where his wife was and was told: "She's in prison, Mr. President." "I'm not surprised," replied Roosevelt, "but what for?"

Although they went their separate ways, as they had since the Lucy Mercer affair, the Roosevelts had a genuine affection and respect for each other.‡ "The Lord only knows where this will catch up with my Will o' the Wisp wife . . . ," he wrote her at one point. And she replied: "We are really very dependent on each other though we do see so little of each other. . . . I miss you and hate to feel you so far away. . . ." In September 1941, Eleanor's brother Hall Roosevelt had succumbed, like their fa-

‡ On Mar. 17, 1933, the Roosevelts' twenty-eighth wedding anniversary, the President sent Eleanor a note and a $200 check:

Dearest Babs:
After a fruitless week of thinking and lying
awake to find whether you need or want undies,
dresses, hats, shoes, sheets, towels, rouge,
soup plates, candy, flowers, lamps, laxation
pills, whisky, beer, etchings or caviar
      I GIVE UP
        !
And yet I know you lack some necessity of life—
so go to it with my love and many happy returns
of the day!
      F.D.R.

ther, to alcoholism. He had always been a trial and a disappointment to her, but she remained with him in the hospital during his last illness, sleeping in her clothes for ten days so as to always be available should he call her. "I remember clearly the day she went to Father and said simply, 'Hall has died,'" James Roosevelt recalls. "Father struggled to her side and put his arm around her. 'Sit down,' he said, so tenderly. I can still hear it. And he sank down beside her and hugged her and kissed her and held her head on his chest. . . ."

Frances Perkins relates that Roosevelt was "enormously proud" of his wife, although he sometimes teased her about her reputation as a do-gooder. "You know, Eleanor really does put it over," he said on more than one occasion. "She's got great talent with people." He had complete confidence in her reports and relied upon her observations in making policy decisions. In cabinet meetings he would often say, "You know my Missus gets around a lot and she says. . . ." No First Lady had a greater effect on policy and public opinion. But it was not a one-way relationship. She learned from him, and under his tutelage became one of the nation's ablest politicians.

Yet there were times when the Roosevelts were in conflict. Eleanor was considerably ahead of her husband—and the nation as a whole—in support of civil rights for blacks and equal rights for women. While the President's record on civil rights is spotty, she tried to persuade him and Jim Farley to appoint blacks and women to ranking places in the Administration and to support antilynching and other laws banning racial discrimination. In 1939, when the Daughters of the American Revolution refused to allow Marian Anderson, the black contralto, to give a concert in Constitution Hall, she resigned in protest, just as she had done when the Colony Club, in New York City, had refused to admit Mrs. Henry Morgenthau because she was Jewish. Ickes, who had been head of the Chicago branch of the National Association for the Advancement of Colored People, arranged for Miss Anderson to sing instead from the steps of the Lincoln Memorial before a crowd estimated at seventy-five thousand people.*

Roosevelt was no racist, but he easily accommodated himself to the segregationist ways of the South, and three of his closest aides, McIntyre, Early, and Watson, were Southerners. The only blacks he knew were servants, and he can best be described as a gradualist on the race issue. He believed that the rising living standards and broadened educational opportunities that were being provided by the New Deal for all Americans would also improve conditions for blacks. For example, whites and blacks

---

* FDR also had a memorable run-in with the DAR. Having avoided the staunchly anti-New Deal organization's annual "Continental Congresses" for four years, he agreed to speak on Apr. 21, 1938. "Remember," he said, "remember always that all of us, and you and I especially, are descended from immigrants and revolutionists."

on relief projects were paid the same wages, something theretofore unheard of in the South. But, worried about losing the support of powerful southern committee chairmen for his legislative program, the President resisted his wife's efforts to force him to take an overt stand against white supremacy. Even so, he allowed her to state her views on the race issue publicly, adding: "I can always say, 'Well, that's my wife; I can't do anything about her.'"

There were occasions, however, when he was exasperated by her insistence on putting across a particular point of view. At dinner one evening, Eleanor told the President that he *must* see a Chinese student who had just arrived in Washington, because he would provide valuable information on the situation in China. Roosevelt replied that he could not take the time to see the young man. Eleanor insisted, and he said he could not do it, if only because of protocol if nothing else. When she continued to press, the irritated President declared: "Send your Chinaman over to the State Department!"

"Franklin," replied Eleanor, "you know perfectly well that the State Department is on the other side politically so far as China is concerned."

"Have the damned Chinaman see Hopkins!"

"Hopkins is too busy."

Finally, the irritated President flatly refused to do anything more about the matter and Eleanor declared: "Well, I will ask him to dinner as my guest."

The President blew up, exclaiming: "Just remember, I want dinner to be a relaxation, not an excuse for doing business!"

Eleanor accepted such rebuffs philosophically. Looking back upon her marriage, following her husband's death, she said: "He might have been happier with a wife who was completely uncritical. That I was never able to be, and he had to find it in other people. Nevertheless, I think I sometimes acted as a spur even though the spurring was not always wanted or welcome. I was one of those who served his purposes."

"One of the worst things in the world is being the child of a president," Roosevelt once said. "It's a terrible life they lead." Unaccustomed to the merciless glare of publicity, the spotlight always seemed to catch the Roosevelt children in an awkward moment. Such mishaps as traffic accidents, speeding tickets, and arguments in public became front-page news. Anna, James, and Elliott were also attacked for supposedly using their father's position to secure favors for those who gave them lucrative positions: Accustomed to the trappings of wealth without being wealthy, they were susceptible to deals designed to make big money quickly. Anna was criticized when John Boettiger was named publisher of the Hearst-owned Seattle *Post-Intelligencer*. Jimmy was accused of using political influence to make huge profits for his insurance agency and of being in league with Joe Kennedy to corner the market for imported scotch when repeal was in the offing. Elliott came under fire for his links to the airline industry and for his ties to a chain of Texas radio stations owned by Hearst.

The President was concerned about the possibility that his family might profit from their position, but his warnings seemed to have had little effect. Jimmy, for one, later realized that despite their protestations about not using family influence, the Roosevelt children had sailed close to the wind in some of their business arrangements. "Possibly I should have been sufficiently mature and considerate enough of Father's position to have withdrawn from the insurance business entirely," he later wrote. "But I was young, ambitious, spoiled—in the sense of having been conditioned to require a good deal of spending money—so I went ahead in pursuit of what seemed to me the easiest solution."

Usually careful about inciting charges of nepotism, Roosevelt couldn't resist naming a member of the family as assistant Secretary of the Navy, a post that had almost become its fiefdom. The fifth of the clan to be appointed was his cousin Henry Latrobe Roosevelt, who had retired from the Marine Corps as a colonel. Jimmy also served briefly on the White House staff, arousing charges of favoritism and mixed reviews on his performance.

The chaotic domestic lives of the Roosevelt children—in all, they have accounted for seventeen marriages—provided considerable ammunition for the President's critics. Elliott was a special trial. The most rebellious of the boys, he refused to attend college after Groton and, like Anna, rushed into an early marriage. At about the time of his father's first inauguration, he left his wife and child in New York and went to Texas, where he announced that he was not only getting a divorce but would immediately remarry. Divorce had become common among upper-class Americans, but this was a first for a presidential family, and Roosevelt's opponents seized upon it. Although he and Eleanor were disappointed by the marital problems of their children, they made little effort to interfere. Perhaps this was a reaction to Sara Roosevelt's insistent meddling in their lives. And having arranged to continue their marriage after Franklin's affair with Lucy Mercer, they may have sympathized with the children's desire for freedom. "I probably carried this thing too far," Eleanor later said of this hands-off policy. And the President, asked if his offspring's problems caused him any political damage, replied: "I believe that a politician should be judged on his politics."

Probably reflecting some of her own anger, Eleanor laid part of the blame for the early marriages of her children upon her husband's failure to make a break with his mother. As a result, she said, the family had always lived in homes that belonged to her and they never had a place of their own. "They were not really rooted in any particular home and were seeking to establish homes of their own," she explained. "This added to their need to make money quickly." And the children may not have had all the parental attention they wanted, she added, because in their formative years Franklin had been preoccupied with his fight against polio; later, his time was taken up with politics and his concentration upon his own objectives.

The children may have joked about having to make an appointment to see their father, but Roosevelt made every effort to maintain close ties to his family. He wrote to them about twice a month, and if they were in Washington, he was available to them as he relaxed before dinner. Although warm and affectionate as always, he was unable to let his guard down, even with his children, and discuss his innermost feelings with them. Upon one occasion, Eleanor recalled, one of the boys came to him for counsel about his personal problems. After listening attentively, the President picked up a paper from his desk and remarked: "This is a most important document. I should like to have your opinion on it." Indignant at being handled in this way, the young man angrily told his mother: "Never again will I try to talk to Father about anything personal."

One of the few persons who claimed to have penetrated the debonair mask was a Washington correspondent who told *Fortune* that he was out walking in the woods with a girl on Campobello one foggy day in June 1933:

> All at once, not five yards off in the fog, there was the President's Ford with big Gus Gennerich, the President's bodyguard asleep against the wheel. And there beside the car was the President. He was sitting on the trunk of a tree, his legs folded out in front of him, his hands over his face. And suddenly, before they could move, the hands came down and there were his eyes looking straight into their eyes just a few steps off and not seeing them at all, the way a man's face will look out at you not seeing you from a flash in the movies; there was a kind of drawn grimace over his mouth and over his forehead like a man trying to see something in his mind and suffering. And then all at once they could see his eyes focusing and it was like a shutter clicking down on a camera the way the smile came back over the look in his eyes and he called out: "Hello there, Billy. Picking flowers?" They turned and got out of there. They could hear his big laugh back of them in the spruce. . . .

XX

A RENDEZVOUS
WITH DESTINY

H UEY LONG WAS angry. Bounding into the White House
one hot summer day, the Louisiana Kingfish plopped down in a chair near
Franklin Roosevelt to complain that he had been bypassed in the handing
out of home-state patronage. Everything had gone to his political enemies
despite his protestations of support for the New Deal. Pointedly, Long
kept his bright-banded straw hat clapped on his head except to periodically whip it off to tap the President on the knee or elbow for emphasis.
Jim Farley and Marvin McIntyre, convinced that he was deliberately baiting Roosevelt, clenched their teeth at this lack of respect. But the
unruffled President enjoyed the performance. Leaning back in his chair,
he pleasantly explained that of course he was solely interested in making
certain that good men were appointed to office. Finally, as if acknowl-
edging defeat, Long removed his hat and kept it off.

"What the hell is the use of coming down to see this fellow?" the
Kingfish snapped to Farley after leaving the Oval Office. "I can't win any
decision over him." Using country terms, he later described Roosevelt as a
"scrootch owl," rather than a "hoot owl." A hoot owl barged into the
chicken roost, knocked a hen off its perch, and grabbed her as she fell, he
explained. "But a scrootch owl slips into the roost and scrootches up to
the hen and talks softly to her. And then the hen falls in love with him
and the first thing you know, *there ain't no more hen.*"

Not long after the White House meeting, open warfare erupted between the senator from Louisiana and the Administration. The Kingfish
had his own plan for recovery: "Share Our Wealth," which promised to
make "Every Man a King." America's great fortunes would be confiscated

through taxation and every family would be given a home, an auto, and a radio. The elderly were promised pensions, the veterans a bonus, and the workers a guaranteed annual wage of about three thousand dollars. Economists scoffed at Long's proposal, but millions of poor people joined his "Share Our Wealth" clubs. As his own following multiplied, Long treated Roosevelt with mounting contempt. He accused the President of selling out to Wall Street and likened the Blue Eagle of the NRA to the Nazi swastika. Roosevelt was ridiculed as "Prince Franklin of the *Nourmahal*," and with equal fervor, Long denounced "Lord Corn Wallace" and "Ickes the Chicago Chinch Bug."

Farley warned Roosevelt that if Long, whose presidential ambitions were notorious, ran as a third-party candidate in 1936, he might do to him what Theodore Roosevelt had done to President Taft in 1912. Roosevelt lost no time in responding to the challenge. The Bureau of Internal Revenue was instructed to start looking into the Kingfish's tax returns, as well as those of his henchmen. "Don't put anybody in and don't keep anybody that is working for Huey Long and his crowd," he told aides. "Anybody working for Huey Long is not working for us."

The Kingfish was not alone in his attacks on Roosevelt as recovery began to falter at the beginning of 1935. The election of the previous November had strengthened Democratic control of Congress and dramatized Roosevelt's popularity, but signs of discontent were multiplying. The New Deal was a promise unfulfilled, a dream deferred. H. G. Wells sensed a "widespread discontent" among the great masses of the American people. "The actual New Deal has not gone far enough and fast enough for them, and that is what the shouting is all about," he said.

The NRA and the AAA had lost their momentum, millions were still unemployed, industrial workers were rebellious, and sharecroppers and marginal farmers had hardly been touched by the New Deal reforms. "The unemployed problem is solved no more here than it is with you," the President wrote an English friend. The American Bankers Association talked of "boycotting" the federal government until the budget was balanced. And while the Liberty League shrilly insisted that the New Deal had already gone too far too fast, other messiahs peddled their own nostrums for recovery.

Leftist intellectuals, recalls Alfred Kazin, dismissed Roosevelt as a "wily, slippery confidence man unable for very long to satisfy 'people of principle.'" Father Coughlin, the Detroit radio priest and one-time Roosevelt supporter, was feeding his huge flock of listeners a litany of vituperation. Week after week, he raged against the New Deal, charging that it was "out-Hoovering Hoover." Coughlin's attacks on "Franklin Double-Crossing Roosevelt" grew increasingly strident, and his speeches were laced with attacks on the "international bankers"—shorthand for the

Jews.* And there were the Townsend Clubs, brainchild of an elderly physician named Dr. Francis E. Townsend. With a touch of the old-time
religion, the elderly were mobilized in support of his plan to pay everybody over sixty years of age a two hundred dollar monthly stipend if they
agreed to retire and to spend the money within the month. These payments were to be financed by a 2 percent tax on all business and commercial transactions—in effect, a general sales tax. Townsend Clubs sprang up
in every city and town, often with prestigious local elders among the sponsors. They met in church basements, peppered the newspapers and their
representatives in Congress with manifestos, and were gaining the ear of
ambitious politicians.

The millions attracted by these three Pied Pipers of radicalism could
hardly have been far from Roosevelt's thoughts as the newly elected
Seventy-fourth Congress convened, in January 1935. Political observers
had confidently predicted that 1935 would be a year of unprecedented
reform, but Roosevelt seemed strangely becalmed. Making one last try to
patch up deteriorating relations with business and fearing that New Deal
legislation would not clear the judicial hurdle of an impending Supreme
Court review, he tried to hew to the middle of the road. Some liberal critics believed he hoped to ward off the threat of Long, Coughlin, and
Townsend in 1936 not by reform measures but by encouraging business to
step up the pace of investment so he could claim to have restored prosperity. The State of the Union address reflected his lack of direction. Roosevelt merely urged the completion of a mild agenda of reforms and expressed his hopes for "a genuine period of good feeling." Major new
initiatives were limited: reorganization of the increasingly inadequate relief program, establishment of a long-awaited pension system for the elderly, a banking bill, and a public-utility holding-company law.

"The federal government must and shall quit this business of relief,"
Roosevelt declared in outlining a new program to replace the old system
of handouts. He described the dole as "a narcotic, a subtle destroyer of
the human spirit," and called for a program of government-created jobs
that preserved not only the unemployed from destitution but also "their
self-respect, their self-reliance, and courage and determination." The plan,
financed by a $4.8 billion appropriation, was to replace direct relief with a
permanent public works program modeled upon the Civilian Works Administration but bolstered by the standards insisted upon by Harold Ickes
and the Public Works Administration. The federal government would provide jobs for 3.5 million people who were able to work, while another 2
million unemployables would continue on direct relief administered by
the states. Workers would be paid more than they received on relief but

---

* To gain sympathy, boys selling Coughlin's organ, *Social Justice*, were trained to start
weeping copiously and when asked what was the matter, to wail: "A big Jew hit me!"

less than the going wage so recipients wouldn't reject opportunities for private employment. Following two months of debate, Congress passed the Emergency Relief Appropriations Act, which gave the President authority to create a new relief agency. The largest single appropriations bill yet approved, it gave Roosevelt a blank check and represented a significant shift in power from Capitol Hill to the White House.

Having obtained the money, Roosevelt faced the problem of establishing an agency to distribute it. Harry Hopkins and Harold Ickes were elbowing each other for the job of top administrator. Both men had aroused controversy and hostility that was likely to rub off on the new agency, but the choice was less between personalities than between programs. Ickes' approach was geared to recovery, rather than relief, with emphasis on large-scale public works projects that would aid industry through expenditures on capital goods; Hopkins wished to put those on relief to work as soon as possible and to rely on the wages pumped into the economy for recovery. Hopkins' approach appealed to Roosevelt because it would have the quickest effect, but he wished to retain Ickes because of his demonstrated ability to keep projects free of graft. Characteristically, he resorted to administrative sleight-of-hand to have it both ways.

The solution was a top-heavy, clumsy bureaucractic monster that was so complicated that it took the President four news conferences to explain it. Roosevelt sat at the top of a pyramid called the National Works Authority, with a troika on the next level below him: Frank Walker, who had the knack of getting along with almost everyone, headed the Division of Applications and Information, which received and screened proposals for spending. From there the proposals were sent to an Advisory Committee on Allotments, headed by Ickes, which had the responsibility of recommending projects to the President. Hopkins was chief of the Works Progress Division, which had a vague assortment of reporting and advisory functions. But Roosevelt had also included a little-noticed clause in his executive order that permitted Hopkins to "recommend and carry on small useful projects designed to ensure a maximum of employment in all localities." Hopkins saw his opportunity and took it. Almost immediately, he altered the name of his division to the Works Progress Administration† and used this seeming afterthought to spend, eventually, nearly $10 billion on WPA projects. Ickes was furious at being outmaneuvered, and the feud that developed between the two men was the longest and lustiest of the New Deal.

A standard cartoon figure of the thirties is the WPA worker leaning

† The name was changed to Work Projects Administration in 1939.

on his shovel. There were charges that many WPA projects were of dubious utility or had been chosen primarily for political reasons and that the agency was a vehicle for reelecting Democrats. The WPA was vulnerable to these charges, but the essential fact remains that it was the largest and most successful relief operation in American history. Millions of people who had previously relied entirely on handouts were provided with a source of income and respect. Talents and skills were preserved until better times arrived. From the summer of 1935 to the end of WPA, in 1941, about 8 million people were on the payroll—about 20 percent of the labor force. The average number of people on the monthly payroll was about 2.1 million, with the peak of 3.2 million reached in November 1938. New highways, airfields (among them New York's La Guardia Airport), playgrounds, schools, and hospitals were built by the WPA, and there were restoration projects that included the rebuilding of Charleston's historic Dock Street Theatre. WPA workers transcribed millions of pages into Braille, taught illiterates to read, served hot lunches to schoolchildren, established dental and medical clinics, and even operated the municipal functions of the bankrupt town of Key West.

Perhaps the most striking feature of the WPA was the inclusion of unemployed writers, actors, and artists. Roosevelt had little understanding of art—in fact, his favorite paintings were those of ships and he judged these by the accuracy of their rigging—but he went along with the idea of including artists in federal relief programs. "Why not?" he said. "They are human beings. They have to live." Thousands of post offices, public buildings, and schools were adorned with murals and other paintings produced by the Federal Arts Project. Many of the artists were mediocre, but Ben Shahn, Willem de Kooning, Jackson Pollock, Aaron Bohrod, and Stuart Davis were among those employed by the WPA at the standard weekly wage of $23.86. The Federal Theatre Project, which produced work of unusually high quality, brought live theater to towns that had never before seen a professional company, and in four years some 30 million people saw productions ranging from Shakespeare through works in Spanish and in Yiddish to those with all-black casts. The Federal Writers' Project, which employed six thousand writers, turned out a variety of nonfiction works, of which the guides to each state and territory attracted the attention of commercial publishers. Some are still in print. Richard Wright, Nelson Algren, and John Cheever were among the new writers who got their start on the project.

The National Youth Administration did for young people what the WPA accomplished for their elders. Nearly a third of the unemployed were in the sixteen-to-twenty-four age bracket, but the Civilian Conservation Corps offered an escape from idleness for only about three hundred thousand youths each year. While it provided some job training, there was no formal education, and the program was closed to girls. The NYA, directed by Aubrey Williams, Hopkins' chief deputy and a preacher turned social worker, created part-time jobs in colleges and schools that helped students complete their education and kept them out of the labor market.‡ These jobs included work as clerks and typists, as assistants in libraries and laboratories, and in campus maintenance. Pay was not high —six dollars a month for high school students, up to twenty dollars a month for college students, and thirty dollars for graduate students—but to many it meant the difference between staying in school and dropping out. Between 1935 and the outbreak of World War II, about 1.5 million young men and women were employed by the NYA.

Although the WPA and its offspring represented the first overt acceptance of the Keynesian doctrine of "pump-priming" to stimulate recovery, it did not go far enough. Roosevelt and his advisers were too conservative to bring themselves to accept deficit spending of the magnitude required to end the depression, so recovery had to wait for the threat of war and a booming armaments program. Nevertheless, the WPA made a lasting contribution to American life.

Passage of the Emergency Relief Appropriations Act was one of Roosevelt's few successes in the otherwise dreary opening months of the congressional session. Despite the overwhelming Democratic victory the previous November, there were wide cleavages in party ranks. Some members were more radical than the President, while others were more conservative. The sizable Democratic majority made members resistant to discipline, and the White House patronage cupboard was now almost bare. The Democratic majority was, in fact, a statistical myth, according to Nevada's Senator Key Pittman.

The various groups at large on Capitol Hill wasted no time in showing the President their independence. Shortly after the session began, Roosevelt proposed that the Senate approve American adherence to the World Court, a step for which there had been considerable sentiment since 1923. Although a warm supporter of the domestic New Deal, Senator Hiram Johnson, a progressive Republican from California, mobilized the isolationist opposition against any involvement in European affairs, and Huey Long, Father Coughlin, and the Hearst press joined in. Johnson warned that as soon as the Court rendered "advisory opinions in which the United States is interested, the whole fabric we have built up since we were a nation goes crumbling to the ground." The opponents

‡ The NYA was also a springboard for a new generation of political leaders, with Lyndon B. Johnson serving as its director in Texas.

were assisted by the charges leveled by a senate committee headed by Senator Gerald Nye of North Dakota that the bankers and arms manufacturers were behind the nation's entry into World War I.

Thousands of telegrams and letters poured in upon the Senate protesting any involvement in another war that would benefit only the bankers and "merchants of death." Not even the acceptance by Roosevelt of an amendment reiterating America's traditional policy of noninvolvement in the affairs of other nations was able to stem the tide. Despite presidential pressures, the Senate fell seven votes short of the two-thirds majority required to approve the resolution. Roosevelt angrily denounced the opponents as "willing to see a city burn down just so long as their own houses remain standing in the ruins." This defeat marked a turning point in American foreign relations, for the World Court fight had stirred the sleeping isolationist giant.

Taking the bit in its teeth, Congress galloped off in its own direction, leaving Roosevelt's priority items gathering dust on the legislative shelf. By May, only the emergency relief bill had been passed, and the New York *Times* observed that Roosevelt's program had been "thrown into a state of confusion bordering on chaos." The President himself was "distinctly dispirited," according to Ickes. "I have never seen him in quite such a state of mind. He looked tired and he seemed to lack fighting vigor or the buoyancy that has always characterized him." Roosevelt even failed to support a bill introduced by Senator Robert Wagner to establish a National Labor Relations Board, designed to preserve the prolabor provisions of the NRA, including the right of workers to bargain collectively.

To friends, he indicated, however, that he was giving the country a breathing space, and a fresh burst of decisive action was waiting in the wings. When Long, Coughlin, and Hugh Johnson engaged in a no-holds-barred radio debate in March, he wrote Colonel House, ". . . it is vastly better to have this free sideshow presented to the public at this time than later on when the main performance starts!" And he told Ray Stannard Baker, Woodrow Wilson's biographer, that "people tire of seeing the same name day after day in the important headlines of the papers and the same voice night after night over the radio. For example, if since last November I had tried to keep up the pace of 1933 and 1934, the inevitable histrionics of the new actors, Long and Coughlin and Johnson, would have turned the eyes of the audience away from the main drama itself. . . . I am inclined to think . . . that the time is soon at hand for a new stimulation of united American action."

And then came the Second Hundred Days.

Early in May 1935, Roosevelt's attempts to court business ended in failure when the U. S. Chamber of Commerce rejected his outstretched hand with a blistering denunciation of the New Deal by speaker after speaker at its national convention. Failing to understand that Roosevelt's objective was to salvage the ailing capitalist system, businessmen reacted blindly to his left-of-center rhetoric, rather than paying attention to his deeds. The President was deeply wounded. "The interesting thing to me is that in all of these speeches made, I don't believe there was a single speech which took the human side, the old age side, the unemployed side," he told Thomas J. Watson, of International Business Machines, who had dissociated himself from the attack. The rich may have believed Roosevelt was "a traitor to his class," but, as Richard Hofstadter has pointed out, he felt justified in believing they had betrayed him, instead.

A few weeks later, on May 27, a date that became known to New Dealers as Black Monday, the Supreme Court declared the NRA and two other pieces of legislation unconstitutional, in unanimous, 9–0 decisions. In the so-called "Schechter sick chicken" case,* the Court ruled that in approving the National Industrial Recovery Act, Congress had exeeded its authority by empowering the President to establish codes for enterprises only marginally connected with interstate commerce. "Extraordinary conditions do not create or enlarge constitutional powers," the Court said in brushing aside the government's attempt to use the economic emergency to justify its actions.

Fear of such a ruling had haunted New Dealers throughout the two years it had taken for the most significant legislation of the Hundred Days to percolate its way up to review by the Supreme Court. Four of the justices—Pierce Butler, James McReynolds, Willis Van Devanter, and George Sutherland—were known as the "Four Horsemen" of arch-conservatism. Chief Justice Charles Evans Hughes and Justice Owen J. Roberts were "swing men," with Hughes being regarded as the more liberal of the two. Louis D. Brandeis, Benjamin N. Cardozo, and Harlan Fiske Stone constituted the Court's liberal wing. But the liberals, particularly Brandeis, who opposed the weakening of the antitrust laws by the NRA, were increasingly disenchanted with the concentration of power in the hands of the federal government.† The decision in the *Schechter* case made it

---

* The formal name of the case was *Schechter Poultry Corporation* v. *U.S.* It originated in 1934, when the Schechter brothers, operators of a Brooklyn poultry business, were convicted of violating the NRA's Live Poultry Code by selling diseased chickens and of disregarding the code's wage-and-hour provisions. The legal battle cost the firm sixty thousand dollars, and Joseph Schechter said he would have gone to jail if he had known this at the start of the action. Nevertheless, in 1936, he announced that he and his brothers were supporting Roosevelt for reelection.

† In April 1934, Brandeis passed the word to Tugwell that he was "declaring war" on the New Deal. Adolf Berle also informed FDR that Brandeis had told him that he "had gone along with [New Deal] legislation up to now, but that unless he could see some reversal of the big business trend, he was disposed to hold the

abundantly clear that the anxiety of the New Dealers had not been misplaced.

The Administration was thrown into disarray, and everyone waited for the President's reaction. Uncharacteristically, he remained silent. Although Roosevelt believed in the principle of the NRA and later made several attempts to reestablish a variant, there are indications that privately he was convinced that it had outlived its usefulness in its present form. "You know the whole thing is a mess," he told Frances Perkins. "We have got the best out of it anyhow." Nevertheless, he was vitally concerned about the implications of the decision for other New Deal legislation. Four days after the ruling had been handed down, he broke his silence by summoning reporters to a press conference. As his wife sat nearby, quietly knitting away on a blue sock, Roosevelt figuratively thumbed his nose at the Supreme Court. Calling the ruling the most important since the *Dred Scott* case, which had helped bring on the Civil War, he declared that the justices had turned the Constitution back to "the horse and buggy days."

Under the goad of the judicial setbacks of Black Monday, business rejection of his offer of cooperation, mounting pressures from progressives, and ominous threats from the demagogues, Roosevelt's five months of indecision and vacillation ended with a dramatic flourish. Congressional leaders were summoned to the White House and handed a list of "must" legislation. Thumping his desk for emphasis, the President insisted that Congress remain in session throughout the summer, if necessary, to pass it. Roosevelt demanded enactment of the social-security, banking, and public-utility holding-company bills, to which he added the Wagner labor bill and a stiff tax bill designed to redistribute wealth and to steal Huey Long's thunder. Leaving a stunned Congress in his wake, he cheerily departed for the Harvard-Yale boat races. "Everyone could see," said *Time*, "that the winter of his discontent had ended."

Senator Wagner's labor-relations bill was the first to benefit from Roosevelt's renewed presidential leadership. By backing the bill, Roosevelt strengthened the provisions of Section 7(a) of the NRA, which put the government stamp of approval on labor's right to organize and bargain collectively and ensured labor support for his campaign for reelection in 1936. With his support, the bill, which had already passed the Senate despite strong opposition, sailed through the House and was signed with much enthusiasm on July 5, 1935. The National Labor Relations Act,

government control legislation unconstitutional from now on." Roosevelt refused to be bullied by such pressure and replied that he expected to soon have "a good long chat" with "our friend on the highest court." There is no record, however, of such a meeting or exchange of views having taken place. Bruce Allen Murphy, *The Brandeis-Frankfurter Connection* (New York: Oxford University Press, 1982), pp. 140–41.

popularly known as the Wagner Act, is regarded as organized labor's Magna Carta and was one of the most important pieces of labor legislation in American history. The National Labor Relations Board, which was established by the law, conducted elections when workers wanted to choose which union to represent them, and forbade employers to discriminate against them because of union activity or refuse to bargain collectively. In return, organized labor, ending its traditional political impartiality, became an annex of the New Deal.

Social security was next. The United States was the only industrial nation in the world without national old-age and unemployment insurance, although some states had inadequate programs. Men and women who had reached old age without financial resources had to depend on their children, private charity, or public almshouses for support. Roosevelt had promised Miss Perkins to do something about social insurance when she became Secretary of Labor, but it had been shunted aside in the effort to meet the emergency. In mid-1934, he was faced with a choice between pressing forward on the problem or chancing the danger that something like the Townsend plan might be enacted by Congress. He announced a commitment to such legislation and appointed a cabinet-level Committee on Economic Security to work its way through the complex technical, legal, and actuarial problems.

> You want to make it simple—very simple, so simple that everyone will understand it [Roosevelt told Miss Perkins]. And what's more, there is no reason why everybody in the United States should not be covered. I see no reason why every child, from the day he is born, shouldn't be a member of the social security system. . . . This system ought to be operated through the post offices. Just simple and natural—nothing elaborate or alarming about it. . . . And there is no reason why just industrial workers should get the benefit of this. Everybody ought to be in on it—the farmer and his wife and family. . . . I don't see why not. Cradle to the grave—from the cradle to the grave they ought to be in a social insurance system.

The program that was introduced in both houses of Congress the following January was a blend of many conflicting ideas and less sweeping than the universal system Roosevelt had envisioned. "I felt sure that the political climate was not right for such a universal approach," said Miss Perkins. Rather than providing an income equal to the needs of the retired, it was designed to provide only a partial replacement for earnings and was to be supplemented by savings and private pensions. Unemployment insurance under joint control of Washington and the states, old-age and survivors pensions under federal control and financed by contributions from the current earnings of workers, and federal grants to the states for aid to the blind and to dependent children were included, but compulsory national health insurance, a feature of European plans, was dropped for pragmatic reasons. The political power of the American Medical Association was strong, and Roosevelt believed that to stir its resistance would endanger the entire package.

Reaction to the bill was generally favorable, but conservatives tried to ambush it in the legislative thickets. Conservatives attacked social security as a violation of the traditional American values of thrift, initiative, and self-help. They claimed every American would have to submit to the indignity of wearing a dogtag bearing his social security number. They charged social security was a case of robbing a thrifty Peter to pay an improvident Paul. "We might as well take a child from the nursery, give him a nurse, and protect him from every experience that life affords," charged Senator A. Harry Moore of New Jersey. Dr. Townsend's followers attacked the proposed benefits as inadequate when compared to the two hundred dollars a month promised by their plan.

In fact, fear that delay might result in approval of more radical demands made the modest administration proposals more palatable and hastened the eventual approval of social security on August 14, 1935. Only about half the work force of some 48 million Americans were eligible for unemployment insurance, and benefits paid the aged were parsimonious, but social security became the most enduring of New Deal reforms. For the first time, the government recognized that it had a duty to protect the social rights of its citizens, and social security was a milestone in the process of grafting a welfare state upon a capitalist foundation.

In sending off his 1935 tax message to Congress, Roosevelt had gleefully told Raymond Moley that Pat Harrison, the conservative chairman of the tax-writing Senate Finance Committee, was "going to have kittens on the spot." Among the most spectacular and controversial of the President's legislative proposals, the tax bill was the first New Deal measure intended to reach directly into the pockets of the wealthy and the large corporations. Roosevelt asked for an inheritance tax, a gift tax to prevent evasion of the inheritance tax, increased individual taxes, and corporate levies scaled to the size of the enterprise. The latter was a response to the refusal of business to cooperate with the New Deal and to the urging of the Brandeisians for an attack on industrial bigness. "Our revenue laws have operated in many ways to the unfair advantage of the few, and they have done little to prevent an unjust concentration of wealth and economic power," Roosevelt declared. Throughout the reading of the President's message in the Senate, Huey Long chortled and at its end piped up with an "Amen."

Roosevelt's tax proposal touched off a whirlwind of protest. From his lordly retreat at San Simeon, William Randolph Hearst ordered his editors to refer to it in their columns as the "Soak the Successful Act" and to call the New Deal the "Raw Deal." Opponents denounced the bill as "un-American," "socialistic," and "a plain, shameless effort to purchase votes" in the 1936 election. J. P. Morgan's family kept newspapers with pictures of the President out of his sight, and in one Connecticut country club, mention of his name was forbidden—to prevent apoplexy. In reality, the tax bill was a fairly mild measure that neither raised revenue nor redistributed wealth, for it closed only a few loopholes and would bring in but $250 million a year—even in 1935 barely enough to run the government for ten days. Before it was passed, on August 15, the corporate tax rate was reduced to insignificance and the inheritance tax was dropped altogether. Nevertheless, Roosevelt had made clear his intention to use taxation as a weapon for social change, and the tax fight marked the real beginning of big-business resentment of the New Deal and "that man in the White House."

None of the President's proposed legislation stirred as much opposition as the Public Utility Holding Company Act. A tribute to Brandeis' argument that the government should exorcise the "curse of bigness" from the utility industry, it marked a departure from the early New Deal philosophy of regulating monopoly, and a return to trust-busting. But Roosevelt needed no proselytizing by the Brandeisians. As governor of New York, he had shared the public outrage at the giant holding companies that pyramided electric utilities, charged exorbitant rates, seized water-power sites, and were often financed by worthless stock issues. Several proposals had been drafted for breaking up the holding companies that dominated the industry, but the President was persuaded to consider the most moderate, drawn up by Ben Cohen and Tom Corcoran. Before he would accept it, however, Roosevelt wanted it to "breathe fire," and the "Gold Dust Twins" added the so-called "death sentence" clause, which would, after January 1, 1940, empower the Securities and Exchange Commission to dissolve any public-utility holding company that could not justify its existence.

Moley reports that no one really expected the death sentence to survive a congressional challenge, that the President originally intended it as a bargaining chip. But Roosevelt became a victim of his own strategy. The utility companies launched a massive lobbying campaign against the bill—particularly against the death-sentence clause—and the Administration was forced into an all-or-nothing struggle. Swarms of lobbyists descended on Capitol Hill, and one newsman calculated they outnumbered the members of Congress. They charged that the proposal was a stalking-horse for a plan to nationalize all public utilities and an attack on their stockholders, who seemed to be composed solely of widows and orphans. The New York Stock Exchange leased a mansion as its headquarters for the fight that was promptly dubbed the "Wall Street Embassy," and there was a whispering campaign that Roosevelt was insane. Later inquiries revealed that the utilities spent well over a million dollars to combat the bill and that a significant portion of the flood of telegrams and letters that poured in upon Washington were fraudulent.

Fictitious or not, the campaign was extremely effective. The Senate beat back an attempt to eliminate the death sentence by only a single vote, and the struggle to preserve it in the House was intense. This battle focused attention on Cohen and Corcoran, who were in and out of the White House day and night as they reported to Roosevelt on the efforts to put the heat on the lawmakers. The two young Harvard Law School graduates complemented each other. Cohen, from Muncie, Indiana, was shy and studious, a former law clerk to Brandeis and a resourceful and precise legal draftsman. Corcoran, "Tommy the Cork" to Roosevelt, was brash and effervescent, an accordionist and singer of Irish ballads. He had come from a Rhode Island mill town to clerk for Justice Holmes, and his court jester's manner masked an ability to manipulate men and policy. Cohen and Corcoran shared a house on Georgetown's R Street that became known as the "little red house"—a play on the "little green house on K Street," which had been the scene of Harding-era revels.

The House of Representatives, usually more inclined to give the President what he wanted than the Senate, showed surprising resistance in the case of the utility holding-company bill. House members, elected every two years, may have feared the retribution of the utilities more than that of the White House. "You talk about a labor lobby," fumed Roosevelt. "It is a child compared to this utility lobby. You talk about a Legion lobby. Well it is an infant in arms compared to this utility lobby."

The principal difference between the bill overwhelmingly approved by the House and eventually by Congress as a whole, and the Senate version, was that the burden of proof lay with the SEC, rather than with the holding company fighting dissolution. Holding companies were required to register with the Commission, and that agency supervised all financial transactions and stock issues. Although many Wall Street lawyers advised their clients to refuse to register with the SEC, the Supreme Court soon upheld the validity of the law. All in all, it was a triumph for the New Deal, rather than a setback, despite the compromise on the death sentence. Most of the great utility empires were broken up within three years, and the Brandeisians regarded the law as a significant victory over bigness. "F.D. gives evidence of appreciation of the 'irrepressible conflict with bigness'—and of growing firmness," Brandeis himself noted with approval.

The Banking Act of 1935 was the final major accomplishment of the Second Hundred Days. The first reform of the Federal Reserve system since 1913, it was the work of Marriner S. Eccles, a nonconformist Utah banker who had been appointed governor of the Federal Reserve Board by Roosevelt. Eccles held views that paralleled those of Keynes—without having heard of the English economist—and believed that prosperity could be achieved and maintained by adjusting the supply of money to fluctuations in the business cycle. To achieve this goal, Eccles sought to remove Wall Street and the private bankers from control of the nation's financial structure and to centralize authority over discount rates and reserve requirements in Washington. The Banking Act was greatly modified as it moved through the legislative process, but it was a precedent-breaking step forward in establishing governmental control over currency and credit. Roosevelt's "must" list was topped off by legislation creating the Rural Electrification Administration, which revolutionized American farm life, and several measures that salvaged provisions of the NRA that had been scuttled by the Supreme Court.

One of the most productive—and grueling—congressional sessions in American history finally ended early in the morning of August 27. Even Roosevelt was weary. "I was so tired," he told Henry Morgenthau, "that I would have enjoyed seeing you cry or would have gotten pleasure out of sticking pins in people and hurting them." New Dealers called it a session of "memorable achievement"; opponents branded it as a time of "ill-advised and extravagant legislation." Few sessions had produced so much legislation of permanent importance: social security, work relief, government guarantees for labor organization and collective bargaining, and tax, banking, and utility holding-company reform. And unlike the accomplishments of the First Hundred Days, those of the second survived the scrutiny of a conservative Supreme Court.

The nation needed "a breathing spell" to absorb the rash of new legislation, said Roy Howard, of the Scripps-Howard newspaper chain, and Roosevelt met the appeal in a spirit of conciliation. "This Administration came into power pledged to a very considerable legislative program," he replied. "This basic program, however, has now reached substantial completion and the 'breathing spell' of which you speak is here—very decidedly so." As if to underscore the message, he left Washington on a transcontinental train trip with a stop along the way to dedicate Boulder (now Hoover) Dam and to be received by "a million eager people" in Los Angeles. With Ickes and Hopkins in tow, he boarded the *Houston* for a leisurely cruise south, returning through the Panama Canal to Charleston.

Faced with the amorphous body of legislation that emerged from the Second Hundred Days, Americans tried to search out a pattern in it. Had there been a significant change in Roosevelt's philosophy during this turbulent period? And if so, where was the President going? Roosevelt's contemporaries saw a shift toward radicalism, nothing less than the creation of a second New Deal. The President, according to this analysis, had leaned over backward to appease business during the First New Deal. Prices were raised, steps were taken to regularize economic activity, and the National Industrial Recovery Act was the key measure of the era. By 1935, Roosevelt had despaired of winning such support and, shifting his base, mounted an all-out attack on business. Measures aimed at punishing business and helping the disadvantaged—such as social security, the National Labor Relations Act, and the Utilities Act—became the legislative hallmarks of the Second New Deal.

More-recent observers, while agreeing that the summer of 1935 was indeed a watershed, have viewed the Second New Deal as a turn toward conservatism. Arthur Schlesinger, Jr., the most eloquent advocate of this thesis, suggests, in *The Politics of Upheaval*, that Roosevelt abandoned his concern with economic and social planning and adopted the restoration of competition as the principal vehicle for regulating the economy. Such planners as Rex Tugwell were expelled from the charmed circle around the President, and neo-progressive Brandeisians like Felix Frankfurter now had his ear. "The First New Deal characteristically told business what it must do," says Schlesinger. "The Second New Deal characteristically told business what it must *not* do."

While laudable in its attempt to impose some sense of structure on the prolix and often contradictory story of the New Deal, this reading of history is misleading. For one thing, a planned economy had not existed during the First New Deal—as Tugwell was the first to acknowledge. The gap between the legislation of 1933 and 1935 is not as wide as it appeared, because such measures as social security, public-utility regulation, and progressive taxation had long been under consideration. The President "is looking forward to a time in the near future when the Government will put into operation a system of old-age, unemployment, maternity, and other forms of social insurance," Ickes noted as early as April 1934. And as Elliot Rosen has pointed out,‡ many of the measures approved during the legislative surge of 1935 were rooted in the Moley memorandum of May 1932. Even more important, Roosevelt himself resisted all efforts to saddle him with any form of ideological orthodoxy. "I always hate the frame of mind which talks about 'your group' and 'my group' among liberals," he told a friend. "Brandeis is one thousand per cent right in principle but in certain fields there must be a guiding or restraining hand of Government."

‡ *Hoover, Roosevelt, and the Brains Trust* (New York: Columbia University Press, 1977), pp. 115–23.

Roosevelt returned from the cruise of the *Houston* refreshed, as always from an ocean voyage. Dr. Foster Kennedy, one of the physicians who had examined him in 1931, came by the White House to look him over again and found him in better shape than before. "Nothing seems able to kill you," laughed Kennedy. "We will have to take you out in the yard and shoot you like an old horse."

"Oh, no, you can't do that!" protested the President, pointing to the guards. "Too many of those fellows out there watching." Turning serious, he asked, "Really, Doctor, do you think this carcass of mine will stand the racket a while longer?"

"Yes, it will," replied Kennedy. "But I have a lot of high-flown Wall Street friends who are quite sure that the country cannot."

The "long, cool swig of political quiescence" promised in the wake of the Second Hundred Days did not survive the approach of the 1936 presidential election. Radicals grumbled about Roosevelt's offer of the olive branch to business as "a sell-out," while conservatives regarded it as a sign of weakness. Encouraged by Republican victories in the New York Assembly and in a traditionally Democratic Rhode Island congressional district, they saw the tide running against the New Deal. Liberty Leaguers such as Al Smith threatened to "take a walk" out of the Democratic party if Roosevelt was renominated. "It's all right with me if they want to disguise themselves as Karl Marx or Lenin or any of that bunch," the one-time Happy Warrior declared, "but I can't stand for allowing them to march under the banner of Jackson or Cleveland." Lorena Hickok told Hopkins that the failure of the WPA to quickly put people to work and the politicization of relief in some states would cost Roosevelt votes. "I should say that the President's situation in Ohio is damned serious," she said. "I don't see how he can carry Ohio if things go on as they are." And in mid-January 1936, the highly regarded *Literary Digest* poll reported 67.9 percent of those polled were anti-Roosevelt.

Even so, the President was optimistic. "We will win easily next year," he told a cabinet meeting, "but we are going to make it a crusade." Roosevelt opened his reelection campaign with his State of the Union address, on January 3, 1936. To obtain maximum exposure, he addressed a joint night session of Congress, the first since April 1917, when Woodrow Wilson had sought a declaration of war against Germany. Roosevelt also proclaimed a state of war—not against a foreign enemy but against "powerful minorities" and "discredited special interests" at home. "We have invited battle," he declared, and "we have earned the hatred of entrenched greed." Yet these fighting words were not accompanied by a demand for further reforms. Trying to avoid stirring further discontent,

Roosevelt emphasized his commitment to a balanced budget by slashing appropriations.

But he had reckoned without the Supreme Court. On January 6, the justices, newly enthroned in a white marble temple across from the Capitol,* plowed under the Agricultural Adjustment Act with a 6–3 vote. The court held that the Congress had no authority to impose the processing tax that was the heart of the measure and ordered the restitution of about $200 million that had been collected. It held, in effect, that neither the federal government nor the states could regulate intrastate commerce—and nothing could be done to mitigate the economic crisis. Sharply dissenting for himself and Brandeis and Cardozo, Justice Stone called this "a tortured construction of the Constitution" that would forestall efforts of other branches of the government to operate effectively.

Roosevelt was meeting with George Dern, the Secretary of War, when an aide brought in the bad news on a slip of paper and laid it before the President. "He just held the sheet of paper in front of him and smiled," Dern later told newsmen. There was no attack on "horse and buggy" justice this time; the President appeared to be biding his time. "It is plain to see . . . ," said Ickes following a cabinet meeting, "that he is not at all averse to the Supreme Court declaring one New Deal statute after another unconstitutional. I think he believes that the Court will find itself pretty far out on a limb before it is through with it and that a real issue will be joined on which we can go to the country."

If this was Roosevelt's strategy, he was successful. The court, in its determination to block the intervention of the executive and legislative branches of the government into the economic and social sphere, scuttled other pieces of New Deal legislation in quick succession, usually on 5–4 votes. Legislation creating a pension system for railroad workers and establishing minimum wages and maximum hours in the coal industry, and a New York State minimum wage law for women were invalidated. If the conservatives continued to have their way, administration supporters said, the court was certain to rule against the Wagner Act, social security, and all the other achievements of the New Deal.

The AAA decision, with its order for restitution of the funds collected by the processing tax and a $2 billion veterans' bonus enacted by Congress over Roosevelt's rather perfunctory veto, played havoc with his plan to balance the budget. New revenue was needed, but as it was impossible to raise income taxes in an election year the President proposed a

---

* The Supreme Court had met in the Old Senate Chamber, on the ground floor of the Capitol, before moving to the new building. It was constructed on the site of the Old Capitol Prison, once a slave market, and where prisoners were held during the Civil War without resort to *habeas corpus*.

levy on undistributed corporate profits. Congress watered it down, but the struggle further fanned business antagonism to the New Deal.

Having anticipated the Supreme Court's action, Henry Wallace produced the Soil Conservation and Domestic Allotment Act as a replacement for the AAA. Farmers were paid to remove land from production that was endangered by erosion and to sow nondepleting crops such as clover and soybeans. These payments were made from regular appropriations, rather than by a processing tax, to avoid conflict with the Supreme Court decision. The second Agricultural Adjustment Act, enacted two years later, embodied many of the features of its predecessor as well as the "ever-normal granary" designed by Wallace to establish a reservoir of surplus in good years for use in bad. Parity payments were set at the prosperous level of 1909–14 agricultural prices, and government protection of farm income became an irrevocable part of the American way of life.

"There's one issue in this campaign," Roosevelt told Moley. "It's myself, and people must be either for me or against me." The President was eager, as always, to be off on the campaign trail, but 1936 was to be different. For the first time in a quarter century in politics, he was without the services of Louis Howe. From the day he had entered the White House, Howe's health had deteriorated, and by early 1935, he was forced to spend most of his time in his room, which was heavy with the smell of incense and cigarette smoke. Eyes more sunken, face more wrinkled, breathing more labored, Howe was wracked by nightlong fits of coughing that taxed his heart. He lived on a diet of Cream of Wheat and coffee but was as pugnacious and irascible as ever. By mid-August, however, the problem of caring for him in the White House had become too difficult, and he was persuaded to enter the Naval Hospital, in suburban Bethesda.

Refusing to be cut off from planning the forthcoming campaign, Howe insisted on a direct telephone line from his bedside to the White House. He grew a scraggly beard that gave him a piratical look and spent hours chatting with young medical corpsmen. Eleanor visited him every day she was in Washington, while the President came out every week or so and they laughed and joked together as before. The little man said he intended to go to New York to take charge of campaign organization even if he had to operate from a bed in the Biltmore Hotel. He planned a Good Neighbor League to play up Roosevelt's sympathy for racial and religious minorities and urged more-intensive use of radio.

In reflective moments, he confided to friends his concern about who would bridle Roosevelt's enthusiasms after he was gone. "Hold Franklin down" were his last words to Vice-President Garner. One day, not long before he died on April 18, 1936, Howe spoke wistfully to John Keller, a young man who had been hired to read to him, of the autumn campaign and how much he would like to be there. "But you will be," Keller assured him. "They can't run it without you."

"No, I shall not be there," Howe replied. "Franklin's on his own now."

"If Roosevelt can be beaten, he can be beaten by a Chinaman," Henry Mencken proclaimed early in 1936.† Roosevelt himself hoped that Herbert Hoover would be his opponent, for it would provide the electorate with a clear alternative. But the Republicans, after gazing longingly at the ex-President during their convention in Cleveland in early June, sadly recognized that his name was too closely associated with disaster, and nominated Governor Alfred M. Landon of Kansas on the first ballot. A Middle Westerner, it was hoped that he would appeal to farmers and to mobilize the growing conservative reaction against Roosevelt.

Alf Landon was described as the "Kansas Coolidge," but he deserved better than that. The only Republican governor elected in 1932 to survive the Democratic landslide two years later, he could boast of a balanced budget in his state. He had made money as an independent oil producer and was flexible and far more liberal than the party that nominated him. Like his vice-presidential running mate, Colonel Frank Knox, publisher of the Chicago *Daily News*,‡ he was an old Bull Mooser, but unlike Knox, he did not see the New Deal as a plot to subvert American institutions. In fact, he had endorsed several New Deal programs—a fact that was to haunt him throughout the campaign. With his pallid delivery and bland manner, Landon had little personal magnetism, but the Republican leaders regarded this as an asset if the voters had wearied of Roosevelt's ever-present smile and transparent slickness. Following one speech by the GOP standard-bearer, Ickes caustically observed: "If that is the best that Landon can do, the Democratic campaign committee ought to spend all the money it can to send him out to make speeches."

Two weeks later, the Democrats gathered in Philadelphia for a convention that was more like a coronation. Despite an attempt by Al Smith to persuade the delegates to put Roosevelt aside for "some genuine Democrat," Roosevelt and Garner were renominated by acclamation. Pulling the strings from the White House, the President forced through a resolution ending the party's century-long bondage to the two-thirds rule. Fittingly, Bennett Champ Clark, whose father had fallen afoul of it in

† Mencken was chagrined to find himself misquoted as saying, "Even a Chinaman could beat Roosevelt"—a statement with the opposite meaning of his actual one, and it cost him considerable prestige as a political soothsayer following the election.
‡ Knox had charged up San Juan Hill as one of Teddy Roosevelt's Rough Riders and proudly exhibited the hat he had worn that day, with two bullet holes through the crown.

1912, had the pleasure of moving the adoption of the majority rule. Southerners were placated by Jim Farley with the promise of additional delegates, but the move helped accelerate urban influence in the Democratic party at the expense of the South.

The platform was also drafted in the White House, primarily by Sam Rosenman and Stanley High, one-time editor of the *Christian Herald*, who had been brought in to counter criticism that Roosevelt was surrounded by Jews and Catholics. Basically, it praised the accomplishments of the New Deal and pledged continuous effort to improve opportunities for all Americans. The volatile Supreme Court issue was fudged by stating that if the Constitution and the court inhibited efforts to take such action, a "clarifying amendment" would be sought.

Rain had been falling steadily, but by the time Roosevelt arrived at Franklin Field to give his acceptance speech, on the evening of June 27, the moon had risen. Making his stiff-legged, halting way through the throng behind the platform on the arm of his son Jimmy, the President recognized Edwin Markham in the kaleidoscope of faces that surged about him. He reached out to shake the white-bearded poet's hand but was jostled off balance. Suddenly his right leg brace snapped open and he toppled over, the manuscript of his speech spinning out of his hand and away into the crowd. There was muffled screams and near panic. Mike Reilly, chief of the Secret Service detail, caught Roosevelt just before he fell to the ground and held him up until the brace was snapped back into place.

Fearing that someone might mistake Markham for an assassin in the confusion, Reilly shouted frantically at the startled poet: "Don't move! Don't move!" White-faced and shaken, Roosevelt snapped, "Clean me up!" As his clothes were being brushed off, he remembered his manuscript and warned those about him to keep their feet off "those damned sheets" until they had all been retrieved. "I was the damnedest, maddest white man at that moment you ever saw," he later recalled. "Okay, let's go," he declared when everything was again in order. He started toward the platform, but catching sight of Markham's tearful face, he stopped again and momentarily took the old man's hand in his.

Roosevelt was greeted by a tremendous roar from the one hundred thousand people gathered in the stadium. He wasted little time before setting the tone of the coming campaign, lashing out at the "economic royalists" and "privileged princes" that threatened America's economic democracy. "The royalists of the economic order have conceded that political freedom was the business of Government, but they have maintained that economic slavery was nobody's business. They granted that the Government could do anything to protect the citizen in his right to vote but they denied that Government could do anything to protect the citizen in his right to work and his right to live. . . . These economic royalists complain that we seek to overthrow the institutions of America. What they really complain about is that we seek to take away their power.

"Governments can err," Roosevelt continued. "Presidents do make mistakes, but the immortal Dante tells us that divine justice weighs the sins of the cold-blooded and the sins of the warm-hearted in different scales. Better the occasional faults of a Government that lives in a spirit of charity than the consistent omissions of a Government frozen in the ice of its own indifference. . . . There is a mysterious cycle in human events. To some generations much is given. Of other generations much is expected. This generation of Americans has a rendezvous with destiny."

Roosevelt had the American people on his side in 1936. In Chicago, some one hundred fifty thousand men and women joined an impromptu procession to escort him from the railroad station to the stadium; in Boston, the crowd overflowed the Common and spilled out into the adjoining streets; in New York, people jammed block after block of mid-town Manhattan to cheer him. As he whistle-stopped across Ohio and Iowa and even in Alf Landon's Kansas, jubilant throngs greeted him. They reached out to touch him and waved and shouted thanks for saving a farm or a home, for getting a factory reopened, or for providing a job on the WPA. Even the weather was on Roosevelt's side, for rain began to fall when he visited the drought-parched Middle West. Wherever he went, he ignored Landon, never mentioning him by name, while vigorously attacking Herbert Hoover and the "economic royalists" of the Liberty League. They were the New Deal's enemies—and thus the people's enemies.

"You look happier than you did four years ago!" was his usual greeting from the rear platform of his campaign train. Wherever he went, he compared conditions in 1936 with those in 1932. Thousands of farms and homes had been saved from foreclosure and new jobs created. The economy was on the upsurge. The number of jobless was down by perhaps six million from the worst of the depression. Auto manufacturers were predicting that 1936 would be the best year since 1929. Corporate profits were the highest since the crash, and the Dow-Jones industrial average was 80 percent over its 1932 level. And with a broad grin, he ridiculed the "powerful leaders of industry and banking who came to me in Washington . . . pleading to be saved" from the results of their own follies:

In the summer of 1933, a nice old gentleman wearing a silk hat fell off the end of a pier. He was unable to swim. A friend ran down the pier, dived overboard and pulled him out; but the silk hat floated off with the tide. After the old gentleman had been revived, he was effusive in his thanks. He praised his friend for saving his life. Today, three years later, the old gentleman is berating his friend because the silk hat was lost.

For the most part, Landon waged a moderate campaign, in keeping with his personality. "Wherever I have gone in this country, I have found Americans," he declared. He attacked the New Deal for reckless spending but backed social security in principle and supported farm subsidies while promising to administer these programs more efficiently and equitably. Frank Knox, his running mate, disdained a policy of "me-tooism," however. "We are not in a political campaign," he thundered. "We are in a campaign to save America" from "fanatics, theorists and impractical experimenters." "Be on your guard," he warned one audience. "Silently in the night they are creeping up, seeking to impose upon us, before we realize it, a new and alien kind of government." Roosevelt and Landon met only once during the campaign, at a Midwestern governors' conference in Des Moines.

"Mr. President," said Landon. "You will not remember the first talk with me when you invited me to Washington in 1933—"

"About the water—" replied Roosevelt.

"You remember that?"

"Yes."

"I am amazed you remember."

Roosevelt was also under attack from the extreme right and the extreme left. The Liberty League, membership rolls bristling with the names of industrial and financial barons, mounted a well-financed stream of propaganda that branded the New Deal as both communistic and fascistic. In the South, the League circulated a leaflet displaying a photograph of Mrs. Roosevelt and two blacks along with the caption that the Roosevelts had welcomed blacks to dine and sleep at the White House. Late in the campaign, notes were slipped into the pay envelopes of factory workers denouncing social-security contributions—which were to begin in January 1937—as a pay reduction. The tactic backfired when organized labor redoubled its efforts for Roosevelt. The Liberty League's efforts to influence voters proved to be so inept that the Republican National Committee finally asked it to cease its efforts in Landon's behalf.

Roosevelt strategists were more worried about the "thunder on the left," even though Huey Long had been removed from the scene by an assassin's bullet and blundering doctors in September 1935. Most Louisiana politicos made their peace with the New Deal after tax-fraud investigations were dropped in what cynics called the "Second Louisiana Purchase," but the Reverend Gerald L. K. Smith, the Kingfish's self-anointed successor as head of Share Our Wealth, refused to go along. Once described by Mencken as the "greatest rabble rouser since Peter the Hermit," Smith joined Father Coughlin and Dr. Townsend in organizing the Union party, which fielded William Lemke as its presidential candidate. A nominal Republican, Lemke was a North Dakota congressman and prominent figure in the radical Nonpartisan League who had soured on the New Deal. Coughlin swore to deliver nine million votes to Lemke or to drop his radio crusade, and some Democratic leaders feared the Union party might cut into Roosevelt's support among Irish Catholics.

Even so, the Roosevelt bandwagon picked up speed as Election Day neared. In Pittsburgh, where, four years before, he had made the embarrassing promise to reduce government expenditures, Roosevelt explained that government had the responsibility "to spend money when no one else had money to spend." Such spending would help revive the economy, thereby increasing government receipts and eventually permitting a balanced budget. This was too much for the normally restrained Hoover. "Boo! Boo," he cried as he listened to a broadcast of the speech along with Landon and a group of newsmen.

At Chautauqua, Roosevelt was at his most eloquent, promising, in a major foreign-policy address, to "isolate" America from the threat of war that was rising in Europe and the Far East. "I have seen war," he declared. "I have seen war on land and sea. I have seen blood running from the wounded. I have seen men coughing out their gassed lungs. I have seen the dead in the mud. I have seen cities destroyed. I have seen two hundred limping, exhausted men come out of the line—the survivors of a regiment of one thousand that went forward forty-eight hours before. I have seen children starving. I have seen the agony of mothers and wives. I hate war."

Roosevelt closed out the campaign on the evening of October 31 with an impassioned speech at Madison Square Garden in which he repeatedly brought the cheering crowd to its feet:

> For twelve years this Nation was afflicted with hear-nothing, see-nothing, do-nothing Government. The Nation looked to the Government but the Government looked away. Nine mocking years with the golden calf and three long years of the scourge! Nine crazy years at the ticker and three long years in the breadlines! Nine mad years of mirage and three long years of despair! Powerful influences strive today to restore that kind of government with its doctrine that Government is best which is most indifferent.
>
> For nearly four years you have had an Administration which instead of twirling its thumbs has rolled up its sleeves. We will keep our sleeves rolled up.

Once again, his tone growing steely, he called the roll of his "old enemies"—"business and financial monopoly, speculation, reckless banking, class antagonism, sectionalism and war profiteering"—those who had long regarded the government of the United States as their fiefdom. "Never before in all our history have these forces been so united against any one candidate as they stand today. They are unanimous in their hatred for me—and I welcome their hatred.

"I would like to have it said of my first Administration that in it the forces of selfishness and lust for power met their match." The audience was on its feet and the Garden was in pandemonium. "I should like to have it said—" but his words were engulfed in a bedlam of cheers, bells, and horns.

"Wait a moment!" cried the President. "I should like to have it said of my second Administration that in it these forces met their master!"

On Election Eve, Roosevelt received Jim Farley's traditional forecast. "After looking them over carefully and discounting everything that has been given in these reports," he wrote, "I am still definitely of the opinion that you will carry every state but two—Maine and Vermont." Eyebrows rose, for even though most experts foresaw a Democratic win, the *Literary Digest* poll predicted that Landon would carry 32 states, with 370 electoral votes, against only 16 states, with 161 electoral votes for Roosevelt.* For a brief moment after reading the *Digest* poll, Landon toyed with the idea that he might win—even considering whom he might have in his Cabinet—but he quickly dismissed it as a delusion.

Family and friends joined Roosevelt at Hyde Park, where he received the election returns, rather than going to Democratic headquarters in New York City. Buoyant and optimistic, the President joined them for a buffet supper in the library. As soon as the returns started to come in, he retired to the dining room, where Associated Press and United Press tickers had been set up, and became engrossed in tallying the figures on a large chart. Periodically, he was in touch with Democratic headquarters by specially installed telephone. From the very beginning, it was obvious that a landslide was in the making. Told that he had carried staunchly Republican New Haven by fifteen thousand votes, Roosevelt refused to believe it and asked someone to check the report. When it proved to be correct, he leaned back in his chair, blew a smoke ring at the ceiling, and exclaimed: "Wow!" One by one, longtime Republican strongholds fell into line: Pennsylvania, Connecticut, and even Landon's Kansas. Not

* The *Literary Digest* poll was so far off because it was based on postcards sent to people whose names appeared in telephone books and on automobile registration lists— hardly a broad sampling of public opinion in 1936. The magazine never recovered from the fiasco and soon suspended publication.

long afterward, he returned to the library, where Tommy Corcoran had unlimbered his accordion and was leading the crowd in song.

Political writers searched for the proper adjective to describe Roosevelt's victory, and most likened it to some irresistible natural force: an avalanche, tornado, tidal wave, or earthquake. As Farley had predicted, he swept every state but Maine and Vermont, creating a caustic new version of the old political saying, "As Maine goes, so goes the nation": "As Maine goes, so goes Vermont." The President won a plurality of nearly 11 million popular votes, the largest yet recorded, and tallied 523 electoral votes to only 8 for Landon, the widest margin since James Monroe's victory in 1820. Roosevelt also carried a top-heavy Democratic majority along with him into Congress. The new House would have 333 Democrats, while the Republican membership was reduced to 103. In the Senate, the Democrats controlled seventy-five seats, so many that when it met in January 1937 it was impossible to squeeze all of them on the Democratic side of the chamber and some had to sit with the Republicans. Lemke garnered only about 882,000 votes—and Father Coughlin announced he was through with politics. Roosevelt had won a smashing victory, and as a New York *Times* writer observed, "If he were to say a kind word for the man-eating shark, people would look thoughtful and say perhaps there are two sides to the question."

The campaign of 1936 saw the birth of a political coalition that dominated American politics for nearly a half century and transformed the Democratic party into a truly national party. Since the Civil War, the Democrats had been a minority, ineffectual except in the Solid South and the cities. The only successful Democratic presidential candidates of the twentieth century had been "accidental" presidents: Wilson, elected in 1912 as a result of a Republican split and Roosevelt himself, who had been propelled into the White House four years before by the Great Depression. In 1936, a significant segment of this strength had remained in the Roosevelt column. Ed Flynn, the Bronx boss who emerged as one of Roosevelt's chief political strategists as Louis Howe faded into his final illness, described the situation to Moley:

> There are two or three million more dedicated Republicans in the United States than there are Democrats. The population, however, is drifting into the urban areas. The election of 1932 was not normal. To remain in power we must attract some millions, perhaps seven, who are hostile or indifferent to both parties. They believe the Republican Party to be controlled by big business and the Democratic Party by the conservative South. These millions are mostly in the cities. They include racial and religious minorities and labor people. We must attract them by radical programs of social and economic reform.

And so Franklin Roosevelt, a man who personified the country squire, who had entered politics as the champion of the farmer and opponent of Tammany, who was essentially a patron of labor, who had nothing against business and disliked cities, became the idol of the dispossessed. Upon the central core of basic Democratic strength in the Solid South and the traditional city political machines, he grafted new elements that were seeking recognition: labor, blacks, the urban masses, academics, and intellectuals. Political bosses such as Frank Hague of Jersey City and Ed Kelly of Chicago found themselves yoked in common cause with such southern Bourbons as Pat Harrison and Joe Robinson; John L. Lewis, of the CIO, and Sidney Hillman, of the garment workers union; Rex Tugwell; and Walter White, of the National Association for the Advancement of Colored People.

Most working men and women had been politically unaffiliated and apathetic until the advent of the New Deal. The NRA, the Wagner Act, and the WPA gave them a stake in the government, and Lewis and Hillman organized Labor's Non-Partisan League to protect it. The organization mobilized support for Roosevelt and contributed about $750,000 to the Democratic campaign chest, offsetting the loss of contributions from business. Labor votes were credited with helping swing Ohio, Illinois, and Indiana to the President, but this victory was probably based less on labor's organizing skills than on the workers' conviction that Roosevelt was their friend. "Mr. Roosevelt is the only man we ever had in the White House who would understand that my boss is a sonofabitch," declared a North Carolina mill worker.

One of the most significant developments of the 1936 election was the dissolution of the traditional black alliance with the Republican party. For the first time since emancipation, blacks voted Democratic. Even in the bleak year of 1932, they had remained loyal to the party of Lincoln, although no segment of American society suffered more painfully from the effects of the depression. The New Deal's relief and work programs were a powerful counterforce that pulled them toward Roosevelt even though his record on civil-rights legislation was weak. For example, Roosevelt denounced lynching but was unwilling to put an antilynching bill introduced by Senator Wagner on his list of "must" legislation. Without his backing, it fell victim to a senate filibuster. He contended that if he angered southern committee chairmen it would endanger vital relief and reform measures. But the President—and especially his wife—made a point of treating blacks without discrimination, and his record of appointing them to responsible office exceeded those of all previous Presidents combined. Blacks scored significant gains throughout the 1930s, which must be credited to the influence of the New Deal. In return, they became an integral part of the Roosevelt coalition and the Democratic party—an allegiance that has remained unbroken.

The urban masses—immigrants and the children of immigrants—also received their first major recognition under the New Deal. While white, Anglo-Saxon, Protestant, small-town America voted Republican, the Jews and the Catholic Irish, Italians, and Poles of the cities who benefited from relief and New Deal patronage became the bulwark of the Democratic party. To them, the New Deal was not an abstraction but a living organism that had helped them or someone they knew. Everyone had a story like that of the young man whose mother, in desperation, wrote a letter to the President asking what to do to save her home from foreclosure. The letter received a prompt reply, a word of encouragement, and an explanation of how to get in touch with the local office of the Home Owners Loan Corporation to refinance the mortgage. Intellectuals were won over by Roosevelt's receptivity to advice from scholars and experts and his willingness to make bold experiments. As propagandists and opinion makers, they were influential far beyond the numerical significance of their votes.

Roosevelt regarded the outcome of the 1936 election as a mandate. "It was the nation that spoke through the voice of an overwhelming majority and [Roosevelt] holds that what this voice declared and imposed was the national will," wrote George Creel in a *Collier's* article published soon after the election. The words appeared under his byline, but they had been dictated by the President. It was Roosevelt's way of announcing that the mandate he had received was a mandate for change.

XXI

THE EDGE OF DARKNESS

A COLD RAIN slashed down upon the sodden crowd that gathered before the Capitol on January 20, 1937, to witness Franklin Roosevelt's second inauguration. Huddled under their umbrellas, the audience looked, from the inaugural platform, like a field of giant black mushrooms. Tension crackled between the President and Chief Justice Charles Evans Hughes as they confronted each other over the pages of the Roosevelt family Bible, which had been covered with cellophane to ward off the rain. Observers noted that Hughes administered the oath with a noticeable emphasis upon the words "to preserve, protect and defend" the Constitution, while Roosevelt replied with equal force. Later, he told Sam Rosenman he could barely restrain himself from crying out: "Yes, but it's the Constitution as *I* understand it, flexible enough to meet any new problem of democracy—not the kind of Constitution that your Court has raised as a barrier to progress and democracy!"

Ignoring the rain that splattered the pages of his inaugural address, Roosevelt threw down the gauntlet to those who thought the New Deal had gone far enough:

> In this nation, I see tens of millions of its citizens—a substantial part of its whole population—who at this very moment are denied the greater part of what the very lowest standards of living today call the necessities of life.
> I see millions of families trying to live on incomes so meager that the pall of family disaster hangs over them every day.

I see millions denied education, recreation, and the opportunity to better their lot and the lot of their children.

I see millions lacking the means to buy the products of farm and factory and by their poverty denying work and productiveness to many other millions.

I see one-third of a nation ill-housed, ill-clad, ill-nourished.

It is not in despair that I paint you that picture. I paint it for you in hope —because the Nation, seeing and understanding the injustice of it, proposes to paint it out. . . .

New Dealers in the crowd cheered Roosevelt's militant humanitarianism. Two weeks before, he had sent Congress a program that included wages-and-hours and slum-clearance legislation, reorganization of the executive branch of the government, renewal of the Reciprocal Trade Agreement, and several regional TVAs. But how would he deal with the Supreme Court, which seemed bent on dismembering the New Deal? The justices had ruled against the Administration in eleven of sixteen cases, and fear was expressed for the Social Security and Wagner acts. No specifics were forthcoming in his second inaugural speech, but Roosevelt urged the American people to "insist that every agency of popular government use effective instruments to carry out their will." Rosenman carefully watched the Chief Justice's face as he took in these words, and came away convinced that Hughes "understood what the President meant when he emphasized the word 'every.'"

For the past two years, Supreme Court reform had hardly been out of Roosevelt's mind. He was particularly galled by the fact that he was the first American President to serve a four-year term without being able to name a single justice, and often discussed this problem with friends and associates. Some urged caution, among them Senator Henry Ashurst, chairman of the Senate Judiciary Committee. Age would take its toll, he said, creating, through death and retirement, vacancies on the court which Roosevelt could fill with his own appointees. "It will fall to your lot to nominate more Justices of the Supreme Court than any President since General Washington," he predicted. Others were more aggressive. "No disinterested student of our Constitutional system and the needs of our society could view with complacency the impasse created by the blind and stubborn majority of the Court," Felix Frankfurter told him. It was obvious that the judicial conservatives were harnessing their legal interpretations to their economic and social prejudices, the professor continued, and the President had every justification for seeking a constitutional amendment as a remedy.

Various amendments were weighed, including those granting Congress the power to reenact laws that had been voided by the Supreme Court and that raised the number of justices required to invalidate an act of Congress from a simple majority to six or perhaps seven. Roosevelt ultimately rejected them all. Two thirds of Congress and three quarters of the state legislatures were needed to ratify a constitutional amendment— and as a former governor he knew how easily legislatures could be influenced or bought. There were reports that the Liberty League had already collected a sizable amount to block this route. "Give me ten million dollars," Roosevelt said, "and I can prevent any amendment to the Constitution from being ratified by the necessary number of states." Besides, the problem lay not with the Constitution but with the justices themselves, and his thoughts turned toward putting his own appointees on the bench. As early as December 1935, he mentioned to Ickes a precedent he admiringly credited to Lloyd George—actually it was Prime Minister Herbert H. Asquith—to pack the House of Lords with new peers to secure passage of a welfare budget in 1910.

The problem was turned over to Homer Cummings, the Attorney General. Cloaked in secrecy, he searched the files of the Department of Justice and dredged up a plan that had been proposed in 1913 by Woodrow Wilson's Attorney General to revitalize the federal judiciary. It empowered the President to appoint a new judge for every one with ten years of service who had reached the age of seventy and failed to retire. Although these provisions had not applied to the Supreme Court, Roosevelt joyfully pounced upon the scheme when it was presented to him. It was, he said, "the answer to a maiden's prayer." Part of his glee resulted, no doubt, from the fact that, ironically enough, Wilson's Attorney General had been none other than James C. McReynolds—now, at seventy-four, one of the most conservative members of the Supreme Court.

There was nothing sacred about the number of justices, and Roosevelt's effort to expand the size of the Supreme Court was justified by both historical precedent and constitutionality. Over the years, strong Presidents had usually clashed with the court and had prevailed upon Congress to alter its size. John Adams cut the original six members down to five; Jefferson increased the number to seven. In 1837, the court was increased to nine justices and to ten in 1863 to prevent it from interfering with Lincoln's war measures. To prevent the detested Andrew Johnson from making two appointments, Congress itself reduced the court to eight members. And in 1869, the magic number was raised again to nine—an early case of court packing in order to ensure approval of the Legal Tender Act, the mainstay of Union finance during the Civil War.

Planning for the assault on the court went forward amid secrecy suitable for a military operation. Congressional leaders, the Cabinet, White House aides, and even close confidants such as Frankfurter were kept in the dark. "Very confidentially, I may give you an awful shock in about two weeks," Roosevelt wrote him. "Even if you do not agree, suspend final judgment. . . ." There was one final touch of drama before the curtain went up on the center stage. With conspiratorial joy, the President played host on the evening of February 3 to the annual White House reception for the judiciary. There were dinner and music, men in white tie and tails, and women in evening gowns. Everyone thought Roosevelt even more ingratiating than usual, and he was seen joking with the Chief Justice.

Two days later, on the morning of February 5, a steady stream of limousines began arriving at the White House. Worried and nervous congressional leaders mixed with members of the Cabinet as they waited to meet the President in the Cabinet Room. "Why are you here?" the chairmen of the Senate and House Judiciary committees asked each other. Both replied that the only thing they knew was that they had been summoned by a telephone call the previous evening. The door from the adjoining Oval Office swung open at ten o'clock and Roosevelt was wheeled to his place at the center of the long table. He was followed by a secretary, who placed a sheaf of freshly mimeographed documents before each of the visitors. Hastily glancing at the material, they ascertained that it was a special message to Congress. What was it about?

Except for a cheery greeting, Roosevelt wasted little time in pleasantries. He reminded the group that, a few weeks earlier, he had sent a message to Capitol Hill recommending reorganization of the executive branch of the federal government. Today, he was following it up with a recommendation for reorganization of the judiciary. Slowly, the full import of Roosevelt's announcement dawned on his audience. He had accepted the challenge to the New Deal offered by the Supreme Court.

For over the better part of an hour, the President read excerpts from his message, ad-libbing here and making comments there, as his audience listened in stunned silence. Instead of a direct assault on the Supreme Court, he contended that the federal courts were unable to keep up with their work. In fact, he said, the Supreme Court had denied 81 percent of the petitions for hearings and appeals that had come before it, without citing any reason. "The personnel of the federal judiciary is insufficient to meet the business before them," Roosevelt said and blamed it on the tendency of judges to remain on the bench "far beyond their years or physical capacity." The question of aged and infirm judges was a delicate matter but one that must be faced, he continued. "A constant and systematic addition of younger blood will vitalize the courts and better equip them to recognize and apply the essential concepts of justice in the light of the needs and facts of an ever-changing world."

Roosevelt's plan for revitalizing the courts was breezily disingenuous.

For every member of the federal judiciary who had reached the age of seventy and did not retire within six months, the President would be empowered to appoint an additional judge. Six Supreme Court justices were over seventy—including its four most conservative members—which meant that if the Judicial Reform Act of 1937 became law, Roosevelt would be able to appoint enough pro-New Deal members to win control of the high court. There was little discussion of the proposal, and the President did not solicit the views of the Cabinet or of congressional leaders.

Returning to his office, he immediately met the press. Few questions were asked, for the reporters were too busy taking notes on the astounding announcement. Several times, Roosevelt was interrupted in his reading of the message by bursts of laughter at his asides, and he heartedly joined in. Later, a Republican congressman asked whether the joke was on the Supreme Court or on the American people.

On Capitol Hill, little groups of legislators gathered in the cloakrooms to discuss the President's message. Vice-President Garner, whom the President expected to play a leading role in winning approval of the proposal, was seen holding his nose and turning down his thumb as he walked out of the Senate Chamber. Later, he slammed his fist against his desk and told some friends that Roosevelt was "the most destructive man in all American history." In the House, word spread that Hatton Sumners, the chairman of the Judiciary Committee, had on the way back from the White House announced to his companions: "Boys, here's where I cash in my chips." But there was also another side. As soon as the clerk had finished droning through the presidential message, Texas' Maury Maverick, a New Deal zealot, grabbed a copy of the bill, scrawled his name across the top, and dropped it into the legislative hopper.

Louis Brandeis, at just over eighty the oldest of the justices, was the first to learn of Roosevelt's proposal. Tom Corcoran had persuaded the President to allow him to provide Brandeis with assurances that the attack on the capacity of elderly judges was not intended as a personal reflection upon him. Corcoran met the jurist in the Supreme Court robing room and they moved out into the hall. As Brandeis' brethren filed past to take their seats in the adjoining chamber, the aide quickly outlined the plan. Brandeis told Corcoran to thank Roosevelt for his consideration but added that he thought the President was making a serious mistake. Not long afterward, a page slipped through the red draperies behind the dais and hurriedly placed a copy of the presidential message before each of the justices. Some merely glanced at what had been given them; others read it through. But, except for this brief distraction, there was no visible reaction. The Supreme Court of the United States appeared as Olympian as ever in its marble palace.

Lines of battle formed quickly, and Roosevelt told Jim Farley that he was "rarin'" for a fight. But in his anger at the Supreme Court for trying to straitjacket the New Deal, the President had seriously miscalculated. While he had expected an outcry from conservatives, even he was surprised by its magnitude and intensity. Nor did he foresee the corrosive effect of the court-packing plan upon the New Deal coalition that had given him the electoral triumph of only two months before. Everyone regarded his announced objective of improving judicial efficiency as a transparent subterfuge to create a "Roosevelt Court," and his Machiavellian slyness troubled even those who normally followed him without question. This lack of candor also worked against the plan's success. Both Congress and the public needed time to become adjusted to the idea of an attack on such a venerable institution as the Supreme Court; yet it was sprung upon them without allowing time for coordination and planning.

Farley, who had been as much in the dark as anyone, asked Roosevelt why such important figures as Senator Joseph T. Robinson, the Senate majority leader, and House speaker John Bankhead hadn't been tipped off as to what was coming. "Jim, I just couldn't," he replied. "I didn't want to have it get out prematurely to the press. More than once when I've had groups of Senators and Congressmen down here, reporters have gathered a detailed account of what went on in 48 hours. I didn't want it to happen again." Perhaps so. Nevertheless, the impression remains that Roosevelt's intoxication with his success and belief in his own infallibility, combined with a delight in pulling rabbits out of hats, overcame the need to consult with the congressional leadership.

Would Roosevelt have committed this political blunder—and others that were to follow—if Louis Howe had been at his elbow? Eleanor Roosevelt, who believed the court-packing plan a mistake, thought Howe would have made a difference. "After Louis' death, Franklin never had a political adviser who would argue with and give him unquestioned loyalty," she said. "Louis gave Franklin the benefit of his sane, reasoned, careful political analysis and even if Franklin disagreed and was annoyed, he listened and respected Louis' political acumen. Whether he ignored Louis' advice or not, at least all the reasons against the disputed action had been clearly stated and argued." Ickes felt the same way. "Howe was the only one who dared talk to him frankly and fearlessly. He not only could tell him what he believed to be the truth, but he could hang on like a pup to the root until he got results."

Harry Hopkins, to whom the President now turned for the companionship he had received from Howe, lacked his predecessor's political skills and independence. Hopkins, who regarded himself as merely an errand boy, was more an executive agent than a confidential adviser. While

FDR arrives in Chicago on July 2, 1932, to address the Democratic convention. Louis Howe is pressing his version of the acceptance speech upon the presidential nominee, while Jim Farley listens with his hand to his ear. (Courtesy FDR Library)

The victors. FDR with Louis Howe and Jim Farley. (Courtesy FDR Library)

FDR and Raymond Moley in the library of the Roosevelt home in Hyde Park, February 26, 1933. (Courtesy FDR Library)

FDR taking the oath as President on March 4, 1933. It is being administered by Chief Justice Charles Evans Hughes. (Courtesy FDR Library)

The myriad faces of FDR at a baseball game. Jim Farley is wearing the derby. (Courtesy George Skadding)

Howe would argue until Roosevelt had heard all sides of a question, Hopkins, an accomplished courtier, trimmed his sails to the presidential mood. Realizing that Roosevelt did not like to be directly contradicted, he frequently agreed with him even if he thought the President was making a mistake. Later, he would bring up the matter again and invite others to reinforce his views. "This was not as valuable a service as forcing Franklin, in the way Louis did, to hear unpleasant arguments," Eleanor noted. Farley would also argue with her husband, but his arguments were not effective, because they were usually solely based on political expediency. Ed Flynn always told him the truth as he saw it, but he was not always on hand to provide advice. "Consequently," as Eleanor observed, "after Louis' death, Franklin frequently made his decisions without canvassing all sides of a question."

Conservative politicians and newspapers immediately pounced on the court-packing plan. Herbert Hoover, looking forward to the 1940 presidential election, in which he hoped to return to the White House from embittered exile, offered the watchword of Roosevelt's opponents: "Hands off the Supreme Court!" The stock market dropped. Tory Democrats like Virginia's Carter Glass assailed the plan as "destitute of moral sensibility and without parallel since the foundation of the Republic." The New York *Herald Tribune* said that if Roosevelt's proposal became law, it "would end the American state as it has existed throughout the long years of its life." The Chamber of Commerce, the Liberty League, the Daughters of the American Revolution, the American Legion, and the National Association of Manufacturers all chimed in. Bar associations, state legislatures, Kiwanis clubs, and women's clubs passed denunciatory resolutions. "Upon what meat doth this our Caesar feed that he is grown so great?" cried Representative Ulysses S. Guyer of Kansas in a wail of Shakespearean anguish. Walter Lippmann solemnly described the plan as "a bloodless coup d'état."

The President had struck a tender nerve. Over the years, the Supreme Court had become in the public mind the bulwark of the Constitution, and any attempt to modify it was regarded as an attack on the tripartite system of government, in which the executive, legislative, and judicial branches served as checks upon each other. Some of this opposition was less than spontaneous, however. Frank Gannett, a newspaper-chain publisher who had originally supported Roosevelt, orchestrated an outpouring of mail. Ordinary citizens, largely unaware of the finer points of Roosevelt's plan, flooded their elected representatives with emotional pleas to save the country from "dictatorship."

Roosevelt's many enemies were also provided with a respectable banner under which they could unite. Longtime opponents not only had their fears and suspicions magnified, but timid supporters of the Administration's emergency legislation saw the episode as an opportunity to cut their ties to the New Deal. Erstwhile congressional supporters who had privately feared the increasing power of the Chief Executive and had been overshadowed by Roosevelt's leadership now felt free to join the opposition. "The President," said one lawmaker, "has left Congress with no more legislative power than Gandhi has clothing." Blacks and Jews were reminded that the Supreme Court was the guarantor of minority rights, while southern senators regarded the challenge to the court as a sinister attack upon white supremacy. Small businessmen, professionals, and middle-class voters were alarmed when thousands of striking auto workers "sat down" in the General Motors plant in Flint, Michigan, raising the curtain on a radical new phase in the struggle for union recognition. Such antiunion congressmen as Michigan's Clare Hoffman accused Roosevelt of encouraging such lawlessness by example in trying to pack the court.

The legislative battle over the court-packing plan was probably the most impassioned since the Civil War. Farley estimated that the Senate —where the major struggle took place, because Hatton Sumners, the chairman of the House Judiciary Committee, refused to hold hearings— was divided into almost equal thirds. One group was in favor of the bill, another was opposed, and the third was sitting on the fence. Although personally distressed by Roosevelt's plan, Senator Robinson led the fight for passage. Some of the Senate's most ardent liberals were among the defectors: Burton K. Wheeler of Montana, one of Roosevelt's earliest supporters for the presidency; Joseph O'Mahoney of Wyoming; and David I. Walsh of Massachusetts. The most disconcerting defection as far as Roosevelt was concerned was that of George Norris. "I am not in sympathy with the plan to enlarge the Supreme Court," the old progressive declared. The Republicans decided that the best strategy was to lie low and let the Democrats tear themselves apart.

Roosevelt sent Tom Corcoran to try to persuade Wheeler, the most articulate defector, to come over to the President's side. If the liberals refused to go along, Corcoran warned his former comrade-in-arms, the President would have to turn to the big-city machines for support, which meant that they would have a say in the naming of the new justices. "A liberal cause," Wheeler said later, "was never won by stacking a deck of cards, by stuffing a ballot box, or packing a court." The Montanan also had personal reasons for opposing the plan. He felt he had not been accorded full recognition for his support of the President and the New Deal. Instead of accepting the olive branch extended by Roosevelt, he took over the leadership of what Joe O'Mahoney, in a reference to the senators who had opposed American entry into the League of Nations, dubbed the "battalion of death to save the Constitution."

Franklin Roosevelt's "Dutch was up" and he took his case to the American people. On March 4, at a hundred-dollar-a-plate Victory Dinner, he called upon all Democrats to close ranks to preserve the gains made over the past four years. Dropping the pretense that he merely intended to improve the efficiency of the judiciary, he declared that the future of the New Deal was at stake. The Supreme Court had "assumed the power to veto" all major New Deal legislation, he declared. Injunctions had paralyzed the enforcement of the Wagner Act and encouraged the great corporations to defy it. Flood and drought swept the country, while injunctions by the lower federal courts paralyzed the TVA. "Here is one-third of a Nation ill-nourished, ill-clad, ill-housed—*now!*" the President continued. "If we would keep faith with those who had faith in us, if we would make democracy succeed . . . we must act—*now!*"

Five nights later, in a Fireside Chat, Roosevelt trained his guns directly on the justices themselves. "Our difficulty with the Court today rises not from the Court as an institution but from the human beings within it," he said. "But we cannot yield our Constitutional destiny to the personal judgment of a few men who, being fearful of the future, would deny us the necessary means of dealing with the present." Roosevelt met the charges that he wished to pack the court with "spineless puppets" head on. "If by that phrase the charge is made that I would appoint . . . justices . . . who understand . . . modern conditions—that I will appoint justices who will not undertake to override the judgment of Congress on legislative policy . . . then I say that I and with me the vast majority of the American people favor doing just that thing—now," he declared.

Roosevelt did not depend solely upon his popularity and oratorical skills, however. The White House carefully choreographed a no-holds-barred campaign designed to persuade the corps of fence-sitters to embrace the plan. The President personally lobbied some senators. Farley dangled promises of public works projects, jobs, and judicial appointments before waverers. Corcoran, Roosevelt's eyes and ears on Capitol Hill, applied muscle and less-than-veiled hints of retribution against defectors. Cabinet members were sent on the road to make speeches. Senator Wheeler complained that his income tax return was suddenly subjected to an audit. Dossiers were compiled on the private lives of some lawmakers, and Roosevelt was said to have ordered an investigation of one anti-New Deal Democrat who was a secret homosexual. Some of these efforts backfired. Corcoran's brashness infuriated senior senators, while Jimmy Roosevelt, who was acting as one of his father's assistants, put in a performance that produced mixed notices. Farley touched off a flurry of adverse publicity when he asked if Democratic senators—and he specifically mentioned Pat McCarran of Nevada and Joe O'Mahoney— could expect any favors from the Administration if they voted against the President. But, in the final analysis, the Nine Old Men of the Supreme Court, themselves, turned the tide against Roosevelt.

On March 10, the scene of battle shifted to the cavernous Caucus Room of the Senate Office Building, where in a chamber haunted by history, the Judiciary Committee opened its hearings on the court reform bill. Little more than a dozen years before, the iniquities of Teapot Dome had been unraveled against the background of its polished marble and glittering chandeliers. Homer Cummings and his assistant, Robert Jackson, made a spirited defense of the President's proposal to enlarge the court in the face of questions tipped with acid from the committee. The interrogation was so intense that it was said that a team of legal experts from the American Bar Association had been brought to Washington to assist the opposition.

Twelve days later, there was a fresh surge of anticipation as Senator Wheeler led off for the opposition. He began with a rambling protest of his "reluctance" to oppose the President but soon turned to the key element of the administration argument: that the lethargy of overage justices had created a logjam of unresolved court cases. Sensing that an important moment was at hand, reporters at the press tables halted their joking among themselves, the spectators stopped their chattering, the members of the committee leaned forward in their seats. With contrived casualness, Wheeler withdrew a sheaf of papers from his coat pocket and announced: "I have here now a letter from the Chief Justice of the Supreme Court, Mr. Charles Evans Hughes, dated March 21, 1937, written by him and approved by Mr. Justice Brandeis and Mr. Justice Van Devanter."

Everyone was stunned, for not within memory had a chief justice taken an active role in a public controversy. Brandeis had played a key role in arranging the surprising statement. Hughes had originally wanted to appear in person before the committee to protest the court-packing plan, but Brandeis convinced him such a move would be demeaning and suggested a letter instead. As veteran progressives, he and Wheeler were old friends, and Brandeis had put the senator in touch with the chief justice, even going so far as to get him on the telephone. "The baby is born," Hughes told Wheeler as he handed the letter over with a mock conspiratorial air. In a brief conversation with the senator, Hughes blamed the situation on the President's misunderstanding of the institutional independence of the Supreme Court and on Cummings' ineptness as Attorney General. "Laws have been poorly drafted, briefs poorly written and arguments poorly presented," he declared.

Factually and unemotionally, Hughes's seven-page letter defended the justices against the charge that they were unable to handle their burden. "The Supreme Court is fully abreast of its work," the chief justice insisted. ". . . There is no congestion of cases upon our calendar." To reinforce his assertion, he produced a detailed statistical table. The addition of more judges would scarcely promote efficiency, he added, for this would simply mean "more judges to hear, more judges to confer, more judges to discuss, more judges to be convinced and to decide." Although some justices later expressed anger that they had not been consulted, Hughes had with consummate political skill demolished the stated objective of the President's plan to expand the size of the court.

Roosevelt was angry at being outfoxed. Certainly the Supreme Court was up on its work, but that did not impress him, for he claimed it was done by refusing to hear cases. He recalled an old police-court magistrate, whom he had known when he was a young lawyer in New York City, who made it a rule to clear his calendar every day by 1 P.M. If he had a heavy docket, he would run the cases through without hearing the defendants. "It was ten dollars or ten days," said the President. "His calendar was not crowded. . . . He was always up with his work."

A week later, the court cut the ground out from under the advocates of reorganization by upholding a minimum-wage law enacted by the State of Washington that was almost identical to the New York statute it had struck down the year before. Justice Roberts had again shifted toward the liberal wing, providing the margin for a five-to-four decision. Radio comedians cracked that "a switch in time saves nine," but the decision had actually been reached back in January, before Roosevelt had unveiled his plan. Nevertheless, supreme court justices do not exist in a political vacuum, and they were aware of the momentous mandate the President had just received from the people. Years later, Roberts acknowledged that he had been "fully conscious" of "the tremendous strain and threat to the existing Court" when he had taken his position.

That same day, the Railway Labor Act and the Frazier-Lemke (farm-mortgage moratorium) Act were also upheld by unanimous decisions. The White House expressed pleasure at this reversal of form but was skeptical. The President's supporters suggested that once the pressure of the presidential reform plan was eased, the court was likely to revert to its usual conservatism. Further rulings revealed that the court had indeed reached a historic turning point. On April 12, it upheld the Wagner Act in a decision that reversed the narrow view of interstate commerce it had enunciated in striking down the NRA. This was followed by a ruling upholding various provisions of the Social Security Act.

Farley telephoned the President after the decision on the Wagner Act and found him jubilant. "We did it," he chortled. "I am very, very pleased. You ought to see Homer Cummings, who's sitting with me now. He looks like the Cheshire cat that swallowed the canary. It's wonderful." But his glee was tempered by the need to make certain that the court would not reassume its old, conservative ways. "I am convinced more than ever that the proposals for reform of the Court are warranted," he told Farley. "It's the same four justices who have dissented all along who are against me this time—McReynolds, Butler, Sutherland, and Van Devanter."

Before the President could regroup his forces to meet the court's new tactics, it delivered another blow to the reform plan. On May 18, the seventy-eight-year-old Justice Van Devanter unexpectedly announced his retirement after twenty-five years on the bench, opening the way for Roosevelt's first appointment. The Old Guard had surrendered, but the President's victory was limited. As a result of the court's surefooted maneuvering, Roosevelt's plan was no longer regarded as necessary. Friends urged a compromise. "The thing to do is to settle this thing right now," Joe Robinson told a White House aide. "This bill is raising hell in the Senate. Now it's going to be worse than ever, but if the President wants to compromise I can get him a couple of extra justices tomorrow. What he ought to do is say he's won, which he has, agree to compromise to make the thing sure, and wind the whole business up."

Roosevelt had no intention of retreating. A compromise might provide him with the substance of victory, but he would be denied the actual triumph needed to restore his bruised prestige. Besides, the fight over court reform had developed into something more than a struggle for supremacy between the executive and the legislative branches of the government. In the President's mind, it was now a duel between liberalism and conservatism. Conservative Democrats such as Harry Byrd, Millard Tydings, and Walter George had long opposed the New Deal, but political traditions extending back to the Civil War and Reconstruction had precluded a coalition with the Republicans. Roosevelt's attempt to pack the court provided them with the issue upon which they could make common cause with the GOP. Although such an old progressive as Burton Wheeler led the alliance, he was merely a front man. Roosevelt reasoned that if he were to give up the fight, it would mean sacrificing the future of the Democratic party to the conservatives. Having already indicated that he would not be a candidate for a third term, he would be unable to name his successor if he lost this battle. So, if he wished to complete his grand design, he could not relent in the fight for a decisive victory over the newly emerging conservative coalition.

Roosevelt was convinced he would win because the people were on his side. "I . . . believe that if the matter was submitted to the country at large and every citizen could vote upon it, your original bill would be heartily endorsed," one federal judge wrote him. Returning from North Carolina, where he had spoken in favor of the reform plan, Ickes reported, "There isn't any doubt that North Carolina is behind you with great enthusiasm." And in traditionally conservative Texas, where the state legislature had gone on record against the President's plan, Lyndon Johnson, who supported Roosevelt on the court issue, won a special congressional election. The President hailed Johnson's victory as a vote of confidence. Corcoran also contributed to the illusion of impending victory by calculating that only twenty-two senators would oppose the court reform plan on the final vote, even though more than that number had already taken a stand against it. Public pressure would force them to switch, the younger New Dealers contended. But the departure of Vice-President Garner on a five-week vacation in the midst of the fight was regarded by the press as evidence of a break with Roosevelt over the court fight.

Nevertheless, the President remained publicly optimistic. "Spring has come to Washington . . . and even the Senators, who were biting each other over the Supreme Court, are saying 'Alphonse' and 'Gaston' to each other," he wrote William C. Bullitt, the American ambassador in Paris. "I, too, am influenced by this beautiful spring day. I haven't a care in the world which is going some for a President who is said by the newspapers to be a remorseless dictator driving his government into hopeless bankruptcy." He also took time out in June to attend the wedding of Franklin, Jr., and Ethel Du Pont. The marriage of the son of "that man in the White House" into a family he had lambasted as "economic royalists" and that had given $325,000 to the Liberty League appealed to his lively sense of humor. Mischievously, Roosevelt brought such arch-New Dealers as Hopkins, Morgenthau, and Miss Perkins to the Du Pont's ancestral enclave in Delaware, enjoyed himself immensely, and would not leave until he had kissed all the bridesmaids.

In Washington, however, there was little to smile about. Senator Robinson, having been promised the Supreme Court seat vacated by Van Devanter, persuaded Roosevelt to accept a face-saving compromise that called for the appointment to the court of not more than one co-justice a year for each member over seventy-five. Although he was optimistic about its chances, opponents denounced this compromise as "no less dishonest, reprehensible and dangerous" than the original plan. The elaborate courtesy of the Senate frayed in the grip of a heat wave, and senators snarled and snapped at each other. And then, on the morning of July 14, the last chance to arrange a compromise vanished. Worn out by his exertions in behalf of the President, Joe Robinson was found dead in his apartment in the Methodist Building, across from the Capitol, the victim of a heart attack. Senators who had made personal pledges to the majority leader to back the compromise now felt free to vote their convictions, and the Administration's support began to fall away.

"How did you find the Court situation, Jack?" Roosevelt asked Garner, who had returned from Texas and taken a private poll of the Senate.

"Do you want it with the bark on or off, Cap'n?"

"The rough way," replied the President with a laugh.

"All right," answered Garner. "You are beat. You haven't got the votes."

With that, Roosevelt decided to throw in the towel. The only thing left was for Garner to arrange a deal that would preserve the tatters of presidential prestige. The battle finally ended on July 22, when the Senate voted by a lopsided margin to send the court-reform bill back to committee—168 days after Roosevelt had first broached the proposal. A week later, Garner gaveled through a weak substitute that provided innocuous procedural reforms for the lower federal judiciary. The Supreme Court was not even mentioned.

Later the President tried, as he had after the Sheehan affair a quarter century before, to turn defeat into victory by describing the court fight as "a lost battle which won a war." In several respects, this assessment was valid. Although it can never be known for certainty, the justices can scarcely have been unaware of the effects of the court-packing plan when they made their sudden switch in outlook. From that time on, the Supreme Court permitted nearly unlimited federal regulation of the national economy. And within little more than two and a half years, Roosevelt appointees formed a liberal majority on the court. The nomination of Senator Hugo Black to fill the seat vacated by Van Devanter stirred controversy when it was revealed that he had joined the Ku Klux Klan as a rising young politician in rural Alabama, but he turned out to be one of the court's staunchest defenders of civil rights for minorities. The "Roosevelt Court" eventually included former Solicitor General Stanley Reed; Felix Frankfurter; William O. Douglas, chairman of the Securities and Exchange Commission; and Frank Murphy, who replaced Homer Cummings as Attorney General. They gave the Supreme Court a liberal cast that was to endure well beyond the New Deal years and produce a revolution in American constitutional law.

Nevertheless, Roosevelt had suffered a humiliating defeat that produced widening ripples. Having for reasons of strategy postponed the fight for his ambitious legislative package until after the battle for judicial reform had been completed, he found Congress in no mood to approve it. Emboldened by their success in bloodying the President's nose in the court fight, Republican and Democratic conservatives cemented their union. Although this conservative alliance controlled only a minority of the seats in Congress, it was able to seriously cripple or to block almost all further progressive legislation proposed by the President. Roosevelt had won control over the Supreme Court, but there would be little New Deal legislation for it to act upon.

On the surface, Roosevelt bore his defeat with astonishing good humor, but Ickes noted, "He is punch drunk from the punishment that he has suffered recently." Not only was he bruised by the Supreme Court fight, but he was buffeted by labor troubles and faced an economic recession that threatened to wipe out all the gains won by the New Deal. No city or state seemed immune to labor unrest in 1937. Strikes and lockouts, and battles on the picket lines and in the courts flared across the nation with the rapidity of an infectious disease. Sit-down strikes spread from the General Motors plant in Flint to automobile factories in Cleveland, South Bend, and Detroit, and to rubber plants in Akron. The Flint workers lived on stockpiled food and supplies smuggled in from outside and stood guard against any attempt by police to drive them out of the plant, while then-Governor Frank Murphy and Frances Perkins tirelessly sought to persuade General Motors executives to negotiate with the newly organized United Auto Workers.

Taking the position that the occupation of its factories was illegal, General Motors ordered the heat turned off in the Flint plant. Police tried to storm it and they were driven off by a storm of nuts and bolts and pop bottles. The company obtained an injunction ordering the strikers to evacuate the plant, and Governor Murphy was urged to declare a state of insurrection and to send in the National Guard to evict them. Murphy, who wished to avoid violence at all costs, asked John L. Lewis, the beetle-browed president of the CIO, what he would do if the troops were called out. "Tomorrow morning, I shall personally enter General Motors plant Chevrolet No. 4," Lewis replied. "I shall order the men to disregard your order. I shall then walk up to the largest window in the plant, open it, divest myself of my outer raiment, remove my shirt and bare my bosom. Then when you order your troops to fire, mine will be the first breast those bullets will strike." The National Guard remained where it was.

Roosevelt was as surprised and bewildered by the wave of sit-down strikes as anyone, but he refused to use force against the strikers. Instead, he urged Miss Perkins to continue to try to persuade General Motors to negotiate with a committee of its workers. "Well, it is illegal, but what law are they breaking?" he told her. "The law of trespass, and that is about the only law that could be invoked. And what do you do when a man trespasses on your property? Sure, you order him off. You get the sheriff to order him off. . . . But shooting it out and killing a lot of people because they have violated the law of trespass somehow offends me. I just don't see that as the answer. The punishment doesn't fit the crime. There must be another way. Why can't those fellows in General Motors meet with the committee of workers? Talk it out. They would get a settlement. It wouldn't be too terrible."

Following lengthy negotiations, Miss Perkins learned that William Knudsen, the president of General Motors, was willing to meet with the workers' committee if he could take shelter behind a face-saving presidential request. Roosevelt was confined to his bed with a bad cold but telephoned Knudsen. He had never met him but turned on his full charm. "Is that you, Bill?" he asked. "I know you have been through a lot, Bill, and I want to tell you that I feel sorry for you, but Miss Perkins has told me about the situation and what you are discussing and I have just called up to say I hope very much indeed that you go through with this and that your people will meet a committee." Shortly afterward, an agreement was reached to recognize the UAW as bargaining agent at General Motors' sixty factories in fourteen states. Chrysler and the smaller auto manufacturers quickly fell into line, but Ford continued to resist until 1941.

United States Steel, the bellwether of the steel industry, was Lewis' next target. The company had long been one of the bitterest foes of organized labor, but Big Steel, as it was known, indicated that it wished to avoid a long and costly strike. Lewis and Myron C. Taylor, the firm's board chairman, quietly reached an agreement on a contract granting union recognition, a forty-hour week, and time and a half for overtime. With U. S. Steel in the bag, Lewis expected the independent steel companies, known as Little Steel, to fall into line, but under the leadership of iron-fisted Tom Girdler, of Republic Steel, they resisted unionization. The worst violence in modern labor history erupted on Memorial Day 1937, when police in South Chicago clashed with pickets at the Republic Steel works and ten strikers were killed.

Fought to a standstill by Girdler, Lewis demanded that the President come to the union's assistance in return for labor's substantial contribution to the 1936 campaign. Roosevelt refused, probably because public opinion had turned against labor. Middle-class professionals and small businessmen were frightened by sit-down strikes and violence, and charged that Roosevelt had condoned this illegal conduct by refusing to use force. The President expressed his anger at both organized labor and Little Steel with a declaration of "a plague on both your houses." Lewis quickly thundered back. "It ill behooves one who has supped at labor's table . . . to curse with equal fervor and fine impartiality both labor and its adversaries when they become locked in deadly embrace," he rumbled.

In the end, the National Labor Relations Board condemned the steel companies for resorting to terrorism against the strikers and ordered them to engage in collective bargaining, but Lewis had soured on Roosevelt. In 1940, he backed the Republican presidential candidate.

To add to Roosevelt's woes, the economy showed unmistakable signs of cracking. Over the past four years, economic conditions had steadily improved, and by the spring of 1937, production and payrolls had been pushed above the levels of 1929. Worried that increasing prosperity might trigger another runaway boom such as that which had preceded the crash, some officials, Henry Morgenthau in particular, urged caution. The time had come to balance the budget, the fiscally conservative Treasure Secretary had strenuously argued—"to take away the crutches to test whether the patient was able to walk by himself." The Federal Reserve Board raised its reserve requirements for member banks by 50 percent, and the President, in his heart a true descendant of his thrifty Dutch Calvinist forebears, resolved upon an end to deficits, and a balanced budget. WPA spending was sharply reduced, farm subsidies curtailed, and PWA pump-priming brought to a standstill in an effort to restore business confidence by balancing the budget. The deficit for fiscal 1936 had been $4.3 billion, but the 1937 budget reduced it to $2.7 billion. In 1938 the deficit was to be cut to only $740 million, and by 1939 the budget would be balanced.

This exercise in governmental frugality did not produce the results that orthodox economists and businessmen had predicted. In August the stock market was jolted by a sharp wave of selling, farm prices fell, unemployment soared, and most of the gains won over the past two years were wiped out. With the coming of winter, breadlines once again appeared in the streets of America's cities. Newspapers in Nazi Germany gloated over the misery of the unemployed and cited the recession as further proof of the degeneracy of democracy. Anti-New Dealers joked about "the Roosevelt Depression" and pointed to the President's exultant statement of two years before: "Yes, we are on our way back . . . because we planned it that way." What had happened? The failure of business and industry to take up the slack resulting from radical cuts in federal spending with increased production was largely responsible for the downturn. Other contributing factors included a speculative buildup in inventories in anticipation of a boom, labor unrest, and the siphoning off of some $2 billion in purchasing power by the new social security tax.

Roosevelt wavered over the choice of remedy to be pursued while the economy continued to deteriorate. One day, he ruefully told a press conference that he had recently received letters from two leading economists. "One says the entire question is one of velocity of capital turnover credit, so do not pay any attention to purchasing power. The other says: forget all the algebraic formula about the velocity of capital turnover credit; the whole question is purchasing power on the part of one hundred and thirty million people." In November, he called Congress into special session. "If private enterprise does not respond to the crisis," he declared, "government must take up the slack." But the program that he presented to Congress was hardly designed to deal with a crisis. Mostly items left over from the previous session, it included a request for new agricultural legislation, a wages-and-hours law, an expanded housing program, and reorganization of the executive branch of the government. Convinced that Roosevelt had lost his magic, the conservative coalition formed during the Supreme Court fight circulated their own recovery program: balanced budgets, states' rights, tax cuts, and encouragement of business. The session adjourned shortly before Christmas, a complete washout.

For the first time, Roosevelt seriously sought solutions from his Cabinet, and became entangled in arguments between the various factions. Morgenthau, Farley, and Dan Roper, the Secretary of Commerce, tried to persuade him to hold the line on the budget and to adopt a more conciliatory attitude toward business, with the hope of ending the "strike of capital" against the government. On the other hand, he was urged to resume pump-priming and spend his way out of the recession by liberals such as Hopkins and Marriner Eccles, of the Federal Reserve Board, who were aided and abetted by Tom Corcoran, Ben Cohen, and Leon Henderson, an economist who had predicted the downturn.

Although almost totally innocent of Keynesian doctrine, the liberals had accepted the British economist's prescription for curing the depression: massive government spending to increase employment, purchasing power, investment, and production. Roosevelt himself was unfamiliar with Keynes's teachings, although they had met briefly in June 1934. "I saw your friend Keynes," the President later told Miss Perkins, shaking his head. "He left a whole rigamarole of figures. He must be a mathematician rather than a political economist." Keynes was no less disappointed in Roosevelt, saying he "had supposed the President more literate, economically speaking."

The advocates of deficit spending received timely support from their mentor when Keynes wrote an unsolicited letter to Roosevelt, in February 1938, pointing out that the key to recovery was a large-scale program of public works. Noting that the Administration was being criticized for neglecting the nation's housing needs, he suggested emphasis be placed on such projects. The President handed the letter over to Morgenthau to prepare an answer, indicating that even though his faith in fiscal conservatism was shaken, he had not capitulated to the spenders.

"As I see it," Morgenthau suggested at lunch in mid-March, "what you are doing now is just treading water . . . to wait to see what happens this spring."

"Absolutely," replied the President.

Within a few weeks, the stock market broke again and recovery seemed as far away as ever to the harassed President. Every index of economic measurement was testimony to the depth of the recession. He met with businessmen in a conciliatory gesture, but they had little to offer. Seizing an opportunity, Harry Hopkins, armed with reports and recommendations prepared by Leon Henderson, descended upon Roosevelt at Warm Springs and made a determined effort to persuade him to launch a massive spending program. Congressional elections were due in November, and unless conditions improved dramatically, the outcome would be fatal to the New Deal and the Democratic party. By the time he returned to Washington, the President had reluctantly agreed to end the experiment in budget balancing. When a grim-faced Morgenthau came to the White House, he found the spenders had carried the day. "They have just stampeded him during the week I was away," he told aides. "He was completely stampeded. They stampeded him like cattle."

Roosevelt unveiled a $3.75-billion package designed to get the economy moving again. Congress was asked to appropriate $1.4 billion for the WPA, the NYA, and the CCC, and $1 billion for a revived PWA. Additional funds were sought for slum clearance and low-cost-housing construction. Fearful of their own future if the recession continued, congressional Democrats of all persuasions quickly approved the presidential request. Additional funds were pumped into the economy by the Agricultural Adjustment Act of 1938, which increased farm subsidies, and by expanded naval shipbuilding and other defense expenditures. This fresh outpouring of government spending reversed the downturn, and by the end of the year, most of the losses had been eradicated. "We are on our way again!" Roosevelt proclaimed in a speech at Bowling Green, Kentucky, in July 1938. But there was a hump of unemployment that no New Deal program seemed able to reduce. A decade after the Wall Street crash, as many as nine million Americans were out of work.

Perhaps the major reason for this phenomenon—the New Deal's most persistent problem and greatest long-term failure—was the contradictions of Roosevelt's personality. Although he had turned to renewed deficit spending to end the recession, he had by no means been fully converted to the Keynesian doctrine of the beneficial deficit. He continued to yearn for balanced budgets, to deplore deficits, and to promise a return to fiscal orthodoxy as soon as possible. Roosevelt was never able to bring himself to make a full-scale commitment to deficit spending, so the amount expended was not large enough to do the job. For the most part, he was content to engage in a salvage operation, rather than a positive program of expansion.

Typically, even as he was priming the pump, the President hedged by asking Congress to approve a wide-ranging investigation, by the Temporary National Economic Committee, into the concentration of economic power. This was matched by the appointment of Thurman Arnold, of the Yale Law School, to head the Anti-Trust Division of the Department of Justice. Arnold launched nearly a hundred new antitrust cases and was one of the most vigorous trustbusters in American history. Trust-busting and investigations of monopoly seemed hardly the appropriate complement to a policy aimed at encouraging the very people and institutions under attack to increase investments.

Paradoxically, even as Roosevelt's plan to restore national prosperity through deficit spending was foundering as a result of his timidity and lack of commitment, he was being condemned by conservatives for adding massive amounts to the national debt. And when limited deficit spending failed to end unemployment, they charged that Keynesianism had not worked. The only way to deal with recession and depression, conservatives said, was through the time-tested orthodoxies of budget balancing, tax reduction, and limited government. In point of fact, Keynesian fiscal policy had barely been tried. A full test had to await the coming of World War II, which saw such an enormous surge in government spending that ended unemployment as the wartime factories absorbed the jobless.

In August 1937, shortly after the end of the Supreme Court fight, sixty Democratic senators attended a dinner in Washington honoring their new majority leader, Senator Alben W. Barkley of Kentucky. The affair was less than a success despite the pledges of cooperation and a cordial message from the President. When a reporter asked one of the guests if harmony had prevailed, the senator snorted and replied: "Harmony, Hell! And don't quote me." Relations between Roosevelt and conservative Democrats had grown even more prickly in the wake of the abortive special congressional session of 1937, and the session that convened the following January was a dismal rerun. With the exception of the second AAA and the Fair Labor Standards Act, which established a minimum wage of twenty-five cents an hour, set a maximum work week of forty-four hours, and abolished child labor, most of the President's legislative program was sidetracked. Particularly galling was the emasculation of his plan to reorganize the executive branch of the government, which had first been submitted the previous year.

On the face of it, the proposal was one of the most innocuous Roosevelt had ever submitted to Congress. As long before as the Wilson era, he had favored increasing administrative efficiency, and the plan, formulated by a team of political scientists and public-administration specialists, called for expanding the White House staff, strengthening the administrative agencies, establishment of cabinet-level departments of social welfare and of public works, and extending civil service to cover almost all nonpolicy-making jobs. The debate that followed had little or nothing to do with the merits of Roosevelt's plan. The opposition, sensing another opportunity to humiliate the President, raised the issue of unbridled presidential authority and dubbed the measure the "dictator bill." Once again, conservative pressure groups mobilized a campaign to preserve the Constitution against encroaching totalitarianism. They charged that the United States was treading the same path to dictatorship as Germany, Italy, and the Soviet Union. Unexpectedly thrown on the defensive, Roosevelt released a statement to reporters called to Warm Springs at two o'clock one morning that was designed to allay public fears:

A. I have no inclination to be a dictator.
B. I have none of the qualifications which would make me a successful dictator.
C. I have too much historical background and too much knowledge of existing dictatorships to make me desire any form of dictatorship for a democracy like the United States of America.

Nevertheless, the temptation to rebuke the President was too great to be denied, and the plan was rejected by a narrow margin. "Jim, I'll tell you I didn't expect that vote," a bewildered Roosevelt told Farley. "I can't understand it. There wasn't a chance for anyone to become dictator under the bill." The defection of so many Democrats from his program after having ridden into office on his coattails also irritated him.

At what point he decided upon a purge of anti-New Deal Democrats is unclear, but he reluctantly concluded that the recalcitrants must be taught that they cannot treat a President with disdain. Also, Roosevelt had long envisioned the Democratic party as a genuine liberal party, shorn of its troublesome conservative wing. Nineteen years before, he had aroused national attention by assailing the Republicans as the party of "conservatism and reaction," while calling upon the Democratic party to become "the party of progress." This speech had marked his arrival as a leader of the party's liberal wing and had helped him win the vice-presidential nomination—and he had never abandoned his vision of the Democrats as the party of "liberalism, common sense idealism, constructiveness, progress. . . ."

Tom Corcoran, for one, urged Roosevelt to make a fight of it, for if he took the defeat lying down, he would have little to look forward to during the remainder of his administration. "It was up to him now to show whether he was going out like Herbert Hoover or like Andrew Jackson," Corcoran told Ickes. Late in the previous year, Hopkins, Ickes, Jimmy Roosevelt, Corcoran, Cohen, and other liberals began meeting informally to consider methods for purging the party of conservative obstructionists and to make certain that the 1940 convention would nominate a liberal presidential candidate. An embittered Hugh Johnson called them the "White House Janizaries." To them, politics was national and ideological in scope, and they had little respect for the views of Farley and the professionals, who cautioned against taking sides in Democratic primaries and becoming involved in local feuds. The impressive victories scored by two enthusiastic New Dealers, Lister Hill of Alabama and Claude Pepper* of Florida, in hotly contested senate primaries encouraged them to believe that similar tactics might be effective elsewhere.

Roosevelt wavered before taking the drastic step of intervening in local elections, however. He had built his career by cultivating political relationships across the spectrum of the Democratic party, and he genuinely liked many of the men who opposed his programs. But the decision was thrust upon him. He was angered by the renomination of the anti-New Deal Senator Guy Gillette in Iowa and was worried by the announcement, by Governor Philip La Follette of Wisconsin, of the organization of a new Progressive party. Roosevelt viewed La Follette's decision as a threat to his appeal to liberals and acted to remove any doubt that the Democratic party was the party of true progressivism.

The opening gun of the purge was fired in a Fireside Chat on the evening of June 24, 1938, in which the President denounced those Democrats opposed to his policy of liberal reform as "Copperheads." To forestall attacks upon him for intervening in local elections, he declared: "As the head of the Democratic party . . . charged with the responsibility of carrying out the definitely liberal declaration of principles set forth in the 1936 Democratic platform, I feel that I have every right to speak in those few instances where there may be a clear issue between candidates for a Democratic nomination involving these principles, or involving a clear misuse of my own name."

The major targets of the purge were Senators Walter George of Georgia, "Cotton Ed" Smith of South Carolina, Millard Tydings of Maryland, Pat McCarran of Nevada, and Alva Adams of Colorado, as well as Representative John J. O'Connor of New York, who used the chairmanship of the House Rules Committee to bottle up New Deal legislation. Roosevelt's tactics were varied. In some cases, he led the attack in person; in others, agents dispensed the presidential blessing or malediction. Favorites were greeted warmly; opponents, snubbed. Party regulars

---

* There were rumors that Pepper had been put over by threatening Florida citrus growers with the withholding of federal funds to combat the Mediterranean fruit fly if they did not support him.

were appalled by Roosevelt's decision, and Farley tried to dissuade him from taking this step. But Farley's star was dimming in the White House firmament.

"The Boss has stirred up a hornet's nest by getting into these primary fights," Vice-President Garner complained to him. "There are twenty men—Democrats—in the Senate who will vote against anything he wants because they are mad clean through, Jim. I think you ought to take exception to the President's attitude."

"John, I just can't do that unless I resign from the Cabinet and the Democratic Committee," Farley replied. "I don't like this purge any better than you do, but the situation won't be helped by my breaking with the Boss."

Leaving Washington on a ten-car train, the President barnstormed across the country. The first major stop was in Kentucky, where he urged the renomination of Senator Barkley, who was opposed in the primary by Governor A. B. "Happy" Chandler. The irrepressible Chandler plumped himself down in an open car between Barkley and the President during the welcoming parade, while the senator did a slow burn and Roosevelt laughed at this impertinence. But the grin tightened on Chandler's face as Roosevelt made the seemingly offhanded revelation that the governor had tried to barter his way into the Senate by persuading him to appoint Kentucky's other senator to a federal judgeship.

Barkley won, but the WPA was a storm center in the Kentucky election. WPA "scandals" had long been fodder for the newspapers and congressional investigators who charged that relief was administered with the aim of building a New Deal political machine.† Hopkins bridled at these accusations, and he claimed that most had been "trumped up" by the Republicans. "How many WPA employees have been involved, even in the charges?" Hopkins asked during a radio speech. "How many have you read about? One hundred? Two hundred? Two hundred and fifty? If it is 250, the total is exactly one one-hundredth of one per cent of the people in the program. That makes us 99.99 per cent pure." Newspapers charged that Barkley's victory had been "bought" with WPA votes, and a senate investigating committee, dominated by anti-New Dealers, turned up evidence of political pressure on some WPA workers to vote for Barkley under the threat of being fired. Others were said to have been shaken down for campaign contributions. When the final tallies were made, it turned out that Barkley had, indeed, gotten some twenty thousand dollars from employees of various federal agencies. But Chandler had outdone him by collecting about seventy-one thousand dollars from state workers. The

† Congressional investigators dug not only for evidence of corruption but for alleged "Reds" who were supposed to have battened on WPA programs for artists, writers, and actors. "Now this [Christopher] Marlowe, is he a communist type, too?" Representative Joe Stearnes of Alabama asked the director of the Federal Theatre Project.

main result of the probe was the passage of the Hatch Act, in 1939, which forbade political activity by federal employees.

In Texas, Roosevelt ignored Senator Tom Connally and Garner and embraced Maury Maverick and Lyndon Johnson. Realizing that he could do little to harm Adams and McCarran, he nevertheless maneuvered to keep them from appearing on the rear platform of the presidential special when he stopped in Nevada and Colorado. In California, he had kind words for the aging Senator McAdoo, who was being challenged by Sheridan Downey, a leader of a pension plan known as "Thirty Dollars Every Thursday."

Everywhere, Roosevelt's personal popularity seemed unimpaired by the setbacks in Washington. In Marietta, Ohio, an old woman bent down and patted the footprint he had left in the dust. And although editorial comment was overwhelmingly critical of the purge, a Nebraska newspaper, the Lincoln *Star*, caught the essence of the struggle from the President's viewpoint: "The issue is not the election of 'yes-men' or men who say they reserve the right to vote their conscience. The issue, in the simplest terms, is the destruction of the New Deal."

Roosevelt opened the main event, the campaign, against Senator George at an outdoor rally on August 10 in the sweltering little town of Barnesville, Georgia. Seated beside him were Harry Hopkins, Lawrence Camp, the Atlanta attorney who had been persuaded to oppose the venerable senator, and a third candidate, gallus-snapping Governor Eugene Talmadge. The President had told a friend that if he couldn't get a proper candidate he would run one of the tenant farmers from Warm Springs—and some thought the colorless Camp little better. Senator George listened impassively as Roosevelt called for his defeat. "Let me make it perfectly clear that he [Senator George] is, and I hope always will be, my friend," the President declared. "He is beyond any possible question a gentleman and a scholar . . . but . . . I am impelled to make it clear that on most public questions he and I do not speak the same language."

As soon as Roosevelt had finished, the senator shook hands with him. "Mr. President," he said, "I want you to know that I accept the challenge."

Roosevelt repeated the performance in South Carolina, where he endorsed Governor Olin D. Johnston over the antediluvian Ed Smith. And then it was on to Maryland. For two days, he stumped the state against Tydings, among the bitterest of anti-New Dealers. Even Farley joined him, for the aristocratic senator had deserted the Democratic fold on almost every important piece of reform legislation. But as in Georgia, the White House had waited until the last minute to choose a candidate, David J. Lewis, a liberal western-Maryland congressman, and Tydings had preempted the usual sources of campaign funds and organizational backing. Tydings shrewdly refused to be drawn into a discussion of his conservative record and lashed out instead at the attempt to dictate to Maryland voters. "Maryland will not permit her star in the flag to be 'purged' from the constellation of the states," proclaimed the senator. During a Roosevelt campaign stop on the Eastern Shore, reporters asked Farley how it was going. "It's a bust," he glumly replied.

And it was. Tydings easily won renomination. In Georgia, the hapless Camp trailed both Senator George and Gene Talmadge. Ed Smith defeated Johnston after both candidates waged a white-supremacy, racist campaign in which there was little difference between liberal and conservative. "It takes a long time to bring the past up to the present," Roosevelt said upon learning of Smith's victory. McAdoo lost, and Maury Maverick was beaten. McCarran and Adams won. Roosevelt's only solace was the ouster of O'Connor from Congress. He tried to put the best face upon the debacle by denying that it constituted a personal rejection, but this was merely whistling in the dark. His attempt to transform the Democratic party into a liberal party had not only eluded him, but in the effort he had strengthened parochialism and conservatism. Once again, it had been forcefully demonstrated that even a popular and powerful leader cannot transfer his strength to other candidates.

By intruding into local elections, Roosevelt lost the moral issue, just as in the Supreme Court fight. The earlier struggle conjured up visions of "court-packing," while the "purge" created the sinister specter of concentration camps, forced labor, and firing squads. The inevitable result of the President's interference was to make martyrs out of those under attack. Some observers even hazarded the opinion that Ed Smith would have been defeated had Roosevelt stayed out of the campaign. In their eagerness to build up a presidential faction, the President's liberal advisers had failed to take into account the homegrown, inbred nature of American politics. They forgot—or ignored—the fact that elections of national importance often turn on local issues.

The disastrous outcome of the purge foreshadowed the results in November. Aided by the recession and the disarray among the Democrats, the resurgent Republicans captured eighty-one new seats in the House and eight in the Senate, along with a net gain of thirteen governorships. Two of the most prominent liberal governors—Frank Murphy of Michigan and Philip La Follette of Wisconsin—were among the casualties. In Albany, Herbert Lehman only narrowly staved off defeat by Thomas E. Dewey, the racket-busting Manhattan prosecutor. The Republicans received a transfusion of fresh talent. In Ohio, Robert A. Taft, the former President's son, was elected to the Senate, while in Minnesota, the thirty-one-year-old Harold Stassen was chosen governor. The Democrats retained control of Congress, but the trend against the New Deal was unmistakable. The alliance of conservative Democrats and Republicans that had hamstrung the Administration's legislative program in the previous session was now stronger than ever.

Roosevelt was surprised by the magnitude of this defeat—he had expected to lose one senator and sixteen congressmen—but he put the best face on it. At a cabinet post-mortem, he attributed the disaster to local party factionalism and a poor selection of candidates. In Massachusetts, he said, the people had not wanted Jim Curley back as governor; there was a racetrack scandal in Rhode Island; a squabble over the Merritt Parkway affected the outcome in Connecticut; in New Jersey, people were fed up with Boss Frank Hague's dictatorship; charges of radicalism had been damaging to Murphy in Michigan; falling farm prices hurt in the Midwest; there was corruption in Ohio. And so it went. Later, a reporter asked if he expected trouble in the new Congress from the conservative coalition.

"No, I don't think so," Roosevelt replied.

"I do!" the newsman shot back amid general laughter.

Yet, to say that the 1938 congressional elections constituted a total repudiation of the New Deal and Franklin Roosevelt would be incorrect. A *Fortune* poll taken early the following year indicated that more than 60 percent of the American people approved in some way of both the President and his policies. And despite the Republican sweep, Roosevelt was the first two-term President since James Monroe whose party did not lose control of Congress before the completion of his second term. The people might have been jaded with the New Deal, but they did not want it dismantled. The sense of emergency engendered by the Great Depression had vanished, and Americans sought a return to the traditional ways of existence. As Woodrow Wilson once noted, American society could not sustain, for more than a very limited time, the tension and turbulence of reform.

Roosevelt acknowledged that the reforming spirit of the New Deal had ebbed, in his annual message to Congress on January 4, 1939. "We have now passed the period of internal conflict in the launching of our program of social reform," he said. "Our full energies may now be released to invigorate the processes of recovery in order to preserve our reforms." For the first time since 1933, he did not send a package of fresh reforms to Congress. The session was primarily concerned with old business. Social security was broadened, and the long-delayed and watered-down Reorganization Act was approved. The Executive Office of the President was established, the Bureau of the Budget was transferred to it, and the President was also given authority to appoint several administrative assistants. For the most part, the session was a stalemate, as conservatives worked to prune relief and public works projects.

But the President was no longer devoting his undivided attention to domestic affairs. More and more, he was absorbed in foreign dangers and American defense as the winds of war began to blow from across the Atlantic and the Pacific.

XXII

THE SEARCH FOR PEACE

MODERN HISTORY PRESENTS few ironies greater than the intertwining of the fates of Franklin Roosevelt and Adolf Hitler. No two men could have been more unlike in personality and policy; yet, for a decade, the shadow of one fell across the path of the other. Roosevelt and Hitler entered office within a few weeks of each other, both having vaulted to power on the wave of despair that accompanied the Great Depression. Both expressed the determination to lift their people out of the malaise of defeat and to restore the national will. Both made eloquent appeals to the emotions, both were daring gamblers, and both passed from the scene in the spring of 1945. There the resemblance ends, however. Roosevelt appealed to the best instincts of mankind, Hitler to the worst. A clash was inevitable.

Exactly at what point Roosevelt sensed the brutal consequences for the United States inherent in the aggression of Hitler and his Italian and Japanese allies is an unresolved question. Early on, he regarded these countries as "bandit nations," and Rex Tugwell claimed he wanted "to do something" about them as early as 1935. But foreign policy did not have high priority in the early New Deal. In fact, Mrs. Roosevelt once invited Anne O'Hare McCormick, of the New York *Times*, to dinner with the suggestion, "I wonder if you would try to get the President more interested in foreign affairs."

With the exception of his unsuccessful attempt to secure American membership in the World Court, Roosevelt made no effort to challenge the pacifist and isolationist mood that prevailed in the United States in the mid-1930s. The transition from isolation to intervention was a long and tortuous process. Numerous trial balloons were sent aloft, and samplings of public opinion were assayed with the intensity of a prospector examining gold-bearing ore. Recalling the failure of Woodrow Wilson to convince the American people to support the League of Nations, Roosevelt realized that an effective policy abroad required a solid consensus at home.

Later on, when he understood the danger Hitler posed to the United States, Roosevelt put all his skills as a showman to work to educate the American people to the grim realities of the international situation, and he was not above resorting to sleight-of-hand. Sometimes, as in the case of the buildup of American military strength, he shrewdly combined within the same measure the isolationist concept of keeping out of war and the interventionist idea of preventing war. Internationalists charged him with vacillation and failing to provide leadership; isolationists accused him of cynical duplicity. Perhaps the razor-tongued Clare Booth Luce best expressed the frustration of both sides. "Every great leader had his typical gesture," she said. "Hitler, the upraised arm; Churchill the V sign." And Roosevelt? She wet her index finger and held it up in the air.

There was no quick and clean break to mark the point at which Roosevelt became absorbed in foreign affairs at the expense of domestic policy. History abhors such attempts at neat compartmentalization. When Japan invaded China, in 1937, the President was involved in the Supreme Court "packing" fight; the recession was uppermost in his mind as Hitler annexed Austria, the following year; the Munich crisis was played out against the background of the "purge." And so it went. When Roosevelt did issue warnings about the gravity of the international situation and sought to increase America's defense capabilities, critics charged that he was trying to cover up his domestic failures by resorting to foreign adventures that were certain to involve the United States in war.

For the most part, Roosevelt operated in the sphere of foreign policy in the same, freewheeling manner in which he conducted domestic affairs. As always, he sought his own information outside official channels. He spent considerable time chatting with knowledgeable visitors and had a network of informants that ranged from Bernard Baruch to Captain Evans F. Carlson, who had commanded the marine security guard at Warm Springs before becoming assistant naval attaché in China. Roosevelt pitted his foreign-policy advisers against each other, as he did on the domestic side, while keeping control of the decision-making process firmly in his own hands. He respected Cordell Hull's knowledge of the ways of Congress, but he sometimes lost patience with the Secretary of State's moralizing and cautious approach to diplomacy, and preferred to work with his old friend and fellow patrician Sumner Welles, who had succeeded William Phillips as under Secretary. Hull was infuriated at being bypassed, and he and Welles were barely on speaking terms. Roosevelt encouraged the tension between the two men as a way to divide the State Department and concentrate control of foreign relations in his hands.

The President distrusted the State Department, regarding it as conservative, rigid, and prone to leaks. He believed that the Foreign Service was filled with deadwood, men who had been appointed merely because of their social standing and instinctively opposed to his policies at home and abroad. "You should go through the experience of trying to get any changes in the thinking, policy and action of the career diplomat and then you would know what a real problem was," Roosevelt once told Marriner Eccles. With dismaying regularity, as far as Hull was concerned, he assigned tasks that belonged to the State Department to the Treasury or to the Navy or to whatever agency he thought might get the job done more efficiently. Important messages were sometimes transmitted through the Navy, because he did not trust the State Department code. Eventually he completely bypassed the State Department and made Harry Hopkins his diplomatic troubleshooter, responsible to no one but himself.

Roosevelt's diplomatic appointments—a grab bag of old friends, career diplomats, campaign contributors, professors, and military men—indicate a disorganized approach to foreign policy. Yet, as Robert Dallek points out, there was an underlying logic to his choice of diplomatic representatives. William E. Dodd, who was sent to Berlin, underscored the President's aversion to Nazism. William C. Bullitt and then Joseph E. Davies, who were sympathetic to the Russians, were sent to Moscow as a sign that the United States wanted improved relations with the Soviet Union. Later, the skeptical Averell Harriman provided a counterbalance to the wartime euphoria about our Soviet allies. And Joe Kennedy was dispatched to London with the expectation that a cool-eyed businessman would be able to provide candid reports about the appeasement policy of the British Government.

The first reaction of the President to a report from his son Jimmy that Kennedy, then chairman of the Maritime Commission, wanted to be named envoy to Britain was one of merriment. "He laughed so hard he almost toppled from his wheelchair," recalled the younger Roosevelt. Nevertheless, this was the type of unexpected gesture that appealed to him, and the more he thought about it, the more he was intrigued by the idea of sending a Boston Irishman to the Court of St. James's. Thinking Kennedy's presence in London might also help overcome the resistance of Irish-Americans to working with Britain in case of war, Roosevelt invited him to the Oval Office one day in the autumn of 1937. The President greeted him and then asked that he step back a bit so he could get a better look at him. Puzzled, Kennedy did so.

"Joe," said the President after a few moments, "would you mind taking your pants down?"

Kennedy was so surprised that he asked the President if he had heard him correctly. He had indeed. Kennedy undid his suspenders and dropped his pants, looking silly and embarrassed as he stood before the fireplace in his shorts.

"Someone who saw you in a bathing suit once told me something I now know to be true," Roosevelt said. "Joe, just look at your legs. You are just the most bowlegged man I have ever seen. Don't you know that the ambassador to the Court of St. James's has to go through an induction ceremony in which he wears knee britches and silk stockings? Can you imagine how you will look? When photos of our new ambassador appear all over the world we'll be a laughingstock. You're just not right for the job, Joe."

"Mr. President," pleaded Kennedy, "if I can get the permission of His Majesty's government to wear a cutaway coat and striped pants to the ceremony, would you agree to appoint me?"

"Well, Joe, you know how the British are about tradition. There's no way you are going to get permission, and I must name a new ambassador soon."

"Will you give me two weeks?"

Roosevelt agreed. Kennedy pulled up his pants and his dignity and left the White House, leaving the President chuckling contentedly to himself.

Two weeks later, Kennedy was back with an official letter granting him permission to appear at the ceremony in striped pants and cutaway. He got the appointment. Later, someone complained about it to Roosevelt, but he threw back his head and laughed. Sending an Irishman to be the ambassador to London was even better than setting a thief to catch a thief in the SEC. "It was the greatest joke in the world," he said.

Few Americans admired Hitler or the Japanese warlords, but they were reluctant to become embroiled in the problems of Europe and East Asia. As much as they sympathized with the victims of aggression, they had no desire to repeat the experience of 1917. Influenced by revisionist historians and the Nye Committee's charges that the United States had been tricked into the First World War by a combination of Allied propaganda, rapacious bankers, and "merchants of death," Americans fervently declared, "Never Again!" College students embraced pacifism, and campuses erupted into strikes aimed at getting rid of ROTC. Many Americans insisted that the United States avoid all "entangling alliances," including commitments to ensure international tranquillity through collective security. Such arrangements, it was argued, might drag America into another foreign war. "The policy of the United States is to remain untangled and free," declared Walter Lippmann in January 1936. "Let us follow that policy. Let us remain untangled and free. Let us make no alliances. Let us make no commitments. . . ."

Roosevelt pursued a foreign policy that mirrored the isolationist mood of the country during his first years in the White House. Except for objections to limitations imposed on his freedom of action, he accepted a series of isolationist-inspired neutrality laws even though they did not discriminate between the aggressor and his victim. He acquiesced in Mussolini's brutal seizure of Ethiopia, Japan's rape of China, and the reoccupation of the Rhineland by Hitler in defiance of the Versailles Treaty, and followed the lead of Britain and France in taking a hands-off attitude toward the Spanish Civil War. Spain became a proving ground for the weapons of World War II as Germany and Italy aided General Francisco Franco's Fascist rebellion while the Soviet Union supplied the government forces, or Loyalists. Like the Europeans, Roosevelt was more concerned about preventing the spread of war than saving Spanish democracy.

Undoubtedly, American isolationism encouraged the dictators, but the appeasement policies of France and Britain were no inspiration to Roosevelt to take a stand against the aggressors. Failing some positive sign from the democracies, it was hardly to be expected that the President would act unilaterally. And in the case of Spain, intervention on the side of the Loyalists, with whom the President privately sympathized, was politically unthinkable in view of the support given Franco by the Catholic hierarchy. An attempt was made in 1938 to lift the arms embargo, which was hurting the Loyalists more than the rebels, but congressional leaders warned the President that it would mean "the loss of every Catholic voter."

Some historians have argued that Roosevelt floated along on the isolationist tide in order to protect his domestic program, and thus failed to fulfill the obligation of leadership. "As a foreign-policy maker," says James MacGregor Burns, "Roosevelt during his first term was more the pussyfooting politician than political leader." Such charges are predicated on the supposition that the President was a closet internationalist and political expediency kept him from exhibiting his true beliefs. Perhaps. But there is much support for the position that Roosevelt was at this time an isolationist in the classic American tradition. In his speeches and letters, he constantly reiterated the conviction that the United States should avoid being drawn into another foreign war.

On Armistice Day 1935, he noted that this generation of Americans "know that the elation and prosperity which may come from a new war must lead—for those who survive it—to economic and social collapse more sweeping than anything we have experienced in the past." America's proper role in world affairs was to provide "the power of good example" to mankind of the virtues of peace and democracy. A few weeks later, he sent a similar message to William Dodd, the American envoy in Berlin. "I do not know that the United States can save civilization but at least by our example we can make people think and give them the opportunity of saving themselves," the President wrote. "The trouble is that the people of Germany, Italy and Japan are not given the privilege of thinking."

Roosevelt dwelt at length upon the threats to peace in various tinderboxes around the globe in his State of the Union speech in January 1936. "A point has been reached," he said, "where the people of the Americas must take cognizance of growing ill-will, of marked trends toward aggression, of increasing armaments, of shortening tempers—a situation which has in it many of the elements that lead to the tragedy of a general war." He urged the continuation of "two-fold neutrality": an embargo on the shipment of arms, munitions, and implements of war, combined with efforts to discourage belligerents from purchasing huge quantities of other American products such as oil and scrap iron that were of assistance to their war efforts. And he reiterated his belief that the United States should serve as a beacon of liberty to mankind "and through example and all legitimate encouragement and assistance to persuade other Nations to return to the ways of peace and good will." Speaking in Dallas at midyear, Roosevelt offered sympathy to the Europeans facing the threat of war but repeated his pledge of neutrality. "We want to help them all that we can," he declared, "but they have understood very well . . . that help is going to be confined to moral help, and that we are not going to get tangled up with their troubles in days to come."

Roosevelt had revealed the roots of his isolationism in his speech at Chautauqua in August 1936. He vividly recalled his visit to the battlefields of France and Belgium in 1918 . . . the wounded . . . the gassed . . . the dead lying in the mud . . . the blasted towns . . . the widows and orphans. "I hate war," he declared. "I have passed unnumbered hours, I shall pass unnumbered hours thinking and planning how war may be kept from this nation. . . . We can keep out of war," he concluded, "if those who watch and decide . . . possess the courage to say 'no' to those who selfishly or unwisely would let us go to war."

These remarks are often dismissed as mere campaign rhetoric, but Sam Rosenman was convinced of the President's sincerity. Roosevelt regarded the Chautauqua speech as one of the most important he ever delivered, according to Rosenman, and he sent friends specially printed and inscribed copies for Christmas. Rather than just a vote-getting campaign speech, it was as clear and as precise a statement of his innermost beliefs as Roosevelt ever presented, says Rosenman.

Roosevelt's fundamental aversion to American participation in a foreign war received its severest test when the Japanese militarists renewed their assault against China in July 1937. Suffering from a population explosion and crowded onto their island empire, the Japanese set out to establish a new order in eastern Asia under their political and economic domination. International opinion, which had proved completely ineffectual in halting the Italian conquest of Ethiopia or their own earlier aggression in Manchuria, was ignored. Preparatory to launching the attack, Japan signed the Anti-Comintern Pact with Germany and Italy, which provided for their assistance should the Soviet Union intervene on the side of China. Japan also renounced attempts at naval limitation going back to the Washington Conference of 1921 and began a massive program of warship construction.

As a result of the historic connection of the Delano family with China, Roosevelt's sympathies, like those of most Americans, lay with the helpless Chinese. They felt a sentimental attachment to China, regarding themselves as self-appointed guardians of the country since the Open Door policy was proclaimed, at the turn of the century. American businessmen, missionaries, and teachers had created an idealized picture of the country, while Japan was viewed with mounting hostility, particularly after Japanese expansionism was seen as a threat to the Philippines and other island outposts in the Pacific. To protest the Japanese attack, Americans boycotted Japanese goods, and some women wore cotton stockings instead of hose made from imported silk.

Roosevelt's immediate problem was whether or not to invoke the Neutrality Act, which had recently been revised and made permanent by Congress. Although isolationists pressed him to declare the law in effect, he was reluctant to do so, because an arms embargo would do more harm to the Chinese, who depended on imported weapons, than to the Japanese. Taking advantage of a provision of the act that stated it was to be applied when the President found a state of hostilities to exist, Roosevelt pointed out that neither side had declared war, and declined to invoke the law. Over the next few months, this expedient hardened into a permanent policy.

Aware that his record of leadership at home and the strength of the nation for which he spoke had thrust a role in world affairs upon him, Roosevelt searched for a policy that would help maintain world order without committing the United States to any action that would upset the isolationists. For a brief moment, he toyed with the idea of economic and trade sanctions against future aggressors, but dropped it. "I now think it is a matter of longtime education," he told Treasury Secretary Morgenthau of the process of weaning the American people from isolationism. "I am not going to do anything which would require a definite response or action on the part of anybody."

Hull and Ambassador-at-Large Norman Davis, the Administration's key foreign-policy adviser, urged Roosevelt to speak out for international cooperation and world order during a fence-mending cross-country tour planned for that autumn. An appearance in Chicago, the capital of isolationism, on October 5, 1937, to dedicate a bridge built with PWA funds was chosen as a suitable pulpit. All that morning, people had gathered along the lakefront, and by the time Roosevelt rose to speak the crowd stretched as far as the eye could see. Little more than half a mile away loomed the tower of the Chicago *Tribune*, the most strident voice of isolationism. The President quickly paid his respects to the new bridge and turned to the "reign of terror and international lawlessness" that had been unleashed upon mankind. "Innocent peoples . . . innocent nations are being cruelly sacrificed to a greed for power," Roosevelt warned.

"If those things come to pass in other parts of the world let no one imagine that America will escape, that America may expect mercy, that this Western Hemisphere will not be attacked and that it will continue tranquilly and peacefully." If the peace-loving nations wished to preserve their freedoms, he continued, they must make "a concerted effort in opposition" to those nations that violate treaties and the rights of humanity. Likening the spread of international lawlessness to an epidemic, Roosevelt said that "when an epidemic of physical disease starts to spread, the community approves and joins in a quarantine of the patients in order to protect the health of the community against the spread of the disease. . . . War is a contagion whether it be declared or undeclared. It can engulf states and peoples remote from the original scene of hostilities. . . ."

Following these eloquent words, everyone awaited action from the President—but none was forthcoming. On October 6, the day after the Chicago speech, he fenced with reporters who asked if a "quarantine" meant economic sanctions against Japan. "Look, 'sanctions' is a terrible word to use. They are out of the window," Roosevelt replied. "The lead is in the last line, 'America actively engages in the search for peace.' I can't tell you what the methods will be. We are looking for some way to peace." And as if to reassure the isolationists, he added that "by no means is it necessary that that way be contrary to the exercise of neutrality."

Roosevelt's refusal to break with the policy of blind neutrality has been blamed on the violent and nearly unanimous repudiation of the speech by the isolationists. Some writers have pictured Roosevelt as having tried to chart a fresh course against the prevailing winds of isolationism but he had found them blowing too strongly against him. "The President was attacked by a vast majority of the press," said Rosenman. "Telegrams of denunciation came in at once. . . . 'It's a terrible thing,' he once said to me, having in mind I'm sure this occasion, 'to look over your shoulder when you are trying to lead—and to find no one there.'"

Yet, no such rejection occurred. With the exception of the isolationist press—"Stop Foreign Meddling: America Wants Peace" proclaimed *The Wall Street Journal*—the majority of the American people seemed to agree that something should be done to "quarantine the aggressors." "The President's speech was magnificent," said Colonel Frank Knox, the Republican vice-presidential nominee in 1936. Foreign reaction was also supportive. A day after the speech, the League of Nations approved a report censuring Japan and convened a meeting in Brussels of the signatories to the Nine-Power Treaty that had been designed to protect the independence and territorial integrity of China.

Having anticipated broad criticism, Roosevelt was surprised by this totally unexpected reaction. He had thought only in general terms about preserving the peace and had nothing to offer in the way of a new policy. As Dorothy Borg has pointed out in her study of the Chicago speech, Roosevelt had dramatized the yearning of the American people for peace, but he was unprepared to proceed beyond it. Nevertheless, Roosevelt did not feel that he had sounded a retreat by refusing to implement the "quarantine." He looked upon the speech as part of the educational process of the American people. "I hope you liked the Chicago speech and the repercussions across the water," he wrote Colonel House a few weeks afterward. "I . . . verily believe that as time goes on we can slowly but surely make people realize that war will be a greater danger to us if we close all the doors and windows than if we go out in the street and use our influence to curb the riot."

Isolationist fears that Roosevelt intended to abandon neutrality were scotched at the Brussels conference. Norman Davis, who headed the American delegation, was instructed to avoid the question of sanctions against Japan and to work for a truce in the Far East. The conference was doomed to failure. Japan refused to attend, and the other parties could not agree on what steps to take against her. When the British and the French, who had refused to support sanctions in the League of Nations, sought to persuade the American delegation to make such a proposal, Roosevelt accused them of trying to protect their own interests in the Far East by deflecting Japanese anger onto the United States. In the final analysis, the Nine-Power conference did more harm than good. The refusal of the Western nations to take a stand against Japanese aggression encouraged the hard-liners in Tokyo, and they did not wait long to show their contempt.

On December 12, 1937, three weeks after the end of the conference, the shallow-draft gunboat USS *Panay* lay at anchor in the Yangtze River about twenty-seven miles above Nanking, the Chinese capital, which was under attack by the Japanese. A handful of American businessmen, diplomats, and newsmen had taken asylum on the vessel, and she was shepherding three small tankers belonging to the Standard Oil Company.

Two large American flags had been freshly painted on the *Panay*'s topside awnings, and each vessel flew the Stars and Stripes. Shortly after 1:30 P.M., a flight of Japanese dive bombers passed overhead and people came on deck to watch them. Suddenly the planes dropped out of the bright China sky. "They're letting go bombs!" someone shouted. "Get under cover!"

Hit repeatedly by bombs and riddled by bullets, the *Panay* slowly settled into the muddy waters of the Yangtze with her flag still flying. As the passengers and crew scrambled ashore in rafts and boats, they were strafed by the Japanese planes. Two American sailors and an Italian journalist were killed, and another forty men were wounded. The tankers, which were also bombed and machine-gunned, were beached before they sank, and their Chinese crews escaped ashore. Several British vessels on the Yangtze were attacked that same day.

Roosevelt and Secretary Hull were outraged by the wanton sinking of the *Panay*. An angry message was sent to Tokyo demanding an apology and compensation for the loss of the vessel and American lives. Morgenthau was ordered to determine what authority would be required to seize Japanese assets in this country as security for payment of the indemnity, and the President discussed the possibility of imposing economic sanctions against Japan. But the reactions of the American people and of the Japanese Government were both less bellicose than expected. Rather than regarding the *Panay* incident as another sinking of the *Maine*, the majority of Americans saw no reason for war, and the Japanese, who seemed genuinely embarrassed, swiftly apologized. Fearing that the crisis might push Britain and the United States into an alliance against them, the Japanese attributed the attack to a mistake by an overzealous officer, paid an indemnity of $2.2 million, and assured Washington that thenceforth the rights of Americans in China would be respected. The *Panay* case quickly faded from public memory.*

Isolationist sentiment received a shot in the arm, however. A long-pigeon-holed resolution calling for a constitutional amendment providing for a national referendum before the President could declare war was brought to a vote in the House. The only thing that prevented it from passing was a strongly worded letter from the President, who argued that the resolution would "cripple" his ability to conduct foreign policy. Even so, the vote was 209 to 188—a clear sign of the strength of isolationism.

One of the President's first official acts of 1938 was to send a special message to Congress requesting increased defense spending. "As Com-

---

* Unknown to the American people, the Japanese sought salvage rights to the sunken *Panay* and suggested that if a replacement were built, the vessel should be constructed in a Japanese yard. Secretary Hull flatly rejected both proposals.

mander-in-Chief of the Army and Navy," Roosevelt said, "it is my constitutional duty to report to Congress that our national defense is, in the
light of the increasing armaments of other nations, inadequate for the
purposes of national security and requires increase for that reason." He
asked Congress for a defense appropriation of $1.04 billion—the largest
since just after the end of World War I—with much of the new money
earmarked for a naval buildup. This decision had the support of everyone
but the pacifists, because the Navy was regarded as the nation's first line
of defense. New battleships, carriers, and aircraft were ordered, with more
to come the following year to match the massive program of warship construction undertaken by Japan. The Imperial Navy had laid down the
largest battleships ever built, the 68,200-ton *Yamato* and *Musashi*, which
mounted nine 18.1-inch guns, compared to the 16-inchers to which the
U. S. Navy had been limited by treaty.

In Europe, the Spanish Civil War was dragging to its tragic end with
the triumph of Fascism, and Hitler, having tested the British and the
French and finding them demoralized, embarked on fresh conquests. In
March 1938, he seized control of his native Austria with a ruthless coup.
European statesmen rationalized the extinguishing of the Austrian state by
pointing to the ethnic and language ties between the two countries. As for
the United States, Austria was a long way off. Roosevelt showed his displeasure by refusing to recognize the annexation, but his main worry at
the time was the deepening economic recession and a balky Congress.

Following the annexation of Austria, the Nazis stepped up the perse-
cution of the Jews. A trickle of German Jews had reached the United
States since Hitler had come to power in 1933, but Congress had refused
to broaden immigration quotas out of fear of adding to the unemployment and relief rolls. American consular officials interpreted the stat-
utes so rigorously that almost three quarters of the German quota went
unfilled. Three thousand Jews besieged the American consulate in
Vienna, and Representative Emanuel Celler, of New York, thought the
State Department's heart was "muffled in protocol." The President, who
was sympathetic to the plight of the Jews but had done little to alleviate
it, was under pressure to do something to assist the refugees. He invited
thirty-two nations to an international conference at Évian, France, to establish a committee to facilitate the emigration of the victims of Nazism,
but he cut the ground out from under it with the declaration that there
would be no changes in American immigration laws.

On November 10, 1938, the Nazis burned 195 synagogues in Germany, savagely beat every Jew they could find, hauled twenty-five thousand people to concentration camps, and shattered the windows of eight
hundred Jewish-owned shops in a fit of rage and destruction that came to
be known as *Kristallnacht*. "I myself could scarcely believe that such

things could occur in a twentieth-century civilization," Roosevelt told the press. The American ambassador to Berlin was recalled, and about fifteen thousand German and Austrian refugees in the United States on visitors permits were allowed to remain. But there was no relaxation of immigration quotas. Public opinion remained a barrier to revision, but the feeling persists that had Roosevelt mounted an effort to permit the victims of Nazism to come to the United States in greater numbers, the nation's humane instincts might have been aroused. Thousands of people who later died in the Nazi gas chambers could have been saved had Roosevelt been more concerned about their fate.

Austria was a prelude, rather than a finale. After parading through the streets of Vienna, the city of his tortured youth, Hitler turned his attention to Czechoslovakia. Established from bits and pieces of the old Austro-Hungarian Empire following World War I, the nation had become a showcase for democracy in Central Europe. Hitler, who envisioned all the Germans of Europe united within the Fatherland, demanded the cession of the Sudetenland, a mountainous region along the Czech-German border where most of the people were of German origin. Nazi henchmen in Czechoslovakia alleged that the Sudeten Germans were being oppressed.

If the Czechs lost the Sudetenland, they would be deprived of their natural defense barrier. Stoutly refusing to give in to Hitler's demand, they called upon France, Britain, and the Soviet Union for help. The crisis reached its height in September 1938 as Hitler promised a frenzied Nazi-party rally in Nuremberg that the Sudeten Germans would have "a party day of their own" by October 15. German troops massed on the frontier. The small but efficient Czech Army was mobilized. The French called a half million men to the colors, and the British dug air-raid shelters in the London parks and distributed gas masks. Black headlines reflected the mounting tension, and for the first time the doom-laden voices of radio commentators delivered an hour-by-hour account of the unfolding of an international crisis.

But the British and the French were reluctant to go to war because of what Neville Chamberlain, the British Prime Minister, described as "a quarrel in a faraway country between people of whom we know nothing." Unprepared for war, the British feared they would be unable to defend their empire from an onslaught that was likely to include Italy and Japan as well as Germany. Chamberlain opted for trying to appease Britain's potential enemies in an effort to keep them from ganging up on her. France's national will had been sapped by the bloodbath of World War I, and the French Army was a hollow shell. Moreover, France was torn by political strife between the left and the right, which made it impossible to reach an agreement on foreign policy. Colonel Charles A. Lindbergh, the famed "Lone Eagle" of the first nonstop solo flight from New York to Paris, contributed to the climate of fear in London and Paris by spreading reports of the invincibility of the *Luftwaffe*, the German Air Force. The Soviets were the most willing to come to Czechoslovakia's assistance. Joseph Stalin, the Soviet dictator, later indicated that he would have done so had the Western powers honored their commitments, but there was no possibility of moving Russian troops across the intervening nations, particularly Poland.

Although Roosevelt was deeply involved in his "purge" of political opponents, he observed the drift toward war in Europe with mounting concern. Regretting his decision to follow the lead of France and Britain in acquiescing in the Fascist takeover in Spain, he now wished them to take a stand against Hitler and decided to make certain that the Germans understood American intentions. "We in the Americas are no longer a far away continent," he told a Canadian audience while on an across-the-border visit. "The vast amount of our resources, the vigor of our commerce and the strength of our men have made us vital factors in world peace whether we choose or not. . . . I give you assurance that the people of the United States will not stand idly if domination of Canadian soil is threatened by any other Empire."

The President added to his series of warning gestures by asking Morgenthau to develop a plan that would allow Britain and France to deposit gold in this country that could be used for purchases of war matériel. Roosevelt was delighted with a proposal developed by the Treasury Secretary and telephoned Hull. "I have hatched a chicken," he said. "Do you want to come over and look at it?" When the Secretary of State arrived at the White House, he told him that he intended to have the plan shown to the German ambassador. "It's a hundred-to-one shot that I will do this if you go into Czechoslovakia," he wished to tell the envoy. Hull scotched the plan. Along with the speech in Canada and a pending trade treaty with Britain, it was "apt to get the American people up on their toes over the European situation."

Whatever efforts the President was willing to make to stiffen French and British backbones soon proved moot. On September 15, Chamberlain flew to Berchtesgaden, Hitler's mountain retreat, where under the dubious assumption that Hitler desired peace as much as he did, he bartered away the Sudentenland. Roosevelt angrily told the Cabinet that Chamberlain was "for peace at any price" and described the surrender as an "international outrage." If the Czechs refused to accept this "betrayal," he said, they would be abandoned by Britain and France, who will "wash the blood from their Judas Iscariot hands." Writing to William Phillips, in Rome, he said that at best the Hitler-Chamberlain meeting would only result in a temporary postponement "of what looks to me like an inevitable conflict within the next five years. Perhaps when it comes the United States will be in a position to pick up the pieces of European civilization and help them to save what remains of the wreck—not a cheerful prospect."†

The Czechs capitulated to the pressure of Britain and France and agreed to the dismemberment of their country, but Hitler precipitated a new crisis by imposing fresh conditions. Fearing an outbreak of war, Roosevelt appealed on September 26 to the Germans, the French, the British, and the Czechs for a continuation of negotiations. "Should hostilities break out, the lives of millions of men, women and children in every country involved will most certainly be lost under circumstances of unspeakable horror," he declared. To prevent a howl from the isolationists, he emphasized that the United States would take no direct part in the discussions. Nothing happened, and the following day Roosevelt asked Mussolini to use his influence to help bring the parties together. He also sent a personal message to Hitler in which he said war was "as unnecessary as it is unjustifiable" and reiterated his call for renewed negotiations to end the crisis.

Having built up tension, Hitler invited Chamberlain, Édouard Daladier, the French Premier, and Mussolini to a conference in Munich on September 29. As soon as he learned that the British Prime Minister had accepted the invitation, Roosevelt sent him a laconic message: "Good man." The President's appeal had had little or no effect upon Hitler's decision, however. The meeting resulted from pressure from Mussolini as well as Hitler's conviction that the British and the French were ready to cave in. He had gauged his opponents well, for without consulting the Czechs, Chamberlain and Daladier acceded to all the German demands. "This is the last territorial claim I have to make in Europe," Hitler told Chamberlain. The elated Prime Minister returned to London proclaiming that he brought "peace with honor . . . peace in our time."

Like most Americans, Roosevelt breathed a sigh of relief that the world had escaped the horrors of war. "I want you to know that I am not a bit upset over the final result" of the conference, the President told Phillips. But Munich was only a way station on the road to war. Within a week, Ambassador Bullitt reported from Paris that Daladier expected new German territorial demands within six months.

Roosevelt's ebullience had not been cooled by the international crisis, the recession, and the failure of the "purge." Although he was sometimes frustrated by the limitations upon his freedom of action, he enjoyed being

† FDR was prescient, for this is exactly what the postwar Marshall Plan set out to accomplish.

President. Nearly six years in the White House had expanded his ego, and he tended to run the country as a one-man show. Nothing counted in the entire Administration, Henry Wallace once said, except for "what went on in FDR's head." Persistent sinus and colds that were aggravated by the dampness of Washington sometimes left him looking gray and washed out, but his spirits were speedily revived by a visit to Warm Springs or a sea voyage. Signs of hypertension appeared, and he once fainted, but by and large, his health was excellent.

"Come on in!" he would boom out to a visitor and wave him in with a sweeping gesture, and his energy was contagious. All those close to him felt invigorated by the glow of his personality. This circle showed a remarkable stability and was still composed of Marvin McIntyre, Steve Early, Missy LeHand, Grace Tully, "Pa" Watson (who was soon to trade the post of military aide for presidential assistant), and Admiral Ross McIntire, the White House physician. Jimmy Roosevelt had left the staff in mid-1938, when persistent stomach problems required hospitalization.

Periodically, Roosevelt escaped from the confines of the White House to drive out to Ickes' country place in Maryland for dinner and a poker game. Within easy reach of the table were bottles of scotch, rye, bourbon, and Irish whiskey, and a washtub full of chilled beer, ginger ale, and soda. There was a dollar limit, and the President, a skillful gambler given to bluff, usually won. On one occasion, Roosevelt's car was spotted by a state trooper and word of the nocturnal visits to Ickes leaked out. Early thought it would create a poor impression if the nation learned that the President was out playing poker, so Ickes was persuaded to say that Roosevelt had come to discuss turning Springwood over to the government after his death.

Christmas was always a merry time in the Roosevelt White House, and the 1938 holiday was even livelier than usual, because Eleanor gave a coming-out party for her favorite niece and namesake, her brother Hall's daughter. Two young English physicians, William Sargant and Russell Fraser, who were visiting Boston at the time, were caught up in the festivities and invited down to Washington. They traveled with a group of Harvard students in a private railroad car and arrived at the White House just in time to dress for dinner. Sargant was seated next to Sara Roosevelt, who talked dotingly about her son during the entire meal. To the Englishman's horror, no wine was served, undoubtedly because of Eleanor's reaction to her brother's alcoholism. The President seemed tired, but he kept up his end of the conversation, telling the doctors that he eventually intended to ask Congress to approve a national medical-insurance program. Later, he brightened and began talking about his experiences as governor of New York. The visitors were amused as he told them how he had tried to stop young girls from hanging around the old soldiers' homes with the intention of marrying the veterans for their pensions.

After dinner, Hall Roosevelt beckoned Sargant and Fraser aside and ushered them up to his room, where he had a cache of liquor. Feeling more relaxed, the English visitors enjoyed the dance that followed. Eleanor captivated them with her kindness and charm, and they observed an example of her innate dignity. She tripped and fell while dancing but gaily made nothing of it except to assure her partner that all was well. After the dance, Hall attached himself to the Englishmen and begged them not to leave. He telephoned a nightclub, persuaded the manager to keep the place open, and led a party to it. They did not get back to the White House until 4:30 A.M.

Throughout the holidays, the President worked over successive drafts of the State of the Union address to be delivered to Congress on January 4, 1939. All lingering traces of the isolationism that had marked his handling of foreign affairs were wiped away with this speech, in which he warned that neutrality and appeasement were no defense against aggression. Although war had been averted, Roosevelt emphasized that peace was not assured and the United States must look to its defense. The President combined a call for repeal of the compulsory-arms-embargo provisions of the Neutrality Act with a request for another $2 billion for defense, much of it earmarked for an expansion of the nation's aerial strength. To reduce isolationist objections, Roosevelt invited the Senate Military Affairs Committee in for a confidential briefing. He candidly revealed his fears that Hitler was bent on dominating Europe, which would imperil the security of the United States. Someone told a reporter that the President had said America's frontier lay on the Rhine, and the isolationists sprang to the attack. Seething with indignation, Roosevelt branded the statement as a lie and attributed it to "some boob."‡

While Roosevelt's efforts to amend the neutrality laws were bogged down in Congress, Hitler struck again. On March 15, 1939, he tore up the agreement he had signed at Munich and occupied the remainder of Czechoslovakia. German troops arrived in Prague in a blinding snowstorm, and the few people who turned out stared at them in a state of shock. From the majestic heights of Hradcany Castle, Hitler looked down through the gloom at the city spread out before him and declared: "Czechoslovakia has ceased to exist!" A few days later, the Germans occu-

‡ Following this incident, FDR asked David Sarnoff, of RCA, to develop a device to record sensitive Oval Office meetings, and it was installed in the late summer of 1940. It was used for less than three months and then allowed to stand idle. The President apparently forgot to turn the machine off upon several occasions and it recorded private conversations. R. J. C. Butow, "The FDR Tapes," *American Heritage*, Feb.–Mar. 1982.

pied Memel, a German city on the Baltic that had passed to Lithuanian control after World War I. Mussolini crossed the Adriatic to seize Albania a month later, and Franco captured Madrid, ending the civil war in Spain. The Japanese, not to be outdone by their Axis allies, occupied the Spratly Islands, placing themselves within striking distance of the Philippines, Hong Kong, and Singapore.

Hitler had won another bloodless victory, but he underestimated the shock caused by the seizure of Czechoslovakia. Until he had extinguished Czech democracy, a case could be made for appeasing Germany. Each of Hitler's moves could be rationalized as an attempt to satisfy grievances resulting from the Versailles Treaty. But in the case of Czechoslovakia, Germany had not merely absorbed a German minority but had crushed a Slav nation. Realizing at last that Hitler's promises could not be trusted, the British and the French committed themselves to the defense of Poland, likely to be Hitler's next target. The pretext for this latest war of nerves was the "Polish Corridor," which had been carved from German territory in 1919, and the determination to regain the Baltic port of Danzig, which had been made a "free city."

The reaction in Washington to the seizure of Czechoslovakia was as grave as in London and Paris. The President was getting "madder and madder" at Hitler, Ickes reported, and he considered breaking relations with Germany. The State Department issued a forceful statement denouncing "the temporary extinguishment of the liberties of a free and independent people" and announced that the United States would not recognize the annexation. Tariffs were raised on exports subsidized by the German Government, and efforts were stepped up to encourage Congress to revise the Neutrality Act.

"We'll be on the side of Hitler by invoking the act," Roosevelt told Senator Tom Connally. "If we could get rid of the arms embargo, it wouldn't be so bad." But he got nowhere. The proposal ran into a rock wall of resistance from isolationists such as Senator Borah. The President invited Borah and other senate leaders to the White House for a personal appeal, but he was unmoved. "We are not going to have a war," Borah declared. Vice-President Garner asked the other visitors if the reform plan had a chance to pass, and they all replied in the negative. "Well, Captain, we may as well face the facts," Garner told the President. "You haven't got the votes, and that's all there is to it."

Roosevelt was not yet ready to give up on the search for peace, however. On April 15, he made a "Saturday surprise" appeal to Hitler and Mussolini to demonstrate their often-repeated statements that they desired peace. He suggested that the dictators pledge that for a period of at least ten years they would not attack any of a list of thirty-one independent nations cited in his message. If such assurances were given, he promised American support for efforts to further world trade and disarmament. This startling proposal met a favorable response from the American public and in London and Paris, but the Axis treated it with scorn.

Hermann Goering, Nazi Germany's No. 2 man, was visiting Mussolini when Roosevelt's message was received. Goering said it suggested an incipient brain malady; Mussolini observed that it might be the result of creeping paralysis. Publicly, the Duce dismissed such "Messiah-like messages" as "absurd." Hitler was even more caustic. In a brilliant propaganda counterstroke, the German Foreign Office asked each of the nations listed by Roosevelt if it felt threatened by Germany. Out of fear and intimidation, most replied in the negative. Hitler told the Reichstag that he had not taken offense at the President's request that he guarantee the integrity and security of all thirty-one—or was it eighty—states listed. Oh, no, he was not offended, even though had he made similar inquiries about U.S. activities in Central and South America, he would have been referred to the Monroe Doctrine. Instead, he had approached all the states mentioned and asked them whether they felt threatened by Germany. "Not all of them have been able to reply," Hitler continued, amid the raucous laughter of the deputies. "In Syria and Palestine, for example, the views of the inhabitants cannot be ascertained due to the occupation of the French and the British—not German—troops."

Rabid isolationists chortled, convinced that Roosevelt had been humiliated for his meddling. "He asked for it," remarked Senator Nye. But the President had not expected a positive response from the dictators. "The two madmen respect force and force alone," he told Henry Wallace. And Hull said Roosevelt's intention was "to put Hitler and Mussolini on the spot for what they were." The "Saturday surprise" helped rouse the American people to the imminence of danger, stigmatized Hitler and Mussolini as disturbers of the peace of the world, and placed Roosevelt in the forefront of the crusade against war. Isolationism was a dead letter as far as he was concerned.

There was a lull that summer as King George VI and Queen Elizabeth of England came to the United States, the first visit by a British sovereign. "I know only three Americans," the Queen told Joe Kennedy. "You, Fred Astaire and J. P. Morgan—and I would like to know more." With Hitler and Mussolini seemingly bent on war, such a visit would help cement the bonds of Anglo-American friendship. Roosevelt was fascinated by royalty, and with the gusto of an impresario he planned a reception that was both dignified and heartily American. The royal couple were cordial and engaging, and they were greeted everywhere by enormous and enthusiastic crowds. The King did not even flinch when Jack Garner slapped him on the back at a British Embassy garden party. Ickes caustically observed that as far as the Vice-President was concerned, "the King was simply a visiting Elk."

The high point of the visit to Washington was a state dinner at the White House that was followed by an entertainment featuring Marian Anderson, Kate Smith, and Alan Lomax, a folk singer who was regarded as something of a radical. The Secret Service and Scotland Yard insisted on "frisking" Lomax, which frightened him so much he could barely sing. All through his performance, Mrs. Roosevelt fervently hoped that he would not reach into his pocket for a handkerchief, for she was certain the security men would immediately pounce upon him. Eleanor arranged for Harry Hopkins' eight-year-old daughter, Diana, who lived in the White House along with her father, to see the Queen in all her splendor. She waited with the child in the second-floor hall until the Queen emerged from her room resplendent in a white gown, jewels, and sparkling tiara. "Oh, Daddy!" Diana told her father, "I have just seen the Fairy Queen."

From Washington, the royal couple went to Hyde Park, with a stopover at the New York World's Fair. The President welcomed his guests to Springwood with a tray of cocktails, while Sara Roosevelt looked on disapprovingly. "My mother doesn't approve of cocktails and thinks you should have a cup of tea," he told the King. "Neither does my mother," George replied gravely as he took a proffered glass. The evening was punctuated with disaster. An overloaded serving table collapsed during dinner and the dishes crashed to the floor. The silence that followed was deadly until the President cracked, "Just an old family custom." And there was a terrible clatter when a White House butler missed the step into the library and fell with a tray of decanters, glasses, and ice.

Later, Roosevelt and the King had a long private talk about the ticklish international situation. "Why don't my ministers talk to me as the President did tonight?" the monarch asked Mackenzie King, the Canadian Premier. "I feel as exactly as though my father were giving me the most careful and wise advice."

The following day, the Roosevelts took their visitors on a typical American picnic. There was a breezy drive in the President's hand-controlled car to the Dutch colonial cottage that had recently been built to his design as a hideaway on a hilltop above Val-Kill.* Cold ham, smoked turkey, various salads, baked beans, and beer were served, along with a plate of hot dogs for the royal couple to sample. Most of the guests were

---

* Elliott Roosevelt lived at Hilltop Cottage for several years after the death of his father, and later sold it. The place is now the home of a Dutchess County oil distributor who complains about FDR's refusal to include closets because Dutch colonial houses did not have them.

ordinary folk—people who worked for the Roosevelts and neighbors from around the surrounding countryside.

Hundreds of people came to the Hyde Park railroad station that evening to bid good-bye to the visitors. They lined the tracks, which run along the shore of the Hudson, and stood on the rocks above, only the glimmer of their cigarettes visible in the descending darkness. The King and Queen waved farewell from the rear platform as the train slowly pulled away in a hiss of steam. Some of the crowd began to sing "Auld Lang Syne," and more and more people joined in, including the President and his wife. Soon everyone was singing. Obviously moved, the royal couple continued to wave until the train disappeared into the night. Eleanor was saddened by the scene: "One thought of the clouds that hung over them and the worries which they were going to face, and turned away with a heavy heart," she said.

XXIII

"AMERICA
WANTS ROOSEVELT!"

THE TELEPHONE AT the President's bedside rang shortly after 3 o'clock in the morning of September 1, 1939. Franklin Roosevelt was awake in an instant.

"Who is it?" he asked.

"This is Bill Bullitt, Mr. President," said the American ambassador to Paris.

"Yes, Bill."

"Tony Biddle has just got through from Warsaw, Mr. President. Several German divisions are deep in Polish territory, and fighting is heavy. Tony said there were reports of bombers over the city. Then he was cut off. . . ."

"Well, Bill, it's come at last. God help us all."

Roosevelt hung up and called Secretary of State Hull, under Secretary Welles, and the Secretaries of War and Navy. Lights went on all over Washington, but there was little the United States could do as Europe hurtled into World War II. Bullitt called back to say that Édouard Daladier, the French Premier, had told him that France would honor her treaty commitments to Poland. Joe Kennedy telephoned from London to report the British would fight.

As he lay awake in the dawn's early light, Roosevelt was startled by "a strange feeling of familiarity—a feeling that I had been thru it all before. But after all it was *not* strange. During the long years of the World War the telephone at my bedside with a direct wire to the Navy Dept. had time after time brought me other tragic news in the night—the same rush messages were sent around—the same lights snapped on in nerve centers of government. I had *in fact* been through it all before. It was *not* strange."

War had been imminent since Hitler and Stalin—who for years had bitterly denounced each other—stunned the world by signing a nonaggression pact, on August 23. Ignored by the British and the French at Munich, rebuffed when he sought an alliance with the Western democracies, and fearing an attack by the Germans, Stalin made his own deal with Hitler. Secret clauses in the treaty divided Eastern Europe between Germany and the Soviet Union. Having isolated Poland, Hitler geared up a campaign of propaganda and faked frontier incidents in preparation for an attack. Submarines and surface raiders were ordered to take up positions athwart the major sea-lanes. The White House went on a permanent emergency routine, to be followed for the duration, and Army and Navy intelligence officers began briefing the President at 2:45 P.M. daily.

"These last two days have given me the feeling of sitting in a house where somebody is dying upstairs," observed a State Department official. "I have a horrible feeling of seeing . . . a civilization dying even before its actual death." The "death watch" ended as German armored columns plunged across the Polish frontier. Two days later, Britain and France reluctantly declared war on Germany.

There was no doubt where American sympathies lay. Eighty-two percent of those responding to a Gallup poll hoped for an Allied victory; only 2 percent favored Nazi Germany. But Americans were wary of being drawn into another European conflict. "I hope the United States will keep out of this war," Roosevelt told the nation in a Fireside Chat on the evening of September 3. "I believe that it will. And I give you assurance and reassurance that every effort of your Government will be directed toward that end. As long as it remains within my power to prevent, there will be no black-out of peace in the United States." To prevent the war from spreading across the Atlantic, he drew a ring of defense around the Americas that extended three hundred miles out to sea, and issued a proclamation of neutrality. Unlike Woodrow Wilson in 1914, he did not ask Americans to remain neutral in thought. "Even a neutral has a right to take account of the facts," the President continued. "Even a neutral cannot be asked to close his mind or his conscience."

Americans were shocked by the speed and ferocity of the German *Blitzkrieg* and by a Russian attack upon the Poles from the rear to make certain of their share of the spoils of the Nazi-Soviet Pact. The President wanted to help the Allies without getting involved in the fighting, but his hands were tied by the arms embargo. British officials told Ambassador Kennedy that it would be "a sheer disaster" if they were unable to obtain munitions and other supplies in America. Realizing that any attempt at repeal would arouse the isolationists, Roosevelt trod lightly. Before

Congress was summoned into a special session, on September 21, the members were canvassed by the telephone to make certain there was sufficient sentiment for amending the Neutrality Act.

Even more care than usual went into the preparation of the speech, to be given to a joint session. Fifteen congressional leaders from both parties were called to the White House the afternoon before to discuss the legislation. The draft prepared by Sam Rosenman and Adolf Berle was revised again and again. Roosevelt went to bed at 11 P.M., but Rosenman and Grace Tully continued work until 2:30 A.M. They were up again at seven o'clock and went to the President's bedroom, where they spent the rest of the morning. Propped up in bed with papers scattered about him, Roosevelt worked over each page, and as he finished, it was given to Miss Tully to be retyped. Hull was consulted several times by telephone. The final version of the speech was not completed until shortly before the 2 P.M. deadline for delivery.

"I give you my deep and unalterable conviction that by repeal of the embargo the United States will more probably remain at peace than if the law remains as it stands today," the President told Congress. "I regret that Congress passed the Neutrality Act. I equally regret that I signed it." Roosevelt carefully avoided any mention of the purpose of ending the arms embargo—to help the Allies—and emphasized the positive effect of repeal upon American industry. And he struck an isolationist note himself by insisting that the proposal would help keep the country out of war by placing all shipments to the belligerents on a cash-and-carry basis. To keep history from repeating itself, American ships—even those carrying nonmilitary cargoes—would be forbidden to enter the war zone, and Americans would not be permitted to travel on belligerent vessels.

The isolationists were not taken in by Roosevelt's maneuver, however, and refused to accept a trade-off of the arms embargo for the ban on American shipping in the war zone. Not long after the President left the Capitol, a group of demonstrators for the Committee for the Defense of Constitutional Rights poured into the building, chanting, "No Cash and Carry!" The demand for repeal came not from the American people, said Senator Borah, but from "the war hounds of Europe." Cash-and-carry would again lead the country down the bloody path to war. Credits, outright gifts, secret agreements, and American troops would certainly follow this opening wedge. Senators Nye, La Follette, and Hiram Johnson agreed. Father Coughlin raged against intervention and inspired a storm of letters that deluged Congress. Colonel Lindbergh suggested that the United States seize the possessions of foreign nations in this hemisphere that had not paid their war debts. "As long as European powers maintain their influence in our hemisphere, we are likely to find ourselves involved in their troubles," the Lone Eagle declared.

Roosevelt kept a low profile and allowed administration supporters to lead the fight for repeal. When Lord Tweedsmuir,* the Governor-General of Canada, suggested that he "slip down innocuously" to Hyde Park to discuss the situation, the President insisted upon a delay. "I am almost literally walking on eggs," he said, "and having delivered my message to Congress, and having good prospects of the bill going through, I am at the moment saying nothing, seeing nothing and hearing nothing." Nevertheless, he orchestrated the campaign from behind the scenes. He encouraged William Allen White to organize a national Non-Partisan Committee for Peace Through Revision of the Neutrality Act, to combat isolationist arguments and to undercut Coughlin's appeal, and personally urged Catholic and labor leaders to support repeal. Six weeks of debate ended with a clear-cut victory for the President. The Allies could now purchase anything they needed in the United States, including guns, aircraft, and tanks, provided they paid cash and carried these supplies away in their own ships.

Isolationists and revisionist historians such as Charles A. Beard have charged that Roosevelt played fast and loose with the truth in arguing that repeal of the arms embargo would help maintain American neutrality. Cash-and-carry was unneutral, they said, because it favored Britain and France; Germany was unable to obtain war matériel from this country, because her enemies controlled the sea-lanes. And if he was untruthful in this instance, his repeated protestations about keeping America out of war were also tainted. Perhaps Roosevelt did dissemble in downplaying his sympathy for the Allied cause, but having grasped the danger from Hitler long before most Americans, he had to wait until public opinion caught up with him. These thoughts were expressed most clearly in a letter to William Allen White: "Things move with such terrific speed, these days, that it really is essential to us to think in broader terms and, in effect, to warn the American people that they, too, should think of possible ultimate results in Europe and the Far East. Therefore, my sage old friend, my problem is to get the American people to think of conceivable consequences without scaring the American people into thinking that they are going to be dragged into war."

As soon as Poland had been crushed, Hitler put out peace feelers to Britain and France but was rebuffed. The Western Front settled down into a stalemate that became known as the "phony war" or "*Sitzkrieg,*" as both sides awaited the coming of spring. Except for the sudden appearance of men and women in uniform, life in the European capitals was little changed from the prewar era, and in the United States there was an atmosphere of complacency. The conventional wisdom held that the Ger-

* John Buchan, the author of *The Thirty-Nine Steps* and other thrillers.

mans would be unable to pierce the Maginot Line, which extended along the French border from Switzerland to Belgium, and that despite an onslaught by Nazi U-boats, Britain would maintain control of the seas. Once again, Germany would be strangled in a war of attrition, isolationists argued, and there was no need for the United States to get involved in the struggle. "The White House is very quiet," the President wrote Joe Kennedy. "There is a general feeling of sitting quiet and waiting to see what the morrow will bring forth."

On October 11, Roosevelt received a visit from Alexander Sachs, an economist with New Deal contacts and friend of Albert Einstein. Sachs brought a letter from the distinguished mathematician and a memorandum from another refugee scientist, Leo Szilard, that warned of German progress in the field of nuclear fission. The President had no knowledge of this arcane area and was preoccupied and inattentive. Fearing that Roosevelt might put the letters aside without giving them careful study, Sachs insisted on reading them aloud. "This new phenomenon," said Einstein, "would also lead to the construction of bombs, and it is conceivable— though much less certain—that extremely powerful bombs of a new type may be constructed." Roosevelt's curiosity was aroused. "Alex, what you are after is to see that the Nazis don't blow us up," he declared.

"Precisely."

"Pa, this requires action," the President told General Watson. Sachs was put in touch with Dr. Lyman J. Briggs, director of the National Bureau of Standards, and an advisory committee on uranium was quickly established, with military and scientific members to study the problem.

Roosevelt's attention was soon diverted by the Russian invasion of Finland, at the end of November. Worried about the possibility of an eventual attack by his German ally, Stalin tried to pressure the Finns into ceding a buffer zone along the frontier to protect Leningrad. When they refused, he launched a massive attack. The Finns, although vastly outnumbered, inflicted heavy casualties on the invaders. American sympathies were with the underdog. Finland had achieved freedom from Russia as a result of Wilsonian self-determination, and the Finns were widely admired for religiously paying their war debt to the United States. Roosevelt was outraged by the "dreadful rape of Finland" and denounced "this new resort to military force." But the United States, paralyzed by fear of becoming embroiled in a foreign war, offered the victims of aggression little more than good wishes.

The Finns sought a $60-million loan to buy armaments and were offered $10 million in agricultural credits instead. "I may be a benevolent dictator and all powerful Santa Claus and though the spirit moves me at times, I still operate under the laws which an all-wise Congress passes," the President replied to a friend who urged him to make the loan available. Congress was having second thoughts after an initial outburst of sympathy for Finland. If the Finns received credits, isolationists charged, the Allies would be encouraged to make similar demands. Angered by the delay in approving even a modest aid package for Finland, Roosevelt told his Cabinet that Congress was "a bunch of Uriah Heeps . . . who did not realize that what was going on in Europe would inevitably affect this country." And he administered a verbal spanking to the Moscow-lining American Youth Congress, which opposed aid to Finland. "The idea that a loan to Finland was an attempt to force America into an imperialist war" was "unadulterated twaddle . . . based on ninety per cent ignorance," Roosevelt told the group. He was booed and hissed. Congress eventually approved $20 million in nonmilitary assistance for the Finns in March—just as they were overrun by the Russians.

The Russian attack on Finland intensified Roosevelt's concern about the defense[†] of the United States, and he expressed his anxiety in his State of the Union message on January 4, 1940. "There is a vast difference between keeping out of war and pretending that war is none of our business," he declared. "We must see the effect on our own future if all the small nations of the world have their independence snatched from them. . . . It becomes clearer and clearer that the future world will be a shabby and dangerous place to live in—yes, even for Americans to live in —if it is ruled by force in the hands of a few. . . . I hope that we shall have fewer American ostriches in our midst; it is not good for the ultimate health of ostriches to bury their heads in sand."

Peering down upon the guests at the annual dinner of the Gridiron Club in March 1940 was a huge papier-mâché reproduction of the Sphinx with the unmistakable features of Franklin Roosevelt. The figure's roguish grin and jauntily tilted cigarette holder taunted the assembled journalists and politicians. The last words of the presidential oath had barely died away in January 1937 before speculation began on whether or not Roosevelt would be a candidate for a third term, but the inscrutable American Sphinx steadfastly refused to answer this riddle. Newsmen who broached the question were told to "put on a dunce cap and stand in a corner." With the approach of the Democratic National Convention, which was to open in Chicago on July 15, trying to fathom Roosevelt's plans became the nation's most absorbing preoccupation. Cabinet members and White House aides were as mystified as the general public, and they eagerly compared notes on relevant snatches of conversation with the President. Not

† In January 1940, the "ready" military force of the United States consisted of an Army of three hundred thousand men, a Navy of two hundred thousand, and a handful of aircraft. Most of the equipment was obsolete, and General George C. Marshall, who was appointed army chief of staff on September 1, 1939, declared the nation was "a third rate power."

even his wife was certain of what he was going to do; as late as the spring of 1940 she thought he would not run again.‡

Roosevelt had a number of reasons for his studied reluctance to put himself on record. If he announced that he would not seek reelection, he would be an immediate "lame duck," shorn of much of his influence with Congress and the politicians of his own party at a time when he had little to spare because of the failure of the Supreme Court packing plan, the purge, and the recession. Yet, if he announced his candidacy, it would arouse virulent antithird-term sentiment that would tie his hands in the conduct of foreign policy. He had to have public opinion on his side if he wished to assist the Allies in their battle against Hitler, and he did not wish to furnish fresh ammunition to his critics.

No legal bar existed to more than two terms, but the tradition had persisted since George Washington had gone home to his beloved Mount Vernon after eight years. Washington once told Lafayette that it would be a gross error to deprive the republic of the services of an experienced leader in a national emergency merely because of his length of service in office, but limitation now had the force of unwritten law.

From almost the time of the second inauguration, White House insiders such as Ickes, Corcoran, and Frank Walker, as well as such city bosses as Frank Hague and Chicago's Ed Kelly implored Roosevelt to run. The New Dealers wanted to remain in power, and the bosses wanted a top vote getter at the head of the Democratic ticket, but Roosevelt remained noncommittal. Upon one occasion when Missy LeHand asked him who would be the nominee, the President replied that the Lord would provide. Well, retorted Missy, God had better get busy pretty soon. Roosevelt's enemies, eager to believe the worst of him, were convinced that he always nurtured third-term hopes and his silence was merely a mask for his dictatorial ambitions. Nevertheless, it is more likely that he kept his options open simply because he couldn't make up his mind.

‡ Grace Tully contributed the following to FDR's birthday party on January 30, 1940:

MY ROSARY
The hours I spend with thee, dear boss,
Are like a string of pearls to me.
I count each hour a gain and not a loss,
A faithful gal, that's me!
Each hour I've toiled I've said a prayer,
I've prayed you'd think my job well done,
Oh, tell me, must this be the end,
Or what about forty-one?
I do not know which way to turn.
I cannot longer bear this cross,
I'd give my head if I could learn
Who'll be my boss next year,
Who'll be my boss!

FDR at work with his secretary, Missy LeHand. The clutter on the President's desk is less than usual. (Courtesy FDR Library)

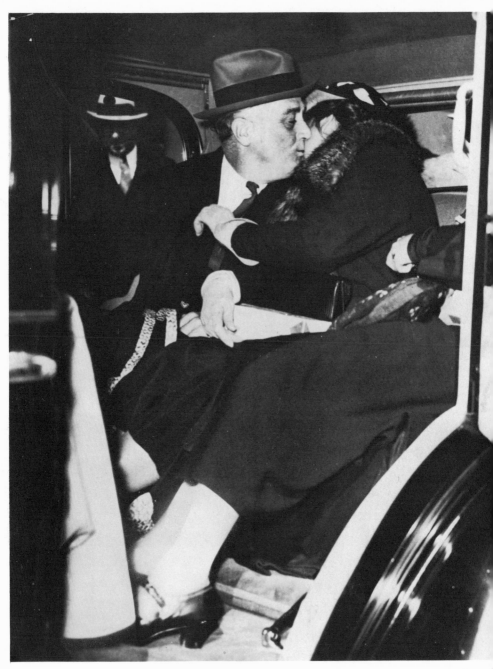

FDR greets Eleanor, following her return from a trip to the Caribbean, on their twenty-ninth wedding anniversary, March 17, 1934. (Courtesy Wide World)

Mr. Roosevelt contemplates the world. The globe was a gift from the U. S. Army. (Courtesy FDR Library)

FDR and Harry Hopkins in June 1942. (Courtesy Margaret Suckley)

Pulled in opposite directions by contradictory impulses, he dawdled and dissembled and resisted every effort to put himself on record until he was forced into a decision by the shock of international events.

On the one hand, he looked forward to retiring to Hyde Park to take up the leisured life of a country squire and to write his memoirs. His place in history was secure and it was time to let others take up the burden. In fact, he signed a contract in January 1940 to become a contributing editor of *Collier's* at seventy-five thousand dollars a year, an amount equal to the presidential salary. Jim Farley, a prospective candidate, said that during the previous summer, Roosevelt had assured him that he would not run again. Rosenman reported that the President tried to persuade him to move up to Hyde Park so they could work together on his papers. And he told Dan Tobin, of the Teamsters Union, that when his term was over, he was going home to Hyde Park for good. "I have to have a rest," he said. "I want to have a rest."

On the other hand, Roosevelt wanted to consolidate the gains of the New Deal and to remake the Democratic party into the party of liberalism. Frustrated by the conservatives, he had no wish to surrender leadership to Harry Byrd or Walter George, who were unconcerned about the one third of a nation "ill-housed, ill-clad, ill-nourished." Roosevelt had a vision of the party as a haven for liberals regardless of their previous political allegiance and wished to redraw the political lines so that the American people would have a clear-cut choice between liberal and conservative candidates. In January 1939, he announced that he could not support any Democrat who was not a New Dealer. The nation, he said, "would be in a sad state if it had to choose in 1940 between a Democratic Tweedledee and a Republican Tweedledum."

There was no shortage of would-be successors. Vice-President Garner and every member of the Cabinet with the exception of Frances Perkins were said to be in the running at one time or another, but Harry Hopkins appeared to be Roosevelt's hand-picked choice. In December 1938, he took the first step to building up Hopkins by naming him as Secretary of Commerce, in hope that he could establish his credentials with the business community, which was alarmed by his free-spending record as WPA administrator.* The President made certain that Hopkins was at his side

---

* Hearings before the Senate Commerce Committee on his nomination provided Hopkins with a forum to deny the widely circulated charge that he had summed up the philosophy of the New Deal as "tax and tax, spend and spend, elect and elect." The story originated with Frank R. Kent, the rabidly anti-New Deal columnist of the Baltimore *Sun*, and was picked up by other columnists, who didn't bother to check it out with Hopkins. Arthur Krock, of the New York *Times*, claimed this was unnecessary, because it seemed "a concentrated gem of Mr. Hopkins' philosophy." Although Kent refused to divulge his source, Robert Sherwood determined that it was Max Gordon, a Broadway producer. Sherwood said that Gordon, Heywood Broun, and Daniel

whenever he appeared in public, and Eleanor mentioned him favorably in her column. But the Hopkins boomlet collapsed because of his poor health. Henry Wallace, William O. Douglas, head of the SEC, and Attorney General Robert Jackson were also encouraged by Roosevelt to run, and Garner, Farley, and Hull had a following among conservatives. Paul V. McNutt, the former governor of Indiana, and Senator Burton Wheeler were also candidates. But Roosevelt's refusal to clearly state his own intentions prevented any of their trial balloons from getting off the ground. The Gallup polls for both January and February 1940 indicated that the President was favored for renomination by 78 percent of Democrats, while Garner, his leading rival, was supported by only 10 percent.

Adolf Hitler did more than anyone to convince Roosevelt to run again. On April 9, the Germans overran Denmark and assaulted Norway without the formality of a declaration of war. The Allied response was too little and too late—soon to be a familiar refrain—and the Scandinavian nations were added to Hitler's expanding empire. Four weeks later, the Western Front exploded into action. With shrieking dive bombers blasting the way, German tanks knifed through neutral Holland and Belgium and outflanked the Maginot Line. The Dutch and the Belgians were overwhelmed almost immediately, and the Germans swept toward Paris. The only ray of light during those bleak weeks was the escape of some three hundred thousand British soldiers from the beaches of Dunkirk. Reeling under the swift sword of the German *Blitzkrieg*, the Allies deluged the United States with demands for planes, ships, guns, and ammunition. The fury of the German onslaught stunned the American people. The comfortable sense of isolation they had enjoyed from Europe's dangers was shattered, and although the debate over policy continued, everyone realized that a Nazi triumph imperiled the security of the United States.

Roosevelt's initial reaction was to strengthen American defenses. He proposed a massive buildup of military and naval forces, including the unprecedented goal of fifty thousand planes a year. Long-range bombers, motorized armies, parachute troops, and the use of traitorous "fifth-columnists" made it mandatory for the American people to "recast their thinking about national protection," he told Congress on May 16.

Over the next few months, an unprecedented $1.7 billion was appropriated for a military buildup. The news from Europe worsened. "All bad, all bad," muttered Roosevelt as he looked over the latest

---

Arnstein, a transportation expert, met Hopkins at the races one summer afternoon in 1938. Broun and Arnstein could not recall Hopkins' having made the "spend and spend" remark. Gordon acknowledged that Hopkins did not use the exact words attributed to him, but "that's what he meant." Sherwood, *Roosevelt and Hopkins*, pp. 102–3.

dispatches. The French Army had collapsed, and Britain would have to fight on alone against hopeless odds. What would happen if the British Fleet, which had been America's bulwark against invasion, fell into German hands?

On June 10, as the President boarded a train for a trip to Charlottesville, where he was to address the graduating class of the University of Virginia, including Franklin, Jr., who was to receive a law degree, he learned that Italy had fallen upon a prostrate France. Roosevelt had originally planned a speech aimed at alerting the students, many of them opposed to intervention, to the gravity of the international situation. Now he decided upon a major foreign-policy address and set to work sharpening the draft provided by the State Department. Ambassador Bullitt reported from Paris that Paul Reynaud, the French Premier, had called the attack "a stab in the back," and the phrase stuck in Roosevelt's mind. He included it in the draft of his speech, but Sumner Welles urged him to drop it to keep from jeopardizing relations with Italy. As his train clattered through the Virginia countryside, Roosevelt could not restrain his anger, and he returned the words to the reading copy of his speech.

"On this tenth day of June 1940, the hand that held the dagger has struck it into the back of its neighbor," the President declared in a cold and biting tone that expressed his contempt even more eloquently than the language itself. The "stab in the back" phrase captured public attention—Winston Churchill, the new British Prime Minister, who listened at midnight with a group of officers in the Admiralty War Room, told Roosevelt that it was greeted with a deep growl of satisfaction—but the Charlottesville speech marked a turning point in the President's conduct of foreign policy. He committed the United States to all-out aid to the Allies, short of war. "We will pursue two obvious and simultaneous courses," Roosevelt said. "We will extend to the opponents of force the material resources of this nation; and at the same time, we will harness and speed up the use of those resources in order that we ourselves in the Americas may have equipment and training equal to the task of any emergency and every defense. All roads leading to the accomplishment of these objectives must be kept clear of obstructions. We will not slow down or detour. Signs and signals call for speed—full speed ahead."

Frantic appeals for "clouds of warplanes" and then for American troops poured in upon Roosevelt from the desperate French, but the United States did not have the aircraft, nor did Americans want to enter the war. France surrendered on June 22, and Hitler had accomplished in six weeks what the Kaiser had been unable to do in four years. To crown his victory, he ordered the capitulation to take place in the same railroad car in which Germany had signed the Armistice in 1918. Only a minority of Americans now expected the British, who stood alone against the Nazi onslaught, to win the war. Privately, Roosevelt thought the chances only one in three. Gloomy reports came from London, where Joe Kennedy, who had always sympathized with Chamberlain's policy of appeasement, was skeptical of Britain's ability to resist. Isolationists in Congress blocked a proposal to transfer twenty motor torpedo boats to the Royal Navy and tightened restrictions on assistance to Britain. Nevertheless, when Henry Morgenthau asked if he would continue to help the British, the President unhesitatingly replied, "Absolutely."

Three days after the German Army entered Paris, Admiral Harold R. Stark, the Chief of Naval Operations, went up to Capitol Hill with a request for $4 billion for a "two-ocean" Navy. It provided for a 70 percent increase in the size of the fleet, or 257 ships, including several battleships and twenty-seven *Essex*-class aircraft carriers. But it would take time to build these ships—"dollars cannot buy yesterday" is the way Admiral Stark put it.

And Roosevelt finally made up his mind to seek reelection.

To prevent the third-term controversy from blemishing the nomination, Roosevelt's supporters planned to have him drafted without the formality of a roll-call vote. This script had problems, however. Garner and Farley, the only candidates still in the race, would have to agree to eliminate themselves. As he drove up to Hyde Park on July 7, a week before the Democratic convention opened in Chicago, Farley was in a sour mood. In recent years, he and the President had drifted apart as a result of what he regarded as Roosevelt's increasing radicalism. He was no longer called to the White House for the morning bedside conferences, and when the telephone rang he did not hear the familiar voice on the other end of the line. The relations between the two men had always been political, rather than social, and Farley professed to be undisturbed about being excluded from the White House inner circle. But, deep down, he was embittered by suspicions that Roosevelt did not consider him a social equal.

Roosevelt was at church when Farley arrived—it was a Sunday—and he was greeted by Sara Roosevelt, who told him she was sorry to read in the newspapers that he was leaving the Administration. "I would hate to think of Franklin running for the presidency if you are not around," the old lady said. "I want you to be sure to help my boy." Lunch was an animated affair, with the President at his best, but when he and Farley adjourned to the study for a private meeting, the two men regarded each other with mutual discomfort. Farley was determined to resist the charm that had beguiled so many others and refused to help ease the tension. Finally, Roosevelt explained his reason for not carrying out his previously expressed intention not to run for a third term: the international crisis. "It would have destroyed my effectiveness as the leader of the nation in the efforts of this country to cope with the terrible catastrophe raging in Europe."

Carefully assessing the effect of his words upon his visitor as he lit up a cigarette, Roosevelt insisted that he wanted to retire to Hyde Park.

"Jim, I don't want to run and I'm going to tell the convention so."

"If you make it specific, the convention will not nominate you," Farley replied.

Having broken his silence, he told the President that he was opposed to a third term as a matter of personal principle and because the Democratic party had always opposed it. There were other men who could be elected in November, and if the convention delegates were given a free hand, they would be chosen. Roosevelt's smile faded. It was obvious that Farley would not withdraw to permit the convention to nominate him by acclamation.

The talk now turned to possible running mates. Garner, McNutt, Sam Rayburn, Senator James F. Byrnes of South Carolina, and Jesse Jones were all discussed and rejected. Farley's own name went unmentioned. Roosevelt brought up Henry Wallace, and Farley noted that the President remained silent when he said many people regarded the Secretary of Agriculture as "a wild-eyed fellow." This convinced him that Wallace had been tapped for the nomination. For the only time in their relationship, Roosevelt mentioned his physical disability. "The man running with me must be in good health because there is no telling how long I can hold out," he said. "You know, Jim, a man with paralysis can have a breakup at any time. . . . Nothing in this life is certain." With that, he pulled up and unbuttoned his shirt and showed Farley a lump of flesh and muscle under his left shoulder which he said was the result of being forced to sit all the time. "It's essential that the man who runs with me should be able to carry on."

The President did not go to Chicago. Reasoning that his presence would be seen as an attempt to force the hands of the delegates and ruin the charade of a draft, he remained in the White House working with Rosenman on the acceptance speech. Washington was even more oppressively hot and humid than usual that summer, but Roosevelt refused to use the newly installed air-conditioning system. He said it irritated his sinuses, and the only concession he permitted was a small fan placed in a far corner of his office. Perspiration poured from the wilted Rosenman, but Roosevelt, tieless and in rolled-up shirt sleeves, mopped his brow and claimed to be comfortable. He kept in touch with the convention by means of a direct line to Harry Hopkins' suite, in the Blackstone Hotel—by coincidence or design the very same "smoke-filled room" from which Warren Harding's name had materialized two decades before. Hopkins kept the telephone in the bathroom, because it was the only place where he could talk with assured privacy.

The delegates, who felt they had been summoned to merely rubber-stamp Roosevelt's nomination, were sullen and angry. Even those who favored a third term were resentful. As professionals, they were angry at the New Dealers, who were trying to shunt them aside. They were angry about the "purge," which had hurt friends. Some had been disturbed by the Supreme Court fight; others had had enough of the New Deal. Roosevelt was urged to come to Chicago to quiet passions. "This convention is bleeding to death," telegraphed Ickes. "Your reputation and prestige may bleed to death with it." Miss Perkins got the President on the telephone. "No, no, I have given it full consideration," he replied to her pleas. "I thought it all through both ways. I know I am right, Frances. It will be worse if I go. People will get promises out of me that I ought not to make. If I don't make promises, I will make new enemies. If I do make promises, they'll be mistakes. I'll be pinned down on things I don't want to be pinned down on *now*."

Roosevelt suggested that his wife might go if she received a personal appeal from Miss Perkins. "You know Eleanor always makes people feel right," he said. "She has a fine way with her." After some wheedling, Mrs. Roosevelt agreed to go, but she did not arrive until after an effort had been made on the second night of the convention to stampede the delegates. Senator Alben Barkley ended his keynote address by reading a long-awaited message from the President stating that he had no desire to be a candidate again and that the delegates were "free to vote for any candidate."

Any candidate?

For a moment, the delegates sat in stunned silence trying to puzzle out the significance of this message. Any candidate? Roosevelt was gambling that his declaration would set off the long-sought draft, but Mayor Ed Kelly was taking no chances. Suddenly the aisles were filled with Chicago ward heelers chanting, "We want Roosevelt! We want Roosevelt!" Barkley was handed a large picture of the President, which he brandished from the rostrum. And from the very bowels of the stadium came a voice that bellowed over and over again: "Chicago wants Roosevelt! . . . Illinois wants Roosevelt! . . . New York wants Roosevelt! . . . America Wants Roosevelt!" The voice was that of Thomas D. McGarry, Chicago's superintendent of sewers, who had been assigned to a basement microphone by Kelly.

The attempted coup failed, but the New Dealers and the city bosses had more than enough votes to put Roosevelt over on the first ballot. Besides the President's, the names of Farley, Garner, and Millard Tydings were placed before the convention, but the balloting was anticlimactic.

Roosevelt received 946 votes, Farley 72, Garner 61, and Tydings 9 (omitting fractional votes). When the figures had been tallied, Farley, his great bald dome glistening under the hot lights, elbowed his way to the rostrum to move that the nomination be made unanimous. There were a few scattered cries of "No! No!" intermixed with a roar of general assent. It was no draft but was as close as most candidates ever get.

An aura of harmony, which had settled over the convention in the wake of Roosevelt's victory, was shattered when it was learned that he had settled upon Henry Wallace as his running mate. Garner was out because of his conservatism, particularly his failure to help during the Supreme Court fight, and his resistance to the third term. Roosevelt's first choice for the vice-presidency had been Cordell Hull, but he had flatly refused the offer. Wallace was a hard worker, was committed to the ideals of the New Deal, supported aid to Britain, and had the backing of farmers and organized labor. Party leaders complained, however, that Wallace was a mystic, a political innocent, and an ex-Republican. "There is going to be a hell of a lot of opposition," Hopkins telephoned Rosenman. "It'll be a cat-and-dog fight, but I think that the Boss has enough friends here to put it over." Roosevelt blamed the opposition upon conservatives and grimly resolved to impose his choice upon the convention. "Well, damn it to hell," he growled, "they will go for Wallace or I won't run and you can jolly well tell them so."

Mrs. Roosevelt arrived in Chicago in the middle of a "stop Wallace" drive spearheaded by such conservatives as Jesse Jones, Paul McNutt, and House Speaker William Bankhead. Elliott Roosevelt, a Texas delegate, was planning to second Jones's nomination. A reporter cornered Eleanor in the turmoil and asked if she was happy about her husband's nomination. "Happy!" she exclaimed. "I don't know how anyone could be particularly happy about the nomination in the present state of the world."

"Henry's my second choice," allowed Governor Leon Phillips of Oklahoma. Asked who topped his list, he replied: "Anyone—red, white, black, or yellow—who can get the nomination." Jimmy Byrnes went from delegation to delegation, imploring votes for Wallace. "For God's sake," he declared, "do you want a President or a Vice-President?" Although unenthusiastic about the choice of Wallace, Eleanor plunged into the task of providing a word of encouragement, shaking hands, sweetening the convention. She cautioned Elliott against putting Jones's name in nomination, and took a place on the rostrum to await her turn to speak. The convention teetered on the brink of chaos, every mention of Wallace's name being greeted by catcalls.

The President played solitaire at a card table set up in the Oval Room as he listened to the proceedings on the radio. Bankhead's nomination was cheered, and McNutt, viewed as most likely to stampede the delegates, received a twenty-minute ovation before he rose to take his name out of the running. The radio commentators left no doubt that a revolt was brewing against Wallace. The nominating and seconding speeches were increasingly bitter. Putting aside his cards, Roosevelt asked Missy LeHand for a note pad and pencil and swiftly covered five pages with a vigorous scrawl. Everyone in the room wanted to sneak up and peek over his shoulder. Finally, he put down his pencil and turned to Rosenman and said: "Sam, take this inside and go to work on it; smooth it out and get it ready for delivery. I may have to deliver it very quickly, so please hurry it up." "Pa" Watson and Missy followed Rosenman out of the room and eagerly crowded about him. "What's in it?" they asked. "Let's see it."

Roosevelt had written a statement, addressed to the "Members of the Convention," declining the presidential nomination if Wallace lost. Missy, who had not wanted the President to run for a third term, was pleased. "Fine, I'm glad," she said with a smile. Watson's reaction was quite different. "Sam, give that damned piece of paper to me," he declared. "Let's tear it up." At first, Rosenman thought he was joking, but the aide was in dead earnest. "He's all excited now in there—and he'll be sorry about it in the morning," Watson said. "Besides, the country needs him. I don't give a damn who's Vice-President and neither does the country. The only thing that's important to this country is that fellow in there. There isn't anyone in the United States who can lead this country in the next four years as well as he can."

When Rosenman returned with his typed draft, Roosevelt looked it over, added a paragraph in longhand, and returned to his cards. In his message, he emphasized that the Democratic party had always been the champion of liberalism and progressivism, but the convention had abandoned these principles. "Under the circumstances," he continued, "I cannot in all honor, and will not, merely for political expediency, go along with the cheap bargaining and political maneuvering which have brought about party dissension in this Convention." The party was going to have to choose the path it wished to follow. "By declining the honor of the nomination for the Presidency, I can restore that opportunity to the Convention. I so do."

Eleanor Roosevelt spoke after the last vice-presidential candidate had been nominated. She was greeted with cheers and applause, perhaps the most genuine expression of affection of the entire convention. Haltingly at first—and without mentioning Wallace—she emphasized that those were not ordinary times and a candidate who was also President would be unable to campaign as usual. "So each and every one of you who give him this responsibility, in giving it to him, assume for yourselves a very grave responsibility because you will make the campaign. You will have to rise above considerations which are narrow and partisan. This is a time when it is the United States we fight for." In Farley's opinion, Eleanor's simple and eloquent words saved the day for Wallace. By the time she finished, the tumult had died down and the roll call was able to proceed in a sober fashion.

Tension was running high in the President's study. Roosevelt looked weary, his face was lined, his clothes rumpled as he tallied the votes through the seemingly interminable process of polling the delegations. Slowly, Wallace's total climbed to the 551 votes needed for victory, and he went on to win with 626. Bankhead had 329 votes, McNutt 68, Jones 59, with a few scattered among various candidates. Everyone in the room was suddenly smiling and laughing, Rosenman recalled, with the exception of Missy, who was in tears. Until the last moment, she had hoped that Wallace would be turned down by the convention and the Boss would bow out of the race. Roosevelt sent word to Chicago that he would address the convention by radio as soon as he had time to freshen up.

Roosevelt did not speak until after midnight, but his voice, which issued from strategically placed loudspeakers, soothed the rebellious delegates. As the President spoke, a spotlight played on a huge portrait which had been unfurled from the steel rafters of the stadium. Smoke and dust eddied in the shifting beam. Sounding like a father talking to his unruly children, Roosevelt explained why he thought it necessary to defy the longstanding tradition against a third term:

> Lying awake, as I have on many nights, I have asked myself whether I have the right, as Commander-in-Chief of the Army and Navy, to call men and women to serve their country or to train themselves to serve, and, at the same time decline to serve my country in my own personal capacity, if I am called upon to do so by the people of my country. . . . Today, all private plans, all private lives, have been in a sense repealed by an overriding public danger. In the face of that public danger all those who can be of service to the Republic have no choice but to offer themselves for service in those capacities for which they may be fitted. . . . I had made plans for myself, plans for a private life . . . but my conscience will not let me turn my back on a call to service.

Henry Wallace was not allowed to give an acceptance speech because of the fire storm of protest likely to greet him.

Winning the nomination was only half the battle. Wendell L. Willkie, the forceful and articulate utilities tycoon who had won the Republican presidential nomination, was likely to be a formidable opponent. Roosevelt's first task was to heal the scars left by a bruising convention, for the Democrats left Chicago more crippled by dissension and defection than at any time since 1928. Southerners felt they had been shunted aside, and party regulars, angry over the prominence of the New Dealers, were disenchanted. All of Roosevelt's persuasive powers were required to convince Ed Flynn to take over the job of national chairman, abandoned by Jim Farley. Assured that he would have a free hand, Flynn accepted—a decision that assuaged the anger of the party stalwarts. Roosevelt planned a low-key campaign in which his only appearances would be "nonpolitical" visits to military installations and defense plants, but the vigorous campaign waged by Willkie eventually forced him to take a more active role.

Willkie was almost as dramatic and appealing a figure as the President. Big, handsome, and friendly, he was as American as apple pie. With his rumpled suits and a shock of hair that fell over his forehead when he spoke, he looked like a country boy from his native Indiana. But he had been president of Commonwealth and Southern, a giant public-utility holding company, and was respected on Wall Street as a shrewd operator. He first came to national attention as a leader in the fight against the Public Utility Holding Company Act, designed to break up such combines. A longtime Democrat—he had voted for Roosevelt in 1932—Wilkie had no intention of scrapping the New Deal but decried its failure to end the depression and believed its programs could be carried out with greater efficiency and less government control. As a young man, he had espoused socialism, which caused him to remark in later life: "Any man who is not something of a Socialist before he is forty has no heart; any man who is still a Socialist after he is forty has no head." Internationally, he was a strong supporter of all-out aid to Britain.

Willkie went into the Philadelphia convention as the darkest of horses, but the leading contenders—Tom Dewey and Senator Robert A. Taft, the conservative favorite—deadlocked. With his strategically placed supporters in the galleries chanting, "We want Willkie! We want Willkie!" he was nominated on the sixth ballot. Old Guard Republicans were reluctant to forgive Willkie his Democratic past, however. "I don't mind the church converting a whore," Senator James Watson told him, "but I don't like her to lead the choir the first night!" To counterbalance his liberalism and internationalism, Senator Charles L. McNary, the conservative senate minority leader, was chosen as vice-presidential candidate.

While Willkie set a dizzying pace—sometimes speaking as many as fifteen times a day and quickly reducing his voice to a hoarse croak—Roosevelt craftily remained above the battle. He ignored his opponent's challenge to a debate, wrapped himself in his familiar navy cape, and acted presidential. His actions and comments on the state of the world overshadowed Willkie's campaign. Most of his attention was focused on the unfolding Battle of Britain. Bombed, besieged, and nearly bankrupt, the British were on the ropes. U-boats operating from newly conquered ports on the French and Norwegian coasts were ripping the hearts out of the convoys that were Britain's lifeline, and the Royal Navy was short of escort vessels. As early as May 15, Churchill appealed for the loan of forty or fifty destroyers left over from World War I which were undergoing refit, but Roosevelt resisted. He was reluctant to provide fresh ammunition for the isolationists, who were accusing him of dictatorial ambitions, and he was certain that Congress would not approve such an unneutral action.

Churchill was insistent, however. At the end of July, he told Roosevelt that Britain's survival might turn on the old destroyers. "The whole fate of the war may be decided by this minor and easily remediable factor," the Prime Minister declared. "Mr. President, with great respect, I must tell you . . . this is a thing to do now." An exchange of the ships for ninety-nine-year leases on a chain of eight air and sea bases ranging from Canada to the Caribbean was suggested to sweeten the deal for the American public. Despairing of the possibility of congressional support, Roosevelt exhibited considerable courage by cutting through political and legal restraints and transferring the vessels to the British by executive order on September 2.

"Congress is going to raise hell about this," the President told Grace Tully, "but even another day's delay may mean the end of civilization." Isolationists charged that he had "committed an act of war," but he justified what was patently an unneutral act on the grounds of self-defense and as retaliation for Hitler's repeated violations of international law. The British not only received badly needed reinforcements but, even more important, the exchange bonded the United States more closely to their cause.

The destroyer deal had the stamp of public approval, but it would have been impossible had not Willkie supported it, even though he condemned Roosevelt for having bypassed Congress. Earlier on, the President had moved to ensure bipartisan support—and left isolationists sputtering in anger—by appointing Henry L. Stimson as Secretary of War and Frank Knox as Secretary of the Navy. These eminent Republican elders were strongly pro-Allied—outdistancing the President in their fervor—and they spoke out in favor of the swap of bases for destroyers as well as the nation's first peacetime draft. They also brought with them into government service such subordinates as James V. Forrestal, Robert A. Lovett, and John J. McCloy, younger Wall Street lawyers and financiers who were to dominate America's national-security policy long after the Roosevelt era.

Although the President favored conscription, he played the artful dodger on the issue because if its political sensitivity and allowed a committee headed by Grenville Clark, his old legal associate, to lead the fight. Willkie supported the draft, but a majority of congressional Republicans refused to follow his leadership even though they belabored Roosevelt for being slack on national defense. With Stimson drawing the numbers, the first draftees were chosen on October 29, a week before the presidential election. The nation was so poorly prepared, however, that many of the new recruits trained with broomsticks for rifles and wooden sawhorses for machine guns.

Unable to goad Roosevelt into taking more than cursory note of his existence, Willkie flailed at the air in frustration. Ickes, who played the role of Democratic hatchet man while the President remained serenely above the battle, derided his folksy manner by calling him a "barefoot boy from Wall Street" and the "rich man's Roosevelt." There was little difference between Willkie's position on social policy and the New Deal, and to many people he merely seemed to be saying, "Me too." "He agreed with Mr. Roosevelt's entire program of social reform and said it is leading to disaster," cracked Norman Thomas, the perennial Socialist candidate for President. Frustrated by a letdown in enthusiasm and prodded by the conservatives who had taken over his campaign, Willkie desperately lashed out at the New Deal's failure to end unemployment and accused Roosevelt of warmongering. A vote for Roosevelt was a vote to send American boys to die on the battlefields of Europe, he charged. If the President was reelected, American troops would be headed overseas by April. Following the election, Willkie acknowledged that some of his inflammatory statements were mere "campaign oratory," but they resulted in an upsurge in his standing in the polls and made Roosevelt "fighting mad."

Late in October, the President, declaring that the time had come "to call the attention of the nation to deliberate or unwitting falsification of fact," embarked on a campaign swing that carried him through the industrial states as far west as Cleveland. "I am an old campaigner, and I love a good fight," he proclaimed. Roosevelt emphasized three major themes in his speeches: (1) The Republicans who were shedding crocodile tears for the working men and women of America in 1940 had been willing to let them starve in 1932; (2) contrary to Republican claims, progress was being made in rearming the nation; and (3) the Republicans had opposed every effort to strengthen America's defenses.

As always, Roosevelt was a master of the art of political ridicule, providing his most skillful performance in a speech at Madison Square Garden. Three of the leading Republican isolationists were Representatives Joseph Martin, the house majority leader and Willkie's campaign manager; Bruce Barton, who was running for senator from New York; and Hamilton Fish, the archconservative congressman from the President's own, Dutchess County district. "Martin, Barton and Fish"—the names chanted by Roosevelt in a sing-song, nursery-rhyme cadence of Wynken, Blynken and Nod—became the symbol of Republican obstructionism.

Roosevelt's audience howled with laughter and crowds began to listen for it. Whenever the President said, "Martin," the crowd gleefully roared back, "Barton and Fish." The Republicans failed to see the humor. "When I heard the President hang the isolationist votes of Martin, Barton and Fish on me, and get away with it, I knew I was licked," Willkie said later.

Under pressure from Democratic strategists alarmed at the apparent success of Willkie's appeal to the "mother vote," Roosevelt sought, in a speech delivered in Boston on October 30, to quiet anxiety about the possibility of America's entry into the war.

> And while I am talking to you mothers and fathers [the President declared], I give you one more assurance.
> I have said this before, but I shall say it again and again and again:
> Your boys are not going to be sent into any foreign wars.
> They are going into training to form a force so strong that by its very existence, it will keep the threat of war away from our shores.

The implied pledge contained in these words was to haunt Roosevelt. At his own insistence, the Democratic platform contained a similar pledge, but it was hedged with the words "except in case of attack," and he had repeated them throughout the campaign. Rosenman and Sherwood wanted to include this qualification in the Boston speech, but Roosevelt insisted that it was not necessary. "It's implied clearly," he said. "If we're attacked, it's no longer a foreign war." Three days later, in Buffalo, he declared: "Your President says this country is not going to war." Undoubtedly, Roosevelt sensed the yearning of the American people for reassurance and he did not want to weaken his reponse to Willkie's charges.

Roosevelt awaited the outcome of the election at Hyde Park with members of his family and close friends. Sara Roosevelt and several elderly ladies knitted and chatted in a small parlor off the front entrance of the house, paying little attention to a radio softly broadcasting the returns. Most of the guests milled about in the library-living room, where there was another radio, while the President, in his shirt sleeves, had set up shop with his tally sheets and news tickers in the dining room. Eleanor moved from room to room, seeing to the needs of everyone and seemingly taking no notice of the radio reports. The early returns indicated unexpected strength for Willkie, and some said Roosevelt was worried about the outcome. If so, he did not show it.

By ten o'clock, however, it was clear that he would win by a sizable margin. Obviously concerned that a defeat might have been considered a victory for appeasement, he told his wife's friend Joseph Lash: "We seem to have averted a *Putsch*, Joe." The President and his guests went out on the porch to greet the traditional torchlight parade of Hyde Park neighbors. Roosevelt was particularly elated that night, for it was the only time he carried the solidly Republican district, and he laughed heartily when he spotted a hastily painted sign that read: SAFE ON 3RD.†

Fifty million Americans had gone to the polls—a record that lasted until the Eisenhower-Stevenson election a dozen years later. Roosevelt received 27,243,466 votes, or 55 percent of the total; Willkie's share was 22,304,755, or 45 percent. Roosevelt's victory was more decisive in the Electoral College; he carried 38 states, with 449 votes, to 10 for Willkie, with 82 votes. Maine and Vermont again went Republican, but most of Willkie's strength was concentrated in the isolationist Middle West. Willkie was handicapped by the backing he received from Nazi sympathizers, and from reactionaries who wished to turn back the clock, although he disavowed such support. His "me too" attitude toward the New Deal offended some Republicans, and the reckless charges at the end of the campaign alienated many independents. Charges that the New Deal had failed to end unemployment had little effect, now that defense industries were beginning to absorb the jobless. And Willkie could not shake off his image of a Wall Street insider, despite his liberalism and a last-minute endorsement by John L. Lewis.

There were defections from the Roosevelt coalition among Irish and Italian Americans, who resented the President's support of Britain and his contemptuous references to Mussolini, but his margin of victory in the cities was off only slightly from 1936. Roosevelt's skill as a campaigner and the closing of Democratic ranks behind him despite the third-term issue were important to his victory. In the final analysis, however, he won because a majority of the American people, confronted by the terrible dangers that lay ahead, turned to him for leadership in a time of crisis.

† The Republicans got their revenge with the Twenty-second Amendment to the Constitution, a posthumous slap at FDR that limits a President to two terms.

XXIV

THE ROAD TO WAR

DID FRANKLIN ROOSEVELT steer the United States into war while cynically professing devotion to peace?

Certainly, in the year between his election to a third term and the Japanese attack on Pearl Harbor, American neutrality became a fiction. Emboldened by his victory, Roosevelt gave Britain unrestricted access to the nation's industrial resources. "We must become the great arsenal of democracy," he said in a Fireside Chat at the end of 1940. "For us this is an emergency as serious as war itself. We must apply ourselves to our task with the same resolution, the same sense of urgency, the same spirit of patriotism and sacrifice as we would show were we at war." Yet Roosevelt was not convinced of the inevitability of American participation in the conflict. With all sincerity, he believed that the best way for America to keep out of war was to help Britain. "There is far less chance for the United States getting into war," he said, "if we do all we can to support the nations defending themselves against attack by the Axis than if we acquiesce in their defeat, submit tamely to Axis victory, and wait our turn to be the object of an attack in another war later on."

Lend-lease was the practical expression of Roosevelt's conviction. Following the election, he had departed for a Caribbean vacation on the *Tuscaloosa*, and on December 9, a navy flying boat touched down beside the cruiser with an urgent message from Churchill. Later described by the Prime Minister as one of the most important letters he ever wrote, it disclosed that Britain faced the imminent exhaustion of her financial resources. "The moment approaches when we shall no longer be able to pay cash for shipping and other supplies," Churchill declared. Under terms of the Neutrality Act and other legislation, belligerents had to pay cash for arms, and loans were prohibited to nations that had not paid their World War I debts. Britain had less than $2 billion on hand to pay for $5 billion in orders from American factories.

Tanned and jaunty, the President returned to Washington in mid-month with an imaginative scheme conceived in what Morgenthau called one of his "brilliant flashes." Why not lend or lease the needed supplies and equipment to Britain? Roosevelt revealed the rough outline of lend-lease with a homely parable at a press conference on December 17. "Suppose my neighbor's home catches on fire, and I have a length of garden hose four or five hundred feet away," he said. "If he can take my garden hose and connect it up with his hydrant, I may help him put out the fire. Now what do I do? I don't say to him before that operation, 'Neighbor, my garden hose cost me fifteen dollars; you have to pay me fifteen dollars for it.' No! What is the transaction that goes on? I don't want fifteen dollars—I want my garden hose after the fire is over."

While the finishing touches were being put on the proposal, the President went before a joint session of Congress on January 6, 1941, to present his annual message. The United States would not be deterred from supplying assistance to the Allies by cries from the Axis that such conduct was a breach of international law and an act of war, he declared. "Such aid is not an act of war, even if a dictator should unilaterally proclaim it so to be. When the dictators are ready to make war upon us, they will not wait for an act of war on our part. They did not wait for Norway or Belgium or the Netherlands to commit an act of war." Victory over the dictators, he added, would result in "a world founded upon four essential human freedoms—freedom of speech, freedom of religion, freedom from want and freedom from fear—everywhere in the world."

The bill to establish lend-lease—H.R. 1776*—went to Congress four days later with the title "An Act to Further Promote the Defense of the United States and Other Purposes." The debate was venomous and spread far beyond the Capitol. "America Firsters" (opposed to intervention) and the Committee to Defend America by Aiding the Allies flooded the country with radio spots, leaflets, and press statements. Tons of mail poured in upon Congress, and militants staged sit-down strikes in lawmakers' offices. Both sides realized that lend-lease marked a point of no return; approval would mean that the United States had been transformed from a cautious neutral to an active nonbelligerent.

Wendell Willkie appeared before a senate committee to endorse the bill, and hostile senators quoted his campaign charges against Roosevelt back at him. "I struggled as hard as I could to beat Franklin Roosevelt,

---

* The symbolic legislative number was said to be the inspiration of an obscure house parliamentarian, although Sherwood notes that it sounds like "a Rooseveltian conception."

and I tried to keep from pulling any of my punches," he retorted. "He was elected President. He is my President now." The audience applauded. Colonel Lindbergh was the star witness for the opposition. Britain's cause was hopeless, he said, and the United States should use its weapons for its own defense. Senator Wheeler compared lend-lease with the plowing up of crops in 1933. "The New Deal's triple-A foreign policy . . . will plow under every fourth American boy," he declared. Roosevelt was livid with anger. "That is really the rottenest thing that has ever been said in public life in my generation," he told newsmen. "Quote me on that."

Two months after the debate began, Congress approved H.R. 1776 by an overwhelming margin, and it was signed into law by the President on March 11, 1941. A triumphant Churchill hailed lend-lease as "the most unsordid act in the history of any nation." The initial appropriation was $7 billion, and by the end of World War II, the United States provided its Allies with some $50 billion in goods and services.

Hitler, who was preparing to unleash an attack on his Russian ally, ignored the unneutral acts of the United States and postponed a show-down to a time of his own choosing. Besides, he had not forgotten the decisive effect of American intervention on the outcome of World War I. Unable to win control of the air over the English Channel despite Lindbergh's claims of the *Luftwaffe's* invincibility, Hitler turned from the invasion of Britain to an attempt to cut her Atlantic lifeline. The submarine campaign was highly effective. During the first half of 1941, German U-boats sank 756 merchantmen bound for British ports and damaged another 1,450 vessels. If this toll continued unabated, the lost tonnage would soon exceed twice the replacement capacity of both British and American shipyards.

Stimson and Knox urged Roosevelt to order the U. S. Navy to begin escorting convoys to ensure the safe delivery of American supplies. Sending ships out to be sunk by submarine wolf packs was like pouring water into a leaky bathtub, observed the Secretary of War. The President was evasive on the convoy issue. Although the possibility of providing escorts was being heatedly discussed within the Administration, he told a press conference no consideration was being given to such a step. "When a nation convoys ships through a hostile zone . . . there is apt to be some shooting . . . pretty sure there will be some shooting . . . and shooting comes awfully close to war, doesn't it? That's about the last thing we have in our minds." Public opinion, as measured by the polls, was not ready to accept such drastic action, so, in characteristic fashion, Roosevelt compromised.

Ever since the beginning of the war, a handful of ships under the command of Admiral Ernest J. King had been patrolling three hundred miles out in the Atlantic to prevent violations of the neutrality of the western hemisphere. On April 10, the President announced that the Atlantic Fleet would be strengthened by transferring ships from the Pacific and that its area of patrol extended halfway across the Atlantic, to the 25th degree of west longitude.† Danish-owned Greenland was immediately placed under American protection, and on July 7, a brigade of marines was dispatched to Iceland—less than a thousand miles from Britain —to relieve British troops that had been occupying the island for a year. These steps were described as measures of hemispheric self-defense. American vessels were not authorized to attack German submarines and surface raiders but were to radio their positions to British convoys. There was nothing, of course, to prevent British warships from picking up these signals and attacking the U-boats.

Roosevelt's hesitation in ordering the U. S. Navy to escort convoys angered Stimson, Knox, and Morgenthau, who believed it essential that the United States immediately enter the war. But the President felt his hands were tied by international and domestic constraints. The United States was already faced with the problem of how to cover two oceans with a one-ocean navy. Even more ships would have to be withdrawn from the Pacific if an effective convoy escort was to be organized, which might encourage the Japanese to seize French and Dutch colonies in Southeast Asia. Allied fortunes were also at a low ebb. The Germans had thrust into the Balkans, overrunning Greece, Yugoslavia, and Crete, and General Erwin Rommel's tanks were hammering the British back upon the Suez Canal. And he was not at all certain that the American people were willing to accept actions that would push the nation to the brink of war. Lindbergh told a rally of "America Firsters" that "we cannot win the war for England regardless of how much assistance we send."

In mid-May, Roosevelt was in a despondent mood. Tugged and hauled by the cabinet warhawks, who wanted him to immediately intervene on the side of the British, and under fire from the isolationists, who were demanding his resignation, he complained of a persistent cold and spent little time in his office. Robert Sherwood had a long talk with him one day and told Missy LeHand: "The President seems in fine shape to me. He didn't cough or sneeze or even blow his nose the whole time I was in there and looked wonderfully well. What is really the matter with him?" Missy smiled. "What he's suffering from most of all is a case of sheer exasperation."

† Seventeen U. S. Navy pilots were secretly assigned as "advisers" to fly American-built PBY Catalina patrol planes with British Coastal Command squadrons. One, Ensign Leonard B. Smith, found the German battleship *Bismarck*, which had dropped out of sight in the Atlantic after sinking the British battle cruiser *Hood*, and alerted the Royal Navy ships and planes that eventually sank her. Smith's role in the sinking of the *Bismarck* remained a secret until 1974.

Roosevelt zigzagged on the convoy issue throughout the summer of 1941. He proclaimed an "unlimited national emergency" on May 27 and informed the American people of the toll of merchant shipping being exacted by the U-boats. "Our patrols are helping now to ensure delivery of the needed supplies to Britain," he added. "All additional measures necessary to deliver the goods will be taken . . . the delivery of needed supplies to Britain is imperative. This can be done; it must be done; it will be done." Telegrams expressing support for this strong stand poured into the White House. "They're ninety-five percent favorable!" the astonished President exclaimed to Sherwood. "And I figured I'd be lucky to get an even break on this speech." Everyone expected him to follow up with an order allowing British ships to join convoys escorted by the U. S. Navy and to seek repeal of the Neutrality Act so American ships could deliver cargoes directly to British ports. But, the very next day, the President said he had no plans for either action.

Stimson urged Roosevelt to seize the psychological advantage presented by Hitler's invasion of Russia, on June 22, and order escorting to begin. Expecting the Russians to collapse within three months, he said the United States should move while Hitler's attention was distracted from the Atlantic. "The door is opened wide for you to lead directly toward the winning of the Battle of the Atlantic," Stimson declared. Once again, however, Roosevelt refused to be drawn toward the vortex. Escorts meant shooting, and shooting meant war—and he did not want an open conflict with Nazi Germany. He still preferred a quasi-belligerency in which the United States provided the tools of war to Britain and other nations willing to resist Hitler.

The question of assistance to the Soviet Union was a ticklish one. Public opinion was hostile, and many Americans preferred to let the twin devils of Nazism and Communism fight to the death. On the other side, left-wingers, who had accused the President of trying to drag the United States into the "imperialist war," now demanded immediate American participation in an anti-Fascist crusade. Within a week or so, Roosevelt instinctively realized that the German invasion of the Soviet Union had altered the course of the war, and regarded it as an opportunity to further his policy of resisting Hitler without direct American involvement. "I deem it to be of paramount importance for the safety and security of America that all reasonable munitions help be provided for Russia," he told Stimson.

Harry Hopkins, who had become the President's chief foreign-affairs troubleshooter, was sent to Moscow to assess the situation. "Give us anti-aircraft guns and aluminum [for building aircraft] and we can fight for three or four years," Stalin told him. Like the British, the Russians also emphasized the need for the United States to take a hard line with Japan to prevent the spread of war in Asia. Hopkins was particularly impressed by the Russian dictator. "I feel ever so confident about this front," he cabled the President. "There is unbounded determination to win."

Early in August, Roosevelt cheerfully announced to the White House press corps that he was going "to take some time off" and go fishing. The presidential yacht *Potomac* cruised idly near Martha's Vineyard for several days and then disappeared as completely as if she had been torpedoed. Not until August 14 did the world learn that Roosevelt and Churchill had rendezvoused for three days in Placentia Bay, off Argentia, Newfoundland, which had been transferred to the United States as part of the bases-for-destroyers deal. Roosevelt arrived first, on the cruiser *Augusta,* and the Prime Minister sailed into the misty harbor the next day on the battleship *Prince of Wales,* which included Hopkins among its passengers.

For nearly two years, Roosevelt and Churchill had communicated with each other by letter, cable, and transatlantic telephone—with the Prime Minister whimsically calling himself "Former Naval Person"—and they agreed the time had come to put their relationship on a personal basis. As soon as his ship anchored, Churchill visited the *Augusta* and the President greeted him at the gangway.

"At last—we've gotten together," said Roosevelt.

"We have."

Roosevelt and Churchill were proud, even vain men, conscious of their responsibilities and places in history, but they took an immediate liking to each other. Sometimes during their meetings over the next four years, the President's garrulity and determination to liquidate the British Empire irritated Churchill, while the Prime Minister's passion for long speeches and late hours ruffled Roosevelt. Yet they were drawn to each other not only by the necessities of policy but by mutual admiration. "It is fun to be in the same decade with you," Roosevelt once cabled Churchill. And Churchill likened Roosevelt's sparkling buoyancy to uncorking a bottle of champagne. It was not a relationship of equals, however. As a chief of state, the President was senior to Churchill, who was head of a government. And Roosevelt held most of the cards. Churchill was forced to woo the President, first to enter the war on Britain's side and then to support British policy. Although he was the older man, he chose to address Roosevelt as "Mr. President"; Roosevelt called him "Winston." When Roosevelt and his advisers objected to Churchill's suggestions, the Prime Minister usually retreated with uncharacteristic grace.

The two leaders came to the Atlantic Conference with differing priorities. Churchill hoped to persuade Roosevelt to enter the war and at least to join Britain in issuing a warning to Japan against an attack on

Malaya or the Dutch East Indies. Rather than spreading the war, this was an effort to contain it. Churchill feared that the Japanese might cut Britain's lifeline to India and Southeast Asia, and believed a firm declaration might force them to have second thoughts. Roosevelt informed the British that he had decided to begin escorting convoys as far as Iceland, which would free forty British destroyers and corvettes for other duties. He also agreed to send a strong note to the Japanese, which was subsequently toned down by Secretary Hull. But he could not commit the United States to war, and as if to underscore the limitations of his power, word was received at the conference that Congress had extended the term of service of draftees for another eighteen months by only a single vote.

Roosevelt's major goal at Argentia was to secure a joint declaration of war aims. Despite his cordial relationship with Churchill, he did not completely trust the British. He believed such a statement would prevent Britain and the Soviet Union from entering the kind of secret agreements that had plagued the post-World War I peace settlement. The resulting Atlantic Charter, which was strongly reminiscent of Woodrow Wilson's Fourteen Points, embraced Roosevelt's "Four Freedoms." It also proclaimed self-determination for all peoples and equitable distribution of the world's wealth, and announced that Britain and the United States sought no new territory. Churchill fought off Roosevelt's anticolonialist attempts to force Britain to relax her imperial role, while the President insisted that all mention of a League of Nations-type international organization be deleted to avoid raising the suspicions of the isolationists. Privately, he preferred a world policed by the United States, Britain, the Soviet Union, and perhaps China—the "Four Policemen"—to make certain that the international organization would not be paralyzed by the inability of its many members to agree.

The emotional high point of the Atlantic Conference occurred on Sunday, August 10, when Roosevelt and several hundred members of the *Augusta's* crew attended church services on the *Prince of Wales*. British and American sailors intermingled under the battleship's guns, sharing the same prayer books and joining together in the familiar old hymns: "Onward Christian Soldiers" and "For Those in Peril on the Sea." Tears flowed down Churchill's cheeks. "Every word seemed to stir the heart," he remembered in later years. "It was a great hour to live. Nearly half those who sang were soon to die."‡

If Roosevelt hoped that the Atlantic Charter would inspire the American people to take up arms against Nazism, he was disappointed. Existing battle lines merely hardened, and polls showed that 74 percent of

‡ Before the year was out, the *Prince of Wales* was sunk off Malaya by Japanese torpedo planes.

the country wished to stay out of the conflict. On the other hand, Roosevelt had apparently made his own commitment to war. The military reverses suffered by Britain and the Soviet Union had convinced him by the fall of 1941 that there was no other alternative to a victory by Hitler. Even so, there can be no certainty as to the depth of his commitment. Some authorities have concluded that he believed the United States would not have to send large armies overseas to fight and that the American military contribution could be limited to naval and air support.

On September 4, the first shots were fired in America's twilight war in the Atlantic. The U. S. Navy destroyer *Greer* was on a mail run to Iceland when a British bomber flashed word to her that a German submarine had been sighted about ten miles ahead. American ships were not authorized to attack U-boats but were to shadow them and broadcast their position, which could be picked up by British aircraft and warships. Racing to the scene, the *Greer* conducted a sweep, and her sonar "locked" on the quarry. After being tracked for three hours, the U-boat commander, obviously tired of the game of hide-and-seek, fired a torpedo at his tormentor. It missed, and the destroyer dropped a pattern of depth charges. Spotting another torpedo coming her way, she evaded it but lost contact with the submarine.

Roosevelt seized upon the *Greer* incident as a springboard for the announcement of his new policy of providing convoy escorts. Of course, the destroyer had placed herself in jeopardy by tracking the submarine in cooperation with British aircraft, and the U-boat captain had no way of determining the nationality of his adversary, but Roosevelt chose to regard the firing of the torpedo, rather than the tracking, as the first shot. A Fireside Chat was scheduled for September 8, and in the meantime the President went to Hyde Park to visit his mother, who, at nearly eighty-seven, had begun to fade.

The old lady perked up at the arrival of her son, but on the evening of September 6, she suffered a circulatory collapse and died the next day without regaining consciousness. Less than five minutes later, the biggest tree on the estate toppled to the ground. There was no storm, no wind, no lightning. Roosevelt gave no outward sign of sorrow at the death of his mother, but associates who knew the tenacity with which he clung to every link to the lost world of his childhood, realized that the loss was deeply felt. Sara Roosevelt was buried in the family plot at St. James' Church beside her husband, who had died forty-one years before. For the first and only time, the President was allowed to appear without a Secret Service man at his elbow. As the funeral party approached the cemetery, Mike Reilly, chief of the Secret Service detail, spoke to Jimmy Roosevelt: "You watch out for him, Jimmy. I don't think we belong in there even if Congress says we do."

Wearing a black mourning band on his sleeve, Roosevelt addressed the nation on September 11. Omitting the fact that the *Greer* had provoked the submarine attack, he denounced it as "piracy—legally and morally" and emphasized that no act of violence would intimidate the United States into abandoning its right to sail the high seas. "We have sought no shooting war with Hitler," he continued. "We do not seek it now." But "no matter what it takes, no matter what it costs, we will keep open the line of legitimate commerce. . . . When you see a rattlesnake poised to strike, you do not wait until he has struck before you crush him. These Nazi submarines and raiders are the rattlesnakes of the Atlantic. . . ."

The President made no false statements, but by ignoring the fact that the *Greer* had provoked the U-boat into firing a torpedo, he exploited the incident. Undoubtedly, he regarded this distortion as necessary to rally the American people behind his "shoot on sight" order to the U. S. Navy. As Lord Halifax, the British ambassador, once observed, Roosevelt "had a fatal gift of manipulation bestowed by a bad fairy." Isolationists railed against this maneuver, but the majority of Americans, although still hanging back from entering the war themselves, shared his conviction that a Nazi victory would endanger the security of the United States.

Two more American destroyers were attacked by U-boats during the undeclared naval war that followed the *Greer* affair. Little more than a month later, the *Kearny* was ripped by a torpedo while on escort duty and eleven of her crew were killed. "America has been attacked," Roosevelt told the nation in an emotional Navy Day (October 27) speech. "The U.S.S. *Kearny* is not just a Navy ship. She belongs to every man, woman, and child in this Nation." Reviving memories of the Zimmermann telegram,* of 1917, he produced documents purporting to show that the Nazis planned to divide South America into "five vassal states." Congress was prodded to eliminate the "hamstringing" provisions of the Neutrality Act so American merchantmen could be armed and allowed to sail to British ports. Four days later, the old four-piper *Reuben James* became the first American naval vessel sunk by a U-boat. She was torpedoed some six hundred miles west of Iceland, with the loss of 115 men.

The situation in the Atlantic had reached the explosive stage. Open warfare was bound to erupt sooner or later, because Hitler could not permit American ships to supply Britain without hindrance unless he was

---

* The Zimmermann telegram was a coded message from the German Foreign Office to the German minister to Mexico urging the conclusion of a German-Mexican alliance before the entry of the United States into World War I. While the Americans were preoccupied with events in Europe, the Mexicans were to cross the frontier and seize the "lost territories" of New Mexico, Texas, and Arizona. British intelligence intercepted the message, and it played a role in the American declaration of war against Germany.

willing to abandon the Battle of the Atlantic. Nevertheless, Roosevelt declined to ask Congress for a declaration of war. Isolationism was still strong—the Neutrality Act had been revised by only the slimmest of margins—and any attempt to secure such a declaration would touch off a ferocious debate that would divide the country and undermine his ability to lead. Besides, the United States was not ready to take up the terrible burden of war. Far from having become the arsenal of democracy, the nation's defense effort was operating on one cylinder.

To unite the country behind his leadership, Roosevelt, like Abraham Lincoln in 1861, had to maneuver his opponent into firing the first shot. These factors may help explain the President's hesitancy in the autumn of 1941. Relatively powerless to shape events, he could do little but wait for Adolf Hitler to provide some dramatic provocation that would unify the American people. "He had no more tricks left," said Sherwood. "The hat from which he had pulled so many rabbits was empty." But as the United States girded for war in the Atlantic, the blow fell in the Pacific with the swift finality of an executioner's sword.

Isolationists, revisionist historians, and Roosevelt-haters—sometimes one and the same—have built an industry based upon proving that the Japanese attack on Pearl Harbor was a monstrous conspiracy hatched in the Oval Office. This devil theory holds that Roosevelt provoked the Japanese in order to drag the United States into World War II through the back door when Hitler would not oblige him with a declaration of war. To unite the American people behind him, conspiracy theorists charge, the master plotter in the White House connived by acts of commission and omission to create an incident in the Pacific. Pearl Harbor rescued Roosevelt from an impossible dilemma, but this is a far cry from proof that he plotted to provoke the Japanese. And even if Roosevelt wished Japan to strike first, it seems hardly likely that he would have offered up the Pacific Fleet as a sacrifice—particularly when he would need these same ships to win the war.

A war in the Pacific was the wrong war at the wrong time in the wrong ocean, as far as Roosevelt was concerned. The basic thrust of his policy was to keep Britain afloat—preferably by all means short of war—and war with Japan would drain off men and matériel from operations against Germany, which was perceived as the main enemy. Roosevelt hoped to deter the Japanese aggression by such moves as transferring the Pacific Fleet to Pearl Harbor from its previous base, at San Pedro, California.† In fact, the ABC-1 Plan secretly worked out by the military and naval staffs

† The transfer, made in the spring of 1940, was strongly protested by Admiral James O. Richardson, and he was replaced by Admiral Husband E. Kimmel.

of the United States, Britain, and Canada in March 1941 established a
"Europe First" strategy. If the United States became involved in a two-
ocean war, Japan was to be held in check through defensive operations
until Hitler had been defeated and the Allies were ready to deal with her.
American policy in the Far East was to tighten the economic screws on
Japan while avoiding a shooting war because of the weakness of the
Pacific Fleet, which had fewer ships of every type than the Japanese Navy,
following the transfers to the Atlantic. "I simply have not got enough
Navy to go around," Roosevelt complained.

The conspiracy theory is also undermined by the lack of any assurance that even if Japan was provoked into an attack against the United
States, war with Germany would result. Nothing in the Tripartite Pact,
which Japan had signed with Germany and Italy, required the signatories
to come to the aid of the others in case of war. Japan used this loophole
to escape joining its Axis partner in the attack on the Soviet Union, so
why should Hitler assist his less than faithful ally? If he had not declared
war on the United States for his own reasons, it would have been a mas-
terstroke. The Americans and British would have been trapped into a war
in the Far East that would have divided British strength and diverted
American arms and supplies from the European front.

In the final analysis, the Pacific war resulted from the miscalculation
by Japan and the United States of the intentions of each other. Both
wanted peace, but they had different definitions of what constituted
peace. To the Americans, it meant a cessation of Japanese aggression in
China and elsewhere; to the Japanese, it meant an East Asia dominated
by Japan. These were the hard-core positions from which the nation could
not retreat. Surely, said the Japanese, the Americans should understand
that a modern industrial nation must have access to raw materials and
markets. The control of Manchuria, China, Southeast Asia—the Greater
East Asia Co-Prosperity Sphere—was absolutely essential to Japan's existence as a first-rate industrial power. American policy, on the other hand,
confused morality with reality. As a result of the popular idealization of
China, the United States allowed the keystone of its policy in the Far
East to be based upon an issue that was extraneous to its basic interests:
the liberation of China. Never believing that Japan would commit national suicide by going to war with the Western powers, Roosevelt was
convinced that through firmness he could force the Japanese to moderate
their course. By the end of 1940, the United States had cut off all shipments of all vital war matériel to Japan except for petroleum.

Would concessions by the United States have placated the Japanese?
Gordon W. Prange, who has made the most complete study of the events
preceding Pearl Harbor, thinks not. Japanese policy had its own dynamic,

he pointed out, and American concessions were regarded as weaknesses that invited further demands. Bogged down in China, Japan desperately needed the oil and mineral wealth of Southeast Asia and the Dutch East Indies to keep its military machine running. The summer of 1941 seemed a favorable time for expansion. British forces were being pushed back in North Africa, the Russians were reeling under the German offensive, and American eyes were fixed on the grim events unfolding in the Atlantic.

The drive to the south began in July 1941, with the occupation of Indochina, including the fine harbor at Camranh Bay, only seven hundred fifty miles from Singapore. The feeble Vichy regime, which ruled a prostrate France, acquiesced without resistance. Warning lights flashed in Washington. The Japanese advance was viewed as a preliminary to an eventual attack on the Philippines, Malaya, and the Dutch East Indies. The Americans knew what was coming, because a code-breaking operation known as Magic was reading the Japanese diplomatic, or Purple, code. Admiral Kichisaburo Nomura,‡ the Japanese ambassador, was summoned to the White House on July 24, where, flanked by Welles, acting Secretary of State in the absence of the ailing Hull, and Admiral Stark, the Chief of Naval Operations, the President issued a stern warning. The Dutch would resist any Japanese attempt to seize the oil of the East Indies, the British would come to their assistance, he declared, "and in view of our own policy of assisting Great Britian, an exceedingly serious situation would immediately result." This bitter pill had a sugar coating. If Japan withdrew from Indochina, the region would be neutralized and the Japanese would be guaranteed free access to its rice and raw materials. Roosevelt had little hope the offer would be accepted but regarded it as "one more effort to avoid Japanese expansion to [the] South Pacific."

Two days later, having heard nothing from Tokyo, the President delivered a body blow to the Japanese economy. He issued an executive order freezing some $131 million in Japanese assets in the United States, which ended trade between the two countries—trade that included 80 percent of Japan's oil consumption. Roosevelt had no desire to strangle Japan, however. Not long afterward, Washington indicated that export licenses would be granted for low-octane petroleum products that were unsuitable for production of aviation gasoline. Fearing that a complete embargo would trigger a Japanese invasion of the East Indies, "the President was still unwilling to draw the noose tight," said Ickes. "He thought it might be better to . . . give it a jerk now and then."

The British and the Dutch followed up on the American embargo by refusing to sell oil to Japan—a move that was viewed by the angry Japa-

‡ Nomura had first met FDR when he served in Washington as Japanese naval attaché during the Wilson years.

nese as the last step in the encirclement of the empire by the Western powers.

Like strategists in all eras, the Japanese had prepared for the next war in terms of the last one. In case of a conflict with the United States, they planned to use their fleet to capture the Philippines, strike for the East Indies, and then confront the advancing Americans in a climactic battle in the Japanese-controlled waters of the Central Pacific. But, early in 1941, Admiral Isoroku Yamamoto, Commander in Chief of the Combined Fleet, conceived a much more daring plan. Having observed America's industrial might at first hand as a student at Harvard and then as a naval attaché in Washington, he declared that Japan had no hope of winning a war with the United States unless the U. S. Pacific Fleet, which was in Hawaiian waters, could be destroyed.

Yamamoto urged that a surprise aircraft-carrier strike be made against the American battleships and carriers as they lay at anchor at Pearl Harbor. Such a move would take full advantage of Japan's superior naval power in the Pacific—ten battleships to nine, and ten carriers to three. There was ample precedent for such a strike. Japan had launched wars against Russia and China with massive surprise attacks, and in November 1940, a handful of British torpedo planes had disabled the Italian battle fleet while it was at anchor at Taranto.*

Yamamoto argued that with the American Fleet out of action, Japan would be able to conquer the Philippines, Malaya, and the East Indies without interference. Then she could retire behind a strong defense line running from the Kuriles to the fringes of Australia, and using interior lines of communication and supply, beat off attacks on this barrier until the Western nations were forced to accept Japan's domination of the Greater East Asia Co-Prosperity Sphere. Yamamoto overcame the objections of the Naval General Staff virtually through the strength of his own personality. Preparations for the attack went ahead under a thick veil of secrecy, with the actual training of the air crews beginning in September 1941.

During the four months between the oil embargo and the Pearl Harbor raid, both sides engaged in a ponderous diplomatic ballet designed to gain time. Roosevelt told Churchill that he hoped "to baby" the Japanese along, for the longer the United States managed to avoid a war with Japan, the better the chances for an incident to occur in the Atlantic. Time was needed to build up defenses in the Pacific, especially in the Philippines, where the armed forces had recently been federalized, with Douglas MacArthur placed in command. Japan's civilian leadership

* Unknown to the Japanese, an American carrier force had successfully surprised Pearl Harbor and "destroyed" the entire Pacific Fleet during fleet exercises in 1932.

sought time to find a diplomatic solution that would appease the militarists and avoid war, while the military in turn used the interval to perfect their preparations for war.

Prince Fumimaro Konoye, the Japanese Premier, requested a summit meeting with Roosevelt, preferably in Hawaii. The President, with his fondness for personal diplomacy, leaned toward accepting the proposal, but Secretary Hull, convinced that Konoye would be unable to offer significant concessions, opposed the meeting. Indeed, he argued that by raising false hopes it would be worse than no meeting at all and would have a crushing effect upon China's will to resist. Most analysts now believe that Roosevelt should have met Konoye, for even if they were unable to reach a settlement, the timetable for the Pearl Harbor attack would probably have been set back. By the time it got on track again, it might have been clear to the Japanese that the Soviet Union was not going to collapse and that an attack on the Allies was a dangerous proposition.

The Konoye government did not survive the American rejection of the summit. In mid-October, the Premier told General Hideki Tojo, the War Minister and a leading militant, that unless Japan agreed "in principle" to withdraw its troops from China, there was no possibility of a diplomatic settlement with the United States. Tojo declared that the Army would never agree to an end to the "China Incident" on such terms, and Konoye resigned. The Army would not agree to a civilian as Premier, and the Emperor appointed Tojo, who also remained as Minister of War. To appease the Emperor, who resisted the idea of war, Tojo dispatched a proposal to Washington on November 5, which constituted Japan's final offer. If no accord was reached by November 25, a deadline extended to November 29, hostilities would begin. The actual date for the raid on Pearl Harbor was fixed for December 7 Hawaiian time.

In Washington, the Magic code breakers read the Japanese proposals before they were presented by Admiral Nomura and Saburo Kurusu, a special emissary sent from Tokyo, and they contained nothing new. Japan expressed a willingness to withdraw its troops from Southeast Asia, but first the United States must agree to cease all aid to China and end the oil embargo. The envoys were met by Hull with sermons on the need for law and justice in the Pacific. Roosevelt told Ickes that "he wished he knew whether Japan was playing poker or not. He was not sure whether or not Japan had a gun up its sleeve." To Ickes, it seemed that "the President had not yet reached the state of mind where he is willing to be aggressive as to Japan." The small circle privy to the Magic intercepts became increasingly nervous as Nomura and Kurusu received repeated warnings from Tokyo that they had only until November 29 to reach an accord, because "things are automatically going to happen" afterward. Security surrounding the Pearl Harbor operation was so tight that neither man was aware that the strike force—six carriers and two battleships— had slipped away into the fog of the North Pacific.

Wishing to make one last attempt to stem the inexorable drift toward war, Roosevelt proposed an accommodation, or *modus vivendi*, with the Japanese, intended to return the situation in the Far East to the status quo of July 1941. The oil embargo would be lifted and talks between China and Japan initiated. In return, Japan would send no further troops to Indochina or along the Manchurian frontier with the Soviet Union and agree not to invoke the Tripartite Pact even if the United States went to war with Germany and Italy. "I am not very hopeful and we must all be prepared for real trouble, possibly soon," Roosevelt told Churchill on November 24. The following day, the President discussed the possibility of a Japanese surprise attack with his War Council: Hull, Knox, Stimson, and his military and naval advisers. "The question was how we should maneuver them into the position of firing the first shot without allowing too much danger to ourselves," observed Stimson. Conspiracy theorists have seized upon the statement as incontrovertible proof that Roosevelt planned to trick the Japanese into attacking the United States, but Stimson later explained that he meant that to have the full support of the American people, it was absolutely necessary to leave no doubt as to who was the aggressor.

Roosevelt's plan for a *modus vivendi* collapsed when the Chinse expressed alarm, fearing that any agreement made with the Japanese would be at their expense. "What about Chiang Kai-shek?" asked Churchill. "Is he not having a very thin diet?" The President might have pressed ahead anyway if he had seen a glimmer of hope, but on the morning of November 26, Stimson barged in, while Roosevelt was still holding bedside court, with the news that a large convoy of Japanese troopships had been sighted steaming south from Formosa. Roosevelt "fairly blew up," Stimson reported. "That changed the whole situation because it was evidence of bad faith on the part of the Japanese," he declared. "While they were negotiating for an entire truce—an entire withdrawal—they should [not] be sending that expedition down there to Indo-China." The truce plan was angrily withdrawn and Hull countered with a ten-point proposal that reiterated principles that Japan had previously rejected. "I have washed my hands of it," Hull said, according to Stimson, "and it is now in the hands of you and Knox—the Army and Navy."†

"War warnings" were sent the next day to American commanders in the Pacific, including Admiral Husband E. Kimmel, commander of the

† Hull denied having made these remarks. *Memoirs*, Vol. II, p. 1080. Stimson may have confused them with a statement by the Secretary of State on Nov. 25, 1941, that "our national security lies in the hands of the Army and Navy."

Pacific Fleet, at Pearl Harbor, and Lieutenant General Walter C. Short, commander of the Hawaiian Department. They were told the negotiations had broken down and a Japanese attack was expected on the Philippines, Thailand, or Borneo within the next few days. "Appropriate defensive deployment" was ordered. Believing Hawaii to be in no imminent danger, Kimmel did not order his fleet on full alert, rig antitorpedo nets, or initiate aerial scouting, which might have detected the approach of the Japanese Fleet. Short, whose primary mission was to defend Hawaii against attack, took no action except to mass his aircraft on their fields to prevent sabotage. Washington officialdom was also at fault by failing to keep Kimmel and Short notified of changing conditions and by failing to make inquiries as to what steps had been taken to meet the crisis.

Most Americans were only vaguely aware that the talks with Japan were near collapse and war might explode momentarily in the Far East. And in case of war, hardly anyone expected a surprise attack on territory under the American flag. Americans tended to regard Japan with contempt. Japanese ships and planes were inferior copies of American equipment, myopic Japanese pilots would be unable to hit their targets, and Japan's teahouse economy would quickly collapse under wartime strain. The New York tabloid PM ran an article on "How We Can Lick Japan in Sixty Days." Most Americans celebrated Thanksgiving without undue concern. Even the President managed to get away, to Warm Springs, although he had to delay the trip until after the holiday. Thanksgiving dinner at the Foundation was postponed until Saturday, November 29, so Roosevelt could be present. Immediately upon arrival, he visited Missy LeHand, who was convalescing from a stroke she had suffered the previous summer and from which she never completely recovered. Returning to the Little White House, the President received a telephone call from Hull, who reported that the situation in the Far East was brittle.

"I think Hull would feel better if I were back in Washington," he told Grace Tully, "but it will be determined tonight if he calls again." Hull telephoned that evening, and the President ordered a return to Washington on Sunday. He paid a farewell call on Missy, who was almost in tears as he left. From her cottage, he slowly drove down to the front of Georgia Hall, where the patients always said their good-byes. It was a solemn farewell, sealed with his closing remark: "This may be the last time I talk to you for a long time."

Throughout the first week of December, there was a feeling in Washington that some implacable machine had been placed in gear and no one knew how to stop it. Hull continued his unfruitful conversations with Nomura and Kurusu as they awaited a reply to the Ten-Point Plan. Congressional leaders were requested not to suspend sessions for more than three days at a time. The President met daily with the War Council. Intelligence reports of Japanese ship movements filtered in, and Magic revealed that the Foreign Office in Tokyo had advised its embassies to burn their diplomatic codes, a sure sign of an impending rupture of relations. But there was no sign of the Pearl Harbor attack force because the ships maintained strict radio silence during the entire voyage.

Hull was even gloomier than usual when the Cabinet met on Friday, December 5. "The Japanese envoys don't mean business," he declared. "I'm sure they don't mean to do anything. With every hour that passes, I become more convinced that they are not playing in the open, that what they say is equivocal and has two meanings to it. . . . They are the worst people I ever saw." With the exception of Stimson and Knox, no one else had much to say except to express consternation at the direction of events. "There was never a flicker of an idea expressed by anybody that the Japanese might at that time engage in war with the United States," according to Miss Perkins.

"Well, you know, Mr. President, we know where the Japanese Fleet is," Knox said. Roosevelt looked about as if to make certain no unauthorized persons were present before permitting the Secretary of the Navy to continue. "Well, we have very secret information that mustn't go outside this room that the Japanese fleet is out. They're out of harbor. They're out at sea."

Under questioning, Knox acknowledged that there was no precise intelligence regarding the movements of the Japanese Fleet but that everything indicated it was headed south, toward Singapore. Roosevelt went around the table asking everyone, one by one, what the United States should do in case of an attack. The President was not seeking strategic advice, Miss Perkins thought, but was trying to gauge public opinion through their reactions. The consensus was that the nation should go to the relief of the British if Singapore was attacked.

"Maybe the fleet is out for maneuvers," someone said hopefully as the meeting broke up.

Knox laughed, a hollow, "how ridiculous" sort of laugh, Miss Perkins recalled.

Roosevelt made a personal appeal for peace to Emperor Hirohito on December 6. Kurusu had told him this was the only way to prevent war. "Both of us for the sake of the peoples not only of our own great countries but for the sake of humanity in neighboring territories, have a sacred duty to restore traditional amity and prevent further death and destruction to the world," he wrote.

"This son of man has just sent his final message to the Son of God," he told some dinner guests after the message was on its way. Lord Halifax, the British ambassador, was assured that in case of an attack on

British or Dutch territory "we should obviously all be together." Later that evening, the President and Hopkins were in the Oval Study when a special courier brought Magic intercepts of the first thirteen parts of a fourteen-part Japanese reply to the American proposal. The message instructed the emissaries to inform the United States Government that the proposal had been rejected. Roosevelt read it through in about ten minutes while Hopkins nervously paced the floor.

"This means war," the President declared as he passed the message along to Hopkins.

"Since war was undoubtedly going to come at the convenience of the Japanese," Hopkins replied, "it was too bad that we could not strike the first blow and prevent any sort of surprise."

"No, we can't do that," said the President. "We are a democracy and peaceful people."

A few hours later, halfway around the globe in the Central Pacific, six aircraft carriers flying the sunburst flag of Japan turned into the wind to launch their deadly brood. As the first plane roared down the flight deck of the flagship *Akagi* into the dawning sky, the crew sped it on its way with three ceremonial *Banzais*. Within fifteen minutes, 183 bombers, fighters, and torpedo planes were headed south toward Pearl Harbor, about two hundred thirty miles away.

XXV

COMMANDER IN CHIEF

RELAXING IN AN old sweater that belonged to one of his sons, Franklin Roosevelt was looking forward to a quiet Sunday afternoon with his stamp albums. He had just finished lunch at his desk and was chatting with Harry Hopkins when the telephone rang, at 1:47 P.M. The operator was apologetic, saying that Frank Knox was on the line and insisted on being put through.

"Mr. President, it looks as if the Japanese have attacked Pearl Harbor!" Knox declared.

"No!"

When Roosevelt told Hopkins about the report, Hopkins couldn't believe it. Surely, Japan would never attack Hawaii.

"It was just the kind of unexpected thing the Japanese would do," the President said. "At the very time they were discussing peace in the Pacific they were plotting to overthrow it." He talked for some time about his efforts to keep the United States out of war and then somberly added, "If this report is true, it would take matters entirely out of my hands."

At 2:05 P.M. the President telephoned Cordell Hull and passed on the shocking news. Hull told him that Nomura and Kurusu had just arrived at the State Department. The final part of the instructions sent to the emissaries from Tokyo—and intercepted by Magic—had specifically told them to deliver Japan's rejection of the American peace proposals at 1 P.M. (7:30 A.M. Hawaiian time). This was shortly before the attack on Pearl Harbor was to begin, and the message was obviously intended as a break in relations. But there had been considerable confusion in the Japanese Embassy, and translation of the note had been delayed. Roosevelt instructed Hull to receive the Japanese but to make no mention of the raid.

He should be formal and "bow them out" coldly. The Secretary was inclined to refuse to see Nomura and Kurusu but decided to follow Roosevelt's orders, because "there was one chance in a hundred" the report was untrue.

Hull refused to shake hands with the envoys and did not invite them to sit down. Having read the Magic intercepts, he pretended to hastily glance through the note which they presented. Usually the model of southern courtliness, he spoke to them with an icy anger: "In all my fifty years of public service, I have never seen a document that was more crowded with infamous falsehoods and distortions—infamous falsehoods and distortions on a scale so huge that I never imagined until today that any government on this planet was capable of uttering them." Bewildered by these harsh words, Nomura tried to remonstrate, but Hull angrily waved the emissaries to the door. "Scoundrels and piss-ants!" he muttered after them. Normura and Kurusu did not learn of the Pearl Harbor attack until they returned to the Japanese Embassy, on Massachusetts Avenue, which was soon surrounded by an angry crowd.

By now, Admiral Stark had telephoned the President to confirm the attack, and reports of extensive damage to the Pacific Fleet were filtering into the White House. The War Cabinet was summoned, and Roosevelt dictated a news release to Steve Early. Various emotions swirled about the President's study. First, there had been shock at the attack, then relief that the question of American intervention had been resolved at last. But as the magnitude of the loss in men, ships, and planes became evident, anxiety and alarm became the predominant mood. Roosevelt managed to get through on the telephone to the military commander in Hawaii and his reaction—"Dammit, you told me that!" repeated over and over—was hardly that of a triumphant schemer. Churchill called from London seeking confirmation of the news, which he had heard on the radio.

"Mr. President, what is this about Japan?" he asked.

"It's quite true," replied Roosevelt. "They have attacked us at Pearl Harbor. We are all in the same boat now."

Grace Tully was summoned to take down the fragmentary reports telephoned in by Stark from the Navy Department and relay them to the President. The noise and confusion were so great she had difficulty in hearing and retreated to a bedroom. "Pa" Watson and Marvin McIntyre hovered over her shoulder as each bit of shattering news was transcribed, and she never forgot the "anguish and near-hysteria" of that afternoon. Some officials expected the Japanese to follow up the devastating raid with an invasion of Hawaii, while others thought the West Coast would be the next target. As the President spoke by telephone with Joseph B. Poindexter, the territorial governor, bystanders heard Poindexter shriek:

"My God, there's another wave of Jap planes over Hawaii right this moment!"

Roosevelt was outwardly calm, but there was rage in his very calmness, according to Miss Tully. "With each new message he shook his head grimly and tightened the expression of his mouth." He sought relief in action. Troop dispositions were discussed with General George C. Marshall, the Army's chief of staff. Hull was instructed to keep the Latin American nations informed and in line. Stimson and Knox were ordered to place guards at all defense plants and key installations. The President, however, refused to permit a military guard around the White House, already a magnet for anxious Americans, who gathered outside the fence looking for reassurance and guidance.

Long winter shadows were falling when Roosevelt called Miss Tully to his study. Everyone had left and they were now alone. "Sit down, Grace," he said, "I'm going before Congress tomorrow, and I'd like to dictate my message. It will be short." He inhaled deeply on his cigarette, blew out the smoke, and began dictating in the same calm tone he used to deal with his mail. He enunciated the words incisively and slowly, carefully specifying each punctuation mark and new paragraph. Running little more than five hundred words, the message was dictated without hesitation or second thoughts.

Thick, black smoke was still rising from the ships that rested on the shallow bottom of Pearl Harbor as the President went to Capitol Hill to ask for a declaration of war against Japan. The anchorage was dominated by the crazily tilted tripod masts of the *Arizona,* a tomb for nearly eleven hundred of her officers and men, and by the capsized hulk of the *Oklahoma,* looking like a giant whale that had tried to beach itself. Small boats moved slowly about, retrieving the bodies of sailors and marines from the oil-coated waters. In all, nineteen ships had been sunk or damaged, including the entire battle line of the Pacific Fleet. An estimated 265 aircraft had been lost, most of them destroyed while neatly lined up on the ground. American casualties totaled 2,403 dead and 1,178 wounded; the Japanese lost twenty-nine aircraft and fifty-five airmen. Pearl Harbor was the worst disaster in American military history.

Wave after wave of applause greeted the President as he made his way to the rostrum of the House Chamber on the arm of his son James, now a captain in the Marines. For the first time in years, the Republicans joined in, because political animosities had faded in the face of a national emergency. Pearl Harbor had united the American people behind Franklin Roosevelt. With one hand grasping the rostrum, he opened a black notebook that looked like those used by schoolchildren. For a moment, his eyes roamed about the room, over the faces of the Cabinet, the justices of the Supreme Court, and the diplomatic corps, in the front row seats, and up to the crowded gallery, where his wife sat with Mrs. Woodrow Wilson. Everywhere across the land, Americans gathered before their radios listening to the familiar voice, which spoke with great deliberation:

> Yesterday, December 7, 1941—a date which will live in infamy*—the United States was suddenly and deliberately attacked by naval and air forces of the Empire of Japan.
> The United States was at peace with that Nation and at the solicitation of Japan, was still in conversation with its government and its Emperor looking toward the maintenance of peace in the Pacific . . . The attack caused severe damage to American naval and military forces. Very many American lives have been lost. . . .
> Yesterday the Japanese government also launched an attack against Malaya.
> Last night Japanese forces attacked Hong Kong.
> Last night Japanese forces attacked Guam.
> Last night Japanese forces attacked the Philippine Islands.
> Last night the Japanese attacked Wake Island.
> This morning the Japanese attacked Midway Island.
> Japan has, therefore, undertaken a surprise offensive extending throughout the Pacific area. . . .
> As Commander-in-Chief of the Army and Navy, I have directed that all measures be taken for our defense. . . .
> With confidence in our armed forces . . . with the unbounding determination of our people—we will gain the inevitable triumph—so help us God.
> I ask that the Congress declare that since the unprovoked and dastardly attack by Japan on Sunday, December 7th, a state of war has existed between the United States and the Japanese Empire.

Within an hour and without debate, the Senate unanimously acted upon the President's request. The House listened to several speeches before following through, with a single dissenting vote.† Britain joined in with a declaration of war against Japan, and three days later, Germany and Italy declared war on the United States.

World War II transformed Roosevelt into a global leader. "Old Dr. New Deal" was replaced by "Dr. Win-the-War," and although many domestic problems remained unsolved, he devoted most of his attention to the war. Always at his best in an emergency, the President assumed the

---

* Examination of the texts of the speech reveals that in the first draft, FDR had dictated, "Yesterday, December 7, 1941—a date which will live in world history. . . ." He struck out "world history" and substituted "infamy" in a later draft.
† The sole vote against war was cast by Representative Jeanette Rankin of Montana, who had also voted against American entry into World War I.

heavy burden of directing military, diplomatic, and domestic policy with the same buoyancy with which the New Deal had been launched. Every line of authority ended in the White House, and he relished the extraordinary expansion of his power. Hull noted that he took special pride in his new role and preferred to be introduced at state dinners as Commander in Chief, rather than as President. Roosevelt's first priority was a military victory; then he wished to avoid the mistakes made by Woodrow Wilson in the making of the peace. Wilson had failed to take sufficient steps to make certain that the Allied coalition would continue into the postwar era and, most important of all, failed to bring about a genuine understanding with the U.S.S.R.

Controversy surrounds Roosevelt's war leadership, just as it does every aspect of his presidency. Two extreme views have appeared. One portrays him as a leader who rallied the free world, won a great victory, and thrust the United States into the center of the world stage. The other, colored by the tendency to look for a scapegoat for the Cold War, presents the picture of a President who blundered into a war, bungled its conduct, and then lost the peace at Yalta. Central to this thesis is the belief that Roosevelt was a naïve politician who, oblivious to the ruthlessness of the Soviet regime, tried to charm Stalin and failed. In point of fact, he was far too cynical and devious for such a strategy of innocence. If anything, he thought he could outwit Stalin, which is a far different thing. Roosevelt realized that Russian cooperation was needed to win the war and keep the peace, and he pursued what he regarded as realistic policy designed to reduce tensions and to assuage Stalin's distrust of the West. Roosevelt's greatness as a war leader lay in his ability to rally the people of the free world. This was the most pressing task confronting him in the dark days following Pearl Harbor. Fanning out from their home islands like the rays of the rising sun, the Japanese conquered the Philippines, Hong Kong, Burma, Thailand, Malaya, and the Dutch East Indies by early 1942. Australia and India were threatened, and Japanese troops had seized a foothold in the Aleutians. China had been isolated by the closing of the Burma Road, Hitler's legions had driven into the outskirts of Moscow and Leningrad, and the U-boats were winning the Battle of the Atlantic. Roosevelt's confident optimism shone like a beacon in the gloom of defeat. He was constantly on the radio, reporting on the progress of the fighting and making certain that the American people never wavered in their determination to fight through to victory. "No matter what our enemies . . . in their desperation may attempt to do to us—we will say as the people of London have said, 'We can take it,'" he declared. "And what's more, we can give it back—with compound interest."

Roosevelt had a small boy's fascination with the secret paraphernalia of war. When he learned that Churchill had a special headquarters where he kept a finger on military operations, he ordered a similar setup for the White House; it was called the Map Room. He went there every day to receive briefings on daily developments on all the fighting fronts. Proud of his naval background, the President told an aide: "I do not need to have military and naval operations explained to me at length." Before the war, he had maintained a proprietary interest in the Navy, even tinkering with the promotions and assignments of ranking officers. General Marshall was fully aware of where his sympathies were likely to lie in any interservice squabble, and upon one occasion, he pleaded good-humoredly, "At least, Mr. President, stop talking of the Army as 'they' and the Navy as 'us.' "

Roosevelt was strongly committed to the principle of civilian control in the making of national policy, and he retained a healthy skepticism in military affairs. Early on, he chose a talented team of military advisers to chart worldwide strategy, and they remained in place throughout the war: General Marshall for the Army, Admiral Ernest J. King for the Navy, and General Henry H. Arnold for the Army Air Corps.‡ Admiral William D. Leahy served as his personal military aide and link to the Joint Chiefs of Staff, which worked out the logistics and directives that sent men, ships, and planes into action. With the assistance of the Joint Chiefs, Roosevelt selected such able theater commanders as General Dwight D. Eisenhower, promoting him over the heads of 366 senior officers; Admiral Chester W. Nimitz; and General Douglas MacArthur. In contrast to Churchill, who harried his staff with often ill-conceived advice, he had the good sense not to interfere, for the most part, with day-to-day military operations.

As Commander in Chief, Roosevelt played the role of mediator between the Army and the Navy, among the various theater commanders, between the needs of the war effort and those of the home front, and between the demands of the British and those of the Russians for scarce supplies. Usually persuading rather than commanding, he exercised a loose control over military strategy, but there was no doubt where the final authority lay. As William Emerson has pointed out, Roosevelt understood the principle that "political leadership must be responsive to technical military opinion and advice, but it must, at whatever the cost, shape and direct the military instrument to support and serve its own purposes." Throughout the blackest days of defeat in the Pacific, he insisted that the war against Germany have the highest priority. Hitler was the most dangerous enemy, he argued in the face of the objections of his own military advisers. Germany could survive without Japan, but the Japanese would not long survive the defeat of Germany. And he pressed ahead

‡ The Air Corps was part of the Army, but Arnold was raised to membership on the Joint Chiefs of Staff to make the American command structure conform to that of the British, in which the Royal Air Force was an independent service.

with the invasion of North Africa in 1942 without regard to the protests of the professionals.

Both Marshall and King were blunt and forthright and had the President's ear and confidence. Quietly assured, reserved, and soft-spoken, Marshall was the exact opposite of the mercurial Roosevelt and privately winced at the President's bantering, first-name familiarity. At first, he doubted Roosevelt's capacity to lead the country during an emergency, until, as Forrest C. Pogue, his biographer, has recorded, he saw him act swiftly and decisively after Pearl Harbor. Marshall was primarily responsible for expanding, training, equipping, and deploying the Army, and Churchill later called him "the true organizer of victory." Roosevelt's growing reliance upon Marshall's integrity and judgment is reflected in his decision not to release the General to command the Allied invasion of Europe in 1944. "I feel I could not sleep at night with you out of the country," the President told him.

Tough, brilliant, and short-tempered, Admiral King embodied Roosevelt's idea of a fighting sailor. Only two years before, he had been passed over for a top command because, it was said, he drank too much, chased other men's wives, and had made too many enemies. "When they get into trouble they send for the sons-of-bitches" is the way he explained his sudden rise to command of the largest navy the world has ever seen. Insisting that the war against Japan be vigorously prosecuted, King aroused the ire of the British, and Churchill regarded him as irascible and intolerant. Most galling of all to the British was that the Royal Navy had become second best to King's Navy—and the Admiral never let them forget it. King also resisted Roosevelt's attempts to dabble in naval operations, and the President, respecting his professional judgment, finally gave up trying to interfere. Roosevelt found at least one naval organization that he could boss without angering King, however. In August 1942, the President's naval aide received the following memo:

> Will you tell the Navy Band that I don't like the way they play the Star Spangled Banner—It should not have a lot of frills in it.
>
> F.D.R.

Roosevelt became the guardian angel of the Grand Alliance and was determined to bring it through the war intact as the guarantor of the peace. Within the broad framework of agreement on the Europe-first strategy, there were significant conflicts among the Allies. Sometimes it seemed as if they were engaged in a war within the war, and all of Roosevelt's skills as a conciliator were put to the test. Not only did the Allies have diverse interests, but they harbored deep suspicions and resentments of each other. The Russians had not forgotten the post-World War I effort, quarterbacked by Churchill, to strangle their revolution, and the

British had not forgiven the Nazi-Soviet Pact, which had given Hitler a free hand in 1939. The Western democracies were also haunted by the fear that Stalin might make a separate peace with Hitler if it proved advantageous to him.

Perhaps the most awkward paradox was that there was no enemy common to them all. The Russians were not at war with Japan, and China was not at war with Germany. Churchill and Stalin were contemptuous of the Chiang Kai-shek regime and had little faith in China as a military force or a political influence. Although he was under no illusions about the Chinese Government, Roosevelt regarded China as a future base for retaliatory strikes against Japan and, alone among the Western leaders, envisioned China as an important postwar influence in the Far East.

The question of the Second Front in Europe dominated Allied relations during the first two years of the war after Pearl Harbor. Stalin, desperately in need of relief from the German assault, pressed for an immediate invasion of Western Europe that would force Hitler to divert troops from the Eastern Front. Haunted by the bloodletting of World War I, Churchill resisted, fearing that a major landing in France would be risky at best and might result in tremendous casualties. He urged instead a peripheral strategy designed to wear down the Germans by attacks through Norway and the Mediterranean while massive bombing raids were mounted against German industry. American planners regarded this strategy as fundamentally irrelevant. Nazi Germany was the center of enemy resistance, and they urged a massive cross-Channel assault on Europe as soon as enough men, shipping, and aircraft were available. Strategically, Roosevelt was thus more in tune with Stalin than with Churchill, but he was unable to make good on the promise of a Second Front until 1944, due to the limits of Allied strength. Stalin contemptuously dismissed such arguments, and his conspiratorial mind seethed with the suspicion that Russia and Germany were being allowed to slaughter each other so the capitalists could dominate postwar Europe.

Global strategy, priorities, and frictions among the Allies were worked out in a series of fourteen summit conferences at which Roosevelt met with Churchill, Stalin and/or Chiang Kai-shek. Roosevelt was convinced that only the President could represent the United States at these crucial negotiations, and he loved the high-level maneuvering and bargaining. At these personal encounters, he utilized his skills in compromise and accommodation to reduce tensions and coordinate the Allied effort to win the war. During the early years of the conflict, most of Roosevelt's meetings were with Churchill, and the relationship between the two men became so close that the Prime Minister seemed like a trans-Atlantic commuter. Eager to confer with the President after America's formal entry into the war, he arrived in Washington only two weeks after Pearl Harbor and remained for nearly a month. Churchill was installed in a big bedroom across the hall from the one occupied by Hopkins and close to Roosevelt's own quarters. There was much informal visiting back and forth, and upon one occasion, according to Hopkins, Roosevelt was wheeled into the Prime Minister's room just as Churchill was emerging naked and dripping from his bath. Embarrassed, the President apologized and started to leave but Churchill declared: "The Prime Minister of Great Britain has nothing to hide from the President of the United States."*

Churchill came to Washington to discuss military plans, but Roosevelt insisted on using the Arcadia Conference, as it was known, to announce political goals. Following considerable discussion interspersed among marathon staff discussions of military affairs, the Declaration of the United Nations—the term "United Nations" was coined by Roosevelt —was signed on New Year's Day 1942 by twenty-six countries waging war against the Axis. They pledged themselves to abide by the principles of the Atlantic Charter and not to sign a separate armistice or peace treaty with the common enemy. Roosevelt pressured a reluctant Churchill into allowing India to sign to make it clear that the war was being waged for the freedom of all nations. And he persuaded Maxim Litvinov, the Soviet ambassador, that adherence to the Charter did not commit his country to a reversal of its antireligious policy. With tongue in cheek, he maintained that freedom of religion included freedom to have no religion. Roosevelt's arguments were so impressive that Churchill whimsically promised to recommend him for appointment as Archbishop of Canterbury when he left the White House.

While in Washington, Churchill pressed for an immediate invasion of North Africa in the area of Casablanca to trap the Afrika Korps between two Allied forces and reopen the Mediterranean to Allied shipping. Roosevelt, eager to have American troops in action against the Axis in 1942, looked with favor upon the proposal. Stimson and Marshall argued forcefully against the project, however, emphasizing the shortage of shipping and equipment, and the President reversed himself. Marshall pushed instead for a massive cross-Channel invasion of Europe in 1943, with the possibility of establishing a limited beachhead as early as 1942—and this became the accepted Allied strategy.

Several events combined to undermine this strategy. In May 1942, Vyacheslav Molotov, the Soviet Foreign Minister, visited Washington and warned Roosevelt that the Russians might not be able to halt a Ger-

---

* When Robert Sherwood asked if the story was true, Churchill replied that he had never received the President without a bath towel wrapped around him. "I could not possibly have made such a statement as that. The President himself would have been well aware that it was not strictly true."

man summer offensive and insisted on an immediate second front. Impressed, the President told him that he could assure Stalin that there would be a second front "this year." Uneasy about this pledge to the Russians, Churchill again met with Roosevelt, this time at Hyde Park. The President picked his visitor up at the airport and took him on a sight-seeing tour of the area in his hand-operated Ford. Churchill was visibly nervous as the President backed the car up near the bluffs overlooking the Hudson and darted into the woods to escape the Secret Service, but he managed to keep up a drumfire of objections to the cross-Channel invasion. Time and again, he warned that a disastrous defeat on the coast of France would be "the only way in which we could possibly lose this war."

The two leaders were continuing their discussions in Washington when word was received, on June 21, that Rommel had captured Tobruk and taken twenty-five thousand British prisoners. Churchill was mortified. Only a thin line of defense at El Alamein stood between the Germans and the Suez Canal and the oil riches of the Persian Gulf.

"What can we do to help?" asked Roosevelt.

"Give us as many Sherman tanks as you can spare, and ship them to the Middle East as quickly as possible."

Making a snap decision, the President issued the necessary orders even though this meant that American troops would have to wait longer for modern tanks. The Tobruk disaster made Churchill even more reluctant to participate in an invasion of France in 1942. Angry over British resistance, the American Joint Chiefs of Staff contemplated redeploying the bulk of their forces to the Pacific, but Roosevelt intervened decisively to end the acrimony. In a sharply worded memorandum to Marshall and King, he ruled out any diversion to the Pacific. Significantly, he signed it "Franklin D. Roosevelt, Commander-in-Chief." An invasion of North Africa had always been the President's "great secret baby," according to Stimson, and he substituted it for the cross-Channel assault. When the British lagged on setting a date for a landing, Roosevelt pressured them into accepting an October 30, 1942, deadline. Elated that the Allies had agreed to go on the offensive at last, he issued orders for "full speed ahead."

Bottlenecks in the production of artillery, airplanes, tanks, and especially landing craft and merchant ships were a major cause of the delay in mounting an Allied offensive. Mobilization had begun long before Pearl Harbor, but the massive war machine which would crush Hitler and the Japanese Empire still ground with confusion and friction. Converting from peacetime to wartime production, the building of new plants and establishing priorities for manpower and matériel required centralized control and planning on a level unprecedented in the American experience.

Some industrialists, particularly the automobile manufacturers, resisted conversion, claiming that Roosevelt was using the emergency merely as a pretext for furthering the radical economic and social policies of the New Deal. And the President, wary of the political repercussions of putting the nation's economy into a straitjacket in peacetime, moved slowly. Like many of the New Deal agencies, the ramshackle system of boards and commissions that he established were the product of short-range pressure, rather than of long-range planning.

Pearl Harbor jolted many of these stuck gears loose. Understanding better than most Americans that modern warfare is as much a duel between rival technologies as one between combat forces, Roosevelt insisted upon production targets that seemed fantastic. While preparing his 1942 State of the Union message, he raised the production figures provided by his staff to 60,000 planes that year, 25,000 tanks, 20,000 antiaircraft guns, and six million tons of merchant shipping to replace those sunk by the U-boat wolf packs that had appeared off the American coast. "Oh—the production people can do it if they really try," he told a protesting Hopkins. This was just the beginning. The goal for the following year was 125,000 planes, 75,000 tanks, 35,000 guns, and 10 million tons of shipping. "These figures, and similar figures . . . will give the Japanese and the Nazis a little idea of just what they accomplished in the attack at Pearl Harbor," he declared.

In an effort to end snarls and foul-ups, Roosevelt, in January 1942, organized the War Production Board, headed by Donald M. Nelson, a former Sears, Roebuck executive, to provide centralized direction for the war effort. The WPB had a short and stormy life marked by frustration and conflict. Following his usual practice when dissatisfied with an agency, the President created a new one to take over its functions without abolishing the old one. "Roosevelt's normal way of organizing a Department," according to one authority, "was to split it down the middle." Finally, in October 1942, he established the Office of Economic Stabilization—later called the Office of War Mobilization—headed by James F. Byrnes, the former South Carolina senator who resigned from the Supreme Court to take the burden of running the domestic economy off Roosevelt's shoulders. Byrnes was called the "Assistant President," with good reason. From an office in the East Wing of the White House, he set policy on priorities, production, manpower, wages, and prices.

Having established ambitious production goals, Roosevelt allowed his subordinates to carry them out, interfering only when disputes threatened to snarl the war effort. "He was the catalytic agent through whose efforts chaotic forces were brought to a point where they could be harnessed creatively," according to Frances Perkins. "He was a creative and energizing agent rather than a careful, direct-line administrator." Stalin was perhaps the best judge of Roosevelt's effectiveness in mobilizing the nation's productive capacity. "Without American production the United Nations could never have won the war," the Soviet dictator declared in one of his more effusive moments. By the end of the war, American factories and shipyards had produced 299,300 airplanes, 72,100 naval ships of all kinds, including 64,000 landing craft, 4,900 merchant ships, 86,300 tanks, 8.5 million rifles, and 14 million tons of ammunition and bombs. This was accompanied by the mobilization of the largest military force in the nation's history. At war's end, the Army and the Air Force numbered 12 million men and women, and at peak strength the Navy and Marine Corps numbered some 3.4 million.

Businessmen thronged to Washington to join the alphabet soup of wartime agencies, and the gulf between business and government that had prevailed under the New Deal was bridged by wartime cooperation. The war created the military-industrial complex, and towns like Seattle and regions such as Southern California became largely dependent on military spending. War spurred the concentration of American industry, and the nation's biggest firms thrived as never before. Fifty-six of the largest companies received three quarters of all federal war contracts. The booming war industries sopped up the pool of jobless Americans left over from the depression, and even women, teenagers, and blacks, previously at the bottom of the labor-market barrel, found work at high wages. Union membership nearly doubled, to some 15 million workers, and although there were some "wildcat" strikes as workers pressed for a greater share of wartime profits, the amount of lost time was comparatively minor. Nevertheless, the belligerence of John L. Lewis and work stoppages by his coal miners provoked considerable public and congressional resentment and passage, in 1943, of the anti-labor Smith-Connally Act, over the President's veto.

Undoubtedly, Roosevelt's greatest failure on the domestic side was his ratification of the decision to uproot some 120,000 Japanese living on the West Coast—two thirds of them American citizens. Panic and prejudice against the Japanese reached hysterical levels following Pearl Harbor. Although there was no evidence of serious disloyalty or cases of espionage, local leaders such as Earl Warren, the attorney general of California and later a liberal chief justice of the United States, pressured the Army to relocate the Japanese. "A Jap's a Jap, and I don't want any of them around here," declared General John L. De Witt, the head of the West Coast Defense Command.

Only a few weeks before, the President had extolled the Bill of Rights on its one-hundred-fiftieth anniversary, but without protest he signed an order authorizing the internment of the West Coast Japanese. Frightened and bewildered, the Japanese were given a week to sell homes, farms, and businesses, usually at a fraction of true value, and were herded into relocation centers in remote desert areas that were little more than concentration camps. There they remained until almost the end of the war. Why did Roosevelt permit an action that bore, in Justice Frank Murphy's words, a "melancholy resemblance" to the Nazi treatment of the Jews? Never a strong civil libertarian, he gave in to public and congressional pressure with little thought of the consequences. Paradoxically, the Japanese living in Hawaii were not interned, even though the islands were under martial law during the entire war.

Roosevelt was also blind to the destruction of six million European Jews by the Nazis. The situation of the Jews had worsened with the coming of the war and the expansion of Hitler's domain, for the State Department actually tightened visa requirements for refugees. The President was curiously ambivalent about the problem. Although personally sympathetic to the plight of the Jews, he left the refugee question in the less-than-compassionate hands of assistant Secretary of State Breckenridge Long. An old Wilsonian and large contributor to the Democratic party, Long had jurisdiction over refugee problems. If not anti-Semitic, he was at least sympathetic to the Jews and feared that letting down immigration barriers would flood the nation with Communist and Nazi spies disguised as refugees. Along with other officials, he thwarted numerous efforts to rescue Jews and suppressed information about Hitler's plans to exterminate them.

By early 1942 details of Hitler's plan for the Final Solution had reached the State Department, but many officials refused to believe the reports. They likened them to the German atrocity stories spread by Allied propagandists to inveigle the United States into World War I. Yet the evidence of death camps and mass murders mounted. Repeated appeals to the Americans and British to bomb the rail lines leading to the camps were unheeded on the ground that such diversions would only delay victory—the best hope for the Jews. Following an Anglo-American conference in Bermuda in 1943 to discuss the refugee problem, Secretary Hull told Roosevelt, "The unknown cost of removing an undetermined number of persons from an undisclosed place to an unknown destination, a scheme advocated by certain pressure groups, is of course out of the question."

It may have been so for Hull but not for Henry Morgenthau. As a Jew he was anguished by the reports reaching Washington, and early in 1944 he instructed Randolph Paul, the Treasury Department's general counsel, to prepare a study of the State Department's handling of the refugee question. Paul produced a bluntly worded indictment, "Report to the Secretary on the Acquiescence of This Government in the Murder of the Jews," which pulled no punches. State Department officials, it charged, "have not only failed to use the Governmental machinery at their disposal to rescue Jews from Hitler, but have even gone so far as to use this Governmental machinery to prevent the rescue of these Jews." Morgenthau personally presented these findings to the President, who appeared surprised. Within a week, Roosevelt created a War Refugee Board outside of the State Department to take over the refugee problem. Representatives of the Board, including Raoul Wallenberg, a Swedish businessman who worked in Budapest, rescued thousands of Jews from the gas chambers. But had Roosevelt acted sooner, other hundreds of thousands of people might also have been saved. As in the case of the Japanese, his sin was not one of commission but omission—with even more tragic results.

Throughout the summer and fall of 1942, Roosevelt impatiently awaited the invasion of North Africa. Eager to go on the offensive and to meet domestic and Russian demands for action, he pressured everyone involved to launch the attack at the earliest possible moment. "Time is of the essence," he declared over and over again. As the year neared its end, the tide of battle showed signs of turning in favor of the Allies. Japanese expansion had been halted in the Battle of the Coral Sea, a Japanese invasion force was turned back at Midway with heavy losses, and the United States had embarked on an island-hopping advance to Tokyo. A German drive into the Caucasus had stalled at Stalingrad, on the Volga, and the Russians were preparing a massive counterattack. And the British had not only held at El Alamein but, reinforced by four hundred Sherman tanks hastily shipped from the United States, crashed through the German defenses on October 23 and sent Rommel's troops reeling backward in disorder.

On November 8, Roosevelt was at Shangri-la, his Catoctin Mountain retreat, in western Maryland. The President seemed on edge—as though he was awaiting important news. Finally, a telephone call came through from the War Department, in Washington. Grace Tully noted that Roosevelt's hand shook as he took the receiver from her. He listened intently until he heard the message through and then burst out: "Thank God! Thank God! That sounds grand. Congratulations."

He dropped the phone and turned to his guests.

"We have landed in North Africa," he told them. "Casualties are below expectations. We are fighting back."

Nearly two hundred thousand American troops had poured ashore at Casablanca, in Morocco, and at Oran and Algiers, in Algeria. The two Algerian ports were quickly captured, but the Vichy French forces resisted for several days at Casablanca. General Dwight Eisenhower, the American military commander, hastily arranged for a cease-fire with Admiral Jean

Darlan, a ranking Vichy official who, by chance, was visiting the region, in exchange for recognizing him as the political authority in French North Africa. Britons and Americans who knew that Darlan was a German collaborator denounced the "Darlan deal" as a sellout of the democratic ideals for which the war was being fought, but Eisenhower regarded the prevention of casualties as more important than politics. Roosevelt, who had already angered liberals by maintaining relations with the Vichy regime, rather than recognizing the Free French organization of General Charles de Gaulle, went along with the arrangement, describing it as "only a temporary expedient, justified solely by the stress of battle." The immediate problem was resolved by the assassination of Darlan, but the episode left a bad aftertaste.

With the Afrika Korps being ground between the advancing American and British forces, the time had come to decide upon future strategy. Roosevelt urged Stalin to join Churchill and himself for a meeting at Casablanca, but the Soviet dictator refused on grounds that he could not leave his country in the midst of a Russian counterattack at Stalingrad. The President was disappointed at being unable to meet Stalin, but he was delighted at the prospect of being the first Chief Executive to fly and the first to leave the United States in wartime.

The principal purpose of the Casablanca Conference, which lasted from January 14 to 24, 1943, was to fix the next Allied target. The Americans were divided. General Marshall wanted to launch the massive cross-Channel invasion of Europe in 1943, while Admiral King argued for more emphasis on the Pacific campaign. The British were united in extolling the virtues of continued operations against the "soft under-belly" of Europe. Although Marshall objected that "periphery-pecking" would drain off resources from the main offensive against Europe, Churchill argued that the Anglo-American armies were not yet strong enough to breach Hitler's Fortress Europe. While a buildup continued, he urged that North Africa be used as a springboard for an attack on Sicily, which might knock Italy out of the war. Excited by the prospect of immediate victories, Roosevelt accepted the British strategy, and the cross-Channel invasion was postponed until 1944. To placate Stalin for the further delay of the long-promised "Second Front," the flow of supplies to Russia would be increased and the aerial bombing of Germany stepped up. Plans were also approved for an intensified campaign against Japan.

The tangled French political situation also intruded into the discussions. Following the collapse of France, in 1940, then-Colonel de Gaulle had escaped to London, where he proclaimed himself and his Free French movement the true symbols of resistance. Proud and stiff-necked as only a man convinced that he embodies the honor of his country can be, De Gaulle irritated Roosevelt and his advisers with his insistence that France be treated as an equal. Roosevelt, however, had no intention of restoring France to great-power status or allowing the French to return as rulers to their former colonies after the war. Although De Gaulle was a rallying point for many patriotic Frenchmen, the Americans selected General Henri Giraud, a brave but unimaginative soldier, to lead French forces in North Africa. Angry at this snub, De Gaulle was persuaded to come to Casablanca only with difficulty, to accept the co-leadership, and then insisted that Giraud must take orders from him. "Yesterday," exclaimed a disgusted Roosevelt, "he wanted to be Joan of Arc. Now he wants to be Clemenceau!" Under pressure from the Allied leaders, the generals reluctantly agreed to work together, but before long De Gaulle outmaneuvered Giraud and he dropped from sight. Eventually, De Gaulle's Free French forces received American military equipment, which they used with skill and courage, but De Gaulle, rankled by the alleged insults of the Anglo-Saxons, nourished a resentment that flowered in the postwar era.

Roosevelt ended the Casablanca conference with something of a bombshell. "Unconditional surrender," he told a press conference, rather than the negotiated armistice of World War I, was the sole condition for ending the war. The announcement appeared spontaneous, with Churchill expressing surprise before agreeing to the doctrine. Roosevelt later claimed that the meeting between Giraud and De Gaulle had reminded him of Grant and Lee and Grant's insistence upon unconditional surrender. "And the next thing I knew, I had said it." In reality, the President had discussed the idea of ending the war with the unconditional surrender of the three Axis partners as early as May 1942. Not even Roosevelt, with his delight in pulling rabbits out of hats, would have casually announced such a momentous policy without consulting Churchill. The Prime Minister's surprise was probably feigned and may well have been an effort to disguise his reluctance to go along.

Roosevelt insisted upon unconditional surrender because he wanted to prevent a recurrence of German claims that Germany had never been defeated on the battlefield in World War I but had been "stabbed in the back" by radicals and Jews. This time they must be forced to admit they had been thoroughly whipped. And he wished to reassure the Soviet Union that the United States and Britain were in the fight to the death and would make no separate peace with Hitler or the Japanese. With the exception of the Yalta settlement, no wartime decision aroused more controversy than the unconditional-surrender doctrine. Critics charged that it fortified Axis resistance, because it left the enemy no option but mass slavery or annihilation, and Axis propagandists used this argument to keep their people fighting. But Roosevelt and Churchill repeatedly emphasized that unconditional surrender meant the punishment of those responsible for the war, rather than the destruction of the vanquished nations. The

Above: FDR, Fala, and Ruth Bie at Hilltop Cottage in 1941. This is one of the very few pictures taken of the President in his wheelchair. (Courtesy Margaret Suckley) Right: FDR and Fala, reproduced here for the first time. (Courtesy Margaret Suckley)

Champion campaigner. FDR in Philadelphia during the 1944 presidential campaign. (Courtesy FDR Library)

FDR, Churchill, and Stalin at Yalta. The civilian behind Stalin's right shoulder is Nikita Khrushchev, one of Stalin's successors as Soviet dictator. (Courtesy FDR Library)

FDR at work at Warm Springs during his final visit to Georgia. Previously unpublished, this may be the last picture taken of the President. (Courtesy Margaret Suckley)

threat of unconditional surrender had little to do with prolonging the war. In reality, the length of the war was determined by the refusal of Hitler and the Japanese warlords to consider any form of surrender at all.

The White House was a cheerless place as the war continued, and Roosevelt was an increasingly lonely man. Eleanor was away most of the time, making speeches or inspection trips, his four sons were overseas, Harry Hopkins had remarried and moved to a house in Georgetown, Marvin McIntyre died in 1943, and Missy LeHand the following year. "See who's home and ask them to stop in," he would tell an usher as he prepared for the evening ritual of cocktails in his study. Some nights he was told: "Sorry, Mr. President, there is no one home." He would have a solitary dinner off a tray and go to bed early. With so many old friends gone, the President tried almost desperately to broaden his circle. As always, he liked to be surrounded by women who offered a touch of frivolity and did not burden him with serious problems.

Two unmarried cousins, Laura Delano and Margaret Suckley, became such frequent visitors that Eleanor called them Franklin's "handmaidens." Miss Suckley, a quiet and gentle woman known as Daisy, was a dog breeder and had given him Fala. Laura Delano was somewhat eccentric and had purple-dyed hair. The President enjoyed teasing her. Once, he convinced her that the sudden darkness that resulted from a total eclipse was the herald of approaching doom. Laura went to her room and returned clutching the one possession with which she intended to meet the end of the world: her jewel case. Roosevelt howled with laughter. "I love it! I love it!" he cried. He also became close to some of the exiled royalty who came to the United States during the war. The Crown Princess Martha of Norway had the run of the White House and Hyde Park, and she and the President enjoyed a mild flirtation. But the lady of his affection now as before was Lucy Mercer Rutherfurd.

Over the years, Roosevelt had maintained loose contact with Lucy, without Eleanor's knowledge. She was provided with tickets for his first inauguration ceremony and was present for his acceptance speech at the Democratic National Convention in 1936. In 1941, while the elderly Winthrop Rutherfurd was slowly dying after a severe stroke, Lucy and Franklin began to meet regularly in Washington. Secret Service agents would drive him out to a rendezvous on Canal Road, beyond Georgetown, where Lucy would be waiting in her car. For an hour or two, they would drive about and talk before the President returned to the White House. Upon one occasion, Lucy saw him at Hobcaw Barony, Bernard Baruch's estate in South Carolina, where Roosevelt had gone for a rest. Lucy offered tranquillity and sought nothing but to be a faithful friend.

In the latter years of the war, after her husband's death, Lucy visited the White House several times while Eleanor was away. Usually accompanied by her daughter or one or two stepchildren, she came to tea or dinner, at which Anna Boettiger served as her father's hostess. "Never was there anything clandestine about these occasions," Anna wrote in her unpublished magazine article. "On the contrary they were occasions which I welcomed for my father because they were light-hearted and gay, affording a few hours of much-needed relaxation for a beloved father and world leader in time of crises. . . . Never was I aware of anything self-conscious in Father's attitude with me about Mrs. Rutherfurd. . . . Never did Father and I discuss or mention any 'relationship' other than one of friendship with which I was familiar. As for me, I still found Mrs. Rutherfurd to be a most attractive, stately but warm and friendly person. She certainly had an innate dignity and poise which commanded respect."†

The President slipped out of Washington on Armistice Day 1943 and boarded the new battleship *Iowa* at Hampton Roads for an Atlantic crossing. The elusive meeting with Stalin had been arranged for Teheran, just over the Soviet border in Iran, and although appalled at having to travel halfway around the world, Roosevelt eagerly grasped the opportunity. It was a time for a "meeting of minds" with the Soviets. In the ten months since the Casablanca Conference, the tide of battle had inexorably turned in favor of the Allies. Sicily had been conquered, Italy had surrendered, a German army of some three hundred thousand men had been destroyed at Stalingrad, the Battle of the Atlantic had been won, and the Japanese were being pressed back upon their home islands. Bickering between the Americans and the British over strategy had ended at conferences in Washington and Quebec, and the massive cross-Channel invasion—Operation Overlord—was fixed for May 1, 1944.

Before the Big Three got together, there was a preliminary meeting at the foreign-ministers level in Moscow in late October 1943. The President intended to send Sumner Welles, but the under Secretary of State was forced to resign because of widespread rumors of a homosexual episode with a sleeping-car porter. Roosevelt was saddened by the departure of a longtime friend whose counsel he valued.‡ Making his only major diplomatic appearance of the war, Hull worked with a dogged tenacity to persuade the Russians to agree to a four-power declaration pledging the es-

---

† Anna originally wrote, "She certainly had an innate dignity and poise which would have precluded any thought of a 'secret romance.'" She crossed out the last nine words.

‡ FDR was so angered at William Bullitt, a Welles rival who was said to have spread the rumors about Welles's indiscretions, that he told him he never wanted to see him again. Bullitt got his revenge with a series of postwar articles and books charging that the President's diplomatic blunders had lost the peace.

tablishment of an international organization to maintain postwar peace and security. Stalin also assured Hull that the Soviet Union would enter the war against Japan as soon as Germany was defeated.

On the way to Teheran, Roosevelt stopped over at Cairo to meet with Chiang Kai-shek in an attempt to prod him into continued resistance to the Japanese. The President thought it vital to keep China in the war to tie down Japanese troops, and Chinese airfields were believed to be indispensable for the bombing of Japan. Repeated efforts to persuade Chiang to reform his corruption-ridden government failed, but Roosevelt had no option but to continue supporting the Generalissimo. American public opinion would never allow him to back the Chinese Communists, who were fighting both Chiang's forces and the Japanese. Roosevelt juggled American military commanders in China, met Chiang's endless demands for money, which always promptly disappeared, and tried to raise his morale by treating China as a great power. These tactics failed in all but the most urgent objective: China remained in the war.

For Roosevelt, the challenge of the Teheran Conference was to develop the same personal relationship with the inscrutable Stalin that he enjoyed with Churchill. "The President's plan," according to Robert Murphy, an American diplomat, "was to make the Russians feel that the Americans trusted them implicitly and valued Soviet-American cooperation in war and peace above any other prospective alliance." Roosevelt's critics charge that his reliance on personal diplomacy and his willingness to go more than halfway to meet Stalin's demands undermined the postwar settlement and resulted in the Cold War. I think not. Although he overestimated his ability to negotiate with Stalin, he was hardly an innocent concerning Russian power and intentions. Recognizing the reality of power as Woodrow Wilson never did, Roosevelt saw that international security had become primarily a police problem for the superpowers. The old European balance-of-power system was bankrupt, and he sought to guide the shift to a new world system in which the Soviet Union, along with the United States would be the arbiters of peace. Roosevelt failed—not through naïveté but because Stalin had different objectives.

The Teheran Conference lasted from November 28 to December 2, 1943—four crowded days in which Roosevelt conferred with Churchill and Stalin at the council table and over meals and met several times with Stalin alone. The President found the Soviet dictator, who wore a beige uniform with the large gold epaulets of a marshal, "very confident, very sure of himself . . . altogether quite impressive." For the first three days, however, he was unable to establish a personal relationship with him. "He was correct, stiff, solemn, not smiling, nothing to get hold of," Roosevelt told Frances Perkins. "I felt pretty discouraged. . . . What we were doing could have been done by the foreign ministers. I thought it over all night and made up my mind I had to do something desperate. . . . On my way to the conference room that morning we caught up with Winston and I had just a moment to say to him, 'Winston, I hope you won't be sore at me for what I am going to do.' Winston just shifted his cigar and grunted."

Roosevelt wheeled himself up to Stalin and through an interpreter engaged him in conversation.

"It appeared quite chummy and confidential, enough so that the other Russians joined us to listen. Still no smile. Then I said, lifting my hand up to cover a whisper (which of course had to be interpreted) 'Winston is cranky this morning, he got up on the wrong side of the bed.'

"A vague smile passed over Stalin's eyes, and I decided I was on the right track. As soon as I sat down at the conference table, I began to tease Churchill about his Britishness, about John Bull, about his cigars, about his habits. It began to register with Stalin. Winston got red and scowled, and the more he did so, the more Stalin smiled. Finally Stalin broke out into a deep, hearty guffaw, and for the first time in three days, I saw light. . . . From that time on our relations were personal, and Stalin himself indulged in an occasional witticism. The ice was broken and we talked like men and brothers."

Later, Stalin made his own assessment of his fellow members of the Big Three in a conversation with Milovan Djilas, a ranking Yugoslav Communist. "Churchill is the kind who, if you don't watch him, will slip a kopek out of your pocket. . . . And Roosevelt! Roosevelt is not like that. He dips his hand only for bigger coins. . . ."

Military matters were quickly disposed of. Roosevelt and Churchill assured Stalin that the cross-Channel invasion would be launched about May 1, 1944, and they were told that a Soviet offensive would be coordinated with the assault. Stalin also reaffirmed the pledge to Hull of Russian participation in the war against Japan, when Hitler was beaten. Political considerations filled a good part of the talks, although decisions were left to a later date, so the President could truthfully say he had made no secret commitments at Teheran. Stalin expressed interest in Roosevelt's "four policemen" concept to monitor the peace after the President outlined in crude form the basic structure of what was to become the United Nations. Stalin also endorsed his proposal that the French be barred from returning to Indochina and other parts of their colonial empire, which would become United Nations trusteeships.* Plans for the dis-

* "Indo-China should not go back to France but . . . it should be administered by an international trusteeship," FDR told Hull in a memorandum dated Jan. 24, 1944. "France has had the country—thirty million inhabitants for nearly one hundred years, and the people are worse off than they were at the beginning. . . . The people of Indo-China are entitled to something better than that."

Nevertheless, there was no official statement of American policy, and the French

memberment of a defeated Germany were also taken up, and the Western leaders signaled their acquiescence to continued Russian occupation of the Baltic States, which had been seized in 1939.

Poland's postwar status proved more of a problem. Pointing out that Britain had gone to war in defense of an independent Poland, Churchill broached the subject of the nation's future political system and boundaries. Stalin effectively blocked discussion of Poland's future government by refusing to have anything to do with the Polish exile regime in London, which he unjustly accused of collaborating with the Nazis. On the territorial question, the Russians insisted on retaining the region overrun by the Red Army in 1939 and argued that the resulting boundary corresponded to the Curzon Line, a frontier proposed by the British after World War I. The London Poles, however, held out for restoration of the nation's pre-1939 boundaries. Stalin suggested that in exchange for accepting the Curzon Line, Poland be compensated for the lost territory with a slice of Germany that would move her western border to the Oder River. Churchill promised to press this solution upon the London Poles. Roosevelt did not take part in these discussions, yet, sympathetic to Soviet demands for security, he privately expressed support for the territorial transfer in a conversation with Stalin. But he emphasized that he could not publicly take part in such an arrangement because it would antagonize millions of Polish-American voters.

Teheran marked the peak of cooperation between the Soviet Union and the West—a cooperation gained by leaning over backward to accommodate Stalin and by postponing difficult decisions. Roosevelt returned to Washington in triumph, certain that the foundation had been laid for a lasting peace. "Britain, Russia, China and the United States and their allies represent more than three-quarters of the total population of the earth," he told the nation in a buoyant Fireside Chat. "As long as these four nations with great military power stick together in determination to keep the peace, there will be no possibility of an aggressor nation arising to start another world war. . . ."

Having set the United States on the path to global leadership at Casablanca and Teheran, Roosevelt revived the liberal agenda of the New Deal with a call for a new Economic Bill of Rights. "Unless there is security here at home there cannot be lasting peace in the world," the Presi-

---

were encouraged to return by some American military and diplomatic officials who saw nothing wrong in assisting the Free French in "liberating" Indochina from the Japanese. The Truman administration, requiring the support of France in Europe as a bulwark against Communism, dropped whatever resistance remained to the return of the French to Indochina. For a full discussion of the origins of the Vietnam imbroglio, see Archimedes L. A. Patti, *Why Viet Nam?* (Berkeley: University of California Press, 1980).

dent declared in his State of the Union address on January 11, 1944.
These rights were to apply to "all—regardless of station, race and creed"—
and they were sweeping:

> The right to a useful and remunerative job . . .
> The right to earn enough to provide adequate food and clothing and
> recreation;
> The right of every farmer to raise and sell his products at a return
> which will give him and his family a decent living;
> The right of every business man, large or small, to trade in the atmo-
> sphere of freedom from unfair competition and domination by monopo-
> lies at home or abroad;
> The right of every family to a decent home;
> The right to adequate medical care . . .
> The right to adequate protection from the economic fears of old age,
> sickness, accident and unemployment;
> The right to a good education;
> All these rights spell security. . . . After the war is won, we must be
> prepared to move forward, in the implementation of these rights, to new
> goals of human happiness and well being.

The Economic Bill of Rights was regarded as a curtain raiser for the
1944 presidential campaign. No one doubted that Roosevelt would be a
candidate for a fourth term except possibly the President himself. "I just
hate to run again for election," he told Admiral Leahy early that year.
The idea of retiring to Hyde Park to assume the role of elder statesman
had considerable appeal. By the time his current term ended, he would be
in the White House for a dozen years, and at the age of sixty-two, he was
showing signs of cumulative weariness. The dark circles never faded from
under his eyes; there was a more pronounced shake in his hand when he
lit a cigarette. Sometimes he would nod over his mail, Grace Tully noted,
and would grin in embarrassment as he caught himself. Always susceptible to respiratory ailments, Roosevelt caught flu at Teheran but failed to
bounce back with his usual resiliency. Wracked by a steady cough, looking gray, and complaining about being tired, he went to the Naval Hospital, at Bethesda, Maryland, for a checkup at the end of March 1944.

The examining doctors were shocked by what they found: high blood
pressure and progressive enlargement of the heart, as well as acute bron-
chitis. They prescribed rest, a reduced work load, less smoking, and a
weight-trimming diet. Lieutenant Commander Howard G. Bruenn, a
heart specialist, was detailed to the White House to maintain a close
watch on the President's health. Roosevelt went along without complaint,
Dr. Bruenn noted, but, strangely enough, he never asked for the results of
the examination or exhibited curiosity about his treatment. Obviously,
he did not want it to influence his decision on whether or not to seek
reelection.

Public obligation and personal vanity won out. The war was still not won—although the long-delayed cross-Channel invasion of Europe was successfully launched on June 6, 1944—and the role of Commander in Chief could not be easily transferred in mid-battle. It was unthinkable that he should not be present to make the peace for which he had so long fought. Nor was he certain that any other American could pick up the threads of the complex relationship with Stalin and Churchill. And so he sent word to Robert E. Hannegan, the new chairman of the Democratic National Committee, that he would run. "All that is within me cries to go back to my home on the Hudson River," he said, but if the people commanded, he would serve "like a good soldier."

The only question for the Democrats to resolve at their convention in Chicago was the identity of their vice-presidential candidate. Roosevelt again wanted Henry Wallace as his running mate, but he was anathema to the party bosses and southern conservatives. There was a crosscurrent of concern about Roosevelt's health, and it was unthinkable, at least as far as they were concerned, that someone as radical and erratic as Wallace should be placed in a position to fall heir to the presidency. Hannegan, who favored his fellow Missourian, Senator Harry Truman, for the nomination, warned the President that Wallace might jeopardize the chances of victory and it would require a major fight to nominate him. Roosevelt conceded. "I am just not going through a convention like 1940 again," he said. "It will split the party wide open and it is already split enough." Unwilling as always to be unpleasant face to face, he delegated to Sam Rosenman the task of breaking the bad news to Wallace.

The next item on the agenda was the choice of a replacement. Various possibilities were trotted out: "Assistant President" James Byrnes, Justice William O. Douglas, House Speaker Sam Rayburn, as well as Senator Truman. None of them aroused much excitement, but Truman seemed the most acceptable. Ever since his election to the Senate, in 1934, he had been an undeviating supporter of Roosevelt's domestic and foreign policies, he had achieved some renown as chairman of a congressional committee that was ferreting out corruption in the war effort, and he was not objectionable to either conservatives or liberals. "It's Truman," the President said with an air of finality. But the endorsement was not unqualified. A letter Roosevelt gave Hannegan to be used at the convention stated that he would be content to run with *either* Truman or Douglas. And to pacify Wallace, who had remained in the race, he sent another letter to Senator Samuel D. Jackson, the permanent chairman of the convention, saying that if he were a delegate he would vote for Wallace.

Wrapping himself in his familiar navy cape, Roosevelt campaigned for reelection as Commander in Chief. Assured of the nomination by all but acclamation, he left for a meeting with the Pacific Theater commanders at Pearl Harbor as the Democratic convention was being gaveled to order. When the presidential train stopped briefly in Chicago on Roosevelt's way to the West Coast, Hannegan came aboard to tell him that Truman refused to believe that he had the support of the President and had agreed to make the nominating speech for Byrnes. Roosevelt promised to deal with the problem. Upon arriving in San Diego, he telephoned Hannegan's suite in the Blackstone Hotel, where Truman was standing by.

"Bob, have you got that fellow lined up yet?" the President asked.

"No, Mr. President," replied the Democratic chairman, who held the phone so Truman could hear the conversation. "He's the contrariest Missouri mule I've ever dealt with."

"Well, you tell him for me that if he wants to break up the Democratic Party in the middle of a war, that's his responsibility."

Hannegan hung up and turned to Truman. "Now what do you say?"

"Oh, shit," said the dazed senator.

Wallace's partisans among liberals and the labor unions put up a fight, but Truman was nominated on the second ballot.

Roosevelt established the theme of the campaign in his acceptance speech, broadcast from a railroad car at the San Diego naval base. "What is the job before us in 1944?" he asked. "First, to win the war—to win the war fast, to win it overpoweringly. Second, to form worldwide international organizations. . . . And third, to build an economy for our returning veterans and for all Americans—which will provide employment and provide decent standards of living. The people of the United States will decide this fall whether they wish to turn over this 1944 job—this worldwide job—to inexperienced and immature hands . . . or whether they wish to leave it to those who saw the danger from abroad. . . ."

The "inexperienced and immature hands" referred to by Roosevelt were those of Governor Thomas E. Dewey of New York, the Republican presidential nominee, and his equally conservative running mate, Ohio's Governor John W. Bricker. Young and aggressive, Dewey hit hard at the "tired old men" of the New Deal. It was "time for a change"—time to end one-man government, time to turn over the business of the nation to more vigorous and more enthusiastic hands.†

Dewey's indictment was cleverly intended to focus attention on the hidden issue of the campaign: the state of Roosevelt's health. Rumors were circulating that the President had collapsed or suffered a heart at-

---

† Dewey learned that the United States had broken the Japanese codes and intended to use the information to prove that Roosevelt had prior knowledge of the Pearl Harbor attack. Acting without the President's knowledge, General Marshall sent emissaries to Dewey to persuade him against taking such action. Marshall revealed that the Japanese were still using the same codes—which was a factor in the American victories in the Coral Sea and at Midway. If Dewey went public, he warned, the Japanese would change the codes. Dewey never revealed the secret of the broken codes. Washington *Post*, Aug. 17, 1981.

tack, and the Republicans gleefully circulated a photograph snapped while he was delivering his acceptance speech that seemed to show a slack-jawed, haggard old man. Rosenman later claimed that it was taken from a bad angle while the President was enunciating a broad vowel and bore no resemblance to the President. Yet, friends who had not seen him for some time were shocked by his ravaged appearance. He seemed so shrunken that his clothes no longer fitted his once-robust torso. Dr. Bruenn states, however, that Roosevelt's gaunt look was not the result of failing health, as most people believed, but was due to the President's insistence on losing weight—over twenty pounds in a few months.

Nevertheless, there were signs of fragility. Jimmy Roosevelt was chatting with his father before a scheduled military review at Camp Pendleton, near San Diego, when the President's face suddenly went white with agony. "Jimmy, I don't know if I can make it—I have horrible pains!" he whispered. Frightened, the younger Roosevelt wanted to summon a doctor, but the President insisted that it was only a digestive problem. He stretched out on the floor of the Pullman car, his eyes closed and his body occasionally convulsed by waves of pain. Ten minutes passed before Roosevelt asked his son to help him up. He arrived at the review, not long afterward, flashing his usual buoyant smile. Upon his return from Pearl Harbor, a few weeks later, the President addressed a large crowd of Bremerton Naval Shipyard workers. Rosenman listened to Roosevelt's hesitating and faltering delivery with a sinking feeling. He feared that the President was finished as a campaigner. Roosevelt told Bruenn that he had suffered severe chest pains that radiated out to his shoulders during the first fifteen minutes of the speech, but an electrocardiogram taken immediately afterward showed no unusual abnormalities.

Following the Bremerton speech, the polls showed a sharp drop in Roosevelt's support and a corresponding upswing for Dewey. Prodded by the whispering campaign about his health, the reports of Republican gains, and his dislike of his self-righteous opponent—whom he privately derided as "that little man"—the President came out swinging. He reiterated the promise of the Economic Bill of Rights and pledged: "We are not going to turn back the clock! We are going forward!" He put to rest much of the concern about his health by touring every borough of New York City in an open car despite torrential rains. And he demolished Republican hopes with a masterful exhibition of campaign oratory. Mischievous twinkle in his eye, he noted that the opposition had spread stories he had left his "little dog Fala" behind on an Aleutian island and had sent a destroyer to retrieve him at an outrageous cost to the taxpayers. "I don't resent attacks, and my family doesn't resent attacks, but Fala *does* resent them," he declared in mock indignation. "You know Fala is Scotch, and

. . . his Scotch soul was furious. He has not been the same dog since. . . ."

Dewey responded with an attack on Roosevelt's claim to indispensability, the most effective speech of the campaign, but once again, the American people placed their confidence in Franklin Roosevelt. As usual, the Electoral College vote was one-sided, 432 votes to 99, but the popular vote was the closest of Roosevelt's presidential races. He received 25.6 million votes to 22 million for Dewey. Perhaps the most comforting thing about the election to the President was the overwhelming repudiation of isolationism. In all parts of the nation, the voters retired senators and congressmen of both parties with isolationist records, including Hamilton Fish, Roosevelt's old enemy from Dutchess County. Always a stickler for proper form, Roosevelt stayed up late to acknowledge Dewey's message of congratulations, but it never came. "I still think he is a son of a bitch," the President finally told an aide.

The inaugural ceremony, in the bitter cold of January 20, 1945—ten days before Roosevelt's sixty-third birthday—was one of the briefest and most somber in the nation's history. Perhaps with a premonition that he did not have much time left, he insisted that every one of the thirteen Roosevelt grandchildren come to Washington for the occasion. There were no parades or glittering balls, and the President took the oath of office on the south portico of the White House, rather than at the Capitol. Wearing neither hat nor overcoat, he spoke for less than five minutes. Looking forward to a forthcoming meeting with Stalin and Churchill, he evoked the principles that were to guide him. "We have learned that we cannot live alone at peace; that our own well-being is dependent on the well-being of other nations—far away. . . . We have learned the simple truth as Emerson said, that 'the only way to have a friend is to be one.'"

Two days later, he left for Yalta.

There were compelling reasons for a meeting of the Big Three early in 1945. Victory over Nazi Germany was at hand. The last desperate German offensive in the west had been beaten back the month before in the Battle of the Bulge. The Red Army had overrun Poland and Eastern Europe and was closing in on Germany from the east. American troops had just liberated Manila, and American bombers were battering Japan from the air. But military professionals believed that nothing short of an Allied invasion of the Japanese home islands—along with perhaps more than a million casualties—would end the war in the Pacific, for there were no assurances that the untested atomic bomb being developed by the supersecret Manhattan Project would work. A time for decision had come on all the problems left unresolved at Teheran: the future of a defeated

Germany, the troubling question of Poland, and the status of other Eastern European nations, the United Nations organization, and the Far East.

Yalta, a resort in the Crimea on the Black Sea beloved of the czars, was chosen for the site of the conference because, once again, Stalin would not leave the Soviet Union. For Roosevelt the trip was an ordeal, although he got a chance to relax on the voyage to Malta on the cruiser *Quincy*, where he transferred to his plane, the *Sacred Cow*, for the flight to the Crimea. "No more let us falter!" joked Churchill. "From Malta to Yalta! Let nobody alter." If the names of all the possible locations for a high-level international conference had been programmed into a computer that was ordered to select the worst, it would unhesitatingly have picked Yalta. The region about Yalta had been plundered by the retreating Germans, and its physical beauty masked primitive conditions. Churchill arrived with a goodly supply of whiskey to counter the typhus, lice, and bedbugs that abounded, a U. S. Navy decontamination team had to spray Roosevelt's quarters three times to make them habitable, and the fifty-room Livadia Palace, where the conference was held, had but a single bathroom.

Roosevelt's goal during the eight days at Yalta was to incorporate the Soviet Union into a world organization for preserving the peace and to obtain a commitment from the Soviets to enter the war then against Japan. For the Soviets, having twice been invaded by Germany in a generation, the overriding consideration was the establishment of a security zone in Eastern Europe. Both Roosevelt and Churchill accepted the legitimacy of Russian control of Eastern Europe. In fact, during a meeting in Moscow in October 1944, Churchill had written the mathematical guidelines for spheres of influence in the Balkans on a slip of paper and pushed it over to Stalin. He suggested that the Russians have 90 percent predominance in Romania, 75 percent in Bulgaria, an equal say with Britain in Hungary and Yugoslavia, and 10 percent in Greece. Stalin accepted on the spot, and Roosevelt later indicated his assent.

Poland, which was not on Churchill's list at Moscow, was the knottiest problem at Yalta and led to six days and nights of haggling among the Big Three. The Curzon Line was designated as the eastern boundary of Poland, ratifying the agreement made at Teheran, but the amount of German territory to be given in compensation was left to be decided after the war. The question of Poland's future government was even more troublesome. The Russians had established a puppet regime at Lublin, in occupied Poland, while Churchill, fearing Soviet domination of Eastern Europe more than Roosevelt, advanced the cause of the London Poles. Worried that the conference might break up over the issue and mindful of the Polish-American voters back home, the President came up with a face-saving formula. He proposed that a provisional government consisting of representatives of the Lublin Poles, democratic elements within the country, and major figures from the London government hold office until a permanent government could be chosen in free elections. Stalin agreed and said the elections could be held in a month.

"Mr. President," observed a worried Admiral Leahy, "this is so elastic that the Russians can stretch it all the way from Yalta to Washington without even technically breaking it."

"I know, Bill—I know it," Roosevelt replied. "But it's the best I can do for Poland at this time."

The Big Three were united in their determination to ensure that Germany would not rise again to plague Europe, although Roosevelt had already backed away from a plan advanced by Henry Morgenthau to turn Germany into an agricultural backwater. The exact boundaries of a defeated Germany were left to a future conference, but the country was to be divided up into four zones of occupation. Roosevelt's dislike of De Gaulle had not abated, but he went along with Churchill's proposal to give France an occupation zone. American public opinion would probably not permit the U. S. Army to remain very long in Europe after the war, the British reasoned, so they wanted a French presence in Germany to help counterbalance the Russians. Berlin was to be divided in the same manner as Germany, but there was little concern about the fact that the Western zones of the city, which itself was deep in the Soviet occupation zone, would be a hostage in the hands of the Soviets.

The basic structure of the United Nations had been laid at a meeting at Dumbarton Oaks, in Washington, during the previous autumn, but the question of how many votes the Soviet Union was to have in the General Assembly had been left to the Big Three. Pointing out that the United States would be able to influence the votes of the Latin Americans and that the British could count on the votes of the Commonwealth, Stalin insisted on votes for all sixteen of the Soviet "republics." Roosevelt countered by saying this would be tantamount to giving every one of the forty-eight American states a vote and persuaded Stalin to withdraw the demand in exchange for votes for the Ukrainian and Byelorussian republics. To protect his own political flanks, Roosevelt exacted the promise of two additional votes for the United States.

Stalin readily agreed to enter the war against Japan within two or three months of the defeat of Hitler. In exchange, the Soviets were granted sovereignty over the southern half of Sakhalin and the Kurile Islands, territory that had been lost forty years before in the Russo-Japanese War. Dairen, in Manchuria, would be internationalized, Port Arthur was to be placed under Soviet control, and the Russians were awarded special privileges in Manchuria. Most of these arrangements were at the expense of China, which was not represented at Yalta, but Roosevelt agreed to intercede with Chiang Kai-shek. The Generalissimo accepted the commitments and later signed a treaty of friendship with the Soviets, who promised not to aid the Chinese Communists.

Yalta was Roosevelt's show. He mediated, conciliated, compromised, jockeyed for position, jollied Churchill and Stalin, and cut corners to ensure the success of the conference. Sometimes, the round of meetings and dinners exhausted his slender reserves of energy and he appeared tired and ashen; at others he glowed with wit and humor. By watching Stalin closely, he discovered the secret of his astonishing capacity to down endless vodka toasts: The wily old Bolshevik surreptitiously watered his drinks during the confusion of standing and hand-clapping. And he enjoyed baiting Churchill about India and the dismantling of the British Empire.

Roosevelt left Yalta on February 11, 1945, in an optimistic mood about the continued unity of the Big Three. "We really believed in our hearts that this was the dawn of the new day we had all been praying for," said Harry Hopkins. "The Russians had proved that they could be reasonable and farseeing and there wasn't any doubt in the minds of the President or any of us that we could live with them peacefully."

Following a tour of the battlefield at Balaklava, where the Light Brigade had charged to glory nearly a century before, Roosevelt flew to Egypt, where he rejoined the *Quincy*. As the cruiser lay at anchor in the Great Bitter Lake, he met with three kings on successive days: Farouk of Egypt, Haile Selassie of Ethiopia, and Ibn Saud of Saudi Arabia. The President, a self-proclaimed Zionist, tried to persuade Ibn Saud to allow more Jewish survivors of Hitler's death camps to enter Palestine, but the grizzled old desert warrior said the Arabs would fight to the death to prevent it.

The euphoria that had followed Yalta faded as the *Quincy* headed through the Suez Canal and into the Mediterranean. Both Hopkins and "Pa" Watson became sick, and Hopkins, who did not relish a long sea voyage, decided to fly home from Algiers. When Hopkins said good-bye to Roosevelt before going ashore, it was the last time the two men ever saw each other. Two days later, Watson died from a cerebral hemorrhage. The President was deeply affected by the loss of another old friend. Louis Howe was gone . . . Marvin McIntyre was gone . . . Missy LeHand was gone . . . and now the always loyal "Pa." Perhaps Watson's death reminded him of his own weakening grip on life, for he slipped into a despondency that lasted for the rest of the voyage. Letting work on a report to Congress go, he read, smoked, and stared at the far horizon. The *Quincy* was not a happy ship as she steamed westward carrying a lonely President and the body of his friend.

"I come from the Crimean Conference with a firm belief that we have made a good start on the road to a world of peace," Roosevelt told a joint session of Congress on March 2, 1945. Instead of standing at the rostrum in his braces, he spoke sitting down at a table in the well of the House. It was a tacit admission of his weariness, a fact confirmed by his lined face and halting, uncertain delivery. For nearly an hour, he ranged over the accomplishments of Yalta and noted that a meeting had been set for April 25 in San Francisco at which a Charter for the United Nations organization would be drafted. Conscious of the parallels with Woodrow Wilson's return from Paris in 1919 with his doomed proposal for a League of Nations, he appealed to Congress for bipartisanship in dealing with the hard tasks ahead. "Twenty-five years ago, American fighting men looked to the statesmen of the world to finish the work of peace for which they fought and suffered," he declared. "We failed—we failed them then. We cannot fail them again, and expect the world to survive. . . . I am confident that the Congress and the American people will accept the results of this Conference as the beginnings of a permanent structure of peace."

Yalta has aroused more controversy than any other aspect of Franklin Roosevelt's foreign policy. He was accused of "selling out" Poland and Eastern Europe to the Russians and betraying China to the Communists. Although these charges reached their pinnacle in the 1950s, they echo down to the present. The common characteristic shared by critics of Yalta is a superior sense of hindsight. They look back upon the settlement in the light of the predatory advance of Soviet power and the Cold War, the expulsion of Chiang Kai-shek from the Chinese mainland, and the altered conditions that vastly reduced the impact of the entry of the Soviet Union into the war against Japan. But the President made the best deal possible under the conditions in which he operated.

As much as Roosevelt and Churchill may have wished for a free and independent Poland, the cardinal fact remains that the Red Army was in complete control of Eastern Europe. The only alternative for the United States and Britain was the use of military force to install a government more to their liking—an unlikely option in the climate of 1945. The most vituperative attacks on the Yalta agreement were leveled at the concessions given the Soviets to get them to declare war on Japan. These concessions are credited with paving the way for an eventual Communist takeover of China, northern Korea, and Indochina. In their eagerness to convict Roosevelt of the ultimate responsibility for having "lost" China, his critics conveniently gloss over the fact that American military leaders, concerned about the casualties to be incurred in an invasion of the Japanese home islands, insisted upon bringing the Soviet Union into the Pacific War. Under these circumstances, Stalin was playing a strong hand

and Roosevelt merely paid the price that he demanded. Even if the President had refused, it is difficult to believe that Stalin would have restrained himself from taking whatever he wanted.

Nothing if not a realist, Roosevelt understood that the political and military events of the years preceding Yalta had already gone a long way toward settling the shape of the postwar world. The Soviet Union and the United States would dominate the globe for the foreseeable future, and he devoutly wished to guarantee that the alliance forged in the fires of war would withstand the strains of peace. To ensnare Stalin in a web of obligations and mutual trust, he compromised, made concessions, and settled for an imprecise and fuzzy consensus—as in the case of the Polish elections—which encouraged the Russians to believe that the Anglo-American representatives were merely seeking a face-saving arrangement. Yet the failure of Roosevelt's policy in Eastern Europe was not the result of naïve optimism or illusions about the nature of the Soviet state. Rather, the President regarded his policy as the height of pragmatism, because it bought time for creation of the long-sought world government.

EPILOGUE

THE GEORGIA COUNTRYSIDE was alive with spring. White, pink, and yellow azaleas clustered near the Little White House, and the peach trees under Pine Mountain were already heavy with budding fruit. Franklin Roosevelt had come down to Warm Springs on Good Friday, March 30, 1945, an exhausted and shrunken figure too tired to even acknowledge the greetings of old friends. During Easter Sunday services, he dropped his glasses and then his prayer book. Not once did he smile. But his spirits were revived by the unfailing magic of his second home. "Within a week there was a decided and obvious improvement in his appearance and sense of well-being," said Dr. Bruenn. The President's appetite was good, he was rested, and he had begun to do a little work—catching up on his correspondence, working over papers, and dictating a Jefferson Day speech.

The news from the fighting fronts was good. The Anglo-American armies had crossed the Rhine and were slashing into Germany as fast as their tanks would go. The Russians were battling in the ruins of Berlin. In the Pacific, American forces had landed on Okinawa, an island of the Ryukyu chain only three hundred fifty miles from Japan. Roosevelt had ceased to think much about the war, however. Most of his thoughts were concentrated on the United Nations Conference, scheduled to open in San Francisco later in the month, which he intended to attend, and upon a state visit to England that he and Eleanor were planning for May. Frances Perkins protested that it would be dangerous to cross the Atlantic while the war was on, but he put his hand to the side of his mouth and whispered: "The war in Europe will be over by the end of May."

Yet all was not well among the Allies. Less than two months after

Yalta, it was obvious that the Russians had no intention of carrying out the promise of free elections in Poland. On April 1, Roosevelt sent a message to Stalin protesting the "lack of progress . . . relating to the Polish question." And he was angered by Soviet charges that the United States and Britain were secretly contriving to arrange the surrender of the German Army in Italy behind their backs. There are indications that Roosevelt was moving in the direction of a tougher policy toward the Soviet Union at the time of his death, although he was still seeking an accommodation. "We must not permit anybody to entertain a false impression that we are afraid," he cabled Churchill on April 6. "Our armies will in a very few days be in a position that will permit us to become 'tougher' than has heretofore appeared advantageous to the war effort." Five days later, in the last message to pass between them, he cautioned Churchill against overreaction to difficulties with the Soviets, but added: "We must be firm . . . and our course thus far is correct."

The President complained to Dr. Bruenn of a slight headache and a stiff neck upon awakening on April 12, but the physician and Roosevelt's cousins Daisy Suckley and Laura Delano thought he looked surprisingly well. He had planned a busy day. Late in the afternoon, he was to be guest of honor at a barbecue and had promised to drop by a dress rehearsal of a minstrel show being put on by some of the younger patients at Warm Springs. Mrs. Rutherfurd had come over from her home in Aiken, South Carolina, a few days before, along with an artist, Madame Elizabeth Shoumatoff, whom she had commissioned to paint a watercolor portrait of the President.

Wearing his navy cape at the artist's request, and sitting at a card table in the simple, pine-paneled living room, Roosevelt dealt with a pouch of official documents from Washington that had been brought by William D. Hassett, "Pa" Watson's successor as appointments secretary. With a flourish, he signed a bill extending the life of the Commodity Credit Corporation and called out to Laura Delano: "Here's where I make a law!" After Hassett left, he worked over papers including the speech he had prepared for broadcast the following evening to mark Jefferson Day. At the end, he wrote out in a shaking hand a summing-up statement: "The only limit to our realization of tomorrow will be our doubts of today. Let us move forward with strong and active faith."

At 12:45, he noted that it was nearly time for lunch and announced, "We have fifteen more minutes to work."

Madame Shoumatoff sketched; Mrs. Rutherfurd sat quietly near one of the windows in full view of the President with a soft smile on her face. Laura Delano bustled about, and Miss Suckley sat on a sofa, crocheting. Along toward one o'clock, she glanced up from her work and saw the President apparently looking for something. His head was forward, his hands fumbling in his lap. She went up to him and, kneeling down, looked up into his face and asked, "Have you dropped your cigarette?"

"He looked at me, his forehead furrowed with pain, and tried to smile," Miss Suckley later recalled. "He put his left hand up to the back of his head and said, 'I have a terrific pain in the back of my head.' He said it distinctly but so low that I don't think anyone else could hear it. I told him to put his head back on his chair, but he could not raise it himself. Laura Delano came back from her room at that moment, and we tilted his chair back, as he was slumping forward. With Mrs. Rutherfurd and Laura holding the chair, I reached for the telephone and asked the operator to get Dr. Bruenn to come to the President's cottage."

Madame Shoumatoff screamed and rushed out of the room for help. Arthur Prettyman, the President's valet, and Joe Espencilla, a Filipino messboy, hurried into the living room. They took the unconscious man up from his chair, and with the cape flowing out behind him on the polished floor, carried him past the frightened women to an adjoining bedroom. He was cold but sweating profusely. Dr. Bruenn arrived about fifteen minutes later. He immediately diagnosed a massive cerebral hemorrhage and administered emergency measures. Roosevelt never regained consciousness, but his strained breathing could be heard throughout the cottage. Madame Shoumatoff and Mrs. Rutherfurd had already left, and a little band of staff members and friends kept an anxious vigil in the living room. No one spoke, but Grace Tully's lips moved in silent prayer. Finally, at 3:35 P.M., the tortured breathing stopped.

Franklin Delano Roosevelt was at peace.

NOTES

PROLOGUE

The New York *Times*, Baltimore *Sun*, and Washington *Evening Star* of Mar. 5, 1933, are the basic sources for this section. Reagan's comment is in *Time*, Jan. 5, 1981. Frances Perkins' comments are in *The Roosevelt I Knew*, pp. 139–40. The Hoover quote is from Smith, *The Shattered Dream*, p. 228. FDR's attempt to make conversation with his predecessor is related in James Roosevelt's *Affectionately, F.D.R.*, p. 206. The comment to Grace Tully is in Tully, *F.D.R., My Boss*, p. 68. The machine-gun quote is from Wilson, *The American Earthquake*, p. 478. The widow taking off her glasses is in ibid., p. 463. I have also viewed the newsreels of the inauguration at the FDR Library.

CHAPTER I

FDR's recollection of his first torchlight parade is in *The Public Papers and Addresses of Franklin D. Roosevelt* (PPA), Vol. XIII, pp. 413–14; SDR's comments on FDR's future are in *My Boy Franklin*, p. 4; for FDR's birth, see ibid., p. 12, and Marx, *Health of the Presidents*, p. 353; for infant care, see SDR, op. cit., pp. 12–13; SDR "detests" the name Isaac, in James Roosevelt, *Affectionately, F.D.R.*, pp. 35–36; christening of FDR is in Kleeman, *Gracious Lady*, pp. 126–27; quotations from SDR's diary, ibid., p. 137; for Roosevelt family history, see Miller, *The Roosevelt Chronicles*; for FDR's views on the family's background, see his sophomore thesis at Harvard, "The Roosevelt Family in New Amsterdam Before the Revolution," in the Franklin D. Roosevelt Library (FDRL) and PPA, Vol. IV, p. 96, also Gerald W. Johnson, *Roosevelt: Dictator or Democrat?* pp. 42–43; for JR and Garibaldi, see *F.D.R. His Personal Letters* (PL), Vol. IV, p. 1224; Lansdowne quote is in Gunther, *Roosevelt in Retrospect*, p. 172; 'Old Miss Delano' is in a letter from SDR to FDR, May 8, 1932; Mrs. TR on JR is in Kleeman, op. cit., p. 101; "avalanche of young men," ibid., p. 82; "beautiful frame," ibid., p. 170; SDR, op. cit., p. 9, for "mind on nice things"; ibid., p. 33, for "we never subjected"; for *Germanic* incident, see Lindley, *Franklin D. Roosevelt*, pp. 47–48, and Kleeman, op. cit., pp. 152–53; first sign of rebellion, SDR, op. cit., pp. 4–6; "laughed with him," ibid., p. 21; "chuck full of tacks," ibid., p. 29; "Steeplechase" game, ibid., p. 19; "all traces of sadness," ibid., p. 9; for Van-

derbilt story, see Hassett, *Off the Record with F.D.R.*, p. 123; for FDR's recollection of his childhood, see PPA, Vol. VIII, p. 580; for Halsey's comments,
see Halsey and Bryan, *Admiral Halsey's Story*, p. 18; South Kensington Mu-
seum story is in SDR, op. cit., pp. 27–28; carrying ER on his back, in Eleanor
Roosevelt, *This Is My Story*, p. 104, and SDR, op. cit., p. 62; "object of sym-
pathy," in McCracken, *Blithe Dutchess*, p. 50; "If I didn't give orders" is in
SDR, op. cit., p. 26; FDR's first letter to his mother is in PL, Vol. I, p. 6;
German letter is in ibid., p. 13; "More than anyone else" is in letter to Mlle.
Sandoz, Mar. 31, 1933; see also Drexel, "Unpublished Letters of F.D.R. to
His French Governess"; "The working people" paper is quoted in full in
Kleeman, op. cit., pp. 183–85; doing "two things at once" is in SDR, op. cit.,
p. 34; FDR's reading is in Kleeman, op. cit., p. 190; "jackdaw" quote is in
Hatch, *Franklin D. Roosevelt*, p. 18; "I go to public school" is in PL, Vol. I,
pp. 19–20; "unusually bright young fellow" is quoted in Freidel, *The Appren-
ticeship*, p. 33; Clinton Roosevelt incident is in Hassett, op. cit., p. 47; visit to
White House is in Kleeman, op. cit., p. 146; background on FDR's entry into
Groton is in ibid., p. 193; for the cycling trip, see ibid., p. 165, and Lindley,
op. cit., pp. 50–51; "It is very hard" is in Kleeman, op. cit., p. 193.

CHAPTER II

FDR's first letter from Groton is in PL, Vol. I, p. 35; others in similar vein
are in ibid., pp. 37, 38, and 42; FDR's description of Groton is in ibid., p. 38;
see also Ashburn, *Peabody of Groton*, p. 77; for description of living conditions and school schedule, see ibid., pp. 92–96; FDR's comments on food at
Groton are in PL, op. cit., p. 45; Harriman is quoted in Freidel, *The Apprenticeship*, p. 39; "If some Groton boys" is in Ashburn, op. cit., pp. 112–13;
Peabody's religious views are discussed in ibid., pp. 177–78; for a discussion of
FDR's religious views, see Tugwell, *The Democratic Roosevelt*, pp. 30–31; "I
count it" letter is in Ashburn, op. cit., p. 349; there is a photograph of FDR's
first report card in PL, op. cit.; "When Father went to Groton" is in Boettiger, *A Love in Shadow*, p. 32; Peabody and football players is from Ashburn,
op. cit., p. 100; "ready to stand on my coconut," PL, op. cit., p. 51; high kick
is discussed in ibid., p. 78; "Uncle Frank" is in ibid., p. 39; for first black
mark, see ibid., p. 97; black attorney's visit is in PL, op. cit., pp. 97–98; TR's
visit is described in ibid., p. 110; for life at Oyster Bay, see Hagedorn, *The
Roosevelt Family of Sagamore Hill*; ER's account of her childhood meeting
with FDR is in Roosevelt, *This Is My Story*, pp. 51–52; "They would go
well" is in PL, op. cit., p. 244; "very good mind" is in Lash, *Eleanor and
Franklin*, p. 100; boxing lessons is in PL, op. cit., pp. 155, 184; for attempt to
enlist in the Navy, see Kleeman, op. cit., pp. 196–97, and PL, op. cit., p. 205;
"wild with delight," ibid., p. 230, and Kleeman, op. cit., p. 203; TR at Groton,
ibid.; "All is confusing," PL, op. cit., p. 332; "gray-eyed, cool," Freidel,
op. cit., p. 50, and PL, op. cit., p. 34; reference to Mrs. Freeman is in ibid.,
pp. 253–55; for FDR's final comments on Groton and Peabody's report, see
ibid., pp. 412–13; for Peabody's exchange with the Old Grotonian, Ashburn,
op. cit., pp. 344–46; Harvard in 1900 is described in Brown, *Harvard Yard in
the Golden Age*, Ch. I; "great fun," PL, op. cit., p. 423; FDR's courses are
listed in ibid., pp. 424–25, also *Harvard Alumni Bulletin*, Apr. 28, 1945, p.
443; "I took economics" is in PPA, Vol. X, p. 460; slipping out of class, in

Freidel, op. cit., p. 54; for FDR's views of a Harvard education, see Looker, *This Man Roosevelt*, p. 32; "I have been in the library" is in PL, op. cit., pp. 464–65; the thesis is on file in the Roosevelt Library; for FDR's relations with Copeland, see Cowperthwaite, "Franklin D. Roosevelt at Harvard," and Brown, op. cit., pp. 132–34; FDR's comments on TR scoop are in PL, op. cit., pp. 456–57; torchlight parade is in ibid., pp. 430–31; Harvard club system is discussed in Davis, *FDR*, pp. 135–36; FDR's comments are in PL, op. cit., p. 469; FDR's disappointment in not making Porcellian was related to author by W. Sheffield Cowles, Jr., in a letter dated Mar. 18, 1980; ER's comments are in Freidel, op. cit., p. 57; "It would be well" is in PL, op. cit., p. 430; Reilly statement is in *Reilly of the White House*, p. 57; LeHand quote is from Boettiger, op. cit., p. 32; "charm and ease" is in PL, op. cit., p. 531; "frictionless command" is in *Harvard Alumni Bulletin*, op. cit., p. 444; SDR diary entries are in Kleeman, op. cit., pp. 209, 213; the Kaiser's pencil story is in Freidel, op. cit., p. 58; "I try to keep busy" is in Kleeman, op. cit., p. 213; "near enough" is in SDR, *My Boy Franklin*, pp. 55–56; Boer refugee clipping is in Kleeman, op. cit., pp. 226–27; FDR's reaction is in PL, op. cit., p. 47; for Princess Alice, see Miller, *The Roosevelt Chronicles*, pp. 259–61; "Great fun" is in FDR diary, Jan. 3, 1902; "I think the President" is in PL, op. cit., p. 481; "Every spare moment" is in PL, op. cit., p. 504; "responsibility to the University," Harvard *Crimson*, Sept. 30, 1903; editorial on political club, ibid., Oct. 8, 1903; men of sufficient brawn, ibid., Oct. 6, 1903; cheering, ibid., Oct. 10, 1903; "felt like a D . . . F . . ." is in PL, op. cit., p. 510; FDR's answer to the anonymous letter is in ibid., Jan. 30, 1904; for TR's speech, see Ashburn, op. cit., pp. 176–77.

CHAPTER III

For the encounter between FDR and ER on the train, see ER, *This Is My Story*, p. 104, and Kleeman, *Gracious Lady*, pp. 233–34; "tea" is in FDR diary, Dec. 23, 1902; "interesting day" is in ibid., Jan. 1, 1903; Kuhn quote is in Lash, *Eleanor and Franklin*, p. 103; "uncivilized English custom" is in PL, Vol. I, pp. 499–500; for ER's account of her childhood, see ER, op. cit., pp. 1–52; for background on Elliott Roosevelt, see Miller, *The Roosevelt Chronicles*; Corinne Robinson is quoted in Lash, op. cit., p. 61; for ER at Sagamore, see ER, op. cit., pp. 49–50; "she was full of duty" is in Lash, op. cit., p. 72; "poor little soul" is quoted in Rixey, *Bamie*, p. 228; for ER at Allenswood, see ER, op. cit., pp. 53–88; "by no stretch" is in ER, op. cit., p. 100; "she was too tall" is in Lash, op. cit., p. 94; for ER and settlement work, see ER, op. cit., pp. 107–9; "You knew a man" is in ibid., p. 110; for FDR's proposal, see ibid., p. 111, and Lash, op. cit., pp. 106–8; ER's acceptance is dated Nov. 25, 1903; "Franklin gave me" is in Kleeman, op. cit., p. 235; "I know what pain" is in PL, op. cit., p. 518; "I know just how" is in ibid., p. 517; for "a man who had made a name," see Kleeman, op. cit., p. 235; "It is dreadfully hard" is in PL, op. cit., p. 523; "F is tired" is in Kleeman, op. cit., p. 235; ER's attitude toward the cruise is in ER, op. cit., p. 112; "I wonder if you know" is in Lash, op. cit., pp. 125–26; cruise activities are in Kleeman, op. cit., pp. 235–38; for the "French lady" episode, see James Roosevelt, *Affectionately, F.D.R.*, p. 33; Choate incident is in Kleeman, op. cit., p. 240; "I am feeling pretty blue" is in Lash, op. cit., p. 128; "I knew your mother" is in ibid., p. 130; TR's letter, dated Nov. 29, 1904, is in FDRL; Alice's comment is in

Teague, *Mrs. L.*, p. 152; "Vallie has been" is in PL, op. cit., p. 531; "I thought he was a better Democrat" is in PPA, Vol. VII, p. 38; TR's inaugural speech is in *Messages and Papers of the Presidents*, Vol. XIV, pp. 6930–32; "I never expected" is in ER, op. cit., p. 123; letter to Peabody is in PL, op. cit., pp. 532–33; "You don't learn much law" is from *The American Boy*, June 1927; "will not find himself" is in Looker, *This Man Roosevelt*, p. 48; wedding ceremony is described in ER, op. cit., pp. 124–26, New York *Herald*, Mar. 18, 1905, and New York *World*, Mar. 18, 1905; "I did not have to display" is in ER, op. cit., p. 127; details of the honeymoon are in ibid., pp. 127–38; the meeting with the Japanese is in PL, Vol. II, p. 7; "We were ushered" is in ibid., p. 10; clairvoyant's prediction is in ibid., p. 66; "You are always" is in ibid., p. 4; and "Goodbye dearest" is in ibid., p. 55; "It certainly shows" is in ibid., p. 73; ER's reaction to FDR's failure is in ibid., p. 64; "It was quite a relief" is in ER, op. cit., p. 139; "sex . . . an ordeal" is in Boettiger, *A Love in Shadow*, p. 53.

CHAPTER IV

"Completely taken care of" is in ER, *This Is My Story*, p. 140; FDR's second-year grades are in Freidel, *The Apprenticeship*, p. 76; exchange with Butler is quoted in ibid., p. 77; family finances are discussed in "Franklin and Eleanor Roosevelt's Fortune," *Fortune*, Oct. 1932; "full-fledged office boy" is in PL, Vol. II, p. 136; mock ad is pictured in Harrity and Martin, *The Human Side of F.D.R.*, unnumbered page; "I went to a big law office" is in PPA, 1941 Vol., pp. 457–58; law-school classmate story is in Looker, *This Man Roosevelt*, pp. 49–52; "you're drunk" is in Busch, *What Manner of Man?* pp. 74–75; "Everybody called him Franklin" is in Harrity and Martin, op. cit.; "always getting over a baby" is in ER, op. cit., p. 163; "I had never had any interest" is in ibid., p. 142; "Father's attitude" is in James Roosevelt, *Affectionately, F.D.R.*, p. 40; cage story is in ER, op. cit., p. 151; wire guards and Anna's tied hands are in Boettiger, *A Love in Shadow*, p. 53; "One of the hazards" is in James Roosevelt, op. cit., p. 40; "Old Battleaxe" is discussed in ibid., pp. 40–41; "If I had it to do over" is in ER, op. cit., pp. 145–46; "Father was fun" is from Boettiger, op. cit., p. 62; Sex education is in James Roosevelt, op. cit., pp. 81–82; death of Franklin, Jr., is in ibid., pp. 164–65; "It's hard nowadays" is in Harrity and Martin, op. cit.; "She thought she was" is in James Roosevelt, *My Parents*, p. 29; "Your mother only" is in ibid., p. 25; "lack of desire" is in Boettiger, op. cit., p. 60; "No one could tell" is in Tugwell, *The Democratic Roosevelt*, p. 66; religious discussion is in ER, op. cit., pp. 149–50; sketch of the new house is in Lash, *Eleanor and Franklin*, p. 161; "What on earth" is from ER, op. cit., p. 162; "kidnapped" is in PPA, 1933 Vol., p. 339; Clark's reminiscences are in *Harvard Alumni Bulletin*, Apr. 28, 1945; Gramercy Park incident is in Perkins, *The Roosevelt I Knew*, p. 9; "Oh, if I could" is quoted in Freidel, op. cit., p. 86, and also see PPA, 1938 Vol., p. 367; "not as a strait-jacket" is quoted in Davis, *FDR: The Beckoning of Destiny*, p. 215; Mack's account of FDR's entry into politics is in interview with George Palmer in FDRL; "On that joyous occasion" is in PPA, 1933 Vol., p. 339; "messy business of politics" is in Kleeman, *Gracious Lady*, p. 252; "I listened" is in ER, op. cit., p. 166; "Franklin ought to go" is in Theodore Roosevelt, *Letters to Anna Roosevelt Cowles*, p. 280; "You'll have to" is in

Lindley, *Franklin D. Roosevelt*, pp. 71–72; acceptance-speech excerpts are in ibid., p. 72; newspaper excerpts are in ibid., pp. 72–73; Mack quotation is in Harrity and Martin, op. cit.; campaign incidents are from Rollins, *Roosevelt and Howe*, pp. 16–22, and Freidel, op. cit., pp. 90–96; "high strung" is from ER, op. cit., p. 167; "Humboldt" is from PL, op. cit., p. 157; "I am not Teddy" is in Freidel, op. cit., p. 93; for background on Lou Payn, see Moscow, *Politics in the Empire State*, pp. 81–82; "You have known what" is from text of speech, Nov. 5, 1910, in FDRL.

CHAPTER V

Howe's remarks are in Louis M. Howe, "The Winner," *The Saturday Evening Post*, Feb. 25, 1933; Warn's dispatch is in the New York *Times*, Jan. 22, 1911; Sullivan is quoted in Lindley, *Franklin D. Roosevelt*, p. 78; "besides the nurses" is in ER, *This Is My Story*, p. 170; "You must be" is in ibid., p. 171; FDR's "horror" is in FDR diary, Jan. 2, 1911; "decision to throw over . . . Grady" is in ibid., Jan. 3, 1911; comments on Wagner are in ibid.; "at least a half a dozen" is quoted in Lindley, op. cit., p. 80; "Shepard is without question" is in FDR diary, Jan. 1, 1911; "Boys, I want" is in FDR, *The Happy Warrior*, p. 4; "Not now" is quoted in Lindley, op. cit., p. 82; "For ten long minutes" is in Edward R. Terry, "The Insurgents at Albany," *The Independent*, Sept. 7, 1911; for the manifesto and Roosevelt's remarks, see New York *Times*, Jan. 17, 1911; "There is nothing" is in New York *Times*, Jan. 22, 1911; Grosvenor letter is quoted in Freidel, *The Apprenticeship*, p. 103; TR letter is dated Jan. 29, 1911, and in FDRL; "roll of honor" is in New York *Times*, Jan. 19, 1911; Cleveland *Plain Dealer* editorial is dated Jan. 23, 1911; New York *Sun* comment appeared Jan. 20, 1911; "There is very little" is in New York *Times*, Jan. 22, 1911; Howe's comments are in Stiles, *The Man Behind Roosevelt*, pp. 25–27; ER's comments are in ER, op. cit., pp. 173–75; Anna Roosevelt's comments are in Boettiger, *A Love in Shadow*, p. 59; "a fizzle" is quoted in Freidel, op. cit., p. 108; "They say that the road" is from Terry, op. cit.; Murphy and nonsinging is in Werner, *Tammany Hall*, p. 564; for accounts of the caucus and legislative session of March 31, see New York *Times* and New York *Herald*, Apr. 1, 1911; Roosevelt's remarks are quoted in Freidel, op. cit., pp. 114–15; "The minority never assumed" is quoted in Lindley, op. cit., p. 97; lampoon of FDR is in Rollins, *Roosevelt and Howe*, p. 31.

CHAPTER VI

Wilson's conversation with Guffey is in Gunther, *Roosevelt in Retrospect*, p. 222; description of Wilson is in Link, *Wilson: The Road to the White House*, p. 93; FDR's reasons for supporting Wilson are in letter to Thomas P. Gore, Oct. 15, 1912; "arrive at convictions" is in Perkins, *The Roosevelt I Knew*, p. 16; "a question of honesty" is quoted in the New York *Times*, Apr. 2, 1911; "pleased with a smaller rattle" is in the New York *Tribune*, Apr. 22, 1911; "I was called some choice names" is in PL, Vol. II, p. 169; comments on the State Highway Commission bill are in Freidel, *The Apprenticeship*, p.

123; "This is the last straw" is in Rollins, *Roosevelt and Howe*, p. 33; comments on the Wappinger's Creek vote are in Lindley, *Franklin D. Roosevelt*, pp. 99–100; Eleanor's comments on votes for women are in ER, *This Is My Story*, p. 180–81; "Awfully arrogant fellow" is in Perkins, op. cit., p. 11; Jimmy Walker: comment is in Fowler, *Beau James*, p. 262; McCabe's remarks are in the New York *Times*, Dec. 25, 1911; pointing finger at Frawley, and Wagner's remarks, are from Freidel, op. cit., p. 119; "I have a vivid picture" is in Perkins, op. cit., p. 11; "You know, I was" is in ibid., p. 12; "Me father and me mother" is in ibid., p. 14; for background on the Triangle fire, see Leon Stein, *The Triangle Fire*; "I took it hard" is in Perkins, op. cit., p. 14; Howe's story of FDR's filibuster is in "The Winner," *The Saturday Evening Post*, Feb. 25, 1933; "Tim Sullivan used to say" is in Perkins, op. cit., p. 13; the Troy speech is on file at the FDRL, the first three pages in longhand; "We like to have" is in PL, op. cit., p. 187; "We may do some good" is quoted in Freidel, op. cit., p. 140; "As masterpieces" is in a letter from Howe to FDR, June 5, 1912; for a full account of TR's campaign, see Mowry, *Theodore Roosevelt and the Progressive Movement*, Chs. 7–10; "Unless the Democrats" is quoted from a broadside issued by the New York State Wilson Conference, June 25, 1912, in the FDRL; the account of the 1912 convention is based on Link, op. cit., Ch. XIII, and the Baltimore *Sun*, June 24 to July 4, 1912; Eleanor's remarks are in ER, op. cit., pp. 188–89; Daniels' remarks are in Daniels, *The Wilson Era*, Vol. I, pp. 124–25; FDR leading the charge is in Lindley, op. cit., pp. 103–4; FDR telegram to ER is in PL, op. cit., p. 192; photograph of "Beloved and Revered Future President" letter is in Stiles, *The Man Behind Roosevelt*; "henchmen" letter is in PL, op. cit., p. 193; Poughkeepsie *Eagle* is quoted in ibid., pp. 194–95; "looking like Robert Louis Stevenson" is in ER, op. cit., p. 191; Howe's comments to James Roosevelt are in James Roosevelt, *My Parents*, p. 85; sources for the profile of Howe are Rollins, op. cit., and Stiles, op. cit.; ER's comments on Howe are in ER, op. cit., pp. 192–93; "more fun than a goat" is in letter from Howe to FDR, Oct. 1912; for account of attempted assassination of TR, see New York *Times*, Oct. 15, 1912; for Daniels' account of the meeting with FDR, see Daniels, op. cit., pp. 124, 126; Root's comment is in ibid., p. 127.

CHAPTER VII

"I am baptized" is in PL, Vol. II, p. 199; Saunders letter is dated Mar. 14, 1913; TR letter is printed in Harrity and Martin, *The Human Side of F.D.R.*; "I get my fingers" is in Daniels, *The Wilson Era*, Vol. II, p. 253; "I now find my vocation" is in a letter to Charles A. Munn, Mar. 26, 1913; incident with navy wife is in Freidel, *The Apprenticeship*, p. 157; "friendly as an airedale" is in *The Independent*, July 17, 1920; quote from Albion is in *Makers of Naval Policy*, p. 385; "Dear Ludwig" letter is dated Mar. 19, 1913; Howe's reply is dated four days later; "The Navy!" is in Stiles, *The Man Behind Roosevelt*, p. 41; O'Brien memo is dated July 14, 1913; for Marvin's remarks, see "Notes on Franklin D. Roosevelt as Assistant Secretary of the Navy 1913–1920," in FDRL; Daniels' comments on Howe are in transcript of an interview with Freidel in the FDRL, and in Daniels, Vol. I, p. 128; data on the size of the U. S. Navy in 1913 are in the *Annual Report of the Secretary of the Navy* for that year; FDR tack memo is in Harrity and Martin, op. cit.; Meyer's advice to Daniels is in Daniels, op. cit., Vol. I, p. 119; Lindley's report is in Lindley, *Franklin D. Roosevelt*, p. 117; Navy League speech is in ibid., p. 119; "The big gray fellows" is in PL, op. cit., p. 221; Daniels on the photograph with FDR is in Daniels, op. cit., Vol. I, p. 129; Jonathan Daniels paints a picture of Washington during the Wilson years in *Washington Quadrille*; FDR's remarks on Wilson are in Perkins, *The Roosevelt I Knew*, pp. 15–16; "the saloon, the salon and the Salome" remark is quoted in Elliott Roosevelt, *An Untold Story*, p. 23; Bryan and the battleship story is in Lindley, op. cit., pp. 115–16; battleship-to-Eastport story is in transcript of an interview with Mahlon S. Tisdale in FDRL; description of the N Street house is from a letter to the author from W. Sheffield Cowles, Jr., Mar. 18, 1980; Henry Adams story is in ER, *This Is My Story*, p. 237; Baker's comments are in Perkins, op. cit., p. 21; Phillips' remarks are in transcript of his memoirs in FDRL; "the handsomest, the strongest" is in James Roosevelt, *Affectionately, F.D.R.*, p. 11; "the punishment simply" is in ibid., p. 74; "There is only" is in ibid., p. 66; "I was really well schooled" is in ER, op. cit., p. 195; exchange between ER and FDR in San Francisco is in Phillips' memoirs, op. cit.; Mrs. Cowles is quoted in ER, op. cit., p. 196; ER's comments on Alice Longworth are in ibid., p. 206; background on Lucy Mercer is in Daniels, *Quadrille*; Anna Roosevelt's unpublished article is in Anna Roosevelt Halsted Papers, FDRL; SDR to ER on Lucy is dated Mar. 24, 1915; greeting the "lovely Lucy" is in Elliott Roosevelt, op. cit., p. 21; speech at the Washington Navy Yard is in Washington *Herald*, June 18, 1913; for the armor-plate controversy, see Melvin L. Urofsky, "Josephus Daniels and the Armor Trust," *North Carolina Historical Review* (Summer 1968); "The passage of a camel" is in Freidel, op. cit., p. 211; FDR to Mahan is dated June 16, 1914; FDR's newspaper comments on the Mexican crisis are quoted in Freidel, op. cit., pp. 231–32; "He was young" is in Daniels, op. cit., Vol. I, p. 129.

CHAPTER VIII

"These are history-making" is in PL, Vol. II, p. 233; "Everyone was asleep" is in ibid., p. 237; "very sad that his faith" is in ibid., p. 238; "Alive and very well" is in ibid., p. 243; "Gee! But these are" is in ibid., p. 245; "These dear good people" is in ibid., p. 238; "Aside from the fact" is in ibid.; "I wrote to you" is dated Aug. 3, 1914; "I hope England" is in PL, op. cit., p. 240; "I just *know*" is in ibid., p. 267; "There can be no compromise" is in New York *Times*, Feb. 10, 1914; Wilson's note is in Freidel, *The Apprenticeship*, p. 180; "I will not run" is in Lindley, *Franklin D. Roosevelt*, p. 131; "representatives of crooks" is quoted in Freidel, op. cit., p. 182; "My senses" is dated Aug. 13, 1914; for FDR's decision to run for the Senate, see Lindley, op. cit., p. 132, and Daniels, *The Wilson Era*, Vol. I, pp. 131–32; "I had no more idea" is in letter to Montgomery Hare, Aug. 31, 1914; Howe's messages are in Stiles, *The Man Behind Roosevelt*, p. 60; "I have been offering up" is dated Aug. 22, 1914; "I have only one possible opponent" is quoted in Gosnell, *Champion Campaigner*, p. 57; "He is quiet and unassuming" is quoted in Freidel, op. cit., p. 187; "ruined us" is in Stiles, op. cit., p. 63; "Our national defense" is in Lindley, op. cit., p. 120; "the truth and even if" is in PL, op. cit., pp. 256–57; "he exhibited" is in New York *Sun*, Dec. 17, 1915; reaction to the *Lusitania* sinking is in Bailey, *A Diplomatic History of the American People*, pp. 626–28; "What d' y' think" is in PL, op. cit., p. 270; "if J.D. gets canned" is in Coletta, *Admiral Bradley A. Fiske and the American Navy.* "I want to tell you" is in Freidel, op. cit., p. 250; "A great many" is in Freidel, op. cit., p. 260; "We spend more" is in ibid., p. 261; "to college boys" and "absolutely democratic lines" are in FDR to Daniels, Feb. 16, 1916; "It's an awful mistake" is in PL, op. cit., p. 317; "I am trying" is in ibid., p. 304; "*Please* kill all" is in PL, op. cit., p. 304; "There is much" and "he is scared blue" are in ibid., p. 325; "the Navy is growing" is in Freidel, op. cit., p. 265; "of the most extraordinary" is in PL, op. cit., p. 338; "a certain distinguished" is in Freidel, op. cit., p. 267; "I hope to God" is in PL, op. cit., p. 339; "It is a curious thing" is in letter to Daniels, Aug. 7, 1915; "I have never been" is in Freidel, op. cit., p. 277; "It was an unforgettable picture" and all other quotes from Marvin are in "Notes on Franklin D. Roosevelt as Assistant Secretary of the Navy 1913–1920," in FDRL; "political considerations" story is in "Trip to Haiti and Santo Domingo, 1917," in FDRL; "No lights" is in ibid.; "I went to see" is in PPA, 1939, p. 117; "I have any amount" is in PL, op. cit., p. 339; nitrate-purchase story is in Lindley, op. cit., pp. 138–39; "999 years" is in ibid., p. 140; "T.R. wanted" is in FDR diary, Mar. 11, 1917; description of scene on Apr. 2, 1917, is in New York *Times*, Apr. 3, 1917, and Millis, *Road to War*, pp. 436–40; ER's reaction is in ER, op. cit., p. 245; FDR's press statement is in Freidel, op. cit., p. 300.

CHAPTER IX

For the arrival of American destroyers at Queenstown, see Taussig, "Destroyer Experiences During the Great War," U. S. Naval Institute *Proceedings*, Dec. 1922; "See young Roosevelt" is in *Time*, May 28, 1923; "Mr. Secretary" is in Freidel, *The Apprenticeship*, p. 304; "Franklin Roosevelt should" is in Langdon Marvin to FDR, July 17, 1917; "completely preoccupied" is in ER, *This Is My Story*, pp. 249–50; "I really think" is in Busch, *T.R.: The Story of Theodore Roosevelt*, p. 314; for Sims and Jellicoe, and Sims and Benson, see Morison, *Admiral Sims and the Modern American Navy*, pp. 338–42; "That decision was" is in "Memorandum for Captain Thomas G. Frothingham—Situation after Declaration of War," in FDRL; for the Navy's growth and operations in World War I, see Miller, *The U. S. Navy: An Illustrated History*, pp. 261–70; FDR memos to Daniels are dated Apr. 18, 1917, July 12, 1917, Sept. 7, 1917; "It is time that they" is in FDR Speech File, May 9, 1917; "turn out mere" is in FDR to Churchill, Apr. 7, 1917; "Our Navy Department" is in Churchill to FDR, June 30, 1917; Churchill's report is in FDRL; "I am encouraged" is in PL, Vol. II, pp. 356–57; "He was a great" is quoted in Davis, *FDR: The Beckoning of Destiny 1882–1928*, p. 496; "If by any perfectly wild" is in PL, op. cit., p. 351; for FDR's account of the North Sea Barrage, see "Memorandum for Captain Thomas G. Frothingham—The Inception of the North Sea Barrage," in FDRL; also see Duncan, *America's Use of Sea Mines*, pp. 47–66; Memorandum to Daniels on barrage, and letters to Wilson and to ER are in PL, op. cit., pp. 363–67; "scuttlebutt" story is in a letter to the author from Admiral John Jay Schieffelin, USNR (ret.), dated June 21, 1980; Camp is quoted in Freidel, op. cit., p. 321; Camalier's remarks are in a transcript in the FDRL; commandeering the generator is in Lindley,

NOTES

op. cit., pp. 144–45; relations between FDR and Kennedy related in Beschloss, *Kennedy and Roosevelt*, pp. 44–46, and Whalen, *The Founding Father*, p. 49; Tammany's offer of the governorship is related in Lindley, op. cit., pp. 164–65; Wilson's instructions to Daniels are in Daniels, *The Wilson Era*, Vol. II. "One of us" is in ibid., p. 263; All quotations from the diary-letter are from PL, op. cit., pp. 375–440; "The bottom dropped out" is in Lash, *Eleanor and Franklin*, p. 220; "I really can't stand" is in PL, op. cit., p. 347; "It seems years" is in ibid., p. 348; *Times* article is in ibid., p. 350; "All I can say" is in ibid., p. 349; letters mentioning trips with Lucy are in ibid., pp. 352, 358; Law's comment on FDR is in Jonathan Daniels, *Washington Quadrille*, p. 89; "I saw you" is quoted in Lash, op. cit., pp. 225–26; "She inquired if you" is quoted in ibid., p. 226; "She was tall and stately" is in Jonathan Daniels, op. cit., p. 157; "unreasonable and touchy" is in PL, op. cit., p. 346; check into Virginia Beach hotel is in James Roosevelt, *My Parents*, p. 101; Anna Roosevelt's unpublished article is in FDRL; "Eleanor was not willing" is in Jonathan Daniels, op. cit., p. 147; Elliott Roosevelt's remarks are in the transcript of an interview on June 20, 1979, in the ER papers, FDRL.

CHAPTER X

For FDR's correspondence with Daniels regarding the European trip, see Kilpatrick, *Roosevelt and Daniels*, pp. 56–57; family relations following the Lucy Mercer affair are discussed in Lash, *Eleanor and Franklin*, pp. 228–29; description of voyage is in PL, Vol. II, pp. 444–46; FDR's comments on death of TR are in Freidel, *The Ordeal*, p. 4; ER's comments are in *This Is My Story*, p. 275, and PL, op. cit., p. 445; Camalier's comments on negotiations with the French are in a transcript in FDRL; French negotiations and the officer's comments are in PL, op. cit., pp. 453–54; for ER's comments on the Covenant, see ER, op. cit., p. 288; meeting with Wilson is in ibid., p. 289; entertainment on the *George Washington* is in ibid., p. 291; near disaster for the ship is in ibid., pp. 291–92, and Freidel, op. cit., pp. 14–15; description of Wilson in Boston is in ER, op. cit., pp. 292–93; for FDR's speeches on the League, see his speech before the League of Free Nations, Mar. 1, 1919, and PL, op. cit., pp. 476–77; for the "Red Scare" and Palmer's activities, see Robert K. Murray, *Red Scare*; for FDR's reaction to the R Street bombing, see James Roosevelt, *Affectionately, F.D.R.*, pp. 56–57; "This business of the President" is in Hatch, *Franklin D. Roosevelt*, p. 115; Hamlin's remarks are in "Some Memories of Franklin D. Roosevelt," in FDRL; "You are not only" is in PL, op. cit., p. 486; for FDR's finances, see James Roosevelt, op. cit., pp. 59–61; "I do not see how" is dated Mar. 5, 1920; "Strictly between ourselves" is dated Dec. 24, 1919; Brooklyn speech is in New York *Times*, Feb. 2, 1920; for the Taussig affair, see *Army and Navy Journal*, Jan. 3, 10, and 24, 1920; for the Newport episode, see Freidel, op. cit., pp. 45–47, and John Rathom to FDR, Oct. 22, 1920; Chicago speech is in FDRL; "It was a humdinger" is quoted in Freidel, op. cit., p. 55; "Being early on the job" is in a letter to Henry Heymann, Dec. 2, 1919; "I do not propose" is in a letter to Nelson Drummond, Feb. 14, 1920; "Hoover is certainly" is in a letter to Hugh Gibson dated Jan. 2, 1920; Wehle's story is in Louis B. Wehle, *Hidden Threads of History*, pp. 81–83; "I know no Democrat" is in Burner, *Herbert Hoover*, p. 152; Mencken on the 1920 convention is in *Heathen*

Days, p. 176; Frances Perkins' account is in *The Roosevelt I Knew*, p. 27; "I am wondering" is dated June 17, 1920; the Roosevelt-Howe platform proposals are discussed in Daniel Fusfeld, *The Economic Thought of Franklin D. Roosevelt*, pp. 73–75; John Mack's account of the convention is in oral-history interview with George Palmer in FDRL; FDR's seconding speech for Smith is in New York *Times*, July 3, 1920; Mencken waving a baton is in William Manchester, *Disturber of the Peace*, p. 147; for Cox's version of Roosevelt's nomination, see James M. Cox, *Journey Through My Years*, p. 232; Ansberry described his meeting with FDR in New York *Sun*, July 12, 1920; Hoover's letter is dated July 12, 1920; Lippmann's letter is dated July 8, 1920; New York *Times* editorial is dated July 7, 1920; Chicago *Tribune* editorial is dated July 15, 1920; "The voters have the right" is in New York *Telegram*, July 10, 1920; meeting between Cox and FDR is described in Cox, op. cit., p. 238; Cox's description of the meeting with Wilson is in ibid., pp. 241–45; FDR's statement to the press is in PL, op. cit., p. 497; comments to ER are in ibid., pp. 494–95; exchange of letters between FDR and Daniels is in ibid., pp. 489–91; "I sympathized" is in ER, op. cit., p. 312; ER's comments on her politics are in the Poughkeepsie *News-Telegraph*, July 16, 1920; FDR's acceptance speech is in PL, op. cit., pp. 499–508; the New York *Post* article is dated Aug. 10, 1920; relations between the Oyster Bay and the Hyde Park Roosevelts are discussed in Miller, *The Roosevelt Chronicles*; FDR's conversation with Lynch is in Lindley, *Franklin D. Roosevelt*, p. 198; for ER and Howe, see ER, op. cit., pp. 313–19; for FDR and Haiti, see Freidel, op. cit., pp. 81–83; Rathom's letter is dated Oct. 22, 1920; ER on FDR's reaction to defeat is in ER, op. cit., p. 320; "Thank the Lord" is in PL, op. cit., p. 514.

CHAPTER XI

"Every war brings" is in a letter to Willard Saulsbury, Dec. 9, 1924; "I am delighted" is in a letter to Frankfurter, Jan. 7, 1921; "younger capitalists" is in Freidel, *The Ordeal*, p. 93; "world beating" is in a letter from Black to FDR, Mar. 2, 1921; "You may be happy" is in a letter from Daniels to FDR, Jan. 22, 1921; "I found all the cards" is in PL, Vol. II, p. 517; FDR's statement is in ibid., pp. 519–22; "looked tired" is in a letter from Missy LeHand to ER, Aug. 21, 1921; FDR's account of the fishing expedition is in Looker, *This Man Roosevelt*, p. 110; "It was a terrifying sight" is in Anna Roosevelt, "How Polio Helped Father," *The Woman*, July 1949; "I'd never" is in Looker, op. cit., p. 111; "I tried to persuade" is in ibid., p. 112; "I don't know what's wrong" is in Stiles, *The Man Behind Roosevelt*, p. 76; for ER's account of FDR's illness, see ER, *This Is My Story*, pp. 330–34; "utter despair" is in Freidel, op. cit., p. 100; "Yesterday and today" is in PL, op. cit., p. 525; "as it is really helpful" is in ibid., pp. 527–28; "I realized that I had" is in Kleeman, *Gracious Lady*, p. 276; "We children were allowed" is in James Roosevelt, *Affectionately, F.D.R.*, p. 120; Anna in clothes closet is in Anna Roosevelt, op. cit.; "Mother told us" is in ibid.; "his whole face" is in Gunther, *Roosevelt in Retrospect*, p. 242; "Mr. Roosevelt was enjoying" is in New York *World*, Sept. 14, 1928; Lynch episode is in Lindley, *Franklin D. Roosevelt*, p. 203; FDR letter to Adolph Ochs is dated Sept. 16, 1921; "He has such courage" is in Gunther, op. cit., p. 244; Daniels incident is in Daniels, *The Wilson Era*, Vol. I, p. 131; "walking on crutches" is in a letter to G. S. Barrow, Dec. 8, 1921; ER's account of her struggle with SDR is in ER, op. cit., pp. 336–40; "I am only being" is in James Roosevelt, *My Parents*, p. 80; "dirty, ugly" is in James Roosevelt, *Affectionately, F.D.R.*, p. 124; "Granny's needling" is in Anna Roosevelt, op. cit.; "He would give us" is in James Roosevelt, *Affectionately, F.D.R.*, p. 124; "somewhat rebellious legs" is in PL, op. cit., p. 530; "See me get into" is in Hamlin, "Some Memories of Franklin Roosevelt," in FDRL; "Now, I don't want" is quoted in Lindley, op. cit., p. 213; "I remember feeling" is in a letter from Sheffield Cowles, Jr., to the author, Mar. 18, 1980; "I cannot walk without a *Cain*" is written on a letter from Charles Ritz to FDR, Dec. 2, 1928; "I have renewed my youth" is in a letter dated Sept. 16, 1921; "Mother told me" is in Anna Roosevelt, op. cit.; "The legs work" is in a letter dated Aug. 10, 1922; "One day he hollered" is in an interview by George Palmer with Depew in FDRL; "I would almost" is in Perkins, *The Roosevelt I Knew*, p. 32; "The legs are really" is in a letter to James Cox, Dec. 8, 1922; "brought to my mind" is in a letter to A. C. Dinkey, June 21, 1922; "Lord knows" is in Howe to FDR, Sept. 1, 1921; "Dear Al" letter is in Gosnell, *Champion Campaigner*, pp. 72–73; "Things in the office" is quoted in Freidel, op. cit., p. 141; "Except for my braces" is in a letter to Glass, Mar. 27, 1923; "I found the growth" is in PL, op. cit., pp. 541–42; "took a motorboat" is in ibid., pp. 543–44; rough draft of FDR's history is in ibid., pp. 546–52; "In regard to my own" is in a letter to George Marvin, Sept. 12, 1922; FDR's peace plan is printed in ER, *This I Remember*, pp. 353–66; "I've often thought" is in Anna Roosevelt, op. cit.; "Franklin Roosevelt underwent" is in Perkins, op. cit., p. 29; "Indeed, I believe that it was not polio" is in James Roosevelt, *Affectionately, F.D.R.*, p. 132.

CHAPTER XII

"Moses, what do you think" is in an interview by George Palmer with Moses Smith in FDRL; "I do not believe in a campaign" is quoted in Freidel, *The Ordeal*, p. 178; "Have something you want to say" is in ER, *This Is My Story*, p. 352; for the Harding scandals, see Miller, *The Founding Finaglers*, pp. 304–49; "like a breeze" is in Claude G. Bowers, *My Life*, pp. 177–78; "The leading candidates" is in Howe to Thomas Mott Osborne, Apr. 1, 1924; for the most complete account of the 1924 convention, see Robert K. Murray, *The 103rd Ballot*; "I'll do it" is in Ernest K. Lindley, *Franklin D. Roosevelt*, p. 222; "As we walked" is in James Roosevelt, *My Parents*, pp. 92–93; Earle Looker's column is in the New York *Herald Tribune*, July 1, 1924; "No matter whether" is in the New York *Evening World*, July 7, 1924; "In the thick of" is in ER, *This I Remember*, pp. 31–32; "In 1920" is in a letter to William Saulsbury, Dec. 9, 1924; sale of naval prints is in New York *Times*, Jan. 4, 1925; "How marvellous" is quoted in Davis, *FDR.: The Beckoning of Destiny 1882–1928*, p. 766; "The pool is really wonderful" is in PL, Vol. II, p. 564; ER's reaction to Warm Springs is in ER, *This I Remember*, pp. 26–27; Warm Springs cocktail-party episode is in Carmichael, *F.D.R., Columnist*, p. 6; "The other partners" is in a letter to Van-Lear Black, Sept. 24,

1924; FDR as a therapist is in Jean Gould, *The Good Fight*, p. 133; FDR's reaction to the regular guests is in ibid., pp. 131–32; "This time I think" is in a letter to Black, Aug. 31 1925; "walked a block" is in PL, op. cit., p. 591; for details of purchase of Warm Springs, see Lippman, *The Squire of Warm Springs*, pp. 41–43; go to some desert land is in ibid., p. 41; "I know you love" is in Lash, *Eleanor and Franklin*, p. 296; for an antagonistic view of FDR's business activities, see Flynn, *Country Squire in the White House*; the account in Freidel, op. cit., Ch. IX, is more evenhanded; "The tendency lately" is in New York *Times*, June 4, 1922; "Our aim" is in a letter to Waldo Adler, May 31, 1923; review of the Bowers book is in New York *Evening World*, Dec. 8, 1925; "We have today" is in a "Memorandum on Leadership," July 6, 1928, in FDRL; for influence of Jefferson on FDR and the New Deal, see Peterson, *The Jefferson Image in the American Mind*, pp. 347–76; "two ladies" is in a letter to William A. Oldfield, Apr. 11, 1925; "My correspondents" is in Lindley, op. cit., p. 225; "You'd almost think" is in Perkins, *The Roosevelt I Knew*, p. 32; Hamlin meeting is in Hamlin, "Some Memories of Franklin Roosevelt," in FDRL; "There are two good reasons" is quoted in Freidel, op. cit., p. 216; "I am very doubtful" is in a letter to Daniels, June 23, 1927; "The campaign is working" is in a letter to Black, July 25, 1928; "Watch the trains!" story is in Moore, *A Catholic Runs For President*, p. 145; "I have had a difficult" is in PL, op. cit., p. 645; exchange of telegrams between FDR and Anna is in ibid.; "Don't you dare!" is in Fleeson, "Missy—To Do This—FDR," *The Saturday Evening Post*, Jan. 8, 1938; for the FDR draft, see Lindley, op. cit., pp. 18–20; REGRET THAT is in a telegram from ER, Oct. 2, 1928; BY WAY OF is in a telegram from Howe, Oct. 2, 1928; "Well, I've got" is in a letter to Frederic A. Delano, Oct. 8, 1928; "I was not dragooned" is in PL, op. cit., p. 647; "A Governor does" is in ibid.; for Rosenman's account of the 1928 campaign, see *Working with Roosevelt*, pp. 15–27; "If I could keep on campaigning" is in FDR speech at Yonkers, N.Y., Nov. 1, 1928; "accepted the ultimate" is in Perkins, op. cit., pp. 44–45; "Well, the time" is quoted in Josephson and Josephson, *Al Smith: Hero of the Cities*, p. 398; Flynn's account of Election Night is in *You're the Boss*, pp. 71–72; Flynn states that FDR went home believing himself defeated, and he called the upstate sheriffs; Rosenman says FDR called them; "You are the hope" is in a letter from Harry Byrd, Jan. 9, 1929.

CHAPTER XIII

"God bless you" is in Lash, *Eleanor and Franklin*, p. 325; "I've got to be" is in Perkins, *The Roosevelt I Knew*, p. 52; "It will always be" is in Lash, op. cit., p. 323; "You see, Al's" is in Perkins, op. cit., p. 55; "One of Franklin's" is in ER, *This I Remember*, p. 51; "Can't you get anything" is in Stiles, *The Man Behind Roosevelt*, p. 161; "It was the Roosevelt habit" is in Tugwell, *The Brains Trust*, p. 52; "In those messages and speeches" is in Rosenman, *Working with Roosevelt*, p. 31; "Being Governor" is in New York *Times*, Dec. 16, 1932; for the fight over the budget, see Bellush, *Franklin D. Roosevelt as Governor of New York*, Ch. II; "I am getting into a grand little fight" is in PL, Vol. III, p. 39; "I raise the broad question" is in New York *Times*, Feb. 28, 1929; "I will not assent" is in *Public Papers of Governor Franklin D. Roosevelt* (PPG), 1929, p. 196; "You are right" is in PL, op. cit.,

p. 24; "If the farming population" is in PPG, op. cit., p. 40; "In the brief time" is in ibid., p. 13; for the power fight, see Bellush, op. cit., Ch. X; "It is probably because of the warm weather" is in PL, op. cit., p. 68, and PPG, op. cit., pp. 710–13; "I want to preach" is in New York *Times*, July 5, 1929; "makes me laugh" is in PL, op. cit., p. 43; "I would tell him" is in ER, op. cit., p. 56; for the stock-market crash, see Galbraith, *The Great Crash*, and Allen, *Only Yesterday*, Ch. XII and XIII; detailed accounts of events on the Stock Exchange floor and outside are in New York *Times* and *Herald Tribune*, Oct. 24–30, 1929, and in Thomas and Morgan-Witts, *The Day the Bubble Burst*; "Little Flurry downtown" is in PL, op. cit., p. 92; "If you had asked" is in Perkins, op. cit., p. 96; "For the love of Mike" is in PL, op. cit., p. 148; "Never let your opponent" is in Rosenman, op. cit., p. 45; "I know the people" is in PPG, 1930, p. 403; "It is not a matter of party" is in ibid., p. 412; "The people of this State" is in ibid., p. 418; "If there are any" is in ibid., p. 437; "I cast" is in Stiles, op. cit., p. 134.

CHAPTER XIV

Moley's letter is in Moley, *After Seven Years*, pp. 10–12; "Whatever you said" is in Farley, *Behind the Ballots*, p. 62; "You can speak too often" is in Farley, *Jim Farley's Story*, p. 8; for the organization of the Roosevelt campaign, see Farley, *Ballots*, pp. 64–76; Howe's card files are in FDRL; "I am not in any sense" is in PL, Vol. III, pp. 161–62; Russell is quoted in Freidel, *The Triumph*, p. 174; Kennedy's visit to Howe is in Stiles, *The Man Behind Roosevelt*, p. 148, and Beschloss, *Kennedy and Roosevelt*, p. 70; for background on Farley's trip, see Flynn, *You're the Boss*, pp. 83–84; for Farley's account of the swing, see Farley, *Ballots*, pp. 80–88; for economic and social conditions in the United States during the depression, see Wecter, *The Age of the Great Depression*, and Bird, *The Invisible Scar*; Hoover's account of the economic revival of 1931 and the European banking crisis is in Hoover, *The Memoirs of Herbert Hoover*, Vol. III, pp. 59–80; "I shall never forget" is in Perkins, *The Roosevelt I Knew*, pp. 107–8; "New and untried remedies" is in PPG, 1931, p. 735; "just can't sit back" is in Rosenman, *Working with Roosevelt*, p. 50; "This is the time" is in ibid.; "The duty of the State" is in PPG, 1931, p. 173; "I am disturbed" is in FDR to L. A. Lincoln, Sept. 2, 1931; "unfed, unclothed" is in PPG, 1932, p. 32; "Where the State itself" is in PPA, 1932, pp. 788–89; Flynn's meeting with Smith is in Flynn, op. cit., pp. 85–86; "What a queer thing" is in PL, op. cit., p. 228; for Howell's talk with Smith, see ibid., pp. 229–32; for the Tammany scandals, see Bellush, *Franklin D. Roosevelt as Governor of New York*, Ch. XII; Lippmann's column originally appeared in the New York *Herald Tribune*, Jan. 8, 1932; "The League of Nations" is in PPG, op. cit., pp. 550–52; "I am devoted" is quoted in Freidel, op. cit., p. 254; letter to Holmes and Wise is in ibid., pp. 290–93; Rosenman's account of the organization of the Brain Trust is in Rosenman, op. cit., pp. 56–58, and Tugwell, *The Brains Trust*, pp. 3–11; "we were off on an exciting" is in Moley, op. cit., pp. 20–21; Berle's comment is quoted in Tugwell, op. cit., p. xxiv; "Forgotten Man" speech is in PPA, op. cit., pp. 624–27; "I will take off my coat" is in the New York *Times*, Apr. 14, 1932; "Wasn't that a terrible" is in ibid., Apr. 15, 1932; background on Oglethorpe

University speech is in Rosenman, op. cit., p. 65; speech is in PPG, op. cit., pp. 639–47; for discussion of Moley memorandum, see Rosen, *Hoover, Roosevelt, and the Brains Trust*, pp. 119–23 and 140–48.

CHAPTER XV

I have used the New York *Times* and the Chicago *Tribune*, June 20 to July 3, 1932, for the convention; conditions in Chicago are in Wilson, *The American Earthquake*, pp. 462–63; "We did nothing" is in Flynn, *You're the Boss*, p. 90; Howe's preparations are in Stiles, *The Man Behind Roosevelt*, pp. 168–69, and Farley, *Behind the Ballots*, pp. 109–10; for details of the charges against Walker, see Bellush, *Franklin D. Roosevelt as Governor of New York*, pp. 274–76; Shouse is quoted in Farley, op. cit., pp. 112–13; Mencken is quoted on Smith in Schlesinger, *The Crisis of the Old Order*, p. 303; Farley's account of the fight over the two-thirds rule is in Farley, op. cit., pp. 116–19; "He looked bewildered" is in Schlesinger, op. cit., p. 299; "It was only the beginning" is in Farley, op. cit., p. 123; "The nervous strain" is in ibid., p. 129; Howe's condition is described in Stiles, op. cit., pp. 177–78; Farley described his meeting with Rayburn in Farley, op. cit., pp. 133–35; "I would have given anything" is quoted in Freidel, *The Triumph*, p. 304; "Mein Gawd!" is in Stiles, op. cit., pp. 181–83; "We presented a strange picture" is in Rosenman, *Working with Roosevelt*, p. 70; FDR's conversation with Long is in ibid., p. 69; this vote "will show" is in Farley, op. cit., p. 143; Farley lying on the floor with Howe is in ibid., pp. 144–45; meeting with Rayburn is in ibid.; Howe's reaction is in ibid., pp. 145–46; Howe's meeting wth Byrd is in Stiles, op. cit., pp. 186–87; "If you don't take Roosevelt" is in Krock, *Memoirs*, p. 330; Brown and Garner is in Schlesinger, op. cit., pp. 308–9; O'Connor to FDR is dated July 7, 1932; "Good—fine" is in Rosenman, op. cit., p. 72; Moley's anger is in Moley, *After Seven Years*, p. 30; "Good old McAdoo" is in Tully, *F.D.R., My Boss*, p. 51; for the flight to Chicago, see Rosenman, op. cit., pp. 75–76; "Dammit, Louis" is in James Roosevelt, *Affectionately, F.D.R.*, p. 185; Acceptance Speech is in PPA, Vol. I, pp. 647–59; "The campaign starts" is quoted in Schlesinger, op. cit., p. 413; "All you have to do" is quoted in ibid., p. 416; campaign organization is discussed in Farley, op. cit., pp. 158–63; for campaign financing, see Louise Overacker, "Campaign Funds in a Depression Year," *American Political Science Review*, Oct. 1933; "Roosevelt so ordered" is in Moley, *27 Masters of Politics*, p. 38; "Tell the Governor" is quoted in Schlesinger, op. cit., p. 416; "to accomplish anything" in the New York *Times*, Sept. 11, 1932; "There's the same goulash of faces" is from John Dos Passos, "The Veterans Come Home to Roost," *The New Republic*, June 29, 1932; for the retreat of the Bonus Army, see the fine account by Lee McCardell in the Baltimore *Evening Sun*, reprinted in Snyder and Morris, *A Treasury of the World's Great Reporting*; FDR's reaction to the crushing of the BEF is in Tugwell, *The Brains Trust*, pp. 357–59; White House incident is in ibid., p. 108; "How would it be" is in Moley, *27 Masters of Politics*, p. 209; "So you'd rather" is in ibid., p. 211; "Campaigning, for him" is in Moley, *After Seven Years*, p. 52; "I have looked" is in the New York *Times*, Nov. 6, 1932; most of FDR's major campaign speeches are in PPA, op. cit.; "Weave the two" is in Moley, *After Seven Years*, p. 48; "chameleon" remark is in Hoover, *Memoirs*, Vol. III, p. 300; Elmer Davis' remarks are quoted in Burns,

Roosevelt: The Lion and the Fox, p. 143; the Frankfurter-Wise exchange is quoted in Smith, *The Shattered Dream*, p. 178; Hoover's speeches are in Hoover, op. cit.; "I simply will not" is in Moley, *After Seven Years*, p. 64; Lindley's comments are in Lindley, *The Roosevelt Revolution*, pp. 3–4; FDR's closing speech of the campaign is in Moley, *After Seven Years*, pp. 401–2; for events at FDR's headquarters, see Stiles, op. cit., pp. 215–17, Rosenman, op. cit., p. 87, Farley, op. cit., pp. 185–88; "This is the greatest" is in the New York *Times*, Nov. 9, 1932; "You know, Jimmy" is in James Roosevelt, op. cit., p. 189.

CHAPTER XVI

Hoover's telegram to FDR with the draft of the reply is in FDRL; the final form was changed in dictating it to Moley; Bernard Baruch's prescription is in Schlesinger, *The Crisis of the Old Order*, pp. 457–58; "Whether his policies" is in Hoover, *Memoirs*, Vol. III, p. 176; transcript of the telephone conversation between Hoover and FDR is in Freidel, *Launching the New Deal*, pp. 26–27; Ike Hoover's account of the meeting between FDR and Hoover is in I. H. Hoover, *Forty-two Years in the White House*, pp. 221–23; Moley's account of the meeting is in Moley, *After Seven Years*, pp. 72–79; "The impression" is in Freidel, op. cit., p. 34; FDR's criteria for selecting the Cabinet are discussed in Moley, *The First New Deal*, pp. 72–73; "I wonder" is in SDR to FDR, Nov. 14, 1932; Rayburn to Moley is in Moley, *After Seven Years*, p. 83; Connally to FDR is in Schlesinger, op. cit., p. 452; FDR on MacArthur and Long is in Tugwell, *The Brains Trust*, pp. 433–34; Moley's account of the attempted assassination is in Moley, *The First New Deal*, pp. 65–67; FDR's account is in Wharton, *The Roosevelt Omnibus*, pp. 160–63; FDR's remarks on the possibility of assassination are in Schlesinger, op. cit., pp. 465–66; ER's comments are in the New York *Times*, Feb. 16, 1933; Moley on FDR's reaction is in Moley, *After Seven Years*, p. 139; "There *is* a star" is in Tugwell, *Roosevelt's Revolution*, p. 4; Coolidge incident is in Smith, *The Shattered Dream*, p. 204; Hoover's letter on the banking crisis is in Hoover, op. cit., pp. 203–4; Moley's account of the incident is in Moley, *The First New Deal*, pp. 140–45; "it means the abandonment" is in Freidel, op. cit., p. 177; "If there was any" is in Moley, *After Seven Years*, p. 110; "Louis can do" is quoted in Russell, *The President Makers*, p. 319; Moley's account of the preparation of the inaugural speech is in Moley, *The First New Deal*, pp. 96–119; for FDR's account of his visit to Hoover, see Tully, *F.D.R., My Boss*, pp. 63–64; Hoover's comments about Tugwell are in Hoover, op. cit., pp. 214–15; Moley's version of the meeting is in Moley, *The First New Deal*, pp. 148–49; for events in Roosevelt's suite and at the Treasury on the eve of the inauguration, see ibid., pp. 151–53.

CHAPTER XVII

"You felt they would" is in New York *Times*, Mar. 5, 1933; "The Presidency is not merely" is in ibid., Sept. 11, 1932; cabinet swearing in is described by Farley in *Behind the Ballots*, p. 209; Starling's comments are in Starling, *Starling of the White House*, pp. 306–7, and see Russell Owen in the New York *Times*, Mar. 19, 1933; "If I fail" is in Peel and Donnelly, *The 1932 Campaign: An Analysis*, p. 312; Tugwell's account of FDR's first day in office is in *The Democratic Roosevelt*, pp. 270–71; "The President outlined" is quoted in Freidel, *Launching the New Deal*, p. 215; "Mr. President, I am ready" is in Moley, *After Seven Years*, p. 148n; "a streak of lightning" is in Lindley, *The Roosevelt Revolution*, p. 82; for personal reactions to the bank holiday, see Allen, *Since Yesterday*, pp. 109–10, and Sherwin and Markmann, *One Week in March*, pp. 107–12; for detailed accounts of the effort to reopen the banks, see Moley, op. cit., pp. 148–55, and Moley, *The First New Deal*, Chs. 10 and 11; first Fireside Chat is in PPA, 1933, pp. 61–65; "Capitalism was saved" is in Moley, *After Seven Years*, p. 155; "Shortly after midnight" is in Lindley, op. cit., p. 88; "For three long years" is in PPA, 1933, pp. 49–51; "I think this would" is in Lindley, op. cit., p. 91; "How do you account" is quoted in Leuchtenburg, *Franklin D. Roosevelt and the New Deal*, p. 62; visit to Holmes is in Schlesinger, *The Coming of the New Deal*, p. 14; "We still have done nothing" is in press conference of Mar. 15, 1933; for FDR and Congress, see Moley, *The First New Deal*, pp. 338–42, and Herring, "First Session of the Seventy-third Congress," *American Political Science Review*, Feb. 1934; "Hunger is not debatable" is in Sherwood, *Roosevelt and Hopkins*, p. 52; "Set a thief" is in Beschloss, *Kennedy and Roosevelt*, p. 88; FDR's remarks on NIRA are in PPA, 1933, pp. 251–56; "Not even the realization" is in Moley, *After Seven Years*, p. 192; "Paralyzing nausea" is in MacArthur, *Reminiscences*, p. 101; joint statement with MacDonald is in PPA, 1933, pp. 145–49; "Put the old organ roll" is in Moley, *After Seven Years*, p. 214; "I think I have" is quoted in Dallek, *Franklin D. Roosevelt and American Foreign Policy*, p. 58; "bombshell" message is in PPA, 1933, pp. 264–65; "That piss-ant" is in Schlesinger, op. cit., p. 231; "magnificently right" is in Harrod, *The Life of John Maynard Keynes*, p. 514; "I'm prouder" is in Freidel, op. cit., p. 489.

CHAPTER XVIII

FDR was like the leader of a newly independent nation is in Leuchtenburg, *Franklin D. Roosevelt and the New Deal*, p. 63; "We stood in the city" is in Moley, *After Seven Years*, p. 128; "he was there, a massive" is in Galbraith, *A Life in Our Time*, p. 29; "A plague of young" is quoted in Schlesinger, *The Coming of the New Deal*, p. 16; "It will be red fire" is in Johnson, *The Blue Eagle from Egg to Earth*, p. 208; "The blood mounted" is in Perkins, *The Roosevelt I Knew*, pp. 202–3; "That makes me personally happier" is in PPA, 1933, p. 299; "He hasn't been" is quoted in Burns, *Roosevelt: The Lion and the Fox*, p. 192; for Hawley's comments, see *The New Deal and the Problem of Monopoly*, pp. 472–90; "But he is so tender-hearted" is in Ickes, *Secret Diary: The First Thousand Days*, p. 195; White House ceremony with Morris and Kleberg is described in Phillips, *From the Crash to the Blitz*, p. 234; "These were not acts" is quoted in Schlesinger, op. cit., p. 63; "No Swank" is the title of an article on Wallace by Sherwood Anderson that appeared in *Today*, Nov. 11, 1933; "flaming one" letter is quoted in Schlesinger, op. cit., p. 33; "There are more brains" is in Carter, *The New Dealers*, p. 75; "You and I understand" is in PL, Vol. III, pp. 360–61; "It's a lucky number" is in Blum, *From the Morgenthau Diaries*, pp. 69–70;

"I am for experience" is in *New Outlook*, Dec. 1933; "The real truth of the matter" is in PL, op. cit., p. 373; "Our troubles will not be over" is in Roosevelt, *On Our Way*, p. 184; "I had I reckon" is in Worster, *Dust Bowl*, p. 58; Hickok letter to ER is in Hickok Papers, FDRL; "You gave us beer" is in Worster, op. cit., p. 39; dust drifting down on the White House is in ibid., p. 38; "My idea is to go" is in Tugwell's Diary, in FDRL, Mar. 3, 1935; "People don't eat" is quoted in Sherwood, *Roosevelt and Hopkins*, p. 52; "sardonic manner" is in Phillips, op. cit., p. 265; "He had the purity" is in Sherwood, op. cit., p. 49; Lunch meeting between Roosevelt and Hopkins is described in Adams, *Harry Hopkins*, p. 57; "If I ever thought" is in Sherwood, op. cit., p. 54; "We cannot carry" is in Seligman and Cornwell, *New Deal Mosaic*, p. 71; "Coming across the continent" is in FDR to Garner, Aug. 11, 1934; "He has been all" is in *Time*, Nov. 19, 1934.

CHAPTER XIX

FDR's conversation with the reporter is in Perkins, *The Roosevelt I Knew*, p. 330; Norman Thomas comment is quoted in Wolfskill and Hudson, *All but the People*, p. 121; Tugwell is quoted in Cramer, *American Enterprise: Free and Not So Free*, p. 219; FDR's remarks to Ludwig are in Ludwig, *Roosevelt*, pp. 229–30; Degler's comment is in Degler, *Out of Our Past*, p. 410; "I'll tell them" is quoted in Cramer, op. cit., p. 448; Democratic-headquarters story is in ibid.; McKenna story is in Lindley, *The Roosevelt Revolution*, p. 277; canary story is in Gunther, *Roosevelt in Retrospect*, p. 91; order to take care of telephoned appeals is in James Roosevelt, *Affectionately, F.D.R.*, p. 207; "one of the people" is in ER, *This I Remember*, p. 74; John R. Boettiger's comments are in *A Love in Shadow*, p. 186; "I always liked that" is in Perkins, op. cit., p. 77; FDR's day is outlined in Geoffrey Hellman, "Roosevelt: From Breakfast to Bed," *Life*, Jan. 20, 1941; also see Henry F. Pringle, "The President," in *The Roosevelt Omnibus*, pp. 56–91; Ickes' remarks are in *Secret Diary: The First Thousand Days*, p. 421; Flynn's comment is in Flynn, *You're the Boss*, pp. 162–63; "You are a wonderful person" is in Ickes, *Secret Diary: The Inside Struggle*, p. 659; Phillips is quoted in Leuchtenburg, *Franklin D. Roosevelt and the New Deal*, p. 167; "the most complicated" is in Perkins, op. cit., p. 3; Morgenthau is quoted in Sherwood, *Roosevelt and Hopkins*, p. 9; young woman's visit is described by Page H. Wilson, New York *Times*, Aug. 14, 1976; "Never let your left" is quoted in Schlesinger, *The Coming of the New Deal*, pp. 583–84; Villard is quoted in ibid., p. 21; Berlin's comments are in *Russian Philosophers*, p. 138; FDR's relations with the press are based upon White, *F.D.R. and the Press*, Ch. I, Smith, *Thank You, Mr. President*, and author's conversations with the late Paul W. Ward; for FDR and the Cabinet, see Schlesinger, op. cit., pp. 518–20, Tully, *F.D.R., My Boss*, Ch. 8, and Perkins, op cit., pp. 134–35; Ickes is quoted in Schlesinger, *The Thousand Days*, p. 308; "Neither has a vote" is in Gunther, op. cit., p. 367; food at the White House is discussed in James Roosevelt, op. cit., pp. 194–96; Hemingway's comments are in a letter dated Aug. 2, 1937, in *Selected Letters of Ernest Hemingway*, p. 460; "During my waking" is in Gunther, op. cit., pp. 35–36; "*Where* does Eleanor" is in Flynn, op. cit., p. 215; "I never wanted" is in Hickok, *Reluctant First Lady*; "Hoover sent the Army" is quoted in Schlesinger, op. cit., p. 15; "I hope Eleanor" is in James Roosevelt, op. cit., p. 221; "I remember clearly" is in James Roosevelt, *My Parents*, p. 113; "You know, Eleanor" is in Perkins, op. cit., pp. 69–70; conversation between FDR and ER is in Gunther, op. cit., pp. 210–11; "He might have been happier" is in ER, op. cit., p. 349; "One of the worst things" is in James Roosevelt, *Affectionately, F.D.R.*, p. 215; "Possibly I should have" is in ibid., p. 179; "I probably carried" is in ER, op. cit., p. 17; "I believe that" is in James Roosevelt, *My Parents*, p. 227; "They were not really rooted" is in ER, op. cit., p. 18; "This is a most" is in ibid.; p. 20; the encounter in the forest is in "The Enigma," in *The Roosevelt Omnibus*, pp. 92–93.

CHAPTER XX

Huey Long and the straw-hat story is in Farley, *Behind the Ballots*, pp. 240–42; "What the hell" is in ibid.; "hoot owl" and "scrootch owl" is in Schlesinger, *The Politics of Upheaval*, p. 56; "Don't put anybody in" is in Seligman and Cornwell, *New Deal Mosaic*, p. 437; Wells's comments are in *The New America*, p. 31; Kazin's comment is in *New York Jew*, p. 15; "The federal government must" is in PPA, 1935, pp. 19–20; for organization of WPA, see Adams, *Harry Hopkins*, pp. 73–74, 78–81, and Sherwood, *Roosevelt and Hopkins*, pp. 66–71; "They are human beings" is in Perkins, *The Roosevelt I Knew*, p. 76; "thrown into a state" is in the New York *Times*, Feb. 24, 1935; "distinctly dispirited" is in Ickes, *Secret Diary: The First Thousand Days*, p. 306; "it is vastly better" is in PL, Vol. III, p. 468; "people tire" is in ibid., p. 467; "The interesting thing" is in FDR to Watson, May 6, 1935; Hofstadter's opinion is in *The American Political Tradition*, p. 330; "You know the whole thing" is in Perkins, op. cit., pp. 252–53; "Everyone could see" is in *Time*, June 4, 1935; "You want to make it" is in Perkins, op. cit., pp. 282–83; "I felt sure" is in ibid., p. 283; "We might as well" is quoted in Wolfskill and Hudson, *All but the People*, p. 226; "going to have kittens" is in Moley, *After Seven Years*, p. 310; "Our revenue laws" and Long's reaction are in the New York *Times*, June 20, 1935; Moley on the "death sentence" is in Moley, op. cit., p. 303; for Corcoran, see Alva Johnston, "White House Tommy," in *The Saturday Evening Post*, July 31, 1937; "You talk about" is quoted in Schlesinger, op. cit., p. 314; "F.D. gives evidence" is in Mason, *Brandeis*, p. 622; "I was so tired" is in Morgenthau, *Diaries*, Vol. I, p. 257; "This Administration came" is quoted in Moley, *The First New Deal*, p. 533; "The First New Deal characteristically" is in Schlesinger, op. cit., p. 392; "I always hate" is in PL, op. cit., p. 561; meeting with Dr. Kennedy is described in Gunther, *Roosevelt in Retrospect*, p. 318; Smith's comments are in the New York *Times*, Jan. 26, 1936; Hickok's comments are in a letter to Hopkins, Oct. 10, 1935; "We will win" is quoted in Burns, *Roosevelt: The Lion and the Fox*, p. 266; "He just held" is in New York *Times*, Jan. 4, 1936; "It is plain to see" is in Ickes, op. cit., p. 524; for Howe's decline, see Rollins, *Roosevelt and Howe*, pp. 432–39, and John Keller and Joseph Boldt, "Franklin's on His Own Now," *The Saturday Evening Post*, Oct. 12, 1940; Ickes' comment on Landon is in Ickes, op. cit., pp. 648–49; Franklin Field incident is in Reilly, *Reilly of the White House*, pp. 99–100, and Tully, *F.D.R., My Boss*, p. 202; "In the summer of 1933" is in Rosenman, *Working with Roosevelt*, pp. 110–11; "We are not in a" is in Wolfskill and Hudson, op. cit., p. 248; meeting between FDR and Landon is in Schlesinger, op. cit.,

p. 610; Hoover's reaction to FDR speech is in Schlesinger, op. cit., p. 622; "After looking them over" is in Farley, *Jim Farley's Story*, p. 65; Election Night at Hyde Park is described in Rosenman, op. cit., pp. 136–39; Flynn's remarks are in Moley, *The First New Deal*, p. 526; "Mr. Roosevelt is the only man" is quoted in Goldman, *Rendezvous with Destiny*, p. 268; "It was the nation" is in *Collier's*, Dec. 26, 1936; quoted in Baker, op. cit., pp. 162–63.

CHAPTER XXI

"Yes, but it's the Constitution" is in Rosenman, *Working with Roosevelt*, p. 144; "emphasized the word 'every'" is in ibid.; "It will fall" is in Ashurst to FDR, Feb. 19, 1936; "No disinterested student" is in Freedman, *Roosevelt and Frankfurter*, p. 272; "Give me ten million dollars" is in Ickes, *Secret Diary: The Inside Struggle*, p. 65; reference to Lloyd George is in Ickes, *Secret Diary: The First Thousand Days*, pp. 494–95; "the answer to a maiden's prayer" is in Baker, *Back to Back*, p. 54; "Very confidentially" is in Freedman, op. cit., p. 377; description of reception for the judiciary is in Alsop and Catledge, *The 168 Days*, p. 64; "Why are you here?" is in Baker, op. cit., p. 3; "the most destructive" is in ibid., p. 14; "Boys, here's where" is in Alsop and Catledge, op. cit., pp. 67–68; "rarin'" for a fight is in Farley, *Jim Farley's Story*, p. 77; "Jim, I just couldn't" is in ibid., p. 73; ER's comments on the loss of Howe are in *This I Remember*, pp. 167–68; for opposition to Supreme Court "packing" plan see Wolfskill and Hudson, *All but the People*, pp. 259–64; Farley's estimate is in Farley, op. cit., p. 78; secret homosexual is in Baker, op. cit., p. 69; Brandeis' role in Hughes's letter is in Mason, *Brandeis: A Free Man's Life*, pp. 626–27; for Wheeler's statement, see the New York *Times*, Mar. 23, 1937; "It was ten dollars" is from press conference, March, 1937; Roberts' acknowledgment is in Baker, op. cit., p. 176; "We did it" is in Farley, op. cit., p. 79; "This bill is raising hell" is quoted in Burns. *Roosevelt: The Lion and the Fox*, p. 304; "I . . . believe that" is in a letter from J. Warren David to FDR, Mar. 15, 1937; "Spring has come" in in PL, Vol. III, p. 676; FDR at wedding is in James Roosevelt, *Affectionately, F.D.R.*, p. 246; "How did you find" is in Baker, op. cit., p. 262; "He is punch drunk" is in Ickes, *Struggle*, p. 182; for the sit-down strikes, see Cramer, *American Enterprise: Free and Not So Free*, pp. 340–42; "Well, it is illegal" is in Perkins, *The Roosevelt I Knew*, pp. 321–22; "Is that you, Bill?" is in ibid., p. 324; "to take away the crutches" is in Morgenthau, *Diary*, Vol. I, p. 388; "I saw your friend" is in Perkins, op. cit., p. 225; Keynes on FDR is in ibid., p. 226; "As I see it" is in Morgenthau, op. cit., p. 415; "They have just stampeded" is in ibid., p. 421; for a discussion of FDR and Keynesian doctrine, see Lekachman, *The Age of Keynes*, pp. 138–43; "Harmony, Hell!" is quoted in Wolfskill and Hudson, op. cit., p. 275; "Jim, I'll tell" is in Farley, op. cit., p. 130; "It was up to him" is in Ickes, op. cit., p. 358; "The Boss has stirred up" is in Farley, op. cit., p. 137; "How many WPA" is in Principal Speeches of Harry L. Hopkins, Oct. 18, 1936, typescript in Library of Congress.

CHAPTER XXII

Tugwell's statement is in the foreword to the paperback edition of *The Democratic Roosevelt*; "I wonder if you" is quoted in Gunther, *Roosevelt in Ret-*

rospect, p. 325; Clare Luce is quoted in Dallek, *Franklin D. Roosevelt and American Foreign Policy, 1932–1945*, p. 336; "You should go through" is in Eccles, *Beckoning Frontiers*, p. 336; discussion of FDR's diplomatic appointments is based on Dallek, op. cit., p. 533 and Langer and Gleason, *The Challenge to Isolation*, pp. 8–9; Kennedy episode is in James Roosevelt, *My Parents*, pp. 208–10; "It was the greatest joke" is in Beschloss, *Kennedy and Roosevelt*, p. 157; Burns's comment is in *Roosevelt: The Lion and the Fox*, p. 262; "I do not know" is in PL, Vol. III, pp. 530–31; Rosenman's comment on the Chautauqua speech is in *Working with Roosevelt*, p. 108; "I now think" is quoted in Dallek, op. cit., p. 147; for background on "Quarantine Speech," see Borg, "Notes on Roosevelt's Quarantine Speech," *Political Science Quarterly*, Sept. 1957; Rosenman's comments are in Rosenman, op. cit., pp. 166–68; for the *Panay* sinking, see Morison, *The Rising Sun in the Pacific*, pp. 16–18; for FDR and the Jews, see Feingold, *The Politics of Rescue*, Ch. I; for background on the Czech crisis, see Taylor, *Munich*; "I have hatched" is in Morgenthau, *Diary*, Vol. I, p. 516; FDR's comments on Chamberlain are in Ickes, *Secret Diary: The Inside Struggle*, p. 468; letter to Phillips is in PL, Vol. IV, p. 810; "I want you to know" is in ibid., p. 818; "what went on" is in Gunther, *Roosevelt in Retrospect*, p. 59; FDR fainted is in Tully, *F.D.R., My Boss*, p. 273; poker game is in Ickes, op. cit., p. 532; Christmas 1938 in the White House is from Farr, *FDR*, pp. 320–21; "madder and madder" is in Ickes, op. cit., p. 597; "We'll be on" is quoted in Connally and Steinberg, *My Name Is Tom Connally*, p. 226; "We are not" is in Langer and Gleason, op. cit., p. 144; for "Saturday surprise," see ibid., pp. 82–90, and Hull, *Memoirs*, Vol. I, p. 620; "You, Fred Astaire" is in Beschloss, op. cit., p. 187; "visiting Elk" is in Ickes, op. cit., pp. 645–46; for the royal visit, see ER, *This I Remember*, pp. 182–98, and Tully, op. cit., p. 318.

CHAPTER XXIII

Conversation with Bullitt is in Burns, *Roosevelt: The Lion and the Fox*, p. 394; "a strange . . . familiarity" is in PL, Vol. IV, p. 916; "These last two days" is from the diary of J. P. Moffat, quoted in Leuchtenburg, *Franklin D. Roosevelt and the New Deal*, p. 293; details on the writing of the Neutrality Act speech are in Rosenman, *Working with Roosevelt*, pp. 189–90; "I am almost literally" is in PL, op. cit., p. 934; "Things move" is in ibid., pp. 967–68; Sachs visit is in Hellman, "The Contemporaneous Memoranda of Dr. Sachs," *The New Yorker*, Dec. 1, 1945; "I may be a benevolent" is quoted in Dallek, *Franklin D. Roosevelt and American Foreign Policy, 1933–1945*, p. 211; "bunch of Uriah Heaps" is in Ickes, *Secret Diary: The Lowering Clouds*, p. 112; for a discussion of the forces determining FDR's decision on the third term, see Parmet and Hecht, *Never Again: A President Runs for a Third Term*, Chs. I and II; for Farley's meeting with FDR at Hyde Park, see Farley, *Jim Farley's Story*, pp. 246–58; Ickes' account of the convention is in Ickes, op. cit., pp. 242–69; Perkins' account is in Perkins, *The Roosevelt I Knew*, pp. 129–34; ER in Chicago is in *This I Remember*, pp. 213–18; FDR during the convention is in Rosenman, op. cit., pp. 215–21; for background on Willkie, see Parmet and Hecht, op. cit., pp. 51–72; "The whole fate" is in Loewenheim, Langley, and Jonas, *Roosevelt and Churchill*, pp. 107–8; "Congress is going" is in Tully, *F.D.R., My Boss*, p. 244; for FDR's campaign, see Gosnell, *Champion Campaigner*, pp. 179–88; for background on "Martin, Barton and Fish," see Rosenman, op. cit., pp. 240–41; "It's implied clearly" is in ibid., p. 242; "We . . . have averted" is quoted in Burns, *Roosevelt: The Soldier of Freedom*, p. 4.

CHAPTER XXIV

"The moment approaches" is in Loewenheim, Langley, and Jonas, *Roosevelt and Churchill*, pp. 122–25; for origins of lend-lease, see Sherwood, *Roosevelt and Hopkins*, pp. 223–25, and Blum, *Roosevelt and Morgenthau*, pp. 340–58; exchange with Wheeler is in press conference of Jan. 14, 1941; for the struggle over whether to escort or not to escort, see Bailey and Ryan, *Hitler vs. Roosevelt*, pp. 109–11; "The President seems" is in Sherwood, op. cit., p. 293; "They're ninety-five per cent" is in ibid., p. 298; "The door is opened" is in ibid., pp. 303–4; "I deem it" is PL, Vol. IV, p. 1202; Hopkins' report on his visit to the Soviet Union is in Sherwood, op. cit., pp. 333–43; FDR's narrative of the meeting with Churchill is in the FDRL, and see Elliott Roosevelt, *As He Saw It*, pp. 28–31; Churchill's account is in *Memoirs of the Second World War*, pp. 489–93; for the *Greer* episode, see Bailey and Ryan, op. cit., pp. 168–87; fallen tree and SDR's funeral is in Reilly, *Reilly of the White House*, pp. 84–85; "He had no more" is in Sherwood, op. cit., p. 383; for a concise critique of the revisionists, see Gordon W. Prange, *At Dawn We Slept*, Appendix "Revisionists Revisited"; "I simply have not" is in Ickes, *Secret Diary: The Lowering Clouds*, p. 567; "the President was still unwilling" is in ibid., p. 588; for Magic operations, see Lewin, *The American Magic*, Ch. II; "he wished to know" is in Ickes, op. cit., p. 649; "I am not very hopeful" is in *Roosevelt and Churchill*, pp. 164–66; "The question" is in Stimson Diary, Nov. 25, 1941, quoted in Prange, op. cit., pp. 371–72; "What about" is in *Roosevelt and Churchill*, op. cit., pp. 166–67; "fairly blew up" is Stimson Diary, Nov. 26, 1941, quoted in Prange, op. cit., p. 396; for FDR's visit to Warm Springs, see Tully, *F.D.R., My Boss*, pp. 249–51; for cabinet meeting of Dec. 5, 1941, see Perkins, "The President Faces War," in Stilwell, *Air Raid: Pearl Harbor!* pp. 113–21; FDR's letter to Hirohito is in Hull, *Memoirs*, Vol. II, pp. 1094–95; "This means war" is in Sherwood, op. cit., pp. 426–27.

CHAPTER XXV

FDR's reaction to the Pearl Harbor attack is in Sherwood, *Roosevelt and Hopkins*, pp. 430–32; "In all my fifty" is in Hull, *Memoirs*, Vol. II, p. 1096; "Scoundrels and" is in Toland, *The Rising Sun*, p. 225; White House atmosphere is described in Tully, *F.D.R., My Boss*, pp. 254–56; "Mr. President, what" is in Churchill, *Memoirs of the Second World War*, p. 505; FDR's role as Commander in Chief is assessed in Burns, *Roosevelt: The Soldier of Freedom*, Greenfield, *Command Decisions*, Baldwin, *Great Mistakes of the War*, Matloff, "Franklin D. Roosevelt as War Leader," and Emerson, "Franklin D. Roosevelt as Commander-in-Chief in World War II"; for diplomatic policy, see Dallek, *Franklin D. Roosevelt and American Foreign Policy 1932–1945*, Smith, *American Diplomacy During the Second World War*, Divine, *Roosevelt and World War II*, Feis, *Churchill-Roosevelt-Stalin*, and U. S. Dept. of State, *Foreign Relations of the United States: Conferences at Cairo and Teheran, 1943*, and *The Conferences at Malta and Yalta, 1945*; "At least, Mr.

President" is in Pogue, *George C. Marshall*, Vol. II, p. 22; "political leadership must be" is from Emerson, op. cit.; Marshall's doubt of FDR's capability is in Pogue, op. cit., p. 23; "I feel I could not" is in Sherwood, op. cit., p. 803; for King, see Buell, *Master of Sea Power*; Navy Band note is in PL, Vol. IV, p. 1343; "The Prime Minister has" is in Sherwood, op. cit., p. 442; appoint FDR Archbishop is in Churchill, op. cit., p. 522; Churchill's reaction to FDR's driving is in ibid., p. 581; "What can we" is in ibid., p. 584; for details on American industrial mobilization, see Janeway, *The Struggle for Survival*; "Oh—the production" is in Sherwood, op. cit., p. 475; "Roosevelt's normal way" is in Janeway, op. cit., p. 51; "He was the catalytic" is in Perkins, *The Roosevelt I Knew*, p. 384; "I do not need" is in PL, op. cit., p. 920; production statistics are in Civilian Production Administration, *Industrial Mobilization for War*, p. 962; FDR and the Final Solution is in Morse, *While 6 Million Died*; "Thank God!" is in Tully, op. cit., pp. 263–64; FDR's version of the origin of the unconditional-surrender doctrine is in Sherwood, op. cit., pp. 695–96; the White House in wartime is in Bishop, *FDR's Last Year*, pp. 19–20; FDR's prank on Laura Delano is in James Roosevelt, *Affectionately, F.D.R.*, p. 257; FDR's relations with Lucy Rutherfurd are in Daniels, *Washington Quadrille*, pp. 287–302; Anna Boettiger's unpublished article is in the FDRL; "The President's plan" is in Murphy, *Diplomat Among Warriors*, p. 210; "He was correct" is in Perkins, op. cit., pp. 84–85; "I just hate" is in Leahy, *I Was There*; nodding over mail is in Tully, op. cit., pp. 273–74; examination of FDR at Bethesda and subsequent medical information are from Bruenn, "Clinical Notes on the Illness and Death of President Franklin D. Roosevelt," *Annals of Internal Medicine*, Apr. 1970; for details of choice of Truman, see Rosenman, *Working with Roosevelt*, pp. 438–51; also Donovan, *Conflict and Crisis*, p. xiii; Rosenman's complaint about the photo of FDR is op. cit., pp. 453–54; "Jimmy, I don't" is in James Roosevelt, op. cit., p. 284; Rosenman's reaction to Bremerton speech is in Rosenman, op. cit., p. 462; details of the campaign are in Gosnell, *Champion Campaigner*, pp. 203–12; "I still think" is in Hassett, *Off the Record with FDR*, p. 294; Churchill at Moscow is in Churchill, op. cit., pp. 885–86; "Mr. President, this is so" is in Leahy, op. cit., pp. 315–16; "We really believed" is in Sherwood, op. cit., p. 870; meeting with Ibn Saud is in ibid., p. 871; the voyage of the *Quincy* is described in Rosenman, op. cit., pp. 522–23.

EPILOGUE

FDR's arrival at Warm Springs is related by Margaret Suckley in transcript of an interview, in FDRL; "Within a week" is in Bruenn, "Clinical Notes on the Illness and Death of President Franklin D. Roosevelt," *Annals of Internal Medicine*, Apr. 1970; "We must not permit" is in Loewenheim, Langley, and Jonas, *Roosevelt and Churchill*, p. 705; "We must be firm" is in ibid., p. 709; "Here's where" is in Hassett, *Off the Record with F.D.R.*, p. 334; "We have fifteen more" and details of FDR's death are in Suckley transcript, *supra*; Bruenn provides details on FDR's final illness and treatment, op. cit.; Hassett, op. cit., pp. 335–37, and Tully, *F.D.R., My Boss*, pp. 361–63 describe the scene in the Little White House.

BIBLIOGRAPHY

Franklin Roosevelt was a collector, and the fruits of his labors crowd the shelves of the Franklin D. Roosevelt Library (FDRL), at Hyde Park. "I have destroyed practically nothing," he said at the Library's dedication, in 1939. "As a result, we have a mine for which future historians will curse as well as praise me." The extent and variety of the material available to the researcher boggles the mind—and is measured by the ton, rather than by the square foot of shelf space. Everything from locks of hair to recently discovered secret recordings of some of Roosevelt's conversations in the Oval Office are available, a truly monumental collection of documents, photographs, films, and transcribed interviews. The life of no President of the United States is more amply documented. The trove is so vast that not even the most conscientious researcher can examine more than selected portions of it in detail.

This book is based upon a wide sampling of Franklin Roosevelt's family, personal, and official papers. Other collections used include the papers of Eleanor Roosevelt, Anna Roosevelt Halsted, Harry Hopkins, Louis M. Howe, Rexford G. Tugwell, and Lorena Hickok. I have consulted the Josephus Daniels papers in the Library of Congress and the records in the National Archives pertaining to Roosevelt's service as assistant Secretary of the Navy. To supplement the manuscript collections, I have also used the four volumes of *Personal Letters* (PL); *The Public Papers and Addresses of Franklin D. Roosevelt* (PPA), in thirteen volumes; and the *Public Papers of Governor Franklin D. Roosevelt* (PPG), in four volumes. The books and articles that follow are those cited in the notes but not all that were consulted.

BOOKS

Adams, Henry H. *Harry Hopkins*. New York: Putnam, 1977.
Albion, Robert G. *Makers of Naval Policy*. Annapolis, Md.: U. S. Naval Institute, 1980.
Allen, Frederick Lewis. *Only Yesterday*. New York: Harper, 1931.
———. *Since Yesterday*. New York: Harper, 1940.
Alsop, Joseph; and Catledge, Turner. *The 168 Days*. Garden City, N.Y.: Doubleday, 1938.
Ashburn, Frank D. *Peabody of Groton*. New York: Coward, 1944.

Bailey, Thomas A.; and Ryan, Paul B. *Hitler vs. Roosevelt*. New York: Free Press, 1979.

Baker, Leonard, *Back to Back*. New York: Macmillan, 1967.

———. *Roosevelt and Pearl Harbor*. New York: Macmillan, 1970.

Baldwin, Hanson W. *Great Mistakes of the War*. New York: Harper, 1950.

Bellush, Benjamin. *Franklin D. Roosevelt as Governor of New York*. New York: Columbia University Press, 1956.

Beschloss, Michael R. *Kennedy and Roosevelt*. New York: Norton, 1980.

Bird, Caroline. *The Invisible Scar*. New York: Pocket Books, 1967.

Bishop, Jim. *FDR's Last Year*. New York: Pocket Books, 1975.

Blum, John M. *From the Morgenthau Diaries*, 3 vols. Boston: Houghton, 1959–67.

———. *The Progressive Presidents*. New York: Norton, 1980.

———. *Roosevelt and Morgenthau*. Boston: Houghton, 1970.

Boettiger, John R. *A Love in Shadow*. New York: Norton, 1978.

Borg, Dorothy. "Notes on Roosevelt's Quarantine Speech," *Political Science Quarterly*, Sept. 1957.

———; and Okamoto, Shumpei. *Pearl Harbor as History*. New York: Columbia University Press, 1973.

Bowers, Claude G. *My Life*. New York: Simon & Schuster, 1962.

Brandenburg, Ernest; and Braden, Waldo. "Franklin D. Roosevelt's Voice and Pronunciation," *The Quarterly Journal of Speech*, Feb. 1952.

Brown, Rollo W. *Harvard Yard in the Golden Age*. New York: Current Books, 1948.

Bruenn, Howard. "Clinical Notes on the Illness and Death of President Franklin D. Roosevelt," *Annals of Internal Medicine*, Apr. 1970.

Buell, Thomas B. *Master of Sea Power: A Biography of Fleet Admiral Ernest J. King*. Boston: Little, 1980.

Bullitt, Orville H., ed. *For the President: Personal and Secret*. Boston: Houghton, 1972.

Burner, David. *Herbert Hoover: A Public Life*. New York: Knopf, 1979.

———. *The Politics of Provincialism*. New York: Knopf, 1968.

Burns, James MacGregor. *Roosevelt: The Lion and the Fox*. New York: Harcourt, 1958.

———. *Roosevelt: The Soldier of Freedom*. New York: Harcourt, 1970.

Butow, R. J. C. "The FDR Tapes," *American Heritage*, Feb.–Mar. 1982.

Busch, Noel F. *T.R.: The Story of Theodore Roosevelt*. New York: Reynal, 1963.

———. *What Manner of Man?* New York: Harper, 1944.

Carmichael, Donald S., ed. *F.D.R., Columnist*. Chicago: Pellegrini & Cudahy, 1947.

Carter, John F. *The New Dealers*. New York: Literary Guild, 1939.

Churchill, Winston S. *Memoirs of the Second World War*. Boston: Houghton, 1959.

Civilian Production Administration. *Industrial Mobilization for War*. Washington, D.C.: Government Printing Office, 1947.

Coletta, Paolo E. *Admiral Bradley A. Fiske and the American Navy*. Lawrence, Kan.: Regent's Press of Kansas, 1979.

Conkin, Paul K. *The New Deal*. New York: Crowell, 1967.

Connally, Tom; and Steinberg, Alfred. *My Name Is Tom Connally*. New York: Crowell, 1954.

Cowperthwaite, L. LeRoy. "Franklin D. Roosevelt at Harvard," *The Quarterly Journal of Speech*, Feb. 1952.

Cox, James M. *Journey Through My Years*. New York: Simon & Schuster, 1946.

Cramer, Clarence. *American Enterprise: Free and Not So Free*. Boston: Little, 1972.

Crowell, Laura. "Roosevelt the Grotonian," *The Quarterly Journal of Speech*, Feb. 1952.

Dallek, Robert. *Franklin D. Roosevelt and American Foreign Policy, 1932–1945*. New York: Oxford University Press, 1979.

Daniels, Jonathan. *Washington Quadrille*. Garden City, N.Y.: Doubleday, 1968.

Daniels, Josephus. *The Wilson Era*, 2 vols. Chapel Hill: University of North Carolina Press, 1944–46.

Davis, Kenneth S. *FDR: The Beckoning of Destiny 1882–1928*. New York: Putnam, 1971.

Day, Donald, compiler. *Franklin D. Roosevelt's Own Story*. Boston: Little, 1951.

Degler, Carl N. *Out of Our Past*. New York: Harper, 1970.

Divine, Robert A. *Roosevelt and World War II*. Baltimore, Md.: Johns Hopkins Press, 1969.

Djilas, Milovan. *Conversations with Stalin*. New York: Harcourt, 1962.

Donovan, Robert J. *Conflict and Crisis*. New York: Norton, 1977.

Dos Passos, John. "The Veterans Come Home to Roost," *The New Republic*, June 29, 1932.

Dows, Olin. *Franklin Roosevelt at Hyde Park*. New York: Am. Artists, 1949.

Drexel, Constance. "Unpublished Letters of F.D.R. to his French Governess," *Parents Magazine*, Sept. 1951.

Duncan, Robert C. *America's Use of Sea Mines*. White Oak, Md.: Naval Research Laboratory, 1962.

Eccles, Marriner S. *Beckoning Frontiers*. New York: Knopf, 1951.

Einaudi, Mario. *The Roosevelt Revolution*. New York: Harcourt, 1957.

Emerson, William E. "Franklin D. Roosevelt as Commander-in-Chief in World War II," *Military Affairs*, Winter 1958–59.

Farley, James A. *Behind the Ballots*. New York: Harcourt, 1938.

————. *Jim Farley's Story*. New York: Whittlesey House, 1948.

Farr, Finis. *FDR*. New Rochelle, N.Y.: Arlington House, 1972.

Feingold, Henry L. *The Politics of Rescue*. New Brunswick, N.J.: Rutgers University Press, 1970.

Feis, Herbert. *The Road to Pearl Harbor*. Princeton, N.J.: Princeton University Press, 1950.

————. *Churchill-Roosevelt-Stalin*. Princeton, N.J.: Princeton University Press, 1957.

Ferdon, Nona S. *Franklin D. Roosevelt: A Psychological Interpretation of His Childhood and Youth*. Unpublished Ph.D. dissertation, University of Hawaii.

"First Session of the Seventy-third Congress," *American Political Science Review*, Feb. 1934.

Fleeson, Doris. "Missy—To Do This—FDR," *The Saturday Evening Post*, Jan. 8, 1938.

Flynn, Edward J. *You're the Boss*. New York: Viking, 1947.

Flynn, John T. *Country Squire in the White House*. Garden City, N.Y.: Doubleday, 1940.

Fowler, Gene. *Beau James: The Life and Times of Jimmy Walker*. New York: Viking, 1949.

"Franklin and Eleanor's Fortune," *Fortune*, Oct. 1932.

Freedman, Max, ed. *Roosevelt and Frankfurter: Their Correspondence, 1928–1945*. Boston: Little, 1967.

Freidel, Frank. *F.D.R. and the South*. Baton Rouge: Louisiana State University Press, 1965.

———. *Franklin D. Roosevelt*, 4 vols. Boston: Little, 1952–73.

Fusfeld, Daniel R. *The Economic Thought of Franklin D. Roosevelt*. New York: Columbia University Press, 1956.

Galbraith, John Kenneth. *The Great Crash*. Boston: Houghton, 1955.

———. *A Life in Our Time*. Boston: Houghton, 1981.

Goldman, Eric. *Rendezvous with Destiny*. New York: Vintage, 1955.

Gosnell, Harold. *Champion Campaigner*. New York: Macmillan, 1952.

Gould, Jean. *The Good Fight*. New York: Dodd, 1960.

Graff, Robert D.; Ginna, Robert; and Butterfield, Roger. *FDR*. New York: Harper, 1963.

Graham, Otis L., Jr. *Toward a Planned Society*. New York: Oxford University Press, 1976.

Greenfield, Kent R., ed. *Command Decisions*. New York: Harcourt, 1959.

Gunther, John. *Roosevelt in Retrospect*. London: Hamilton, 1950.

Hagedorn, Hermann. *The Roosevelt Family of Sagamore Hill*. New York: Macmillan, 1954.

Halsey, William F.; and Bryan, Joseph. *Admiral Halsey's Story*. New York: Whittlesey House, 1947.

Harrity, Richard; and Martin, Ralph G. *The Human Side of F.D.R.* New York: Duell, 1960.

Harrod, R. F. *The Life of John Maynard Keynes*. New York: Avon Books, 1971.

Hassett, William D. *Off the Record with F.D.R.* New Brunswick, N.J.: Rutgers University Press, 1958.

Hatch, Alden. *Franklin D. Roosevelt*. New York: Holt, 1947.

Hawley, Ellis W. *The New Deal and the Problem of Monopoly*. Princeton, N.J.: Princeton University Press, 1960.

Hellman, Geoffrey. "The Contemporaneous Memoranda of Dr. Sachs," *The New Yorker*, Dec. 1, 1945.

———. "Roosevelt: From Breakfast to Bed . . . ," *Life*, Jan. 20, 1941.

Hemingway, Ernest. *Selected Letters of Ernest Hemingway*. Carlos Baker, ed. New York: Scribner, 1980.

Herring, E. Pendleton. "First Session of the Seventy-third Congress," *American Political Science Review*, Feb. 1934.

Hickok, Lorena. *Reluctant First Lady*. New York: Dodd, 1962.

Hofstadter, Richard. *The American Political Tradition and the Men Who Made It*. New York: Knopf, 1949.

Hoover, Herbert. *The Memoirs of Herbert Hoover*. Vol. III. New York: Macmillan, 1952.

Hoover, I. H. *Forty-two Years in the White House*. Boston: Houghton, 1934.

Howe, Louis McHenry. "The Winner," *The Saturday Evening Post*, Feb. 25, 1933.

Hull, Cordell. *Memoirs*, 2 vols. New York: Macmillan, 1948.

Ickes, Harold L. *The Secret Diary of Harold L. Ickes*, 3 vols. New York: Simon & Schuster, 1953–54.

Janeway, Eliot. *The Struggle for Survival*. New Haven, Conn.: Yale University Press, 1950.

Johnson, Gerald. *Roosevelt: Dictator or Democrat?* New York: Harper, 1941.

Johnson, Hugh. *The Blue Eagle from Egg to Earth*. Garden City, N.Y.: Doubleday, 1935.

Johnston, Alva. "White House Tommy," *The Saturday Evening Post*, July 31, 1937.

Josephson, Matthew; and Josephson, Hannah. *Al Smith: Hero of the Cities*. Boston: Little, 1969.

Kazin, Alfred. *New York Jew*. New York: Knopf, 1978.

Keller, John; and Boldt, Joseph. "Franklin's on His Own Now," *The Saturday Evening Post*, Oct. 12, 1940.

Kemler, Edgar. *The Irreverent Mr. Mencken*. Boston: Little, 1950.

Kilpatrick, Carroll, ed. *Roosevelt and Daniels*. Chapel Hill: University of North Carolina Press, 1952.

Kleeman, Rita H. *Gracious Lady: The Life of Sara Delano Roosevelt*. New York: Appleton-Century, 1935.

Krock, Arthur. *Memoirs*. London: Cassel, 1968.

Langer, William L.; and Gleason, S. Everett. *The Challenge to Isolation, 1937–1940*. New York: Harper, 1952.

———. *The Undeclared War*. New York: Harper, 1953.

Laqueur, Walter. *The Terrible Secret*. Boston: Little, 1980.

Lash, Joseph. *Eleanor and Franklin*. New York: Norton, 1971.

Leahy, William D. *I Was There*. New York: McGraw, 1950.

Lee, Susan; and Passell, Peter. *A New Economic View of American History*. New York: Norton, 1979.

Lekachman, Robert. *The Age of Keynes*. New York: Random House, 1966.

Leuchtenburg, William. *Franklin D. Roosevelt and the New Deal*. New York: Harper, 1963.

Lewin, Ronald. *The American Magic*. New York: Farrar, Straus & Giroux, 1982.

Lindley, Ernest K. *Franklin D. Roosevelt*. New York: Blue Ribbon Books, 1934.

———. *The Roosevelt Revolution*. New York: Viking, 1933.

Link, Arthur S. *Wilson: The Road to the White House*. Princeton, N.J.: Princeton University Press, 1947.

Lippman, Theo, Jr. *The Squire of Warm Springs*. Chicago: Playboy Press, 1977.

Loewenheim, Francis L.; Langley, Harold D.; and Jonas, Manfred; eds. *Roosevelt and Churchill: Their Secret Wartime Correspondence*. New York: Dutton, 1975.

Looker, Earle. *This Man Roosevelt*. New York: Brewer, Warren & Putnam, 1932.

Ludwig, Emil. *Roosevelt*. New York: Viking, 1938.

MacArthur, Douglas. *Reminiscences*. New York: McGraw, 1964.

McCracken, Henry N. *Blithe Dutchess*. New York: Hastings House, 1959.

Manchester, William. *Disturber of the Peace*. New York: Harper, 1950.

Mangione, Jerre. *The Dream and the Deal*. Boston: Little, 1972.

Marx, Rudolph. *The Health of the Presidents*. New York: Putnam, 1960.

Mason, Alpheus T. *Brandeis: A Free Man's Life*. New York: Viking, 1946.

Matloff, Maurice. "Franklin D. Roosevelt as War Leader." In H. L. Coles, ed. *Total War and Cold War*. Columbus: Ohio State University Press, 1962.

Mencken, H. L. *The Days of H. L. Mencken*. New York: Knopf, 1947.

Miller, Nathan. *The Founding Finaglers*. New York: McKay, 1976.

————. *The Roosevelt Chronicles*. Garden City, N.Y.: Doubleday, 1979.

————. *The U. S. Navy: An Illustrated History*. Annapolis, Md.: U. S. Naval Institute, 1977.

Millis, Walter. *The Road to War*. Boston: Houghton, 1935.

Moley, Raymond. *After Seven Years*. New York: Harper, 1939.

————. *The First New Deal*. New York: Harcourt, 1966.

————. *27 Masters of Politics*. New York: Funk, 1949.

Moore, Edmund A. *A Catholic Runs for President*. New York: Ronald, 1956.

Morison, Elting E. *Admiral Sims and the Modern American Navy*. Boston: Houghton, 1942.

Morison, Samuel Eliot. *The Rising Sun in the Pacific*. Boston: Little, 1948.

————. *Strategy and Compromise*. Boston: Little, 1958.

Morse, Arthur D. *While 6 Million Died*. New York: Ace Books, 1968.

Moscow, Warren. *Politics in the Empire State*. New York: Knopf, 1948.

Mowry, George E. *Theodore Roosevelt and the Progressive Movement*. Madison, Wis.: University of Wisconsin Press, 1947.

Murphy, Robert. *Diplomat Among Warriors*. Garden City, N.Y.: Doubleday, 1964.

Murray, Robert K. *The 103rd Ballot*. New York: Harper, 1976.

————. *Red Scare*. Minneapolis: University of Minnesota Press, 1955.

Neustadt, Richard E. *Presidential Power*. New York: New American Library, 1960.

Nourse, Edwin G. *Three Years of the AAA*. Washington, D.C.: Brookings Institution, 1937.

Overacker, Louise. "Campaign Funds in a Depression Year," *American Political Science Review*, Oct. 1933.

Parmet, Herbert S.; and Hecht, Marie B. *Never Again: A President Runs for a Third Term*. New York: Macmillan, 1968.

Paterson, Thomas G.; Clifford, J. Garry; and Hagan, Kenneth J. *American Foreign Policy*. Lexington, Mass.: Heath, 1977.

Patti, Archimedes. *Why Viet Nam?* Berkeley: University of California Press, 1980.

Peel, Roy V.; and Donnelly, Thomas C. *The 1932 Campaign: An Analysis*. New York: Farrar, 1935.

X Perkins, Dexter. *The New Age of Franklin Roosevelt*. Chicago, Ill.: University of Chicago Press, 1957.

Perkins, Frances. *The Roosevelt I Knew*. New York: Viking, 1946.

Peterson, Morrill D. *The Jefferson Image in the American Mind*. New York: Oxford University Press, 1962.

Phillips, Cabell. *From the Crash to the Blitz: 1929–1939*. New York: Macmillan, 1969.

Phillips, William. Transcript of memoirs in FDRL.

Pogue, Forrest C. *George C. Marshall*, Vol. II. New York: Viking, 1966.

Prange, Gordon W. *At Dawn We Slept*. New York: McGraw, 1981.

Rauch, Basil. *The History of the New Deal.* New York: Creative Age, 1944.
———. *Roosevelt: From Munich to Pearl Harbor.* New York: Creative Age, 1950.
Reading, Don. "New Deal Activity in the States 1933 to 1939," *Journal of Economic History,* Dec. 1973.
Reilly, Michael F. *Reilly of the White House.* New York: Simon & Schuster, 1947.
Rixey, Lillian. *Bamie.* New York: McKay, 1963.
Robinson, Edgar E. *The Roosevelt Leadership 1933–1945.* Philadelphia: Lippincott, 1955.
Rollins, Alfred B., Jr. *Roosevelt and Howe.* New York: Knopf, 1962.
Roosevelt, Anna. "How Polio Helped Father," *The Woman,* July 1949.
Roosevelt, Eleanor. *Franklin D. Roosevelt at Hyde Park.* Washington, D.C.: Government Printing Office, 1949.
———. *This I Remember.* New York: Harper, 1949.
———. *This Is My Story.* New York: Harper, 1937.
Roosevelt, Elliott. *As He Saw It.* New York: Duell, 1946.
———; and Brough, James. *An Untold Story: The Roosevelts of Hyde Park.* New York: Dell, 1973.
Roosevelt, Franklin D. *F.D.R. His Personal Letters,* ed. Elliott Roosevelt, 4 vols. New York: Duell, 1947–50.
———. *The Happy Warrior.* Boston: Houghton, 1928.
———. *On Our Way.* New York: Day, 1934.
———. *The Public Papers and Addresses of Franklin D. Roosevelt,* ed. Samuel I. Rosenman, 13 vols. New York: Macmillan, 1938–50.
———. *The Public Papers of Governor Franklin D. Roosevelt,* 4 vols. Albany, N.Y.: J. Blyon Co., 1930–39.
Roosevelt, James; and Shalett, Sidney. *Affectionately, F.D.R.* New York: Avon Books, 1959.
Roosevelt, James; and Libby, Bill. *My Parents.* Chicago: Playboy Press, 1976.
Roosevelt, Mrs. James, as told to Isabelle Leighton and Gabrielle Forbush. *My Boy Franklin.* New York: Crown, 1933.
Roosevelt, Theodore. *Letters to Anna Roosevelt Cowles.* New York: Scribner, 1924.
Rosen, Elliot. *Hoover, Roosevelt, and the Brains Trust.* New York: Columbia University Press, 1977.
Rosenman, Samuel I. *Working with Roosevelt.* New York: Harper, 1952.
Russell, Francis. *The President Makers.* Boston: Little, 1976.
Schlesinger, Arthur M., Jr. *The Age of Roosevelt,* 3 vols. Boston: Houghton, 1957–60.
Secretary of the Navy, *Annual Report: 1913.* Washington: Government Printing Office, 1913.
Seligman, Lester G.; and Cornwell, Elmer E., Jr. *New Deal Mosaic: Roosevelt Confers with His National Emergency Council.* Eugene: University of Oregon Press, 1965.
Sherwin, Mark; and Markmann, Charles L. *One Week in March.* New York: Putnam, 1961.
Sherwood, Robert E. *Roosevelt and Hopkins.* New York: Harper, 1948.
Smith, Gaddis. *American Diplomacy During the Second World War.* New York: Wiley, 1965.

Smith, Gene. *The Shattered Dream*. New York: Morrow, 1970.

Smith, Merriman. *Thank You, Mr. President*. New York: Harper, 1946.

Snyder, Louis L.; and Morris, Richard B. *A Treasury of Great Reporting*. New York: Simon & Schuster, 1949.

Starling, Edmund W. *Starling of the White House*. New York: Simon & Schuster, 1946.

Steeholm, Clara; and Steeholm, Hardy. *The House at Hyde Park*. New York: Viking, 1950.

Steel, Ronald. *Walter Lippmann and the American Century*. Boston: Little, 1980.

Stein, Leon. *The Triangle Fire*. Philadelphia: Lippincott, 1962.

Stewart, William J., compiler. *The Era of Franklin D. Roosevelt*. Hyde Park, N.Y.: FDR Library, 1974.

Stiles, Lela. *The Man Behind Roosevelt*. New York: World Pub., 1954.

Stilwell, Paul. *Air Raid: Pearl Harbor!* Annapolis, Md.: U. S. Naval Institute, 1981.

Stimson, Henry L.; and Bundy, McGeorge. *On Active Service in Peace and War*. New York: Harper, 1948.

Straight, Michael. "A Dutchess County Boy," *The New Republic*, Apr. 15, 1946.

Taussig, Joseph K. "Destroyer Experiences During the Great War," U. S. Naval Institute *Proceedings*, Dec. 1922.

Taylor, F. J. *The United States and the Spanish Civil War, 1936–1939*. New York: Bookman Associates, 1956.

Taylor, Telford. *Munich*. Garden City, N.Y.: Doubleday, 1979.

Teague, Michael. *Mrs. L.; Conversations with Alice Roosevelt Longworth*. Garden City, N.Y.: Doubleday, 1981.

Terry, Edward. "The Insurgents at Albany," *The Independent*, Sept. 7, 1911.

Thomas, Gordon; and Morgan-Witts, Max. *The Day the Bubble Burst*. Garden City, N.Y.: Doubleday, 1979.

Toland, John. *The Rising Sun*. New York: Random House, 1970.

Tugwell, Rexford G. *The Brains Trust*. New York: Viking, 1968.

———. *The Democratic Roosevelt*. Garden City, N.Y.: Doubleday, 1957.

———. *In Search of Roosevelt*. Cambridge, Mass.: Harvard University Press, 1972.

———. *Roosevelt's Revolution*. New York: Macmillan, 1977.

Tully, Grace. *F.D.R., My Boss*. New York: Scribner, 1949.

Urofsky, Melvin L. "Josephus Daniels and the Armor Trust," *North Carolina Historical Review*, Summer 1968.

U. S. State Department, *Foreign Relations of the United States: Conferences at Cairo and Teheran, 1943*. Washington, D.C.: Government Printing Office, 1961.

———. *Foreign Relations of the United States: The Conferences at Malta and Yalta, 1945*. Washington, D.C.: Government Printing Office, 1955.

Wecter, Dixon. *The Age of the Great Depression*. New York: Macmillan, 1948.

Wehle, Louis B. *Hidden Threads of History*. New York: Macmillan, 1953.

Werner, M. R. *Tammany Hall*. Garden City, N.Y.: Doubleday, 1928.

Whalen, Richard J. *The Founding Father*. New York: New American Library, 1964.

Wharton, Don, ed. *The Roosevelt Omnibus*. New York: Knopf, 1934.

White, Graham J. *F.D.R. and the Press.* Chicago: University of Chicago Press, 1979.

Wilson, Edmund. *The American Earthquake.* Garden City, N.Y.: Doubleday, 1958.

Wohlstetter, Roberta. *Pearl Harbor: Warning and Decision.* Stanford, Calif.: Stanford University Press, 1962.

Wolfskill, George; and Hudson, John A. *All but the People.* New York: Macmillan, 1969.

Worster, Donald. *Dust Bowl: The Southern Plains in the 1930s.* New York: Oxford University Press, 1979.

PERIODICALS

New York *Times*
New York *Herald*
New York *Herald Tribune*
New York *Sun*
New York *Daily News*
New York *World*
Baltimore *Sun*
Washington *Post*
Washington *Evening Star*
Poughkeepsie *Eagle*
Los Angeles *Times*
The American Boy
Harvard Alumni Bulletin
Harvard *Crimson*
Life
Newsweek

Chicago *Tribune*
Liberty
The Saturday Evening Post
The New Republic
The Nation
Political Science Quarterly
U. S. Naval Institute *Proceedings*
American Heritage
New Yorker
Military Affairs
Annals of Internal Medicine
The Quarterly Journal of Speech
Parents Magazine
American Political Science Review
Journal of Economic History

INDEX

Coolidge, Calvin, 159, 168–69, 201, 202,
206, 215, 219, 236, 237, 300, 302
election of 1924, 207, 207n
as governor of Massachusetts, 159, 161
Puritan image of, 202
Copeland, Charles Townsend, 32, 33–34
Coral Sea, Battle of the, 490, 500n
Corcoran, Thomas G., 327, 375, 376, 395,
398, 399, 403, 408, 411–12, 444
Cornell University, 228
Costigan, Edward P., 285n
Coué, Dr. Émile, 194
Coughlin, Father Charles E., 292, 386, 388,
440
attacks on "international bankers,"
365–66
Council of National Defense, 144
Council of Parks, 227
Covenant of the League of Nations, 157–58,
160–61
Cowles, Mrs. Anna Roosevelt, 42, 45, 48n,
49, 51, 62, 64, 109–10, 112
Cowles, Admiral W. Sheffield, 110, 140
Cowles, W. Sheffield, Jr., 190
Cox, James M., 167, 192, 195, 247
campaign of 1920, 171–72, 175, 176
nomination of, 169–70
Craig, May, 354
Creditanstalt (bank), 251
Creel, George, 390
Crete, Nazi invasion of, 462
Croly, Herbert, 67, 89
Cross, Mrs. Lillian, 298
Crumwold (estate), 19, 20
Cuba, 130, 176
Cuff Links Club, 177n, 302
Cummings, Homer S., 268, 302, 307–8, 309,
393, 400–1, 402, 404
Curley, James M., 267n, 416
Curry, John F., 241, 267, 273
Curzon Line, 497, 503
Cutting, Bronson, 310n
CWA. See Civilian Works Administration
Czechoslovakia, 429–31
Nazi occupation of, 433, 434

Daily Bugle, 348
Daladier, Édouard, 431, 438
Dall, Anna Eleanor (Sisty), 346
Dall, Curtis (Buzzy). See Roosevelt, Curtis
Dall, Curtis B., 221n, 346
Dall, Mrs. Curtis B. See Roosevelt, Anna
Eleanor
Dallek, Robert, 320, 420
Dana, Frances, 42, 42n
Dana, Richard Henry, 42n
Daniels, Jonathan, 107n
Daniels, Josephus, 93, 100–1, 180, 187, 201,
217, 219, 268, 296
as ambassador to Mexico, 107n
as Navy Secretary, 102, 103, 104–5, 104n,
106, 115, 116, 119–20, 124, 125n, 126,
127, 128, 128n, 129, 132, 134, 156, 161,
165, 170, 171, 172, 214
penal system reforms, 164–65

relations with FDR, 107, 115, 117, 138
World War I, 137, 139, 140, 141, 141n,
142, 147, 151, 152, 155–56
Dante, 384
Danzig, 434
DAR. See Daughters of the American
Revolution
Darlan, Admiral Jean, 490–91
"Darlan deal," 491
Daughters of the American Revolution
(DAR), 351, 397
FDR's run-in with, 360n
Davies, Joseph E., 170, 249, 338, 420
Davis, Elmer, 286
Davis, John W., 206, 207n, 217, 266, 281
Davis, Kenneth S., 141n
Davis, Norman, 321, 424–25, 426
Davis, Richard Harding, 32
Davis, Stuart, 368
Debating Society, 29
Debt Commission, 294
Declaration of the United Nations, 485
De Gaulle, Charles, 20n, 491, 504
Degler, Carl N., 345
De Kooning, Willem, 368
Delano, Franklin Hughes, 8
Delano, Frederic, 184, 185–86
Delano, Laura, 493, 509, 510
Delano, Warren, 8, 13–15, 14n, 18, 19
Delano, Warren, Jr., 8
Delano family, 13–14, 15, 18, 19, 43, 48, 59,
424
Delaware and Hudson Railroad, 11
Democratic Finance Committee, 129
Democratic League, 71
Democratic National Committee, 166, 200,
220, 258, 262, 268, 270, 280, 499
Democratic national convention of 1912, 81,
82, 83, 90–94, 100, 268
Democratic national convention of 1920,
167–68, 169–72
Democratic national convention of 1924,
203–6, 271
Democratic national convention of 1928,
219–20
Democratic national convention of 1932,
265–80
acceptance speech, 270, 272, 278–79,
279n, 303
balloting, 273–74, 276
campaign songs, 266, 272, 276
Credentials Committee, 270
Hyde Park strategy sessions, 268, 270
keynote address, 269–70
number of delegates, 269
"stop Roosevelt" movement, 267, 268,
269, 270, 273
two-thirds rule fight, 268–69
Democratic national convention of 1936,
283–84, 493
Democratic national convention of 1940,
443, 448, 449–53
keynote address, 450
third-term controversy, 448, 453